The IDG SECRETS™ Advantage

Hard Disk SECRETS is part of the *InfoWorld SECRETS* series of books, brought to you by IDG Books Worldwide. The designers of the *SECRETS* series understand that you appreciate insightful and comprehensive works from computer experts. Authorities in their respective areas, the authors of the *SECRETS* books have been selected for their ability to enrich your daily computing tasks.

The formula for a book in the *SECRETS* series is simple: Give an expert author a forum to pass on his or her expertise to readers. A *SECRETS* author, rather than the publishing company, directs the organization, pace, and treatment of the subject matter. *SECRETS* authors maintain close contact with end users through column feedback, user group participation, and consulting work. The authors' close contact with the needs of computer users gives the *SECRETS* books a strategic advantage over most computer books. Our authors do not distance themselves from the reality of daily computing, but rather, our authors are directly tied to the reader response stream.

We believe that the author has the experience to approach a topic in the most efficient manner, and we know that you, the reader, will benefit from a "one-to-one" relationship, through the text, with the author. The author's voice is always present in a *SECRETS* series book. Some have compared the presentation of a topic in a *SECRETS* book to sitting at a coffee break with the author and having the author's full attention.

And of course, the author is free to include or recommend useful software, both shareware and proprietary, in a *SECRETS* series book. The software that accompanies a *SECRETS* book is not intended as casual filler. The software is strategically linked to the content, theme, or procedures of the book. We expect that you will receive a real and direct benefit from the included software.

You will find this book comprehensive whether you read it cover to cover, section to section, or simply a topic at a time. As a computer user, you deserve a comprehensive and informative resource of answers that *Hard Disk SECRETS* delivers.

— David Solomon
Publisher

InfoWorld Hard Disk SECRETS™

INFO WORLD

Hard Disk SECRETS™

by John M. Goodman, Ph.D.

Foreword by Steve Gibson
President, Gibson Research Corporation
Creator of SpinRite and InfoWorld Columnist

IDG BOOKS

IDG Books Worldwide, Inc.
An International Data Group Company

San Mateo, California ♦ Indianapolis, Indiana ♦ Boston, Massachusetts

Hard Disk SECRETS

Published by
IDG Books Worldwide, Inc.
An International Data Group Company
155 Bovet Road, Suite 310
San Mateo, CA 94402

Text and figures copyright © 1990, 1993 by John M. Goodman, Ph.D. Interior design and icons copyright © 1993 by IDG Books. All rights reserved. No part of this book may be reproduced or transmitted in any form, by any means (electronic, photocopying, recording, or otherwise) without the prior written permission of the publisher.

Library of Congress Catalog Card No.: 92-74306

ISBN 1-878058-64-9

Printed in the United States of America

10 9 8 7 6 5 4 3 2 1

Distributed in the United States by IDG Books Worldwide, Inc.

Distributed in Canada by Macmillan of Canada, a Division of Canada Publishing Corporation; by Woodslane Pty. Ltd. in Australia and New Zealand; and by Computer Bookshops in the U.K. and Ireland.

For information on translations and availability in other countries, contact Marc Jeffrey Mikulich, Foreign Rights Manager, at IDG Books Worldwide; FAX Number 415-358-1260.

For sales inquiries and special prices for bulk quantities, write to the address above or call IDG Books Worldwide at 415-312-0650.

Limit of Liability/Disclaimer of Warranty: The author and publisher have used their best efforts in preparing this book. IDG Books Worldwide, Inc., International Data Group, Inc., and the author make no representation or warranties with respect to the accuracy or completeness of the contents of this book and the accompanying disk, and specifically disclaim any implied warranties or merchantability or fitness for any particular purpose, and shall in no event be liable for any loss of profit or any other commercial damage, including but not limited to special, incidental, consequential, or other damages.

Trademarks: All brand names and product names used in this book are trademarks, registered trademarks, or trade names of their respective holders. IDG Books Worldwide is not associated with any product or vendor mentioned in this book. SpinRite is a trademark of Gibson Research. InfoWorld is a registered trademark of InfoWorld Publishing, Inc. ...SECRETS is a trademark of IDG Books Worldwide, Inc.

Dedication

I dedicate this book lovingly to my parents, who set me on the right track in the first place and then realigned me to it as necessary. In particular, I have learned from my father a passion for how things work and for stating ideas with precision, clarity, and accuracy.

In addition, I dedicate this book to a very plucky young woman who has shown great strength and internal beauty in coping with what life has dealt her: my daughter, Sabrina.

Credits

Publisher
David Solomon

Acquisitions Editor
Janna Custer

Managing Editor
Mary Bednarek

Project Editor
Diane Graves Steele

Editor
Gregory R. Robertson

Technical Reviewers
Linda Slovick
Victor R. Garza

Production Manager
Beth J. Baker

Production Coordinator
Cindy L. Phipps

Text Preparation
Dana Sadoff
Mary Ann Cordova

Proofreader
Charles A. Hutchinson

Indexer
Ty Koontz

Book Design and Production
Peppy White
Francette M. Ytsma
Tracy Strub
(University Graphics, Palo Alto, California)

Acknowledgments

This book could not have been created without the generous help and cooperation of a great many people. Foremost among them is Steve Gibson. SpinRite is Steve Gibson's program. He created Gibson Research as a means of bringing SpinRite to the public. Through these experiences he has become one of the acknowledged experts on hard disks for PCs. He shared with me all that he knows about hard disks, holding back nothing. This is a most uncommon event in an industry that is rife with paranoia and where nearly all entrepreneurs hide whatever they perceive as the source of their competitive advantage.

Steve served as the initial technical reviewer for the manuscript. He studied my drafts carefully, picking out everything from simple typographic errors to the most subtle errors of reasoning or fact. Thank you, Steve!

At a later stage, Linda Slovick and Victor R. Garza of the *InfoWorld* Review Board assumed the role of technical reviewers. Linda is the one who read most of the final manuscript and pointed out a number of points that required further checking, clarification, or correction. Thank you, Linda and Victor.

Naturally, I could not depend on any one person's knowledge of this field, so I called on many of the industry's leaders, and almost all of them proved to be most gracious and helpful.

I want to acknowledge with much thanks the many hours that Brad Kingsbury, project chief for Calibrate at Peter Norton Computing, took to explain that product's features, his company's goals, and more general aspects of the hard disk industry. Along the way he managed to further enlighten me about some of the fundamentals of hard disk operation and other DOS arcana.

Don Brunnett, a senior engineer at Brand Technologies, was similarly generous with information on the latest developments in hard drive manufacturing technology. His special expertise is in servo design. Brand Technologies are leaders in the effort to bring vertical recording to the PC mainstream. Much of what you will find in this book about hard disk servos and about vertical recording I learned from Don.

Dal Allan has become a legend in the PC industry, especially in the sub-area concerned with peripheral interconnections, for his work on a number of standards that have been critical to the explosive growth of the PC marketplace. Talking with Dal helped me gain valuable perspective on the developments in the IDE/ATA and SCSI standards, in particular.

Tom Hanan at Western Digital is another of the moving forces in PC standards. His special area has been in the integration of the IDE/ATA standard with the PCMCIA standard. Tom both answered my questions and supplied me with official standards documents, for both of which I thank him very much.

Others who helped me included Norman Ivans, President of Prime Solutions; Mark Kolod, President of Kolod Research; Dave Bushong, author of IAU; and Bart Dangerfield, Marketing Director for Gazelle Systems.

Richard Evins shared his knowledge of the industry and introduced me to some helpful people and interesting products. Johnny Tseng at UltraStor helped me understand their fine disk controllers. Howard Chan at Wyse Technologies explained some of what has made Wyse DOS special.

Thanks also are due, of course, to the companies and individuals who graciously supplied the software that is included on the *Hard Disk SECRETS* disk. Special thanks are due Vasu Raman and Douglas Anderson at Micro House — they rewrote the Micro House utilities many times to incorporate my suggestions.

My research assistant, John Lunsford, has read this book more times than he cares to remember, at every stage from rough draft through the page proofs. He caught many errors and places where my explanations needed improvement. Thank you very much, John.

The final manuscript was copy edited by Greg Robertson. Diane Steele was the project editor for this book. Greg and Diane were particularly fine editors. Each gave loving attention to every paragraph and each idea, and were faithful advocates for the readers throughout the process.

In the end, all the responsibility for the final text and figures is mine. Still, I sleep a lot more soundly knowing I have had knowledgeable, careful, competent, and meticulous readers going over everything I wrote.

Thanks also to Mary Bednarek, Bill Hatfield, Dana Sadoff, and Chuck Hutchinson for their contributions to the editorial process.

I also received a great deal of support and encouragement from John Kilcullen, IDG Book's President, and David Solomon, IDG Book's Publisher.

I used Microsoft Word for DOS to prepare the manuscript, and CorelDRAW! to prepare the figures. These fine programs made easy work out of some potentially arduous tasks.

(The publisher would like to give special thanks to Patrick J. McGovern, without whom this book would not have been possible.)

About IDG Books Worldwide

Welcome to the world of IDG Books Worldwide.

IDG Books Worldwide, Inc., is a division of International Data Group (IDG), the world's largest publisher of computer-related information and the leading global provider of information services on information technology. IDG publishes over 190 computer publications in 60 countries. Thirty million people read one or more IDG publications each month.

If you use personal computers, IDG Books is committed to publishing quality books that meet your needs. We rely on our extensive network of publications, including such leading periodicals as *PC World, InfoWorld, Computerworld, Macworld, Publish, Network World,* and *SunWorld,* to help us make informed and timely decisions in creating useful computer books that meet your needs.

Every IDG book strives to bring extra value and skill-building instruction to the reader. Our books are written by experts, with the backing of IDG periodicals, and with careful thought devoted to issues such as audience, interior design, use of icons, and illustrations. Our editorial staff is a careful mix of high-tech journalists and experienced book people. Our close contact with the makers of computer products helps ensure accuracy and thorough coverage. Our heavy use of personal computers at every step in production means we can deliver books in the most timely manner.

We are delivering books of high quality at competitive prices on topics customers want. At IDG, we believe in quality, and we have been delivering quality for over 25 years. You'll find no better book on a subject than an IDG book.

John Kilcullen
President and C.E.O.
IDG Books Worldwide, Inc.

IDG Books Worldwide, Inc. is a division of International Data Group. The officers are Patrick J. McGovern, Founder and Board Chairman; Walter Boyd, President; Robert A. Farmer, Vice Chairman. International Data Group's publications include: **ARGENTINA's** Computerworld Argentina, InfoWorld Argentina; **ASIA's** Computerworld Hong Kong, PC World Hong Kong, Computerworld Southeast Asia, PC World Singapore, Computerworld Malaysia, PC World Malaysia; **AUSTRALIA's** Computerworld Australia, Australian PC World, Australian Macworld, Reseller, IDG Sources; **AUSTRIA's** Computerwelt Oesterreich, PC Test; **BRAZIL's** Computerworld, Mundo IBM, Mundo Unix, PC World, Publish; **BULGARIA's** Computerworld Bulgaria, Ediworld, PC World Bulgaria; **CANADA's** Direct Access, Graduate Computerworld, InfoCanada, Network World Canada; **CHILE's** Computerworld, Informatica; **COLUMBIA's** Computerworld Columbia; **CZECH REPUBLIC's** Computerworld Elektronika, PC World; **DENMARK's** CAD/CAM WORLD, Communications World, Computerworld Danmark, Computerworld Focus, Computerworld Uddannelse, Lotus World, Macintosh Produktkatalog, Macworld Danmark, PC World Danmark, PC World Produktguide, Windows World; **EQUADOR's** PC World; **EGYPT's** PC World Middle East; **FINLAND's** Mikro PC, Tietoviikko, Tietoverkko; **FRANCE's** Distributique, GOLDEN MAC, InfoPC, Languages & Systems, Le Guide du Monde Informatique, Le Monde Informatique, Telecoms & Reseaux; **GERMANY's** Computerwoche, Computerwoche Focus, Computerwoche Extra, Computerwoche Karriere, edv aspekte, Information Management, Macwelt, Netzwelt, PC Welt, PC Woche, Publish, Unit; **HUNGARY's** Computerworld SZT, PC World; **INDIA's** Computers & Communications; **ISRAEL's** Computerworld Israel, PC World Israel; **ITALY's** Computerworld Italia, Lotus Magazine, Macworld Italia, Networking Italia, PC World Italia; **JAPAN's** Computerworld Japan, Macworld Japan, SunWorld Japan; **KENYA's** East African Computer News; **KOREA's** Computerworld Korea, Macworld Korea, PC World Korea; **MEXICO's** Compu Edicion, Compu Manufactura, Computacion/Punto de Venta, Computerworld Mexico, MacWorld, Mundo Unix, PC World, Windows; **THE NETHERLANDS'** Computer! Totaal, LAN Magazine, MacWorld Magazine; **NEW ZEALAND's** Computer Listings, Computerworld New Zealand, New Zealand PC World; **NIGERIA's** PC World Africa; **NORWAY's** Computerworld Norge, C/World, Lotusworld Norge, Macworld Norge, Networld, PC World Ekspress, PC World Norge, PC World's Product Guide, Publish World, Student Data, Unix World, Windowsworld, IDG Direct Response; **PANAMA's** PC World; **PERU's** PC World; **PEOPLES REPUBLIC OF CHINA's** China Computerworld, PC World China, Electronics International; **IDG TECH BEIJING's** Electronics New Product World; **IDG SHENZHEN's** Computer News Digest; **PHILLIPPINES'** Computerworld, PC World; **POLAND's** Computerworld Poland, PC World/Komputer; **PORTUGAL's** MacIn; **ROMANIA's** InfoClub Magazine; **RUSSIA's** Computerworld-Moscow, Mir-PC, Sety; **SLOVENIA's** Monitor Magazine; **SOUTH AFRICA's** Computing S.A.; **SPAIN's** Amiga World, Autoedicion, Computerworld Espana, Macworld Espana, NeXTWORLD, PC World Espana, Publish, Sunworld; **SWEDEN's** Attack, ComputerSweden, Corporate Computing, Lokala Natverk/LAN, Lotus World, MAC&PC, Macworld, Mikrodatorn, PC World, Publishing & Design (CAP), Datalngenjoren, Maxi Data, Windows World; **SWITZERLAND's** Computerworld Schweiz, Macworld Schweiz, PC & Workstation; **TAIWAN's** Computerworld Taiwan, Global Computer Express, PC World Taiwan; **THAILAND's** Thai Computerworld; **TURKEY's** Computerworld Monitor, Macworld Turkiye, PC World Turkiye; **UNITED KINGDOM's** Lotus Magazine, Macworld, Sunworld; **UNITED STATES'** AmigaWorld, Cable in the Classroom, CD Review, CIO, Computerworld, Desktop Video World, DOS Resource Guide, Electronic News, Federal Computer Week, Federal Integrator, GamePro, inCider/A+, IDG Books, InfoWorld, InfoWorld Direct, Laser Event, Macworld, Multimedia World, Network World, NeXTWORLD, PC Games, PC World, PC Letter, Publish, SunWorld, SWATPro, Video Event, Video Toaster World; **VENEZUELA's** Computerworld Venezuela, MicroComputerworld Venezuela; **VIETNAM's** PC World Vietnam

About the Author

John M. Goodman has a doctorate in physics and has been teaching technical topics to both specialists and the lay public for nearly 30 years. He is a Course Director for the Center for Advanced Professional Development, a best-selling author, and past-president of the Orange Coast IBM PC Users Group (OCIPUG) — one of the largest PC users groups in the United States.

Contents at a Glance

Introduction 1

Part I: The Hard Disk Companion 11

Chapter 1: Why Hard Disks Matter So Much 13
Chapter 2: Magnetic Storage of Information 33
Chapter 3: Some Important Engineering Issues 69
Chapter 4: Messy Hard Disk Details 101
Chapter 5: Disk Caching 151
Chapter 6: Hard Disks Under DOS 169
Chapter 7: Bumping Up Against and Breaking Barriers 207
Chapter 8: Preparing a Hard Disk to Store Information
  Step One: The Physical (Low-Level) Format 227
Chapter 9: Preparing a Hard Disk to Store Information
  Step Two: Partitioning 237
Chapter 10: Preparing a Hard Disk to Store Information
  Step Three: The Logical Format 259
Chapter 11: How Hard Disks Die 287

Part II: The SpinRite Companion 325

Chapter 12: Reinterleaving Software: A New Category of Utility
  Program 327
Chapter 13: Preventing the Slow Death of Your Hard Disk 343
Chapter 14: Details of SpinRite's Operation 365
Chapter 15: SpinRite's Evolution 389
Chapter 16: Advanced User's Guide to SpinRite 407

Part III: Appendixes 445

Appendix A: Genesis of a Product: How SpinRite Was Born 445
Appendix B: The *Hard Disk SECRETS* Disk 449

Index 529
Installation Instructions for the *Hard Disk SECRETS* Disk 561

Figures at a Glance

Chapter 1 13
Figure 1-1: A worthwhile thought to hang over your computer. 20

Chapter 2 33
Figure 2-1: A cutaway view of a typical hard drive. 36
Figure 2-2: Tracks and sectors. 38
Figure 2-3: Location and numbering of disk heads and cylinders. 40
Figure 2-4: A typical read/write head design. 43
Figure 2-5: A magnetized hard disk platter. 45
Figure 2-6: A naive data-encoding scheme. 48
Figure 2-7: Data-encoding strategies. 54
Figure 2-8: Flow chart for 2,7 RLL data encoding. 59
Figure 2-9: The "orchard model" of ECC. 63

Chapter 3 69
Figure 3-1: Anatomy of a hard disk sector. 70
Figure 3-2: Sector interleave values. 72
Figure 3-3: Head skewing. 79
Figure 3-4: Essential hardware parts of a PC hard drive subsystem. 83
Figure 3-5: Popular PC hard disk interfaces. 95

Chapter 4 101
Figure 4-1: A simple electric motor. 102
Figure 4-2: A multipole motor. 104
Figure 4-3: A stepper motor head positioner. 106
Figure 4-4: A loudspeaker is a motor. 107
Figure 4-5: A voice-coil (servo) head positioner. 110
Figure 4-6: An external servo head-positioning system. 113
Figure 4-7: An example of a Gray code. 117
Figure 4-8: A dedicated platter servo system. 119
Figure 4-9: Servo track details. 120

Figure 4-10: A wedge servo. 123
Figure 4-11: An embedded servo. 125
Figure 4-12: An inductive read/write head. 129
Figure 4-13: A thin-film (inductive) head. 131
Figure 4-14: Longitudinal recording. 133
Figure 4-15: The critical dimensions for longitudinal recording. 134
Figure 4-16: Perpendicular (vertical) recording. 137
Figure 4-17: The critical dimensions for perpendicular (vertical) recording. 139
Figure 4-18: Read/write head-switching circuits. 145

Chapter 5 151
Figure 5-1: Memory cache versus disk cache. 152

Chapter 6 169
Figure 6-1: How DOS block and character devices differ. 174
Figure 6-2: Layers of programs in a PC. 177
Figure 6-3: Steps in processing a file request (part 1 of 4). 180
Figure 6-4: Steps in processing a file request (part 2 of 4). 181
Figure 6-5: Steps in processing a file request (part 3 of 4). 182
Figure 6-6: Steps in processing a file request (part 4 of 4). 183
Figure 6-7: How interrupt vectors and interrupt service routines are used to handle events. 185
Figure 6-8: A TSR program "hooks" an interrupt (part 1 of 2). 188
Figure 6-9: A TSR program "hooks" an interrupt (part 2 of 2). 189
Figure 6-10: Some numbers stored in the interrupt vector table point to the hard disk parameter tables. 192
Figure 6-11: The structure of the hard disk parameter table. 193
Figure 6-12: An installable block device driver. 205

Chapter 7 207
Figure 7-1: Head and sector translation example. 216
Figure 7-2: Hooking an interrupt to intercept error messages. 222

Chapter 8 227
Figure 8-1: An analogy to how information is stored on a hard disk. 229

Chapter 9 237
Figure 9-1: The regions into which partitioning divides a hard disk. 239
Figure 9-2: A typical master boot record (MBR). 241
Figure 9-3: The partition table structure. 243
Figure 9-4: Extended partition tables and logical drives. 248

Chapter 10 259
Figure 10-1: The parts of any DOS logical drive. 260
Figure 10-2: The DOS boot record. 261
Figure 10-3: A 12-bit file allocation table (FAT). 266
Figure 10-4: A 16-bit file allocation table (FAT). 266
Figure 10-5: The details of a DOS (root) directory. 271
Figure 10-6: A couple of ways to view a directory tree. 273
Figure 10-7: The beginning of a DOS boot sector. 275

Chapter 11 287
Figure 11-1: The essential hardware parts of a PC's hard disk subsystem. 288
Figure 11-2: The essential information "parts" of a PC's hard disk subsystem. 289
Figure 11-3: How head drift can cause drive malfunction. 294
Figure 11-4: Bumping a hard disk while low-level formatting can cause
  a wavy track. 295
Figure 11-5: Pinhole surface defects can appear to come and go. 296
Figure 11-6: An error to avoid when mounting a hard drive. 307
Figure 11-7: The new DEFRAG program from MS-DOS 6. 310

Chapter 12 327
Figure 12-1: Tracks and sectors. 329
Figure 12-2: Three examples of different sector interleave values. 330
Figure 12-3: The problem with reinterleaving without data-integrity testing. ..336
Figure 12-4: The anatomy of a hard disk sector. 338
Figure 12-5: Head Drift and Read Errors. 339

Chapter 13 343
Figure 13-1: A sample of the table of bytes. 350
Figure 13-2: A thin spot (or similar defect) in the platter coating. 354
Figure 13-3: The SpinRite data test patterns for MFM drives. 358
Figure 13-4: The SpinRite data test patterns for RLL drives. 359

Chapter 14 365
Figure 14-1: When SpinRite detects a bad sector. 384

Chapter 15 389
No figures

Chapter 16 407
Figure 16-1: The SpinRite clean boot diskette approach. 4122
Figure 16-2: The CONFIG.SYS file for the SpinRite clean boot diskette. 412
Figure 16-3: The AUTOEXEC.BAT file for the SpinRite clean boot diskette. 413
Figure 16-4: Running SpinRite from a clean boot diskette. 427
Figure 16-5: The CONFIG.SYS file from a clean boot diskette. 428
Figure 16-6: The AUTOEXEC.BAT and MENU.BAT files from
a clean boot diskette. 429
Figure 16-7: The CHK.BAT file from a clean boot diskette. 430
Figure 16-8: The SR.BAT file from a clean boot diskette. 431
Figure 16-9: The two principle hard disk head-parking strategies. 435

Tables at a Glance

Table 3-1: The performance penalty incurred by having an incorrect sector interleave value. 77
Table 5-1: DOS 5 default numbers of buffers. 165
Table 5-2: DOS recommended values for buffers. 165
Table 10-1: Cluster Sizes for Various Size Disks or Logical Drives and Versions of DOS. 269
Table 15-1: The names, sizes and dates and times of all SpinRite versions. 390

Table of Contents

Figures at a Glance xvi

Tables at a Glance xx

Introduction 1

Read the Introduction to find out what reading this book can do to help make your life with computers better and easier and your data safer. The Introduction also contains some tips to help you discover all the ways this book can help you — with the least effort and in the shortest time.

Is This Book Meant for You? 1
    Those who need it, now! 1
    Those who want to know all there is to know 1
    Those who are curious 2
    Those who don't have a PC or don't use DOS 2
What You Need to Know Already 3
    Every author makes assumptions 3
    You may need to know how to open your PC 4
    What to do if you don't know those things 5
How You Can Use This Book to Best Advantage 5
    What's where: the big picture 5
    Three ways to read the book the first time through 6
    Conventions used to help you 7
What the Hard Disk SECRETS Disk Adds to the Book 8
An Invitation 9

PART I: The Hard Disk Companion 11

Chapter 1: Why Hard Disks Matter So Much 13

Why should you read a whole book on how hard disks work and how they die? This chapter explains how a little knowledge can enable you to create powerful protections for your data. If your disk has already died, you learn what to do next.

A Hard Disk Is Not Just Another Peripheral Device 13
    Hard disks are the most expensive pieces of hardware in your PC........14
    Hard disks die more frequently than other parts 14
    Hard disks hold something even more valuable 15
Often a Broken Hard Disk Can Be Fixed — Sometimes Easily 15
A Little Knowledge Can Be a Powerful Thing 16
    Carelessness is bad — panic is worse 16
    Don't throw out the baby with the bath water 17
    Get help when you need it 17
Data Cannot Be Insured; You Have to Provide Your Own Protection 19
    All disks die; it's only a matter of when 19
    Be prepared: have a perfect backup 19
    More ways to protect against your own mistakes 21
Make Your Hard Disk Run Better As Well As More Safely 22
    Good organization helps both you and DOS 22
    Speeding up your disk also helps 22
Recovering from Disaster — Some Suggestions 23
    Be prepared: create a safety boot diskette 23
        Start with the system files 23
        Add some customization files 25
        Add some optional files 26
        Now, fill up the diskette 26
        Test your new safety boot diskette 27
    Keep other useful diskettes handy 29
    Creating a safety boot diskette when your hard disk is already dead...30

Chapter 2: Magnetic Storage of Information 33

This chapter covers the fundamental physical and mathematical principles behind magnetic data storage technologies. It starts with a discussion of the lowest level of data storage — bits and flux reversals. A description of the clever strategies used to "encode" data for reliable storage and retrieval follows. The chapter ends with a discussion of real-world imperfections in magnetic data storage and how practical disk systems deal with those realities.

Fundamentals 33
    Three important physical facts 34
    The basic construction of a hard disk 36
        Platters and heads 36
        Tracks and cylinders 37
    The importance of cleanliness 41
    How the heads write and read information 42

Bit size 44
    Minimum magnetic flip-flop length 46
    Theoretical versus practical bit densities 49
Data-Encoding Strategies 51
  A simple-minded pulse approach 52
  FM 55
  NRZ 55
  MFM 56
  RLL 57
  ARLL and other encoding methods 60
A Problem of Imperfection and Some Solutions 61
  A partial solution: error detection 61
    Parity 61
    Cyclical redundancy checks 62
  A better solution: error correction 62
    The orchard model for ECC 63
    Real ECC 64
    What DOS does when ECC comes into play 66

Chapter 3: Some Important Engineering Issues 69

Knowing the fundamental principles is not enough. Building a good, working hard disk requires some attention to a number of critical engineering issues. This chapter explains what those issues are and some of the ways they have been addressed. It also explains the difference between the popular interface standards used in PC hard disks. The chapter ends with a review of what you have learned thus far and a new way to look at the structure of data on a hard disk.

Improvement of Hard Disk Performance by Sector Interleaving
    and Head Skewing 69
  Anatomy of a disk sector 70
  Sector interleave 71
    How DOS stores and retrieves files 73
    The simplest (and sometimes the worst) case 74
    How sector interleave solves the problem 74
    Interleave is a system-level problem 75
  Head skewing 78
  Where sector interleave and head skew information is stored 80
  How to alter interleave and skew 81
  When and how to set the interleave wrong 81
  Inconsistent interleave values 81
  A special case of varying interleave values 82

Popular Products and Standards	82
ST412/ST506	84
ESDI	87
SCSI	88
Connecting SCSI devices to a PC	88
Trouble in SCSI-land	89
Making the fictitious perfect drive	91
IDE	92
Hard disks on an option card	93
PCMCIA	94
Drive Geometries: Two Contrasting Views	96
A review of heads, cylinders, and sectors	96
Logical structures of information	97

Chapter 4: Messy Hard Disk Details 101

The preceding chapter introduces some important engineering issues. This chapter carries that theme a good deal farther. Here you will learn the intimate, "gory" details of how various parts of your hard disk function. You'll find out why servo drives are better, and more costly, than stepper-motor drives. And you'll understand what the newest wrinkle in magnetic data storage, vertical recording, is all about. The chapter closes with an explanation of some very scary things your hard disk may do — and what you need to do about them.

What the Physical Parts of the Drive Do	101
Steppers are simple	102
Voice coil motors are better	111
Head positioning	113
External servo systems	113
Use Gray code to find out where you are	114
Use other reliable ways to find out where you are	116
Dedicated platter servo systems	118
Wedge servo systems	123
Embedded servo systems	124
Hybrid servo systems	125
Buried servo systems	126
Sector headers	127
Read/write head details	128
Longitudinal recording	129
Thin-film heads	130
Flux-sensing read heads	132

Table of Contents

A limitation to bit density in longitudinal recording	133
Critical dimensions in longitudinal recording read/write heads	134
MIG and double MIG heads	135
Vertical recording	136
Critical dimensions in vertical recording read/write heads	138
What we can look forward to	140
What Happens in the Drive Electronics	141
Spindle-motor drive circuit	141
Head-positioner drive circuit	142
Switches and amplifiers	144
Interface electronics	145
What Happens in the Controller Electronics	145
Recalibration and Other Strange Sounds in the Night	147

Chapter 5: Disk Caching 151

If you don't have a disk cache now, you should. In this chapter you learn why. You also discover that there are many different kinds of cache, some more effective than others. Some are very powerful — and also dangerous. Learn what to watch out for, and how to protect yourself if you choose to use a dangerous kind of cache.

The Purpose of a Disk Cache	151
The Varieties of Caches	153
Track buffer	154
Read cache	154
Write-through cache	156
Advanced write-through cache	157
Deferred-write cache	157
Elevator cache	159
The Right Options for Your Cache Program	159
A Different Dimension of Difference	160
Fully associative cache	160
Direct-mapped cache	161
Set-associative cache	161
How do you know what you have?	162
Buffering Controllers Versus Caching Controllers	162
Caching Software Versus a Hardware Cache	162
DOS Disk Buffers	164
The "Correct" Value for Your CONFIG.SYS BUFFERS = Statement	166

Chapter 6: Hard Disks Under DOS 169

Disk drives on PCs do not operate in a vacuum. Most PCs run the MS-DOS, PC DOS, or DR DOS operating system. This chapter details the fundamentals of how MS-DOS defines and uses hard disk drives. It also shows you how to use a hard disk of any capacity in any PC, XT, AT, or other MS-DOS computer — something that is not always easy to accomplish.

An Introduction to DOS 169
The Relationship Between Hard Disks and DOS 171
DOS Devices: Block Versus Character 172
How DOS Makes Things Happen 176
    The layers of programs in a PC 176
    Interrupts 179
    Terminate-and-stay-resident (TSR) programs 184
    Device drivers 187
    Hard disk parameter tables 190
Drive-Type Determination 194
    Original XT and similar older controller cards 194
    The newer autoconfiguring XT controller cards 195
    AT and higher PCs 196
    AT drive-type table 197
    Hard disks on an option card 200
    ESDI hard drives 200
    IDE/ATA hard drives 200
    SCSI hard drives 202

Chapter 7: Bumping Up Against and Breaking Barriers 207

There are many limits on how large a hard disk can be. Learn what they are and how you can sometimes evade those limits. This chapter ends with a discussion of error messages from the disk controller, the BIOS, and DOS, telling what makes them happen and what you need to do about them when they occur.

Logical Size Limits Imposed by DOS 207
Physical Size Limits Imposed by the BIOS 209
Evading the Logical Limits 210
    Large sectors 211
    Disk partitions 212
Evading the Physical Limits 213
    The pure software-evasion technique 214

Table of Contents

Sector mapping 214
Other controller-mapping strategies 217
RAID and Related Strategies 219
Error Messages 221

Chapter 8: Preparing a Hard Disk to Store Information Step One: The Physical (Low-Level) Format 227

A disk drive fresh from the manufacturer is useless for data storage. This chapter and the following two detail the three steps necessary to prepare the drive for use and describe some strange methods used by certain manufacturers to accomplish these steps.

What Is Disk Formatting? 227
A Three-Step Process (and an Analogy) 228
Three Ways to Do Physical Formatting 230
Only the controller can do it 231
Some weird alternative formats 233
Certain disk/controller combinations 234
Some autoconfiguring hard disk controllers 235

Chapter 9: Preparing a Hard Disk to Store Information Step Two: Partitioning 237

After the physical format is complete, the disk could be used to store information. But the PC architectural design demands that the disk first be divided into regions. This chapter explains why and how that is done.

Why PC Hard Disks Need to Be Partitioned 237
Carving Up the Disk 238
The master boot record and partition table 238
The diagnostic cylinder 244
The "secret" cylinder 245
Where Files Are Stored 245
The active, or bootable, partition 245
Primary DOS partition 246
DOS extended partition 247
Other kinds of partition 247
Non-DOS operating systems that can use the DOS primary and
extended partitions 249

The Partition Table 249
   Steps to partitioning a new disk with FDISK 251
      An important WARNING 251
      How to get full use of a large hard disk 251
      When you choose to have more than one volume on a single
         disk drive 252
   Third-party disk-partitioning software 254
   A recommendation 254
A Suggestion (Only for Brave Readers!) 255
Another Recommendation 256

Chapter 10: Preparing a Hard Disk to Store Information Step Three: The Logical Format 259

The final step in preparing a hard disk for use with DOS is the logical format. This part is the only one done by using the DOS FORMAT program. In this chapter you learn what that program does. When you understand the details of the DOS data structures on your disk, you can understand how they can get messed up and have at least some idea what to do when that happens. The chapter ends with a brief discussion of some alternative kinds of logical format.

What Is a Logical Format? 259
The Logical Organization of a DOS Partition 259
The DOS boot record 260
   The data area 262
      Clusters 263
      Slack space 265
   The file allocation table 265
      The two kinds of FAT 267
      How big is your FAT? 269
   The root directory 270
   Subdirectories 272
   The volume label 274
   Recap of the structural parts 274
   How clusters become "lost" and related problems 274
   Some other ways DOS can mess things up 275
The Rest of What FORMAT Does 276
   Disk initialization 276
   A simple-minded disk test 276
   Interpretation of the DOS boot record data table 277
   How the floppy diskette format process is different 280

Alternatives to the DOS high-level format 280
UNIX 281
OS/2 and the HPFS 281
Windows NT and the NTFS 282
Novell NetWare 283
How Bad Spots Are Found and Avoided 284

Chapter 11: How Hard Disks Die 287

In this chapter, you learn all the many ways your disk drive can fail. In some of these cases, some lost data can be recovered. In other cases, you can even reverse the damage. Other options are described for dealing with the rest of the failures.

Failure Modes 287
    How to distinguish hardware failures from information
        pattern failures 291
    Simple things that sometimes go wrong 291
    Slow death by growing misalignment 294
    Data accidents 297
        A source of data accidents you may not have considered 298
        How to fix damaged data, and some popular disk utility
            packages that make it easier 299
        Destructive FORMAT programs 300
    Sudden death by drive hardware failure 301
        Stiction 301
        Spindle-bearing failure 302
        Drive electronics failures 303
        Temperature-related problems 303
        Head crashes 305
    Controller death 306
    A form of degradation that does NOT signal impending hard disk
        death — file fragmentation 308
That Laundry List of Failure Modes Is Fine, but I'd Rather You
    Just Told Me How to Fix My Ailing Hard Disk 311
    Why this assignment is tough 311
    When you can make an explicit troubleshooting chart 313
    An approach that may help 314
Data Recovery — The Hope Versus the Reality 315
Backups: What, Why, and How 316
    Three kinds of backups 317
        Full backups 317

Hard Disk SECRETS

      Incremental backups 317
         Differential backups 318
   What makes a good backup strategy "good?" 319
   How often should you back up? 319
   A good backup strategy 319
   One case where a different approach to backing up may be needed ..320
   Another use for good backups 321
Is Disk Mirroring a Substitute for Backups? 321
Some Stern Warnings and Strong Suggestions 322

PART II: The SpinRite Companion 325

Chapter 12: Reinterleaving Software: A New Category of Utility Program 327

Through a concise description of both the old and the new ways to reinterleave your hard disk, this chapter introduces one of the two main values of SpinRite. The chapter closes with a brief indication of the other benefits that such a program can have, the details of which are covered in the next chapter.

The Good Old Days 327
The Old Method 329
   Back up your data 331
   Redo the sector interleave 332
   Redo the partitioning and high-level format 332
   Restore your data 332
   Test to see whether you chose the right
      interleave value 333
   Do it again (and again) until you get it right 333
An Early Attempt to Make It Easy 333
A Better Way..334
   The essential insight 334
   A few pitfalls along the way 335
The Side Benefits (Now the Main Point of These Programs) 337
   Refreshing the sector headers 337
   Recovering "unreadable" data 340
   Moving data to safety 340
   Incidental testing of RAM and other parts of your computer 341

Chapter 13: Preventing the Slow Death of Your Hard Disk 343

This chapter explains the traditional factory analog disk surface analysis and contrasts it with the testing done by SpinRite and similar programs. After detailing how SpinRite does its tests, the chapter concludes with some recommendations for when to rely on defect information provided by the disk manufacturer and when it may safely be ignored.

How to Catch Problems Before They Become Problems 343
    A common misconception 344
    Benefits of rewriting the data 345
    Benefits of refreshing the low-level format 346
Surface Analysis — Finding the Bad Tracks, Sectors, and Clusters 347
What the Factory Tells You 349
    How they test 349
    How they report defects 351
    Why this is less helpful than it appears 352
Digital Surface Testing 353
    Worst-case paradigm 353
    What makes a case "worst" 354
    Disk surface tests 355
    An important first step 355
How the Encoding Technology Affects the Choice of
    Worst-Case Patterns 356
SpinRite's Digital Tests 356
    The test patterns 357
    Why these patterns were chosen 360
        Low-frequency test 360
        High-frequency test 360
        MFM mixed-frequency test 361
        Rapid low-high alternation test 361
        Scrambled-bits test 361
        Isolated-ones test 361
        RLL narrow-band and wide-band mixed frequency tests 361
    How the patterns are used 361
Which Way Is Best? 362

Chapter 14: Details of SpinRite's Operation 365

In this chapter, you "go under the hood" and learn in detail the algorithms that SpinRite uses to accomplish its wonders.

Getting Ready to Work 365
    SpinRite checks its own health 365

Hard Disk SECRETS

Choosing what to do and where 366
Making sure that the system memory is good enough 366
    SpinRite's scratch pads 366
        Checking the scratch pads 367
Testing the hard disk controller 367
Catching active caching 368
Watching for device driver weirdness 368
The Quick Surface Scan 369
Further Testing Before Doing Anything Serious 371
Seek and maybe you'll find a problem 371
When you may not want to do this test 372
Scoping Out the Drive — It's All a Matter of Timing 372
Breaking the code 374
Checking your interleave 375
Other calculations 375
SpinRite's Disk Analysis 375
What interleave is best? 376
Setting the interleave 377
When SpinRite can't reformat your drive 377
Data-Integrity Testing and Data Recovery 377
Reading the data 377
Low-level reformatting 379
Pattern testing 380
Recording problems 380
    On the screen and in the report 380
    In the Detailed Technical Log 381
    In the sector headers 381
Putting the data back 382
Moving data to safety 382
    Where should your data go? 383
    How will DOS find the data it moved? 383
    Telling the user where the data went 385
When the bad becomes good 385
Interrupting SpinRite 386
What is stored and where 386
When you resume 387

Chapter 15: SpinRite's Evolution **389**

This chapter describes all the versions of SpinRite and offers some recommendations regarding upgrades.

A Short History of SpinRite 389
    Various versions 389
        SpinRite Version 1.0 390
        SpinRite Version 1.1 391
        SpinRite Version 1.2, 1.2A, and 1.2B 393
        SpinRite II Version 1.0 394
        SpinRite II Version 1.1 398
        SpinRite II Version 2.0 399
    Should I upgrade? 400
The future: SpinRite 3 401
News At Deadline — SpinRite 3 Update 401
A Funny Thing Happened on the Way to Market 405

Chapter 16: Advanced User's Guide to SpinRite 407

This chapter is a guided tour that helps you learn the best ways to use SpinRite in both interactive and batch modes. Along the way, you learn much more than is contained in the product literature about how to interpret the information presented by SpinRite on-screen and in its log files. This chapter also details the need for head parking utilities and describes some that are safe and some that are dangerous. The chapter concludes with some hints and tips for achieving greater data safety and easier operation of SpinRite.

Become a SpinRite Power User 407
Get Out of Its Way! 408
The SpinRite Clean Boot Diskette Approach 411
Using DOS's CHKDSK First 414
    Why CHKDSK is needed 415
    What CHKDSK can tell you 415
    What CHKDSK might do for you 416
    What CHKDSK might do TO you 417
    How to use CHKDSK safely 417
When You Can't Fix the Problems 419
Interactive Use of SpinRite 419
    Whether to low-level reformat 420
    Should you let bad clusters become good? 420
    When to perform the seek test 420
    Choose a pattern-testing depth 421
    Create a report 422
    Something you can't do interactively 423
Batch Mode Operation 424

Hard Disk SECRETS

    Your choices and their default values 424
    Fundamental command-line options 424
    Functional command-line options 425
    Cosmetic command-line options 426
    An example of batch file usage 427
Getting Around Some Limitations 433
What Is Head Parking? 434
    Some horror stories 435
    Self-parking drives 436
    Head-parking programs 438
        Safe park programs 438
        Impolite park programs 439
        Destructive park programs 439
    Resident park utilities 441
Hints and Tips 442
    Some things to remember, always 442
    An unusual way to use SpinRite 442
    It might not be your disk 443

PART III

Part III: Appendixes 445

Appendix A: Genesis of a Product: How SpinRite Was Born 445

This appendix tells you not only how SpinRite came to be but also gives you a brief biography of its creator, Steve Gibson.

Appendix B: The Hard Disk SECRETS Disk 449

This appendix explains what the programs and data files on the Hard Disk SECRETS disk can do for you, as well as how to install and use them.

What Is on the Disk? 449
    Freeware 450
    Shareware 450
The Programs 451
    DAZZLE your eyes 451
    LIST, the much enhanced TYPE command 453

Table of Contents

  The basic LIST program 454
  Getting fancy 454
  The accompanying files 454
 The Micro House utilities 455
  MH-ESDI and MH-IDE 456
  MH-SAVE and MH-RESTR 457
  MH-SYS 458
 MOVEHDD.SYS for when disk controllers put important data in an
  imprudent place 459
 Steve Gibson's head parking program, PARK.COM 459
 TIMEPARK.COM, a head parking in time... 460
The Really Great Information File — HDINFO 460
Shareware Documentation 460
DAZZLE 461
 Registration 491
LIST 492
 Registration 528

Index 529

Installation Instructions for the *Hard Disk SECRETS* Disk 562

Reader Response Survey .... Back of Book

Foreword

Why are hard disks so hard to understand? It is true that they are very complex electro-mechanical devices, and their design involves a large number of engineering compromises. That is part of the reason. But more importantly, up until now, no one has written a book that explains simply all of that complexity and describes clearly the subtle issues behind those compromises. Now, John Goodman has written just such a book and you are holding it in your hands.

I think that you will find that his straightforward writing style moves with just the right mixture of speed and detail. The result is a readable and worthwhile book — one that fills a void in a market currently overflowing with rehashed owner's manuals and ghost-written hearsay.

A quick look through the Table of Contents reveals that this book is something different. If you have even a passing interest in the mechanisms of modern hard disk storage on IBM compatible PCs, this book is for you.

Of course, I also am delighted and flattered that John Goodman chose to focus Part II of this book on SpinRite. Although I've developed other commercially successful products in my time, none of them ever had a book written about them! I enjoyed working with John as an information source and, on the predecessor to this book, as its technical editor.

Hard disk drive reliability has been a casualty of extreme pricing pressure. The hard disk is the only complex mechanical component in the typical PC. As such, it has not been nearly as amenable to manufacturing economies of scale as mass produced solid state electronics. Many sharp engineering pencils have been dulled by the job of making hard disk drives cheaper.

The good news is also the bad news: Engineers the world over have succeeded in cheapening hard disk drives. Unfortunately they did so in both senses of the word!

The sad fact is that contemporary personal computer hard disk drives are not as reliable as they need to be to deliver years of error free operation. In the pursuit of ever-lower manufacturing costs, the engineering tolerances which create safety margins and allow handling the inevitable errors have continually been shaved. SpinRite's surprising success in the marketplace is one testament to the fact that hard disks do die daily.

Whether you're reading John's book casually for background information or from a more urgent need to find out how to recover from a recent hard disk disaster, I'm sure you'll find that the information here is presented clearly and accurately.

Here's to a future of long-term hard disk health through simple periodic maintenance and understanding.

Steve Gibson, President
Gibson Research Corporation
November, 1992

Introduction

By reading this Introduction, you can find out what reading the rest of this book can do to help make your life with computers better and easier, and your data safer. This Introduction also contains some tips to help you discover all the ways this book can benefit you, with the least effort on your part and in the shortest time.

Is This Book Meant for You?

Is this book meant for you? What a good question to be asking at the outset! If you are browsing through this Introduction in the bookstore, you want to find out as quickly as possible whether you can benefit from reading this book.

I wrote this book for three main groups of readers, and a fourth group of readers may want to read it even though I did not write it explicitly for them. From the following descriptions, you should be able to figure out whether you are in one or more of these groups.

Those who need it, now!

The first group of readers are those who really need the information in this book immediately. Members of this group have a PC, a hard disk, and — right now — a problem with that disk for which they are seeking a solution. If you are in this group, reading this book will help. You will find steps you can take that will enable you to identify and solve almost any hard disk problem.

In addition, you will find a great deal of useful and interesting information about how hard disks work. And you will get some guidance on how to make any future disk problems less serious.

Those who want to know all there is to know

You may be looking at this book because you are an information omnivore. You want to know *everything!* You will not find all you can know about everything in here, but you will find nearly all you can possibly want to know about PC hard disks somewhere in this book.

Hard Disk SECRETS

Whether you are new to PCs or have been using them for years doesn't matter. The entry-level requirements on your knowledge are very modest. On the other hand, there are enough obscure details here to satisfy the most technically inclined readers.

Those who are curious

The story of how hard disks for PCs are designed and how they work is a fascinating one. Hard disk design is built solidly on a foundation of fundamental physics, includes some very clever engineering insights, and has been molded by powerful economic considerations. The story of hard disk design history includes some accidents and many development steps, both orderly and chaotic.

This book is not an historical treatise, but it does provide the basic information you need to understand the history of these marvelous engineering achievements. You also will find a few anecdotes that connect the development of hard disks with their creators.

Those who don't have a PC or don't use DOS

Some of this material appeared previously in an IDG book called *The Official SpinRite II and Hard Disk Companion*. I was surprised to learn that some people who owned only a Macintosh or other non-IBM-style personal computer bought and read that book and found the information quite useful.

Perhaps I shouldn't have been so surprised. Hard disks in Macintosh, Amiga, Atari, NeXT, and similar small computers are the same as hard disks in PCs. In fact, hard disks in minicomputers and mainframe computers are essentially the same also. Only the operating system software support differs in these different computers.

If you are in this group, you should know that the material in Chapters 1 through 5 applies to any hard disk in virtually any modern computer, as does the material in Chapters 8 and 11. Only about one-quarter of Part I does not have that wide applicability. If yours is a non-DOS computer, even in the nominally irrelevant chapters of this book you may find a number of core ideas that apply to your computer. Those ideas simply are expressed somewhat differently by the operating system in your computer than they are by DOS.

Part II is focused directly on one class of utility program for PCs. If you don't have or use a PC, you can skip Part II.

Introduction   3

What You Need to Know Already

You wouldn't be reading this Introduction if you could not understand the language in which it is printed. That is true for any book (except pure picture books!). You will not be surprised to learn that you need to know at least a little bit more than just how to read to get much benefit from this book.

Every author makes assumptions

I am assuming that you have some knowledge of personal computers. Further, I assume that you are interested in knowing more about IBM-compatible PCs and the hard disks in them.

In this book, whenever I use the term *PC,* I mean a computer that is essentially the same as some model of personal computer built by IBM. This sameness means that the computer uses as its *central processing unit* (CPU) chip some member of the Intel 80x86 family of integrated circuit microprocessor chips or a clone of one of those chips made by a competing chip manufacturer (including AMD, Cyrix, Harris, NEC, Phoenix, and others).

[HISTORICAL ASIDE] PC stands for *personal computer*. The first personal computers were not made by IBM; they were made by companies you may never have heard of, such as MITS, IMSAI, and Southwest Technical Products.

One name you are sure to have heard is Apple Computer. Apple introduced the Apple II personal computer in April of 1977. Tandy (the parent company of Radio Shack) started selling its TRS-80 line of computers in June of 1977. These companies are two of the most widely known of a whole flock of companies that made small computers in the late 1970s and early 1980s.

In August 1981, IBM introduced its first personal computer, which was called simply the IBM Personal Computer. Shortly, the IBM Personal Computer became known as the PC. So many of them were sold that the IBM PC quickly established a new standard of computing.

IBM also told the world quite openly how its engineers had built the PC. IBM sold rather complete technical specifications for a very modest price. The company offered this information to encourage other companies to make PC-compatible add-on products and programs.

Many companies did create these products, which contributed greatly to the success of the PC. But something else also happened. Some companies did not merely make compatible add-on products; they made *clones* of the IBM PC and its younger sibling, the PC/XT. These clones, or PC-compatible computers, were so nearly identical to the original models that the standard defined by IBM became an industry-wide standard.

Hard Disk SECRETS

Two more definitions are important: one for DOS and one for PC. DOS, in this book, means any version of MS-DOS, PC DOS, or DR DOS, including any of the proprietary versions of MS-DOS created by the manufacturer of a PC-compatible brand of personal computer.

HISTORICAL ASIDE

Microsoft created PC DOS as the original operating system for IBM's PC. DOS stands for *disk operating system*. The disk operating system is the essential set of programs that activate the hardware and enable you to run *application* programs, which you use to do things such as word processing, spreadsheet analysis, communications, and database management.

Microsoft also licensed a version of PC DOS, called MS-DOS, to the makers of PC-compatible computers. Digital Research created a functionally equivalent operating system called DR DOS. (For almost all the purposes of this book, it doesn't matter which of these three brands of operating system you are using.)

For the purposes of this book, then, a PC is a machine that can run the MS-DOS operating system. (The PC need not be used in that way. Many of them are used to run UNIX, OS/2, or some other operating system; still, they can run MS-DOS if their owners want to do so.)

And I assume that you know how to turn on a PC; that you can run some simple DOS commands and PC programs; that you know what the DOS prompt is and how to create and change directories; and that you have the other basic skills needed to use a DOS-based computer.

Of course, you may not know some of these things. If you don't, read on for some suggestions about how you can help yourself get the full benefit of this book anyway.

You may need to know how to open your PC

IBM designed its PCs with the expectation that the owners of those boxes would be working on the components inside the box from time to time. You don't have to be some special sort of technical wizard to do that. Most clone makers also have that expectation, and they, as well as IBM, provide adequate documentation on how to open the case and perform tasks such as inserting or removing option cards and disk drives.

You will not find very many places in this book where I suggest that you open up your PC. If you are not comfortable with opening your PC, you can skip those parts or you can get someone else to do it for you.

If you are going to open your PC and try out some of the more advanced tips you will find here, please be sure to read carefully the advice on how to do so safely (near the end of Chapter 1 in the section "Test your new safety boot diskette"). You cannot hurt your PC by anything you type on its keyboard. You *can* hurt it by doing the wrong things — or doing the right things in the wrong ways — inside the system unit.

What to do if you don't know those things

You at least need to know the rudiments of DOS, which you can get very nicely in Dan Gookin's *DOS For Dummies.* A more thorough reference is *PC World DOS 5 Complete Handbook* by John Socha and Clint Hicks.

You also may find that you want additional information about PC hardware. This book contains all you need to know about the hard disk subsystem of your PC (that includes the hard disk controller, the cables, and the drive itself) and how that subsystem works with the rest of your PC. If you want information on other subsystems, an excellent basic resource is *PCs For Dummies* by Gookin and Andy Rathbone. All these books are published by IDG Books Worldwide and are available at your local bookstore.

How You Can Use This Book to Best Advantage

The table of contents for this book is very complete, which is intentional. You can use the table of contents as a road map to the information contained in the various chapters. The Figures at a Glance and Tables at a Glance lists may lead you directly to some crucial information you are seeking.

What's where: the big picture

You may want a very broad brush stroke version of what you can find where in this book. Here is that overview:

The Introduction you are reading now is a guide to how to use this book and to what sorts of information you can expect to find here. Chapter 1 serves two purposes: telling you why you should study the rest of the book and giving you some important safety tips.

The rest of Part I (Chapters 2 through 11) explains all that you are likely to want to know about PC hard disks, including how they work, the many ways they can die, and how to recover from most of those deaths. (When a hard disk dies, it often is merely exhibiting its underlying imperfections — imperfections that have been hidden up until then by some very clever engineering tricks that also are explained in Part I.)

Part II is an in-depth look at the popular hard disk utility SpinRite, from Gibson Research. This part describes what that program does and why it is important. Part II also goes into a great deal of detail about how the program does its job. When you finish Part II, you will know more about this program than is known publicly about almost any other commercial PC software other than DOS itself.

Three ways to read the book the first time through

You may think that you are holding just one book in your hands. Actually, you can view this book as three or four different works, all bound into one.

The first path through this book is for anyone with a moderately high level of curiosity about hard disks, a willingness to study them in detail, and enough time to do that. This path is the obvious one: just read every paragraph, one after another.

The second path through the book is for people who are not necessarily very knowledgeable about PCs or who don't have much time or patience for nitty-gritty details. If that describes you, simply skip over any sections that are marked as Technical Secrets. These technical sections are included to provide additional detail for readers who want to understand hard disks more fully. A Technical Secrets signpost marks the start of each section of technical text, and a vertical rule extends the length of the technical text. The design makes it especially easy for you to skip directly to the next paragraph after such a section.

The Technical Secrets design especially aids the technical experts who want to use the third path through this book — those who are in a hurry to see what new and very technical information they can glean from the book. These readers should do exactly the opposite of those who are following track two. If you are one of these readers, go directly to each Technical Secret signpost, read the text, and then jump on to the next such section.

Those approaches are the three main ways to read this book initially. The fourth way to use this book is as a reference work, reading wherever you see something you want to learn about, and jumping out again after you have satisfied that particular need to know. I expect that most readers will use the book in this fourth way after going through it once by following one of the first three paths. The index has been prepared with particular care to help you find places in the book that may help you learn anything you wonder about in the general subject area of hard disks and PCs.

Introduction   7

Conventions used to help you

You have been introduced to the Technical Secrets design. In addition, this book includes design elements (you have already encountered the Historical Aside icon) to assist you in locating specific kinds of information. The following descriptions provide a brief rundown on how these "visual aids" can assist you:

TECHNICAL SECRET

The Technical Secret signpost flags those sections containing the highest level of detail and jargon. You may want to avoid, or go directly to, these paragraphs, depending on who you are and what you want from this book.

The Caution icon alerts you to hazardous possibilities. Please read the caution paragraphs very carefully! You really want to know this information; if you don't, you may end up irreparably harming your data or your PC hardware.

The Tip icon leads you to helpful suggestions. Tips are intended for every reader.

Paragraphs marked with the Historical Aside icon are tangential to the main story this book tells, but they are too interesting to leave out. You don't need to read them, but you probably will enjoy doing so.

The Disk icon points out references in the text to programs contained on the *Hard Disk SECRETS* disk that accompanies this book.

Sidebars

Sidebars offer background information, an expanded discussion, or an interesting sidelight to a topic under discussion in the body text.

New terms, variables, and words that carry emphasis appear in *italic* type.

Commands you are to type appear in **bold** type.

On-screen information appears in a `special typeface`.

What the *Hard Disk SECRETS* Disk Adds to the Book

The disk accompanying this book has three kinds of files on it. The first is a collection of hard disk utility programs created by Micro House. These programs include some capabilities you will find nowhere else. The second is an extensive listing of hard disk drives, which was created by Ray Martin and Martin Development Services. In addition to these highlights of the *Hard Disk SECRETS* disk, I have included a copy of the superb file-viewing utility LIST, which was written by Vernon Buerg, and a couple of Mr. Buerg's other programs. Finally, you will find on the disk a small device driver that may help you free up to 16KB more upper memory for other programs and three different head-parking programs (one of which also is a marvelous screen saver). You can find details on how to install these programs and how to use them in Appendix B.

You can use some of the Micro House utilities in creating your own personal safety-boot diskette (see Chapter 1 for details). Other utilities help you learn more about your hard disk (at least if you have an IDE or ESDI drive; see Chapter 3 for details).

Because Ray Martin's HDINFO files are pure ASCII (that is, they contain no special graphics or formatting information), you easily can view them by using the LIST program. That program also has a search capability that can help you find exactly those lines or columns of information of most interest to you. (The HDINFO file is large enough that this help is most welcome!)

The Micro House utilities are *freeware,* which means that they are copyrighted works, and the author has made some very special stipulations about how you are allowed to use these products. You can share these utilities with anyone, and the author does not expect any payment from you or those with whom you share them. The same applies to Ray Martin's HDINFO files. Both authors only ask that you not modify the files and that you supply the full set of them (either the HDINFO set or the MH utility set) to whomever you choose to share them with.

The LIST and DAZZLE programs are *shareware,* which means that you are entitled to use them on a trial basis without charge. You also are free to give them to anyone else. (Again, please don't modify the files, and give the whole collection to your recipient.) The difference between shareware and freeware is that if you choose to continue using the shareware programs, you are obliged (legally, ethically, and morally) to pay the authors a registration fee.

Please do register any shareware you use. Everyone benefits when you do so. The authors get paid, which means that they can afford to continue to create and support good shareware. And that means you and everyone else will have even more great, affordable software to use in the future.

Introduction

An Invitation

I want to hear from you. Please write to me with your reactions to this book, including any corrections you want to offer me.

I also want to hear either your horror stories or your glory stories. In other words, I want to hear about the times you really hated your PC's hard disk for what it did to you, but I also want to hear about the times you loved how well you were able to do something with or to it because you understood how a PC's hard disk works.

Send your letters to:

John M. Goodman, Ph.D.
P. O. Box 746
Westminster, CA 92684-0746

PART I

The Hard Disk Companion

Page

- **13** | **Chapter 1**
  Why Hard Disks Matter So Much

- **33** | **Chapter 2**
  Magnetic Storage of Information

- **69** | **Chapter 3**
  Some Important Engineering Issues

- **101** | **Chapter 4**
  Messy Hard Disk Details

- **151** | **Chapter 5**
  Disk Caching

- **169** | **Chapter 6**
  Hard Disks Under DOS

- **207** | **Chapter 7**
  Bumping Up Against and Breaking Barriers

- **227** | **Chapter 8**
  Preparing a Hard Disk to Store Information
     Step One: The Physical (Low-Level) Format

- **237** | **Chapter 9**
  Preparing a Hard Disk to Store Information
     Step Two: Partitioning

- **259** | **Chapter 10**
  Preparing a Hard Disk to Store Information
     Step Three: The Logical Format

- **287** | **Chapter 11**
  How Hard Disks Die

Chapter 1
Why Hard Disks Matter So Much

In This Chapter
- The true value of your PC's hard disk
- Accidents aren't necessarily disasters
- How to protect your valuable data
- How to improve your hard disk's performance
- How to use MH-SAVE to save your sanity when your PC glitches
- How to help make your next encounter with a hard disk death a mere annoyance, not a major disaster

A Hard Disk Is Not Just Another Peripheral Device

Why, you may be wondering, should you read a book all about hard disks? Do you really need to know all that much about them? Maybe you are just curious about how your hard drive works. In that case, you don't need any convincing. You could jump directly to Chapter 2, but please don't. You may need to learn some of the information in this chapter to properly protect your disk and its data.

Probably you can get away without a full understanding of your PC's hard disk, but the more you know about how it is designed and how it works — and the more you know about how it can fail — the more successful you will be when you have to cope with a failure of that disk drive. And make no mistake, such a failure will happen someday, maybe some day very soon.

Or worse, perhaps that day already has come. In that case, you probably started reading this book at Chapter 11. Perhaps you returned here because that chapter suggests that you'd do well to read this chapter first. In this chapter, you may find some helpful reassurance and gain some valuable perspective on your problem. Of course, the hard disk is not the only part of your PC that can die. Why is it so much more important that you understand the failure potential of your hard disk than that of, say, your video card or printer port card?

Hard disks are the most expensive pieces of hardware in your PC

You can find one answer to that question by looking at the cost of the various parts of your PC. In most cases, the hard disk turns out to be the most expensive single piece of hardware in the PC. Yes, some very highly integrated computers have more value in the motherboard, especially if the hard disk in such a PC is not a large capacity one. But even then the hard disk costs almost as much as the motherboard.

A printer port card, on the other hand, certainly can be replaced for less than $100 — quite probably for much less. But perhaps your PC has a very highly integrated motherboard that includes serial and parallel ports. If one of those ports fails, you are looking at the cost of a new motherboard. Your prospects, even in this extreme case, are not quite that grim. Usually, if a port on that motherboard fails, you can disable the dysfunctional port and replace its functionality with a new, inexpensive plug-in option card.

Hard disks die more frequently than other parts

Hard disks have moving parts. They run constantly, whenever your PC is turned on. Things that have moving parts generally wear out more quickly than those that don't. Hard disks are *not* an exception to this rule.

Floppy disk drives also have moving parts; however, they only run when you use them, which for most of us is not all that often. The fan in the power supply is the only other moving part that often fails in a PC. (And when the fan dies, the power supply is effectively dead. Replace it. Don't even think of repairing it because the repair is simply not feasible or cost effective these days.)

After these moving parts, the components in your PC that are most likely to fail are any large electrolytic capacitors that are mostly found in the power supply. The life of these capacitors is drastically curtailed when they are forced to work at a higher temperature, so you can help them last longer by keeping the PC's ventilation holes uncovered.

Some portable PCs offer special *power management* features. These features likely include the option of specifying a time interval after which the hard disk "goes to sleep." In other words, the PC turns itself off any time you have not accessed it for more than the specified time interval. If your PC offers this option, and if you run it on its internal batteries a lot, you can benefit a great deal from activating the option. Be aware, though, that you are not necessarily extending the hard disk's life by using this option — indeed, you could be shortening it! The hardest moments in your hard disk's life happen each time it is turned on, so you may want to choose a relatively long interval of inactivity before the power management feature puts your PC to sleep.

Hard disks hold something even more valuable

A hard disk is a valuable piece of hardware. But even more valuable is the information that you store there. This value stems from all the time and work you have invested in the creation and maintenance of the information.

Your data are irreplaceable. You can go out and buy another copy of any commercial programs you use, but the data you generate by using the programs is uniquely yours.

HISTORICAL ASIDE

Fire insurance companies say that most small businesses that suffer a fire and thereafter go out of business do so *not* because they lose buildings or furnishings and equipment; they fail as businesses because they lose their data (especially if they lose their accounts receivable).

Your first line of defense is a very good set of back-up copies of your data. It is also a good idea to create and save copies of your programs exactly as you installed them on your disks. In this chapter, the section "Be prepared: have a perfect backup" tells you what constitutes a very good set of backups.

But sometimes human frailty strikes. You may find that you haven't got a perfect set of backups and your hard disk has quit working. When that happens, you truly come to appreciate the value of your hard disk, or, more particularly, you appreciate the value of the information it contains.

If you choose to have data recovered from a really badly crashed hard drive, you need the expert (and costly!) services of some very specialized companies. Chapter 11 includes information on how to contact a couple of them.

Often a Broken Hard Disk Can Be Fixed — Sometimes Easily

Because your most valuable computer possession is your data, and because your data exist on your hard disk, you may be excused for feeling a touch of panic when your hard disk fails. That feeling happens to all of us.

Of course, if you are absolutely certain that your backups are totally current and completely reliable, you may be quite unruffled by even the most dramatic disk failure. Actually, you can be somewhat reassured, even if your backups are less than perfect, just by knowing that the odds are with you. The very good news is that often you can fix whatever went wrong with your hard disk. Frequently, fixing the problem isn't even difficult. Not all disk failures are forever.

First of all, data failures are the most common of all disk problems. And those failures are "merely" a case of some bit of information stored somewhere in your PC getting messed up. Put it right again, and bingo! your PC's disk will work perfectly once more.

Naturally, before you can apply that insight, you have to learn how to tell whether your PC hard disk problem is a data failure or actually reflects a real hardware failure. And after you know the kind of failure you are faced with, you need to know exactly what to do about it.

A Little Knowledge Can Be a Powerful Thing

The details of all the many ways hard disks can die and what to do about each kind of hard disk death are the subjects of Chapter 11. You will be better prepared to understand what is in Chapter 11 if you first read Chapters 2 through 10. And before you read that background information, you should read the following sections to learn how another aspect of the knowledge you will gain can be of great help to you.

Carelessness is bad — panic is worse

Most PC accidents happen when the user does something ill-advised. Yes, hard disks do break all on their own, but that isn't nearly as common as incidents of the user deleting some files imprudently or making any of a number of other simple mistakes.

When something happens to your PC, especially if that something means you can't get at all the data on your hard disk, panic is a likely consequence. If you find yourself in that situation, get up, go away from your PC, and take some time to calm down. Call a friend. Talk out your troubles. Don't try to be macho and tough it out. When you are panicky, you aren't a very good repair person.

Remember, too, that in all likelihood, you *can* solve your problem — or find someone else who can solve it for you. You really don't have any good reason for panic. Just remembering that fact can do a lot to help you calm down.

Chapter 1: Why Hard Disks Matter So Much

Don't throw out the baby with the bath water

Most failures of a hard disk subsystem in a PC are caused by really minor things. Just changing the wrong number in the wrong place the least little bit is enough to render your whole hard disk inaccessible. Sure, major, catastrophic hard disk failures do happen, but they are relatively rare.

Too often, a person's first impulse when facing a problem with a hard disk is to assume that the worst possibility has, in fact, occurred. The next thought is that the disk needs low-level reformatting. (Maybe that thought has never occurred to you — for the simple reason that you don't know what the phrase means. In Chapter 8, you learn both what low-level format means and why performing one usually is *not* the right thing to do at such a time.)

Try the easy things first. Only if you cannot revive your disk after you have tried all the easy solutions is it time to go to the next level and try the medium-hard things. After you have exhausted the medium solutions is plenty soon enough to consider the really tough, drastic steps.

Low-level reformatting is one such drastic step, which should be something you consider only after you have checked out a whole host of simpler remedies. Indeed, you cannot always do a low-level format unless you have first attended to those earlier steps. (And with some disk drives, you cannot do low-level reformatting at all.)

The final recourse is to replace some of or all the hardware pieces in your PC's hard disk subsystem. Some of those pieces are much cheaper than others. Changing certain of them means you will lose your data for sure. Changing others may allow you to recover your data. Again, knowledge is the key to doing a wise job of troubleshooting and repair.

Get help when you need it

Sometimes, what you most need to recognize is that you don't know enough to solve your current problem. What you next need to know is how to find someone who *can* solve it. That knowledge is all you really need to have (as long as you use it).

Where can you turn to find an expert to help you? If you have someone who regularly solves your PC problems you are in luck. You know who to turn to. But if you don't have someone in mind, you can ask your friends for their recommendations. If your company has a PC coordinator, ask that person for advice.

An uncommon PC fixer

Aside from those tips that are the usual pieces of common wisdom about finding PC fixers, here is one that is far too uncommon, yet often is much better: Find a PC user group in your area. Seek help there.

User groups are voluntary associations of people with a shared interest. Among the members are people who know more than you do, as well as some who know less. Share what you know and learn from those who know more. As with any all-volunteer group, user groups work best when everyone involved gives as well as expects to get.

Many user groups operate BBSs that are free to their members, or maybe even free to anyone. Post a message on such a BBS and you very likely will get a lot of advice in just a few days. Because most of the callers to these bulletin board systems are from the immediate vicinity, you may even find a competent helper among those who answer your query.

Be careful. Not all self-proclaimed PC experts know how to solve hard disk problems. After you have read this book, you may know as much as or more than many of them. Listen to the advice you get: sound out the people you are considering relying on to see what approaches they plan to use and why. If you are uncomfortable with what you hear, seek another opinion from someone else before you let anyone mess with your valuable data.

If you bought your computer from a dealer, ask the dealer for help or a recommendation of someone good to rely on. If you are sure your problem is with the hard disk in your PC, the company that made the drive may be able to help you or steer you to someone who can. Call the manufacturer's technical support line or check out the information on any electronic bulletin board system (BBS) the company may operate.

Another valuable resource is the CompuServe Information Service. CompuServe and other on-line services have forums in which you can ask questions and get answers from some highly competent folk. (Many manufacturers sponsor forums on CompuServe. In those cases, you can get help from the very people who made the drive, the PC, or the programs you may be worried about. You also can hear from experts not associated with the makers of those pieces of hardware and software. Outside experts can give you advice that is not tinged with the self-interest of those who work for the manufacturers.)

If you are bashful, browse among the questions others have posted. Maybe your question has already been asked and answered. You pay something to use CompuServe and most other subscription information services of that type, but the information you find there can easily be worth the cost.

Data Cannot Be Insured; You Have to Provide Your Own Protection

By now you know that your hard disk itself is probably not nearly as valuable as the data you have on it. You may have an insurance policy to protect your investment in hardware. Some insurance policies even protect your investment in commercial software. But *you* have to protect your custom programs and your data. No insurance company can help you get those programs and data back if you really, truly lose them.

Even floppy disks fail. Keeping important files only on a floppy disk is no solution, unless you have multiple copies of each one and keep the copies in different buildings.

All disks die; it's only a matter of when

If you have only one copy of your data and that copy is on your hard disk, you will lose your data someday. Be perfectly clear about this fact. Remember this adage:

> There are only two kinds of hard disk: those that have died, and those that will die.

Be prepared: have a perfect backup

The very best protection you can have is a perfect set of backups of all your programs and data files. If you have those backups, when your hard disk dies, you have a way to recover all the information the disk sent to "bit heaven" as it died.

Be sure that you don't become a victim of false security. Check to make sure that your backups work. Do this check periodically. All too often, people don't test their backups until they need them. Then they find out that they cannot actually restore their files — or not all of them — from those backups. If even one file cannot be restored accurately, and if it is one of those you really needed, then the backups have failed to serve their purpose.

Of course, you shouldn't leap to the conclusion that your disk has died. Don't needlessly throw away what may be a perfectly serviceable piece of rather expensive hardware. First, determine for sure that you cannot revive your hard disk.

If, after suitable checks, you discover that your hard disk really is dead, you can replace it with a new one. (A piece of nice news: you probably can buy a new hard disk with a larger capacity than your old disk and still pay no more for it than you originally paid for the old one.)

After you have gotten a new disk installed in your PC, you just have to restore your programs and data from your (presumably nearly perfect) backups. Then you are ready to go back to work. With such a perfect set of backups, a hard disk death is an annoyance and an expense to be sure, but it is nothing worse than that. Without perfect backups, however, a hard disk failure can be anything from a major headache to a full-fledged disaster.

TIP: Use this opportunity to reorganize how you use your hard disk. Very likely you will have some better ideas now than you did when you first set up this disk's predecessor.

As Figure 1-1 states, a perfect backup is whatever it takes to get you back up and running after a hard disk failure, in the minimum amount of time and with the minimum amount of grief. As a reminder, you can copy Figure 1-1 and put it where you will see it often.

Chapter 11 includes a further discussion of the different kinds of backup (full, incremental, and differential) and how to use them. That chapter also describes some programs you may find helpful in creating and maintaining your backups.

> **A perfect backup is whatever it takes to get you back up and running after a hard disk failure, in the minimum amount of time and with the minimum amount of grief.**

Figure 1-1: A worthwhile thought to hang over your computer.

More ways to protect against your own mistakes

Most losses of data on a hard disk are not consequences of any failure of the hard disk system. They are, instead, consequences of user mistakes. You can develop a number of simple habits to minimize those mistakes.

Use programs that help you do what you intend with your files and not what you don't intend. One type of program that many people find very helpful is a DOS shell program. Starting with Version 4, DOS includes one such program, DOSSHELL. Only with Version 5, however, has that program become good enough to be acceptable to most users. Fortunately, many excellent third-party programs, such as XTreeGold, are available to do this job.

If you run Windows, you can get similar benefits from a good Windows file manager. The one included with Windows 3.0 (called, you won't be surprised to know, File Manager) was widely perceived to be inadequate. In Windows 3.1, the file manager has been very much improved — enough that you may not need an alternative. But if you want one, you can choose from many good alternatives, including Norton Desktop for Windows.

> **TIP** If you use any DOS shell program or Windows file manager, be sure to permanently turn on the feature that asks you for confirmation before it deletes a file or directory.

Save copies of critical disk information structures. Again, there are many ways to accomplish this task. Starting with Version 5, DOS includes a program called MIRROR that can perform this task. Used without any parameters, MIRROR saves most of the critical information. (You have to rerun MIRROR on each of your logical drives.) Used with the /PART option, MIRROR saves another portion of the critical information. And used as a "terminate-and-stay-resident" (TSR) program with the /T*d* option (where *d* is a drive letter), MIRROR can keep the saved information up-to-date.

The MIRROR program was dropped from DOS 6. Most of its functions are now in UNDELETE. The partition table saving feature (/ PART) is not, however. Fortunately, you now have an even better way to deal with this possible problem.

> **DISK** The program MH-SAVE.EXE included on the disk that accompanies this book can do all this and more. Appendix B describes MH-SAVE.EXE.

Finally, be sure to study carefully and follow the suggestions in the section "Be prepared: create a safety boot diskette" later in this chapter.

Make Your Hard Disk Run Better As Well As More Safely

While you are developing good habits that help you protect your files, you may as well also do some things to help you improve your productivity with the files and increase the speed with which DOS can help you, too.

Good organization helps both you and DOS

Organizing your hard disk is a very large topic and somewhat tangential to the main focus of this book. Many books and articles have been written to show readers how to organize programs and data on their hard disks. I simply want to alert you to the importance of organization and suggest that you refer to one or another of the many excellent references and guides that may help you. One of those publications is the *Official XTree MS-DOS, Windows, and Hard Disk Management Companion*. This book by Beth Slick, now in its 3rd Edition, is published by IDG Books Worldwide.

One reason for bringing up this topic here is that you need to consider it before you can make an intelligent decision about how to partition your hard disk. In Chapter 9, you learn all about what disk partitioning is and how to do it. Chapter 9 does not cover, however, *all* the things you need to consider when deciding how large to make each partition. You also must take into account how you are going to organize and access your files.

Indeed, as you continue to work with your PC and accumulate more and more programs and data files, you may find that you need to redo the partitioning of your hard disk. When that happens, review Chapter 9 and whatever other sources you value on the topic of hard disk organization. That information will help you do the repartitioning in the easiest and most helpful manner.

You can do several things to help keep track of all the files you have. One such task is to organize your files into meaningful groups and then place each group into a subdirectory of its own. Another is to group related subdirectories under some other subdirectory.

What may surprise you is that not only will this organization help *you* keep track of your files, it also will help DOS find and deliver files more quickly. You learn why later in this book, especially in Chapter 10.

Speeding up your disk also helps

You can do two more useful things, besides organizing your files and directory structure, for optimum performance. One of these things is to defragment your disk periodically. The other is to get the sector interleave value (and possibly the head and cylinder skew) set correctly. (*Defragmenting* your disk means rearranging the chunks of information it holds so that all the pieces that make up each individual file are stored next to one another. *Interleave* and *skew* refer to how the physical sectors get numbered going around one track and how that numbering pattern shifts from track to track.)

The first of these topics, disk fragmentation, is covered in Chapter 11. That chapter also points out some of the better programs you can get to help you defragment your hard disk.

Sector interleave and head and cylinder skewing are pretty arcane ideas. You may never have heard those terms before. They can be important ones for you to understand, though, and fortunately, that understanding can be accomplished quite easily. Chapter 3 explains these concepts in terms almost anyone can understand, although it does require some careful reading and thought. Chapter 12 explains both the traditional and a more modern way of deciding what the optimum values are for these numbers on your hard disk. That chapter also describes how to change those numbers.

Recovering from Disaster — Some Suggestions

I have said it before, and I will say it again: *If your hard disk has not yet died, be warned that it will. All hard disks die eventually.* Even if you are among the lucky ones whose disks are working just fine (so far), you, too, will benefit from reading this section carefully and following its suggestions.

Be prepared: create a safety boot diskette

Perhaps the most important tool in your arsenal when you have any kind of problem with your PC's hard disk is your *safety boot diskette*. A friend of mine calls it the "save your fanny" diskette. By any name, a safety boot diskette is a wonderful aid.

A safety boot diskette is a diskette with which you can boot your PC no matter what happens to your hard disk. This diskette also enables you to access your hard disk in the case of all but the most serious kinds of hard disk failure. In its simplest form, a safety boot diskette is a bootable DOS diskette with a few extra important files on it; however, it is much more than that.

Start with the system files

As you may know, a diskette is bootable only if it was formatted properly and has some *system files* on it. (The system files are essential parts of the DOS operating system that are contained in some special files on the disk. These files have been entered in the directory in a way that keeps them from showing up when you use DIR to list the disk's contents. You can tell they are there by using the CHKDSK command and reading its report of hidden files and the bytes they contain.)

The easiest way to create such a bootable diskette is to use the command **FORMAT A: /S.** If you create this diskette after you have booted your computer from the hard drive, you can be sure that the version of DOS on the diskette is the same as the version you just booted from. This exact match is very important.

TECHNICAL SECRET

A bootable DOS diskette has, at a minimum, a boot sector, two hidden system files, and a command interpreter — all created by, or a part of, the same version of DOS. If you format a diskette and make it bootable by using MS-DOS, or one of most of the clone versions of DOS, the hidden files are called MSDOS.SYS and IO.SYS. If you use PC DOS or DR DOS, the hidden filenames are IBMBIO.COM and IBMDOS.COM. Some of the clone versions of MS-DOS use other, proprietary names.

The *boot record* is created when the disk is formatted. Among other things, the boot record contains the names of the system files it expects to find on the disk. If you merely format the diskette, without also putting the system files on, you can make the diskette bootable at a later time by copying those files to the diskette.

You can add the system files by using the DOS command SYS. But watch out. If you use one brand of DOS to do the formatting and a different brand of DOS to "SYS" the disk, you may find that it is not a bootable DOS diskette if the system filenames in the two brands differ. Because you cannot see the filenames on a DIR listing of the disk contents, you might not catch this slip right away. And catching it only by finding out that your supposed safety boot diskette won't boot when you need it is a horrible time to learn about the problem!

All versions of DOS use the file COMMAND.COM as the command interpreter, although you can replace COMMAND.COM with any of a number of alternatives. Perhaps the most popular alternatives are the shareware product 4DOS.COM and NDOS.COM, which is a part of the Norton Utilities (Version 6 and later). To change the command interpreter, you must have a CONFIG.SYS file on the disk from which you will be booting, and the disk must have a SHELL statement that specifies the command interpreter's name and location.

Your safety boot diskette should use whatever command interpreter you normally use. Naturally, this requirement means that the safety boot diskette must have a suitable CONFIG.SYS file if you use anything other than a copy of COMMAND.COM in the root directory.

> ### Be prepared for disaster
>
> You want your safety boot diskette to bring you back from the brink of disaster. Creation of this diskette is no time to be messing around with nonstandard techniques of dubious reliability!
>
> If you have a low-density drive A (one that can read and write only diskettes that hold 360KB [5-¼"] or 720KB [3-½"]), you must use a low-density diskette. If you have a high-density drive A (one that can read and write diskettes with capacities of 1.2MB, 1.44MB, or 2.88MB), you may think you can use either a low- or a high-density diskette for your safety boot diskette; read on.
>
> Although high-density drives can read and write low-density diskettes, they are not quite as reliable when doing that as when reading the diskettes for which they were primarily designed. (Even worse is using a low-density diskette as if it were a high-density one. Some drives may let you get away with this method, but then reliability really suffers.)

It also is important that you use drive A when creating your bootable floppy diskette. If drive B is a different size, a disk prepared in it cannot be used later to boot your computer because, typically, a PC can boot only from either drive A (the first floppy disk drive) or drive C (the first hard disk drive). You might be tempted to use drive B if its capacity is the same as drive A. That choice could be okay, but it might not be. Some drives are not quite properly aligned. A disk written in such a drive can be read in the same drive; however, another nominally identical but differently aligned drive may or may not be able to read the disk.

Add some customization files

In addition to the system files necessary for booting, your safety boot diskette should include special versions of the CONFIG.SYS and AUTOEXEC.BAT files that you normally use on your hard disk. The CONFIG.SYS and AUTOEXEC.BAT files tell DOS how to customize itself each time your PC is booted. You want them on your safety boot diskette to be sure that DOS is built the way you expect and need it for optimum disaster recovery.

The special files you create will have some details in common with the original files, but they should be different for two important reasons:

- When your PC is acting up, a good strategy is to get very simple in your dealings with it. Simplify your CONFIG.SYS and AUTOEXEC.BAT files as much as you can for the version you use on your safety boot diskette. Don't invoke some fancy memory manager. Only load the truly necessary device drivers and TSR programs.

- You want to be able to use the safety boot diskette to access your PC even when the hard disk is totally inaccessible. To have that capability, all files referred to in the CONFIG.SYS and AUTOEXEC.BAT files must be on your safety boot diskette. Further, the path references to those files must point to them on drive A.

Add some optional files

One other group of files that are not necessary for a simple bootable DOS diskette but belong on your safety boot diskette are those that store and can help you restore the contents of your PC's configuration CMOS memory. Two ideal choices are MH-RESTR.EXE (on the *Hard Disk SECRETS* disk) and the data file created by MH-SAVE.EXE (on the same disk) for your PC's hard drive.

MH-SAVE can save just the configuration CMOS contents (including the extended CMOS contents if your PC has them), or it can save that information and much more. Be aware of the following conditions when you choose what to save:

- If you save only the CMOS information, you do not need to update your safety boot diskette unless you change either the brand or version of DOS you use on your hard disk, or change some setting in the CMOS (which normally is done only if you are changing the hardware configuration of your machine).

- If you use MH-SAVE to create a full safety backup data file, that file becomes out of date as soon as you alter some of the files on your hard disk. You have to re-create this backup data file frequently if you want to gain the full protection it can offer. See Appendix B for details.

TECHNICAL SECRET

The MH-SAVE program normally creates a data file that describes all the important parts of one physical hard drive. If you have two physical drives, MH-SAVE creates such a file for each drive.

Depending on the number of logical drives (DOS drive letters) you have in your system, these files can get quite large. They can become so large that they won't fit on the safety boot diskette along with the other files you must have. In that case, you can use one or more options on the command line to tell MH-SAVE to store less information about your hard drive. See Appendix B for the details on how to accomplish this task.

Now, fill up the diskette

Fill up the rest of the space on your safety boot diskette with various useful utility programs. Some of the most useful are the DOS programs CHKDSK, FDISK, and FORMAT. (Be sure that they are from the same version of DOS as the hidden system files.) If you cannot fit all that you want on the safety boot diskette, you can put the overflow onto another diskette. This point is more fully covered later in this chapter in the section, "Keep other useful diskettes handy."

Chapter 1: Why Hard Disks Matter So Much

Additional utility programs that you may consider adding to the safety boot diskette are MH-SYS, which you can find on the *Hard Disk SECRETS* disk, and the Disk Editor program (called NU in Version 4.5 and earlier) from the Norton Utilities.

Test your new safety boot diskette

The last three steps in creating a safety boot diskette are very important: Write-protect the safety boot diskette. Test the safety boot diskette. Using DISKCOPY, make a copy of the diskette, write-protect that copy, and keep one copy next to the PC and the other copy in another building. Don't fail to follow each step. Until you have completed all three steps, your level of protection is minimal.

A fairly good test of your safety boot diskette is to boot off this diskette. If you have a typical desktop PC, you can do better. (The following instructions assume that you have a clone PC of the usual design. If you have an IBM PS/2 or other Micro Channel Architecture machine, some of the details on removing or disconnecting the hard drive's power may be slightly different. Consult your PC's documentation for the details.)

Before working inside your PC's system unit, make sure that you park your PC's hard disk and then turn off the PC. Unplug all the cables and power cords connected to the PC system unit. Then you may open it up safely. (The reason for unplugging every cable is to be sure that electricity has no path to flow back from the PC to ground, in addition to being sure that you have no way to come into contact with line voltage. This precaution protects you from electrocution and gives an additional measure of protection to your PC from possible damage by static electric discharge.)

Your PC is much more vulnerable after you open it up. Be very sure that *each and every time you reach inside* the system unit (which you do in the next few steps), you touch the power supply or the PC chassis before you touch anything else. This touch ensures that any static electric charge you deliver to the PC is safely carried to its case and does not flow through some integrated circuit chip. If such a discharge did flow through a chip, the electricity easily could fry that chip.

If your only hard disk is mounted on an option card (or if that one is drive C), unscrew the hold-down screw and carefully remove the hard-disk card from the PC. If, on the other hand, your hard disk is mounted separately from the option cards, you simply can unplug the cable that connects your hard disk to the PC power supply. (You have to unplug this cable where it connects to the hard disk; ordinarily, the other end is attached permanently to the power supply.)

Put your new safety boot diskette into drive A. Turn on your PC. Be sure that the computer can boot correctly and that you get no unexpected error messages during that process. Look especially for any messages about DOS not being able to find some device driver. (If you have an AT or higher level computer, you will get one message that says something like Bad or missing C

Part I: The Hard Disk Companion

drive. Because you know you removed or disabled your hard drive, you expect that error message.) When you finish with the test, turn off power, reconnect the hard disk power cable, and close up the PC.

The following steps summarize the procedure you should use when creating a safety boot diskette. Follow these steps and then keep that diskette close at hand at all times:

1. Boot your computer from the hard disk. Get to a DOS prompt on drive C.

2. Put a floppy diskette into drive A. Use a diskette that matches the maximum capacity of that drive. (If you have a 1.2MB drive, for example, use a 1.2MB floppy; don't use a 360KB diskette.)

3. Type **FORMAT A: /S /V** and press Enter. Give the diskette any name you want; just make sure that you do give it a name. (If you are using DOS 5, add a colon and a name after the *V* to give the disk a volume label. In earlier versions of DOS, if you include the */V* switch on the command line without a name or colon after it, DOS prompts you for the name when it finishes the formatting.)

4. Create minimal CONFIG.SYS and AUTOEXEC.BAT files on the floppy diskette. (Remember that your goal is to allow access to your hard disk. Make sure that you include any device drivers or TSR programs you need for that purpose. Don't include any device drivers or TSR programs that are not necessary, nor any memory-management programs.) Include these lines in your AUTOEXEC.BAT file:

   ```
   PATH=A:\DOS;A:\UTIL;A:\VIRSTUFF
   PROMPT $P $G
   ```

5. Create DATA, DOS, UTIL, and VIRSTUFF directories on your floppy diskette.

6. Copy the DOS programs CHKDSK, FDISK, and FORMAT to the A:\DOS directory.

7. Copy the programs MH-SYS and MH-RESTR from the *Hard Disk SECRETS* disk to the A:\UTIL directory. (If you have the Norton Utilities, Version 5 or later, copy Disk Editor to this directory also.)

8. Copy your favorite virus-scanning utility program to the A:\VIRSTUFF directory.

9. Type **MH-SAVE /BA:\DATA\DATA.FIL /C** and press Enter. (This procedure assumes that you have put the *Hard Disk SECRETS* disk programs into a directory on your hard disk that is currently on the PATH.) Optionally, you may choose to let MH-SAVE store more information about your hard disk, at the cost of more room on your safety boot diskette. (See Appendix B for a complete discussion of this point.)

10. Copy as many other utility programs of your choice as will fit into A:\UTIL.

Chapter 1: Why Hard Disks Matter So Much

> **⚠ CAUTION**
>
> **DOS and OS/2**
>
> Some people have installed both DOS and OS/2 on their PCs. Starting with OS/2 2.0, this installation can be accomplished in two dramatically different ways. IBM calls one method their Dual Boot method and the other Boot Manager method.
>
> The difference is important, especially in the context of a safety boot diskette. If you use the IBM OS/2 Dual Boot strategy, your PC will always boot to the same operating system it was last using. If your hard disk dies while OS/2 is the current operating system, and especially if you had installed OS/2 into an HPFS (High Performance File System) logical drive, you may need to have a second safety boot diskette prepared with the essential OS/2 boot files. (Some OS/2 CMD files [similar to DOS batch files] are available from IBM and on various BBSs to help you create the second OS/2 safety boot diskette.)
>
> If you use IBM's Boot Manager strategy (which you can use for multiple versions of DOS as well as for DOS and OS/2, and you can use a variety of programs to do it), you don't need to worry. You can recover from a hard disk failure with only one (DOS-based) safety boot diskette.

11. Test your safety boot diskette.

12. Make a backup copy of this diskette by using DISKCOPY.

13. Write-protect both copies.

14. Put one copy near the PC and the other copy in another building.

15. Update your safety boot diskette (by following these steps) each time you change the brand or version of DOS you use on your hard disk. You also need to update the DATA.FIL file *at least* each time you make any significant change to your hardware configuration (which means you changed the contents of the configuration CMOS). If you have chosen to let MH-SAVE store more information about your hard disk, update the data file each time you change any aspects of what is stored on your hard disk. (Appendix B explains this issue in more detail.)

16. Repeat this procedure for each PC you have. Each PC needs a safety boot diskette that is prepared especially for that PC.

17. If you ever find that you cannot boot your PC normally from its hard drive, you need to whip out your safety boot diskette. Then open this book to Chapter 11, where you can find a detailed list of steps you take to discover just what sort of problem you have and fix it.

Keep other useful diskettes handy

You probably cannot fit all the utility programs that you might find useful onto one diskette, no matter what its capacity. The obvious solution is to prepare a software toolkit of diskettes for use in any hard disk emergency. The custom safety boot diskette for each PC is always a part of the emergency toolkit for that PC.

One very good group of programs to include in your emergency toolkit is the Norton Utilities. (Versions 5 and later include the Disk Editor — a superb tool for exploring hard or floppy disks and for fixing some of the problems that commonly strike them. As I recommended earlier, if you know how to use Disk Editor well, it is so valuable that it deserves a place on your safety boot diskette.) The other Norton Utilities that I recommend you include in your toolkit are Disk Doctor, File Fix, Unerase, and Unformat.

You also may want to have a complete set of DOS diskettes, including all the DOS external command files. If you followed the suggestions earlier in this chapter, you already have copied at least CHKDSK, FDISK, and FORMAT to your safety boot diskette. Most of the rest of the external command files can prove useful under certain circumstances. Particularly useful are the programs DISKCOPY, COMP, and DISKCOMP, plus the SYS command that comes with DOS (if you did not copy MH-SYS to the safety boot diskette). Users of DOS Version 5 may find MIRROR, UNFORMAT, and UNDELETE useful, too.

Finally, having a recent copy of a good antivirus program can give you considerable peace of mind. One good one is VIRUSCAN by McAfee. Most hard disk problems are not caused by a computer virus, but some are. And being able to check to see whether your PC is infected can reassure you (if it is not infected) or tell you what you must do next (if it is). Be sure to update this program often. Most antivirus programs use knowledge of the current strains of computer virus, and they are nearly useless after they are seriously out of date.

Creating a safety boot diskette when your hard disk is already dead

What if your PC died before you read this chapter? Are you out of luck? Not necessarily. You just have to work a bit harder (and you have to know a few things about your PC that you may have to ferret out).

First, do you know which version of DOS you were using before your PC died? Go to some other PC that is running that same version and create the basic bootable diskette, using the command **FORMAT A: /S**. (Remember the earlier tip about diskette density.)

Next, do you know whether you needed any special device drivers to access your hard disk? For example, did you use any special third-party disk partitioning software like Disk Manager (with the device driver name of DMDRVR.BIN)? Or any on-the-fly disk compression software like Stacker (with the device driver name of STACKER.COM)?

Don't worry if you need these drivers only to access the D or higher lettered logical drives. If you can get to the files on drive C, you can read your old CONFIG.SYS and AUTOEXEC.BAT files and probably recover the device drivers you will need.

Chapter 1: Why Hard Disks Matter So Much

If you do need any such device driver or TSR program, create minimal CONFIG.SYS and AUTOEXEC.BAT files that include lines to load those programs, and put these files and those programs onto your new diskette. This simple, bootable DOS diskette, supplemented with the minimal set of device drivers needed to access drive C, can stand in for a real safety boot diskette in almost all situations.

The one problem for which this diskette is not sufficient is when your PC has a configuration CMOS and its contents have been lost. That information includes a record of what types of hard and floppy drives are in your PC. You may know what the capacities are for your floppy diskette drives. You are less likely to remember the drive type for your hard disk. (The drive type is a number which is stored in the configuration CMOS memory that points to a table of drive descriptions in your motherboard BIOS ROMs. Most often it is a number between 1 and 47, although other values are possible. Drive type 47 often stands for a *user-defined drive type*. If your drive is this type, its description is also stored in the CMOS.) Each PC with a configuration CMOS has a table of drive types, and you need to know which one the CMOS entry identified as yours.

If you have lost the configuration CMOS information and you don't know the hard disk type, one workaround is to go into the setup program and try choosing each possible hard disk type in turn. After each new choice, you have to reboot the computer and see whether you can successfully access your drive C. Eventually, you probably will stumble across the right value.

This situation becomes even more difficult if the correct type for your drive is not listed in the table of drive types. You may have been using any of several strategies for getting around this limitation, and if someone else set up the hard drive for you, you may not know the strategy that person chose. Depending on which strategy was used, the loss of the CMOS information may be only a slight nuisance or may be a profound difficulty.

These strategies include the user-defined drive type supported by some motherboard BIOS ROMs, an autoconfiguring hard disk controller, or a loadable device driver. If you have no idea which of these techniques was used before, rather than trying to guess, your best bet may be to use a special utility designed for — among other things — just this eventuality. The special utility is a Micro House commerical program called DrivePro. (The MH utility programs on the *Hard Disk SECRETS* disk are from Micro House.)

After you have your substitute safety boot diskette in hand, if you are having hard disk problems, turn to Chapter 11 for more advice. If you find that advice difficult to understand, read Chapters 2 through 10 and then try Chapter 11 again.

Summary

To reiterate a point made at the beginning of this chapter: not all hard disk failures are forever. You often can fix things quite easily, after you know enough about how hard disks work and how they can die. In this chapter, you learned the following:

- Your hard disk is valuable, in itself as a piece of expensive hardware, and even more so for the data it contains.

- Simple preparation can make the inevitable problems with your hard disk much more tolerable. When you don't take those precautions, you put your data, and potentially all the work you did to create that data, at serious risk.

- You can follow the prescriptions in this chapter to create a safety boot diskette for your PC. Creating this diskette is the beginning of building a survival kit for that PC.

Before you attempt to use the survival kit to identify and solve hard disk problems, read the rest of the material presented in this book, beginning with the next chapter. You will be a much more capable diagnostician and repair person after you understand that material.

Chapter 2
Magnetic Storage of Information

In This Chapter

▶ The three fundamental physical principles underlying all magnetic data recording
▶ The essential parts of any hard disk, and how they use those fundamental principles to accomplish data storage
▶ The meanings of the terms *track, sector,* and *cylinder*
▶ The size of one bit of data as it is stored on a disk and why it cannot be any smaller
▶ Why sometimes bits are given more than the minimum room necessary, for some very good economic reasons
▶ A very interesting game mathematicians and engineers play to "hide" your data so that you can find it again with great accuracy and reliability
▶ The differences between the FM, MFM, and RLL data encoding strategies
▶ How storing just a small amount of extra information can make a disk appear to be hundreds of times more reliable than it really is
▶ How *error correction codes* sometimes can keep you from knowing about problems until it is too late to fix them without losing some of your data

Fundamentals

A hard disk serves as a depository for data between the times the computer is processing them. The hard disk's essential purpose is to store information and, upon request, to deliver that information back. Hard disks function similarly to audio tape recorders: both use patterns of magnetization in a thin film of magnetic material on some supporting material (called a *substrate*) for their information storage.

The two technologies differ in that tape drives use as their recording substrate long strips of plastic that are wound on spools, and hard disks use rigid metal disks. A more important difference is that audio tape stores information in *analog* form, which means that the magnetic signals directly mimic the audio information being stored. Hard disks are *digital* devices: Their magnetic signals are used to store numbers that represent the data to be stored.

The magnetic recording media used in both cases are only able to support two levels of magnetization: all one way or all the other way. In other words, the media are fully *saturated* at every point. To record analog information, one adds the analog signal to a bias oscillator signal and records that composite. The resulting magnetization flips between its two saturated levels with a duty cycle that reflects the analog value being stored. To read this signal, the read head commonly is designed to average out the bias oscillator signals, thus recovering the original analog signal.

Digital data storage is quite different. As you learn in this chapter, digital data is a bunch of numbers, which are encoded and stored as transitions in the magnetization at certain well-defined locations on the disk surface. The read head sees each of these changes, and the decoding electronics converts the changes back into copies of the original numbers.

A final difference is that in analog audio tape recordings, tolerating minor imperfections, such as some extra noise or small gaps of missed information, is easy. In contrast, a hard disk subsystem in a computer is expected to store digital data absolutely perfectly. An error in just a single bit (a binary one or zero) out of many billions of bits can significantly impair your computer's operation.

Real hard disks are not perfect, of course, so some errors do creep in. To minimize the impact of these errors, disk makers incorporate some very clever strategies for defect masking and error correction in their products. These strategies enable those products to appear to be much more nearly perfect than they actually are.

To understand how hard disks work and how they die, you first must understand how digital data is recorded magnetically. This information includes learning the special steps that hard disk manufacturers have taken to make their products appear to have the perfection their customers insist on. After you understand these facts, you are ready to learn how this strategy sometimes breaks down, or how hard disks die, which is the subject of Chapter 11.

Three important physical facts

Both audio tape recorders and hard disk drives depend on the same physical principles. You need to know just three facts to understand how any magnetic recorder works at the most fundamental level. (These three facts suffice to explain the workings of magnetic recorders that use *inductive read/write heads* — nearly all the magnetic recorders that are built. The few that use a different technique for reading, and for which a fourth physical fact is important, are discussed in Chapter 4 in the section titled "Flux-sensing read heads.")

Chapter 2: Magnetic Storage of Information

1. Pass a current through a coil of wire, and you generate a magnetic field.

2. Impose a strong enough magnetic field on a ferromagnetic or ferrimagnetic substance and that field will "stick"; that is, part of the material becomes magnetized in the same direction, and that *remnant* magnetization lasts until another sufficiently strong magnetic field comes along and magnetizes the substance in some other direction. This process is how magnetic information is recorded.

3. Change the magnetic field that is passing through a coil of wire, and a voltage appears across the ends of the coil. If, for example, you pass a permanent magnet over a coil, you can detect the magnet's field from the voltage induced in the coil. This process is how magnetically recorded information is read.

In Chapter 4, you learn about some disk drives that use a different read strategy, one that depends on a different physical fact. Most disks in PCs today, however, use inductive read/write heads, and they depend on the three preceding facts.

Two kinds of magnetic substances are used in magnetic recording systems. The first kind of substances are those that concentrate and conduct magnetic field lines (*magnetic flux*) but do not retain any appreciable magnetization after the external magnetic field is removed. In this book, these substances are called simply *magnetic materials*. (The notion of conducting a magnetic field means that those fields exhibit a strong preference for traveling through magnetic materials rather than through a nonmagnetic material.) In other books, you may see these materials referred to as being *softly magnetic*.

The second kind of substances are materials that can be *permanently* magnetized. These materials not only concentrate and conduct magnetic fields, they also retain some magnetization after the external field is removed. Technically, this group can be broken into two subgroups: *ferromagnets* and *ferrimagnets*. (The difference between them is not important to the discussion in this book, but those are the proper names for them, and members of both groups are used in magnetic hard disks.) To avoid using the awkward phrase "a ferromagnetic or ferrimagnetic material," any such substance is hereafter referred to as a *magnetizable* material. In other books, you may see them referred to as *hard* or *permanent* magnets.

Now that you know the three basic physical phenomena behind the magnetic storage of information, you are ready to learn how they are applied in the design of a hard disk drive.

The basic construction of a hard disk

Figure 2-1 illustrates the principal parts of a hard disk drive. One or more circular metal platters, coated on both sides with a very thin layer of a magnetizable material, are mounted on a spindle that rotates them at a constant, high speed. For each surface (the top and the bottom of each platter), the drive has a *read/write head*. These heads are mounted on a *head assembly* that moves them in toward the spindle or out toward the edge of the platters.

Platters and heads

Recently, some drive manufacturers have begun to make hard disk drives that use glass platters. Glass platters can be made flatter and smoother more easily, and they have higher rigidity. This latter quality is especially important in some new drives that turn faster than the usual 3600 revolutions per minute (rpm). So far, only a few drives are made with glass platters, but they may become more common in the near future.

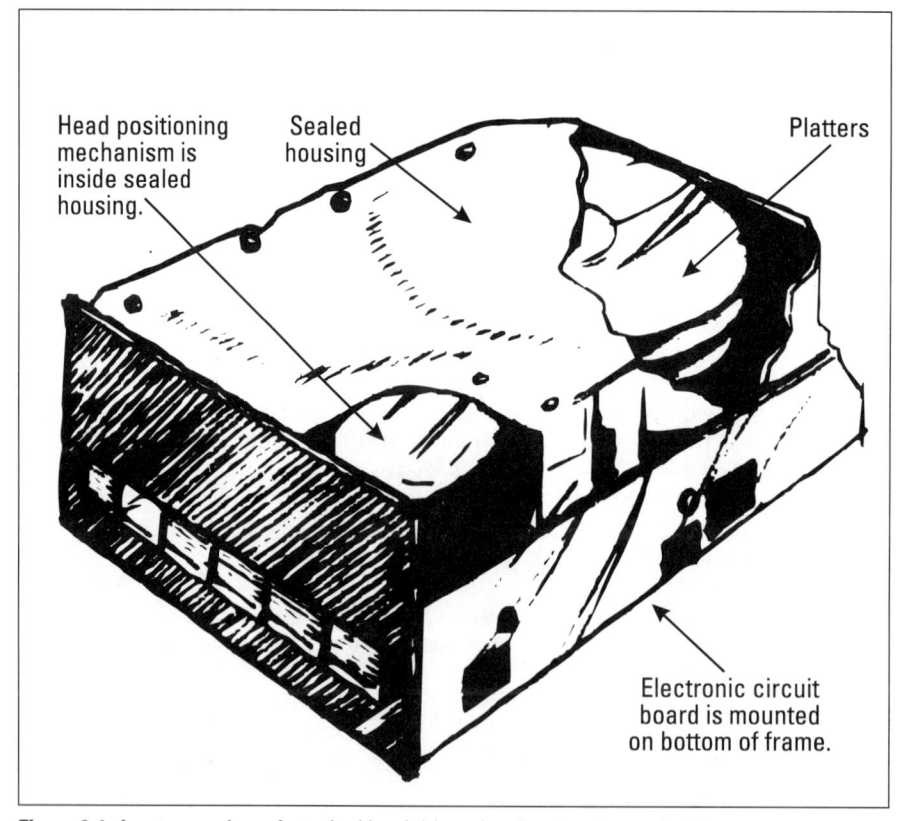

Figure 2-1: A cutaway view of a typical hard drive, showing the platters inside.

Chapter 2: Magnetic Storage of Information

When the disk is not turning (when the drive is turned off), weak springs hold each head in contact with the platter surface. When the disk is turning, the heads *surf* on the wind created by the turning disk. The air flowing past the head is strong enough to lift the heads away from the surface, though only by a very small distance.

/ TECHNICAL SECRET /

Early disk drives were designed to keep the heads flying several microns (millionths of a meter) above the surface. More modern designs keep the heads about 0.1 to 0.5 micron above the surface. This latter range is 0.000004 to 0.00002 inch, which is a mere one-thousandth the diameter of a typical human hair.

The air flow both holds the head away from the surface and keeps it close to the surface. The air flow thus keeps the head flying in a tightly controlled way, following quite closely any up or down motion of the platter surface.

The head must fly above, rather than on, the surface — this position prevents the head from wearing out the magnetic coating by rubbing and, even more importantly, it keeps the coating from wearing away the head. The head must not fly too far above the surface, though, or it cannot magnetize the surface strongly enough or read the magnetization that is there.

In Chapter 4, you learn much more about the issues involved in head design and how flying height affects the head's function. You also learn there how the new perpendicular recording technology is dramatically changing the old rules.

Tracks and cylinders

As the disk spins, with the head assembly held in one position, each head traces out a circular ring on the surface of its platter. These rings are called *tracks*. Information is recorded in these rings in bursts called *sectors*.

The data in each sector is read or written as a unit, all at once. Figure 2-2 shows one platter and one head and indicates where these tracks and sectors are. (This figure greatly exaggerates the size of the head relative to that of the platter, so the width of the tracks shown also are greatly exaggerated. Instead of just seven tracks, which is all that would fit if the tracks were as broad as shown in this figure, a typical hard disk has anywhere from a few hundred to a few thousand tracks on each platter surface.)

These tracks are not normally visible because they are simply regions of the surface that have been magnetized in a special way.

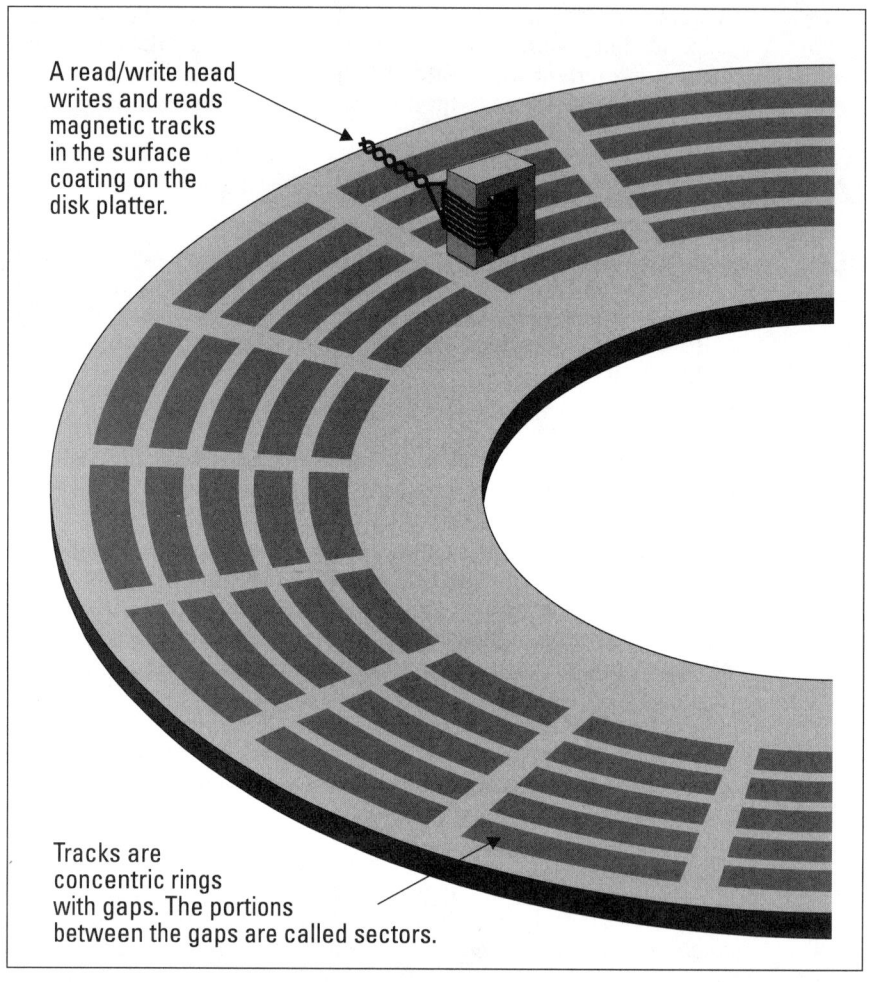

Figure 2-2: As the disk platters spin under the read/write heads, those heads pass over the surface along tracks.

A read/write head writes and reads magnetic tracks in the surface coating on the disk platter.

Tracks are concentric rings with gaps. The portions between the gaps are called sectors.

These tracks would look, if only you could see them, almost like the grooves on a record — which they almost are, but not quite. An important difference between the tracks on a hard disk and the groove on a record is that the tracks on a disk are circular and separate. A record usually has only one groove, which spirals in from the outside to the center. When playing a record, the needle moves continuously from the outside toward the center. When reading or writing data on a hard disk, the heads are held still. They only move when you need to go from one track to another and then the moving of the heads happens between bursts of reading or writing.

> ### An unusually groovy record
>
> You may question my suggestion that a record can have more than one groove. Some novelty records have been made with more than one spiral groove. For example, there might be four such grooves, starting at four equally spaced points on the outer edge of the record and spiraling in together. That means that when you put the needle on the record surface you have no way of knowing which of the several tracks you will be playing. That design allows some randomness in the experience of playing the record, which is exactly what the creators of the records desired to give to their audience.

The *actuator* is the component that moves the head assembly in and out. Two types of actuator are common: a *stepper motor actuator* that drives a *rack and pinion,* and a *voice coil actuator.* The first is a dead-reckoning positioner. The latter uses servo feedback to home in on the correct position. For more details on how these two actuator types function and how they differ, see Chapter 4.

The head assembly actuator moves the head assembly in or out in small, equal-size steps. For any given position of the head assembly, each head traces out a circle on its platter surface as that platter turns under it. Each of these circles is called a track. Each time the heads are moved to a new position, they sweep out a new set of tracks. (The heads actually form the tracks at the time the disk is low-level formatted. Therefore, when you position them and then turn the platters, the heads trace out, or sweep out, a path that is the set of tracks they will record there on the platters.)

Starting from the outside edge of the platter, the tracks form concentric circles and are numbered, beginning with 0 at the outside edge (see Figure 2-3). (This figure shows a cutaway view of a four-platter hard disk that has had the vertical dimensions drastically exaggerated for clarity. Also, the tracks are shown as being much wider than they really are.) Tracks with the same number (all the tracks on all surfaces for a single head assembly position) form what is called a *cylinder.* **Note:** The maximum number of platters is 14; more common numbers are between 2 and 8 platters.

The significance of a cylinder is simple to explain. A cylinder's tracks pass under their respective heads simultaneously. This arrangement means that the computer can write data to or read data from any of the tracks in the cylinder currently passing under the read/write heads, merely by electronically switching to the appropriate head. Such electronic switching can be done very quickly — much faster than physically moving the heads to a neighboring cylinder.

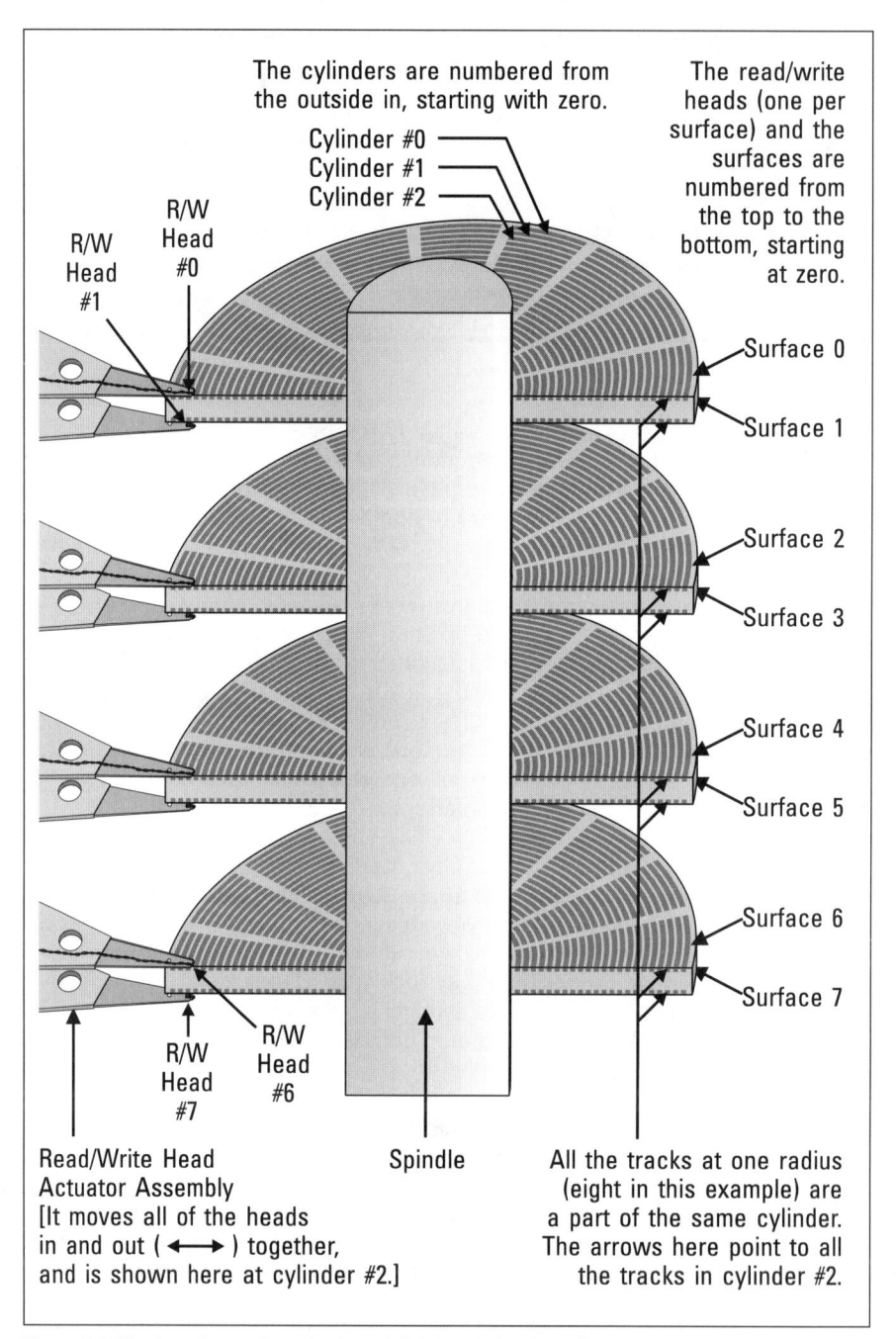

Figure 2-3: The location and numbering of disk heads (surfaces) and cylinders.

There are as many tracks per cylinder as there are heads, or, because each platter has two heads, the number of tracks per cylinder equals twice the number of platters. (In some drives, one or two of those heads is reserved for use by the servo-positioning mechanism. The existence of drives that have one head reserved for the servo system is the reason you will see an odd number of heads listed for some drives in tables of drive dimensions.) The heads are numbered, starting with zero for the head on the top surface of the uppermost platter. (Computer engineers like to count starting with zero instead of one — the reason is not easy to explain.)

The number of cylinders (or tracks per platter) that any given hard drive has depends both on how narrow each track is (which in turn depends on how small the head is) and on the size of the track, to track steps that the head actuator is able to make. Remember, the drawing in Figure 2-3 has been greatly exaggerated; typical real hard drives have anywhere from a few hundred to several thousand cylinders.

The importance of cleanliness

Because even minute dust specks can cause disastrous failures of the drive, all the moving parts are sealed in a chamber filled with very clean air. This chamber must never be opened except by qualified technicians in a suitable "clean room." Opening this chamber otherwise will void the manufacturer's warranty and almost certainly lead to destruction of the drive.

TECHNICAL SECRET

The chamber that contains all the moving parts of a hard drive is not hermetically sealed. The chamber simply has a fan pulling air into it through a very fine pore filter with holes only a small fraction of a micron (less than a dozen millionths of an inch) in diameter. The air escapes out the inevitable leaks in the housing. This system makes the air pressure inside higher than that on the outside, which helps keep dirt from coming in through those same leaks.

If you were to open up a hard drive and look inside, its "fan" would be easy to overlook. The fan actually is simply an aspect of the design of the housing and the disk spindle and platters. Whenever the disk is spinning, those platters pull some air along with their motion and in the process fling the air off the outside edges. This *centrifugal fan* action pulls air in through the vent and filter located above the top of the spindle.

How the heads write and read information

Each head is a small coil of wire wound around a magnetically conductive core. Figure 2-4(a) shows one design. Notice the small gap in the core. That gap is where all the action is, as far as the magnetic coating on the platter is concerned. As the read/write head sweeps over the platter, the head writes regions of magnetization along its track (see Figure 2-4a). Magnetic field lines from current in the head coil form a permanent magnet in the platter surface coating (see Figure 2-4b). The permanent magnets in the coating have field lines that close on themselves. The magnet next to the head gap closes its field lines through the head core and coil (see Figure 2-4c).

One more important fact is that all magnetic fields are closed loops. Whether they are created by a current passing in a coil of wire or by a permanent magnet, the field lines loop around and connect back on themselves. For a permanent magnet, the loop goes through the magnetic material, comes out its "north pole" and, after looping around outside, goes back into its "south pole." In the case of a coil of wire, the loops go through the coil, around the outside, and back in the other side of the coil.

Magnetic field lines also strongly prefer to travel through a magnetically conductive material. For that reason, an electromagnet often has a core made of some magnetic material. The core both guides and concentrates the magnetic field.

When a read/write head in a hard disk writes information to the disk, the head acts as a tiny electromagnet with a magnetic core. But that core does not extend all the way around the loops that the magnetic field lines want to follow. The core has a small gap. The field lines themselves cannot have any gaps, so they have to leave the core material and somehow cross the gap.

If any magnetic material is nearby, the field lines will detour through that material instead of going straight across the core gap. In a hard disk, the nearby material is the surface coating on the platter, as illustrated in Figure 2-4(b). In making that detour, the field lines from the coil's magnetic field force the surface material to become magnetized. Reverse the current in the coil, and its magnetic field lines reverse direction; this change will record a reversed magnetic field in the surface of the platter.

As the disk platter turns under the head, the current in the head coil is rapidly changing from one direction to the opposite and back again, causing the current to record a magnetic field on the disk surface that also changes frequently. This field points forward along the track for a short distance and then backward and then forward again. These changes provide the means to store information, as the example in Figure 2-4(a) shows.

Chapter 2: Magnetic Storage of Information

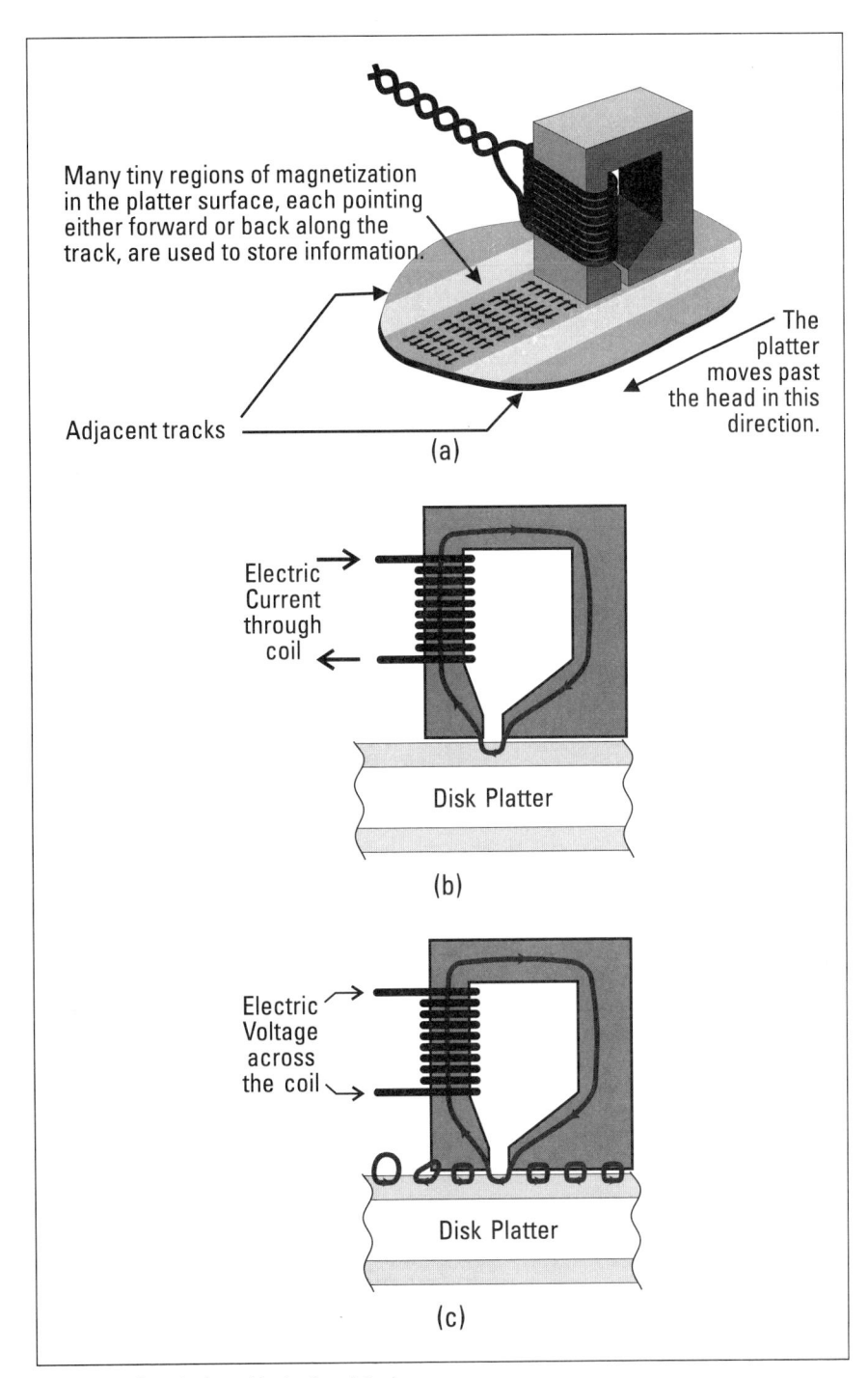

Figure 2-4: A typical read/write head design.

When the coil is not carrying any current (and so is not making any magnetic field of its own), it can read the magnetic fields in the platter surface. If a portion of the platter surface next to the core gap is magnetized, the magnetic field lines passing over that portion will close on themselves through the core, and thus through the coil, rather than simply curving back around that magnetized region over the gap (see Figure 2-4c).

After data has been written to it, the part of the platter that passes under the head contains, in effect, a string of permanent magnets, some pointing one way and some the other. As the head passes over each magnet, it closes that magnet's field lines through the head coil. Consequently, when the head passes from on top of a magnet pointing in one direction to on top of a neighboring magnet pointing the other way, the magnetic field passing through the head's coil changes. According to the third important physical fact, for just a brief moment, a pulse of voltage appears across the ends of the coil. These voltage blips enable the hard disk to sense recorded information.

Besides the platters, spindle, spindle motor, read/write head, head assembly and actuator, and the sealed chamber that contains and protects all those parts, all hard disk drives must have one more part — an electronic circuit card. This circuitry is connected on one side to the head actuator, the heads, and the spindle motor. On its other side, the circuit board is connected to the computer or to a disk controller card in the computer, as well as to the computer's power supply. The function of the circuitry on that board is described in the section "What Happens in the Drive Electronics" in Chapter 4.

Bit size

PC users want their hard disks to store as much information as possible. Information is stored in units called bits. Each *bit* can be either a one or a zero. Eight bits make up a *byte*. A word processing document, for example, commonly uses one byte for each symbol or formatting code in the document. The number of bits of data a given drive can store depends on how much magnetizable platter surface it has (how may platters and how large each one is) and how much of that surface area must be used to store each bit.

Bits are recorded as patterns of magnetic fields along the tracks, with the fields pointing either forward or backward. As the platter turns under the head, the current through the head is reversed, which in turn reverses the recorded magnetic field in the surface. Think of this process as a flipping and flopping of the permanent magnets in the surface as you go along the track. Figure 2-5 shows schematically how the magnetic particles in the surface of the platter are aligned circumferential and the way the read/write head leaves regions

Chapter 2: Magnetic Storage of Information

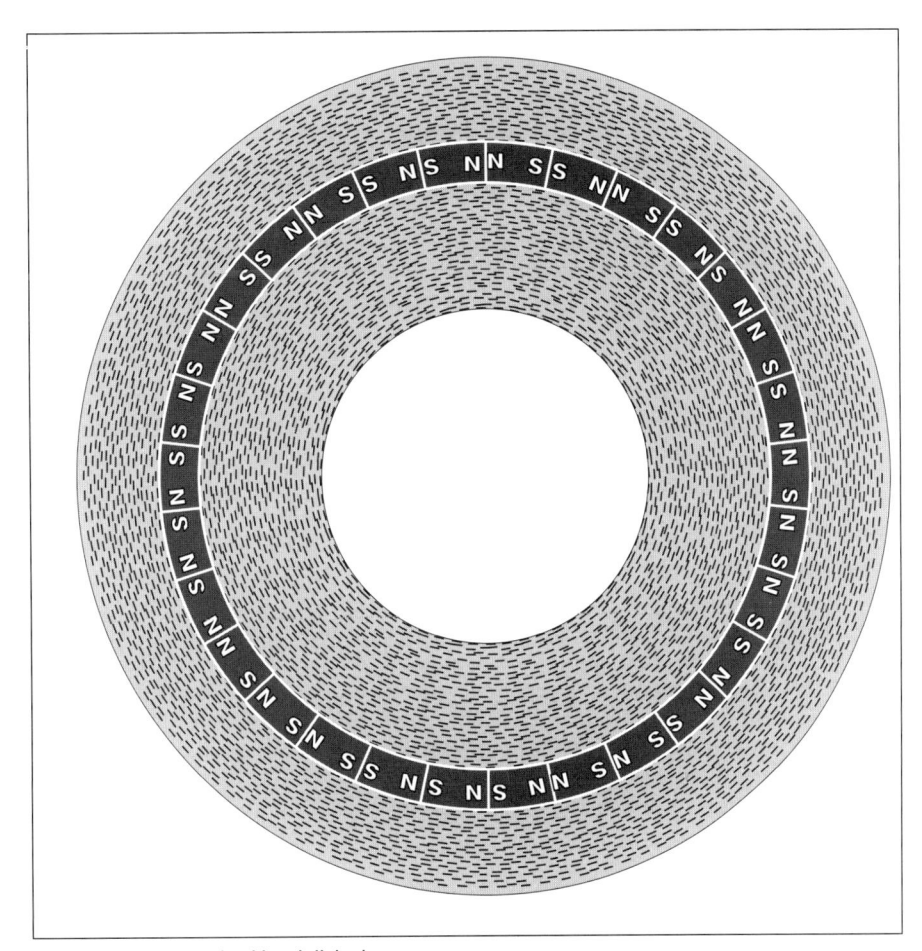

Figure 2-5: A magnetized hard disk platter.

magnetized forward and backward along the path of its motion (the track). (On an actual disk platter, there are many more and much smaller individual magnetized regions than are shown here.)

The size of a bit is its width times its length. The width of a bit equals the width of its track, which is simply the width of the read/write head. To prevent the writing of one track from also overwriting a portion of the adjacent tracks, and to keep the read head from sensing information from more than one track at a time, engineers have found it prudent to leave a small gap between the tracks. That buffer zone space adds to the space used up by each bit so that the effective width of a bit is the track-to-track distance rather than just the (slightly smaller) width of each track.

> **TECHNICAL SECRET**
>
> Actually, the tracks are just a tiny amount wider than the heads. This difference exists because there are some magnetic field lines that leak out the sides of the gap and affect parts of the platter surface that merely pass very near a head, rather than under it. This "leakage" would affect the accuracy of what the head reads if you tried to place the tracks too close together; the minimum track spacing is set to avoid that circumstance.
>
> Video recorders manage to suppress *crosstalk* (adjacent track interference) by using two or more read/write heads and aligning those head gaps so that they are not parallel (called the *azimuth* alignment). Those recorders, therefore, can put tracks down immediately next to one another. That technique is not used in typical hard disks primarily because of how the heads move from track to track, which almost forces use of the same head for each track. VCRs, having the spinning head with the tape wrapped around it in a spiral fashion, are much more easily capable of using multiple heads with differently aligned gaps for successive tracks.

The length of a bit is a little more difficult to describe. Three factors affect a bit's length. First, there is some limit to how closely the flips and flops of the magnetic field along the track can be spaced. Second, more than one such flip-flop length may be needed to store a bit of information. Multiplying the *minimum magnetic field flip-flop length* by the required number of such lengths yields the absolute minimum length of a bit for any particular hard drive. Third, the hard disk's designers may have had some good reasons for making the bit storage regions larger than the absolute minimum size.

The minimum magnetic field flip-flop length turns out to depend on a complex combination of the properties of the platter's magnetic surface, combined with the size of the core gap in the head that does the writing and the distance that the head flies above the surface. The number of these flip-flop lengths needed to encode a bit of information depends on the method used to encode the data into magnetic signals. The last factor, whether the disk designer uses the minimum possible space per bit, is decided by a compromise between efficiency and simplicity in the design of both disk drives and disk controllers.

Minimum magnetic flip-flop length

How small can the magnetic flip-flop length be? Again, the answer to this question can be broken down into three parts.

First is the nature of the surface material. In drives with *oxide coatings,* the surface consists of small particles of magnetic material suspended in a binder. (The binder is a special type of paint. Common paint is made of particles of a colored substance suspended in a material that sticks when applied to whatever you want to paint. The type of paint used for hard disks simply substitutes magnetic stuff for colored stuff.) In *plated media* drives, a deposited film of pure

Chapter 2: Magnetic Storage of Information

magnetic material composes the surface. With either surface, there is a minimum size region that can be magnetized, which is called a *grain* or *domain size*. The flip-flop length cannot be any shorter than this size.

The second limitation on the minimum distance between magnetic transitions is a consequence of the orientation of the recorded regions. Notice in Figure 2-6(b) that adjacent regions of opposite magnetization have a "north pole" next to another "north pole" or a "south pole" next to another "south pole." The bits on the disk repel each other in the way magnets push each other away when you hold them together; the closer you place them, the stronger the magnetic field of one region (or bit) pushes onto those of adjacent regions. If the regions are too close together, the field of one region can reverse the field of an adjacent region, causing the two regions to become one. The minimum flip-flop length, then, must be large enough to prevent that from happening.

Figure 2-6(a) shows a perspective view of the head and track; Figure 2-6(b) is a side view, but not to scale; and Figure 2-6(c) is a graph of magnetization in the surface — + is forward along the track; – is backward along the track. *Note:* This is too simple a data encoding scheme to use for real data storage. See the next section for an explanation of the more complex schemes actually used.

The third limiting factor is the size of the gap in the head's core. Usually, the flip-flop length is made at least as long as the width of this gap. Although you can record regions smaller than this, doing so is not advisable — fields generated by more than one region will simultaneously pass through the head's coil, making it difficult separately to detect the magnetic field of each region. Also, when writing to the disk, the coil current will magnetize an entire core gap length of the track in the same direction, possibly wiping out bits adjacent to the one you wanted to write.

Modern disk manufacturing techniques enable the disk designer to set all these size limits to be about the same. Thus, the grain or domain size in the surface, the minimum-size regions that will not demagnetize one another, and the head gap width are comparable to each other.

TECHNICAL SECRET

The minimum-size region of the platter coating that is independently magnetizable is one of the two most important physical parameters describing the recording medium. The other critical parameter is the threshold magnetic field strength required for magnetizing the surface coating (its *coercivity*). As you might expect, much research has been done over many years to learn how to control these numbers in the manufacturing process. The minimum size of an independently magnetizable region has been made ever smaller, so more bits can be packed into a given length of track. The coercivity has been raised, leading to more firmly locked-in magnetic regions on the disk surface.

Part I: The Hard Disk Companion

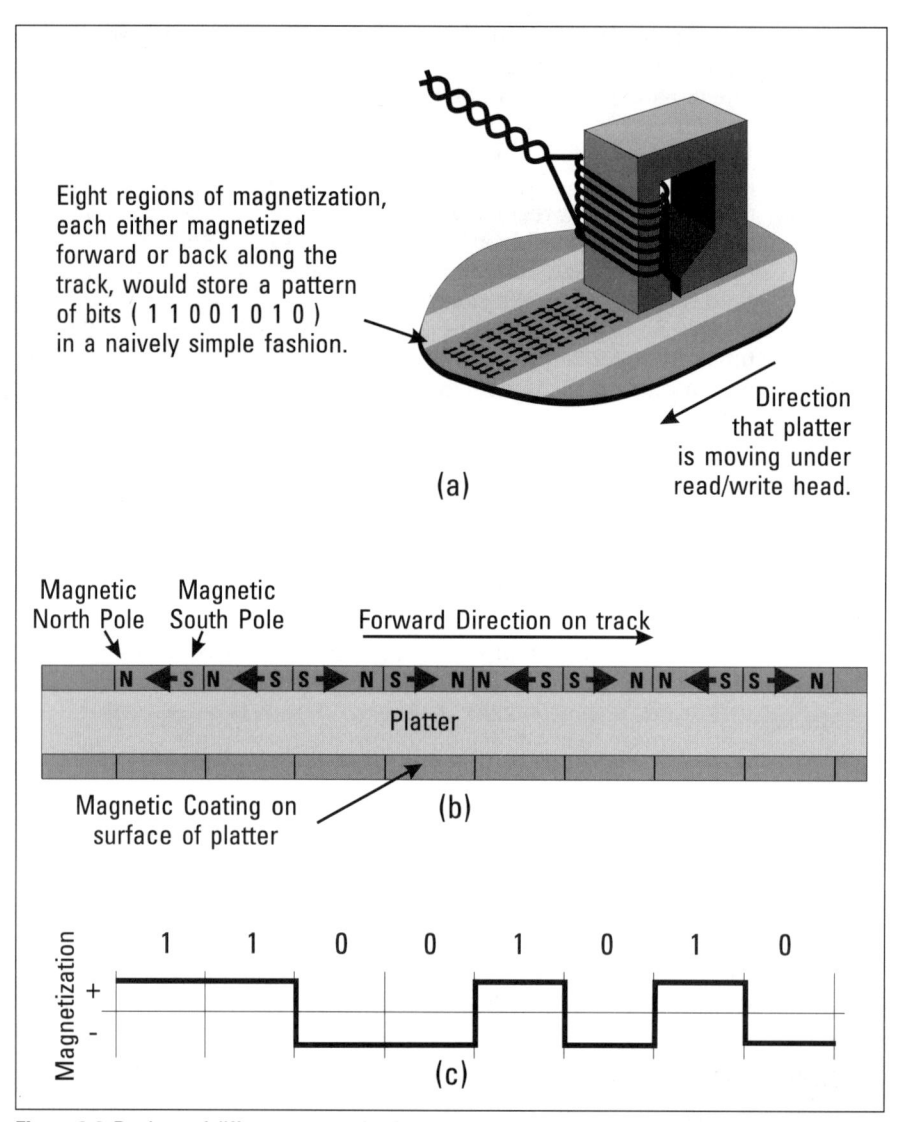

Figure 2-6: Regions of different magnetization are used to store information on the hard disk platter surface.

The magnetizable surface coating can be made in several ways. In the earlier disk designs, tiny needle-shaped magnetic iron oxide particles (so-called gamma Fe_2O_3) are dispersed in an epoxy binder and coated on the platter surfaces. The platters are often spun under a strong magnet as the epoxy cures (becomes hard) so that the particles will be aligned along the tracks. This process ensures that the magnetization is always in the plane of the disk surface and either forward or backward along the track direction (see Figure 2-5).

Later improvements led to coatings that are more nearly pure magnetic material, sometimes sputtered or plated on the platter surface. The material is oriented so that the magnetization is the same as that for the oxide-in-binder surfaces. The advantages of the plated media are primarily that they can be thinner and still have enough magnetic material in them to make the same strength signals. This thinness in turn makes possible smaller regions in which information can be stored.

The oxide-in-binder surfaces permit the recording of up to about 20,000 bits per inch along the track. The plated media can support perhaps four times as many bits. Also, the plated media are used mostly with heads that are narrower and thus with tracks that can be closer together, leading to total capacities per platter for plated media around ten times that of the oxide-in-binder surfaces.

These factors limit the minimum possible size of an independently magnetizable region on the disk surface (the magnetic flip-flop length). The form of data encoding used determines how many of these flip-flop lengths are necessary to store one bit. That subject is covered in the next section; for now, it is enough to know that you need some fixed number (not necessarily an integer) of these regions (up to two) per bit.

Theoretical versus practical bit densities

The length of track used to store one bit can be called a *bit cell* length. Real hard-disk bit cells are not always as small as they could be (that is, one minimum magnetic flip-flop length times the number of flip-flop lengths needed to code a bit), for reasons having more to do with economics than with physics. The tracks near the spindle are shorter than those closer to the outer edge, which means that there is more room for bits on the outer tracks. That's physics. Because the spindle turns at a fixed speed, independent of the head assembly position (which, by the way, is not true in some floppy disk drives — though not those used in PCs), the time it takes for an entire track to pass under the head is the same for every track. The longer, outer tracks simply move under the head faster.

In other words, the head reads the data without regard to the speed of motion of the platter surface. All that counts is the frequency of magnetic field transitions the head sees. The bits out near the rim are stretched out longer than those in near the center. It is easiest to treat each track as if it were the same length as every other track. Each track occupies the same length of time passing under the head as every other track. The read-and-write electronics then do not have to consider which track the head is passing over.

Part I: The Hard Disk Companion

> **TECHNICAL SECRET**
>
> This discussion has glossed over a subtle point. If you put the same number of bits on every track, those on the inner tracks will be closer together. To get as much information as possible on the drive, the bits on the innermost tracks will be jammed together as tightly as feasible. Something interesting happens when the bits are put this close together. The magnetic transitions actually move even closer together on their own. The name for this phenomenon is *bit shifting*, or *pulse crowding*. (By *magnetic transitions* I mean the boundaries between regions that are magnetized in one direction and those in which the magnetization is in the opposite direction.) On the other hand, depending on the data encoding strategy used and the particular data being recorded, it is possible to see bits moved farther apart than normal.
>
> These effects can make the signals picked up by the read head come at slightly wrong times, possibly confusing the controller about what information has been recorded at this place on the disk. A common way of preventing this problem is to anticipate the bit shifting and correct for it before it happens.
>
> The signals sent to the write head are forced to have their current reversals positioned either just before or just after their nominal times. Which way to shift a given transition may depend on many things, but in a given drive (with a given data-encoding strategy and fixed physical properties), the rules are determined and well known. If this positioning is done just right, the read signals will be spaced exactly as you would have thought they would be without all this fuss. This technique is called *write precompensation*.
>
> Write precompensation only needs to be done for the cylinders that are close to the spindle. The outer cylinders have their bits spread far enough apart that the bit-shifting effect does not occur. The best possible precompensation would be some function of cylinder number, but the more economical approach is to do a fixed amount for all cylinders closer than a certain distance to the spindle and not to do any for the rest.
>
> Older hard disk controllers will do write precompensation for a range of cylinders if asked. More modern controllers perform write precompensation automatically, without instructions from you.

If you are willing to build a substantially more complex drive or controller, you can put more bits on the outer tracks, but the process is more expensive. That's where the economics comes in. The designers of the smaller and less expensive PC disk drives built today settle for putting an equal number of bits on each track, regardless of the length of the tracks. Designers of the more expensive, larger capacity drives may or may not do this.

Chapter 2: Magnetic Storage of Information 51

TECHNICAL SECRET

> Because until very recently almost all drives stored a constant amount of information on each track (possibly a different constant for different drives), the standard drive controllers do not allow for any other possibility. You can put more data on the outside tracks than on the inner ones, therefore, only if you forego the use of a standard controller.
>
> The Small Computer System Interface (SCSI) and integrated drive electronics/AT attachment (IDE/ATA) drives contain their own controllers. (See the discussion in the section "Popular Products and Standards" in Chapter 3 for more on this point.) Some manufacturers build SCSI and IDE/ATA drives that take advantage of the geometrical fact that the outer tracks are longer than the inner ones and put more data on the outer tracks. These manufacturers divide the tracks into *zones*. The tracks in the outer third of the platter, for example, will be zone #1; the middle third, zone #2; and the innermost third, zone #3. The amount of data per track within each zone is a constant, but that constant changes from zone to zone. One name for this technique is *zone bit recording*. Some of the proprietary format MFM and RLL drive/controller combinations and hard disks on an option card also use this technique.

Although the size of a bit on the disk surface depends on the drive, it is likely to fall into the following range: The length along the track is at least 0.00002 inch (0.5 microns) and at most 0.0001 inch (2.5 microns). The width of the track is anywhere from about 0.0005 inch (12 microns) up to 0.003 inch (75 microns).

These ranges put the minimum area at somewhere between about 6 square microns and about 200 square microns. Taking the reciprocal of these numbers, you can see that the *areal density* of bits can range from about 5,000 per square millimeter (which is the same as 3 million per square inch) up to about 170,000 per square millimeter (100 million per square inch).

To put those numbers in terms of something you may be able to visualize, the area on the disk platter occupied by one bit is at most about the cross-sectional area of one typical human hair. At the greatest density now used in hard disks, 30 or so bits could be stored in that same space.

Data-Encoding Strategies

The purpose behind a hard disk's complex structure is to store information, specifically a bunch of binary numbers. A *binary number* is just a collection of ones and zeros. To read and write the data, these ones and zeros, or *bits*, somehow must be *encoded* as magnetic signals on the disk's surface. You might imagine that the individual bits can be stored one right after another along the track, assigning each bit one of the two magnetic field directions, depending on whether the bit is a one or a zero. If this arrangement were possible, just one magnetic flip-flop length would be necessary to store each bit.

Figure 2-6(a) and (b) show what this encoding strategy would look like for a particular data pattern. Figure 2-6(c) is a graph of the magnetic field strength versus distance along the track for that same data pattern. When you consider the third important physical fact listed at the beginning of the preceding section, you see why this strategy will not work. For a voltage to appear across the coil, the magnetic field in the coil must *change,* which will not happen when using this encoding scheme if all the bits you record happen to be identical (such as all zeros or all ones). Consequently, there will not be any signal for the head to read.

In addition, if the disk turns at an even slightly different speed when it is reading than it did when writing, the head will traverse the bits at a different rate. If you could see each bit as it went by, you could take this different rate into account, but if you are sailing over identical magnetic fields and thus getting no signals at all, you have no way of knowing just how many of those identical bits you have passed over. To ensure that the drive can reliably read the information, a more complicated method of recording data is needed.

Think of data encoding as a game in which the goal is to find a way to "hide" the bits of information in the flips and flops of the magnetic field in such a way that the drive can reliably "find" them again when it is time to read the data. An obvious solution is to make each bit stand out in some way. Perhaps the simplest way of achieving this result would be to put a region of no magnetization between each of the bits of data. Unfortunately, that is not easy to do. The grains, or tiny needles, that comprise the disk surface will be strongly magnetized one way or the other. All you can easily influence is which way each needle is magnetized.

A simple-minded pulse approach

Here is a simple way that will work: Make each binary one into a bidirectional pulse and make each binary zero a similarly long absence of pulse (see the upcoming caution). Finally, intersperse between each of the data bits a dummy pulse, or *clock* signal, that is just like the binary one pulses.

If you look in other books on this subject and compare their discussion with this one, you may become quite confused. *Pulses* are signals that go up and down. Many authors, though, speak of recording "pulses" when they really mean the recording of a transition in the magnetic field, either from minus to plus *or* from plus to minus (and *not* back again).

Chapter 2: Magnetic Storage of Information

These recorded transitions will result in corresponding pulses of voltage across the read head later on when the drive reads the information. (When a transition from minus to plus magnetization is passed, the voltage rises briefly to some positive value and then goes back to zero, which is a positive pulse. When a transition of the opposite sign is traversed, the voltage on the read head briefly goes down to some negative value and then back to zero, which is a negative pulse.)

There is another way those other authors may confuse you. Sometimes they use *1*s and *0*s to stand for both transitions and lacks of transition and for data bits, without clearly distinguishing between them. In this book, you will not run into either of these confusions.

Figure 2-7 shows a number of graphs of magnetic field strength versus position along the track for the same data pattern shown in Figure 2-6. The several graphs in this figure show a variety of encoding strategies, each applied to the same data byte (11001010).

There are eight bit cells in each graph in Figure 2-7. In each case, the cell boundaries are indicated by a lightweight line, and the bit (a *1* or a *0*) that is stored in that bit cell is printed to the left of the cell. The vertical dimension represents distance along the track. The gray lines connect the bit cell boundaries in one graph with those in the next graph. You can see that each newer, better data-encoding strategy dramatically shrinks the size of the bit cells. Why this happens is explained shortly.

In Figure 2-7(a), you see the pattern obtained by using the interspersed clock and data pulses just described. The pulses for the one bits show up clearly as they pass under the head, but those for the zero bits, because they still have no changing magnetic field, do not. But the clock pulses always show up and enable the head to detect even long strings of zero bits. This method makes it easy to write and read data but is unnecessarily inefficient.

Figure 2-7 shows the following data-encoding strategies:

- (a) Bidirectional frequency modulation
- (b) NRZ frequency modulation (commonly called FM)
- (c) Modified frequency modulation, or MFM
- (d) Idealized voltage signal across the read head when the pattern in (c) passes under it
- (e) 2,7 RLL (run-length limited)

Part I: The Hard Disk Companion

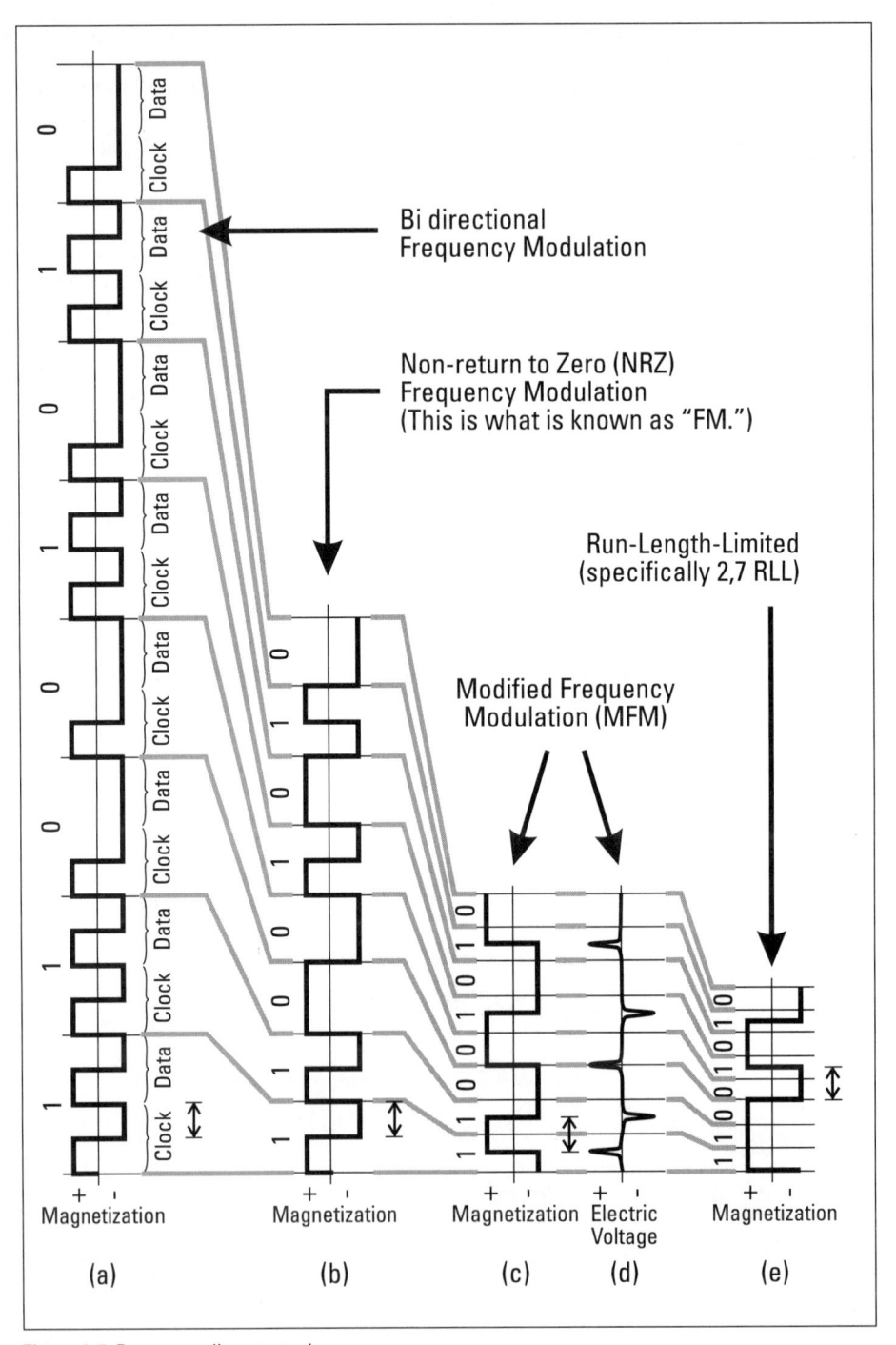

Figure 2-7: Data-encoding strategies.

Chapter 2: Magnetic Storage of Information

FM

Up to this point, data encoding has been described in terms of the distances along the track from one region of magnetization to the next. Another way to look at the same information is in terms of the times between the passage of those regions under the read/write head or — by dividing those times into one second — in terms of the frequencies with which those regions pass the head.

Figure 2-7(a) can be viewed as a square wave with a varying frequency. There is one cycle per bit cell when it is storing a zero, and two cycles per bit cell when it is storing a one. This method is similar to the one used to put information on radio waves at an FM radio broadcast station, although radio requires a whole range of frequencies to encode the subtleties of music and speech, and computer disk drives need only two frequencies to encode ones and zeros. This method of representing data is called *frequency modulation* encoding, or *FM*. Although this approach works, disk system designers soon realized that they could create a considerably more efficient strategy.

NRZ

The scheme outlined in Figure 2-7(a) gives exactly two changes in the magnetization of the medium for each item that is being stored: a transition as the field goes from backward (negative) to forward (positive) and as it returns. When the head passes over the first transition, a positive voltage pulse appears across the coil, and when it passes over the reverse transition, a negative voltage pulse appears. To use this data-encoding scheme, the electronics for reading the data will use only the positive voltage pulses, ignoring the negative ones.

This overkill exacts a severe penalty. Remember that the field cannot be reversed along the track any more often than the minimum magnetic flip-flop length. In Figure 2-7, a short, double-headed arrow to the right of each magnetization graph represents the minimum distance between magnetic field transitions for that encoding scheme.

At best, the bytes of data can be shrunk down until that double-headed arrow distance equals a minimum magnetic flip-flop length. (In the figure, this has been done; all the double-headed arrows are the same length. The decrease in size of the bit cells in the figure, therefore, correspond to the actual increase in bit density that results from using each of these encoding strategies.)

In Figure 2-7(a), you see that this minimum distance is one-quarter of the bit cell size; for the bidirectional pulse version of FM encoding, therefore, four minimum flip-flop lengths are needed just to store one bit of data and its associated clock pulse.

A simple way to halve the track length needed to store a given amount of data is to ignore the direction of each transition when reading the data (the direction shows up as the sign of the voltage pulse on the coil as it passes over that transition) and then count every transition as significant. How the data are written also must be changed.

Figure 2-7(b) shows that change. Compare this diagram with the pattern in Figure 2-7(a). Every time the signal in (a) goes from minus to plus, the signal in (b) changes, either up or down; when in (a) the signal goes from plus back to minus, that in (b) does not change. There are exactly half as many transitions in (b) and thus just half as many voltage pulses on playback, yet all the information is there. This is called a *Non-Return-to-Zero* (NRZ) approach to data encoding. By using this approach, one can convert any pattern of pulses into an identical series of half pulses without any loss of information.

Because this approach yields half as many transitions (and those that there are get spaced exactly twice as far apart), this pattern can be stored in half as much track length. The increased efficiency is well worth the slight extra bother required to store and retrieve data this way. Because nobody uses the simple-minded version of FM anymore, future references to FM here (and in most works on this subject) really mean this NRZ variation of the most simple-minded frequency modulation.

TECHNICAL SECRET

Many more data-encoding strategies have been used from time to time than are described in this chapter. They have been called NRZ, NRZI, PE, ZM, and other names. The NRZ variation of FM discussed here actually goes by the name FM in most books; NRZ and NRZI are two other, different schemes that also incorporate the Non-Return-to-Zero idea.

MFM

Early makers of magnetic tape and disk drives used FM; then some clever engineers and mathematicians figured out a way to double the system's efficiency. This simple variation on FM data encoding, initially called *double-density* encoding and now mostly known as *modified frequency modulation* (MFM), essentially has replaced FM in the world of PC hard drives.

HISTORICAL ASIDE

When you buy diskettes that are labeled DSDD, it means that they have been certified for use on both sides (*Double-Sided*) with *Double-Density* data encoding. That is the data encoding used in all PC floppy diskette drives, and it was the one used in the original hard disks that IBM shipped with the PC/XT, as well as in any other hard disk subsystem that is labeled MFM.

Chapter 2: Magnetic Storage of Information

The notion behind MFM is that clock transitions are only needed when there are no nearby data transitions. Many of the clock signals, therefore, can be eliminated. Still, it must be possible, somehow, to tell reliably which transitions are data and which are clock information.

Figure 2-7(c) shows the MFM pattern of magnetization used to encode the same data as Figure 2-7(b). Changes from a high to a low level or vice versa indicate field transitions. Figure 2-7(d) shows the voltage pulses that will be seen when this pattern of magnetization moves under the read head.

TECHNICAL SECRET

Notice that in Figure 2-7(b), the FM case, there is a transition (clock) at the start of every bit cell, and another transition in the middle of every cell that stores a binary one. MFM just gets rid of as many of the clock transitions as seems safe.

The rule for MFM encoding is simple. Start with FM and then omit each clock pulse associated with a bit cell, unless that cell and the previous cell hold *zeros*. All bit cells holding *ones* and the cells immediately following them are close enough to a transition that no additional transitions are needed just for clock purposes.

The rule for separating clock and data signals when reading is also simple. You need only be able to tell whether the signal came at the start of a bit cell, indicating a clock pulse (between two zero bits), or in the middle of a cell, indicating a one bit.

The minimum and maximum spacing of the transitions in this method of data encoding are exactly twice that in FM. Because the minimum spacing is doubled, MFM-encoded data fits into half as much track length — hence the term double density. Looked at in frequency terms, FM has just two frequencies (f and 2f), but MFM has three (f, 1.5f, and 2f). The requirement that the controller shall be able to discriminate among more frequencies means that the electronic circuitry and disk motors must be more stable than for FM, requirements that, it turns out, are not particularly difficult to meet.

RLL

Although very popular and effective, MFM is not the most efficient way to encode data. Using MFM reduces the bit cell size down to the same size as the minimum magnetic flip-flop length, but it is possible to do even better if the number of clock signals is cut back even more. How far one can go depends on how steadily the disk turns and how precisely the spacing of the voltage pulses coming out of the head coil can be timed.

Disk system designers have tried many different schemes to lower the average number of clock signals per data bit and thus increase the maximum density of bits on the disk surface. The most popular plan, at least for hard disks used in PCs, has the name *2,7 RLL (run-length limited)*. This process uses no clock signals at all! This deficiency is made up for by recording on the disk patterns that are different from the ones in the data to be stored. If these patterns are chosen correctly, the controller can reverse that process when it is time to read the data.

TECHNICAL SECRET

Mathematicians and engineers refer to 2,7 RLL as an example of *group-coded recording* (GCR). The idea is that a group of data bits is replaced by a specially chosen larger group of bits to be recorded. ("Why," you may well ask, "would you want to spend space recording more bits than you have data?" Patience. The answer will emerge shortly.)

The usual form of 2,7 RLL is further distinguished by being a variable-length GCR method. That is, the size of the groups of bits of data to be replaced depends on what the actual data bits are.

The idea behind RLL is that there are two constraints on any pattern of magnetic field transitions that can be usefully recorded on the disk surface. First, the magnetic field transitions must not come any more often than the minimum magnetic flip-flop length (which avoids the risk of erasing the preceding field when recording a new field). Second, spaces without transitions must not be so long that the disk controller will lose track of the current position on the disk.

There is, therefore, a maximum and a minimum frequency that can be tolerated for the magnetic field transitions. (Or, viewed in terms of distances along the track between magnetic field transitions, there is a maximum and a minimum acceptable length without any transitions. *Run-length limited* means that these "runs" of track between transitions are limited to no more and no less than certain values.)

TECHNICAL SECRET

As in both FM and MFM, in 2,7 RLL, transitions occur only at the beginning or center of any bit cell. Rather than simply translate the incoming data bits into transitions, though, the controller examines them in small groups at a time, and for each group, a specially chosen sequence of transitions and lack of transitions gets stored. In this explanation, the letter *T* stands for a transition and the letter *O* stands for an open space. Both a *T* and an *O* take up exactly one-half bit cell of distance along the track.

Chapter 2: Magnetic Storage of Information

In 2,7 RLL, the sequences of Ts and Os must be chosen such that, no matter what the incoming data stream, there will always be at least two and never more than seven Os between any two Ts. By thinking about these rules, you can see that the minimum spacing of transitions is three half-bit cells, and the maximum spacing is eight half-bit cells.

Figure 2-8 shows a flow chart for generating the sequence of Ts and Os from the incoming stream of data ones and zeros. Look at the sequences at the right side of that figure. Notice that some start with a T and some have some Os before a T. Some have more than one T inside them, but always they have at least two Os between any two successive Ts. Finally, every sequence has at least two Os at the end. No matter which of the sequences is put after any other, then, there will always be at least two Os between successive Ts.

Similarly, you can see that no sequence has more than three Os at the end nor more than four Os at the beginning. No matter which sequences are put next to each other, then, there will never be more than seven Os between successive Ts.

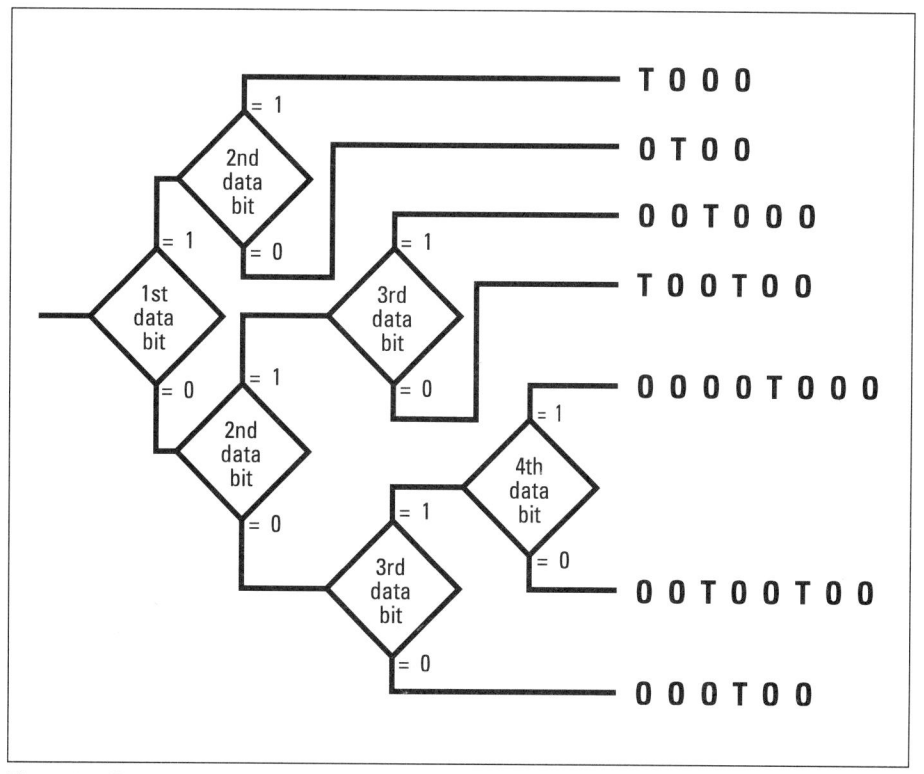

Figure 2-8: Flow chart showing how to convert a data-bit stream into magnetic transitions (Ts) and spaces between them (Os) by using 2,7 RLL encoding.

Every sequence of *T*s and *O*s has exactly twice as many symbols as the sequence of ones and zeros it is encoding. Because of the minimum of three symbols from *T* to *T*, three symbols can fit into one minimum magnetic flip-flop length. Because two symbols equal one bit, that means that the bit cell size has been reduced to two-thirds of a flip-flop length. This size enables the drive to put half again (150 percent) as many bits into a length of track as was possible with MFM, and three times the number possible with FM.

To summarize, with 2,7 RLL, special patterns of transitions are substituted for the actual data patterns to be recorded. These patterns have been chosen so that the maximum-to-minimum spacing of field transitions will be 8 to 3. Using this approach makes it possible to store 50 percent more data in the same space. Because most hard disks turn at the same rate, that also means it takes only two-thirds as much time to write or read any given information. Figure 2-7(e) shows how 2,7 RLL encoding of that same data byte looks compared to the other encoding methods. Although it is possible to improve upon RLL, the process is not easy, nor, at this point, is it reliable enough for most users. As it is, RLL pushes the limits of practicality.

Because RLL encoding puts down magnetic field transitions no closer than MFM does, people thought at first that they could use any MFM drive as an RLL drive just by hooking up the MFM drive to an RLL controller. Unfortunately, when first introduced commercially several years ago, RLL data encoding asked more of the disk drives and controller electronics than they could be depended on to do reliably. The drives and controllers failed over time — often quite soon and quite dramatically.

Manufacturers of RLL controllers have since learned better methods, and the makers of disk drives have devised ways to test their drives for this more demanding application. As a result, many drives are now available that are "certified for RLL use," though others still are not. Teaming an RLL-certified drive with an RLL controller makes for a fairly reliable combination.

HISTORICAL ASIDE Before testing for RLL compatibility was introduced by the drive makers, you may have had as much as a 50 percent chance of getting an MFM drive to work with an RLL controller at least tolerably well. Almost all the drives that can do this are now marked *RLL-capable;* any that are marked *MFM* are very likely *not* RLL-capable.

ARLL and other encoding methods

Some people like to live dangerously. Some manufacturers have introduced versions of RLL that go well beyond 2,7 RLL, to what is sometimes called *advanced run-length limited* (ARLL). The essence of these schemes is that they allow an even larger ratio of maximum-to-minimum spacing of the magnetic field transitions, enabling you to pack data on the tracks even more closely — almost twice as densely as MFM.

Drives attached to Enhanced Small Device Interface (ESDI) and SCSI controllers are sometimes referred to as using *enhanced run-length limited* (ERLL) data encoding. Actually, they commonly use 2,7 RLL data encoding, but because they record at a higher bit rate, they also put more bytes of data on a track than is the case with the standard RLL controllers and drives.

When a drive and controller do use a special form of data encoding, it is important that they be closely tuned to each other. This tuning is something that cannot be done unless one manufacturer creates both parts of the combination. Because ESDI, SCSI, and IDE/ATA drives, and hard disks incorporated on an option card all include their controllers with the drive inseparably, this tuning is possible in those cases. Anytime a controller is sold separately from the drive and yet claims to offer much higher data density than RLL, it is most likely an invitation to a data disaster. *Note:* ESDI drives do use a separate controller, but the data encoding for writing and the clock and data separation on reading are done on the drive. For the purposes of this discussion, then, they are in the same category as IDE/ATA, SCSI, and hard disks on an option card.

A Problem of Imperfection and Some Solutions

You now understand the way in which data can be stored on a hard disk. These schemes depend on being able to read exactly the pattern of magnetization written to the disk. Nothing in life is perfect. To cope with the inevitable errors, disk and controller makers have come up with some clever additional features that they regularly build into their products. This section describes what those manufacturers do to make our disks act as if they were perfect, or, at the very least, to allow them to inform the computer to which they are attached whenever they are unable to appear to be perfect. This latter capability, in turn, allows the PC to keep from using bad data as if it were good.

A partial solution: error detection

Your computer stores more than just the information it needs to get back. It also stores extra bits to help it determine whether the retrieved information can be trusted.

The simplest form of error detection, commonly used in a PC's system RAM, is the use of parity bits. A slightly more complex and more powerful technique, used on disk drives, is the cyclical redundancy check.

Parity

In almost every PC's system RAM, every data byte (8 bits) is accompanied by a ninth bit called a *parity bit*. When writing each byte of information to RAM, the PC computes its parity by counting the number of ones in that byte. If the number of ones is even, the corresponding parity bit is set to a one; otherwise, it is set to a zero. Looking at all nine bits, you will always find an odd number of bits set to a one, unless an error has occurred. This sitation is what is meant by the term *odd parity*. If any one bit is read or stored in error, the parity will come out wrong and the PC will know about the error. The computer will not know, however, which bit is in error.

/ TECHNICAL SECRET /

If an even number of bits flip, the parity will check out okay, even though the information has been damaged. Fortunately, in RAM, the most common errors by far are single-bit errors, and even these occur rarely. Because the PC cannot fix bit errors, it simply alerts you to the problem and then halts the computer. This problem is the source of the infamous `PARITY CHECK ONE` and `PARITY CHECK TWO` messages.

Some clone PCs give you a little more information when this sort of problem arises. They may display a message worded something like `I/O memory error at XXXXX`. The `X`s in this sample message are replaced by some hexadecimal symbols. That hexadecimal number is the address the PC was attempting to read when it found the parity error. As with IBM brand PCs, after presenting this parity error message, the clone PC will probably just stop.

Cyclical redundancy checks

When MS-DOS writes information to a floppy disk, it uses a similar protection scheme. First, it groups the information into sectors of exactly 512 bytes of data. It then adds two more bytes to the end of that information. MS-DOS computes this 16-bit binary number by combining the values of each of the 512 data bytes in the sector in a special fashion called a *cyclical redundancy check* (CRC).

Like parity, a CRC provides a means to test for corrupted data. CRC can spot any single-bit, and some multibit, corruptions but cannot detect just which bits got flipped. The message `Error reading drive A` most likely means that the machine read a sector with an invalid CRC value.

A better solution: error correction

Hard disks can store a great deal more data much more rapidly than floppy disks, making errors a lot more likely. Without some means of catching and correcting errors, users would experience an intolerable failure rate when the computer reads their hard disks, encountering errors as often as several times per day.

Fortunately, some clever engineers and mathematicians have devised *error correction codes* (ECC). All modern hard disk controllers include special logic to generate and use these ECC numbers. Most of the time, the PC's user doesn't even know disk errors have occurred; the disk controller simply fixes the errors automatically through the use of ECC.

Chapter 2: Magnetic Storage of Information

The orchard model for ECC

To understand the magic of ECC takes a bit of patience. Before discussing how ECC works in a hard disk controller, it is useful to look at a simpler model that is easier to understand. Suppose that you have 16 bits of information that you want to protect. Arrange those ones and zeros into an "orchard of data," with four rows and four columns. For each row and each column, if there are an even number of ones, add another one bit; add a zero bit if the row or column already contains an odd number of ones; and add a final bit where the additional row and column meet, choosing a one or a zero to make an odd number of ones in the bottom row (see Figure 2-9).

This arrangement gives each row and column odd parity. If any single bit flips anywhere, you can detect it because the row and column that bit is in will no longer have odd parity. Not only can you detect any single-bit error, you can correct it with total certainty!

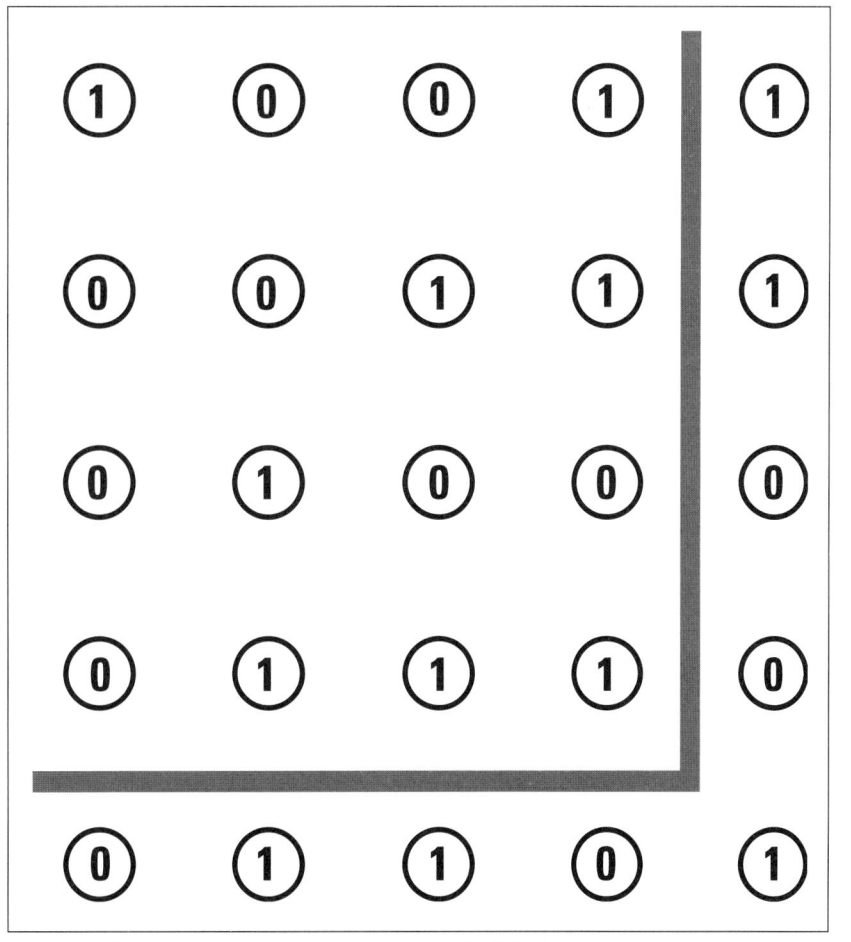

1	0	0	1	1
0	0	1	1	1
0	1	0	0	0
0	1	1	1	0
0	1	1	0	1

Figure 2-9: The orchard model demonstrates the principles behind error correction codes (ECC).

This capability may seem almost like magic. Most people, if confronted with the challenge of devising some way to be sure some data were stored correctly, would say that one has to store at least one additional copy of every bit. Then, if the two copies disagreed, you would know for sure that one of them was wrong. Actually, this approach is still not enough for error correction because you then would be unable to say which of the two copies was the correct one.

The idea of being able to detect and correct errors with only a modest amount of redundant information (and less than a full copy of the original data) is both marvelous and unexpected. But that is exactly what ECC permits our computers to do.

The orchard model has these lovely properties, albeit only for single-bit errors. For this reason, it serves as a good demonstration of the essence of ECC. Notice that, by using the orchard approach, you were able to protect 16 bits of data against any single-bit error with an overhead of only 9 bits. This is quite efficient, and the efficiency rises dramatically if you choose to use this approach to protect a larger number of bits.

Suppose that you set out to protect one entire sector of information from a hard disk. A sector is 512 bytes, or 4096 bits. This size means that you would create an "orchard" with 64 rows and 64 columns. To complete the orchard, you only need to add another 129 bits, thereby getting full protection against all single-bit errors.

Although this orchard approach is not yet a practical ECC, it shows the principle behind any useful ECC. Two things are missing in this model. First, this method cannot deal at all with multibit errors. Second, although quite efficient, the orchard approach is not nearly as efficient as possible.

A useful way to look at the construction of the orchard model's protective bits is to consider what it would take to create an explicit formula for each one. Those formulas would be sums of groups of bits, with each group chosen differently. (In calculating these sums, you just ignore any carry you encounter. This is what mathematicians call *modular arithmetic*.) A real ECC is much like this, only it uses more groups of bits, combines them in a slightly more complex manner, and those groups are chosen in some very arcane ways.

Real ECC

Manufacturers incorporate ECC circuitry in their hard disk controllers, each in slightly different ways. They say that their methods are proprietary, so you cannot discover what they are in detail or even whether they really are different from one another.

This is probably one of the reasons that a new controller often cannot read data on a hard disk previously formatted with a different controller. Because they were written in a different way, the sectors on the drive look strange to the second controller, so it considers the hard disk unformatted.

Chapter 2: Magnetic Storage of Information

Typically, any controller's ECC can detect and correct any pattern of errors in an entire sector containing 512 bytes (4096 bits) of data, as long as all the errors are contained within a single burst no longer than some specified length. IBM's standard for its original MFM drives for the PC/XT allowed for error bursts up to 11 bits in length to be corrected with total accuracy. To do this, they need only store 32 bits (4 bytes) of ECC at the end of each sector. That same amount of ECC also allows a very high probability of detecting any longer error burst or group of bursts, though those errors cannot be corrected just by using the ECC information.

> **TIP**
> Just knowing about the existence of those larger errors can be very helpful. First, you could order the disk drive to try again to read the data you sought. Often, doing so is all that is necessary to retrieve them with full accuracy. If the errors persist, at least you will know enough not to use this version of your data as if it were a perfect copy.

Because RLL stores 50 percent more data than an MFM drive in the same space, a spot defect in the platter coating that will damage 11 adjacent bits on an MFM drive will damage about half again that many on an RLL drive. RLL controllers, therefore, often use more bits of ECC. Many RLL controller makers choose to use 56 bits (7 bytes) to protect against any error contained within 17 consecutive bits of data. (This amount still is only a very tiny fraction of the bytes of data it is protecting.)

TECHNICAL SECRET

Although it's possible that error patterns may span more than 11 consecutive bits (or 17 bits on an RLL drive), such patterns are rare. Most errors on hard disks occur because of some spot defect that makes it impossible to store information reliably over a very small portion of a sector, usually much less than 11 bits long.

The bad news is that if you do have two or more regions of error within one sector, the ECC may occasionally *seem* to be adequate for fixing the damage, yet the fix suggested by the ECC will turn out to be incorrect. There are several possible ways to deal with this problem (none of which are yet in common use in PC hard disks, unfortunately).

One scheme that is used in the most advanced mainframe disk drives includes a multilayer scheme of error detection and correction. Each region of the disk to be protected (typically a whole track) is divided into many subregions, and each subregion is further divided into small sections, each of which is protected by some ECC. The whole scheme is further protected by some embedded CRC values.

If, upon reading the region, some of the small sections are found to contain errors, those errors will be corrected by using their ECC. Because of the way the CRC values protect the subregions and the total region, if the correction suggested by the ECC turns out to be incorrect, that fact will be detected at the CRC level. This method does not allow for correcting that error, but almost certainly detects it. In this way, the problem of incorrect fixes can be virtually eliminated. Future disk designs in PCs may incorporate some such scheme, but for now you must simply hope that such mistakes will rarely crop up on your machine.

What DOS does when ECC comes into play

When the disk controller tries to read a sector of data from a hard disk, three things can happen: the computed ECC matches the ECC on the disk; the controller finds the data to be inconsistent with the ECC, but the ECC suffice to show what the data should have been (known as a *correctable read error*); or the error in data is so large that the ECC is not sufficient to pinpoint the corrupt bits (called an *uncorrectable read error*).

TECHNICAL SECRET

When errors occur during the reading of data, the disk controller may use the ECC to correct the data it got and go on to the next sector, or it may attempt to read the questionable sector again and again, perhaps many times, to see whether it can get a perfect read. Whether the controller attempts to reread the data may depend not only on which controller you have, but also on the BIOS on your PC's motherboard, and perhaps on the version of DOS and what application program you are running.

The disk controller then hands the data to the computer with one of three messages. Put colloquially, these messages are as follows:

1. "Here is your data. I read it perfectly."

2. "Here is your data. I could not read it, but I figured out what it should have been."

3. "Here is what I got reading your data, but I am pretty sure this is *not* what it is supposed to be."

DOS was designed to take care of disk business without bothering the computer user any more than necessary. You don't have to tell DOS, for example, where on the disk to store information; you let it figure that out for you. When you want your information back again, you just tell DOS the filename and let it figure out where to find the data. This design philosophy makes computers much easier to use, in general. But one aspect of this design is less than wonderful.

The messages from the disk controller come into your PC and are received by its BIOS (basic input output system), a very low-level set of programs for dealing with the hardware. The BIOS then hands the data and the status message to a higher level program, the operating system (which in most cases is DOS).

Chapter 2: Magnetic Storage of Information

When DOS gets any of the three preceding status messages, it does one of two things. For either message 1 or 2 (success in reading; or failure to read, but the data were apparently successfully reconstructed by using the ECC), DOS simply accepts the data and hands it off to your application program without comment. Only if the disk controller could not read or reconstruct the data will DOS let you (or your application program) know that there was a problem. By that time, however, the problem is so severe that you have lost some of your data.

This situation is most unfortunate, for disk errors often are progressive. What today is a correctable read error can develop over time into an unrecoverable error. If DOS would inform you of a recoverable error when it occurs, you could move your endangered data to some safer place on the disk, or otherwise deal with this incipient data loss before it creates more trouble.

This circumstance is where programs like SpinRite shine. These programs can go behind DOS and the BIOS to decipher what really takes place when data are written to and read from your hard disk. Through such an intimate, down-to-the-platter look at your disk, these programs can detect problems before they become disasters and either move the data out of harm's way or actually repair the damage.

HISTORICAL ASIDE A curious side note: Several makers of products like SpinRite claim that they or their competitors "turn off" ECC. Actually, none of them do because they cannot really force hard disk controllers not to use ECC. The best they can do is notice the use of ECC. Gibson says his claim to "turn off" ECC is phrased that way "partly to confuse our competitors." Chapter 14 describes SpinRite's particular strategy.

Part I: The Hard Disk Companion

Summary

This chapter introduces you to the following concepts:

▶ Hard disks and audio tape recorders depend on the same basic magnetic principles both for recording and for retrieving digital data (in the case of hard disks) or music or voice (in the case of an audio tape recorder).

▶ Hard disks spin one or more platters coated with a magnetizable substance past an array of read/write heads — one head per surface. These heads move in and out radially to access different tracks where information can be recorded.

▶ All the heads at one radius form a cylinder. The importance of a cylinder is that all the tracks in that cylinder, which means all the tracks that pass in front of one of the heads in this position of the head assembly, are accessible at electronic speeds (requiring only a switching of the read or write circuitry from one head to another); accessing tracks in other cylinders requires moving the head assembly in or out — a process that takes a much longer time.

▶ PC hard disks use a changing current through one of the heads to form a changing magnetic field that, in turn, creates many tiny permanent magnets in the platter surface. The locations of these magnets determine what information is stored.

▶ The disk reads information recorded on the platter surface by detecting the boundaries of those permanent magnets as they pass under the read head.

▶ Binary data cannot simply be recorded on the surface in exactly the form it arrives at the disk controller. It first must be packaged, or encoded, in some fashion. The most common encodings for PC hard disks are MFM and 2,7 RLL. The newer RLL encoding is 50 percent more efficient, but it requires a higher grade of disk and controller to be reliable.

▶ All hard disks have problems of reliability which generally are simply hidden from the consumer by a very powerful set of error detection and correction strategies.

▶ Error correction codes are an essential part of error detection and correction strategies. They permit the drive and controller to detect, almost without fail, any time the data in a sector have been damaged. These codes also allow reconstructing what those data were in many cases.

▶ DOS, unfortunately, hides all the efforts of your disk controller to recover flawed data. This circumstance often keeps you and your application programs from knowing about trouble until it is too late — which may lead to substantial data loss.

To build on the basics of magnetic data recording, in the next chapter you learn about some tricky technical innovations in this technology, and about the most popular forms taken by hard disks in PCs.

Chapter 3
Some Important Engineering Issues

In This Chapter
▶ Sector interleaving: what it is, why it is often needed, and how to adjust it if your hard disk is not set correctly
▶ Head and cylinder skewing: what they are and when skewing may need to be readjusted
▶ The differences between the popular PC hard disk interface standards (ST412/ST506, ESDI, SCSI, and IDE)
▶ How hard disks on an option card compare to other PC hard disks
▶ The distinction between the physical and logical addresses for data stored on a hard disk

Improvement of Hard Disk Performance by Sector Interleaving and Head Skewing

One way to speed up your hard disk is to buy a much more expensive, higher performance drive. Such a purchase is not always necessary, however, and if the drive isn't installed with careful attention to its sector interleave value and possibly also its head skew, you may be wasting your money.

There are two things people normally quote about a hard drive in attempting to express how quickly it works. One number is called the *access time,* which means, roughly speaking, how long it takes for the controller to find a file on the disk. The other number is the *data transfer rate,* which refers to how quickly the controller can read the file once it has been found.

You cannot do much to lower the access time of your hard disk. (Well, one thing you can do is partition your hard drive into several different logical drives; this option is discussed near the end of Chapter 9.) In many cases, you *can* do something to dramatically improve your hard disk's data transfer rate: be sure that its sector interleave (and head skew) are set to their optimum values.

Anatomy of a disk sector

In Chapter 2, you learned that MS-DOS stores information on disk drives in sectors, each of which contains 512 bytes of data. The sectors contain those data bytes as well as some other things. A hard disk straight from the factory must be properly prepared before an MS-DOS computer can store data on it (see Chapters 8 through 10). To create the sectors, a suitable pattern of bits must be recorded for each sector on every track on each surface on the disk drive. A sector has two main parts: its identifier and the segment where the data will be stored (see Figure 3-1).

The sector header contains the three-dimensional address of this sector: Cylinder, Head (surface), and Physical Sector. It also contains a "bad sector" flag and it may contain various other things such as a pointer to a replacement sector.

The sector header ends with a CRC value. This is used to be sure the sector header was read correctly.

Gap between sector header and data portion of sector (to allow time for head to switch from reading to writing)

Inter-sector gap (to allow time for head to switch from writing to reading)

Error Correction Codes (ECC)

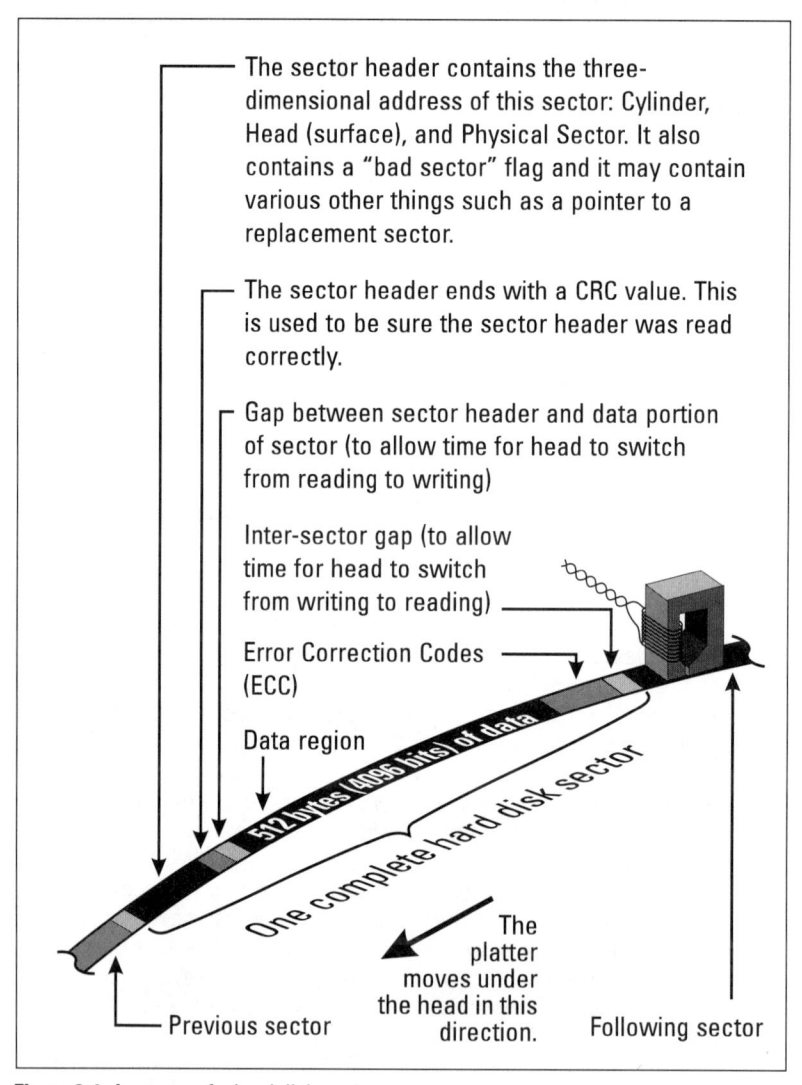

Data region

512 bytes (4096 bits) of data

One complete hard disk sector

The platter moves under the head in this direction.

Previous sector

Following sector

Figure 3-1: Anatomy of a hard disk sector.

Chapter 3: Some Important Engineering Issues

The identifier, or *sector header*, contains three numbers that together make up the sector's address: the head (or surface) on which this sector is located, the track (or cylinder) number, and the position of the sector on the track. The header also contains a field in which a mark shows whether the sector can store data reliably or if some defect has been found that makes its use inadvisable. Some hard disk controllers also record pointers in the sector headers, to direct the disk to an alternative sector or track if the original sector is faulty. Finally, the sector header ends with a *cyclical redundancy check* (CRC) value, which the controller uses to make sure that it has read the sector header correctly.

The second major part of the sector, where the computer stores data, can be divided into the data itself and the *error correction codes* (ECC) that protect that data. During the initial preparation, the computer fills this area with 512 dummy information bytes — placeholders for the real data — and ECC values that correspond to those dummy information bytes.

Sector interleave

The sector header contains a sector number that identifies that sector on the track. These numbers do not have to be assigned in any particular order. The design of a sector header allows sector numbers from 1 up to some maximum value, in some cases as high as 256.

The disk controller doesn't care what number in this range gets placed in any particular sector header; sectors can share the same number, although that situation would be most unusual. The disk controller doesn't even care how large the data area is. The disk controller just reads whatever it finds or writes whatever it is told to write.

One fairly common use of even the most bizarre of these possibilities is on the floppy diskettes used to distribute certain copy-protected programs. These diskettes have a few very nonstandard sectors on at least one track. The DOS commands COPY and DISKCOPY cannot duplicate such sectors, which is how the copy protection works. Such programs will run only if they see those special, oddly numbered and possibly odd-sized sectors on the diskette in drive A.

The disk-preparation program, on the other hand, assumes that the sectors will be numbered in some simple order. The sectors can be numbered 1, 2, 3, 4, 5, and so on, for example, but they don't have to be.

An alternative strategy for numbering the sectors goes by the name *sector interleave*. The name comes from the fact that in this scheme groups of sectors with adjacent numbers are interleaved between other groups of sectors with different adjacent numbers. Or, to look at it another way, after numbering one sector, instead of assigning the next sector number to the next sector, you jump over some number of sectors and then assign the next number.

Part I: The Hard Disk Companion

The amount of interleaving you are using is specified by a sector interleave value, or ratio, expressed as two numbers separated by a colon. If the value is 3:1, for example, after the first sector on the track is given sector address 1, two intervening sectors get skipped over and the fourth sector on the track is given address 2. Then two more sectors are skipped over, and the seventh sector is given sector address 3. This process continues until all the sectors have been given an address. (This method may seem like an arbitrary and unreasonable way to do things, but the reasoning behind this scheme will become clear as you read the following several paragraphs.)

To see why you might benefit from choosing a particular value for the sector interleave, consider the three cases shown in the three tracks on the disk in Figure 3-2. This illustration shows 17 sectors per track, which is typical of

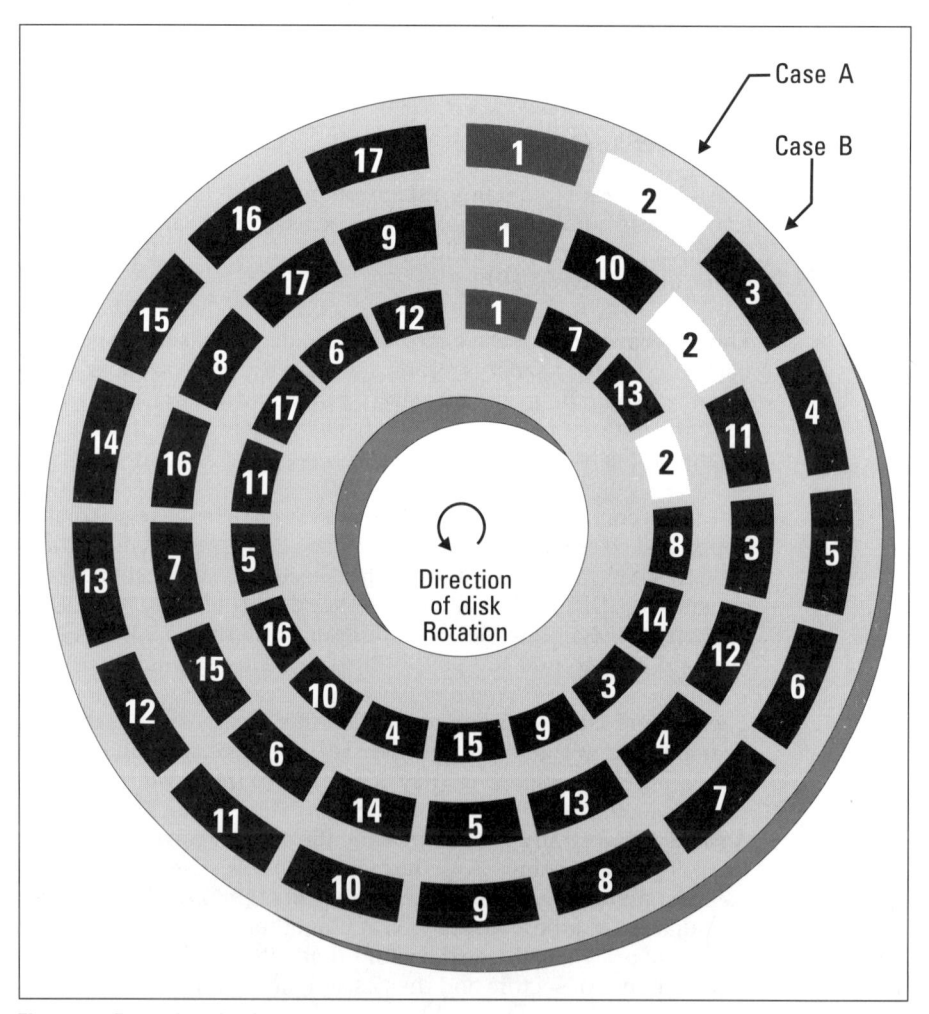

Figure 3-2: Examples of different sector interleave values.

almost all MFM hard disk drives; the tracks appear as they might actually be recorded on an MFM hard disk, except that the tracks in the figure are shown as very much wider than the tracks on an actual hard drive. (More modern hard disk designs have more sectors per track — anywhere from 23 to 75 sectors — and sometimes a given disk drive doesn't even have the same number of sectors on each track.)

The sectors in the outermost track (cylinder 0) in this figure have been numbered in the simplest order possible (sequentially), corresponding to a sector interleave value of 1:1. As the disk turns, the sectors present themselves under the read/write head in the order 1, 2, 3, 4, 5, and so on. The sectors in the next to outside track (cylinder 1) have been numbered using a sector interleave value of 2:1. The next track in from that (cylinder 2) has had its sectors numbered using a sector interleave value of 3:1.

Now consider what happens when the disk turns and the disk controller tries to read sector number 1 and immediately after that tries to read sector number 2. The arrows marked Case A and Case B point to two possible places where the head might start reading after it has finished "digesting" the data from reading sector 1. In Case A, the second sector on the track has already partly gone past the read/write head by the time the head is ready to start reading the second sector, but the third sector has not. In this case, an interleave of 2:1 is optimum. In Case B, even the third sector has at least partially passed the head before the head is ready to read that sector, but in this case the fourth sector has not yet arrived at the head. In this case, an interleave of 3:1 is optimum.

How DOS stores and retrieves files

If you ask DOS to store a file on the disk and if all the sectors in that region are available, DOS will store each set of 512 bytes sequentially in sector number order. DOS switches to the next head in the same cylinder when the first track is full, again filling each sector sequentially.

This process continues until the cylinder is full. At this point, if there is still more data to be stored, DOS will ask the disk controller to move all the heads at once to the next cylinder (which the controller does by stepping the head assembly in by one track spacing). This whole process continues until DOS has written the entire file to the disk. Similarly, DOS will read the sectors back in the same order. DOS reads a sector by telling the disk controller the cylinder, head, and sector numbers (the three components of the physical address) of the sector to read.

The disk controller in turn simply steps the head assembly to the appropriate cylinder, turns on the correct head, and waits for the desired sector to come under the head. The disk controller reads every sector header as it comes along, comparing the address information in those headers with the head and cylinder it is supposed to be looking at (to be sure that its head actuator and head switching circuitry work correctly), and looking for the desired sector number. When the controller finds that sector header, it either switches on the write circuitry or it reads the data and trailer, depending on whether it is writing or reading a sector.

After finding the sector, the disk controller must "digest" that sector's information before going on to the next sector. If it is reading data, the controller must compute the ECC for the data as read and then compare that ECC with the recorded ECC; if it is writing data, the controller must compute the ECC to store with the data. The disk continues to turn during the time the controller does the necessary processing of the information in that sector. Because digesting the information can take a considerable time, the disk may have turned an appreciable amount during that time.

The simplest (and sometimes the worst) case

Remember that in the example under discussion, the sectors are numbered sequentially around the track. If during the time the controller is digesting one sector's data, the disk turns farther than the (small) intersector gap, the next sector that the controller wants to read from or write to will already have gone past the head — possibly quite a distance past. In this case, the disk controller must wait until the disk has gone almost all the way around again before the desired sector comes into view.

Notice that the sectors are numbered differently in each of the tracks. For now, focus on the outer track. Its sectors are numbered sequentially, just as in the current example. (The other tracks in this figure will be explained shortly.)

The arrow labeled Case A points to a place on the disk where the system might start reading just after it finishes digesting what it read from sector 1. Notice that this arrow points to the middle of the sector on the outer track (sector 2). This example represents the situation just described, in which the disk controller is not ready to start reading sector 2 until after that sector has already passed at least part of the way under the head. Because the controller must wait until it sees the sector header of sector 2 pass under the head, it must wait almost an entire revolution before it can resume reading.

In this situation, the hard disk controller only manages to read one sector on each revolution of the disk. At this rate, data cannot be read or written to a hard disk any faster than to a floppy disk. Fortunately, you can do very much better with only a little change in how the sectors are numbered.

How sector interleave solves the problem

Many years ago, an ingenious engineer at IBM figured out a way around this problem. He did not want to make the intersector gaps any larger, for that would waste space on the disk and reduce its storage capacity. Instead, he renumbered the sectors in a nonsequential manner. To establish a 2:1 interleave on a track with 17 sectors, for example, the sector is numbered in this

Chapter 3: Some Important Engineering Issues

fashion: 1, 10, 2, 11, 3, 12, 4, 13, 5, 14, 6, 15, 7, 16, 8, 17, 9, and then back to 1 again (see the middle track in Figure 3-2). For a 3:1 interleave, the pattern is 1, 7, 13, 2, 8, 14, 3, 9, 15, 4, 10, 16, 5, 11, 17, 6, 12, and back to 1 (see the innermost track in Figure 3-2).

The sector interleave number, therefore, is greater by one than the number of sectors you must skip between each sequential sector (for a 2:1 interleave, for example, you skip one sector). The interleave number also equals the number of times you would have to go around the track to read all the sectors in order, assuming that none of the sectors passed by before the controller was ready for it. Reading all the sectors on one track when your computer has a 1:1 interleave, for example, requires just one revolution — *if* the disk controller can digest the information fast enough. If the disk controller is not that fast, it will need as many revolutions of the disk as there are sectors in one track in order to read one track's worth of data.

Increasing the interleave to 2:1 means that the track *must* go around at least twice for the head to read or write all the sectors sequentially. This process slows down the sectors' arrival at the head enough that the disk controller may be ready when each new sector arrives. If a 2:1 interleave is not slow enough, though, the disk will have to make 17 or even 18 revolutions to read the full track (on a disk with 17 sectors per track, and correspondingly more revolutions on disks with more sectors per track).

The middle track in Figure 3-2 shows that if the delay between reading one sector and before the system is ready to read another sector is represented by the arrow marked Case A, an interleave of 2:1 will be just right. The very next sector to appear after the system is ready to read (after digesting sector 1) will be the sector numbered 2.

The inner track in Figure 3-2 shows that if the delay is enough longer that the head is positioned where the arrow marked Case B points when the controller is first ready to read the next sector, an interleave of 3:1 is best. In this case, an interleave of 2:1 is just as bad as 1:1 because both of those interleave values will force the controller to wait a full revolution to get the contents of each successively numbered sector.

Interleave is a system-level problem

When deciding what the ideal interleave value is for a given hard drive, you have to consider several factors. In addition to looking at the disk controller speed, you also need to consider the clock speed of the motherboard and, in particular, the speed at which the *input-output bus* slot into which the controller is plugged can operate. After most disk controllers have read a sector, they must hand off those bytes of data to the computer before they are ready to read the next sector. Similarly, the disk controllers will not accept another sector's worth of data to be written until they have finished writing the sectorful they already have. The speed at which the computer's input-output bus operates, therefore, also can limit the correct interleave value.

All these factors mean that the correct interleave value can only be decided at the system level — the person who assembles the disk, controller, and computer is the only one who can determine this value correctly.

Because of the subtlety of the issue of finding and setting the correct sector interleave value and the effort required to resolve it properly (especially before the introduction of programs like SpinRite), until quite recently, nearly all PCs' hard disks were interleaved incorrectly. With the rise in popularity of IDE and SCSI drives, which usually are built to work correctly with a 1:1 interleave, this problem is beginning to vanish. If you have an older drive design, however, your hard disk may very well not have an optimum sector interleave value.

TECHNICAL SECRET

Many modern disk drives, especially IDE and SCSI drives and hard disks mounted on an option card, incorporate a track buffer. This buffer enables these drives to read an entire track at once, without having to digest each sector before reading the next one.

In some cases, a problem may still exist, but only when going from reading one track to the next. Because that occurs much less often than going from one sector to the next, the problem is not significant. (To the extent that it is a problem, it can sometimes be dealt with by an appropriate value for head skew, an idea that is described in the next section.) Some controllers even have two track buffers: one to hold what is being read or written and the other to digest or prepare the preceding or following track's worth of data.

One practical result of this approach is that these drives are able to handle a 1:1 interleave, no matter how fast or slow the system unit may be. All that the speed of the system unit influences is how much time must elapse after finishing with one track before going on to the next track.

Some ST412/ST506 and ESDI controllers also have track buffers. They, too, can support 1:1 interleave for any disks that they control.

If your disk's interleave value is set too high, you have to wait only a small extra amount of time to get your data on or off your disk. If your disk's interleave value is too low, on the other hand, you will pay an enormous penalty in reduced disk performance. (See the shaded portion of Table 3-1.)

Table 3-1 shows just how much an incorrect interleave value will cost you for several common cases. The only way to be sure that your interleave is set correctly is to run a program that will evaluate the disk performance in your system for each of several different interleave values. This feature is standard with SpinRite and most other reinterleaving programs.

Chapter 3: Some Important Engineering Issues

The performance penalty incurred by having an incorrect sector interleave value

Peak data transfer rate in kilobytes per second

Minimum sector interleave ratio your system can handle without missing any sequentially numbered sectors:	1:1	2:1	3:1	4:1	5:1
MFM (17 sectors per track)					
If sector interleave is set to 1:1	510	30	30	30	30
If sector interleave is set to 2:1	255	255	30	30	30
If sector interleave is set to 3:1	170	170	170	30	30
If sector interleave is set to 4:1	128	128	128	128	30
If sector interleave is set to 5:1	102	102	102	102	102
RLL (26 sectors per track)					
If sector interleave is set to 1:1	780	30	30	30	30
If sector interleave is set to 2:1	390	390	30	30	30
If sector interleave is set to 3:1	260	260	260	30	30
If sector interleave is set to 4:1	195	195	195	195	30
If sector interleave is set to 5:1	156	156	156	156	156
ESDI (34 sectors per track)					
If sector interleave is set to 1:1	1620	30	30	30	30
If sector interleave is set to 2:1	810	810	30	30	30
If sector interleave is set to 3:1	540	540	540	30	30
If sector interleave is set to 4:1	405	405	405	405	30
If sector interleave is set to 5:1	324	324	324	324	324

NOTE:
The above figures were calculated using the following information:

Data on different encoding schemes

	MFM	RLL	ESDI
Revolutions per second	60	60	60
Kilobytes per second	0.5	0.5	0.5
Sectors per track	17	26	54
Maximum possible data transfer rate	510	780	1620
Data transfer rate for one sector per revolution	30	30	30

(Some RLL drives have as few as 23 or as many as 27 sectors per track. ESDI drives range from 34 to 56 sectors per track. Some SCSI and IDE drives have up to 75 sectors per track, often with variable numbers of sectors in different zones of the drive.)

Table 3-1: Performance penalties for incorrect sector interleave values.

HISTORICAL ASIDE: Even before programs like SpinRite existed, there were some other programs, such as HOPTIMUM, that could help you determine both what your hard disk's current interleave value was and what it should be for optimum performance. Unfortunately, programs in this earlier generation did their work by destructively reformatting one or more tracks, wiping out data if you weren't very careful and knowledgeable. These programs were not suitable for the fainthearted or the uninitiated PC user. SpinRite and the other modern reinterleaving programs are, in contrast, perfectly safe programs for anyone to use.

CAUTION: All modern reinterleaving programs are safe, with one exception: IAU, also known as the Interleave Adjustment Utility. See the discussion in Chapter 12 to learn why this program is dangerous.

Head skewing

Sector interleaving is a subtle concept that many people have difficulty grasping. This next topic, *head skewing*, is similarly subtle, but your knowledge of sector interleaving should help you comprehend it.

Remember the steps that DOS goes through to write a file to the disk? First, DOS fills one track and then goes to the next head in the same cylinder; when the cylinder is full, DOS goes on to the next track. Each transition from one track to another and from one cylinder to another takes time, during which the disk inexorably keeps on turning. Considering this fact, you can see that you can incur a similar penalty in disk performance every time you read or write a file that goes across a track or cylinder boundary. This point is where head skewing comes in.

The idea of head skewing is simple enough. Suppose that you have just finished writing to the last sector on one track. Because you presumably have already set the interleave to its optimum value, you are now ready to write to the first sector of the next track. But you must wait until you get the head switched and get the head assembly repositioned over the correct, next track. If that operation takes more than just a very little time, the head will arrive there just too late, despite the interleaving. The solution is to move all the sector numbers for the new track around by one (or more) positions, relative to where they were on the previous track.

To see what this all means, consider a simple example. In almost any hard drive and controller combination whose overall performance is good enough to warrant worrying about skew, the optimum sector interleave value for each track will be 1:1. For simplicity, assume that when going from one head to another, the optimum performance will be obtained if the track on the next surface is

Chapter 3: Some Important Engineering Issues

displaced from the one just read by a single sector. Moving the heads takes longer than switching from one head to another one. Again, for simplicity, assume that a displacement of three sectors is what is needed when switching from one track to an adjacent one.

Figure 3-3 shows this simple example for a particular drive geometry — a two-platter (four-head) hard disk with a 1:1 sector interleave value on each surface, a head-to-head skew of +1, and a cylinder skew of +3. Notice that there are only two platters; the tracks on the bottom of each platter are shown as if you could see through the platter. Imagine writing (or reading) a file into contiguously numbered sectors and assume it is a file that will require many tracks before you are finished.

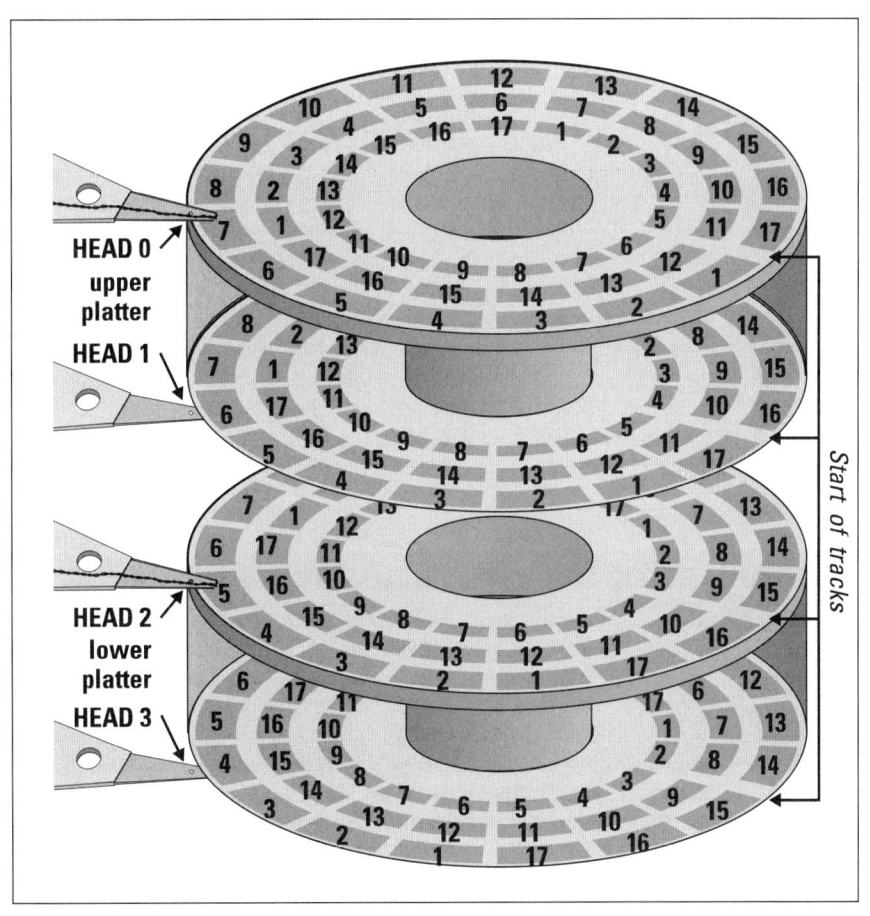

Figure 3-3: Head skewing.

- The first track (Head 0, Cylinder 0 — at the outside of the disk on the top surface of the upper platter) has its sectors numbered sequentially starting right after the end of the track gap, starting with sector number 1. The next track to be read or written is in the same position on the opposite side of the top platter — that is, it is Track 0 for Head 1. Notice that its sector numbers start with 17, which is followed by 1, 2, and so on. This offset of one sector in going from the top to the bottom of that platter is an example of a *head skew* of +1.

- Once all the sectors in the track at Head 0, Cylinder 0 have been read, and all the sectors in the next track (at Head 1, Cylinder 0), the next track to be read is on the top of the lower platter, at Head 2, Cylinder 0. Notice that this track has its sectors starting (just after the end of track gap) with numbers 16, 17, and then 1, 2, and so on. These sector numbers are offset from those in the preceding track by exactly one sector — again, a head skew of +1.

- This pattern continues until you reach the end of the last track in Cylinder 0 (using Head 3). The last track in Cylinder 0 starts with sector number 15.

- Now the head assembly must be moved in, to Cylinder 1, and writing will resume at the top of the disk, using Head 0. In this case, to allow for the time needed to move the heads, the outer track is numbered starting with sector 12. You can see why this is so by remembering that the last track (Head 3, Cylinder 0) started with sector number 15. Subtract 3 for the *cylinder skew* and you get 12 for the starting sector number of this track.

> **TIP:** Some high-performance disk controllers permit the user to set the head skew, but most disk controllers do not. Head skew is not yet a commonly understood idea in the marketplace, although it will no doubt become more important, and therefore discussions about it, as well as controllers and programs that help you set skew, will become more prevalent as the industry moves to ever faster disk drives.

Where sector interleave and head skew information is stored

The sector numbers are stored in the sector headers, which means that the interleave and skew values are set by whatever writes those sector headers. Initially, the disk-preparation program (the low-level formatter) performed this task by simply invoking a special function of the disk controller to do the work. Because this process destroys all the data on the tracks that are low-level formatted, it was done as infrequently as possible.

In the old days, if you wanted to reinterleave your disk, you first had to back up all the data, redo the low-level format, re-create the partition table, redo the high-level format, and then restore all your data. This process very likely would take you at least a full working day. (All these terms and processes are discussed in detail in Chapters 8, 9, 10, and 12.)

How to alter interleave and skew

The advent of SpinRite and other nondestructive reinterleaving programs made it possible to alter your sector interleave value at any time. Now you can easily test different values and then set up your disk for the best one for your PC.

TIP Although it is always a good idea to do a full backup of your system before the first time you use any utility program that messes with your hard disk at such a deep level, it is most unlikely that you will need that backup. After you have proven the compatibility of your system and your reinterleaving program once, you may reuse it anytime you want without doing a full backup first.

The head and cylinder skew are more difficult to change. Fortunately, because they come into play only when you are reading or writing a file that extends across the end of a track, you pay a much lower time penalty than you do with an incorrectly set sector interleave value. If you are technically sophisticated and daring, you can experiment with different skew settings by use of the HTHF program, available from Kolod Research, 1898 Techny Court, Northbrook, IL 60062-5474; 708-291-1586.

When and how to set the interleave wrong

If you are going to set your interleave to anything other than the optimum value, you certainly should set it too high. Remember that when 3:1 is optimum, setting it to 4:1 means you will have to wait only 4 revolutions to read a full track of data that at best would take you 3 revolutions. On the other hand, setting the interleave to 2:1 means you will have to wait 17 or maybe even 18 revolutions.

But why might you want to set the interleave to a nonoptimum value? Remember another fact: The optimum value depends on several factors, including how fast your computer bus operates. If the bus operates at different speeds at different times (a Turbo XT, for example, may run at 4.77 MHz or 10 MHz), the optimum interleave value most likely will not be the same for both. You therefore should set the interleave to the optimum value for the lowest bus speed, unless you know you will not be using your computer at that speed much.

Inconsistent interleave values

Because the sector interleave value is set by numbers written into the sector headers, each track can and does have its own sector interleave value. On most drives, all tracks have the same interleave value, but this circumstance need not be so.

If you interrupt the operation of a reinterleaving program, then some of the tracks will have been changed and others will not. This inconsistency will not adversely affect your computer's operation. The tracks that are optimally interleaved just will work faster than the others.

A special case of varying interleave values

The detailed discussion of SpinRite's operation in Chapter 14 includes mention of some curious facts. Although it normally redoes the low-level format and resets the sector interleave value for almost every track in a DOS partition, SpinRite is sometimes very careful not to do so in the very first track.

SpinRite also may skip the track whose location is cylinder 100, head 0. Finally, it uses a track in the diagnostic cylinder to experiment with different sector interleave values. When it is finished, it restores the sector interleave value for that track to its original value. The result is that there will be at least one and maybe several tracks on your disk for which SpinRite does not permanently alter the sector interleave value. Chapter 14 covers the SpinRite details.

This information becomes more than a bit of trivia when you learn that several of the popular disk-performance-testing programs, such as the CORETEST program from Core International and the SI program in the Norton Utilities, use the very same tracks that SpinRite carefully leaves alone for much of their testing. If you run those programs on a disk that has had its interleave changed by SpinRite to the optimum value, the programs will not correctly report the improvement in disk speed.

Popular Products and Standards

When IBM introduced the PC in 1981, a hard disk was not a standard option. IBM made this choice not because there weren't any hard disks available for personal computers; some already had been used with a few Apple II, CP/M, and S-100 bus systems. Hard disks were just considered too expensive for an individual's home computer.

By 1983, IBM realized that it could successfully sell PCs to small businesses and that people wanted and would pay for the added storage capacity and convenience of hard disks. The IBM PC/XT, introduced that year, therefore, came with a 10MB hard drive as standard equipment.

HISTORICAL ASIDE — The fact that IBM specified the XT as having a "5-year design life (8,000 hours Mean Time to Failure)" reveals that it thought these machines would not be used even as much as 40 hours per week, let alone around the clock, as so many PCs now are.

Chapter 3: Some Important Engineering Issues

IBM implemented the hard drive by means of an *option card* that you could plug into one of the bus slots on the PC/XT motherboard. This card, christened the Fixed Disk Adapter, in turn was connected to the drive by two ribbon cables (see Figure 3-4).

As Figure 3-4 illustrates, in a typical PC hard disk drive subsystem, the controller card plugs into the system unit's input/output bus (one of the slots on the motherboard). One or two hard disk drives are mounted in a drive bay. The drives are connected to the controller via ribbon cables. The drives are also connected directly to the power supply. (This pattern of mounting and cables is not the only one used in PCs, but it is the most common.)

The XT used a four-wire cable from the power supply to the drive, similar to that powering a floppy disk drive. Many later versions of disk drives for PCs receive their operating power in a similar fashion. One exception to that rule is that some modern designs have only two wires in their power cable. Another exception is that hard disks mounted on an option card, as well as some IDE drives, get their power from the PC's input/output bus.

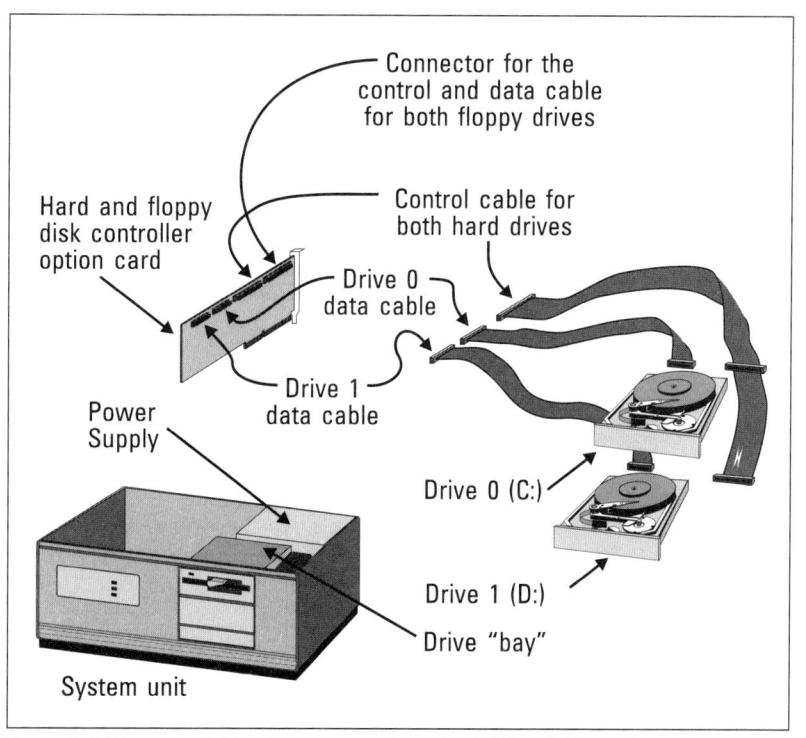

Figure 3-4: The essential hardware parts of a typical PC hard drive subsystem.

Part I: The Hard Disk Companion

/ TECHNICAL SECRET /

You can put IBM's original XT hard disk controller and hard disk into an IBM PC, but first you have to be sure that the PC's power supply is able to provide enough power to operate the disk; the power supply IBM put in the original PC is not powerful enough.

If you want to perform this task, you also have to be sure that your PC does not have one of the very earliest ROM BIOS chips. It is likely your ROM BIOS is too early if your PC can accept only up to 64KB (kilobytes) of RAM on the motherboard. If yours is one of the older ROM BIOS chips, you can upgrade to one dated October, 1982. This chip and all later versions of the ROM BIOS for the IBM PC include a procedure called the option ROM scan, without which the hard disk controller (and several other plug-in cards) will not work. All PC clones and all other IBM-brand personal computers already have a sufficiently up-to-date ROM BIOS. (Many diagnostic programs, such as CheckIt, will display the date of the ROM BIOS. Or you can use the DOS program DEBUG, using the command d FFFF:5 C <Enter>. Follow that command with Q <Enter> to get out of DEBUG.)

As with many of the parts in the PC and XT, IBM bought off-the-shelf technology for its hard drives. It made its own controllers, which were very similar to some existing controllers, and had the drives made to its specifications by experienced drive manufacturers.

Because the IBM PC, XT, AT, and PS/2 models have sold so well, their basic design has become a standard. These computers define what is meant by a personal computer today. (Well, yes, there are other important designs, but the lion's share of the personal computer market is for "IBM compatibles.")

The way IBM chose to implement its first hard disk controllers and disk drives, therefore, defined by example an important standard for these products. IBM never gave a name to that design standard. Because the design for the first IBM PC/XT hard drives bears a very close resemblance to a couple of earlier designs by the Seagate Technology Company, blending features of both of them, the design is now known by the numbers of those models — the ST412/ST506 interface. (You may see it written as ST412/506, ST506/412, or even just ST506.)

ST412/ST506

This model-number designation describes a particular variety of hard disk interface, indicating in detail how the disk drive and its controller "talk" to one another. How the controller talks to the computer is described in the definition of the PC input/output (I/O) bus that connects to all the motherboard slots because the hard disk controller plugs into that bus.

Chapter 3: Some Important Engineering Issues

The specification of this (or any) interface has several aspects. The first concerns the physical description of the cables through which the controller and drive conduct their conversation, and the connectors at the ends of those cables. Another is the electrical aspect, giving the voltage levels and signal timings on each wire. Yet another is the logical aspect in which the function of the signal on each wire is described. Finally, there are usually some critical timing issues that must be specified, such as how long various signals may or must linger and how rapidly they can change from one state to another. When you mention a standard, like ST412/ST506, you are implying all these aspects.

TECHNICAL SECRET

The hard disk controller is connected to each hard drive by two ribbon cables. One cable has 34 wires in it (with a 34-pin connector, so the wires are sometimes referred to as *pins*). This cable carries a number of control signals to and from the drive.

Among the signals going from the controller to the drive are those used to command the head actuator to move one track in or out, those to set the level of write current for the heads, and a signal saying whether the drive is next going to read or write. Signals from the drive include those to tell the controller that it has done what was asked or signals about any problems it encounters. Other uses for this cable include the drive reporting back to the controller on its success or failure in carrying out a controller command and on its readiness for further work.

Digital in nature, these signals change slowly for the most part. If you have two hard drives attached to the same controller, this cable will be routed from the controller to the first hard drive and then to the other drive. (This pattern of running a cable from one device to another and then on to yet another is called a *daisy chain*.)

The second cable contains 20 wires, most of which are connected to electrical ground and serve as shields for the other wires. All the bits of data the controller writes to the drive travel on just one of these 20 wires, with the complementary signal traveling on another specific wire. (Complementary means that when the first wire is carrying a binary zero, the other wire is carrying a binary one and vice versa.) Yet another pair of wires carries the read signal and its complement from the heads to the controller. These are high-frequency signals, up to 5 million bits per second. These signals are much more susceptible to noise contamination than those on the 34-wire cable. To keep these signals clean, if you have two drives attached to one controller, each drive gets its own 20-wire cable, which you should keep as short as possible.

Significantly, only one bit of data can travel in the data cable at a time, even though the cable has 20 wires. Because the data bits travel at 5 million bits per second, then, and because one byte requires eight such bits, the bytes of information can only go in or come out at most one-eighth that fast (625 kilobytes per second). This speed is in contrast to, for example, parallel-cable SCSI drives, in which the data cable carries the information at least 8 bits, and sometimes up to 32 bits, at a time. For SCSI parallel cables, the byte data-transfer rate is at least as large as, and can be as much as four times, the maximum bit-frequency on the cable (in a cable with 32 data wires). (A recent innovation in SCSI involves connecting devices via a SCSI serial cable in which data flows one bit at a time, just as in ST506/ST412 data cable.)

The name ST412/ST506 does not imply any particular data-encoding strategy, although manufacturers at first used it to describe an MFM drive with 17 sectors per track. Because encoding data when using 2,7 RLL leads to the same maximum frequency of magnetic field transitions (but with a lower minimum frequency), the signals on the wires in the cable between an RLL controller and its drive look very much like those for an MFM controller and drive combination. You can say, then, that an RLL drive also has an ST412/ST506 interface.

TECHNICAL SECRET

Because RLL packs more data into less distance along the track, an RLL drive ordinarily has 25 or 26 sectors per track instead of the 17 typical of an MFM drive. Also, because an RLL drive has more bits encoded into a given number of field transition times, even with no higher frequency signals than on an MFM drive, the RLL drive can convey 50 percent more bits per second across the cable (780 kilobytes per second for 26 sectors per track, and in some cases up to 937 kilobytes per second with 31 sectors per track).

The more daring ARLL controllers also are sometimes described as using this interface. But because they use signals to and from the head that exceed the standard's frequency specification, their interface ought to be given some other name.

The ST412/ST506 interface design was simple to build in 1983 with available hardware. This design also adequately met the needs of PC owners when the largest hard drives available were 10MB models and the maximum PC bus speed was 4.77 MHz. It did not take long for that happy situation to change, however. Prices of hard drives began to plummet, available disk sizes grew, and new PCs ran at ever higher clock speeds. The interface limits soon became, at the very least, annoying. Hard disk manufacturers quickly proposed two different solutions to this problem.

ESDI

One hard disk maker, Maxtor, began to push for an Enhanced Small Device Interface (ESDI) standard in the early 1980s. This standard evolved from the ST412/ST506 interface. Only a few subtle, yet very important, changes were made. This solution still works with a disk controller card plugged into the PC bus and connected to the drive with the same two ribbon cables, one with 34 wires (going from the controller to the first drive and then on to the second drive, if you have two) and one with 20 wires (or two 20-wire cables if you have two drives).

TECHNICAL SECRET

The most important change from ST412/ST506 standard to ESDI is that the circuitry called the clock-data separator is put on the drive itself instead of on the controller. (The *clock-data separator*, as its name implies, separates the signals from the drive into signals representing clock information and signals that carry the actual data being read. See Chapter 2, and especially the discussion of Figure 2-7 for more details.) This approach has at least a couple of very important advantages.

The companies that make hard drives generally do not also make controllers. With the ST412/ST506 interface, therefore, MFM or RLL controllers had to incorporate clock-data separators that had a somewhat "vanilla" design — they were able to work with anyone's ST412/ST506 hard drive. Now, with an ESDI interface, the drive makers can incorporate a data separator that has been very finely tuned to their own disk designs.

The other important advantage is that, because the data is recovered from the head signals before entering the cable, the bit-transfer rate can be raised without undue degradation. The maximum frequency of bit information transfer for the ESDI design is 24 MHz (or 24 million bits per second). Drives now on the market go up to at least 15 MHz. Proposed extensions to the ESDI standard would raise the maximum frequency to around 50 MHz.

Don't forget, though, that this is still a standard that sends data along the cable one bit at a time, so the maximum byte information rates are one-eighth of these values. Thus the ESDI drives on the market today offer at most about a 2-million-byte-per-second data-transfer rate.

In the ESDI standard, some other minor changes from its predecessor include new commands that can be issued by the controller and new status reports that the drive can give to the controller. For example, the controller can tell the drive to go to a certain track by giving its track number (instead of having to tell it to step in or out some number of steps). Also, the controller can command the drive to perform some diagnostic tests upon itself and to report the results.

SCSI

The Small Computer System Interface (SCSI, pronounced "scuzzy") is a very different kind of disk interface. Properly speaking, SCSI is not a disk interface at all.

The SCSI standard was first developed in the late 1970s under the name SASI (Shugart Associates System Interface). Over the past dozen years, disk makers have upgraded it several times. Many current drive and controller designs adhere to the version of the standard called SCSI-2. The committee that writes these standards is currently working on SCSI-3.

SCSI differs in many important ways from the other interfaces already described. The most important idea is that this interface presupposes that only rather intelligent devices are attached to its interconnecting cable (the SCSI bus). There may be up to 7 SCSI slave devices and one SCSI master sharing a single cable.

Note: The notion of a *master* and a *slave* in this connection is just about what you may have imagined it would be. The master device tells the slave what to do, and the slave does it. There can be only one master because somebody has to decide what is going to happen next. A master can tell a slave to take control of the bus and use it for a while, but eventually the slave must give back control to the master once more.

The nature of these SCSI devices may be quite diverse. You can attach large and fast hard disk drives, tape drives, optical disks, laser printers, and even slow devices such as a mouse, so long as each device has the appropriate SCSI interface electronics between it and the SCSI cable. In many ways, SCSI is more of a small local area network (LAN) than a normal PC-to-hard-disk interface.

Connecting SCSI devices to a PC

To attach a SCSI bus to a PC, you must have a *SCSI host adapter*. This adapter is a circuit card you plug into your PC's input/output bus and to which you can attach a SCSI bus cable.

TECHNICAL SECRET

Most SCSI devices communicate via a ribbon cable with 50 pins (or, in one aspect of the SCSI-2 standard, a 50-pin cable plus an auxiliary 68-pin cable). All the signals are digital. The data is carried 8 (or 16 or 32) bits at a time in parallel. There are relatively few control signals in the cable.

It is possible for each of seven SCSI slave devices to have up to 8 *logical units* within them. In principle, then, you could have one SCSI host adapter in a PC communicating with up to 56 logically separate subdevices.

Chapter 3: Some Important Engineering Issues

> The data-transfer rate in the original SASI interface was only 12 megabits per second, or 1.5MB per second over 8 parallel wires. In the latest version of the SCSI standard (often called SCSI-2), the bit rate may be as high as 10 MHz, with a corresponding data rate as high as 40MB per second (using 32 parallel wires).

The SCSI host sends a command to one of the slaves, which in turn possesses enough intelligence to execute the sequence of operations by using the SCSI cable (in other words, the slave becomes a temporary master). When the slave completes its task, it relinquishes the cable, and the original SCSI host may permit some other slave device to control the cable for a time.

A SCSI hard disk actually consists of three parts. First is the disk drive. Next is the electronics package that in earlier designs would have been put on the disk controller. And finally, there must be a special *SCSI slave interface*. This last part is another piece of electronics designed to "talk SCSI" across the SCSI bus.

Apple Macintosh computers popularized the SCSI interface. (All but the earliest Macintosh computers came with a SCSI port built in.) The PC world showed little support for SCSI until recently. Now that IBM has introduced a SCSI host adapter and some SCSI peripherals, this approach is rapidly gaining favor.

TECHNICAL SECRET

> Originally, the SCSI interface was designed to use a wide ribbon cable and to carry at least eight bits of data in parallel. One of the features in SCSI-2 was support for even wider cables, carrying up to 32 bits simultaneously. SCSI-3 actually reverses the trend. More accurately, SCSI-3 supports both wide and narrow versions. In addition to the parallel, wide-cable form, SCSI-3 supports a serial cable that transfers just one bit at a time.
>
> This capability may seem like regression, but it isn't. To see why, you need to realize that much of the power of SCSI is in the command set it supports. The serial version of SCSI-3 was included to allow the use of all the advanced features (other than the parallel data transfer) of the SCSI interface in very small computers, such as palmtops, that could not possibly accommodate the large connectors needed for parallel SCSI.

Trouble in SCSI-land

The hardware interface for SCSI is pretty well-defined. Unfortunately, the software support for SCSI in the PC marketplace (primarily the device drivers contained in installable device driver files and in option ROMs on SCSI host adapters) is anything but standardized. There are at least three competing approaches being pushed by different manufacturers.

Microsoft is sponsoring the Layered Device Driver Architecture (LADDR). A group of companies headed by Adaptec favors the Advanced SCSI Programming Interface (ASPI). But the American National Standards Institute is about to approve yet another standard, the Common Access Method (CAM).

Not all hardware vendors of SCSI host adapters offer device drivers in all three flavors. Most commonly, manufacturers support only one. And programs that access SCSI devices may be written based on a particular one of these three methods of access. The upshot is that you may have to have up to three different SCSI host adapters in your PC, each with its own device driver (one each for LADDR, ASPI, and CAM).

TECHNICAL SECRET

The problem is that a given SCSI host adapter needs to be controlled by, and respond through, one interrupt request level (IRQ). Therefore, to support multiple SCSI devices — with some of them needing to be talked to according to each of the three standards — three host adapters would be required with three device drivers talking to them (and it would use up three of your IRQ levels).

Ideally, you would have only one SCSI host adapter for any number of SCSI devices, but that is not yet possible with an arbitrary mix of device types. If all your devices conform to one of the three access standards (and you have no more than seven physical devices and no more than 56 logical units) you can have the ideal now. Otherwise, you must have multiple SCSI host adapters in your PCs.

This is not to say that one could not have more than three SCSI host adapters in one PC; you can have about as many as you can find open slots to plug them into. It is possible, at least in some cases, to have multiple SCSI host adapters using the same access method (such as ASPI) and a single device driver. (One user has reported using four SCSI host adapters and an ASPI driver to control 28 different SCSI tape drives at once. Using logical unit numbers off each SCSI slave interface, this arrangement could allow controlling up to 224 devices.)

Until recently, if all you wanted to do was add one or two high-performance hard disks to your PC, the easiest way was to use an ESDI controller and disk drive. This method worked almost without any effort at all. But it didn't offer any help when you needed to add still other peripheral devices, such as CD-ROM or a tape drive.

Now that the SCSI software support issues are beginning to get worked out, ESDI is falling from favor. Almost all new designs for high-capacity, high-performance disks are either SCSI or IDE.

Making the fictitious perfect drive

In effect, a SCSI hard disk contains its own disk controller electronics. The SCSI host adapter merely manages the SCSI bus, which acts as a sort of mini-LAN. One important implication of this layered approach to controlling the drive is that many of the physical details of the drive may, and indeed must, be hidden from the computer.

No longer does the computer, or a disk controller plugged into the computer bus, command the drive to step one track in or out. The computer does not know how many tracks a SCSI drive has. Instead, a SCSI drive appears to the computer as an idealized, large group of logical blocks in which data may be stored. The SCSI host addresses each of those blocks by its *logical block address* (LBA). To make the PC think that a SCSI hard disk is just like any other hard disk, the host adapter presents the SCSI hard disk to the PC as if it were a conventional, three-dimensional disk. But the host makes up the number of heads, cylinders, and sectors per track for that fictitious disk in whatever way is most convenient.

TECHNICAL SECRET

> A large, high-capacity SCSI drive might actually have 5 platters with 10 heads, of which one or two heads are used for servo-positioning of the head assembly. The drive may have a couple thousand tracks. The inner tracks may have more than 30 sectors and the outer tracks more than twice this number, with some of the intermediate tracks having some intermediate numbers of sectors.
>
> The SCSI slave interface reduces all this complexity to a simple, one-dimensional array of storage blocks. The SCSI host adapter, for its part, creates from that linear array of logical blocks the appearance of a fictitious, or *logical*, drive with 64 heads, 32 sectors per track, and just a few hundred cylinders. That arrangement is something your PC's BIOS can deal with.

SCSI drives always appear to be perfect. You never will see any bad sectors if you run CHKDSK on this type of drive. The reason is contained in the very smart SCSI slave interface.

When a SCSI drive is initially prepared for use, it tests each location where it could store data and rejects those that have defects. The remaining locations are given logical block addresses. That feature solves things at the outset. What about defects that come into being later on?

Many SCSI drives watch the disk's performance, and if any sectors develop "badness," the drive moves the data they contain to a nearby spare sector, without the PC user (or, for that matter, the SCSI host adapter) having any inkling of what is going on. Drives that work this way are said to support *hot fixes*.

This process is an extreme example of *head translation* and *sector translation,* which are discussed in more detail in Chapter 7. Because of the air of unreality that SCSI drives present, they significantly limit the function of a program like SpinRite (although SpinRite still can do some wonderful things with these drives).

IDE

Currently, the most popular hard disk interface for the PC is the so-called *integrated drive electronics* (IDE) drive. The drive maker Conner Peripherals has popularized this approach, which includes an entire RLL or MFM controller on the drive itself, eliminating the need for a controller card. To connect to the computer, IDE drives do not take up a bus slot — one of the IDE drive's most attractive features. Instead, they use a special connector on the motherboard, which is, in effect, a minislot that carries only those bus slot signal lines that the IDE interface needs.

TECHNICAL SECRET

The formal name for this sort of connection strategy is *AT Attachment,* or ATA. A formal ATA standard has been adopted by the computer industry. This standard calls for a 40-pin connector of a particular design, with signals taken from the standard (ISA) PC input/output bus.

Many hard disks that have their controller electronics built onto the drive, technically speaking, are a kind of IDE drive. Yet they often are more commonly called by some other name. All SCSI drives have their drive electronics integrated onto the drive. IBM puts a form of ESDI drive, with its controller mounted on the drive, into some of its PS/2 models. In both these cases, therefore, you could say they are IDE drives. They are not IDE/ATA drives, however, because they do not use the 40-pin bus connector defined in the ATA specification. Using the designation SCSI or ESDI in these cases is more useful because it tells you something about the drive's capabilities rather than merely about its physical construction.

Many places in this book, as in much common parlance in the industry, IDE will be used as shorthand to refer to hard disks that have IDE with an ATA interface (see the preceding technical secret).

It is possible to put an IDE hard disk into a PC that does not have the ATA-specified connector on the motherboard. You accomplish this task by getting a so-called "IDE paddle card." This card is an option card that plugs into the system input/output bus and has the proper ATA connector on it. For convenience, because many AT hard disk controllers of the other types have a floppy disk controller on them, some paddle cards do also.

Because IDE drives, like SCSI drives, incorporate the entire drive controller on the drive, they can and many times will do some nonstandard things, such as sector translation. Indeed, most IDE drives have the capability of appearing to have any dimensions that you might want to give them. In other words, IDE drives can pretend to have whatever number of heads, cylinders, and sectors per track that your PC is expecting, provided that set of numbers describes a drive with no more capacity than the physical drive's actual capacity.

This capability is possible because at the lowest level, an IDE drive works just like a SCSI drive. Its interface electronics creates a single linear pool of blocks, addressed by their logical block addresses. Then the electronics translates this scheme into the three-dimensional one the PC is expecting.

IDE and SCSI hard disks share so much in common that you may be wondering what their differences are. First, of course, they differ in that they have different interfaces. You cannot plug a SCSI drive into an ATA connector, nor an IDE drive onto a SCSI bus.

In many cases, that is the only significant difference. You often can buy the same model of hard drive in a SCSI or an IDE version. But they are not all the same. In general, the industry provides the smaller drives in the IDE format and the larger ones in SCSI (with, as noted, a substantial range of overlap in which drives come in both flavors). The larger drives, and therefore mostly SCSI drives, tend to have more "intelligence" built in. That means, for example, that although it is quite common for a SCSI drive to support hot fixes, only a few IDE drives do.

How does the design of IDE and SCSI drives impact programs that work with the disk at a very low level, such as SpinRite and other disk reinterleaving programs? If the disk appears to the computer exactly as an MFM or RLL drive, SpinRite often can treat it like one. But if, as is more common, the disk masks some of its real personality, it will prevent SpinRite and any other low-level reformatting programs from performing all their functions. These programs may still provide useful services, just not everything they can do for MFM, RLL, and most ESDI drives.

Hard disks on an option card

Several years before the introduction of IDE hard disks, the Plus Development Corporation (now Quantum Corporation) made a similar departure from the usual approach, but in the opposite direction. The company wanted to integrate the drive and its electronics, but instead of doing so on a drive to be mounted in the usual manner, they moved the hard disk onto the controller card. Since Quantum's first Hardcard was introduced in 1985, many other drive makers have introduced similar products. Quantum's models have evolved from an initial 10MB capacity to units able to store several hundred megabytes, yet each one still fits into a single slot in a PC.

Hardcard is a registered trademark of Quantum, but some people use it as a generic term for similar products from any manufacturer. In this book, the phrases "hard disk on an option card" or "hard-disk card" (all lower case letters) are used for generic references.

The makers of hard-disk cards often have opted to take advantage of the same tight integration of controller and drive as the makers of SCSI and IDE drives, using zone-bit recording (see Chapter 2 for details), sector translation, and other nonstandard approaches to get the maximum capacity into the minimum space. Hard-disk cards appear to the computer as more-or-less standard MFM drives, but they deny the computer the lowest levels of control that it could expect for such drives. Again, SpinRite and similar programs can do only some of their usual work on a hard-disk card.

Figure 3-5 presents in summary form some of the information covered in this section about each of the most popular types of PC hard-disk subsystems.

PCMCIA

The very latest wrinkle in hard disk interfaces is to mount the drive on a PCMCIA card. This name stands for the PC Memory Card International Association. That organization was formed to define and promote a standard means of interconnection between a special design of plug-in modules and a number of different electronic systems. The target systems initially included handheld, laptop, and some portable computers plus some MIDI machines. Now the PCMCIA slots are appearing in desktop computers and a variety of other types of appliance.

The PCMCIA standard defines three sizes of PCMCIA card. All of them are about the size of a thick credit card; the differences between Types 1, 2, and 3 are only in the thickness of the card. They all use the same 68-pin connector design.

One of the nicest features of PCMCIA is that cards built to this standard can be safely plugged in and unplugged from a computer's PCMCIA slot at any time. So you can change these cards while you are computing as freely as you now change floppy diskettes.

At first, these cards were used only to hold RAM or ROM chips. But the design of the PCMCIA interface is essentially a superset of the AT Attachment interface, which means that it was possible from the outset to put on a PCMCIA card almost any kind of peripheral device that one could put on an option card designed to plug into the AT bus.

The originators of the PCMCIA standard were all makers of memory chips. They built such a good design for a peripheral interface that now makers of other products want to get in on the game. At least three variations on the PCMCIA standard have been proposed to allow putting IDE/ATA hard disks on these cards.

Chapter 3: Some Important Engineering Issues

Hard (and floppy) disk controller card

These drives are normally connected to the controller with a 20-wire data cable (one per drive) and a 34-wire control cable (one for both Drives 0 and 1). They receive power from the power supply via a separate 4-wire cable.

Hard disk

ST412/ST506 (MFM and RLL) and ESDI

IDE drives with the AT Attachment interface can plug directly into the special ATA interface jacks that are built into some PC system units. These 40-pin jacks simply extend the bus of the system unit for the use of an ATA device. In other PCs an IDE drive is hooked up by use of a "paddle card" plugged into the system bus. That card has the ATA jack (and possibly a floppy disk controller).

Hard disk & controller electronics

Integrated Drive Electronics with an AT Attachment interface (IDE/ATA)

A hard disk on an option card (such as the Hard Card from Plus Development) puts all the controller electronics and all the moving parts on a single plug-in card. Power for these drives comes from the power supply through the bus slot where the option card is plugged into the system unit.

Hard disk with its controller electronics

Hard-disk card

A SCSI host adapter is a bridge between two buses: the PC system unit's I/O bus and the SCSI bus. The latter is often a 50-wire cable and can connect up to seven peripheral devices (and up to 56 logical units) to one host adapter in a "daisy chain" fashion.

SCSI host adapter (interface to the SCSI bus)

Hard disk, controller, and SCSI slave interface

Small Computer System Interface (SCSI)

Figure 3-5: Several popular types of PC hard disk subsystems.

The lowest level of compatibility is when the cards conform to the Type 2 PCMCIA card-form factor, use the standard PCMCIA 68-pin connnector, and have the electrical signals on the pins of the connector that are compatible with PCMCIA signals. The meanings of these signals are not, however, the same as under the real PCMCIA specification.

This level of compatibility, which was developed by Hewlett-Packard for its 1.3 inch Kittyhawk hard drives, allows a PC maker to incorporate a slot of an industry standard design (PCMCIA) and yet connect a single IDE/ATA hard drive in that location. It was the first way PCMCIA slots were used with hard drives. Close on its heels came the second modification to the PCMCIA standard.

This modification offered full ATA compatibility on the PCMCIA connector. With a slot built to conform to this standard in a PC, it would be possible to plug in a PCMCIA memory card, a PCMCIA modem card, or an IDE/ATA drive on a PCMCIA card and have each of them function flawlessly. Still, cards designed to this standard do not support all the features of the PCMCIA standard. You'd need to have loaded a device driver that knew you might be loading a hard drive there before you could access the device. This version of the specification was developed jointly by Western Digital and Hewlett-Packard.

The final variation is a full implementation of the ATA specification for hard drives on a PCMCIA card that fully supports the PCMCIA specification (Release 2.0). When hard drives are built to this specification, it will be possible to use them interchangeably with memory cards as removable storage devices for PCs that have normal PCMCIA sockets. This version is a product of the PCMCIA committee.

All three of these standards are wending their way through the standards approval process. None is final as I write this. Already, though, the first drives built to these various standards have started to appear, as have PC add-ins that will provide suitable sockets into which these drives may be plugged.

Drive Geometries: Two Contrasting Views

All of the discussion of hard disk drive geometries so far has been in terms of their physical dimensions (number of heads, number of cylinders, and number of sectors per track). But the physical aspect is not the only useful way to view a hard drive. In fact, DOS doesn't view disks that way at all.

A review of heads, cylinders, and sectors

In Chapter 2, you learned that a hard drive is built with platters and heads. The heads (one per surface of a platter) are attached to a head assembly and are moved in toward the spindle or out toward the edge of the platters by an actuator. For each position of the actuator and head assembly, each head reads or

Chapter 3: Some Important Engineering Issues

writes a track on its respective platter surface. The collection of tracks for a single head assembly position is called a cylinder (refer to Figure 2-3).

The cylinders are numbered starting at zero at the outer edge of the platters. The heads are numbered also, starting at zero on the top surface. Some drives use one of the heads for a servo-feedback head-positioning system, and thus they appear to have an odd number of heads as far as data storage is concerned.

The tracks are divided into sectors, each storing 512 bytes of data (plus sector header and ECC information). The sectors are numbered starting at 1.

Therefore, if you want to send some information to a particular spot on the drive, you would expect to have to tell the drive controller to put it on some particular head (surface), in a certain cylinder, and into some numbered sector.

That is exactly what the BIOS does. But it definitely is not what DOS does. The DOS view of any disk drive is much simpler. We call it a logical view.

Logical structures of information

What is described in the preceding paragraphs is a *physical* way of addressing data on the disk, a method the hardware ultimately must follow. Programmers and users of hard disks seldom want to be bothered with this point of view, however, because it is much easier to think of the disk in a simplified, *logical* sense instead.

After all, MS-DOS is designed to relieve us (and our programs) of the need to know any great detail about the disk drive. Instead, DOS attempts to manage that resource so that we and our programs need give DOS only the simplest of instructions to save and retrieve our information.

TECHNICAL SECRET

The operating system of your PC is divided into several parts: (1) the *BIOS ROMs* (Basic Input Output System Read-Only Memory chips) on the motherboard and on various option cards that contain very low-level hardware control programs; (2) the *BIOS program,* which is contained in one of the two hidden system files on bootable disks; and (3) the highest level *DOS program,* which is contained in the other hidden system file on bootable disks. The BIOS programs, both those that live in ROM and that which comes off the disk, deal with the hardware in a way that usually is quite close to the physical reality. The DOS program tends to abstract the hardware into some simpler, logical form.

Chapter 9 includes a discussion of the various parts into which a disk drive's space gets divided when it is prepared for use with DOS. At this point, suffice it to say that there is a region before the DOS information storage area and there may be another region after it. For now, you may ignore those non-DOS regions.

DOS, in its highest level form, regards the portion of the disk in which it may store data as just a large number of logical sectors. It numbers these sectors in a simple list, starting at logical sector number 0.

TECHNICAL SECRET

The DOS numbering scheme for logical sectors is not to be confused with the numbering scheme for physical sectors, which starts over with sector number 1 on each track.

Also, do not confuse this numbering of logical sectors with the (very similar) logical block addresses used in IDE and SCSI drives. Both the DOS logical sector number and the LBA approach use a single dimension to refer to a storage area. The difference is that the LBA numbers start at the very beginning of the disk. The DOS logical sector numbers start at the beginning of each DOS-accessible partition or logical drive on the disk.

Almost every program that runs under DOS is thereby relieved of much complexity in its dealings with the disk. Even many disk utility programs deal only with this abstract, logical disk drive instead of with the actual, physical drive. Precisely these properties of DOS allow programs to work with so many different kinds of hard disk drives. DOS has hidden their diversity from our view and from our programs' views.

For some of its purposes, SpinRite can work with a disk in this abstract way too, but to deliver all its potential benefits, SpinRite must get behind DOS and see the physical reality by talking directly to the controller. Unfortunately, if the controller, rather than DOS, is hiding reality, even SpinRite may not be able to penetrate this veil, which may limit its capability to fix certain problems.

Chapter 3: Some Important Engineering Issues

Summary

▶ Data-transfer rate is one of the most important measures of how fast your hard disk is. Setting the sector interleave value to its optimum level often can boost this important number dramatically.

▶ Setting the sector interleave to a too-small value can make your hard disk dramatically slower than it could be.

▶ Getting the right value for sector interleave cannot be done by the manufacturer of the drive or controller. Only the person who integrates the drive and controller has even a hope of doing it right (unless the controller incorporates a track buffer).

▶ Head and cylinder skewing are the next level of optimization after sector interleave. So far, not many disk subsystems support this level of fine tuning, but as disks continue to improve in speed, more of them will.

▶ There are six popular varieties of disk subsystems used in PCs. They are MFM and RLL (both using the ST412/ST506 interface), ESDI, SCSI, hard-disk cards, and IDE/ATA drives. The most popular new designs are all SCSI or IDE, with SCSI preferred for larger capacity drives and IDE for smaller drives.

▶ The very newest wrinkle in hard drive interfaces is to mount the drive on a PCMCIA card. This will allow using removable hard drives in anything from a handheld to a desktop PC.

▶ The location of a block of information on a drive can be specified in any of four ways: the actual physical address (head, cylinder, and physical sector number), a logical block address, a fictitious physical address, or a logical sector number. The drive and its controller ultimately must use the first. IDE and SCSI drives may accept locations in either of the next two forms from the BIOS. DOS uses only the last way of specifying locations on the disk.

This chapter and the one before it cover the most critical physics and engineering issues in hard disk design. The next chapter gives even more detail on the design of hard disk drives — a level of detail that was not previously available except from a technical book store or in a professional engineering journal.

Chapter 4
Messy Hard Disk Details

In This Chapter
- How stepper motors and voice coil motors differ
- How servo feedback makes a disk's head positioning mechanism work better
- The two kinds of information stored on your hard disk and the two systems that use this information to help the computer find and recover data stored on disk
- Several ways that read/write heads can be constructed
- How longitudinal and vertical recording differ and how they are similar
- The roles played by the electronics mounted on a hard disk drive and in a hard disk controller
- What *recalibration* means and what it means to you when your disk starts doing it too often

What the Physical Parts of the Drive Do

The disk platters turn, the head assembly moves in and out, and the heads read and write data to the platter surfaces. That much of what goes on in a hard disk is covered in Chapter 2.

The main drive motor turns the platters at a constant speed, usually 3,600 revolutions per minute (60 revolutions per second). The motor achieves this speed by driving the spindle with a specially designed multipole DC motor. The torque the motor delivers is very nearly constant, making the speed at which the platters turn nearly the same at every part of a revolution, as well as from minute to minute.

How the heads move in and out gets a bit more complex, but it's a fascinating story. How the read/write heads work requires a bit more explanation as well.

Many designs exist for the actuators that move the head assembly in and out, but they can be classified into two common types: dead-reckoning positioners and servo-feedback positioning systems (servos). The dead-reckoning positioners use stepper motors. The servos use *voice coil* motors. Because stepper-based systems tend to be cheaper, slower, and less accurate at positioning the heads than those that use voice coil motors, stepper-motor systems are used in the less expensive, smaller-capacity drives.

Steppers are simple

Any electric motor works by having two magnets pushing or pulling on one another. One of the magnets is bolted to the frame of the motor (the part that stays put), and the other one is mounted on the portion that moves (see Figure 4-1). Depending on the motor's design, one or the other magnet may be permanent, but at least one must be an electromagnet so that it can be turned on and off at just the right times.

When an electric current passes through the field coil, a magnetic field is generated in the gap. This field pulls the rotor into alignment with that field. When the current in the coil is reversed, the field in the gap reverses direction. This reversal forces the rotor to flip around to the opposite orientation. If, just as the rotor is arriving at its new orientation, the current is again reversed, the rotor will continue to turn back around to the original orientation. Continue reversing the field current at just the right moments, and the rotor can be kept spinning steadily, even against some opposing friction.

You can think of how an electric motor works as being a little like the way you make a child's swing go by pushing it each time it passes a certain point in its path back and forth.

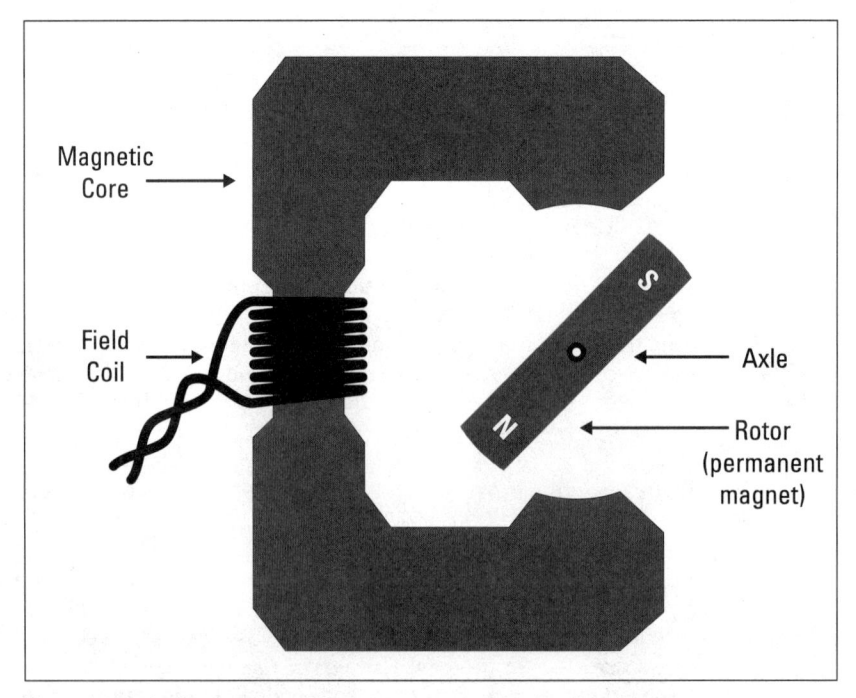

Figure 4-1: A simple electric motor.

Chapter 4: Messy Hard Disk Details

TECHNICAL SECRET

For smoother operation, some motors incorporate several magnets attached to the frame; these magnets take turns pushing on the magnet mounted on the shaft. In making such a "good" motor, the designer attempts to make the pushes merge into one another as smoothly as possible. This capability is especially true for the spindle motor of a hard disk, where the constancy of rotation speed is critical to the drive's performance.

It is possible to get the effect of many magnets and yet get away with using just two of them mounted on the frame. This trick requires that these magnets be made and mounted in a special way. One possible design is shown in Figure 4-2(a). Figure 4-2(b) shows a pattern of current in the two phases that will make the rotor turn.

The proper term for this sort of motor is a *multipole electric motor*. In the kind of motor shown in Figure 4-2(a), there are two field coils, each wrapped around a core that has four heads where the core meets the rotor. As the rotor turns, it sees the heads from the two cores alternating with one another. This type of motor will run when current is turned on first in one field coil and then in the other. Then the current is reversed in the first coil and then in the second one. This current pattern is called *two-phase excitation* and is diagrammed in Figure 4-2(b).

Consider what happens in each of these steps: In the first step, the rotor's magnet is drawn near one of the poles of the first magnet (phase A). In the next step, the rotor "feels" the pull of both the phase A magnet and the phase B magnet, which means that the rotor turns to a position midway between two adjacent poles. (This position is the one shown in Figure 4-2(a).) In the next step, the field from the phase A poles reverses, which pushes the magnet away from the pole toward which it was first attracted. As the magnet passes the phase B pole, it is also drawn toward the next pole of phase A, so again the magnet goes to a point midway between poles (a clockwise rotation of 45 degrees in the example). In the successive steps of the two-phase current in the coils, the rotor must step around by a fixed angle each time the current in either coil reverses.

Repeating that alternating pattern of current reversals in the two field coils will cause a multipole motor to turn continuously. There is another way to use such a motor: simply turn on current in one or both of the field coil magnets and leave it on. If you do so, the motor makes part of a turn and then stops, its rotor "locked" either directly in front of one of the poles (if only one field coil is carrying current) or midway between two (if both coils are energized). If the current through either coil is reversed or changed from off to on or vice versa and then the currents are again held steady, the motor's shaft will turn to a different position and stop. You learn how this sort of motor is used in hard disk drives later in this chapter.

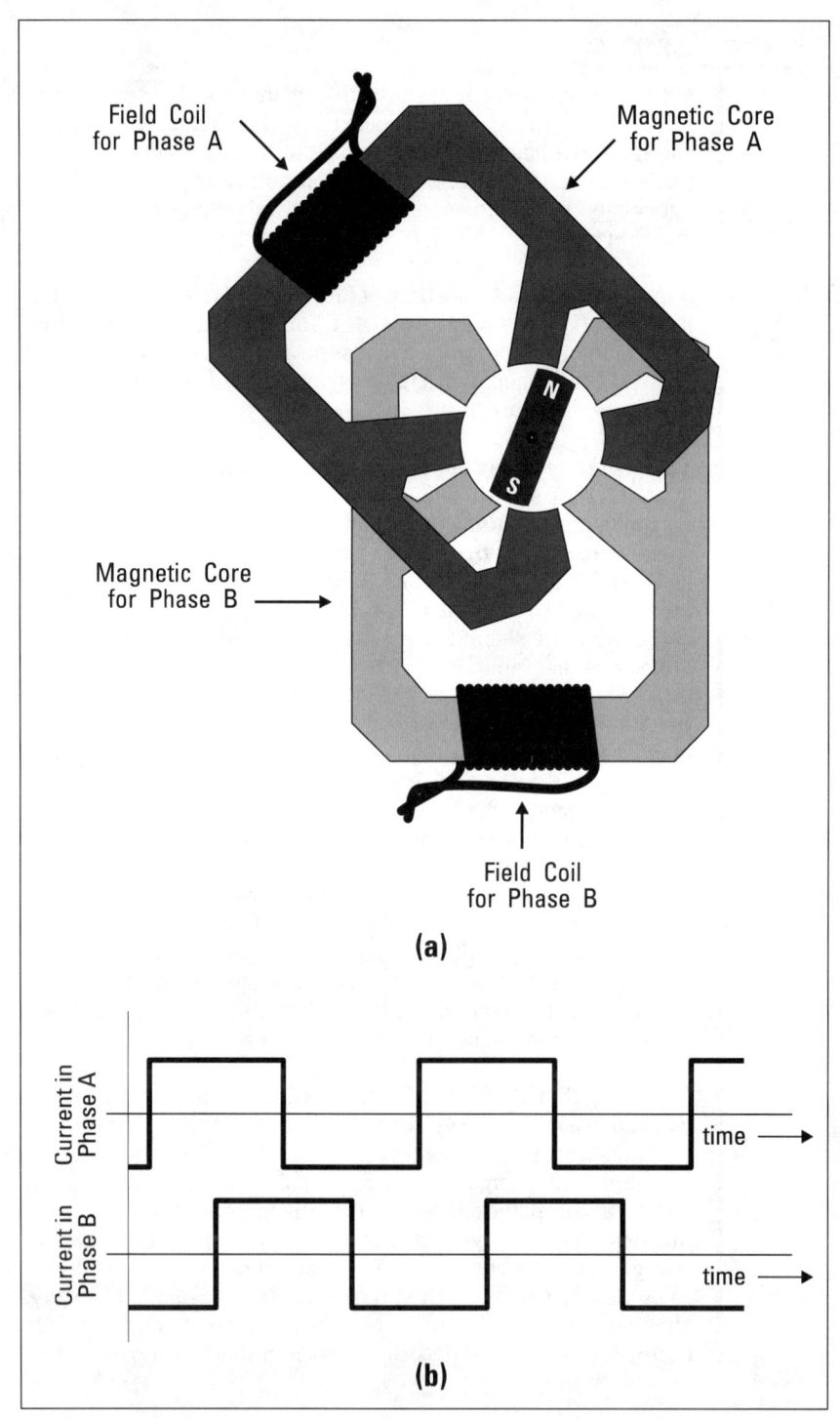

Figure 4-2: A multipole motor.

Motors that are not carefully designed will tend to *cog,* which means that they will tend to jump from one of these preferred positions to the next and, as they reach each position, try to pause there (refer to preceding technical secret). Though considered a defect in a normal motor, it is the whole point behind a stepper motor.

A stepper motor is one that can be operated by simple, all-on or all-off DC signals to turn its shaft to a succession of positions a step at a time.

TECHNICAL SECRET

Think about what happens if the motor in Figure 4-2 has very many poles for each of the magnets. By driving one or both of the electromagnets in the frame with a succession of steady (DC) current patterns, you can move the motor shaft to any of a very large number of positions in small, well-defined steps. Because this strategy involves just turning the magnets all the way on or off at each step, it is inherently a digital technique. The distance the motor turns for each step is fixed by the construction of the motor. A step's size does not depend on the electric signals at all; the signals govern only *when* the motor will take a step. So, without having to be overly concerned with how the driving electronic circuitry is built, you can rely on a stepper motor to step to a definite (angular) position.

If a small gear with a few fine teeth (called a *pinion*) is mounted on the shaft, and if the pinion engages what amounts to a large gear with many fine teeth that has been sort of unwrapped (the name for such a gear is a *rack*), then as the motor steps, the rack will be moved back and forth in a straight line, also in steps. This procedure is the essence of a *rack-and-pinion, stepper-motor head-positioning actuator.* Such an actuator was included in the first IBM-PC/XT hard disk drives, and it has been common in most of the lower-cost drives built since then.

When a stepper motor is used with a rack-and-pinion gear arrangement, it can move something (in this case, a head assembly) in a straight line in small, well-defined steps (see Figure 4-3). Such an actuator design puts the heads into one of a large number of predefined places. Exactly where one of these places falls relative to the disk platters depends solely on how the mechanism was constructed (and how it may have altered its shape or size through aging, wear, or in response to gravity or some other external force).

This approach of forcing the heads to one of a number of predetermined positions sometimes is referred to as *dead reckoning.* This mechanism is simple and inexpensive to build, and it works (at least pretty well), which is why it is the kind of head positioning mechanism used in all the early PC hard disks. The dead-reckoning method continues to be used in many of the smallest-capacity drives today.

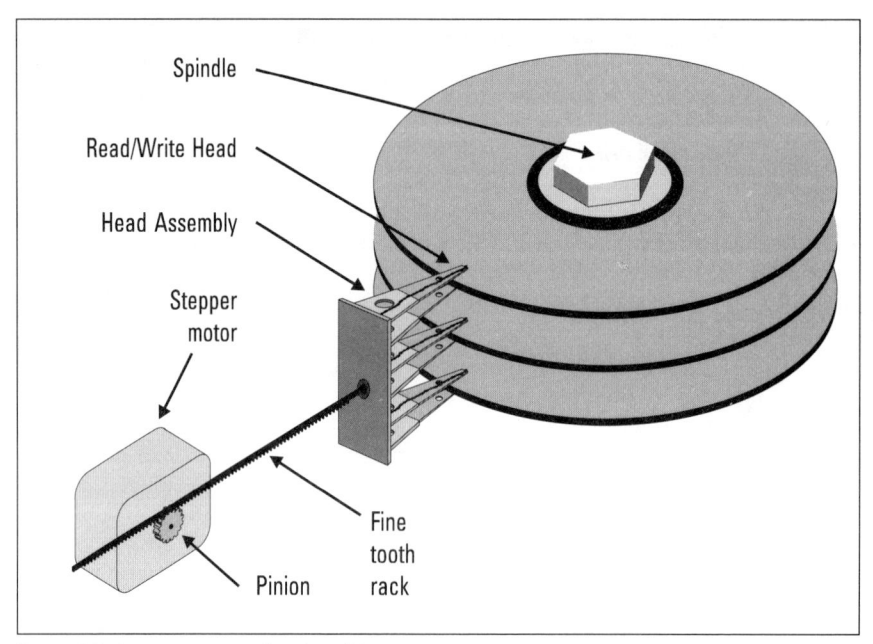

Figure 4-3: A stepper motor head positioner.

Dead-reckoning, however, is not the best approach. A better idea is to put the heads about where you think they belong, notice where the heads actually are, and then make any necessary fine adjustments to that position. This better approach is the basis of all the servo-positioning techniques discussed later in this chapter.

Several variations on the dead-reckoning technique have been used in disk drives. A helical groove cut into a shaft that is mounted on the stepper motor, which then has a carriage ride along in the groove (you may know this arrangement as a *lead screw*) is one variation. Another variation is replacing the rack with a portion of a large round wheel and transferring its rotation to the head assembly through a taut metal band. All these different mechanical arrangements share the stepper motor's capability to move in small, clearly defined steps.

You have just read a description of one of the most common ways to build in a head-positioning system. The motor that is at the heart of the system is also very typical of a large class of electric motors.

There is another, very different way to build a motor. The motors built in this different way have some very different properties — including some that turn out to be extremely useful in building high-performance head positioners.

You surely have encountered motors of this other kind but probably in a context in which you did not recognize them as motors. A loudspeaker in a radio or home entertainment system is simply a cone of paper attached to a linear electric motor of a special kind. Once again there are two magnets, one permanent and the other an electromagnet, that push against each other. One of these magnets — the permanent one — is fixed, and the other one is able to move (see Figure 4-4). Figure 4-4 shows a cutaway view that clearly reveals the essential working parts of a loudspeaker.

Unlike the usual electric motor that rotates a shaft, this kind of motor can move only a short distance because a linear motor can move only until its voice coil moves out of the permanent magnet (or until it runs into something). This limitation is in sharp contrast to a rotary motor, whose shaft can turn for as many revolutions as you want without the magnetic field of the moving part becoming disengaged from the fields produced by the fixed magnets.

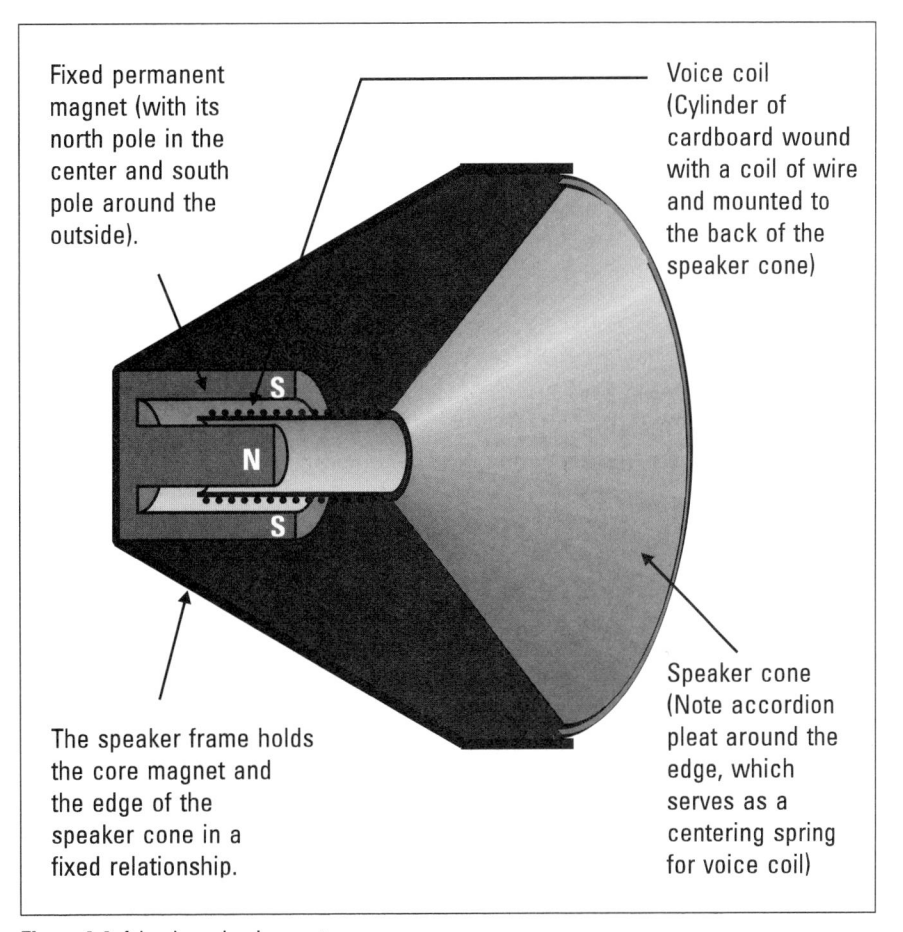

Figure 4-4: A loudspeaker is a motor.

TECHNICAL SECRET

Normally, a physical stop is built into a linear electric motor at each end of its working range of motion. A positive current in its coil pushes the moving part in one direction, and a negative current pushes it in the other direction. The stronger the current, the larger the force, and the more rapidly the moving part accelerates in one direction or the other.

Often a spring is included, which attempts to hold the moving part near the center of its range of motion. In a loudspeaker, this "spring" is just a pleat near the outer edge of the speaker cone. In a loudspeaker, the spring forces are comparable to the forces generated by the currents passing through the coil.

In a head positioner built with a voice coil motor, the spring is insignificant compared to the magnetic forces when currents flow in the coil. This weakness allows the head assembly to be driven very firmly in either direction toward a desired location. Still, the spring forces are sufficient to slowly return the coil to its normal "home" place when the current is off.

Because this sort of motor was first used in radio speakers, the moving part (the electromagnet) is commonly called a *voice coil.* The voice coil pushes the speaker cone in and out to make sounds you can hear.

Notice that in a stepper motor, current is applied steadily and the motor moves to a new position and stops. In a voice coil motor — at least those used in head positioners with their relatively weak springs — the moving part accelerates as long as the current is applied. After the motor is moving, the only way to stop the movement short of the end of its range of motion is to send a reverse-direction current through the coil for a time comparable to that used to accelerate the head assembly.

There is an important difference between the rack-and-pinion, stepper-motor way of moving things and the voice-coil method. In the first case, the motion is in steps, with the size of the steps being a built-in feature of the stepper motor and its gear arrangement. All one can influence with the electric signals is *whether* (and when) a step will be taken and *in what direction.* This system is inherently a *digital* system. With the voice coil, in contrast, the technique for moving something a particular distance in a straight line depends directly on *how much* electric current passes through the coil and for *how long* that current is applied. The voice coil positioner, therefore, is inherently an *analog* system.

Note: *Analog* and *digital* are used here as opposites. In common speech, analog refers to anything that is analogous (that is, very much similar to) something else. Digital refers to the fingers (digits). In the context of computers and hard disks, analog signals are signals that can assume any value within some range. Digital signals, in contrast, are signals that can assume only certain, discrete

Chapter 4: Messy Hard Disk Details

> **HISTORICAL ASIDE**
>
> ### Why the permanent magnet turns in some motors and stays fixed in others
>
> You may have wondered why in a conventional stepper motor the rotor is normally the permanent magnet, but in the linear motor the fixed element is the permanent magnet. The explanation is really quite simple.
>
> Hooking flexible wires to the voice coil in a linear motor is easy. There is no problem with keeping them connected while the motor moves through its full range of motion. And making the voice coil the moving part keeps its mass low, which enables the voice coil to accelerate very rapidly.
>
> In contrast, a stepper motor shaft may turn many revolutions in one direction before it starts turning back again. If these motors used connections wired directly to a coil on the rotor, the wires would become hopelessly tangled long before the rotor had turned the required number of times. The much easier task, therefore, is to build stepper motors with a permanent magnet rotor and make the fixed magnet the electromagnet.
>
> Another possibility is to make both magnets electromagnets. For a DC motor, this method requires the capability to reverse the connections to the rotor's coil as the rotor turns. That reversal commonly is done with a special switch called a *commutator*. Many alternating current (AC) motors use a rotating transformer to couple AC power signals to the rotor in a contactless manner. Neither of these designs is used in disk head positioners, so they are not discussed in any more detail in this book.

values. Mathematically speaking, analog signals are continuously variable. Digital signals are like the counting numbers (1, 2, 3...from the concept of counting on one's digits) and thus can only change in steps of a fixed size. In the preceding paragraph, the words *whether* and *in what direction* refer to concepts that have simple, yes/no, left/right sorts of answers — that is to say, digital values. *How much* and *how long* refer to quantities that can assume any of a continuous range of values and thus are analog values.

If such a voice coil "motor" is attached to a head assembly for a disk drive, the heads can be positioned to any cylinder just by passing an appropriately varying current through the coil for exactly the right amount of time (see Figure 4-5). But if the current is too strong or too weak, or persists too long or not long enough, the heads will move somewhere else. To make sure that the current is supplied in exactly the right way, the control circuitry uses *negative feedback,* also called *servo feedback.*

You may find it useful to think of a servo head positioner as a system that acts very much the same as the driver of an automobile. In both cases, there is some target course to be followed (a cylinder in the case of the head positioner, and a traffic lane for the automobile driver). And in both cases, after putting the controlled object (head assembly or vehicle) into the desired path, the control

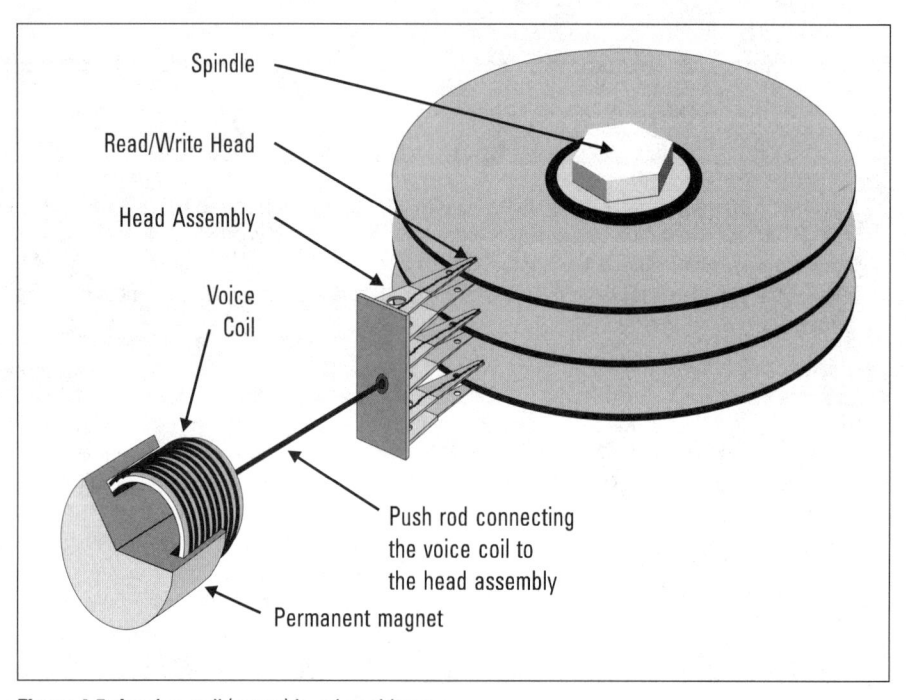

Figure 4-5: A voice-coil (servo) head positioner.

system monitors where the controlled object is at each moment; it makes many small adjustments, as necessary, to keep the controlled object on path (the heads on or near the cylinder centerline or the vehicle safely inside the traffic lane).

A fairly new name for a very old idea

The first industrial uses of negative feedback were in control systems developed during World War II. These systems were called servo-mechanisms. From this usage, the shorthand name *servo* was derived, and now it is applied to any similar system.

The first uses of negative feedback by humans are lost in prehistory. Everyone uses negative feedback constantly simply to keep from falling down, for example, or to walk to an intended location instead of wandering off target. In that usage, negative feedback is so ubiquitous that many centuries passed before anyone thought to give it a name.

Voice coil motors are better

A servo system has several advantages over a stepper motor positioner. First, as the head actuator parts age and wear, the servo system has a built-in tendency to compensate for that wear. This tendency occurs because the system constantly "looks" to compare the current position of the heads with the desired position. This comparison also helps compensate for any tendency of the head assembly to sag under gravity in different orientations, such as if you turn your PC on its end and place it on the floor to free up your desktop.

The servo system also has the advantage of being quicker than a stepper positioner. This speed difference occurs in part because you simply can pour a very large current into the voice coil — briefly — to push the heads more forcefully. With the stepper system, the sizes of the currents in the coils are fixed.

Finally, the servo system has a certain degree of built-in disk-surface protection. These designs come standard with circuitry that *parks* the heads (that is, forces the heads in toward the spindle) whenever you turn off power. In contrast, a stepper positioner may not do anything special when you turn off the power. As a result, the heads in stepper drives often stay in whatever position you last put them.

This difference is described by saying that servo drives are inherently *autoparking* or *self-parking*. Most stepper drives must be parked by the deliberate use of a special head parking program before the computer is turned off.

TECHNICAL SECRET

A stepper motor takes a step and stops. When a stepper motor loses power, it does not move. A voice-coil motor is likely to be moving in or out a little bit all the time. When a voice coil loses power, then, it will tend to continue moving in whatever direction it was moving just before the power loss. To ensure that when power is turned off the voice coil motor used in a hard drive will do something predictable, the machine stores up some energy. (Some drives do this in electrical form, using a capacitor; others use the energy already stored mechanically in the spinning platters.)

Then whenever power to the drive is turned off, special shut-down circuits dump that energy through the voice coil, causing the motor to slam the head assembly all the way in toward the spindle until it hits the mechanical stop, or out all the way off the platters. Often you can hear this happen when you turn off your PC (although with modern disk drives you have to listen very carefully).

Part I: The Hard Disk Companion

Alternatively, the drive may force a normal "seek" to some preselected landing zone (a cylinder where no data is kept). Sometimes, after moving the heads to their parked position, a pin is dropped into the head actuator to lock it in that position. This behavior — in whichever of these many variations it may occur — is called *auto-parking*.

You may have wondered why disk heads usually are parked near the spindle. There are some very good reasons for this parking location.

The best place to put the heads to protect them and the disk surfaces would be somewhere completely off the platters. Some drives do just that; these drives pull the heads out away from the spindle until they actually come off the edge of the platters. Then, typically, they push a small fork or wedge between the pairs of heads to keep them from bumping into one another. Separating the pair of heads that go on each platter also makes it possible to push them back onto the platter when power to the disk is turned on again.

That strategy may be the best technically, but it certainly is complicated. The alternative that is used by most disk makers is to drive the heads in about as far as possible toward the spindle.

There are at least three good reasons for using this alternative method. One is that there may be very little room on the outside of the platter between the edge of cylinder zero and the edge of the platter. A drive manufacturer who tries to park the heads there would run the risk that they would either fall off the edge or would slip back over cylinder zero, which is where the very most valuable information of all is stored — the information needed for access to all the rest of the information stored on the disk.

Another reason for pushing the heads in toward the center is that wherever the heads will be parked is a cylinder that ordinarily will not be used to store data. Giving up a group of short length tracks rather than long ones makes sense because the storage of data is more reliable when the bits are not overly crowded together. The shorter tracks are, of course, those in the innermost cylinders.

Finally, think of the disk platters as cymbals. Like those musical instruments, when they are struck by some impact, the edges will flutter up and down. The center of each platter is clamped to the spindle and will not move at all. If the heads are out near the edge, they will be more likely to crash into the fluttering surface than they would be when positioned near the spindle.

Chapter 16 includes a section that discusses in some detail just why parking the heads on a disk drive is *vital* to your data's safety. That chapter also describes some *dangerous* park programs you should never use.

Head positioning

There are many different ways to build a servo-controlled head-positioning system. This section describes six designs that have been used or proposed for hard disk drives.

External servo systems

The essential requirement for a servo-controlled head positioner is that there be some way to find out where the heads are at any given moment. Then the electronics can compare that position with the desired one and can send an error signal to the voice-coil actuator to force the heads closer to the desired location.

One way to provide the position information is to use an optical encoder attached to the head assembly. Figure 4-6 shows one possible design. In this design, a plate of glass with a special pattern of markings on it passes between an array of light-emitting diodes (LEDs) and an array of photosensors. The arrays are fixed in position relative to the disk spindle. The glass plate is fixed in relation to the head assembly.

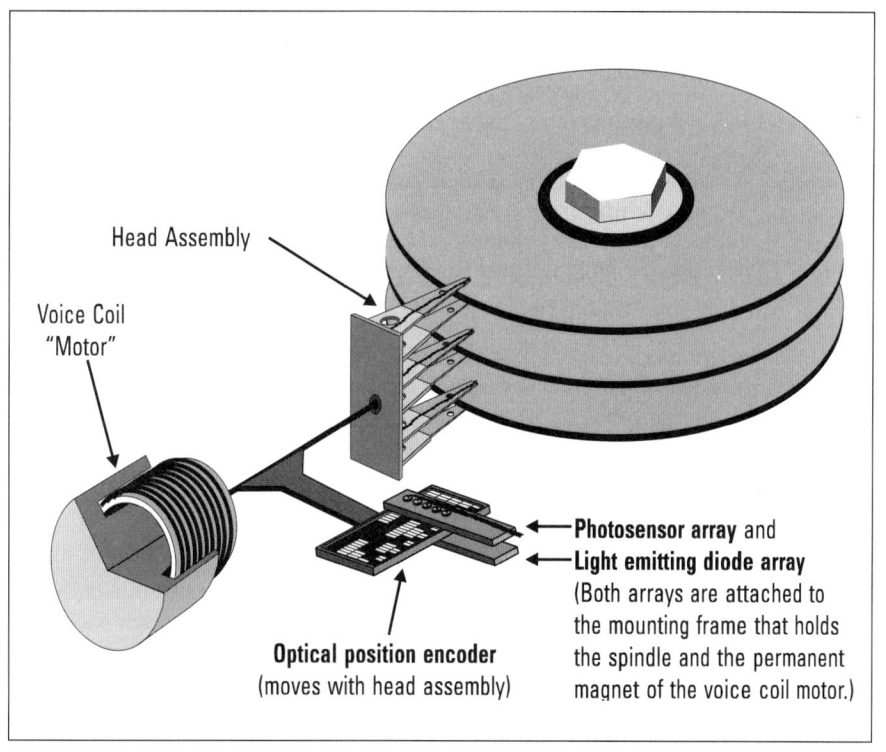

Figure 4-6: An external servo head-positioning system.

One advantage of this system is that all the added hardware is external to the disk platters (unlike the rest of the designs discussed in this section). The makers of the Plus Development (now Quantum Corporation) Hardcard chose this strategy to help them make their disk drives on an option card carry as much data as possible.

The disadvantage of this system is that the LED and photosensor arrays, must not move relative to the disk spindle, and the optical encoder plate must move exactly synchronously with the heads. That is almost true in practice but not quite. No mechanical system ever can be relied upon to move exactly as you expect. There are always minute deviations from the nominal path in the motion. The systems you read about next attempt to deal with those minor discrepancies in several ingenious ways.

Wait a minute. You aren't ready to learn about those alternative approaches. You don't yet know, really, how this external servo system works. In particular, you probably don't have any idea what pattern of marks are required on the optical encoder plate, nor how these marks can be used to infer the head locations.

Use Gray code to find out where you are

You may think you know how these marks are used. Perhaps you guessed that the marks on the plate are simply clear or black to indicate zeros or ones. That is a good guess, and true as far as it goes, but it is not the whole story.

The disk drive needs to know where the head assembly is to a considerably better accuracy than the intertrack distance. Because a disk drive may have about a thousand cylinders, this necessity means that there are at least several thousand significant positions where the heads might be at any given moment.

One way to provide the disk drive's control circuits with the required information is to assign an *address* to each of the possible and significant head positions. This address is just a number, from 0 to some maximum value. The address can be expressed as a binary number, which is simply a collection of bits that are each either a one or a zero. If you use 12-bit binary numbers, you can express addresses from 0 to 4,095. Then you must arrange for the disk's control circuitry to be able to learn reliably at which of those addresses the head assembly is at any moment.

The plate shown in Figure 4-6 has several parallel columns of black and white marks (five in that example) and an LED-photosensor pair for each one. You may have assumed that at each position on the plate, the corresponding address was coded as a binary number and then the ones and zeros of that binary number were written in the various columns on the plate. That guess is close but not good enough.

Chapter 4: Messy Hard Disk Details

The problem is not that there aren't 12 columns of marks and 12 photosensors. You could build a system that had that many. Alternatively, as explained a little later in this section, you can design a system that does not need to record all the bits of each address. The real problem is with binary numbers themselves.

Here are the first 21 binary numbers (those whose decimal names are 0 through 20):

0	0 0 0 0 0
1	0 0 0 0 1
2	0 0 0 1 0
3	0 0 0 1 1
4	0 0 1 0 0
5	0 0 1 0 1
6	0 0 1 1 0
7	0 0 1 1 1
8	0 1 0 0 0
9	0 1 0 0 1
10	0 1 0 1 0
11	0 1 0 1 1
12	0 1 1 0 0
13	0 1 1 0 1
14	0 1 1 1 0
15	0 1 1 1 1
16	1 0 0 0 0
17	1 0 0 0 1
18	1 0 0 1 0
19	1 0 0 1 1
20	1 0 1 0 0

Notice that as you go from the binary number for 7 (00111) to that for 8 (01000), four of the five bits change at the same time. The change from 15 (01111) to 16 (10000) is even worse: all the bits change at once. Look more carefully, and you will see that half the time when you go from one number to the next at least two bits change at once.

As the encoder plate moves under the sensors, any time that going from one address to the next requires changing more than one bit, you could have a serious problem. To see why, imagine that one of the sensors is just a wee bit out of alignment. It may sense the change of its bit just a tad later than its neighboring sensors. So when the address is changing from, for example, 15 (01111) to 16 (10000), if the third (middle) sensor changes a bit later than the others, there will be some time in which the output will be 10100, which indicates position 20. The servo system will think the head assembly was four or five places out of position (briefly) and it could become very confused. This problem is one that servo mechanism designers faced and solved many years ago. The solution is quite elegant.

It is possible to rearrange the binary numbers into a pattern so that each time you go from one number to the adjacent one, only a single bit changes. Any such pattern is called a *Gray code*.

At first glance, you might have thought this arrangement was impossible. After all, in fully half the transitions from a normal binary number to the next one, more than one bit changes. It is a marvelous, and for servo designers a most fortunate, mathematical fact that you always can rearrange the binary numbers to form a Gray code. In fact, there are many ways to make a Gray code, using all the binary numbers with any given number of bits.

Figure 4-7 shows one such code for five-bit binary numbers. In this figure, you see 36 rows. Focus your attention on the central 32 rows. (The top two rows are a repeat of the bottom two rows of the central 32. Similarly, the bottom two rows are the same as the top two of the central section. These added four rows, shown in gray, are included to show how this pattern fits with repetitions of itself, which is how it gets used in certain applications.)

To the right of each row is a five-bit binary number. These numbers are hardly in what one would normally call numerical order, but they are in a Gray code order. This order means that the successive locations of a servo system's position encoder could be given this pattern of successive binary numbers as their addresses. As long as the servo-feedback system that reads the patterns of black and white blocks knows the order in which they were recorded, it can reliably translate any of those patterns into the corresponding position.

Now consider what happens if you use a Gray code on the encoder plate instead of normal binary numbers representing the address of each position. Again the sensor may be somewhat misaligned. But as you move the plate from one position (corresponding to one binary value) to another, only one sensor will see a change from dark to light or from light to dark. Therefore, multiple sensors seeing transitions at the same point in the movement isn't an issue.

When this strategy is used in a hard drive, it allows the drive to tell with perfect certainly where the heads are (to a resolution equal to the spacing of the marks in the least significant bit column). No matter how much the photosensors may be out of line, they will still show an increase of one address every time the head assembly moves an amount equal to the spacing of the marks in the least significant bit column, with no extraneous "phantom" positions popping up in between.

Use other reliable ways to find out where you are

There are alternatives to using a full Gray code. In fact, you can get away with just a single row of black and white marks and two photosensor/LED pairs. One pair of sensors is positioned so that it is over the middle of a stripe when the other pair is over the boundary between marks.

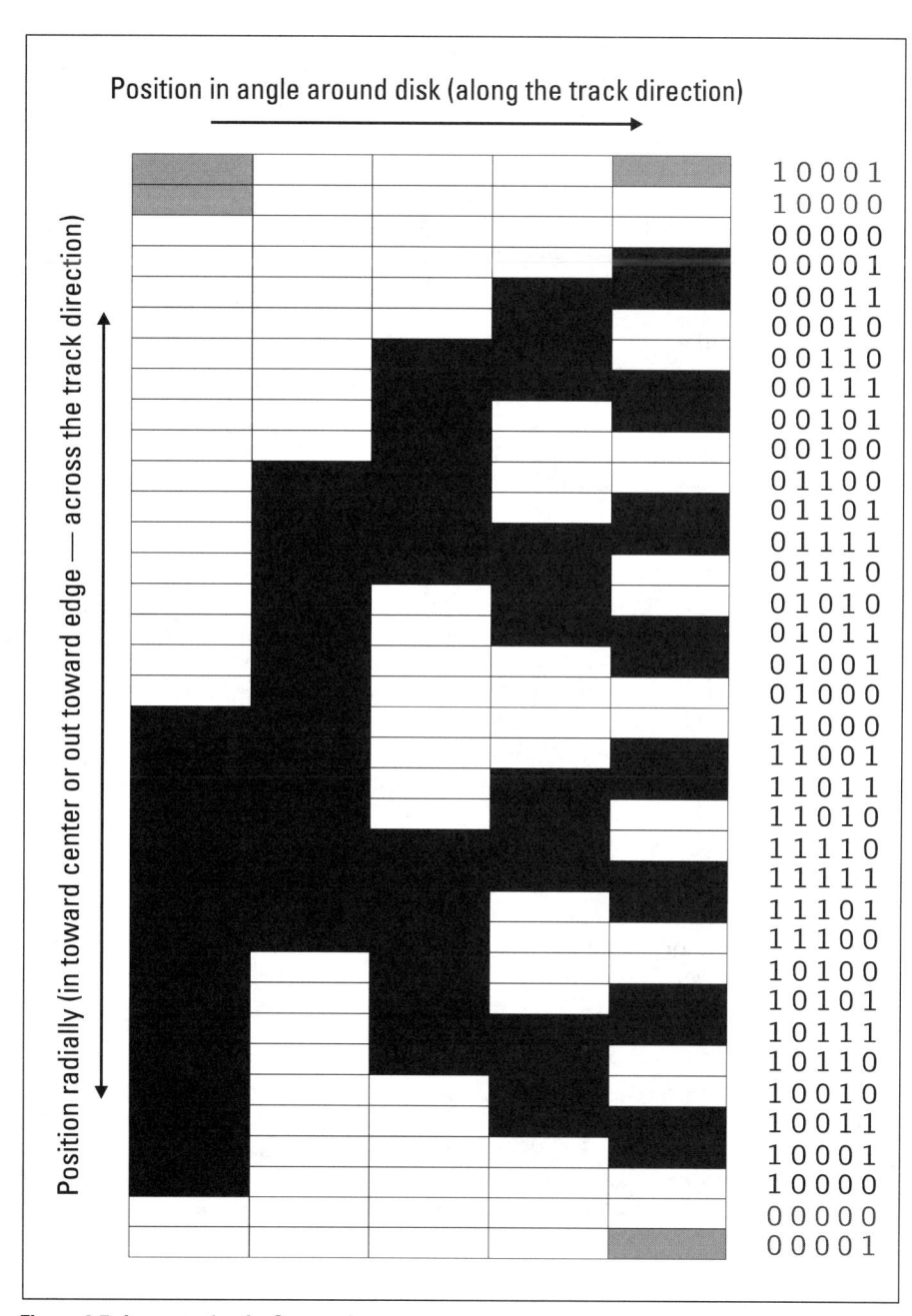

Figure 4-7: An example of a Gray code.

This setup is the minimum optical hardware that will allow you to detect each time the head moves by as much as the space between marks and to know unambiguously which way it moved. If you know where you started from and if you never lose count of the number of stripes passed over and the directions in which they went by, you can tell where you are at all times.

This simplest-possible optical encoding strategy has been used in commercial hard disks, such as in some Hardcard drives. Its proper functioning requires absolute perfection in keeping track of the signals from the encoder.

A middle ground approach is to encode several bits of each position's address (using a Gray code) but not all the bits in that address. Curiously, the ones you can most safely ignore are the very ones mathematicians would call the most significant bits. The reason is that you know the heads will never leap instantaneously from one address to another one far away. You always should see each and every address in between.

If you assume that you will never fail to notice any motion that is larger than, for example, 100 tracks, you could use only the seven least significant bits of the address to indicate where you are. This scheme saves some space on the encoder plate (or, more significantly, on the disk surface if the signals are recorded there) at the cost of at least a possibility of getting quite lost without knowing it. The more of the bits you encode (starting with the least significant bit and progressively including more significant ones), the more reliably you will know where you are at all times. The simplest scheme, described previously, amounts to using only the two least-significant bits.

Dedicated platter servo systems

External servo systems work pretty well. But as disk cylinder densities climb, their imperfections show up more and more. One solution is to put the feedback information on the same structure as the data. That way, even if the whole disk frame were to become distorted or, more likely, if the head assembly were to bend or sag a little, the feedback would accurately show you where the heads actually were relative to the data.

An early implementation of this approach, and one that is still in use, is to dedicate one or two of the surfaces of a multiplatter hard disk to servo information. Typically, the top or the bottom surface — or sometimes both of them — will be prerecorded at the factory with some very special *servo signals*. The rest of the surfaces (all those in between the top and bottom platters) are used to store your data.

Chapter 4: Messy Hard Disk Details 119

TECHNICAL SECRET

The dedicated surface approach explains what is otherwise a very mysterious fact: Some disk drives are listed in tables of disk drive dimensions as having an odd number of heads. Because every platter has a top and a bottom, you would think that all disk drives would have an even number of heads. The answer to the mystery is that those tables don't count the heads devoted to reading servo information; they count only the heads used to record and read a user's data.

Figure 4-8 shows a block diagram of a dedicated platter disk system. In this case, the top surface of the top platter (only) is used for servo information.

That's fine, you say, but what exactly is recorded as the servo signals? A fair question. Some of what gets recorded is obvious, and every manufacturer does it in much the same way. Some of what is recorded is special and proprietary to each manufacturer, and they aren't about to let you know what that information is.

These two parts are shown schematically in Figure 4-9. The first part is a Gray code similar to that shown in Figure 4-7 (the only difference is that this is a six-bit Gray code). The second, proprietary part, is shown simply as a gray band to

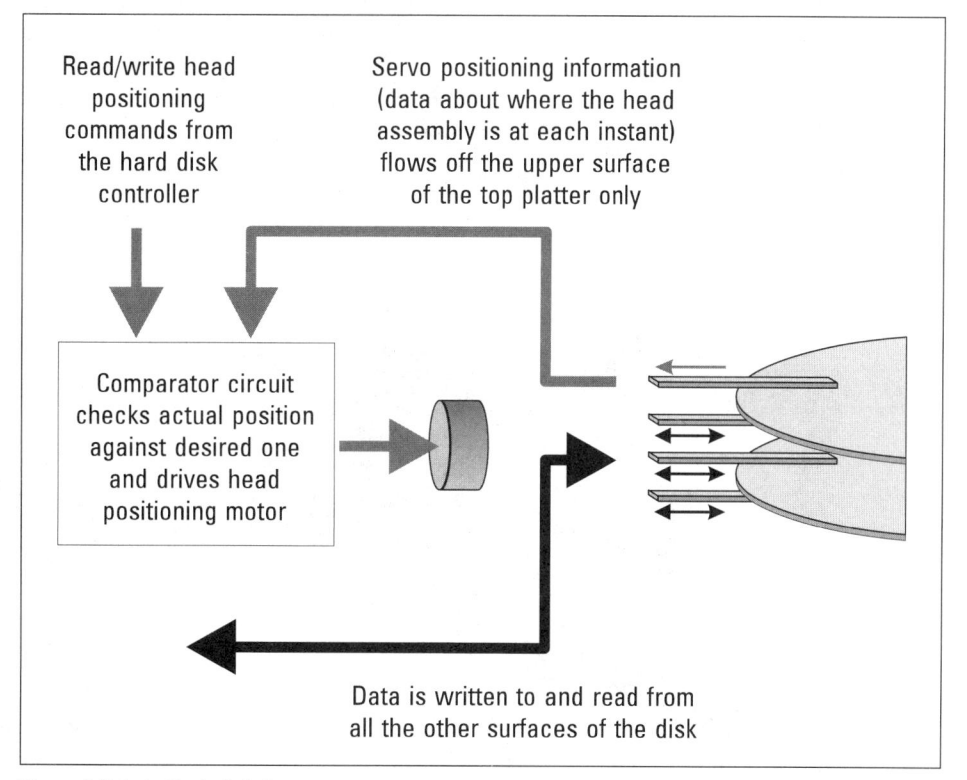

Figure 4-8: A dedicated platter servo system.

Part I: The Hard Disk Companion

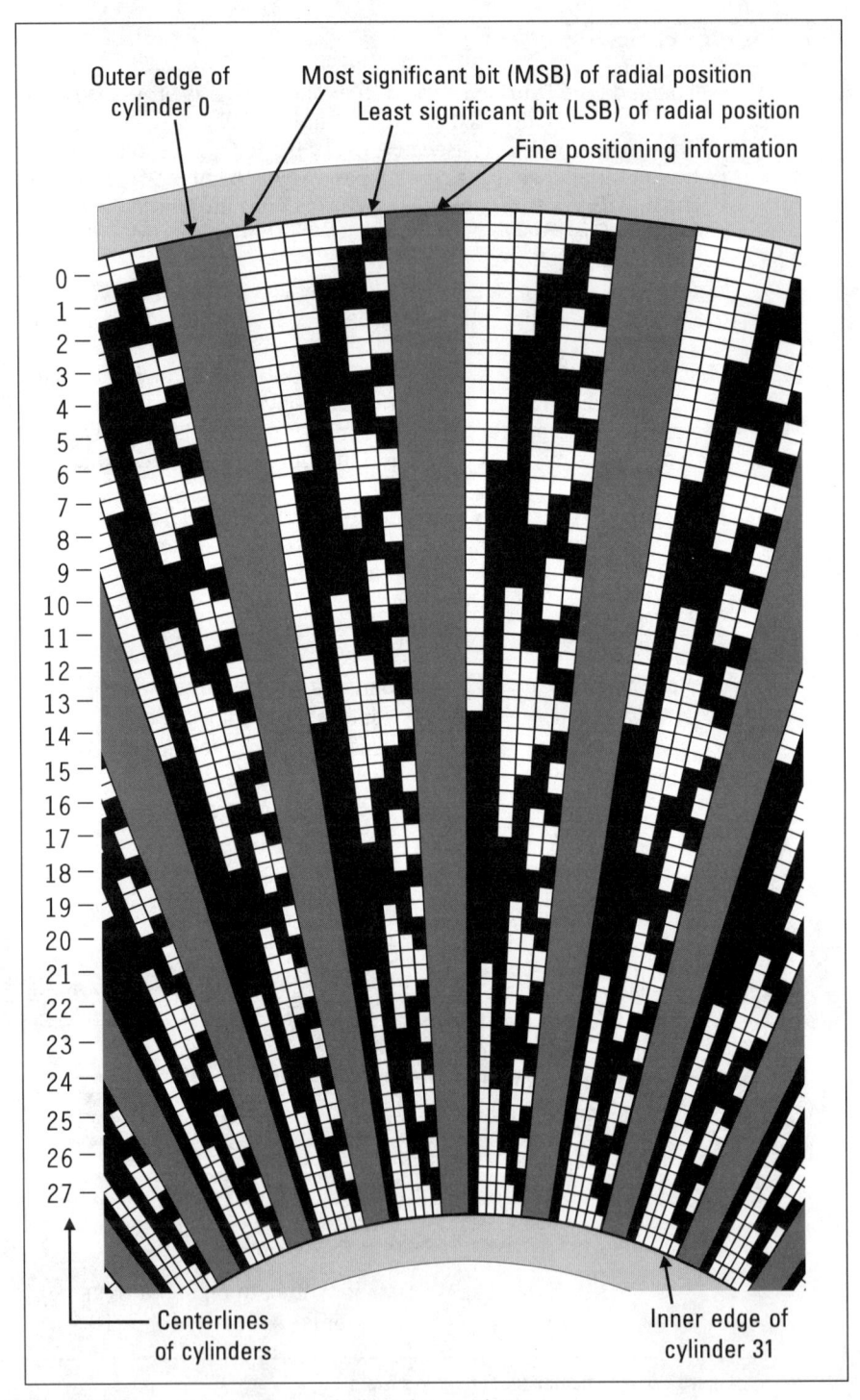

Figure 4-9: Servo track details on a dedicated servo platter.

indicate that we don't know what it contains. All the way around the surface are repeated recordings of the same two-part pattern. The number of repetitions of this pattern has nothing to do with the number of sectors per track. The manufacturer simply repeats this pattern as many times as possible. Each time one repetition of the pattern passes under the servo head, the disk control mechanisms get another reading of where the heads are.

If you were to look at the dedicated servo platter in an actual hard disk, it would not, of course, look exactly like Figure 4-9. For one thing, there would be many more bits to the Gray code. But most important, the information is not painted on the surface in a way that people can see; this information is recorded magnetically in the surface coating. Wherever you see a black square in Figure 4-9, think of it as a region that is magnetized in the forward direction along the track (the way the head passes over that place). The white squares also are magnetized but in the reverse direction.

The several bits of each position number are recorded on the surface one after another. Instead of using many sensors, one per bit, as shown in the optical encoder in Figure 4-6, the magnetically recorded bits are read by a single read head similar in design to those used to read and write data on the other surfaces.

Some manufacturers save a bit of disk real estate by recording only the least-significant few bits of the radial position numbers. This method works but has the disadvantage of requiring the drive to *recalibrate* (force the heads to cylinder 0) and then step back to the desired cylinder whenever it is unsure just where the heads are.

The problem of misaligned sensors in a multitrack sensor array that led to the idea of a Gray code is now replaced by what happens if the head assembly moves in or out just a little way during the time it is passing over the digital position code. Again, using a Gray code is the only way to ensure that the servo-control system will never get a confused picture of where the head assembly is at each instant.

The servo information pattern is recorded at every radial position, including on-track and in-between track locations. The digital data suffices to tell the disk control circuits where the heads are, to an accuracy of at least half an intertrack distance (which is the same as the intercylinder distance).

The portions of the pattern in Figure 4-9 that are marked "Fine positioning information" are the ones that are done differently by each manufacturer. After the digital position information has been processed and the head assembly has been moved into place according to that information, the heads are known to be somewhere over the desired cylinder. The fine-positioning information is designed to help keep the heads in the center of that cylinder as accurately as possible and to restore them to that location as quickly as possible any time they get out of place.

> ### Analog versus digital feedback signals
>
> In the early days of servo-mechanism design, servo positioning systems used feedback in the form of an analog signal; that is, the signal representing position varied in *amount* rather than being a digitally encoded position *value*. Some early hard disk designs used analog servo signals.
>
> The industry generally has moved away from an analog servo approach for the same reasons that audio recordings are now mostly done digitally (on CDs or digital audio tape) instead of in the analog manner (on vinyl records or analog audio tape). That change has come about because digital systems are inherently more tolerant of noise — thus, capable of more accuracy and consistency — and developments in microprocessor chips have made digital systems affordable.

A dedicated platter servo system has one big advantage over most of the other head-positioning systems, and a couple of big disadvantages. The advantage is that there is always some servo information flowing to the control system so that whenever the disk gets bumped or the head assembly moves relative to the platters for any other reason, that fact can be detected almost immediately.

The first big disadvantage is that the servo information takes up a whole platter surface (or two of them). That necessity means that you have that much less disk real estate in which to store your data.

The other big disadvantage, which this system shares with the external servo system, is that it assumes that the heads will move precisely together. (This system must assume only that the heads don't move relative to one another; the external servo system also must rely on the spindle and external sensor array not moving relative to each other.)

The heads are meant to move together, but of course they don't do so exactly. Like all mechanical systems, at least some tiny variations will occur from time to time.

A dedicated platter servo-feedback system guarantees that when the controller asks the disk to position the heads to cylinder number 85, for example, the servo head will be traveling accurately over the center of track 85 on the servo surface. What the system cannot guarantee is that all the other heads also are traveling precisely over the center of track 85 on their respective surfaces.

One way such an error can arise is if the data tracks are initially recorded (in what is called a low-level format — see Chapter 8 for details) when the disk is upright. Later on, the PC user may turn the system unit on its side. This change in orientation may cause the head assembly to twist or tilt some. This twist or tilt will put all the heads that read and write data off track some small amount. The name for this sort of defect is *tower tilt*.

Wedge servo systems

An early attempt to deal with tower tilt involved moving the servo information off the dedicated platter and onto the same surfaces as the data. In other words, a portion of every surface holds servo information and the rest of the surface holds data. (Changing from a dedicated platter servo to a wedge servo means that you gain one more surface for data storage, but you must give up a portion of every surface for servo signal use. What you gain and what you lose roughly balance each other.)

Figure 4-10 shows a wedge servo platter schematically. As usual, the figure cannot show a realistic number of cylinders, nor do all wedge servo drives have only 17 sectors per track. These early designs used a single burst of servo position information for each revolution of the disk.

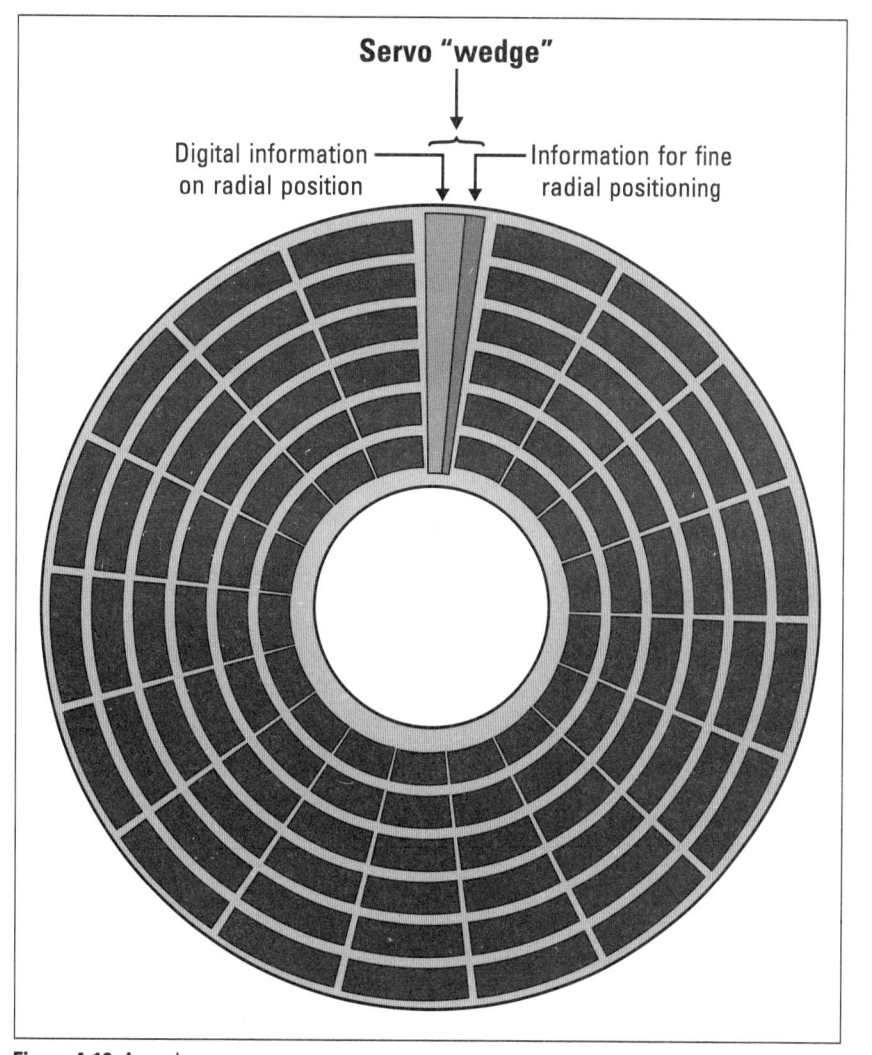

Figure 4-10: A wedge servo.

Because not much servo information is contained in a single burst, the drive may have had to wait until several revolutions had gone by before it was able to lock onto the desired cylinder location accurately. Furthermore, there is no way to know about any drift that might occur until the next time the servo wedge comes around.

Both of these problems limit the usefulness of this approach. Now that better designs have been invented, no major disk manufacturers are using a pure wedge servo approach any more.

Embedded servo systems

One better design is called an *embedded servo disk drive*. This drive is very much like the wedge servo, except that there is a burst of servo information recorded on each platter in front of each sector. This design is shown in Figure 4-11.

This figure illustrates a disk drive with only 17 sectors per track and only 13 tracks. Real drives usually have more than 17 sectors and always have many more tracks.

TECHNICAL SECRET

> Some drives have different numbers of sectors per track in different regions of the disk. The outermost zone may have 75 sectors per track, a middle zone 50, and an inner zone only 25. On these disks would be a wedge of servo information spanning the whole range of radial positions (on-track and off-track) for a given zone recorded in front of each sector within that zone. In this example, there would be 75 bursts of servo information per revolution whenever the heads were in the outer zone but only 25 per revolution in the inner zone.

The advantage of embedded systems is clear. The heads can never get off-track without the drive control electronics learning about that fact quite soon (before the next sector is read or written). No amount of tower tilt will matter at all.

Most modern disk drives use embedded servo signals. This use has almost entirely done away with the need to redo low-level formatting to realign the data tracks with the heads that read and write them.

There are, however, a couple of weaknesses of the embedded servo design. One is that there is simply not very much servo signal. The fact of these brief signals means that it can take longer for the servo system to move the heads back on track whenever they get off (or whenever they are moved to a new track). The other disadvantage is that even with a burst of servo information before each sector, there is no way to know while you are in the middle of reading or writing a sector whether the heads get knocked off track.

The solution to both these problems is a hybrid approach, combining the best of both the dedicated platter and the embedded servo approach.

Chapter 4: Messy Hard Disk Details

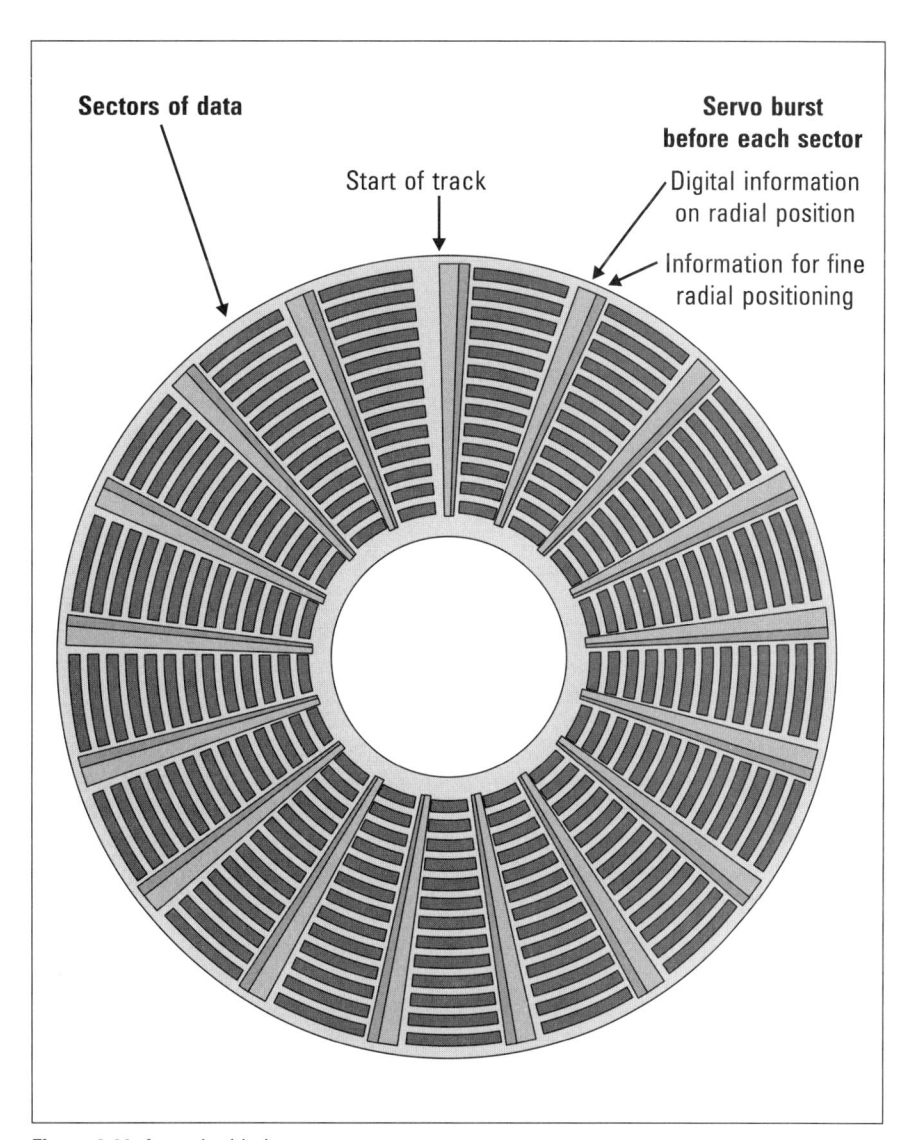

Figure 4-11: An embedded servo.

Hybrid servo systems

The very best of modern hard disk designs use two dedicated platter surfaces (the top and bottom surfaces) plus embedded servo information in front of every sector on each of the data-bearing surfaces. This arrangement enables the drive to go rapidly to any desired cylinder by using the dedicated platter information. If there are two dedicated surfaces, the drive will average the positions indicated by each, which partially compensates for tower tilt.

If the head assembly simply tilted (as the name tower tilt suggests), using two dedicated platters would provide a means of compensating perfectly. If the shift from head to head is not linear (a graph of head shift from nominal position versus head number is not a straight line), something more needs to be done.

In fact, such non-linearities do occur. So the best drives have both the two dedicated platter surfaces and embedded servo information on every platter. The dedicated platters allow quick, coarse positioning. The embedded servo information is used to fine-tune the head position for the particular platter surface on which reading or writing is currently taking place.

This combination approach creates a significant improvement in the *settling time* (how soon after being told to go to a new cylinder the drive actually succeeds in locating the heads there). This translates to an improvement in the disk's *average access time* to the data stored on it.

Perhaps the most striking advantage of these systems is that they can monitor the head position continuously and thus know even in the middle of writing a sector whether the head assembly has been knocked out of place. The best drives use that information to suppress writing and reading during any such transient movement. This temporary suppression of activity keeps the heads from recording wavy tracks and helps keep them from misreading a sector's contents (see Figure 11-4 in Chapter 11).

As seems always to be true in life, you must pay something to get these benefits. In this case, you have to give up two of the platter surfaces for the dedicated servo signals in addition to giving up the area on the remaining surfaces for the embedded servo signals.

Buried servo systems

The absolute ideal system would be one in which servo position information flowed off the disk through the very same heads as those reading and writing data, and in which it flowed off those heads even while they were reading or writing data. That system would be ideal, and it seems as if it would also be impossible.

Some engineers were not convinced. They devised just such an ideal (and seemingly impossible) system called a *buried servo drive*. This design involves recording the servo information underneath the data (deeper into the magnetizable surface coating on the platters). Special heads and electronics permit separating the servo information from the data stream.

This method has all the advantages of the best of the other servo systems. It can put the heads on track quickly, and it can hold them there reliably. This system can detect almost immediately when the heads are thrown off track. And it uses up no platter real estate.

The buried servo system has only one salient disadvantage: it is more complex and, therefore, more costly than any of the other schemes. Its advantages over the hybrid systems are not sufficient to justify this extra cost, however, so no major disk manufacturer is now using this approach in a commercially available PC hard disk drive.

Sector headers

So far in this section, you have learned much about how the heads get positioned over the tracks. That positioning is important, for without proper positioning it is impossible to read the data stored on the tracks (or to write new data in those locations). But it is not the whole story about how the disk drive manages to find your data and return them to you on demand.

In Chapter 3, you learn that information is recorded on the disk in sectors, each containing 512 bytes of data and each preceded by a sector header. That sector header includes a three-dimensional address (head, cylinder, and physical sector number).

The information in the sector headers is recorded in the same fashion as the data (using the same encoding strategy, for example) and is read by the same electronic circuitry that reads the data. This circuitry is entirely different from the set of circuits that read and process the servo information. (This difference is true even in wedge, embedded, and hybrid servo systems in which the same heads read the data and the servo information.)

One group of circuits, then, keeps the heads flying over the tracks of recorded information, and another set finds the information you desire among the heads that fly past. (A third servo mechanism in every hard disk drive — one that keeps the disk turning at a constant speed — is described in a later section of this chapter.)

To return to the analogy of driving a car down a highway traffic lane, the head-positioning servo corresponds to the driver. The data-reading circuits correspond to the navigator. That person (in this analogy) reads the road signs and tells the driver when to change lanes, and the driver is responsible for getting to the requested lane and staying there until the next lane-change request.

The circuits that read and make sense of the stored data also must notice whether the head is at this very instant passing over the sector whose information you want to read or write. If so, the circuits either must pay attention to the contents of the data section of this sector or must turn on the write circuitry to the head to record new data in that section.

Read/write head details

You already have learned that the read/write heads are small electromagnets, one for the top and one for the bottom of each platter, that write information to and read information from the disk. You know that as the disk turns, the heads skim along just a fraction of a micron above the platter's surface. When the disk stops turning, the heads sit down on the platter.

Perhaps the most important thing to know about the read/write heads is that they almost certainly will acquire some permanent magnetization. This magnetization can be useful, for if it is properly engineered into the head design, it can increase the sensitivity with which the head can pick up the magnetic fields from the platter surface. Unfortunately, such magnetization also can play a negative role.

The problem is that because the heads are *always* magnets — not just when the computer is using them to record signals on the platter surface — sweeping them over the platter tends to weaken the recorded signals on the platter surface, perhaps by wiping out small portions of those signals. This problem leads to one form of premature hard disk death and is, therefore, one reason that you should *always park the heads* over a safe cylinder before you turn off the disk drive motor.

You don't actually have to know much more about how read/write heads are built other than this: The heads have coils of wire wound on a magnetic core; that core has a small gap, which is where the magnetic field lines leak out and go through the platter's magnetic coating. The most common configuration is shown in Figure 4-12. This arrangement is called an *inductive* read/write head.

But if you want to understand the nuances of head design, and in particular if you would like to make sense out of advertisements for drives with MIG, dual-MIG, thin-film, and flux-sensing heads, you must learn a lot more about head design. The newest wrinkle in disk technology, vertical recording, also involves a subtlety of disk head design and function.

If you are satisfied with the simple explanation of how magnetic heads work, you may want to skip ahead to the section, "What Happens in the Drive Electronics." If, on the other hand, you are curious about head-design subtleties, read on.

Chapter 4: Messy Hard Disk Details

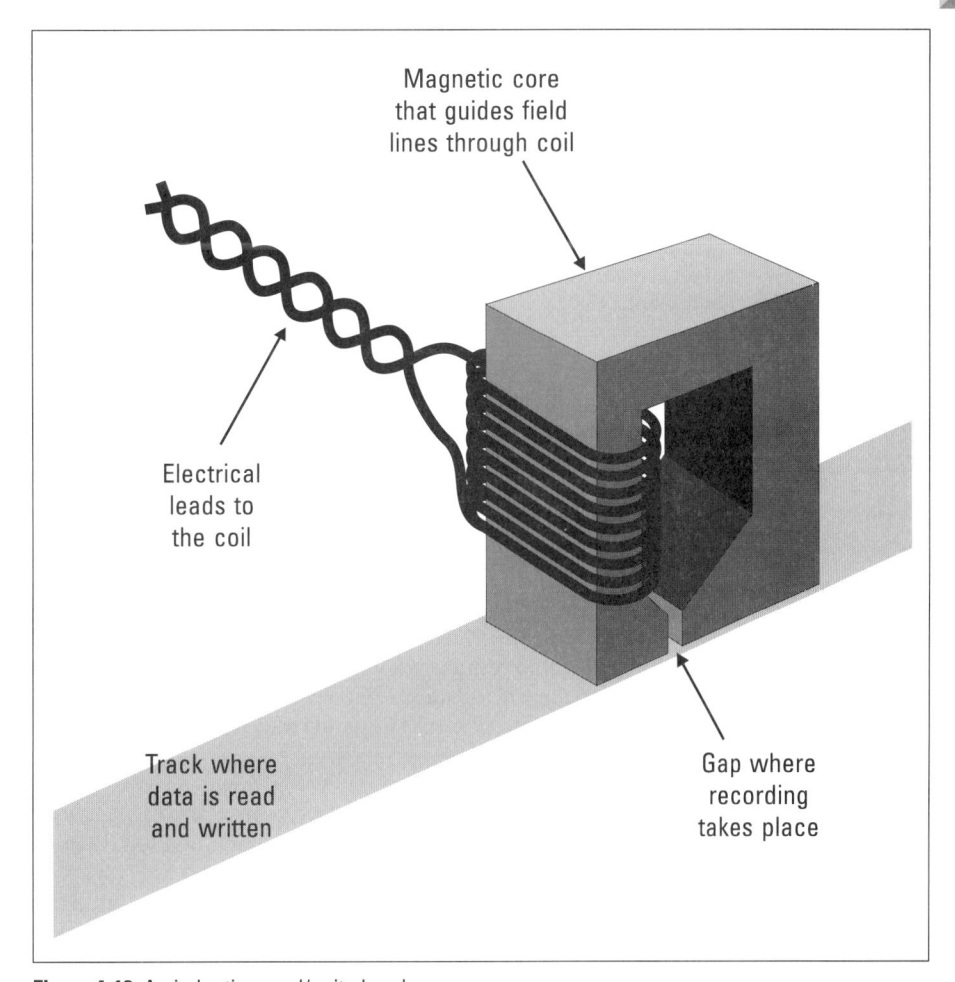

Figure 4-12: An inductive read/write head.

Longitudinal recording

The Chapter 2 explanation of how a head records or reads data (illustrated in Figure 2-4) applies only to a particular type of read/write head used in a particular way with a particular kind of magnetizable platter surface. This combination goes by the name of *longitudinal recording using an inductive-ring head*.

The name comes from the fact that the magnetic field lines that go into the platter surface from the core gap mostly travel in the platter surface parallel to the surface and parallel to the track's length (thus longitudinal). The core in the head is a (distorted) ring-shape (thus it is called a ring head).

It is possible to design read/write heads that are quite different. Some use a thin-film design instead of a tiny machined core wound with wire. Some make the magnetic field lines go into the platter at right angles to the surface. Some record in the usual manner but read by a totally new mechanism. Each of these possibilities is briefly discussed below.

Figure 4-12 shows a larger image of one design for an inductive-ring head. Many different shapes have been used; the particular shapes mainly influence ease of manufacture and sensitivity. In their essence, all ring heads are like that shown in this figure.

Thin-film heads

Computer users constantly hunger for more and more data-storage capacity, so disk drive makers are forever trying to increase the storage capacity of their products. They also are constantly trying to shrink the actual, physical size of those drives. Accomplishing these aims requires doing two things. One is to shrink the spacing of the cylinders so that more of them can fit on a platter. The other goal is to cram the bits more closely together on the tracks.

Accomplishing the first of these (putting the tracks closer together) hinges largely on developing improved servo systems that can position the heads more accurately. It also requires developing heads that are narrower, or at least heads that record narrower tracks. Accomplishing the second goal (cramming more bits per unit length of track) depends almost entirely on improvements in the design of heads and platter surfaces.

In both cases, shrinking the head size is one essential step. One way this shrinkage has been accomplished is to change from machined ferrite cores with wire coils wrapped around them (which is what is pictured in Figure 4-12) to *thin-film heads*. The thin-film heads come in many different designs, but a typical one is shown in Figure 4-13.

This design starts with a ferrite back plate. This plate serves as both the physical support for the other components of the head and as one half of the magnetic circuit.

All the other parts of the head are constructed in a manner similar to that used to prepare modern, integrated electronic circuits. The gap indicated in Figure 4-13 is created by depositing a very thin layer of some nonmagnetic material on the back plate under the bottom end around the coil windings and under the bottom end of the front pole.

This approach allows shrinking the heads to a very tiny size, and it also allows making vast numbers of the heads quite inexpensively. Thin-film heads are rapidly becoming the standard in the industry.

Chapter 4: Messy Hard Disk Details

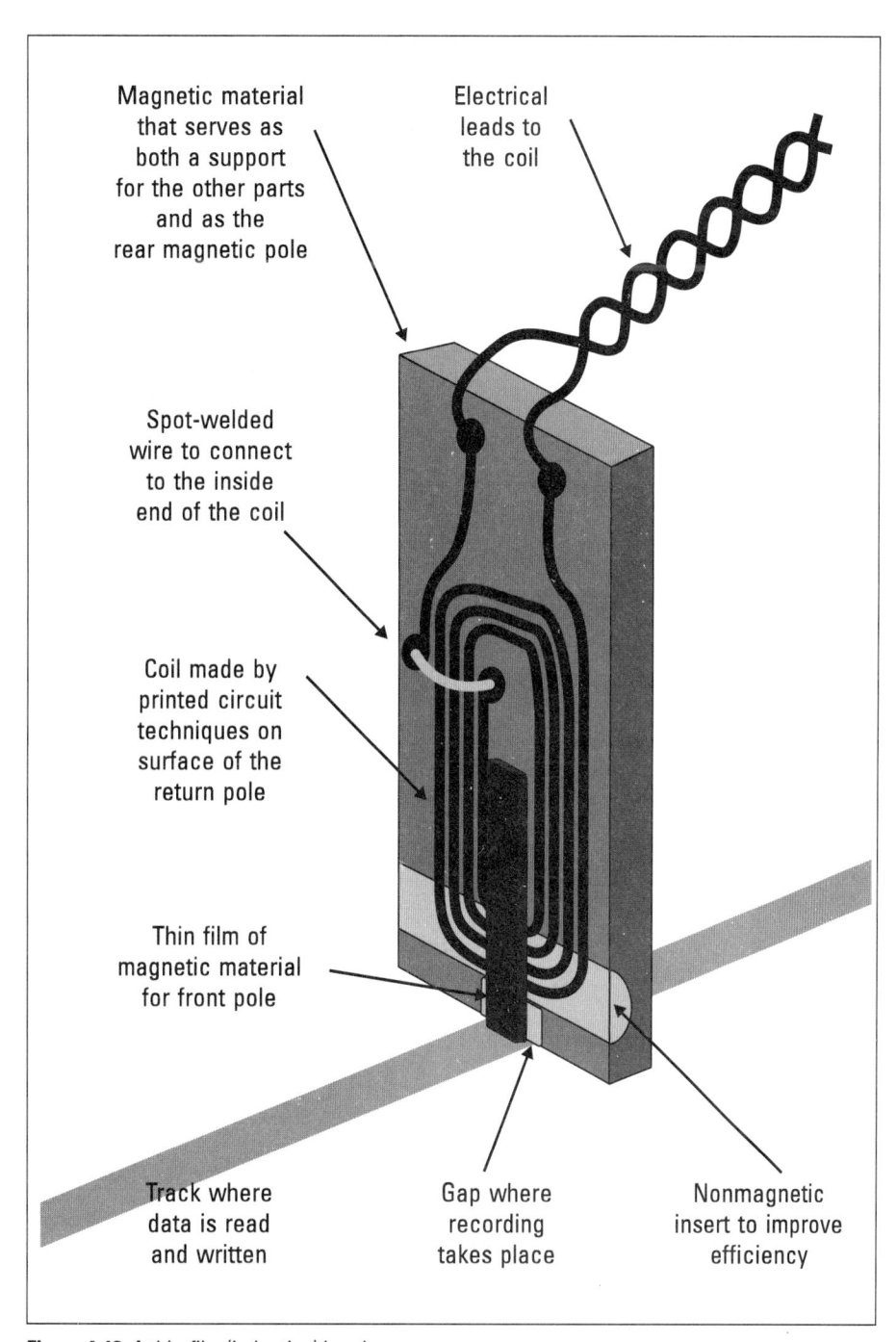

Figure 4-13: A thin-film (inductive) head.

Flux-sensing read heads

All disk *write* heads operate according to the same physical law: They create a magnetic field by passing an electric current through a coil. (In thin-film heads, the "coil" may have only one turn, but it still functions as a coil.) This current causes a magnetic field that is concentrated and directed by a core made out of some magnetic material. The field coming out of the core pole pieces magnetized regions in the platter surface, thus storing information.

All disk *write* heads work in the same way, but the same cannot be said of all disk *read* heads. Most of the read heads are inductive heads, but a few are flux-sensitive. (Magnetic flux is a measure of the amount of magnetic field passing through a particular region. You may think of it as the number of field lines. Equivalently, it is the strength of the magnetic field — called the magnetic intensity — times the area of the region in question.)

The inductive heads are only able to sense a *change* in the magnetization of the platter surface over which it is passing. Each time such a head passes over a magnetized region, it passes a portion of the field from that region through its coil. If the region is magnetized differently from its neighbors, the field through the coil changes, which causes a voltage pulse that can be detected.

A few read heads, called *flux-sensitive heads,* work entirely differently. These heads produce an output that depends only on the *size* of the magnetic field through their sense element and not on how rapidly the magnetigation changes. There are several different physical principles that have been exploited in the design of a flux-sensitive sensor element. These designs include magnetoresistive strips, Hall effect sensors, and flux-gate amplifiers.

Because these sensors can be used only to read a magnetic field and not to generate one, they must be combined with a conventional inductive write head. This combination head is then mounted in a *slider* and attached to an arm of the head assembly, exactly like a conventional inductive-ring read/write head. (The idea of a slider is explained later in this chapter in the sidebar "Head crashes — a real problem?")

These exotic flux-sensitive read heads are certainly interesting and they have found application in some other kinds of magnetic recording, but they are not yet commonly used in hard disks for PCs.

Despite the radically different way in which such a head is manufactured, it works very much the same way a ring head does. In particular, the information is recorded in regions of the track that have their magnetization oriented either forward or backward along the track. The name for this method is *longitudinal recording*.

A limitation to bit density in longitudinal recording

An alternative scheme in which the regions of magnetization in the platter surface have their magnetization pointing up or down, into or out of the surface, is called either *perpendicular recording* or *vertical recording*. The details of how this type of recording differs from longitudinal recording are given in the next section.

Figure 4-14 shows a close-up view of a cross section of the platter along a track that has been recorded by using longitudinal recording technology. Notice that the arrows representing the magnetization are either pointing to the right or to the left. Notice also that the boundaries of the differently magnetized regions are very jagged.

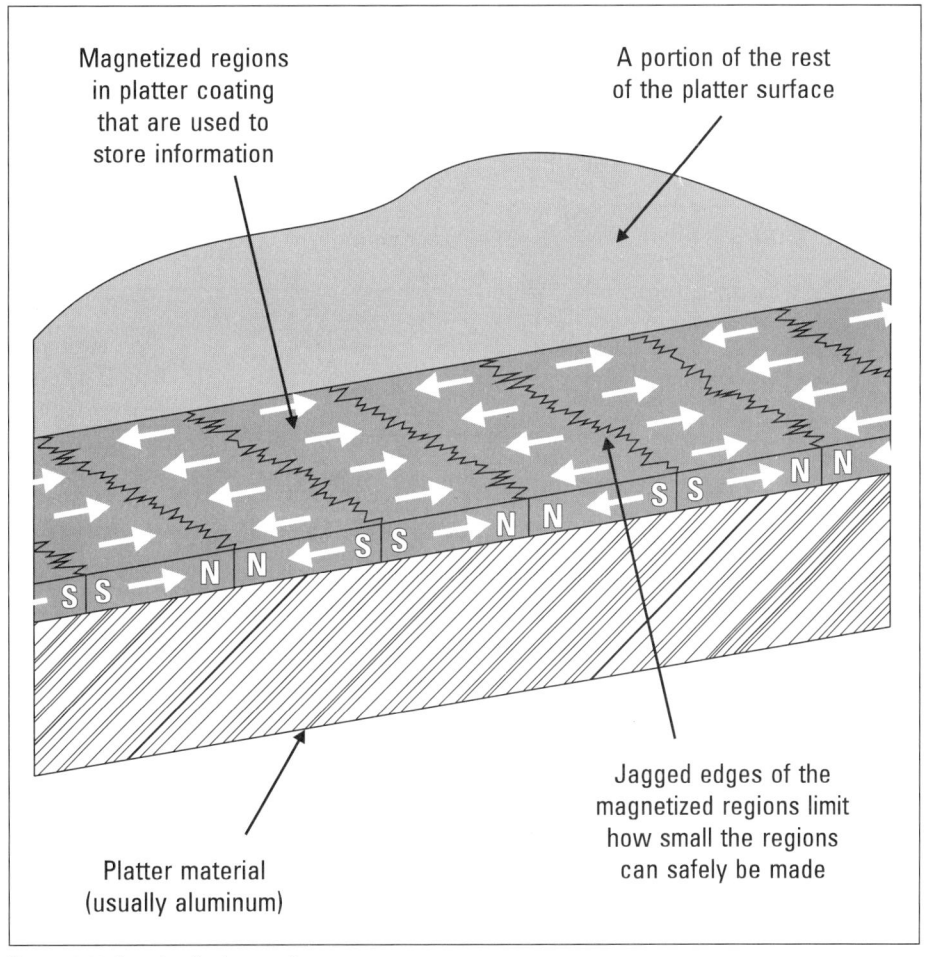

Figure 4-14: Longitudinal recording.

There are some very good physical reasons for those jagged edges and one important consequence. You must not make a longitudinally recorded region arbitrarily small. If you make it too small, it will simply disappear. This requirement provides one limitation on the number of bits per unit of track length that can be recorded on such a disk.

Critical dimensions in longitudinal recording read/write heads

The other limitation on how many bits can be recorded per unit of track length is an aspect of the read/write head's design. Specifically, the minimum size of a magnetic flip-flop length is set by some critical dimensions of that head. Figure 4-15 shows a side view of a ring head for longitudinal recording and a cross section of a portion of the platter. The figure shows three places where size is critical to the performance of such a head.

The most basic limitation on the size of a recorded region is provided by the gap size. The field lines leave the core there and detour through the nearby coating, which is how a region of that coating becomes magnetized.

Another very important distance is the height at which the head flies above the surface. The magnetic field pattern around the gap spreads and weakens very rapidly with distance away from the gap. Because the relevant distance is from the gap to the magnetizable platter coating, the design must include both the

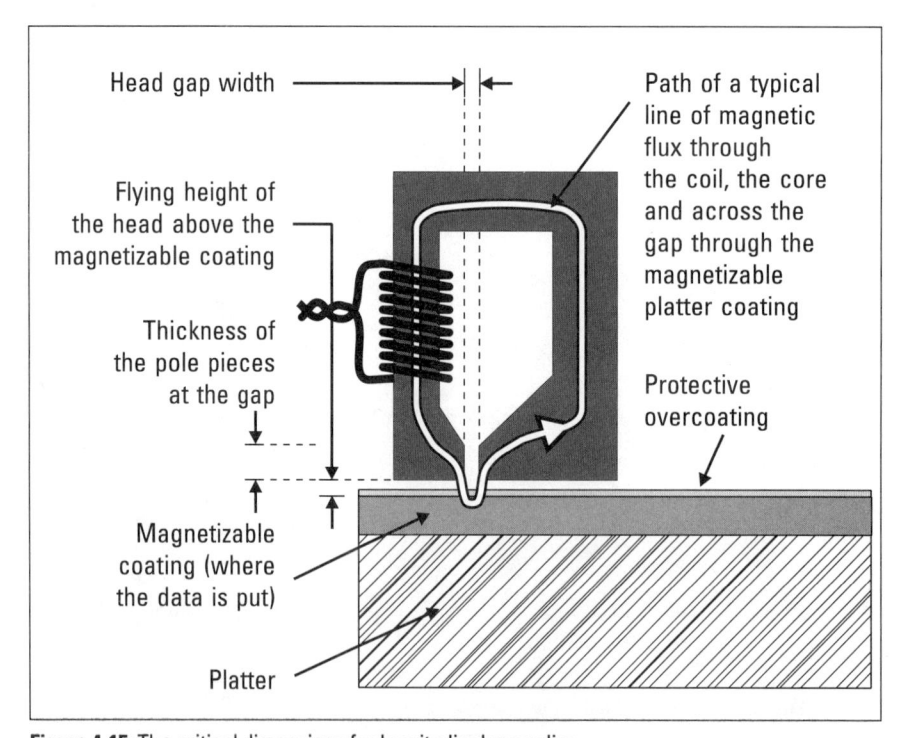

Figure 4-15: The critical dimensions for longitudinal recording.

air gap (the actual height at which the head flies above the upper surface of the platter) and the thickness of any protective or lubricating overcoating that may have been applied to the platter.

Finally, the thickness of the pole pieces right next to the gap is also critical. Why this thickness is so important may not be obvious at first. If the pole pieces are very wide at the gap, a significant portion of the magnetic field lines will jump straight across the gap. They will not detour through the platter surface and, therefore, will not contribute to magnetizing it. Conversely, if the pole pieces are too narrow, the field lines will crowd together so much in the pole tips that the core material will reach its maximum possible magnetization. The term to describe this situation is *saturation*. After the core is saturated, it will be unable to further concentrate the field lines.

The effective thickness of the pole pieces is either their actual thickness at the tip or their thickness at the place where the core material becomes saturated. The field lines will start to leak out of the tip where it becomes saturated, in effect making the gap appear to be wider than it really is.

This information may seem like a bit of really arcane knowledge, but it isn't. This fact, more than anything else, is the reason it is common to use flying heads. You may have thought that hard disk heads were made to fly in order to protect the surface from being abraded. That is true to a degree, but more to the point, the heads are made to fly to keep them from being worn down. If the pole thickness were made equal to its optimum value at the outset, any wear would translate immediately into an effectively wider gap and thus to lower recordable bit densities. This condition is in sharp contrast to the situation for heads designed to work by vertical recording, as will be made clear later in this chapter.

There is one other critical dimension of a read/write head that is not shown in Figure 4-15: the width of its pole pieces in the direction across the track. That distance is, in fact, what determines the width of the track that this head will record on the platter surface. (Because of fringing fields at either end of the gap, the track width is slightly greater than the head width. Furthermore, to provide a margin of safety, the manufacturers of drives typically leave at least half a track width of space between adjacent tracks. The average track spacing, therefore, is nearly twice the width of the pole pieces.)

MIG and double MIG heads

One way that head manufacturers have found to narrow the effective gap size and help keep the pole tips from saturating is to coat the interior surface of the ring on one or both sides of the gap with a magnetizable metal film. Such a head is called a *MIG (metal in gap) head* or a *double MIG head* (for two layers of metal in the gap). This approach helps because metal films are available that can support higher levels of magnetization than is common for the ferrite materials used in normal ring head cores.

Part I: The Hard Disk Companion

TECHNICAL SECRET

An interesting, although not essential, fact is that the head core gap is not just a space. Normally, the gap is filled with some hard, nonmagnetic material that not only ensures that the gap will remain the same size but also makes sure that there will be no sharp edges on the heads to scrape the surface when the heads land (which happens each time the disk platters slow down and stop turning).

Manufacturers make the heads (and the assembly that holds them and connects them to the actuator) as lightweight as possible and yet as rigid as possible. This way, the assembly can be moved quickly and easily and yet will put each head in a predictable place for any given position of the actuator.

Vertical recording

Wouldn't it be nice if hard disks could hold about 10 times as much information and yet be as inexpensive and easy to build and as reliable as present designs? That is the promise of what is called *vertical recording* or *perpendicular recording*.

The essential idea is easy to grasp: simply arrange to record the magnetic regions in such a way that the little magnets created in the magnetizable coating stand on end, pointing into or out of the platter surface. There are several ways this result can be accomplished. The one that is now receiving the most attention, and which can be most easily implemented by only a minimal alteration in the current technology, is diagrammed in Figure 4-16.

Compare Figure 4-16 with Figure 4-14. You can see just three important differences. The one that gives the vertical method of recording its name is that the white arrows, representing the direction of magnetization in each region, are all vertical. The surface of the track in each region is covered with N and S symbols to indicate either the heads of the arrows or their tails at that point in the region's surface.

The second difference is that there is another coating layer in Figure 4-16. This underlayer is made up of a magnetic, but not a magnetizable, material. That is, this layer channels magnetic field lines just as the core material in the head does. During recording, this layer serves as an essential part of the head's magnetic circuit. The rest of the time, the fields passing through this layer form closed loops through the magnets that have been formed in opposite directions (up and down) in two adjacent regions of the platter's magnetizable surface coating.

Chapter 4: Messy Hard Disk Details

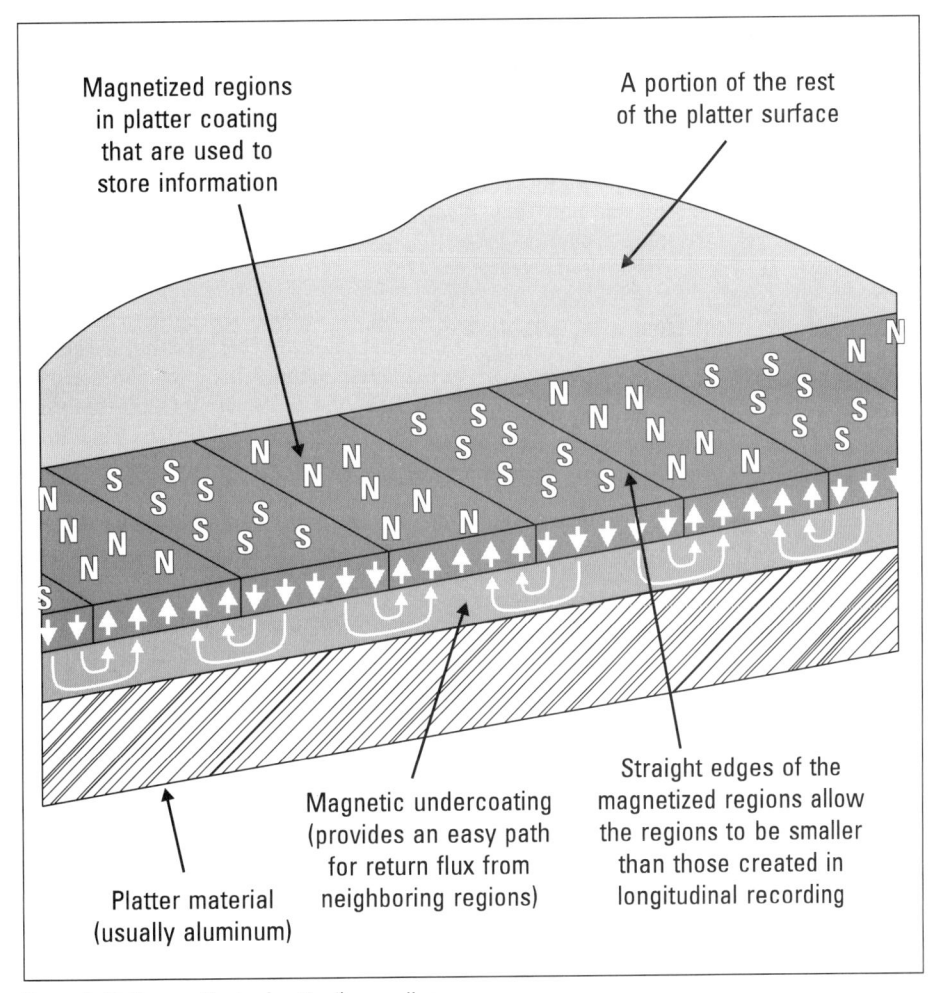

Figure 4-16: Perpendicular (vertical) recording.

The third difference in the comparison between the two figures is a consequence of the second one: the very much straighter boundaries between adjacent regions with opposite magnetization. You can understand why this difference occurs by thinking about what happens if you put two magnets down on a table and try to push them close together.

If you push their north poles toward each other, the magnets will repel each other. This action creates an unstable situation, and it is precisely what longitudinal recording creates in the platter's magnetizable surface coating. But if you put the two magnets down on the table side by side, with the north pole of one next to the south pole of the other, they will attract one another. This attraction creates a very stable situation, and it is what vertical recording produces in the platter's magnetizable surface coating.

Part I: The Hard Disk Companion

> ### It's easy to become confused
>
> The very close similarity of a platter created for longitudinal recording and one made for vertical recording has led to some amusing instances of confusion at various disk drive manufacturing plants. If you pick up a platter and look at it, there is literally no way to see which kind of platter you are holding. The underlayer used for vertical recording is completely covered up and thus out of sight. The surface layers (both the magnetizable one and the protective overcoating) are the same in both types of platter.
>
> The only sure way to know what kind of platter you have is to install it in a disk drive and test it. If you attempt to record some data by using a longitudinal recording platter with a vertical recording head, you will get at most a very tiny signal when you attempt to read the data. This weakness is because — lacking the underlayer — the platter is unable to efficiently return the field lines from the recording head's front pole to its back pole. Therefore little, if any, signal will be recorded.
>
> Conversely, if you attempt to record data by using a longitudinal recording head on a platter meant for vertical recording, you also will get no output when you try to read the data. In this case, the underlayer steals all the field lines from the magnetized regions of the platter surface layer that otherwise would have to return through the air above the platter. Only lines that are in the air can be trapped by a passing read head into returning through the read head core and coil (see Figure 2-4).
>
> Any company that makes both types of disk drive (drives using vertical recording as well as those using longitudinal recording) must keep very careful control of its inventory of disk platters!

As a result, it is possible by using vertical recording to make much smaller magnetized regions than are practical with longitudinal recording. To take full advantage of this last fact requires making heads whose critical dimensions are smaller than present technology permits and to fly those heads closer to the surface than is done in any hard disk made today. Once head manufacturing technology advances sufficiently, vertical recording will most likely become the dominant form used in disk drives.

What are the critical dimensions in a vertical recording head? How do they differ from those in a longitudinal recording head?

Critical dimensions in vertical recording read/write heads

The size of one of the pole pieces is critical in a vertical recording head, but the size of the other one is not (see Figure 4-17). The head that is very narrow will do all the recording. The other head is merely a path for the magnetic field lines to close back upon themselves. Because the return head is very broad and the field lines can go a substantial distance through the underlayer quite easily, the density of those lines where they enter the return pole is so low that it does not affect the magnetizable coating appreciably.

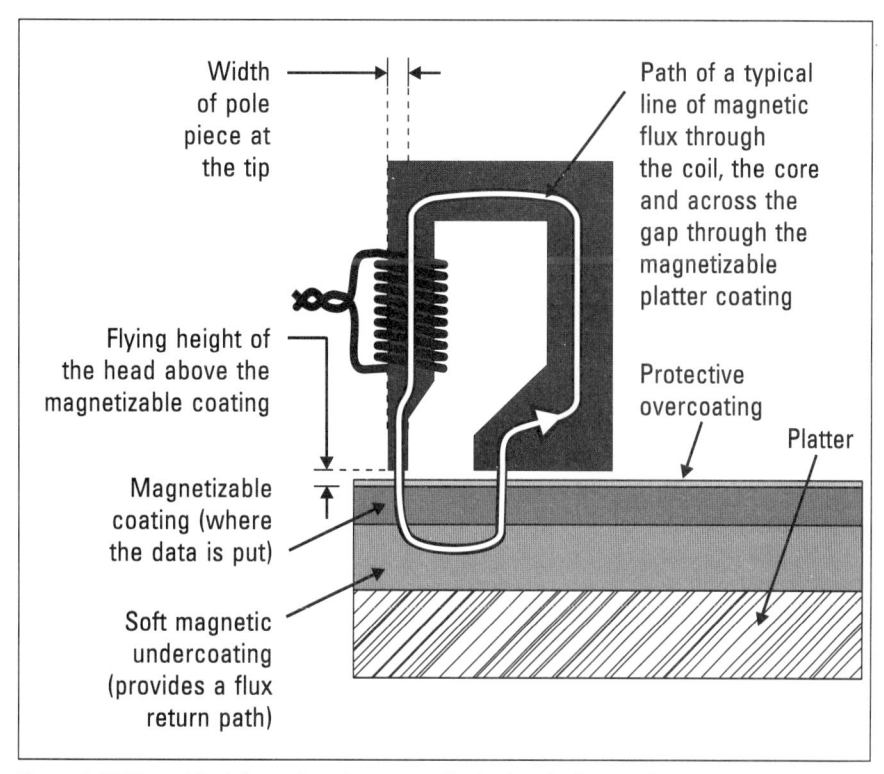

Figure 4-17: The critical dimensions for perpendicular (vertical) recording.

You may have worried that the field lines are shown as closing back on themselves through the immediately adjacent region and thought that perhaps that could not always happen. In fact it might not, but exactly where the field lines close back is not important. They will find a suitable place. The length of the field lines is unimportant. Only their density (number per square centimeter) matters.

The flying height of the head and, of course, the width of the pole tip (which sets the track width) are the only other important dimensions for this kind of head. The thickness of the return pole tip is totally unimportant.

As long as the thin tip is of a nearly constant cross-sectional shape, its length is not important. As the tip wears down it will still have the same cross-sectional size and shape. Therefore, a vertical recording head can safely be operated in actual contact with the platter surface! This is totally unlike the situation with a longitudinal recording head.

> ### Head crashes — a real problem?
>
> Many of us have heard lots of bad stories about hard disk head crashes. Years ago, head crashes were a major problem. Now that problem has mostly been solved.
>
> If the head crashes into the platter surface too hard, it will damage that surface (and possibly the head also). Certainly if a portion of the magnetizable coating gets scraped off the platter, you will lose whatever data were stored in that vicinity.
>
> Modern disk designs and manufacturing practices have nearly eliminated head crashes as a source of hard disk death. In fact, the heads must be able to "crash" gently every time the disk is turned off. After the platters slow down enough, the air currents that had been lofting the heads will cease supporting them, and the heads will land on the surface — softly, one hopes — and skid until the platters come to a complete stop.
>
> Modern hard disk heads are always mounted on a slider, which is a specially designed mounting block. The design of these blocks enables them to take advantage of even quite gentle air currents entrained by the spinning disk and fly above the surface, and to slide on the surface without causing appreciable wear to the coating whenever the disk is not turning fast enough to loft the heads. Furthermore, modern disk designs often include an overcoating that protects the magnetizable layer and lubricates the slider where it contacts the surface.
>
> Today's disk drives are much more likely to fail by either a failure of the spindle bearing or of an electronic component on the circuit card than they are to experience a destructive head crash.

In the vertical head, a modest amount of pole tip wear doesn't change anything important. In the longitudinal type, on the other hand, any wear that reduces the head thickness near the pole tip will drastically degrade the head's performance. And, of course, if it is safe to operate the head in contact with the surface, the head flying height can be reduced to simply the thickness of the platter surface's protective overcoating.

What we can look forward to

Now that thin-film heads are being made in much the same way as integrated circuit (IC) chips, progress in head-size reduction can be expected to follow the same pattern as that for IC chip-size reduction. It is only a matter of time before heads can be made with very much smaller dimensions than is presently possible. When this size reduction is combined with the minimum possible head-flying height (none!), the result will be even narrower tracks and higher bit densities along the tracks.

How far might this progress go? In the next several years, you can expect to see bit densities along a track go up quite dramatically through the use of vertical recording and heads that ride in contact with the surface. (Because these heads will be allowed to wear down during use, we may see drives in the future that permit — or even require — periodic head replacement as an aspect of their routine maintenance!)

Chapter 4: Messy Hard Disk Details   **141**

Track densities could be pushed up equally dramatically, which is to say that the magnetic materials and head design could support doing so. Unfortunately, the technology for making head positioners that are about ten times as accurate as present ones (and yet are economical to build and adequately reliable in long-term use) will be quite difficult to develop.

The product of the track density and the bit density along the track is the *areal recording density*. Modern disk designs have gone as high as about 80 thousand bits per square millimeter (which is 50 million per square inch). We may plausibly expect to see this amount increased by at least a factor of 5, but probably not by more than a factor of 20, in the next decade.

What Happens in the Drive Electronics

Near the start of Chapter 2, the function of the electronic circuit board that is attached to every hard disk drive is described in general. What the circuit board does in detail depends on the kind of drive in question. All of them must have some circuitry to control the spindle-motor. All of them have some kind of head-positioning circuitry. All of them have some switches and signal amplifiers. Some have special interface circuitry as well.

Different manufacturers have implemented each of these common elements in any of several ways. In the following sections you learn about some of the different strategies used in these common elements.

Spindle-motor drive circuit

In all PC drives, this board contains circuitry to drive the spindle motor (thus turning the platters at a constant speed). The board can use one of three strategies to keep the spindle turning at the desired rate. The simplest, conceptually, is the synchronous motor drives. A slightly more complex version is the phase-locked loop drives. The fanciest (and best) use servo feedback to regulate not the turning speed itself but rather the actual rate at which the sectors go past the heads.

TECHNICAL SECRET

Some spindle motors are *synchronous motors* — they turn synchronously with an oscillating electric signal, much like a kitchen clock that uses the frequency of the AC power line to keep accurate time. The circuit card has an oscillator whose frequency is crystal controlled (like a "quartz" wrist watch) and an amplifier to make that signal strong enough to drive the spindle motor.

The second kind of spindle motor is more tightly integrated into the driving circuitry. It forms a part of the oscillator, called in this case a *phase-locked loop*. Again, the frequency is controlled by a quartz crystal. The only essential difference is that, in this case, the oscillator will not oscillate unless the motor is turning.

The third strategy is like the second, only instead of having just a quartz crystal to set the frequency of the oscillator, these drives also monitor the rate at which sectors appear under the read/write head. This capability allows them to slightly alter the motor speed as necessary to keep constant the rate at which sectors appear, rather than keep the disk RPM constant.

You can find significant similarity between these strategies and those described earlier in this chapter for positioning the heads: The first of these three strategies is the equivalent of the dead-reckoning, stepper-motor head positioners. The second is like an external servo, in which feedback is used, but not from the actual data on the disk. The third approach is like the more advanced servo head positioners that use information about the actual data (or their associated servo bursts) on the disk platters that are passing under the heads at any instant.

Head-positioner drive circuit

The electronic circuitry built onto the drive also controls the head-positioning actuator. Just what it does depends on two factors. One is the kind of positioning mechanism the drive has (stepper motor or servo feedback). The other is the kind of interface used with that drive (ST412/ST506, ESDI, SCSI, IDE/ATA, or a hard-disk card).

Once again, for most purposes it really doesn't matter if you know what kind of head-positioning circuitry your drive has. There is one reason to be cautious, though. If your drive uses a servo feedback head positioner, you can hurt it by using the wrong kind of head parking program. If you should run such a program on that sort of drive, you will hear it going *bang, bang, bang, bang,* until you turn off power to your computer. Better turn off power quickly in this case, or your drive will be destroyed! (You can learn more about what these programs are doing in the following technical note. Chapter 16 has additional information on head parking programs.)

TECHNICAL SECRET

ST412/ST506 controllers (used with MFM and RLL drives) simply tell the drive to step in or to step out some number of cylinders. Unlike ESDI and SCSI controllers, they do not specify the destination cylinder by number.

Stepper-motor drives are naturals for the ST412/ST506 approach. After all, these motors take a step whenever they get a suitable pulse of electric current, and they have no means of knowing what cylinder number the heads are over. There is a buffer on the drive circuit card that can store up several step commands, but nothing to keep track of absolute cylinder number. If you command a stepper-motor drive, for example, to go in 4,000 cylinders, it will cheerfully go in as far as it can and then simply push the heads against some physical stop several thousand times, not noticing that it isn't moving them at all.

In a servo-motor drive, things are different. Again, if you are talking about a drive with the ST412/ST506 interface, the controller will command it to step in or to step out by a single cylinder at a time. Again, the drive electronics will store up a number of those commands in a buffer until it has time to carry them out.

Unlike the stepper drives, though, servo drives *must* keep track of where (over which numbered cylinder) they are supposed to have put the heads. This information is necessary because the only way they properly position the heads is to read the special servo signals, see which cylinder number the signals say the heads are sailing over, and then compare that with the desired cylinder number.

If you tell this sort of drive to step in 4,000 cylinders, it will compute some huge cylinder number that it is supposed to find and then turn on the voice coil current in the appropriate direction, looking at the servo head signals all the while to see whether it is yet where you commanded it to go. Because no PC drive today has that many cylinders, it will inevitably fail to find what it is looking for. What happens then?

The circuitry is clever enough to notice that it didn't get where it was going even by using a large, long pulse of voice coil current. Noticing that, it tries again. First, the circuitry will reverse the current and hold it there until it sees cylinder number 0, out at the very edge of the platter. Then it reverses the current again and goes back to looking for the cylinder you have requested. Again, of course, it will fail.

The drive will continue this process forever, or until it completely destroys itself. Unfortunately, there are some head parking programs that are just dumb enough to ask a servo drive to do this.

Because ST412/ST506 controllers (used with MFM and RLL drives) only command the drive to step in or to step out by one cylinder at a time for some number of times, they are well matched to the stepper design of head positioner. The higher performance MFM and RLL drives, though, have the extra circuitry needed to operate a servo-feedback head positioner.

All ESDI drives must have that circuitry because those kinds of controller will typically send to the drive a command to go to a particular cylinder by its number. As it happens, these drives are high-performance models that use servo-feedback head positioners, which means that they have the absolute cylinder-number positioning capability built-in anyway.

IDE/ATA drives and hard-disk cards are essentially combinations of a drive (usually an RLL or ERLL drive) and a controller card. They, too, include the absolute cylinder-positioning circuitry.

SCSI drives (and some of the most modern IDE drives) accept commands to seek to a logical block address (LBA). They must have even more electronic circuitry mounted on the drive because they first must compute what physical address (head, cylinder, and physical sector number) the LBA corresponds to and then use the usual servo strategies to go there.

Switches and amplifiers

Finally, the electronics card on the drive must have some circuits connected to the read/write heads. The three parts to these circuits are a set of switches that let the circuit choose which head to turn on and whether to set that head to reading or writing; a write amplifier that takes the signals from the controller and makes them strong enough to record information on the platter surface; and the read amplifier circuitry, whose job is to strengthen and clean up the signals coming off the heads when data are being read (see Figure 4-18). In addition, some drives, such as ESDI, SCSI, IDE/ATA, and hard-disk cards, have a clock-data separator circuit on the electronics card.

TECHNICAL SECRET

A clock-data separator circuit takes the analog signals from the heads (after they have been amplified and somewhat cleaned up) and converts these pulses into binary digital data. If the drive is using MFM data encoding, it figures out which pulses are clock signals and which are data signals and then separates them (hence the name clock-data separator). If RLL data encoding is used, the job is more complicated, but the circuitry that accomplishes it is still called a clock-data separator.

For ESDI drives, that is the end of the story. For SCSI, IDE, and hard-disk cards, there is one more part.

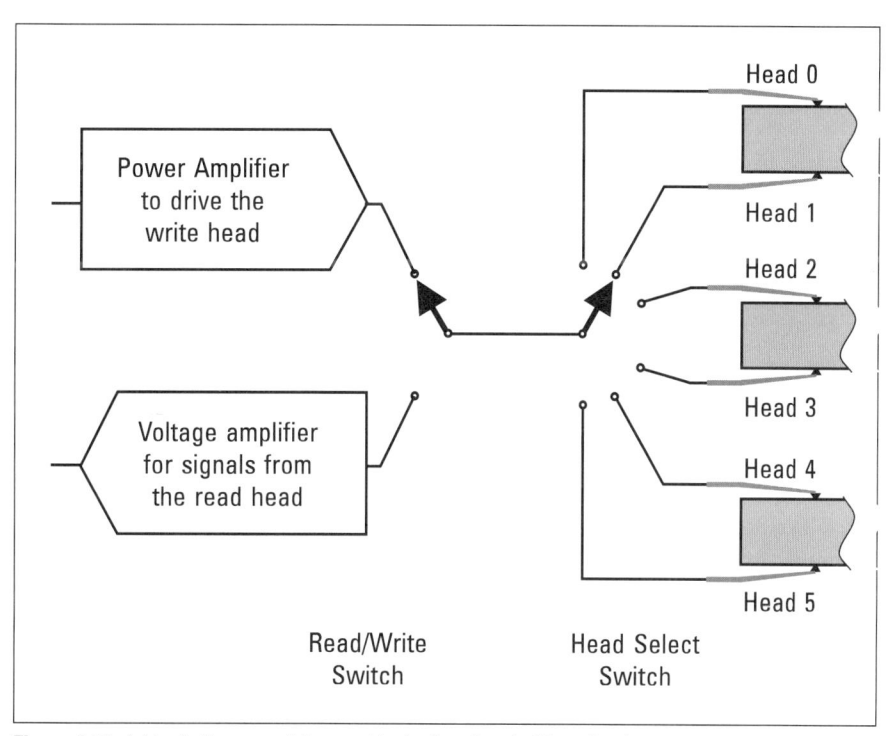

Figure 4-18: A block diagram of the read/write head-switching circuits.

Interface electronics

IDE/ATA and hard-disk cards are each essentially a complete controller plus hard disk all in one. The basic drive design is most likely similar to RLL drives. In any case, these drives must have circuitry that is able to talk to the PC input-output bus, in addition to performing the tasks already described.

SCSI drives have the full circuitry of a controller plus drive, as well as the SCSI interface circuitry, which gives them the "intelligence" to conduct a proper conversation with the SCSI host adapter and to control the SCSI bus when permitted.

What Happens in the Controller Electronics

MFM, RLL, and ESDI drives connect to controller cards plugged into the PC's input-output bus. Those controller cards take commands from the PC and translate them into the language understood by the drives and then do the reverse from the drives to the PC.

Part I: The Hard Disk Companion

TECHNICAL SECRET

The controller cards' job includes packaging the data as it comes from the computer by adding the error correction code (ECC) bytes. In the case of ST412/ST506 interface controllers (for MFM and RLL drives), this task also includes encoding the bytes of data plus ECC, according to the chosen data-encoding strategy (MFM or RLL). For ESDI drives, that job is done on the drive.

Going the other way, an ST412/ST506 controller must separate clock and data signals or otherwise infer the actual binary data from the string of pulses coming off the drive's heads. ESDI systems do this separation on the drive. Any of these controllers (ST412/ST506 or ESDI) then must compute the ECC and compare that result with what was read, attempt to reread the data if there is a discrepancy, and deliver the data to the PC (with the ECC removed and perhaps with the data corrected by use of the ECC). Finally, the controller must send a message to the PC to describe the level of confidence it has in the data just delivered.

The most important thing to know about the workings of disk controller cards is that each one does its job in a unique manner. This uniqueness means, first, that you always must use the right sort of controller for the drive. MFM drives do not generally work correctly when attached to RLL controllers (even though both use the ST412/ST506 interface), and certainly neither controller can be used with an ESDI drive, or vice versa.

Also, as already mentioned, you cannot format and fill a drive with data by means of one controller and then necessarily expect another controller, even the same kind of controller, to be able to read the data. Only if the two controllers are of the same model and revision number, and were made nearly simultaneously by the same company, can you be assured that such a swap will work.

What some people think of as a SCSI controller (which is more properly called a SCSI host adapter) is completely different. The disk controller *per se* is located on the SCSI drive along with the SCSI slave-interface circuitry.

Drives that have their own controllers mounted on them (which include all IDE/ATA drives, hard disks on an option card, and SCSI drives), of course, cannot get mismated to an inappropriate controller.

Chapter 4: Messy Hard Disk Details

Recalibration and Other Strange Sounds in the Night

Sometimes horrible grinding noises may emanate from your computer. Clearly the disk drive is doing it, but what, exactly is it doing and why? Should you be worried?

Some unusually noisy disk drives *always* make strange sounds. If they work once, you may assume that they will continue to work more or less as long as any other, similar drive. For such drives, you can safely ignore the strange noises. You should worry about drives that make inconsistent noises, however, such as when a drive that was working quietly suddenly starts grinding away. This noise scares people, as it probably should.

TIP

Naturally, you will be scared of strange noises only if you *notice* the sounds your hard drive is making and if you realize that they are not the usual sorts of sounds it makes. Many disk drives make idiosyncratic sounds. Learn what the normal, "good" sounds are that your drive makes and listen for any sounds that are different from the normal ones.

There are two main reasons for these strange noises. In both cases, the drive is doing a *recalibration*. These noises mean the disk is having some trouble carrying out the orders it was given; you are right to be concerned. If some of the sectors lie in places on the disk where it cannot reliably store information, perhaps it is enough to mark those sectors as bad and then avoid trying to write or read data there. Of course, if you already have written some data there, that strategy may not suffice.

TECHNICAL SECRET

The first of the main reasons for the recalibration noises is that the drive has lost its sense of where it is — in particular which cylinder its heads are traveling over. Perhaps it is a servo-feedback drive, and the servo-head signals tell the drive electronics that it is no longer over the track it meant to be over. Perhaps it is a stepper drive, and the signals read from the sector headers on a data track tell it the same thing. This situation can occur even when the drive is neither reading nor writing any information (that is, you could be sitting at the DOS prompt or in some application program that was waiting for your input).

The usual ploy the drive electronics will use to get (literally) back on track is to go first to the outermost track (cylinder 0) and then come in from there. This method makes the most sense in a stepper drive, in which the most obvious way to find cylinder number 12, for example, is to go to cylinder number 0 and take 12 steps in toward the spindle. This method also is used in servo drives to confirm which way they should be looking.

The second reason a drive may make these strange noises is that the drive may be trying to read a bad sector. Either it could not find a sector header with the right address numbers in it, or the CRC value for that sector header did not agree with the header's contents. Here the drive may be quite sure which cylinder it is over, yet it again tries to reread the sector by going first back to the start of the disk (cylinder 0) and then returning to the desired track to look for the desired sector. The drive uses this method to ensure that it is not failing to read the sector simply because it was looking in the wrong place.

Some modern IDE drives will try again and again to read a bad sector, and while they are doing so will approach the right cylinder first from one side and then from the other, or in other ways attempt to "jigger" the heads around a bit to see whether that makes it possible to read the sector.

You also may hear these noises when you first prepare a hard disk. Both in the low-level and in the high-level formatting, the machine does a cursory test of every sector on the disk to assure itself that those sectors can be used reliably to store and retrieve information. When it finds a bad spot, the program will tell the controller to try again and again and again. Only after a very large number of failures will it give up and mark that place as bad so that DOS will never try to store information there.

You very likely will hear these noises when you run a disk surface testing program like SpinRite, too. These noises happen because the testing program may test even places that have previously been declared bad, just in case they are no longer defective.

The worst time to hear these noises is when some ordinary DOS program is trying to read or write information on the disk. These are the times when you may lose some data if you are not careful (and a bit lucky).

If you hear these noises while you are running an ordinary DOS program, you should immediately back up any active files to a floppy disk or tape cassette. If DOS doesn't allow you to back up, telling you it cannot find a sector or that it discovered an error when reading the drive, you may be able to recover your data by running SpinRite. See Chapter 11 for additional details.

Chapter 4: Messy Hard Disk Details

Summary

▶ Stepper motors are simple, digital actuators. They are used in less expensive, smaller-capacity disk drives to position the heads by dead reckoning.

▶ More expensive disk drives use negative feedback to constantly readjust the position of the heads to keep them traveling over the centers of the tracks. Another name for this strategy is a servo-control system.

▶ Voice coil motors are able to push or pull over a wide range of force and thus can be used to create very quick responding head-positioning mechanisms. They are not able to put the heads into place without help from a servo system that monitors where the heads are.

▶ Several kinds of servo systems have been used in hard disk head positioners. The most popular now are the embedded servo and the hybrid approach. The latter combines the virtues of the dedicated platter and embedded strategies.

▶ Most hard disk read/write heads are variations on the inductive-ring head and use longitudinal recording. Newer fabrication methods produce heads that can record and read many more bits per unit of track length and narrower tracks.

▶ Vertical (or perpendicular) recording is a new approach to data storage in a magnetized platter surface. It has the potential for storing vastly increased densities of data. Practical vertical recording hard disk systems are only now reaching the marketplace, but this area is likely to be a very active one for development in the next several years.

▶ The electronics mounted on a hard disk drive, and those in any separate controller card it may have, do a number of tasks: control the rate at which the disk platters turn; move the head assembly to the desired cylinder; combine data and clock information (encoding) and append ECC information before storing the data on the disk.

▶ A complementary part of the electronics reverses those last steps when the data are read from the drive, separating the data and clock information and judging the accuracy of the recovered data, reconstructing the data when necessary by use of the recorded ECC information.

▶ Drives that conform to the different interface standards (ST412/ST506, ESDI, IDE/ATA, SCSI) and hard disks on an option card (which are simply a variation on the IDE/ATA approach) each distribute these functions differently, but drives of any type must perform every one of those functions.

▶ One way a drive can fail is if it forgets to which cylinder it has moved the head assembly. When this situation occurs, the drive will recalibrate by moving the heads out to cylinder 0 and then back to where they belong. If your disk starts doing this frequently, spontaneously, it may be telling you that it is about to die. Pay attention to this warning! You may not get another one.

In the next chapter, you learn all about a way to make your disk seem to work a whole lot faster. Disk caching can be quite complex, but don't let that keep you from using this most valuable technique. (In reading the next chapter, you also will learn the concepts behind memory caching — another valuable technique to make the fastest PCs run even faster.)

Chapter 5
Disk Caching

In This Chapter
- What disk caching is
- How disk and memory caching differ and how they are similar
- Why all PC users will benefit from adding a disk cache if they don't already use one
- How six common cache-management strategies differ and which is best for you
- A kind of cache difference worth knowing about
- When getting a hardware caching disk controller makes sense
- The correct value to use on the line in your CONFIG.SYS file that sets the number of BUFFERS that DOS will use

The Purpose of a Disk Cache

A disk cache, at its most fundamental level, provides a place to store information on its way to or from a disk drive. Its purpose is to speed up disk reading and writing.

In this way, a disk cache resembles memory cache, which is used in some computers as a special place to store information on its way between the central processing unit (CPU) chip and the computer's main RAM. Conceptually similar, the two differ in detail (see Figure 5-1). This book covers the details of disk caching only.

The difference between disk and memory caching, stated in a bit more detail, is this: A *disk cache* is a temporary storage location (some RAM) for data moving between the PC's main RAM and its disk drive. A *memory cache* is a temporary storage location (some very fast RAM) between its central processing unit (the 8088, 8086, 80286, 386, or 486 chip) and its main RAM. Your PC might have both (the fastest PCs do), one or the other, or neither.

Any computer is an information processor. For your PC to process any information, both the data and the program to process it must reside in the PC's RAM. When you turn off your PC, it loses all the information in RAM. Consequently,

Part I: The Hard Disk Companion

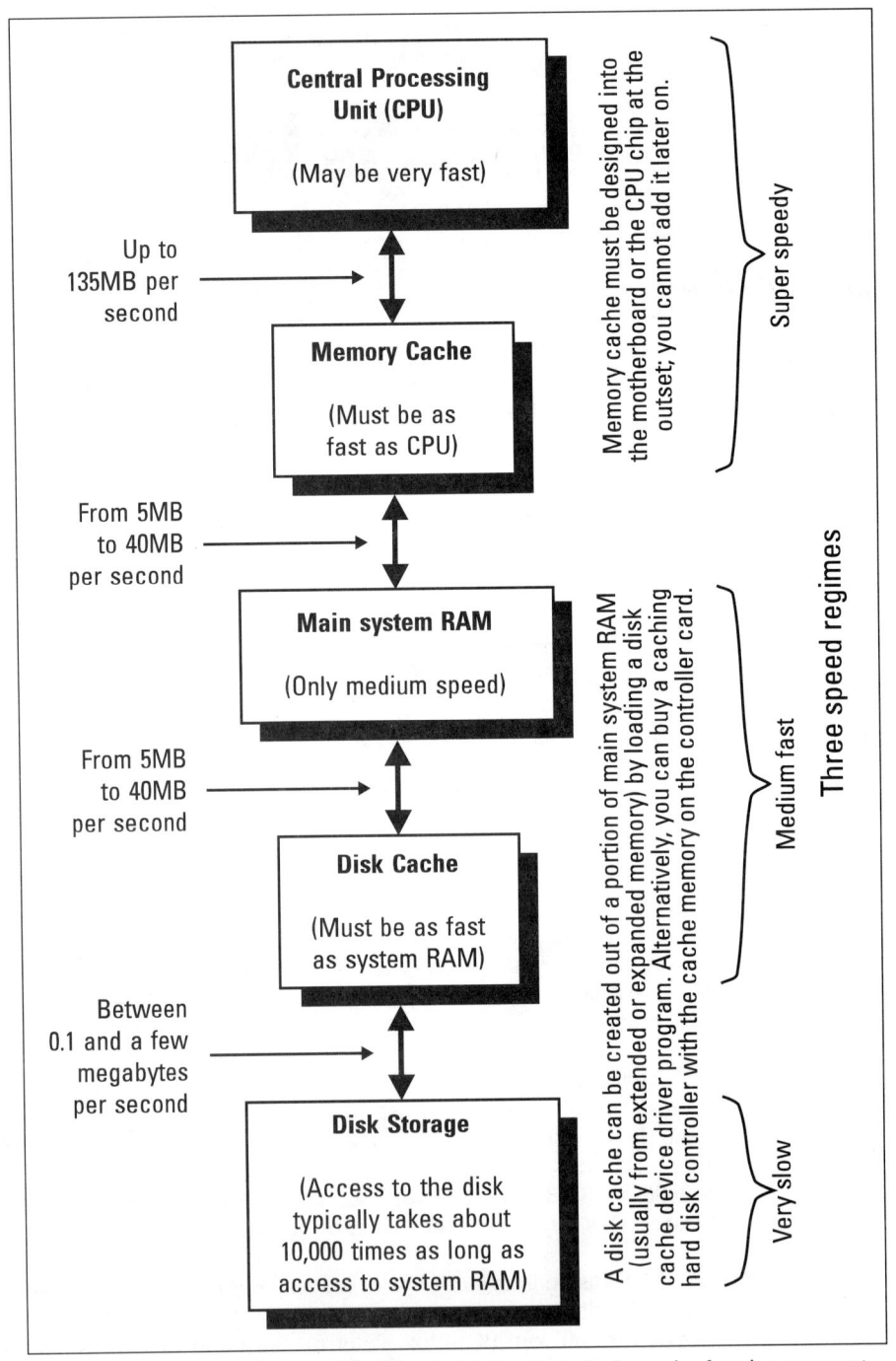

```
                  ┌─────────────────────┐  ┐
                  │  Central Processing │  │
                  │      Unit (CPU)     │  │
                  │                     │  │
                  │  (May be very fast) │  │  Super speedy
                  └──────────▲──────────┘  │
      Up to                  │             │
      135MB per ───────►     │             │
      second                 ▼             │
                  ┌─────────────────────┐  │
                  │    Memory Cache     │  │
                  │                     │  │
                  │    (Must be as      │  │
                  │    fast as CPU)     │  │
                  └──────────▲──────────┘  ┘
      From 5MB              │
      to 40MB ────────►     │
      per second             ▼
                  ┌─────────────────────┐  ┐
                  │   Main system RAM   │  │
                  │                     │  │
                  │  (Only medium speed)│  │
                  └──────────▲──────────┘  │  Medium fast
      From 5MB              │              │
      to 40MB ────────►     │              │
      per second             ▼             │
                  ┌─────────────────────┐  │
                  │     Disk Cache      │  │
                  │                     │  │
                  │   (Must be as fast  │  │
                  │    as system RAM)   │  │
                  └──────────▲──────────┘  ┘
      Between               │
      0.1 and a few ──►     │
      megabytes              ▼             ┐
      per second  ┌─────────────────────┐  │
                  │    Disk Storage     │  │
                  │                     │  │
                  │  (Access to the disk│  │  Very slow
                  │  typically takes    │  │
                  │  about 10,000 times │  │
                  │  as long as access  │  │
                  │  to system RAM)     │  │
                  └─────────────────────┘  ┘
```

Memory cache must be designed into the motherboard or the CPU chip at the outset; you cannot add it later on.

A disk cache can be created out of a portion of main system RAM (usually from extended or expanded memory) by loading a disk cache device driver program. Alternatively, you can buy a caching hard disk controller with the cache memory on the controller card.

Three speed regimes

Figure 5-1: Memory cache versus disk cache, indicating the typical speeds of each component and the data-transfer rate between them.

you must store the programs and information on a hard disk or some other less-volatile medium. Naturally, because only information in RAM is processed, you must have a method of loading everything from the disk into RAM and back again.

DOS routes information on its way to or from a disk drive through something called the *DOS disk buffers,* which are special regions of RAM set aside for this purpose. These buffers are described in detail later in this chapter. First, you need to learn more about hardware disk caching and software disk caching. An important point to remember is that the PC will ask for information from or send information to the disk drive one entire sector — and only one sector — at a time.

/ TECHNICAL SECRET /

Versions 3.3 and above of MS-DOS and PC DOS offer an exception to the one sector rule. These versions of DOS can request that the hard disk controller read or write multiple sectors at a time. Most programs, however, do not take advantage of that capability. Also, some controllers are not able to handle those requests correctly if there is any error, even a fully correctable one, in the data that is being read or written more than one sector at a time.

An even more important point to remember is that the disk drive has moving parts. This fact means that a disk drive handles data far slower than the CPU can shuffle data around in RAM. (The speed ratio is at least 1,000:1 and can be many tens of thousands to one.)

The Varieties of Caches

A *hardware disk cache* consists of a chunk of RAM on the disk controller, in which information can be parked temporarily before it is sent on to the disk drive or to the computer. A *software cache* is a program that uses a portion of your main computer RAM to simulate a hardware disk cache.

Both hardware and software disk caches have another aspect that you need to understand: they somehow must manage the use of their memory cache. In the case of a hardware cache, a separate small computer on the disk controller handles this job. In the case of a software cache, a resident program in your PC's main memory handles it.

There are many different strategies used by disk-cache managers (either the hardware or the software kinds). The next sections describe the most popular ones.

Track buffer

A *track buffer* is a chunk of cache RAM whose data capacity matches that of one full track on the disk. When DOS asks for a sector of information from the disk drive, the cache controller reads not only that sector but also the rest of that track, anticipating that DOS will ask next for another sector out of the same track, which it generally does. Whenever that happens, the controller can supply the data right away, without waiting for the disk to turn and bring that next sector into view again.

TECHNICAL SECRET

The presence of a track buffer located on the disk controller (a kind of hardware disk cache) can greatly mitigate the effect of an improper interleave on the disk drive. For optimum performance, though, you want to have the appropriate interleave *and* a cache buffer of some sort on the disk controller.

Because the typical MFM drive has 17 sectors, each holding 512 bytes, a track buffer requires only 8.5KB of RAM. For an RLL drive, that number may be about 13KB, and for an ESDI or SCSI drive, it could be as high as 38KB. These days, this much RAM is not very expensive, so more and more disk controllers are including at least a track buffer. IDE/ATA and SCSI drives (which have their controllers built onto the disk drive) always have a track buffer.

This kind of disk buffering can speed up disk reading enormously, especially if you are reading a file that is stored in successive sectors on the disk. A track buffer does nothing to speed up disk writes.

Read cache

A slightly fancier sort of disk cache, the *read cache,* has more RAM and uses that RAM a bit more cleverly. This version of disk cache may provide enough RAM to store several tracks' worth of data. Typical amounts of RAM cache range from 32KB to 16MB.

Each time the computer wants to read a sector's worth of information from the disk, the request goes to the cache controller. First, the cache controller checks to see whether the information already is stored in the memory cache. If it is, the cache controller returns the requested information to the CPU and its job is finished. If not, the cache controller gets the data from the disk and supplies it to the CPU, and it keeps a copy of the data and a record of where on the disk it came from in the memory cache.

Chapter 5: Disk Caching

This process continues until the disk cache's memory is full. After the read cache starts to fill up, the chances increase greatly that DOS will ask for sectors that are already in the cache, causing the effective speed of your disk to soar.

TECHNICAL SECRET

The technical term for finding what you are seeking in the cache is a *cache hit*. The percentage of hits is a measure of how effective the cache is. In favorable circumstances, a large cache can achieve hit rates over 90 percent. Because whenever you get a hit, the cache returns the data in almost no time, but when you get a miss, an actual disk access is required. A 90 percent hit rate (which means a 10 percent miss rate) will make your drive appear to operate about ten times as fast as usual.

Most of the time, such favorable circumstances will not prevail, and then the cache will not do nearly that well. Still, even if the cache only doubles the speed of your disk drive and just occasionally makes it appear to run ten times as fast, the cache is a real boon.

Each time the controller is asked for a sector whose contents are not already in the cache, the controller must go to the disk and read it. At the same time, if the disk cache's memory already has been totally filled, it will discard the *least-recently-used* entry in the cache, replacing it with the contents of the sector or track that it just read from the disk. (By the way, you as a user don't have any choice about the replacement strategy the cache will use. That choice is exercised solely by the manufacturer.)

It is not easy to know what is the "right" choice of cache element to replace. The least-recently-used entry means the one that has been kept in the memory cache for the longest time since it was last referenced, but it is only one common means of choosing what cache element to replace. This entry may not be the one that was put into the memory the *longest* time ago; that would be called the *oldest* entry. If the oldest entry has been used any time more recently than the last reference to some other entry, the best strategy would be to keep that oldest, but not least-recently-referenced, entry around; it may well be used yet again.

Some cache controllers will discard the oldest entry instead of the least recently used one. This method is, however, uncommon. Many controllers do not bother to keep accurate records of each access to every item in the cache; they can at best approximate the ideal least-recently-used-item replacement strategy.

You may have seen the term *look aside read cache*. This is a read cache that, when asked for the contents of a sector on the disk, will look simultaneously in the cache and on the disk and will return the information from whichever place it finds it first. Because the disk is so very much slower than RAM, the difference between this and the strategy that waits to go to the disk until the cache controller is sure that the information is not in the disk cache's memory is negligible. In the case of a memory cache, the speed difference between main memory and the disk cache's memory is not so dramatic, so this strategy difference may be important.

Another variation on this theme is the *read ahead cache*. This is a read cache that always reads a full track of information from the disk. This method combines some of the benefits of a track buffer with those of a general read cache. This variation is most likely to be found in a hardware disk cache implemented on a disk controller. As with a track buffer, a read ahead cache does nothing for disk *writing* speed; it speeds up disk *reading* only.

Write-through cache

A *write-through cache* speeds up disk writing by setting aside some fraction of the memory cache to remember recently written information. The remaining portion of the memory cache is used for read caching, and that part works just like the read caches already described.

The difference between a read cache and a write-through cache shows up when the CPU needs to write some information to the disk. A write-through cache intercepts those actions, as well as reads requests.

The cache controller first checks to see whether the data now to be sent to the disk already resides in the cache and whether it was previously written to the same destination on the disk. If so, it tells the CPU it has finished writing the information, even though it didn't actually have to do any writing to the disk at all. That way, the CPU gets back to its other work without the delay that an actual disk write would cause.

If the information to be sent to the disk was not already sent there (and kept in the cache), the controller must go ahead and do an actual disk write. At the same time, the controller will keep a copy of the data (and a record of where on the disk it was written) in the cache, just in case it may be asked to repeat that write some time soon. In this case, the CPU will have to wait until the disk write is accomplished, but if it ever wants to rewrite the same information in the same place (and if the copy of that information in the cache hasn't yet been discarded), it will not be at all delayed at that time.

A write-through (and read) cache is the most commonly used disk cache strategy. And for many people it is the most sensible choice. There are several other cache strategies, and each is just right for some users. So read on to see whether one of them might better fit your needs.

Advanced write-through cache

Mostly marketing hype, an *advanced write-through cache* is a caching disk controller like the one already described but with either more cache RAM or a "better" cache control method.

One improvement on the basic write-through cache that is significant is a version that sorts all pending writes so that the disk drive can execute those commands in the least possible time. No requests to write to disk are delayed artificially, but because the CPU can generate write requests (and deliver the data to the cache) far faster than the disk can accept them, it is possible for many requests to be queued up, waiting for the disk to have time to process them. In this case, if those requests are sorted according to their locations on the disk, the drive will be able to move through all the requests in a minimum amount of time.

This process closely resembles the elevator cache described later in this chapter (and gets a substantial portion of the advantages of that strategy) but without the dangers of deferred writing. (When a cache defers writing information to the disk for more than just a brief instant, you run the risk of losing some data or, worse, of ruining the integrity of an entire database. This point is covered in detail in the next section.)

The popular Super PC-Kwik program offers ordered writes under the name PowerWrite. The PC-Kwik company stresses that PowerWrite is not a deferred-write strategy but just a more efficient write-through strategy.

A subtle, but significant, further improvement in the write strategy is used in some commercial cache programs. In this scheme, not only are the pending writes sorted, they also are deferred (briefly) until either the system is not busy reading from the disk or until some specified small fraction of a second has elapsed. This subtle delay often allows the disk to be used to read information that the CPU needs to keep busy and yet does not delay writing the information to the disk long enough to be subject to very much risk of loss.

Deferred-write cache

A *deferred-write cache,* on the other hand, is really a very different sort of caching disk controller. Such a cache differs from a write-through cache in one extremely significant way: a deferred-write cache doesn't write information to the disk when it receives it; it writes the information later on, whenever the cache controller is good and ready, which may be as much as several seconds later.

This sort of cache tells the CPU that the disk write is finished right away, so the computer can go back to whatever it was doing far sooner than if it had to wait until the data actually had been written to the disk drive. That is good. But sometimes the data never makes it to the disk drive. That is very bad.

For some people, a deferred-write cache is ideal. On the other hand, this kind of cache can be so dangerous that many other people don't want to fool with it.

When the CPU asks for information from the disk, this kind of controller acts just like the other disk-caching controllers with a lot of RAM. It looks to see whether it already has the sector the CPU wants. If it does, it gives that sector to the CPU immediately. If not, the controller goes out and reads either just that sector or the whole track containing that sector, keeping in the cache whatever it reads in case the CPU will soon request more of it.

The difference comes when the CPU asks the cache to write information to the disk drive. The deferred-write cache, as its name suggests, simply takes the information and puts it in the cache — for the moment. It writes it to the disk drive some time later on.

This method provides the fastest performance of any of the caching disk controllers. It speeds up even the first write, whereas any other caching controller doesn't improve performance until the CPU asks it to reread or rewrite something it recently read or wrote (and remembered).

These controllers are fast! But make no mistake, they have a dark side: possible data loss if power fails before the deferred-write cache has written the data from RAM to disk or if your computer "hangs" from some problem with the other programs it is running. If the data you meant to store to the disk was a part of your accounts receivable, you could be in big trouble.

You can force the controller to *flush its buffers* (write the information in the cache to the drive) in various ways. In some cases, the buffer flushing will occur automatically whenever you leave an application and go back to DOS. In others, you may have to press some special hot-key combination to force the flush. Otherwise, the controller may wait until the buffer is full or perhaps until the disk drive is free for some preset time period before it writes the cached information to the drive. Whatever the case, just remember that until the controller flushes its cache buffers, you remain vulnerable to data loss.

SMARTDrive is a disk-cache program that Microsoft includes for free with all recent versions of MS-DOS and Windows. Prior to Version 4 (which shipped first with Windows Version 3.1), SMARTDrive was not a very good disk-cache program. With Version 4.0, SMARTDrive made a giant leap forward.

The major disadvantage to SMARTDrive Version 4.0 is that it either does read- and write-deferred caching of a drive or no caching at all. You have no way to control it more subtly than that. And for many users, neither of those two choices is very good.

With Version 4.1, shipping with DOS 6, SMARTDrive finally is as good as its competitors. It has almost all the flexibility and performance of the best disk caches on the market.

If you choose to use a deferred-write cache, a very smart thing to do is to get and use an uninterruptible power supply (UPS). Then you will at least keep from losing any data that was in the cache (but didn't get written to the disk) because of an inopportune power failure.

If yours is a software deferred-write cache, you have another possible problem to worry about: having your computer get stuck (hang). A software deferred-write cache is not a very good idea if your computer is prone to hanging often, whether because it has some flaky hardware components or because you run a weird and possibly incompatible set of programs.

Elevator cache

An *elevator cache* is an especially elegant version of the deferred-write cache. This variation not only speeds things up as much as possible, it even makes the actual disk drive work less hard.

The elevator-caching controller will organize in cylinder order all the accumulated data in the cache that it has not yet written to disk. Then when it goes to write the information to disk, it will have to move the head assembly from outside to inside only once, writing all the sectors of data in the order they go on the disk drive, instead of in the order that they were delivered to the controller by the CPU. This method is the fastest, but remember the vulnerability of your data.

The Right Options for Your Cache Program

Setting up a disk-caching program can be a daunting task. There are so many options (at least with the better programs). How do you know what will work best for you?

The fact is, you won't know unless you do a lot of experimentation. You can let the program use its default settings, and very likely you will get a lot of benefits from it. But if you really want to tune your system and make it perform at its very best, you have no choice but to do many experiments until you discover the way that works best.

Remember to do those experiments while using the sorts of software you normally use. Sometimes a cache manufacturer will supply a *benchmark* program to help you evaluate their product. Other benchmark programs are supplied with various utility packages. Be very dubious about accepting the recommendations of any benchmark programs for how you should set up your cache. They only show you how well your current cache settings help speed up the benchmark programs and not necessarily how much it will speed up your ordinary work.

A Different Dimension of Difference

The essence of any cache is having a pool of reusable memory where information can be kept temporarily. Up to this point, the discussion about the differences between different cache strategies has been about when items get stored in the cache and when they get copied out of the cache into permanent storage on the disk.

There is another important dimension of difference in cache design. This difference has to do with how the cache controller decides which portions of its memory cache to use for storing any given item to be cached.

Fully associative cache

The best caches are *fully associative*. This term means that any item to be stored can be stored anywhere in the cache, along with a record of the full address on the disk where that information originated or is finally destined to go.

These cache designs are best, but they also are the most expensive to build. The cache controller must look in every location each time it is about to read or write anything, just in case that item already is in the cache. And deciding just which item it would be best to discard when the cache is full also takes quite a bit of work. For these reasons, fully associative caches are generally implemented in hardware, allowing all locations to be queried simultaneously by parallel hardware. This technique is, so far, too expensive to use in PCs.

Direct-mapped cache

The opposite extreme in cache designs is *direct mapped*. A direct-mapped cache assigns every disk location to a unique location in the cache. Of course, because the memory cache is much smaller than the disk drive, many disk locations are assigned to each cache location. (Mathematicians call this a many-to-one mapping.)

Here is the usual way that disk locations are mapped to cache locations in a direct-mapped cache: Successive locations on the disk are assigned to successive locations in the cache, until you run out of cache locations. The next location is assigned to the first cache location and the process is repeated until all the disk locations have been assigned to cache locations. This strategy spaces the disk locations assigned to each cache location as far apart as possible, which is the optimum mapping to use in most cases.

Each time a sectorful of information is to be read or written, this type of cache controller has only one place to look for whether it has that item cached. And if not, it knows immediately which item in its cache will be replaced by the newly read or written item. The direct-mapped cache is the simplest kind of cache to build, but it also is least effective.

Set-associative cache

A *set-associative cache* (two-way set associative and four-way set associative are names you may hear used) is, in effect, a large number of very small fully associative caches. The disk space is divided into an equally large number of sets of locations, with each disk location assigned to one of these small minicaches. A four-way set-associative cache, for example, stores four data items (and a record of where they belong on the disk) in each of its tiny, fully associative caches.

The mapping of disk locations to caches is done in a way very similar to that used in direct mapping. Again, the different locations on the disk that are mapped to the same minicache will be as widely spaced as possible.

When a four-way set-associative cache needs to read or write a sector, it has only four places to check for whether it already has that item in the cache. And when those four locations are already filled with other data, it only has to decide which one of the four to discard. This design is much simpler than a fully associative cache but somewhat more complex than the direct-mapped cache. Its cost to build is, of course, also in between that of the other two designs.

A one-way set associative cache is just another name for a direct-mapped cache. An *n*-way associative cache, in which *n* is the same as the number of items that can be stored in the total cache, would be another way to describe a fully associative cache.

How do you know what you have?

How do you find out what kind of disk cache you have? You probably can't. All the cache manufacturers use whatever strategy they think is best, and generally they won't tell you what that strategy is in any detail. (One exception is when there are user-settable parameters to enable or disable various options. Manufacturers *will* tell you those parameters so that you can know what they do.)

Each of the cache manufacturers will give you data to prove that their strategic choices are the best ones. They probably are — for the test situations they have analyzed. The diversity that abounds in the marketplace suggests that the "best" solution for your computer depends on your particular system and the particular ways you use it.

Buffering Controllers Versus Caching Controllers

Some manufacturers of disk controllers may tout that one of their products has a cache, when all it has is a more-or-less-large buffer: a mass of RAM that the controller can fill at one end and empty at the other. Such a buffer also may be accessible in the middle, but it is all one block of data. If the buffer doesn't hold what you ask for, the controller will fill the whole block with new data.

Functioning like a super track buffer, this kind of buffer may be much larger than a track buffer, yet not offer much, if any, improvement in speed. Its main drawback is that it lacks the flexibility to cope well with the tendency of DOS to dart around the disk drive.

Caching Software Versus a Hardware Cache

Hardware-based caching disk controllers may soup up performance, but they will lighten your wallet, too. A software disk cache offers a much cheaper solution that often works just as well. Such a program takes advantage of some otherwise unused RAM in your PC, in much the same way that the caching controllers use their RAM.

Chapter 5: Disk Caching

TIP

A disk-cache program might store the information in extended memory (on an AT or higher model PC) or in expanded memory. It would be a very bad idea to ask the disk-cache program to store the information in the system RAM (the bottom 640KB of RAM in a DOS machine); you should reserve that memory for other purposes.

With a software cache program, such as Super PC-Kwik from the PC-Kwik Corporation (15100 SW Koll Parkway, Beaverton, OR 97006; 800-274-5945; 503-644-5644) — to name just one good one — you get most of the benefits of all but the deferred-write hardware disk caches. The latest version of SMARTDrive, from Microsoft, even offers deferred-write disk caching. These programs cost only a fraction of what a hardware disk cache costs, even when you include the cost of the extra RAM you may have to add to your computer.

TECHNICAL SECRET

You may have wondered how it could possibly be true that a software cache could be as effective as a hardware cache. After all, the hardware-based caching disk controllers have a separate processor on them devoted to managing the cache, whereas the software cache programs must use the PC's main CPU for that job.

The reason that the software cache programs can compete effectively with the hardware caches is that the speed of the input/output bus limits both of them. Unless you have a PC with a fast, 32-bit (or wider) input/output bus, you may as well stick to a software disk-caching program. (The fast, 32-bit bus refers to an MCA [Micro Channel Architecture] or EISA [Extended Industry Standard Architecture] computer or to a computer with a special "local bus" or proprietary slot and a matching disk controller.)

Extend or expand? A memory quandary

Many people are confused about the distinction between expanded and extended memory in PCs. Briefly, *expanded memory* was an early strategy devised when all PCs were built with 8088 or 8086 CPU chips. Its purpose is to help circumvent the infamous DOS 640KB barrier. It uses a paging scheme to make up to 16MB of memory appear (only a little bit at a time) within the CPU's 1MB memory address space.

Extended memory, on the other hand, is only a possibility with 80286, 386, or 486 based PCs. It is memory that has real, physical addresses beyond the 1MB maximum available in the earlier PCs. The problem with this memory for PCs running DOS is that DOS was not designed with expanded memory in mind. So only by using some extraordinary means can DOS or DOS programs use extended memory. (For a long explanation, refer to *Memory Management for All of Us,* by John M. Goodman, Ph.D., published by Sams, 1992.)

Well, if you want the absolute maximum possible performance, you might buy both! (But the performance gain you will achieve will be only a few percentage points better than either of them by itself.)

There is one important way in which a hardware-caching disk controller is better than a software-caching program. If you have information waiting in the cache that has not yet made it to the disk, and if your PC hangs (becomes totally confused about what to do next), the software-caching program will be unable to finish writing your data to the disk; the hardware-caching disk controller will do so.

DOS Disk Buffers

Now turn your attention back to the buffers that all PCs have: the DOS disk buffers. If you do not have a line in your CONFIG.SYS file that says BUFFERS = nn, where *nn* is some number, DOS will assign a default number of disk buffers.

With early versions of DOS, that default number was only 2 for PCs and XTs and just 3 for ATs, 386, and 486 computers. Although reasonable back when a minimum PC might have only 16KB of RAM total, or at most 64KB of RAM, these levels are now definitely *un*reasonable.

Such a small number of DOS disk buffers makes sense only if you also have a large, fast buffer or cache on the disk controller or a disk-caching program running in your PC's RAM. In those cases, follow the cache manufacturer's suggestion. Otherwise, you will have to assign your own value to the BUFFERS statement.

Later versions of DOS have more generous default values, at least if you have more than a minimal amount of RAM in your PC. The default values for MS-DOS 5.0 and the number of buffers that Microsoft recommends are shown in Tables 5-1 and 5-2. Notice that the default depends only on how much RAM you have. The recommended values depend on the size of your hard disk.

MS-DOS 5.0 default number of DOS disk buffers

PC Configuration	Buffers	Bytes of RAM used
Less than 128KB of RAM with only a 360KB diskette drive	2	–
Less than 128KB of RAM with a greater than 360KB disk drive	3	–
Between 128KB and 255KB of RAM	5	2672
Between 256KB and 511KB of RAM	10	5328
Between 512KB and 640KB of RAM	15	7984

Table 5-1: Default numbers of buffers

Microsoft recommended values to use in the BUFFERS = n, m statement in CONFIG.SYS file

Size of hard disk	Number of DOS disk buffers (n)	Number of secondary cache buffers (m)
Less than 40MB	20	8
40MB through 79MB	30	8
80MB through 119MB	40	8
More than 120MB	50	8

Table 5-2: Recommended values for buffers

The "Correct" Value for Your CONFIG.SYS BUFFERS = Statement

At last you are ready to decide what the correct number is to put in the BUFFERS = statement in your CONFIG.SYS file. There is no one right answer for all PCs, but in all cases the considerations are the same.

You want to have enough disk buffers to let your PC work efficiently. On the other hand, you don't want to use up any more of your precious first 640KB of RAM than you must for this purpose.

You also have to take into account any special demands that your application programs may make on the number of DOS disk buffers. And, above all, you need to be sensible about your choice. Those are the general issues. Now look at each issue in detail.

DOS can't function without at least one disk buffer. And if it has only one, that one will be reused constantly — not the most efficient way to do things.

The legal values for the numbers you may use in the BUFFERS statement in your CONFIG.SYS file are from 1 to 99 for the total number of buffers and from 1 to 8 for the secondary cache. Almost always, the legal maximum of 99 DOS disk buffers is a mistake. The main reason is that choosing that value would force you to use up about 50KB of lower memory (the first 640KB) for this purpose.

If you are also using any other disk-caching strategy (a software disk-cache program and/or a hardware-caching disk controller), you can just as well specify a very small number of DOS disk buffers. A good choice in this case might be **BUFFERS = 3**. And in this case, you also want to have the minimum possible number of buffers in the DOS secondary cache. Because the default for that value is always 1, you needn't specify anything; you'll get that right value automatically.

If, for some reason, you aren't using a disk-cache program or caching disk controller, you surely will want to increase the numbers of total DOS disk buffers and secondary cache buffers. See Table 5-2 for Microsoft's recommendations.

Some programs demand that you have some minimum number specified in your BUFFERS = line, but most programs (correctly) don't care. They assume that you have done something intelligent in setting up your DOS disk buffers and any other disk-caching you may have. Only if you use one of the too-fussy programs do you need to accommodate its demands.

There are some special considerations if you are using DOS 5 or a later version. If you use MS-DOS or PC DOS and you have specified **DOS = HIGH** and loaded the HIMEM.SYS device driver, your DOS disk buffers will be put into the high memory area (HMA) that lies just above 1MB in memory address space. That is, your DOS disk buffers will be put there *if they fit*.

Any number of buffers up to about 35 or 40 will fit. Watch out, though: if you specify even one too many buffers, *all* of them will land back in lower memory. If you are using DR DOS 6, you can load some or all of your DOS disk buffers into either the HMA or any available upper memory blocks.

As is the case for the parameter settings for a third-party cache program, the only way to decide the for-sure best number of DOS disk buffers in a particular situation is by conducting a careful (and time-consuming) test. If you don't choose to do that, you may as well accept Microsoft's recommendations (or Digital Research's recommendations if you use DR DOS) or the recommendations made by the vendor of your third-party disk cache program.

Summary

- A cache is a reusable block of memory where some information is put temporarily. Its purpose is to speed up the transfer of information between devices whose inherent speeds are very different.
- A disk cache is a wonderful addition to any PC. Anyone can have a disk cache; you only have to add a suitable line to your CONFIG.SYS or AUTOEXEC.BAT file to load a disk-caching software program.
- Hardware-caching disk controllers are also available and in some cases are an even better choice (although not often).
- Caches come in many types. One kind of difference is how they choose which information to store and whether they pass all new information they store to the final destination immediately or do so later on.
- The most common disk cache is a read and write-through cache. Super PC-Kwik is one very popular example of this group.
- The next most common disk cache is a read and deferred-write cache. Microsoft's SMARTDrive is an example of this group.
- Another way that caches differ is in the strategy they use to choose where in their memory cache to keep each new data item. The three names associated with this difference are fully associative, set associative, and direct mapped.
- The BUFFERS = statement in your CONFIG.SYS file controls how many disk buffers and secondary cache buffers DOS creates. Probably the best advice is to set those numbers very low (for example, to 3 and 1 respectively) and then use a good disk-caching program. If you cannot do this, choose values in accordance with the Microsoft recommendations or — if you have the time — run some tests and see what the optimum values are for your PC when running your programs.

Now you know all you need to know about the structure and function of hard disks. With this background, you are ready to learn how these disk design details interact with the design of MS-DOS.

Chapter 6
Hard Disks Under DOS

In This Chapter

▶ What DOS is and why you need it (or some equivalent)

▶ How DOS treats disk drives and how that treatment differs from how DOS treats devices such as keyboards or printers

▶ The many layers of programs that exist in your PC and how those programs work for you and your applications

▶ How the PC's interrupt mechanism works and how that helps the layers of programs in your PC do their jobs

▶ How a TSR program or a device driver can modify the way your PC works and why you often want or need to use them

▶ The way DOS is able to support such a fantastic variety of hard disks, including many that weren't conceived of when DOS was first designed

▶ The very clever (and sometimes almost too clever) ways that disk designers have extended the concept of sector translation in IDE and SCSI drives

An Introduction to DOS

What is DOS? Why do I need it? What, exactly, does it do for me? How does it do that? These are all important questions to which you need good answers. This book is not primarily about DOS, but in this chapter, I give you some useful, if brief, answers to each of these questions.

You bought your computer to perform some task, or perhaps many tasks. You bought programs, called applications, that help you do those jobs. (Examples of applications are programs such as WordPerfect, Excel, or Lotus 1-2-3.) So why do you also need DOS?

The writers of your application programs don't know, nor want to know, exactly what hardware you have. Instead, they want to write programs for a hypothetical "standard PC." Furthermore, they don't want to have to know anything about what other programs you also may want to run in your computer along with their applications.

DOS stands for *disk operating system*. It is the name of a program, or actually a collection of programs. The job of these programs, collectively, is to manage your PC's resources to your benefit and to the benefit of all the different application programs you may choose to run. That capability lets the designers of those application programs concentrate on making them work well, without much worrying about how to activate the PC hardware or about what other programs may be running on the same PC at the same time.

To a very large extent, dividing the programming work for a computer into work involved in creating an operating system and work involved in creating applications works out very well. It is still true that the application program writer must know something about the range of hardware possibilities and, in some cases, must even write specific drivers for certain classes of hardware — most notably video displays and printers.

The greatest separation between the operating system software writers' job and that of the application programmers' occurs in some alternative operating systems and in certain extensions to DOS. Windows, GeoWorks, OS/2, and Windows NT are all examples of programming environments (hardware and software context in which a program is to be run) which exhibit a great deal of device independence. This means that programs written to work in one of these environments need not be written with very much particular knowledge of the devices that will be attached to the PC on which those programs ultimately will run. The applications can ask the environment for information, such as what resolution the video screen or printer supports, and then tailor their output to match those values.

Commonly, people speak of DOS as if it were a single entity. In fact, DOS consists of several layers, each with different responsibilities. One useful division breaks the overall operating system into two parts, the BIOS and, confusingly enough, DOS. (Yes, DOS is the name of one part of a larger whole whose overall name is also DOS. There's not much I can do to clarify that for you; it's simply a confusing fact. At least I will try to distinguish clearly which of the two meanings I have in mind in what follows.)

The first set of programs, called the *Basic Input Output System* or *BIOS,* embodies the designers' knowledge of exactly how the hardware pieces of your PC work and what commands are needed to activate those parts. The other portion (DOS) embodies a strategy for managing resources, disk drives in particular.

Any PC has much in common with all other PCs, so the standard pieces of hardware can be activated by a very standard set of BIOS routines. Many PCs also have some relatively unusual hardware pieces. Specialized additions to the BIOS are needed to activate those pieces.

All PCs use a standard strategy for managing files. That is what the higher level part of DOS (the one called DOS) is all about. DOS doesn't have to change when the hardware changes, although it may need to be augmented if you add a network connection or a CD-ROM drive, or certain other kinds of new hardware.

The details of how DOS and the BIOS view the hardware, and thus how they are able to do their jobs, will become clearer as you read the rest of this chapter and Chapters 7 through 10. The bottom line for why you need DOS is that your application programs need it. And for that you can be very grateful. The industry is able to produce far more and far better software by separating the jobs of writing applications and writing operating software, with different teams of specialists working on each part.

The Relationship Between Hard Disks and DOS

Why, you may be wondering, all this emphasis on DOS in a book about hard disks? The answer is that exactly how your hard disk appears to work depends a lot on the programs used to access it. And those programs are, in a PC, a big part of what we call DOS. At least that is true in most PCs, the exceptions being those PCs that run only OS/2, UNIX, or some alternative.

All IBM PC or compatible computers (which is what *PC* means in this book) can run MS-DOS (the Microsoft Disk Operating System). DOS comes in many forms. In addition to the original PC DOS from IBM (which is essentially just MS-DOS renamed), and the plain-vanilla MS-DOS you can buy directly from Microsoft, there are a host of brand-specific versions of MS-DOS (such as COMPAQ DOS), which have been modified to work with hardware that in some way differs from the IBM design. Digital Research (a division of Novell) has a product called DR DOS, which is functionally almost the same as MS-DOS. Lumping together all these varieties of DOS, it is fair to say that most PCs run DOS every day.

To run DOS, a computer must be designed around an Intel 80x86 microprocessor chip (also called the *central processing unit,* or CPU), and it must follow the Microsoft additions to the Intel design. Further, to be an IBM PC compatible, a computer must follow some design aspects of the IBM PC and PS/1 or PS/2 families. The label *PC,* then, implies more than merely that a computer uses an 80x86 microprocessor. **Note:** The notation 80x86 is how Intel refers to its 8088, 8086, 80186, 80286, 386, and 486 microprocessor chips and other members of that family. (It is possible to emulate a PC in another computer and therefore to run DOS programs. The Amiga can have a PC Bridge Board added to it and a Macintosh or NeXT computer can run a SoftPC emulator program.)

Some people use a different operating system on their PCs. Scientific computing and design work is often done on PCs running UNIX. Larger business systems sometimes run OS/2. The most popular PC network, Novell NetWare, uses a custom operating system on its file servers (with DOS as the usual operating system for the workstations). Microsoft has recently announced a new operating system for use on PCs: Windows NT. (In Chapters 9 and 10, you can find some brief descriptions of how OS/2, Windows NT, UNIX, and NetWare differ from DOS in their use of hard disks.)

Because most of us use MS-DOS, this book focuses on how that affects hard disk operation. Also, SpinRite and the other reinterleaving programs discussed in Part II work only on PCs running DOS. (Sector interleave and reinterleaving are explained in Chapters 3 and 12.)

The general information about hard disks in the earlier chapters of this book applies to any hard disk in any computer. But from here on, the focus quite clearly will be on hard disks in PCs running DOS. (The troubleshooting information in Chapter 11 is mostly applicable to all hard disks, but the discussion of error messages applies only to DOS machines.)

That is enough on the generalities of why; now on to the details of what and how. Here is how DOS deals with hard disks in PCs.

DOS Devices: Block Versus Character

First, you need to understand that DOS is largely concerned with the flow of information from place to place in your PC. Sometimes information comes in from a keyboard. Other times the information comes in from a disk drive. Sometimes its destination is a video screen or a printer, and still other times it is on its way to a disk or tape drive.

DOS treats all these possible sources or destinations in a very similar manner. The class name for these places is a *device*. DOS classifies all devices into two subclasses: *character devices* and *block devices*. DOS then deals with any character device in one way and with any block device in a different way.

A *character device* is any device that can accept or deliver only one character of information at a time. The screen and the keyboard are both character devices. You press one key and the computer gets one keystroke. That same keystroke is then sent to the screen for display, which informs you that the computer noticed your action. A mouse, a modem, and a printer are also character devices.

Chapter 6: Hard Disks Under DOS

A *block device* only handles information in blocks of some fixed size that contain many characters. All disk drives are block devices, as are tape drives. Any block device must have a buffer in RAM where the computer can assemble information to be sent to it or into which the device can dump the current block of information it is delivering.

(An analogy that may be useful to you is to say that a disk drive is like a warehouse for data. The buffer is the loading dock, where a truckful of data can be assembled before it is loaded onto a truck and shipped out, and where data can be unloaded from incoming trucks before being put away inside the warehouse.)

You must have at least a couple of DOS disk buffers. DOS allows you to create as many or as few of these disk buffers as you want, from 2 to 99. The last couple of sections in Chapter 5 go into detail on what the default number of DOS disk buffers is in various situations and how to decide what value probably would be best for your system.

TECHNICAL SECRET

Under DOS, a disk buffer normally holds 512 bytes of data — just enough to fill one disk sector. Each buffer actually uses up a bit more memory than that — 528 bytes is the usual amount; DOS uses the extra 16 bytes to help manage the buffer.

Some manufacturers have created special programs to allow users of early versions of DOS (before Version 3.3) to access large hard disks (those with more than 32MB of total storage capacity). In some cases those special programs are customized versions of DOS. Others are some of the third-party disk partitioning programs. When one of these special programs is loaded into memory, it actually modifies how DOS views the hard disk in whatever ways it must to achieve its purpose. Sometimes this modification is done by enlarging the apparent size (the *logical size*) of the hard disk's sectors.

There are also some peripheral devices you can attach to your PC that look much like a disk drive but which use larger sectors. Some rewritable-optical disk drives use disks with either 512- or 1024-byte sectors. This is an actual, physical sector size increase — not merely a convenient fiction, as is the case with the programs mentioned in the preceding paragraph.

Whenever you have a block device that uses a physical or logical sector size greater than 512 bytes, the DOS disk buffers will be enlarged so that they each will still hold one (logical) sector's worth of data.

Part I: The Hard Disk Companion

When your program wants to read some information from the disk, even if it only wants to read a few bytes, it must ask DOS to get the entire sector containing those bytes into a disk buffer. Then your program can extract the information it wants from that buffer.

Similarly, if your program wants to write some information to the disk, it actually writes that information to a disk buffer. The content of that buffer will normally only be written to a sector on the disk when the buffer is full. If the program has more to write, it will repeat this process, filling the buffer and having it written to the disk, sector by sector, until it is finished.

When your program finishes writing the last of its information to the buffer, even if that doesn't exactly fill the buffer, the program somehow must force the buffer to be written to the disk anyway. The program accomplishes this task by telling DOS that the program is finished with the file (which is called, technically, "closing the file"). DOS then writes the final buffer load to the disk no matter what it contains.

Here is a light-hearted restatement of how DOS devices work: Character devices accept or deliver information "retail" and block devices only deal in information "wholesale" (see Figure 6-1).

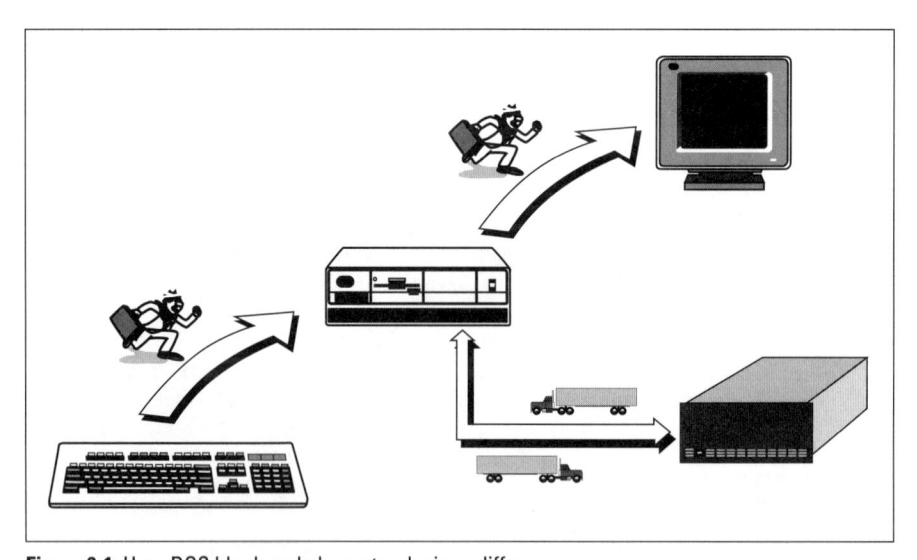

Figure 6-1: How DOS block and character devices differ.

A little-known and well-hidden security risk

Because each time a program writes information to the disk, the last buffer load of data is written to the disk in whatever state it happens to be; it very likely will contain something besides information generated by your program. The beginning of the buffer certainly holds the end of your program's output. The end of the buffer holds whatever it held the last time it was used, whether it was used for reading or for writing some other sector.

The result of this situation is that any file on the disk that does not exactly fill the last sector it has been allocated will probably have some unrelated information tacked onto its end. Furthermore, because DOS allocates space on the disk in units that are multiples of a sector, there may be additional sectors at the end of a file's allocated space that have never been written to by your program at all. What they may contain could be anybody's guess.

Ordinarily, this fact does not cause any problems because DOS records in the disk directory exactly how long each file is, right down to the byte. Most programs use that information to read only the information you intend them to read. But that only means that they know enough to ignore the remaining junk. DOS will deliver the entire last sector of the file's data, at least, and possibly the rest of the sectors in that allocation unit; it is up to the program that uses that information to ignore anything it deems to be irrelevant.

Various disk utility programs exist that let you look at what really is stored on the disk. They can show you whatever garbage may be stored after the end of each of your files. (A very good one is the Disk Editor program that became a part of the Norton Utilities collection starting with Version 5. The Norton Utilities are published by the Peter Norton division of the Symantec Corporation.) This capability could be important if the security of your information is a high priority to you. Someday you might give a file to someone else without knowing that some crucial, confidential information was tagged onto its end.

If this possibility concerns you, and especially if you find from some snooping that it is happening on your disk in ways you cannot stand, there is an easy (enough) way to deal with the problem. Run the WipeInfo program (also from the Norton Utilities) and ask it to "Wipe slack space at end of files" by using its /K command line option. You also might choose to use the /E option to wipe all the erased spaces on your disk. This option will permanently erase anything stored in those places. (Of course, it also will prevent you from undeleting any files you had erased before you ran WipeInfo.)

Certain databases have an additional vulnerability: irrelevant data can get inserted into the middle of the file in a way that makes it totally invisible as long as the file is only used with the application that created it but which can be seen by using a disk-snooping utility.

Another way you might get to see this sort of garbage is when a file is sent by modem from one computer to another. Often the information is sent in blocks, and the exact length of the file is not sent along, so the PC on the receiving end records the length rounded up to the end of the last block. The block sizes used vary from less than 100 bytes to several kilobytes. Some communications programs pad the end of the last block with some innocuous "fill character"; others just send whatever was in the disk buffer after the end of the file. In the latter case, the end of the file as it gets stored on the remote PC could easily include some quite visible and perhaps embarrassing information.

How DOS Makes Things Happen

As you learned earlier in this chapter, PCs have many layers of programs. You may only be aware of the very highest couple of layers, but those layers could not function without help from other programs operating at the lower levels.

In the next three sections you will learn more about these programs. In particular, you will be introduced to the lowest level programs, called the BIOS routines; to the very important interprogram communication strategy called interrupts; and to the ubiquitous programs called TSRs. Understanding these ways in which PCs function is essential if you want to understand how DOS deals with hard disks.

The layers of programs in a PC

Some of the programs used to activate your PC are built into the hardware. (The usual term for software that is built into hardware is *firmware*.) These programs are contained in various read-only memory (ROM) chips on the motherboard and possibly on some plug-in option cards.

Other programs come into RAM from one or more disk drives. When you *boot* your computer from a disk, you are loading several layers of programs into your PC's RAM.

Figure 6-2 shows some of these layers in a fairly simple case. This figure is shown to scale and shows the actual memory allocations in one particular, real PC running MS-DOS Version 5.0. Notice that the bottom 64KB section has been expanded to an eight-times larger scale so that you can see the individual layers near the bottom of the CPU's memory address space.

This figure shows only the first megabyte of the CPU's memory address space. That is all the memory space there is in an original PC or an XT. In an AT or later design in the PC family, there can be more, *extended* memory, but DOS cannot normally access it. The first 640KB of the first megabyte is called *lower memory* or *system RAM*. The region from 640KB to 1MB is called *upper memory*. (Programs that have been DOS-extended, such as Windows 3.*x*, Lotus 1-2-3 Release 3.*x*, and AutoCad Release 10 or later, are able to use extended memory, as are the VDISK and RAMDRIVE device drivers included with PC DOS and MS-DOS respectively. Beginning with Version 5, DOS includes EMM386, which can be used to convert extended memory into simulated expanded memory or into upper memory.)

The PC represented in Figure 6-2 could be any PC. The checkerboard pattern in the upper end of memory address space represents the built-in programs in the motherboard BIOS ROM. The shaded checkerboard in the region from address C0000h to E0000h indicates that this region could have some additional BIOS ROMs in it. These would be BIOS additions in ROMs on option cards.

Chapter 6: Hard Disks Under DOS

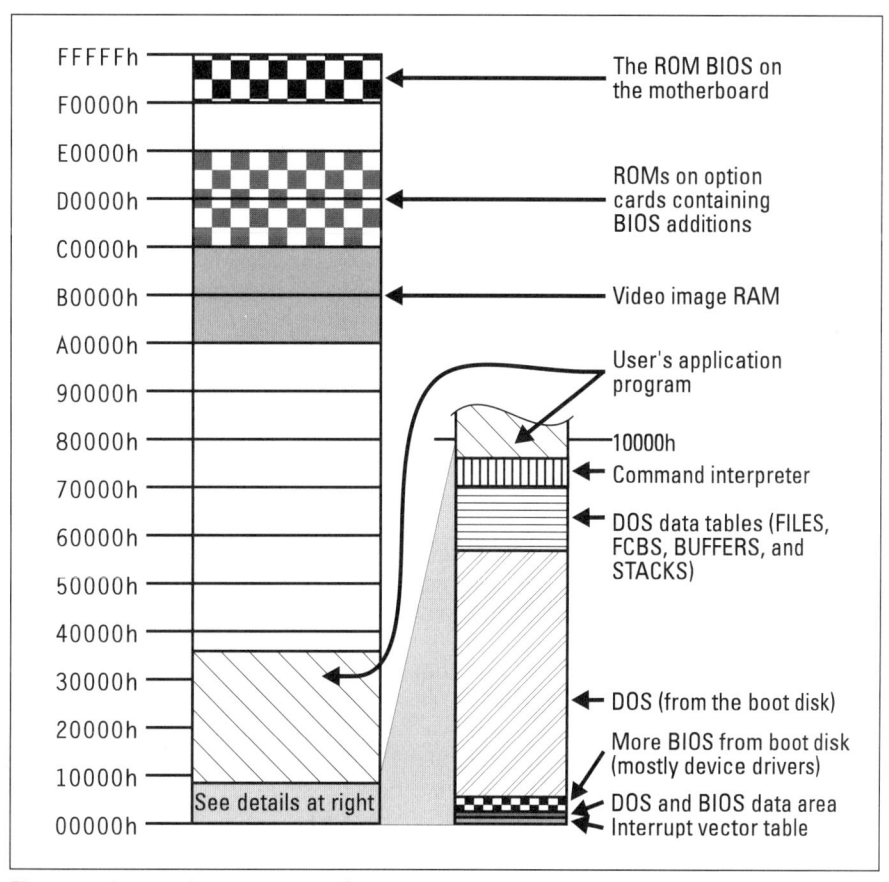

Figure 6-2: Layers of programs in a PC — what goes where in a typical computer running MS-DOS Version 5.0.

The gray shaded area from A0000h to C0000h indicates that this region is used by various kinds of video cards for RAM in which image information may be stored. Not all of that region is in use at any one time (usually), but all of it may be used by a video card potentially.

The regions in lower memory (below address 40000h) that are shaded in various ways are the layers that are loaded when you boot DOS and run your first application program. The size of the region occupied by that application program, of course, will vary, depending on what program it is. The empty space above the application program and below the video RAM area is just that: empty, or free RAM. (The very top of that range is used by the transient part of COMMAND.COM, but it can also be taken over by any application program that wishes to use that space. If it is overwritten, its contents will be refreshed by the permanent part of COMMAND.COM the next time you get back to the DOS prompt.)

To keep this example as simple as possible, the boot disk had no CONFIG.SYS or AUTOEXEC.BAT file. This is, therefore, the simplest possible picture you will see on a PC running DOS.

This figure is also the basis for the discussion later in this chapter of how *interrupts* work (see the section "Interrupts"). The complexity of adding just one *terminate-and-stay-resident* (TSR) program is also covered later in this chapter.

In that discussion, you will learn about the bottom layer, marked the "Interrupt vector table." The DOS and BIOS data area is simply a scratch pad area in which the BIOS and DOS can record information about the PC's configuration and operating modes. The checkerboard region marked "More BIOS from boot disk" contains additional BIOS routines loaded from one of the hidden system files on any bootable DOS diskette. The region marked "DOS" comes from the other hidden system file on the bootable diskette. The command interpreter is normally the program COMMAND.COM, which is the only piece of DOS that many people know about because it is a visible file on all bootable DOS disks.

(One comment about this figure: No special memory-management software is loaded — including that provided with DOS; if any such tools were used, DOS would take up less lower memory than is shown here.)

You will have to refer to a book devoted to DOS or to memory usage and management in PCs for more details on how the various layers of software are constructed in lower memory. For the purposes of this book, just knowing these layers are there is enough. Well, almost enough. What is really important for the purposes of this book is how those layers are used when you or your programs access information on the disk. (You can learn more about how these layers are formed and what they contain in *Memory Management for All of Us,* by John M. Goodman, Ph.D., Sams, 1992.)

When you load a document into your word processor, for example, you just press some keys and specify the filename. Neither you nor your word processor needs to know exactly how the document is loaded; the program just asks another, lower level program to do the actual work of loading the document.

Your word processor turns your request over to DOS (this time, DOS refers to just the higher level portion of the larger entity called DOS that also includes the BIOS). DOS understands requests in terms of filenames. It translates your request into a series of more detailed requests to the BIOS (the basic input output system), which is a collection of those lower level programs. DOS must phrase each of those requests to the BIOS in terms of the actual disk location where the file's data is stored (the particular cylinder, head, and physical sector values).

Before making those requests, DOS first must find out where on the disk the file is stored. To do this, it must ask the BIOS to get copies of the disk's FAT (file allocation table) and one or more of the disk's directories. By inspecting these tables, DOS can pinpoint your file on the disk.

The BIOS translates these low-level requests further into a series of yet lower level and more-detailed requests to the hard disk controller. To read any one sector, for example, the BIOS tells the controller to position the read/write head assembly to the correct cylinder, to turn on the correct head, and finally to notice when the desired sector comes into view and read it. Figures 6-3 through 6-6 show just a few of the very many steps in this process. (Figures 6-3 and 6-4 are the left and right halves of the top of a larger, four-panel figure. Figures 6-5 and 6-6 are the left and right halves of the bottom of that same overall figure.)

These layers allow a person or team of people writing a particular layer to focus on just that specialized level of the PC's inner workings, which is a big advantage both for them and for us. If you later want to modify how the PC does things at one level, you need only replace the program that works at that level by switching word processor applications, for one example, or by changing printer drivers for an example of a change at a different level.

Interrupts

The multilayer programming strategy covered in the preceding section could not work without a standardized method of passing messages between the different layers. PCs communicate in this way by using *interrupts*.

Interrupts are events that cause whatever program is running to be suspended while some other program takes over to handle that event. When the event-handling program ends, it returns control of the PC to the first program, which then resumes operation.

Hardware events cause some interrupts. The hard disk controller, for example, may need to signal the PC's BIOS program that the controller has finished reading a sector and has the data ready for use. Or the disk controller might, in other circumstances, have to tell the BIOS program that the requested sector could not be read.

Software causes other interrupts. DOS, for example, will cause an interrupt each time it wants the BIOS to do something for it. Many application programs cause a software interrupt any time the program wants DOS to do something for it.

The Intel microprocessors in PCs were designed to make the interruption procedure work easily and well. When a hardware or software interrupt occurs, the microprocessor finds a subprogram created for handling that event and lets it do its thing. This method may seem roundabout, but it has proven to be extraordinarily flexible and powerful.

Part I: The Hard Disk Companion

Word Processor (or any other application program)

Open file named
C:\MINE\MYFILE.DOC

→ Open file named C:\MINE\MYFILE.DOC

High level part of DOS

Request root directory
(32 separate requests for one sector each time)

→ Request logical sector #127 (and later on sectors up to logical # 158)

← Here are the data you requested

Examine root directory for subdirectory named MINE

Found at cluster number 65. Convert to logical sector number and request it.

→ Request logical sector 411 (and perhaps several more following it)

Examine MINE subdirectory for file named MYFILE.DOC

← Here are the data you requested

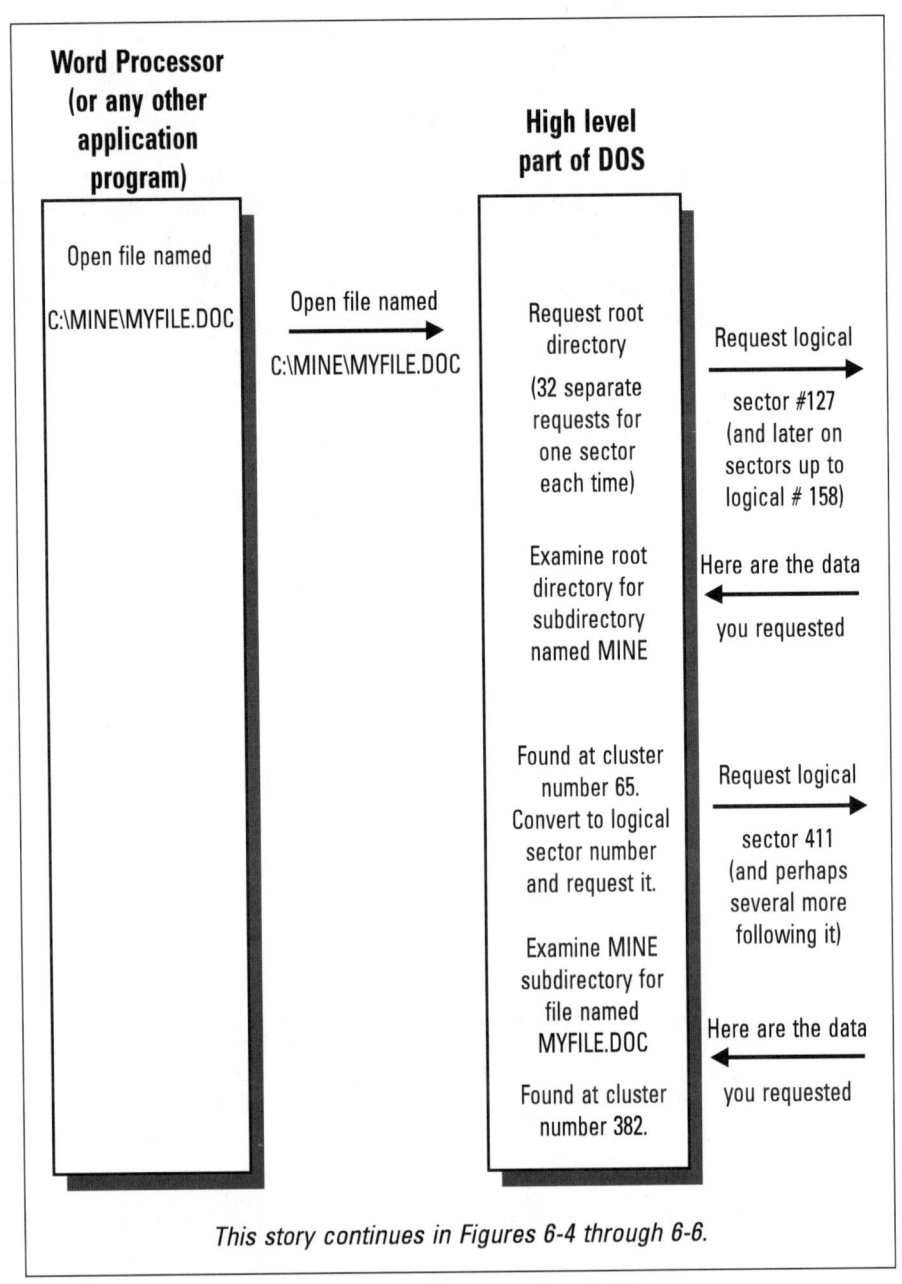

Found at cluster number 382.

This story continues in Figures 6-4 through 6-6.

Figure 6-3: Some of the steps in processing a file request (part 1 of 4).

Chapter 6: Hard Disks Under DOS

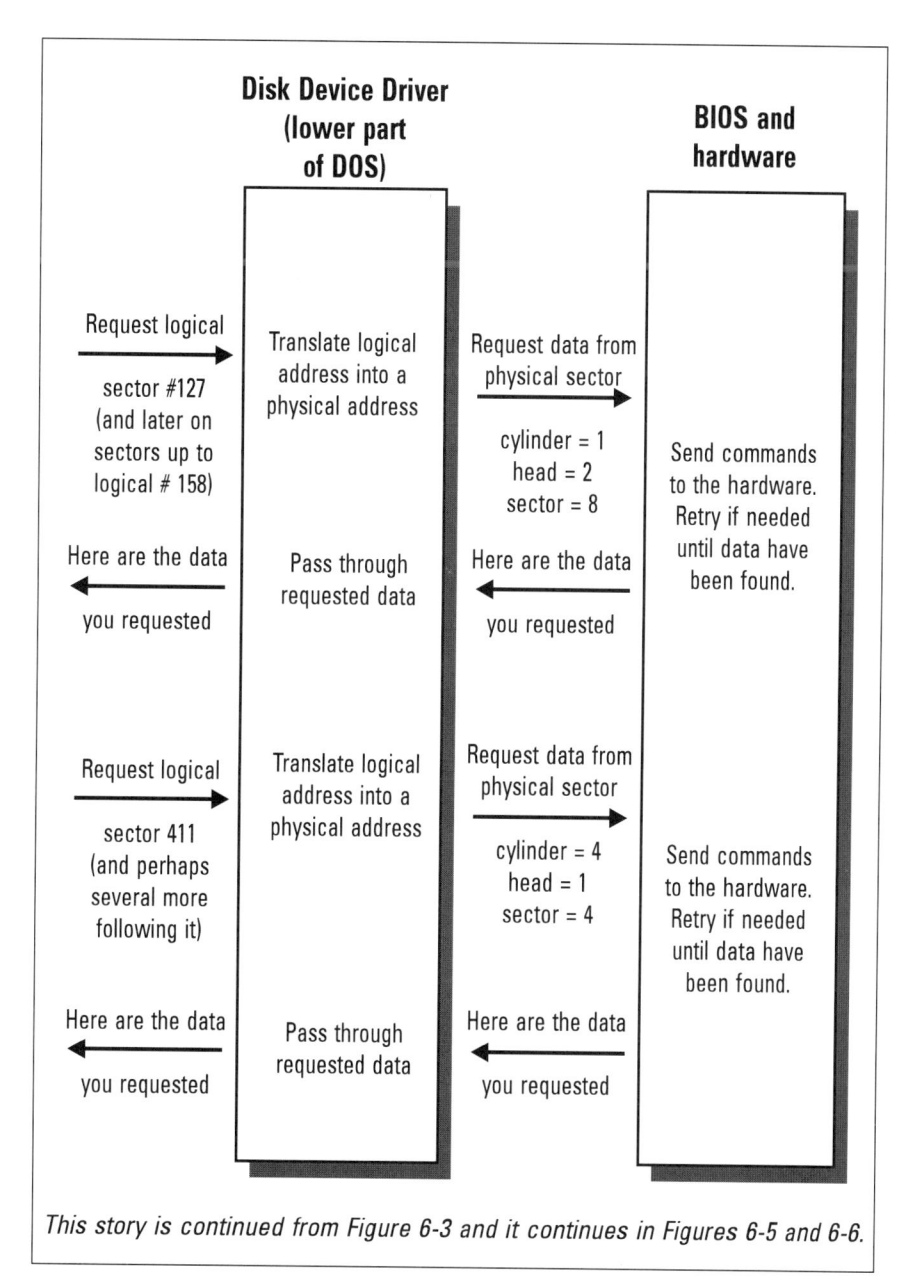

```
Disk Device Driver                          BIOS and
(lower part                                 hardware
of DOS)

Request logical    Translate logical    Request data from
─────────────▶    address into a       physical sector
sector #127        physical address     ─────────────▶
(and later on                           cylinder = 1        Send commands
sectors up to                           head = 2            to the hardware.
logical # 158)                          sector = 8          Retry if needed
                                                            until data have
Here are the data  Pass through         Here are the data   been found.
◀─────────────    requested data       ◀─────────────
you requested                           you requested


Request logical    Translate logical    Request data from
─────────────▶    address into a       physical sector
sector 411         physical address     ─────────────▶
(and perhaps                            cylinder = 4        Send commands
several more                            head = 1            to the hardware.
following it)                           sector = 4          Retry if needed
                                                            until data have
Here are the data  Pass through         Here are the data   been found.
◀─────────────    requested data       ◀─────────────
you requested                           you requested
```

This story is continued from Figure 6-3 and it continues in Figures 6-5 and 6-6.

Figure 6-4: Some of the steps in processing a file request (part 2 of 4).

Part I: The Hard Disk Companion

Word Processor (or any other application program)

Now file is open. Request data from it by offset into file in bytes.

Request 407 bytes starting at offset 5,025 bytes into MYFILE.DOC →

← Here are the data you requested

Eventually, this application must ask DOS to close the file.

High level part of DOS

File MYFILE.DOC found, starts at cluster 382. Convert cluster number to logical sector number and request that sector's data.

← I have found your file

Pass through requested data

From directory listing we know file is in more than one sector. Request part of FAT to find rest of clusters in file.

Examine chain of clusters in FAT. Request other clusters as needed to give program data it wants.

Request logical sectors 1679 (and following) →

← Here are the data you requested

Request logical sector 2 →

← Here are the data you requested

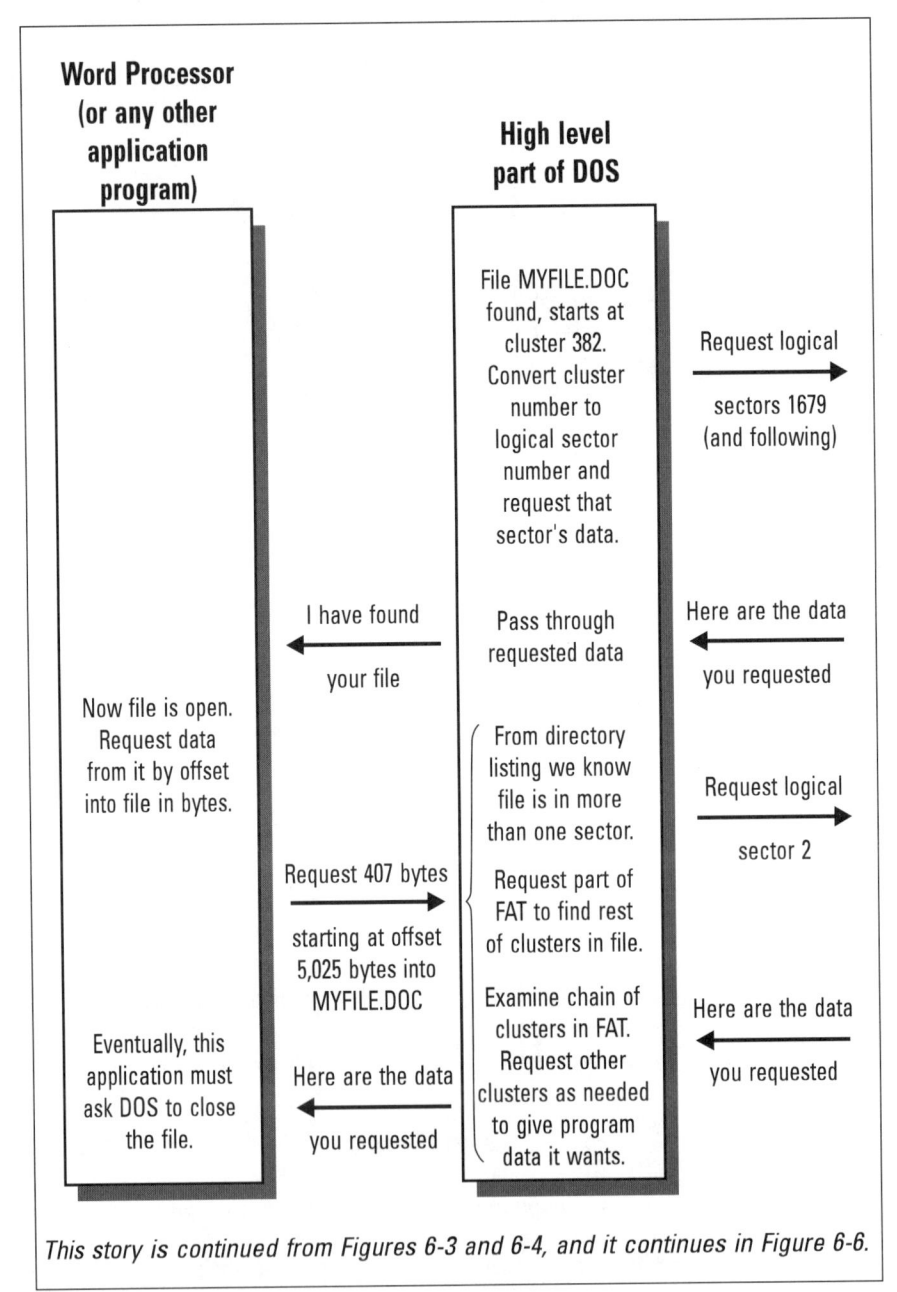

This story is continued from Figures 6-3 and 6-4, and it continues in Figure 6-6.

Figure 6-5: Some of the steps in processing a file request (part 3 of 4).

Chapter 6: Hard Disks Under DOS

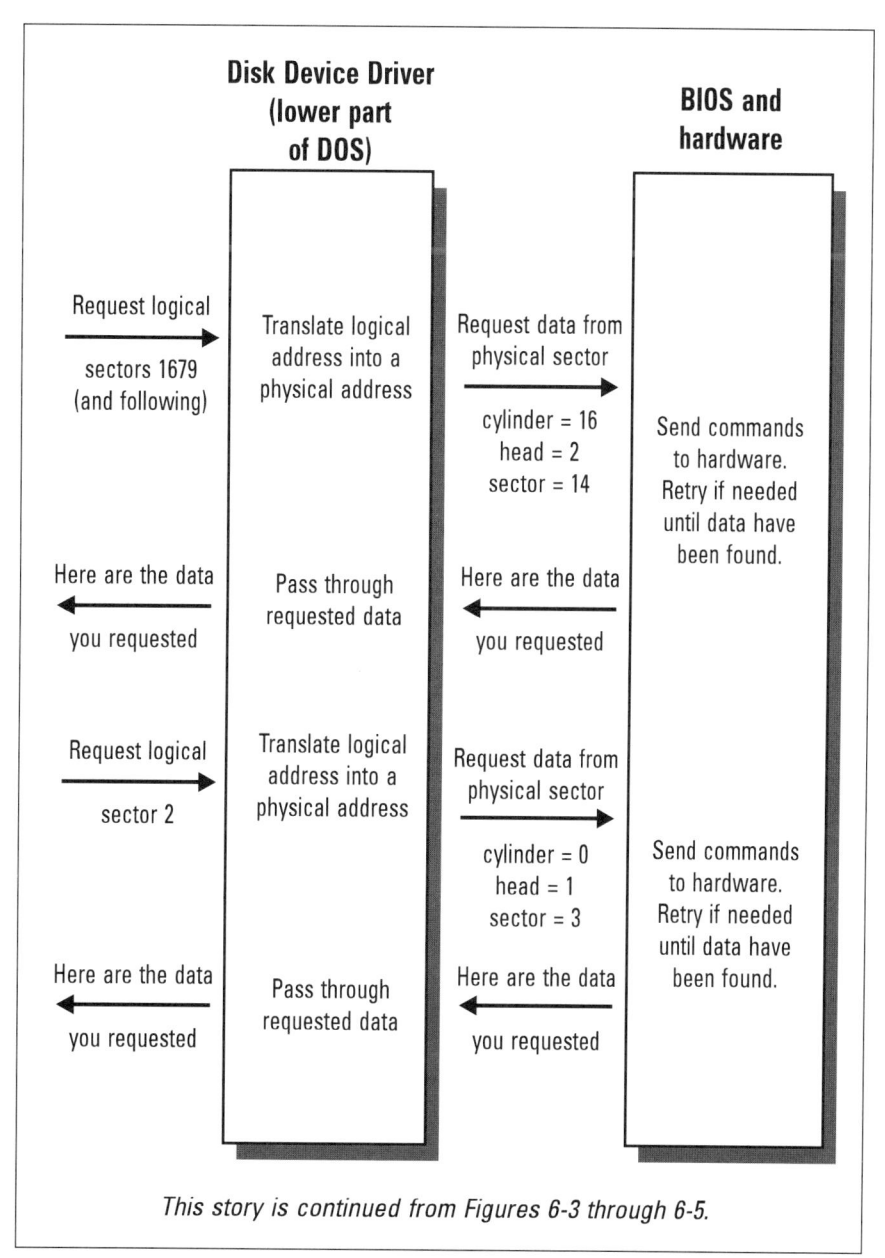

Disk Device Driver (lower part of DOS)	BIOS and hardware

Request logical sectors 1679 (and following) → Translate logical address into a physical address → Request data from physical sector

cylinder = 16
head = 2
sector = 14

Send commands to hardware. Retry if needed until data have been found.

← Here are the data you requested ← Pass through requested data ← Here are the data you requested

Request logical sector 2 → Translate logical address into a physical address → Request data from physical sector

cylinder = 0
head = 1
sector = 3

Send commands to hardware. Retry if needed until data have been found.

← Here are the data you requested ← Pass through requested data ← Here are the data you requested

This story is continued from Figures 6-3 through 6-5.

Figure 6-6: Some of the steps in processing a file request (part 4 of 4).

Part I: The Hard Disk Companion

TECHNICAL SECRET

The Intel 80x86 chips reserve the first 1,024 bytes of RAM for a table, called the *interrupt vector table*. This table holds 256 addresses, four bytes per address. The first two bytes store a segment value and the next two bytes store an offset into that segment. The addresses stored there are those of miniprograms, called *interrupt service routines* (ISRs), that will be called upon to handle events of types 0 to 255.

The primary purpose of DOS is to provide various services to programs. The programs request these services by calling one or another interrupt. From this point of view, DOS is simply one huge collection of ISRs.

When an event of a certain type occurs, the microprocessor interrupts whatever else it is doing and looks in the interrupt vector table for the address that goes with that particular type of interruption. The microprocessor then runs the program stored at that address, which it assumes is the proper way to deal with that event. After that program finishes its work, it tells the microprocessor to return to its original task.

Figure 6-7 shows this process schematically. It is based on the layered model shown in Figure 6-2, and uses the actual addresses and sizes for each layer that were measured in the PC described earlier.

When your computer first boots, the start-up program in the motherboard BIOS ROM fills in some entries in the interrupt vector table, causing them to point to interrupt service routines located elsewhere in the motherboard BIOS ROM. Later, DOS, as it loads itself from the disk, will fill in other entries (and change a few of the ones filled in by the BIOS start-up program). Other programs can alter the entries in the interrupt vector table at any time. Doing so is often part of a very powerful way of customizing your PC. (This customizing starts when you first load DOS and it processes your CONFIG.SYS [custom configuration] file. It continues every time you load a terminate-and-stay-resident program, and it can happen in the middle of an application program's execution.)

There are two main classes of programs that alter the contents of the interrupt vector table: TSR programs and device drivers.

Terminate-and-stay-resident (TSR) programs

A *terminate-and-stay-resident* (TSR) program is a program that you can run from the DOS prompt, cause to run by means of a line in your AUTOEXEC.BAT file (or any other batch file), or cause to run by means of an INSTALL line in your CONFIG.SYS file. (The latter option is only available if you run DOS Version 5 or later.)

Chapter 6: Hard Disks Under DOS

```
1000h ─┐
       │        ← 77.43K
0000h ─┘
CPU Memory
address space
```

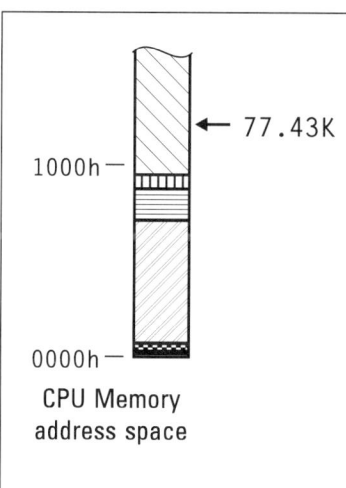

Assume that before an interrupt occurs the CPU is running the user's program. This means that the *code segment* (CS) and the *instruction pointer* (IP) combined give a *current program address* somewhere in the user's program region of the CPU's memory address space. (For the purposes of this example, assume CS:IP is pointing to 0F36:4257, which is a linear address of 135B7h [hexadecimal], or 77.43K [decimal] as shown by the arrow.)

When an interrupt occurs, the CPU first saves the current program address and contents of the FLAGS register on the stack. Then it jumps to whatever address is contained in the Interrupt Vector Table for that type (number) of interrupt. In this example, an interrupt of type 9 (caused by a character coming in from the keyboard) will cause a jump to CS:IP of 0D99:0045, which is a linear address of 0D9D5h or 54.46K (see the arrow in the next diagram).

A	F000:EF6F
9	0D99:0045
8	0D99:003C
7	F000:EF6F
6	F000:EF6F
5	F000:FF54
4	0070:06F4
3	0070:06F4
2	0D99:0016
1	0070:06F4
0	002A:91FB

Contents of the Interrupt Vector Table

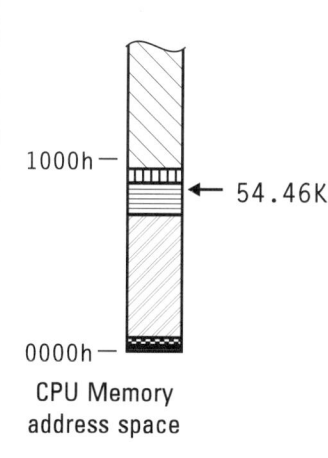

```
1000h ─┐
       │        ← 54.46K
0000h ─┘
CPU Memory
address space
```

Now the current program address points to an Interrupt Service Routine (ISR) that is, in this case, located just below the command interpreter. This ISR is one loaded by DOS to provide its standard console (keyboard and screen) handling services.

When that ISR program finishes its work it will execute an IRET (Interrupt Return) instruction. This causes the CPU to retrieve the saved "current program address" and FLAGS values. Using them causes the CPU to resume working on the user's program.

Figure 6-7: How interrupt vectors and interrupt service routines are used to handle events.

Part I: The Hard Disk Companion

These programs get the name terminate-and-stay-resident from the last thing they do when you load them. They tell DOS that they are through working, so some other program can have control of the PC, but that they are not through with their memory. Thus, they are terminating (ending their control of the PC) but staying resident (remaining in memory). The significance of this action will become clear to you in the following sections.

There are at least four things that any TSR program must do. First, it must copy at least one entry from the interrupt vector table to someplace within itself. Next, it must put the address of some miniprogram it contains into that place in the interrupt vector table (or into those places if it is "hooking" more than one interrupt). Just before it goes to sleep, the TSR must tell DOS which portions of the memory that it was using can be reused by other programs and which portion it needs to keep. The last step is for the TSR to tell DOS, in effect, "I am through for now, but leave me around — I have more work to do later on."

The interrupt vector table changes made by the TSR are the only means it has of getting control of the PC again. Without that step in its initialization, no TSR could ever do anything useful for you.

TECHNICAL SECRET

Before a TSR program is first run, the interrupt vector table will contain entries that point to various interrupt service routines (ISRs). When you first run a TSR program, it will examine certain entries in the interrupt vector table. It will then copy some of those numbers into a safe place inside itself. Next, the TSR puts some other addresses into those places in the interrupt vector table. These addresses are pointers to still other places within itself. At each of those places, the TSR has a miniprogram.

Finally, the TSR causes a special software interrupt that tells DOS that the TSR is finished running but asks DOS to please leave it in memory and protect it from being overwritten by any other program. As was pointed out earlier, this is where the name TSR comes from.

Now, if one of the events that this TSR has "hooked" occurs, the PC will stop whatever program it is running. The CPU (central processing unit, or microprocessor chip) will put a marker in memory that tells it where it was working. Then it calls on the program pointed to by the entry in the interrupt vector table corresponding to that kind of event, expecting that to be the appropriate program to handle this kind of event. If the TSR replaced the numbers originally in that location in the interrupt vector table, the CPU will not invoke the original ISR but will instead run the corresponding miniprogram inside the TSR.

Like any other ISR, that miniprogram can do whatever it is designed to do. When it is finished, the ISR may do something a bit different. A normal ISR will end by telling the microprocessor to go back to running whatever program it was in when the interrupting event occurred. A TSR could do this (if it had fully "handled" the event that caused the interrupt), or it may instead turn around and call the ISR whose interrupt vector table address it stored inside itself and replaced in the interrupt vector table with its own address.

At that point, the original ISR can do whatever it normally does. When it finishes, it will tell the TSR to go back to what it was doing, and then the TSR will tell the main program to resume.

That is what happens when one TSR hooks itself between the normal ISR and the main programs. It is even possible for several TSRs to hook themselves together in that way. Called "chaining off an interrupt," this has proven to be a very powerful way to make PCs do many useful things.

That may sound more complicated than it is. Figures 6-8 and 6-9 explain how a single TSR is hooked into one interrupt. Actual TSRs often hook many interrupts, and you may have several TSRs loaded in memory at once. That situation is much too complex to show easily in a diagram. Your PC manages amazingly well to keep track of what to do even in such complicated cases.

Device drivers

The other kind of program that routinely alters the contents of the interrupt vector table is a *device driver*. A device driver is a program that takes standard commands from DOS to transfer information to or from a device and translates those standard commands into whatever form this driver's particular device requires. You may cause this program to be loaded through a DEVICE or DEVICEHIGH line in your CONFIG.SYS file, or it may masquerade as a TSR program, and thus be loaded through any of the ways any other TSR is loaded. (Those ways are, you will recall, via an INSTALL line in CONFIG.SYS, a line in AUTOEXEC.BAT, a line in some other batch file, or by being directly executed at the DOS prompt.)

The major difference between device drivers and normal TSR programs is that in addition to altering the entries in the interrupt vector table, device drivers build themselves into another part of the operating system.

DOS maintains something called the *device driver chain*. Any time DOS wants to send a request for service to a device, that request is routed through the device chain. The first device in the chain that recognizes the service DOS is requesting can and probably will take the request and perform it. Any messages about the success or failure of its attempt will be sent back along the same chain.

Part I: The Hard Disk Companion

A TSR program first acts like any other program. Loaded right above the command interpreter, it may occupy a fairly large amount of memory. While initializing, it saves inside itself the address(es) of one or more ISRs from the interrupt vector table. In this example just the address for INT9 is saved. Then it replaces that value (or each of those values) with a pointer to itself, releases as much memory as it can, and tells the command interpreter that it wants to "terminate and stay resident" (which is where the name TSR comes from).

A	F000:EF6F
9	0D99:0045
8	0D99:003C
7	F000:EF6F
6	F000:EF6F
5	F000:FF54
4	0070:06F4
3	0070:06F4
2	0D99:0016
1	0070:06F4
0	002A:91FB

Interrupt Vector Table entries when TSR loads

The user's application loads, as before. Only this time it is loaded slightly higher in memory than it was when the TSR was not present. Notice the new address for INT9 (0F40:04EC = 62.27K) in the interrupt vector table. That is the TSR's entry point.

A	F000:EF6F
9	0F40:04EC
8	0D99:003C
7	F000:EF6F
6	F000:EF6F
5	F000:FF54
4	0070:06F4
3	0070:06F4
2	0D99:0016
1	0070:06F4
0	002A:91FB

Interrupt Vector Table entries after the TSR is loaded

Once again, consider what happens when a keyboard interrupt occurs. First the user program is executing at, for example, address 10AB:4257. (This is exactly the same address as in the previous example, except that the segment value has been increased by the amount of memory retained by the TSR program.) The arrow to the left shows this current program address, 83.26K.

This story continues in Figure 6-9.

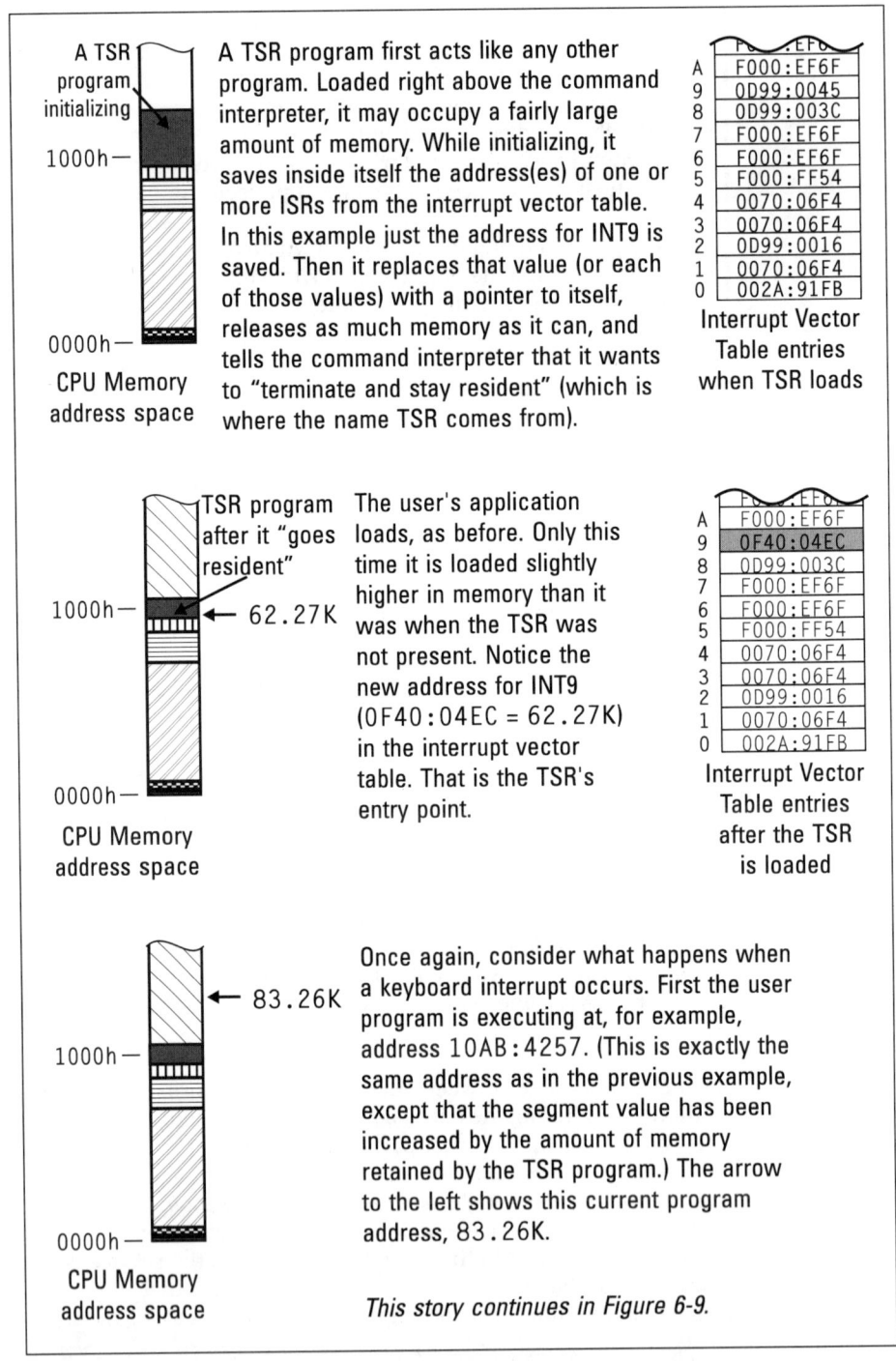

Figure 6-8: A TSR program "hooks" an interrupt to handle some events, but not others, that are otherwise handled by the original interrupt service routine (part 1 of 2).

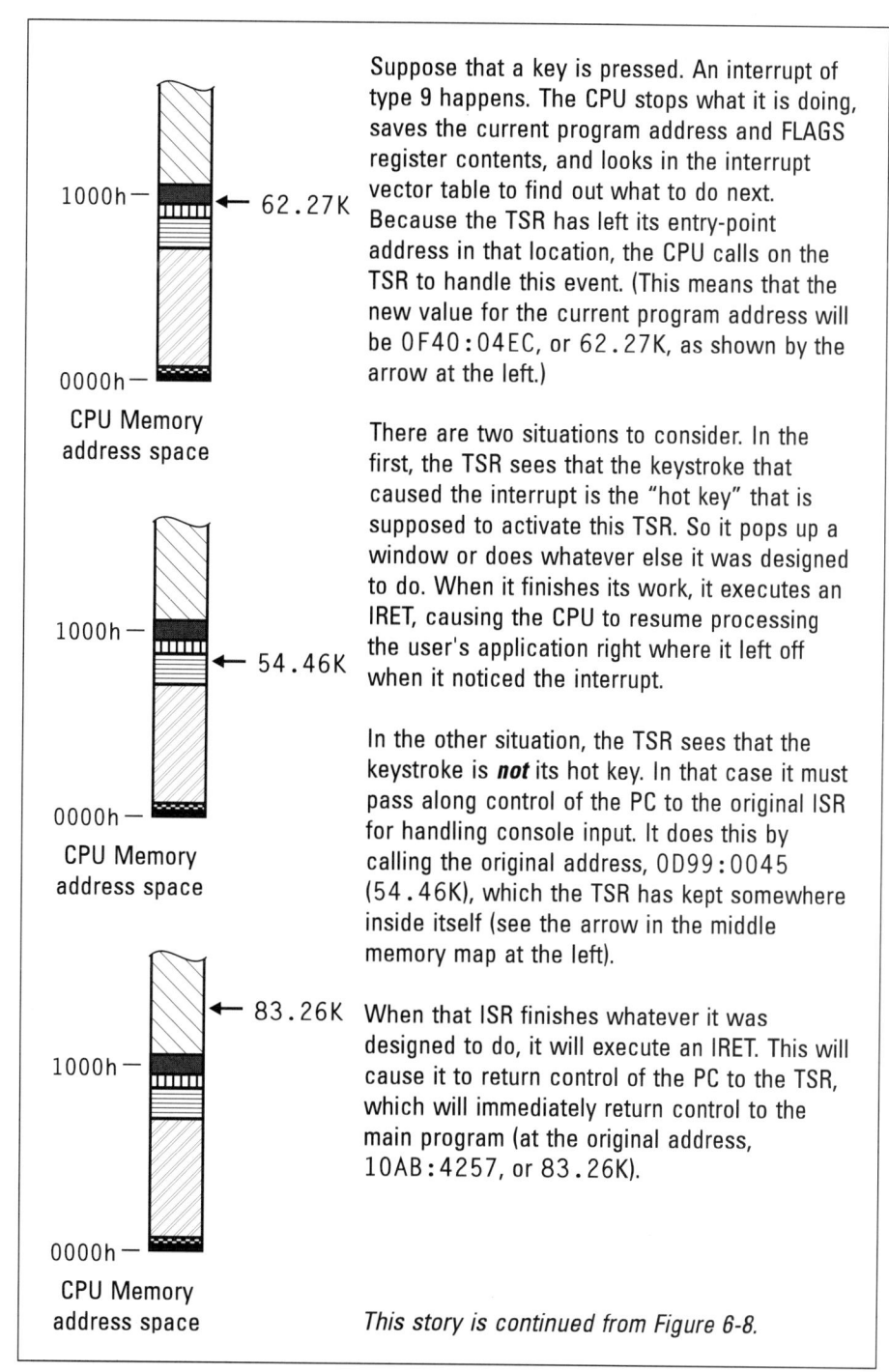

Suppose that a key is pressed. An interrupt of type 9 happens. The CPU stops what it is doing, saves the current program address and FLAGS register contents, and looks in the interrupt vector table to find out what to do next. Because the TSR has left its entry-point address in that location, the CPU calls on the TSR to handle this event. (This means that the new value for the current program address will be 0F40:04EC, or 62.27K, as shown by the arrow at the left.)

There are two situations to consider. In the first, the TSR sees that the keystroke that caused the interrupt is the "hot key" that is supposed to activate this TSR. So it pops up a window or does whatever else it was designed to do. When it finishes its work, it executes an IRET, causing the CPU to resume processing the user's application right where it left off when it noticed the interrupt.

In the other situation, the TSR sees that the keystroke is *not* its hot key. In that case it must pass along control of the PC to the original ISR for handling console input. It does this by calling the original address, 0D99:0045 (54.46K), which the TSR has kept somewhere inside itself (see the arrow in the middle memory map at the left).

When that ISR finishes whatever it was designed to do, it will execute an IRET. This will cause it to return control of the PC to the TSR, which will immediately return control to the main program (at the original address, 10AB:4257, or 83.26K).

This story is continued from Figure 6-8.

Figure 6-9: A TSR program "hooks" an interrupt to handle some events, but not others, that are otherwise handled by the original interrupt service routine (part 2 of 2).

This strategy allows new device drivers to be built into the chain, and, if they come in front of any similar device drivers that were previously installed, the new ones will get priority access to the messages DOS sends. This priority means that the new device drivers will preempt the other, similar drivers.

This is how the ANSI.SYS driver can replace the default console-handling routine with its own, more extensive program, to name just one example. The console is a character device. Likewise, one can add a new block device driver. It is also possible, though more difficult, to replace the DOS default block device driver. At the end of this chapter, you will learn about why it is sometimes very important to replace the DOS default block device driver, and you will learn a little bit more about how to do it.

Intel allowed for up to 256 different kinds of interrupt. Because no PC has to respond to that many kinds of events (and because, in some cases, many events are grouped under a single interrupt), some space in the interrupt vector table regularly goes unused. DOS puts some of that "waste space" to use by storing address pointers that point to tables of information, instead of to interrupt-handling programs, as you will learn in the next section.

Hard disk parameter tables

DOS can talk to a vast variety of disk drives by using some stored parameters that describe key aspects of particular drives. The name of the main parameter table is the *hard disk parameter table* (HDPT). Because most PC hard disk controllers can control either one or two hard disk drives, the design of DOS provides for two hard disk parameter tables. (Starting with Version 5, MS-DOS allows for more physical drives — up to seven — though very few PC users have taken advantage of that fact so far.)

TECHNICAL SECRET

You may think your PC has more than two hard disk drives. You may call them C:, D:, and E:, for example. These drives are called *volumes*, or *logical drives*. They act logically as if they were separate disk drives, but in fact they are usually only different partitions of one, or at most two, physical hard disk drives. Down deep, DOS knows which of these volumes belongs to each physical drive.

In addition to the hard disk parameter table or tables, each of which describes one *physical* drive, DOS maintains for each logical volume two other tables (the *drive parameter block* and the *BIOS parameter block*). They are described a bit more in Chapter 10, in the section "Interpretation of the DOS boot record data table."

Partitioning a hard disk into volumes is one step in preparing it for use. The details of how to do that are covered in Chapter 9. Chapter 7, in the section "Evading the Logical Limits," covers one reason that you may want to create such volumes.

For interrupts number 41h and 46h, DOS uses the locations in the interrupt vector table that would normally point to ISRs to point instead to the first and second hard disk parameter tables. If both drives have the same dimensions, DOS can get away with only one hard disk parameter table by putting the same sets of numbers in both these locations in the interrupt vector table (see Figure 6-10).

If your PC only has one physical hard drive, the entry in the interrupt vector table for INT 46h probably will be pointed to some one of the HDPTs in the motherboard ROM BIOS; which one is of no importance because the configuration CMOS memory entries will show that no second hard disk is installed.

Translating to decimal notation, 41h becomes 4 times 16 plus 1, or the decimal number 65. Similarly, 46h becomes 4 times 16 plus 6, or decimal 70. Thus the two entries in the interrupt vector table that point to the HDPTs are at the 65th and 70th slots in that table. Because it takes four bytes to specify an address for an ISR program, the actual addresses at which these particular interrupt vectors are stored are just four times these numbers, or 00104h (260 decimal) and 00118h (280 decimal). Actually, each of those addresses only points at the first of four bytes needed to specify the corresponding table's address. The next three addresses hold the rest of that address.

In the hard disk parameter tables, DOS stores the number of cylinders and heads (or surfaces) for each drive, as well as the numbers telling it how large an error the error correction codes (ECC; stored with the data in each hard disk sector) can correct and how many times to retry reading a sector that it cannot read correctly the first time. DOS also stores some timeout values (to govern when the controller should give up trying certain operations that aren't succeeding) and a couple of very arcane numbers: the cylinder at which to start *reduced write-current* and that at which to start *write precompensation*.

TECHNICAL SECRET

Each hard disk parameter table is 16 bytes long. Figure 6-11 shows what each byte is used for. Not all hard disk controllers will use every number in this structure, but because DOS can't tell which type of controller it's working with, it will fill in every number.

The hard disk parameter tables can be placed almost anywhere in the first megabyte of the CPU's memory address space. Any program that wants to move the tables need only update the pointers to them in the interrupt vector table; DOS will not be any the wiser.

Part I: The Hard Disk Companion

```
FF (255)
FE (254)
FD (253)
   ⋮
49 ( 73)
48 ( 72)    Pointer to second Hard Disk
47 ( 71)    Parameter Table (or back to
46 ( 70)    the first one if the drives
45 ( 69)    are identical)
44 ( 68)
43 ( 67)    Pointer for first hard
42 ( 66)    drive to Hard Disk
41 ( 65)    Parameter Table with
40 ( 64)    values describing
3F ( 63)    that drive
3E ( 62)
3D ( 61)
   ⋮        } The DOS
              Interrupts
21 ( 33)
20 ( 32)
1F ( 31)
1E ( 30)
   ⋮        } The BIOS
              Interrupts
02 (  2)
01 (  1)
00 (  0)
 ↑
Interrupt Vector Table slot numbers,
given in both of the common ways of
specifying numbers: hexadecimal (decimal)
```

These slots contain addresses of programs (called Interrupt Service Routines) which are designed to "handle" various interrupting events.

Second Hard Disk Parameter Table

First Hard Disk Parameter Table

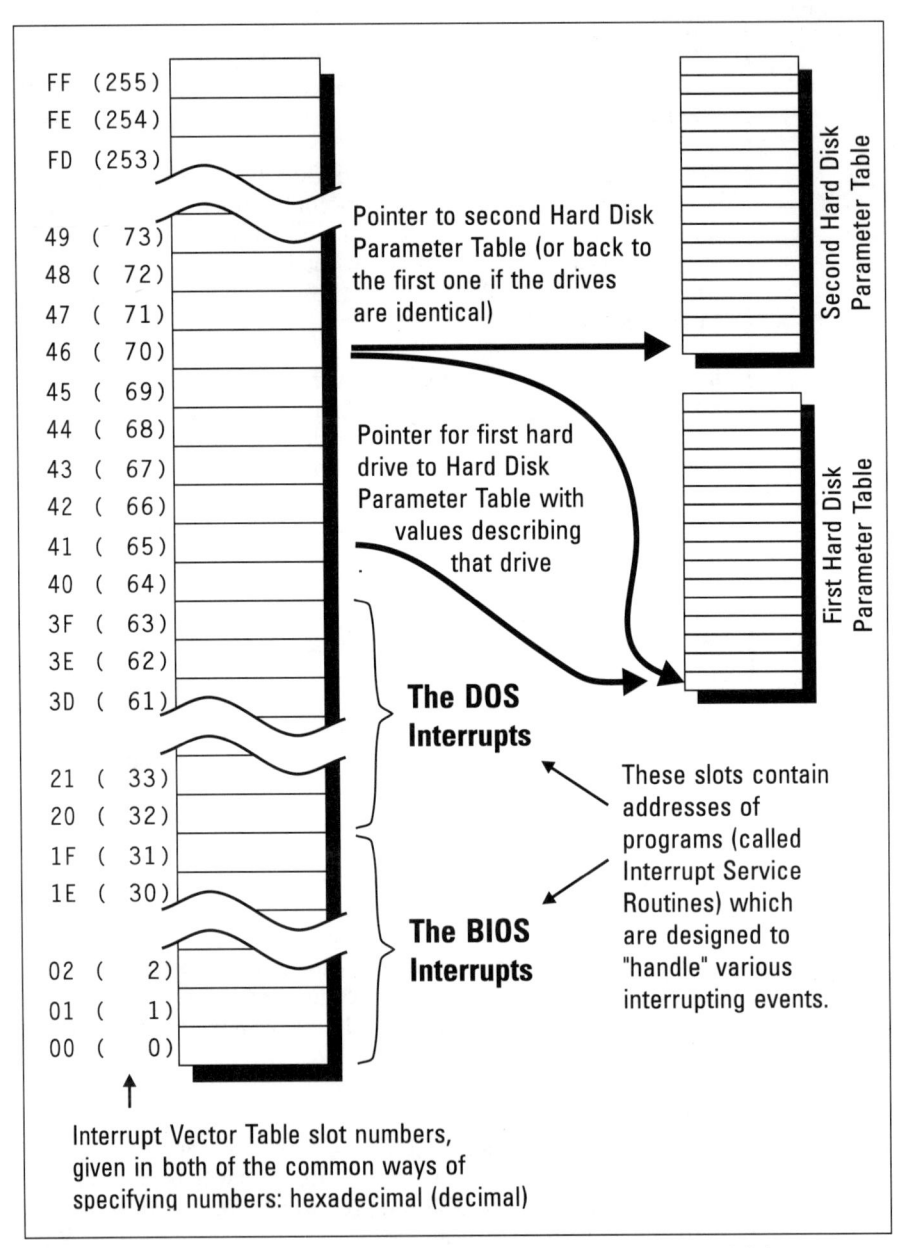

Figure 6-10: Some numbers stored in the interrupt vector table point to the hard disk parameter tables instead of to interrupt service routines.

Chapter 6: Hard Disks Under DOS | **193**

```
                                    Translating the values
                                    in this particular Hard
                                    Disk Parameter Table

    00   ← Reserved for future use   0 hex  =   0 decimal

    3F   ← Number of sectors         3F hex =  63 decimal
           per track

    02   ⎫ Cylinder number at
         ⎬← which to "park"          029A hex = 666 dec.
    9A   ⎭ heads (landing zone)

    00   ← Check drive               0 hex  =   0 decimal
           timeout value
    00   ← Format disk        (*)    0 hex  =   0 decimal
           timeout value
    00   ← Standard                  0 hex  =   0 decimal
           timeout value

    08   ← Drive step options        8 hex  =   8 decimal
           and flags

    07   ← Maximum length error      7 hex  =   7 decimal
           burst correctable
           using ECC

    FF   ⎫ Cylinder number at
         ⎬← which to start write-    FFFF hex = 65536 dec.
    FF   ⎭ precompensation

    00   ⎫ Cylinder number at
         ⎬← which to start reduced   0 hex  =   0 decimal
    00   ⎭ write-current (*)

    10   ← Number of Heads           10 hex =  16 decimal

    02   ⎫
         ⎬← Number of cylinders      029A hex = 666 dec.
    9A   ⎭
```

The numbers in slot 41 (hexadecimal = 65 decimal) or 46H (= 70 decimal) in the interrupt vector table point to this location (the lowest memory address in this table).

Actual values for a large (335 MB) ESDI drive (a Micropolis 1664-7 with an UltraStor 12F controller)

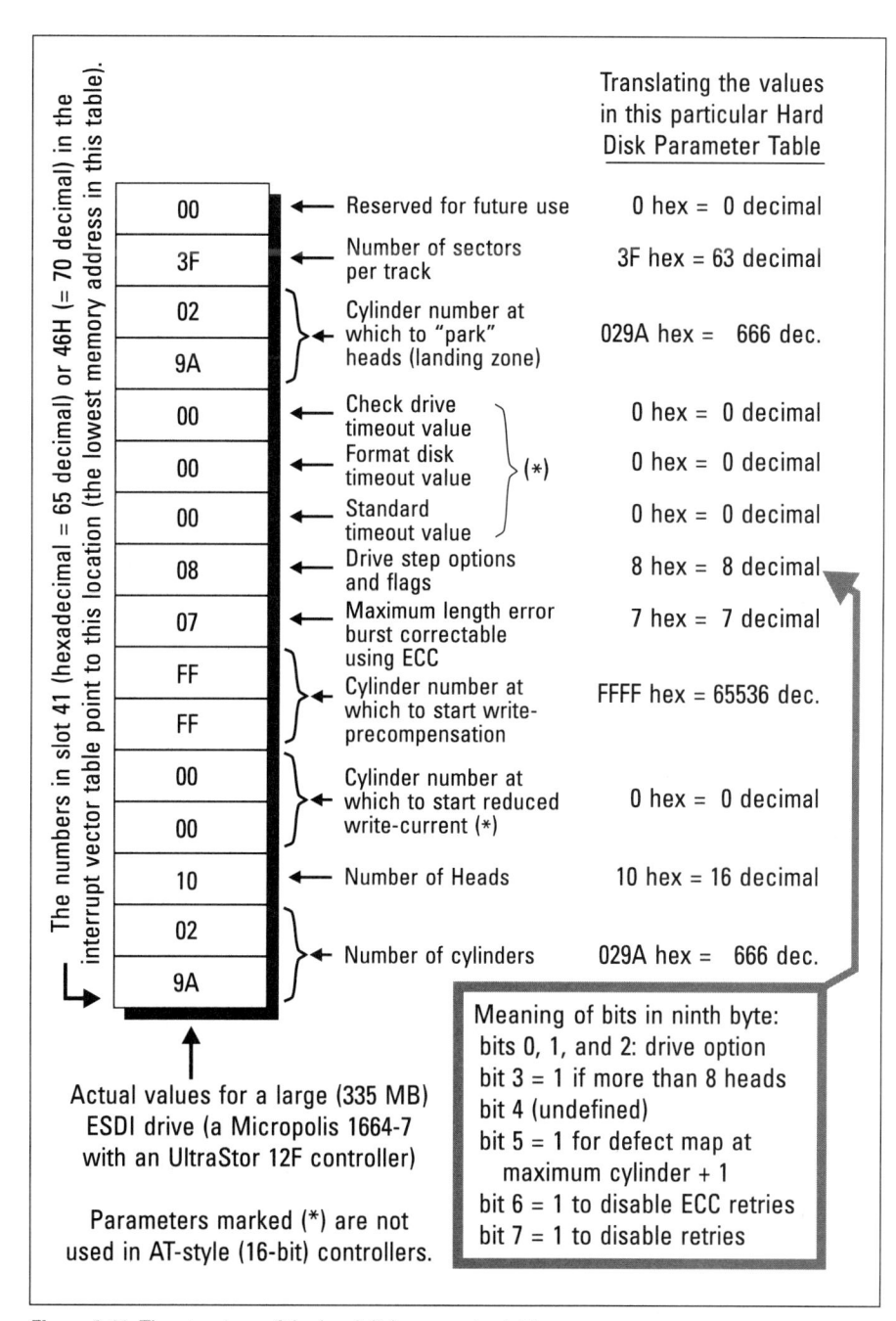

Parameters marked (*) are not used in AT-style (16-bit) controllers.

Meaning of bits in ninth byte:
bits 0, 1, and 2: drive option
bit 3 = 1 if more than 8 heads
bit 4 (undefined)
bit 5 = 1 for defect map at maximum cylinder + 1
bit 6 = 1 to disable ECC retries
bit 7 = 1 to disable retries

Figure 6-11: The structure of the hard disk parameter table.

> ### Hexadecimal Notation
>
> The hexadecimal number notation used in this book: a number followed by the letter *h* means a number expressed in base 16, or *hexadecimal notation*. Some authors use an uppercase H after the number or place 0x before it, but in this book, only the trailing lowercase *h* is used. (Any time you encounter what otherwise appears to be a number — some string of characters containing mostly numerals 0 through 9 but with some letters A through F mixed in — you can pretty well assume that it is a number in hexadecimal notation. The worst problems occur when the hexadecimal number contains only letters. Then it is hard to know that it is not a word, instead. To deal with this case, some authors insist that any hexadecimal number start with some one of the usual ten numerals. They put a zero in front of any hexadecimal number that starts with a letter. But again, in this book I have relied upon the trailing *h* to signal any hexadecimal numbers.)

This is an important point, for without some such means of easily altering the HDPT, it would not be nearly as easy for PCs to make use of the vast variety of hard disks now on the market. In the next section, you will learn some of the situations in which a hard disk parameter table is moved or a new one created and made active by placing a pointer to it in the interrupt vector table.

Drive-Type Determination

Your PC may employ any one of several methods to make sure that the DOS hard disk parameter tables get filled with the right numbers. The next several sections give the most popular strategies, roughly in historical order.

Original XT and similar older controller cards

The original XT hard disk controller had a couple of jumpers that you set to specify the kinds of first and second drives you were attaching. There were just four places for the jumper to go for the first drive and four for the second. This approach, therefore, could accommodate only a very small set of choices.

When you boot your XT or XT clone, the initial program that takes control does many things, including reading the position of these jumpers. That information tells the program what numbers to put into the interrupt vector table to point to the correct hard disk parameter tables.

Chapter 6: Hard Disks Under DOS

The newer autoconfiguring XT controller cards

More modern XT hard disk controllers will work with a wide variety of drive types. When you low-level format the drive (see Chapter 8), you tell the controller what the drive's dimensions are (the number of heads, cylinders, and sectors per track), as well as the numbers for the cylinders at which to start write precompensation and reduced-write current. As a part of the low-level format, these controllers record all this information somewhere on the drive itself.

When you boot your PC, these types of controllers eventually get charge of the computer. The controller then reads the dimensions of the first drive off the drive itself, builds the first hard disk parameter table, and puts its address into the interrupt vector table, repeating the process for a second drive if you have one. This ability to automatically configure themselves to work correctly with whatever drives they are attached to is what gives these controllers the name *autoconfiguring disk controllers*.

Where does such a controller put the HDPTs? There are several choices. One is in some unused portion of the interrupt vector table. Another is in some RAM on the controller card that is mapped into the CPU's memory address space somewhere within the same general range of addresses as the BIOS ROM on that controller card.

The first of these possibilities is a bit problematic. Sometimes, the space in the interrupt vector table that the hard disk controller manufacturer thought was unused is, in fact, used by some other piece of hardware in your PC. If so, you will have a serious conflict. The second choice is okay for an XT-class computer, but is not so wonderful for most higher level computers (ATs, 386, and 486 machines).

Perhaps the most common conflict will be between an expanded memory specification (EMS) card and a second physical hard disk. If you should find that your second hard disk seems to go all screwy just after the expanded memory manager (EMM) program loads, you have exactly this problem.

The solution is to load another device driver, MOVEHDD.SYS, from Washburn and Associates, which is on the *Hard Disk SECRETS* disk. If it finds that your HDPTs are either in the interrupt vector table or in the C or D pages (addresses between C0000h and E0000h) of the CPU's memory address space, MOVEHDD.SYS will reserve a very small amount of memory well above DOS but below the command interpreter, and it will move the HDPTs to that region.

AT and higher PCs

If you have an AT or higher level PC, then as a standard part of the design your PC will have something called the *configuration CMOS memory,* which stores several facts about your PC, including the number and type of disk drives (both floppy and hard) that you have attached to your PC.

/ TECHNICAL SECRET /

CMOS stands for *complementary metal oxide semiconductor* and refers to a process for making integrated circuits that require very little electric power to operate. The CMOS chip in your AT is a small RAM chip made by means of that process. Like all other RAM, it would ordinarily lose any resident data when you turn off your PC, were it not for the small attached battery that provides its power.

The CMOS stores the date and time of day, the amount of memory (RAM), the type of video display, and some other information about your computer's configuration. A crystal-controlled oscillator, powered by the same battery, constantly updates the CMOS record of date and time. This is why ATs, but not XTs (which do not have CMOS), usually "wake up" knowing the correct date and time.

When you turn on your AT, it may complain that the CMOS values are invalid, for one of two reasons: the date or time is invalid, or the configuration information (which includes the record of what drives you have) is invalid.

How can your computer know whether the date or time it has stored is wrong? Likewise, if that is where it keeps track of what equipment you have, how could your computer know whether that information was wrong? The answer in both cases is that your computer keeps a checksum with the configuration information and another checksum with the date and time. When you turn on your computer, it recomputes those checksums and compares them to the saved values. If either value is incorrect, your PC can safely conclude that there is a problem with that aspect of the information stored in the configuration CMOS memory chip.

If the date and time are off, and if you are running MS-DOS (or PC DOS) Version 5, you can easily fix things. At the DOS prompt, type **DATE** and press Enter. Answer the question. Do the same thing by using the TIME command.

If you are using an earlier version of DOS, you will find that following these steps only sets your DOS clock and not the real-time clock. That is, your PC will only know the correct time and date from then until the next time you reboot.

In that case, or if the configuration checksum was in error, you need to run your computer's *set-up* or *reference* program to correct those values. For some computers, you can do that by pressing some special hot-key combination, possibly during the boot process, or possibly at any time. Other computers have the set-up program on a special set-up or reference diskette (as it is for IBM PCs and PS/2s).

If the data in the CMOS are chronically wrong, you may need to replace its battery, or perhaps the CMOS RAM chip itself is bad.

The *Hard Disk SECRETS* disk that comes with this book contains a program called MH-SAVE.EXE. That program can save the information in the configuration CMOS memory and much more. Its companion program, MH-RESTR.EXE, can selectively restore different portions of the saved information.

To save space in the CMOS chip, it usually holds just a single number for each drive, called the drive type. The computer stores the actual dimensions of that type of drive in the *AT drive-type table* in the BIOS ROM chips on the PC's motherboard.

Some BIOS designs include the possibility of one or more of what is called a *user-definable drive type*. Entering this number, usually 46 or 47, signals the BIOS that you want to tell it about some nonstandard drive. Then you get to enter the actual physical dimensions of that drive and have them stored in the CMOS along with the drive-type number.

AT drive-type table

The AT drive-type table in the motherboard BIOS ROM is a collection of many possible hard disk parameter tables, one for each type of drive that the AT has information about. This strategy lets the start-up program merely inspect the CMOS to see which types of drives are installed (by type number) and then put into the interrupt vector table the addresses of the appropriate places in the AT drive-type table. The hard disk parameter tables are then ready to go.

The original design of the AT assumed that all possible PC hard disk drives were known and included among the many HDPT copies included in the BIOS ROM. That, of course, was ridiculous.

When IBM first introduced the AT, it had a very modest table, listing only 14 different types of hard drive. (That is a lot more than the four accommodated by the XT controller, however.) Later IBM models and AT clones extended the BIOS ROM AT drive-type table substantially, some listing nearly a hundred different types of hard drive. This is still not enough.

What if the drive you have isn't listed in the HDPT master table in your motherboard BIOS ROM? You have several choices. One choice is to replace your motherboard BIOS ROM with an updated one whose drive-type table includes at least one new entry — describing a drive with the dimensions of the drive you plan to install. That works, but you might end up having to buy a new BIOS ROM set every time you change hard drives. Not a pleasant prospect.

Some hard disk controllers, especially those for RLL drives, use a clever way to get around the limited number of drive types in the AT drive table. Their approach is essentially the same as that of the XT autoconfiguring hard disk controllers described in a previous section. These controllers expect you to tell your AT set-up program that you have a type 1 drive installed (the smallest possible size).

This means that the BIOS start-up program will initially put in the interrupt vector table's pointers to the hard disk parameter table in the BIOS ROM for a type 1 drive. Later in the boot process, during what is commonly called the *option ROM scan*, the hard disk controller's BIOS extension program will get control of the PC. At that time, it reads the actual drive dimensions off the drive itself, creates in RAM new hard disk parameter tables, and repoints the interrupt vectors to the new tables.

TECHNICAL SECRET

Shortly after you turn on power to your PC, the start-up program checks to see whether you have a special video card. It usually checks at address C0000h to see whether there is a valid *option ROM* there. Another name for such a ROM is a *video BIOS extension ROM* because it contains programs that are, in effect, additional pieces of the BIOS (a common shorthand name that you may encounter is *video ROM*).

If the start-up program finds a video BIOS extension ROM, that ROM's initialization program is run. This sets up the BIOS to be able to print things on the screen correctly. (All EGA and VGA video plug-in cards for PCs have such a video BIOS extension ROM on them.)

Next, the start-up program finds out how much RAM the PC has, what disk drives, what video display, and possibly some other information. Then the set-up program tests all those parts, at least briefly, in a process called the *power on self test* (POST).

After the POST is complete, the start-up program will look at several more places in memory address space to see whether it can find any additional ROM BIOS chips containing extensions to the main ROM BIOS. (The possible places are at each multiple of 2KB, starting either at C0800h or at the next multiple of 2KB after the video BIOS ROM, if it previously found one of those, and ending at E0000h.)

Chapter 6: Hard Disks Under DOS

Each time it finds any such ROM BIOS extensions, the start-up program issues a call to that BIOS extension's initialization program, which is always at a standard place within such a BIOS. That program may do anything it likes. When it is finished, it must give control of the computer back to the start-up program so that the start-up program can go on looking for other option ROMs and eventually try to load an operating system from a disk drive.

The BIOS extension ROM chips are most often located physically on plug-in cards (also called *option* or *add-in* cards). Normally, each option ROM initialization routine announces its presence with a message on the screen and then does whatever it needs to do to make all accesses to its special hardware work.

Every XT has an option ROM to enable the PC to use a hard disk. That is because when the original IBM PC was designed, a hard disk was not among its standard features. The AT and all later PC designs include support for a hard disk in the main BIOS ROM on the motherboard. Still, even in these PCs, you might have a hard disk controller with an option ROM on it.

The minimal sort of option ROM would simply be an extension to the main AT drive-type table. The more likely, and a much more flexible, possibility is that the controller is *autoconfiguring,* meaning that it can accommodate a disk drive with almost any dimensions by recording those dimensions on the drive itself.

You probably can find out whether you have an autoconfiguring hard disk controller by watching the messages that come across the screen during the boot process. Very few option ROMs do not announce their presence as they are initializing their hardware and bonding themselves into the BIOS.

There is one not-so-wonderful thing about these autoconfiguring hard disk controllers that you need to be aware of: Some of them put the HDPTs into an unfortunate place. Both the choice of some unused space in the interrupt vector table and the use of some RAM in the same region of memory address space as the option ROM are not very nice.

The discussion in the section "The newer autoconfiguring XT controller cards" applies here as well. In fact, because the motherboard BIOS ROM has support for hard disks, many times you only need to have access to the option ROM during the boot process. Thereafter you could, if you had an advanced PC (386 or later model), remap some extended memory on top of the option ROM and thereby get some useful RAM in upper memory space. But you can't do this if the HDPT is located there. Once again, the best way to deal with this is to load the MOVEHDD.SYS device driver first. It will move the HDPTs to a better place.

Hard disks on an option card

Hard disks mounted on an option card have their controllers inseparably joined to them. These controllers know all about the hard disks attached to them. You don't have to tell them anything special at all.

You do have to inform the PC that you have installed a hard drive, but as with the AT autoconfiguring hard disk controllers, you can tell a small lie. You simply say you have a type 0 drive. At boot time, the hard-disk card will figure out what the truth is and build the appropriate HDPT for it.

ESDI hard drives

ESDI drives and controllers are much smarter than MFM or RLL drives and ST412/ST506 controllers. The drives routinely store their dimensions on themselves and are prepared to answer a standard-format query by the controller as to what those dimensions are.

Installing an ESDI drive, therefore, is very simple. You either declare that you have a drive of type 1 or of type 0. (Type 0 is the same as no drive installed.) Which choice you use depends on whose ESDI hard disk controller you are using and is clearly spelled out in the instructions that come with it.

IDE/ATA hard drives

The most popular drives sold for PCs today are called IDE drives. More accurately, they should be called IDE/ATA drives. The name means *integrated drive electronics with an AT attachment interface* (see the section "Popular Products and Standards" in Chapter 3 for more details).

TECHNICAL SECRET

Strictly speaking, any drive with its own controller is an IDE drive. That includes all SCSI drives, all hard disks on an option card, and some ESDI drives (such as those built for installation into certain PS/2 models). It even includes some drives built for very different sorts of computers — say, a Macintosh. But none of these is what most people mean when they refer to an IDE drive.

If you add to the name the letters *ATA*, the designation specifies very clearly a drive meant for a PC that has as its interface just those 40 wires taken from a standard AT's I/O bus and connected to the standard ATA connector. That connector and the signals carried on its pins are spelled out in a formally adopted industry standard, called the AT attachment specification. Only drives that are designed to work when plugged into that interface can properly be called IDE/ATA drives.

These drives, like hard disks on an option card, have their controller built onto them. Unlike the hard-disk cards, these drives mount in a normal drive bay. You can connect them to the PC's input/output bus in either of two ways. One is via a special 40-pin AT attachment connector. The other is by using a paddle card that plugs into the bus and sports the AT attachment 40-pin connector. (The paddle card may also have a floppy disk controller on it.)

So far they don't sound very remarkable. Keep reading. These drives have one very unusual trait, and one that can easily trip you up if you are not aware of it.

IDE/ATA drives are real chameleons. They can pretend to have almost any dimensions you care to propose. (Naturally, an IDE/ATA drive has some definite maximum capacity, but you can apportion that capacity among cylinders, heads, and sectors per track in most any way you want.)

When installing an IDE/ATA drive, you get to choose any drive type you like, so long as it represents a drive with no more total capacity than the IDE/ATA drive you are installing. You enter that drive type number into the configuration CMOS memory. The next time you boot your computer, the start-up program will place into the interrupt vector table entries 41h (and 46h, if you have told the CMOS you have two physical drives) pointers to HDPTs for the drive types you have set in the CMOS.

Now, when the IDE/ATA drive comes to life, it will check those pointers and look at the appropriate HDPT. Then it will set up a *sector mapping* (also called a *sector translation*) that makes it look as if it were the type of drive you said it was. (Sector mapping is described in detail in the next chapter. You also will find a quick summary of what happens and how it is done in the next section of this chapter, "SCSI hard drives.")

That is wonderful, as far as it goes. It means you don't have to know the true dimensions of an IDE/ATA drive to install it and use it. All you need to know is its true maximum capacity.

And it is terrible. Especially if you forget what drive type you chose and if your configuration CMOS memory gets wiped out. Unlike all the other drive types, an IDE/ATA drive cannot help you know what its apparent dimensions were the last time you used it. If, when you reboot your computer, the CMOS entry for your hard disk has changed to indicate some different drive type, the IDE/ATA drive will cheerfully assume that you now want it to do a different kind of sector translation, and it will do what it assumes you want.

The sad result is that you will not be able to access any of the data on that disk until you figure out what drive type you used when you put the data there. Chapter 11 goes over the ways you can attempt to get out of this pickle if you should find yourself in it.

Part I: The Hard Disk Companion

TIP: The best way to protect yourself is, of course, to write down which drive type you chose when you installed the drive. Write it on a label and stick it on the drive itself. Also record that information in an overall summary sheet describing all the parts of your PC hardware and keep that sheet close to the PC, where it will be easy to find when you need it.

The reason for writing this information in two places is so that when you forget about or lose one of them, you will still have the other. The label on the drive is harder to look at than something outside the PC, but it also will not get lost unless you lose the drive!

SCSI hard drives

A SCSI hard drive is an IDE drive (in the broad sense of the term) plus a SCSI slave interface. SCSI drives connect to a PC through one of three sorts of SCSI host adapters, each of which looks very different to DOS.

TECHNICAL SECRET: All option cards that control a DOS block device can come in any of the three forms described here, not merely SCSI host adapters. Examples of other such option cards include proprietary optical disk-drive controllers and some tape-drive controllers.

Fundamentally, SCSI treats a hard disk as simply a large number of sectors, just like the high-level DOS logical view of a disk drive. This method requires only one number to point to a location on the drive — a *logical block address* (LBA). (This number is equivalent to the logical sector number used by DOS, except perhaps for an offset to account for the portion of the disk not used by DOS.)

DOS and the BIOS talk to a hard disk on a much more physical level, using the cylinder, head, and physical sector numbers to specify a place on the drive. The three types of SCSI host adapters differ mainly in how they convert information on the hard drive from the BIOS's way of addressing to that used by the SCSI standard.

The simplest type of SCSI host adapter to install and use is a register-compatible controller. To the computer, it looks exactly like a standard AT hard disk controller for an MFM drive. This sort of host adapter may have an option ROM, but when that program takes control of the PC, it does not hook any of the interrupts.

TECHNICAL SECRET: Because a register-compatible SCSI host adapter presents the full appearance of a standard AT hard disk controller, the PC can and does give commands to it exactly as if it were talking to an MFM controller. The adapter differs from the standard AT controllers, however, in that it doesn't

Chapter 6: Hard Disks Under DOS

have to make the drives it controls look like any of the drives in the AT drive-type table. To accomplish this, it must be an autoconfiguring controller and build its own hard disk parameter table somewhere in some RAM during the option ROM scan portion of the boot process, instead of using the AT drive-type table entries in the motherboard BIOS ROM.

Some very common SCSI host adapters are not register compatible, but they are *INT 13h compatible.* These controllers have an option ROM that repoints the interrupt 13h (INT 13h) entry in the interrupt vector table to a program within itself. Thus the controller does not use the BIOS program in the motherboard ROM of an AT at all. (The number 13h is the same as decimal 16+3, or 19, so the INT 13h interrupt vector is that stored in the 20th location in the table [INT 0 being the first location].)

TECHNICAL SECRET

An INT 13h-compatible SCSI host adapter presents the computer with a fictitious drive having some convenient number of cylinders, heads, and physical sectors per track. It then translates all INT 13h requests into a logical sector number and sends those translated requests on to the SCSI slave adapter. The slave adapter will, in turn, translate the logical block addresses back into real cylinder, head, and physical sector numbers, using the actual dimensions of the drive. (The figure in the section "Sector mapping" in Chapter 7 shows an example of sector translation.)

The third variety of SCSI host adapter is neither register- nor INT 13h-compatible with the standard AT hard disk controller design. To use an adapter of this sort for hard disk access requires an *installable device driver*. This driver is a program that may be in the option ROM on the host adapter, or it may be loaded into RAM off the boot disk. The purpose of any installable device driver is to replace a low-level part of DOS. In this, the device driver resembles many TSR programs, but it hooks itself into DOS in a different way.

SCSI host adapters are not the only kind of hardware that can force you to use an installable device driver. A CD-ROM drive, for example, also requires the use of an installable device driver. The difference is that the installable device driver for a SCSI drive may have to preempt the normal DOS default block device driver (the one that DOS normally uses to access drive C). There are some peculiarities as to how DOS does its disk access that make creating such an installable device driver a bit tricky.

Whichever kind of SCSI host adapter you have, installing a hard disk is done in a similar manner. Normally, you tell the set-up program that writes to your configuration CMOS memory that you have no hard disk at all. (Or, if you are adding a SCSI hard drive to a PC that already has another hard drive in it, you simply leave the settings in the CMOS alone.)

When DOS doesn't follow its own rules

DOS includes two interrupts for accessing the disk at the logical level. They are INT 25h (for reading a sector) and INT 26h (for writing). Strangely enough, DOS does not use them. Any other program may use them, in which case it will get the same result that DOS gets by its different strategy.

The higher level part of DOS (or an external program) does this to be able to get at a spot on the disk by specifying only the logical sector number. The DOS-resident block device driver normally converts such requests into requests that use the actual physical addresses (cylinder, head, and physical sector numbers). Finally, that driver calls on the BIOS through INT 13h to do the actual disk access.

DOS gets to the device driver by an absolute call to an address known to itself. Changing any of the entries in the interrupt vector table (such as those for INT 25h or INT 26h) will *not* allow you to interfere with this action.

The lower level part of DOS maintains a linked list of device drivers. That means that DOS holds the address of the first one, and then each driver points to the next one in the chain. There is a standard way of inserting character devices at the head of the chain and block devices at the end. There is no standard way to insert a block device except at the end.

Because DOS searches the chain in order when looking for a device driver that can perform whatever task it has to do, an installed character device can easily supersede a resident one. An installed block device normally cannot. Anyone wanting to replace the DOS resident block device must learn how to do some very nonstandard things.

Makers of the third kind of SCSI host adapter must create installable device drivers that insert themselves in front of the normal DOS resident block device driver (see Figure 6-12). They usually also hook INT 13h so that they can respond to requests for disk service at that level too.

Because a SCSI controller looks at a disk as a one-dimensional string of sectors, its special block device driver has a very easy task at the INT 25h or INT 26h level. It merely adds some offset to the DOS logical sector number to get the corresponding logical block address. When it intercepts an INT 13h BIOS call, it must do the inverse of the job normally done by the DOS resident block device, this time converting from a three-dimensional disk address back into a one-dimensional disk address.

The host adapter's BIOS ROM or the installable device driver will ask the SCSI drive what size it is. The host adapter will tell the BIOS that you have a hard disk with 32 sectors per track and 64 heads. That works out to a capacity per cylinder of 1MB, so the host adapter gives however many MB that drive can store as the number of cylinders. (The way the host adapter tells the BIOS these things is to put them into a hard disk parameter table and point the appropriate interrupt vector to it.)

Chapter 6: Hard Disks Under DOS

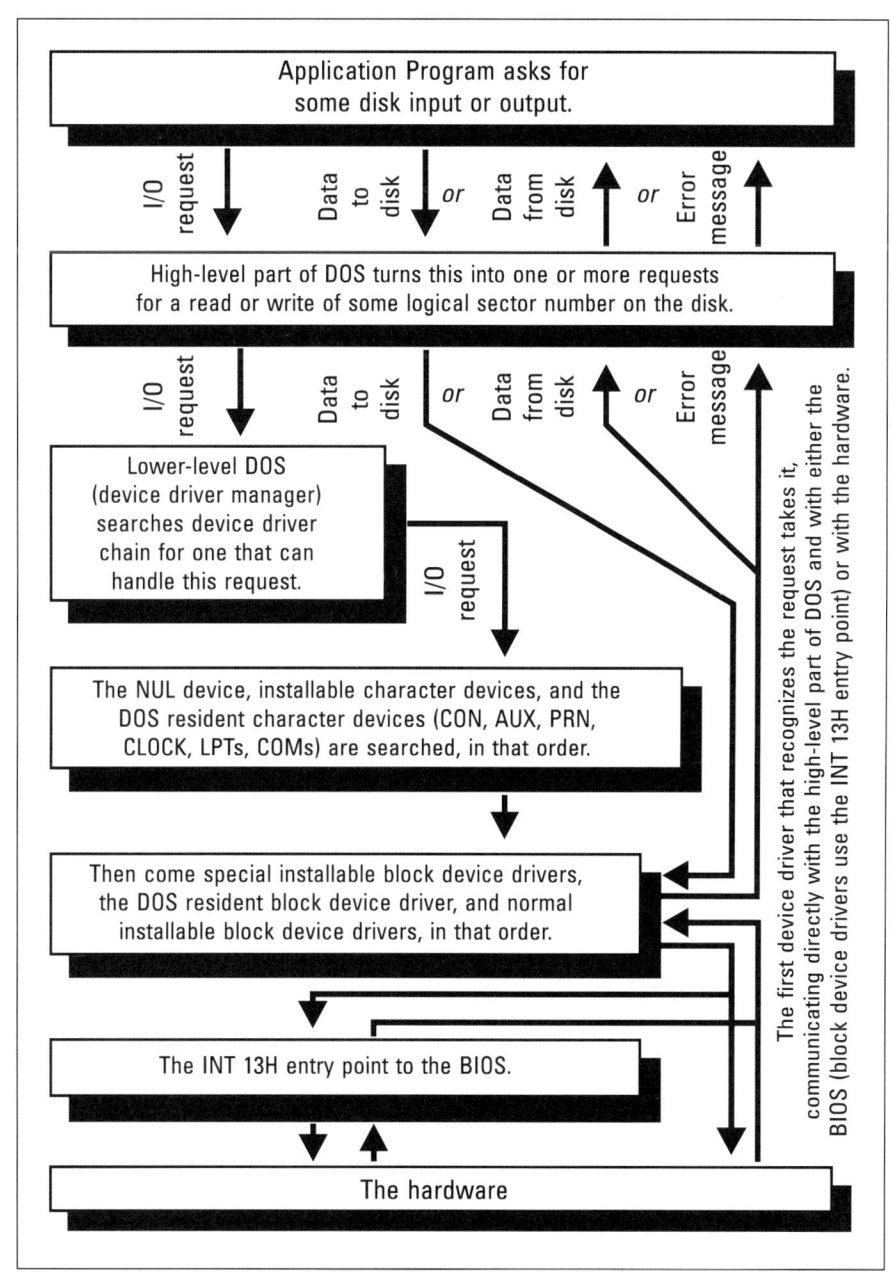

Figure 6-12: How an installable block device driver designed to replace the original DOS block driver inserts itself into DOS.

Summary

- MS-DOS is an operating system for the PC (as are its close kin, PC DOS and DR DOS). DOS provides a layer of software that goes between the hardware and your application programs. Its job is to manage access to the hardware by all the different programs you may be running and to activate the hardware upon the request of those programs.

- What is commonly called DOS can be broken down into two broad parts, the BIOS and the "real" DOS. The former part, which is partially embodied in ROMs and partially comes from files on the disk from which you booted, activates the hardware. The "real" DOS part is what views data in terms of files and manages usage of the disk and other hardware resources.

- All the sources and destinations for data flowing in or out of a PC are viewed by DOS as devices, and they are treated in one of two ways, depending on whether they are character or block devices.

- Character devices handle information a single byte (character) at a time. The keyboard, screen, mouse, modem, and printer are some examples of character devices.

- Block devices handle information in blocks, usually blocks that contain 512 bytes. All disk drives are supported under DOS as block devices, as are tape drives, CD-ROM drives, and several other PC peripherals.

- Programs get layered in your PC, with the lower layers serving to support the higher ones. Application programs call on DOS to do various tasks for them. DOS, in turn, calls on the BIOS, which directs the hardware to do the actual work.

- Device drivers and terminate-and-stay-resident programs (TSRs) can interpose themselves in this structure. In this way, they can modify how DOS does things for your programs.

- The primary mechanism for communication between the layers of programs in your PC is the interrupt. A secondary method is via the device driver chain.

- DOS also uses various data tables. One of critical importance for hard disk access is the hard disk parameter table (HDPT). There is one HDPT per physical drive, and it holds information about the dimensions of that drive (number of heads, cylinders, and sectors per cylinder).

- The original IBM PC/XT and PC/AT had information in their hard disk BIOS ROMs about all the possible types of drives that could be installed in them. More modern PCs use any one of several strategies to learn about the dimensions of the drives they contain.

- The best strategies put the disk dimensions on the drive itself and have the controller retrieve them at boot time. This method allows you to use any drive whose interface is compatible with that controller.

- IDE/ATA drives are chameleons. They make themselves seem to have whatever drive dimensions you want. Sometimes this is wonderful, but it can also lead to great grief if you forget what you previously told the drive; then you may have great difficulty getting at your data.

Now that you know how DOS works with disks, you are ready to learn how those techniques limit the size of disk you can use. In the next chapter you learn the limits and also how those limits can sometimes be evaded or broken.

Chapter 7
Bumping Up Against and Breaking Barriers

In This Chapter

▶ The several ways in which the design of DOS, and of the original PC, limit the maximum size of the hard disks you can use in a PC

▶ Which limits apply to logical drives (drive letters) and which apply to physical drives

▶ How to get around the limits if you are using a version of DOS prior to 3.3

▶ DOS 3.3 introduced a better way to get around these limits; learn why and how to change to this strategy if you were using the older method

▶ DOS Version 4 offered a still better way to get around the limits; learn why you don't need to take advantage of it, and if you want to, how to do so

▶ The various error messages that are generated by the disk controller and the BIOS when an access to your hard disk goes awry, and why and how some of them are suppressed by DOS so that you normally never learn about them

▶ How a sufficiently clever program can get behind DOS and intercept *all* the disk error messages, and why that can be important to you

Logical Size Limits Imposed by DOS

Prior to Version 4, DOS could not handle a hard disk volume larger than 32MB. (A disk volume, in this context, means what appears to DOS as a disk drive — that is, an entity to which DOS assigns a drive letter.)

DOS at its higher levels looks at the disk drive as just a long string of sectors. It numbers those sectors, starting at 1. This is the *logical* view of the disk drive. Later, when DOS is ready to command the hardware to read or write something, it must translate each logical sector number into a real physical address (head, cylinder, and physical sector number).

Part I: The Hard Disk Companion

The higher levels of DOS have a designed-in limit on the number representing the *logical sector number*. This limit implies a maximum size for any logical volume that DOS can handle. The lower level routines (in the BIOS) have another set of limits which together impose another maximum size for any physical drive you attach to a PC. Nothing requires that these two maximum sizes for a disk be the same, and in general they are not the same. In this section you learn precisely how the DOS limitation arises and what maximum size it implies. In the next section, you learn about the BIOS limits and the size they imply.

In all versions of DOS before 4.0, the logical sector number had to fit into a 16-bit number. This requirement meant that there could be no more than 65,536 (2^{16}) sectors in a DOS-addressable portion of a disk drive (a single disk volume).

Under DOS, the standard size for sectors is 512 bytes. This size times the maximum number of sectors equals 32MB, which was the maximum storage capacity that DOS could address in one disk volume before Version 4.0.

DOS 4.0 raised the size limit on the sector number. Instead of only a 16-bit number, the sector size can now be a 32-bit number (up to 4,294,967,296). This implies a maximum disk size, with the standard 512-byte sectors, of 2 terabytes (2TB, which is 2 megamegabytes, or approximately 2.2 million million bytes). That seems like a large enough limit — at least for now!

The restriction to a 32-bit sector number sets the maximum logical size to a disk (or really to a logical volume) under DOS. Another set of limits, called the physical limits, are much more binding, no matter what DOS version you use. In the next section, you learn that the limit to the size of a disk, based on the official BIOS limits on the physical addressing, is 504MB. There is a commonly used technique for increasing this size, but even then there is a limit for any PC's hard disk of 7.875GB. Either way, it is a far smaller limit than the logical size limit for a disk volume under the most recent versions of DOS (Version 4 and later).

Years ago, long before DOS 4.0, people began to want to exceed the 32MB storage-capacity limit. Various people found a variety of ways around this limit. Using one of these nonstandard methods may bring on some unpalatable consequences, a point that is discussed later in this chapter in the section "Evading the Logical Limits."

Chapter 7: Bumping Up Against and Breaking Barriers

Physical Size Limits Imposed by the BIOS

Whenever a program wants to have some information read from or written to the hard disk, that request must eventually get translated down to the physical level. It may start as a request for a file, which DOS will translate into some number of accesses to some particular clusters or logical sectors on the drive. Eventually, before the hardware can be commanded to do the needed read or write, each of those logical addresses must be resolved to a particular cylinder and head (thus specifying one track) and then to the particular sector on that track.

This translation is done by a block device driver. There is a default block device driver that is a part of the BIOS code loaded by DOS from the disk, and it may be replaced or its actions modified by an installable device driver loaded either during the CONFIG.SYS file processing or later on.

TECHNICAL SECRET

The highest level part of DOS does this translation by calling a device driver (either the resident block device or an installed replacement). In either case, the called program translates the request to a physical address and then calls the BIOS through INT 13h, subfunction 5 or 6 (see Figure 6-12).

(When a program calls for interrupt services, the interrupt number specifies which interrupt service routine [ISR] will handle the request. To accommodate many more services without risking running out of interrupt numbers, it has become common practice to write interrupt service routines that can do any of a large number of different things. These different activities are called the ISR's subfunctions. A program calling an ISR indicates which subfunction it wants by placing the number of that subfunction in the AX register in the CPU before issuing the interrupt call.)

The numbers that this device driver uses to do this translation are the dimensions of the drive. The device driver learns those dimensions at boot time by another call to INT 13h, this time to subfunction 8.

Once the location has been translated to an actual, physical address, the request for data transfer must be given to the BIOS, which will, in its turn, give the request to the actual disk controller hardware.

The interrupt call that DOS uses to give the translated information to the BIOS (INT 13h) has some severe limits on the size of the numbers it can accept for the physical address components. It only allows the use of a 10-bit binary number to specify the cylinder number. It limits head numbers to 4 bits and sector numbers to 6 bits. This limitation means that you can have cylinder numbers from 0 to 1,023 ($1,023 = 2^{10}-1$), heads from 0 to 15 ($15 = 2^4-1$), and sectors from 1 to 63 ($63 = 2^6-1$). Anything beyond that could perfectly well exist, but you couldn't get information about it to the hard disk controller through the BIOS.

Part I: The Hard Disk Companion

If you multiply these numbers (1,024 cylinders times 16 heads times 63 sectors per track times 512 bytes per sector), you get a total maximum capacity for any physical hard drive in a fully standard PC of 504MB (about 528 million bytes).

TECHNICAL SECRET

Actually, the head number is only *supposed* to be kept in the range 0 to 15. The places in DOS and the BIOS that hold the actual maximum head number can take numbers up to 255. Nothing in DOS or the BIOS checks to see whether the number of heads is lower than 16; the documentation just says it is *supposed* to be. This is an important loophole in what would otherwise be a painfully tight set of size restrictions. You will read more about this loophole and about other ways people have devised to evade both the DOS (logical) and the BIOS (physical) size limits in later sections of this chapter.

Even if you allow a maximum of 256 heads, the maximum size of a hard disk in a PC works out to 7.875 gigabytes (7.875GB, which is about 8,455 million bytes). This is not very much larger than the largest hard drives being installed in PCs today. More and more people are going to find themselves running up against this limit in the very near future.

When PCs were new, the BIOS limits on hard disk size did not seem to be a particularly severe restraint. With the latest, largest hard drives, they are positively unacceptable. Though you can evade these limits by using clever techniques, doing so has some serious consequences. These consequences are discussed in this chapter in the section "Evading the Physical Limits." Before discussing ways to evade the physical limits, let's return to the logical limits and see some of the ways they have been evaded.

Evading the Logical Limits

In the first section of this chapter, you learned that DOS used to limit the logical size of drives to 32MB. Starting with DOS Version 3.3, it became possible to use larger drives but only by partitioning them into multiple logical volumes, each of which was no more than 32MB in size. Starting with DOS Version 4.0, it finally became possible to use virtually any size disk drive as a single logical volume or to break it up into multiple volumes any way you might like.

These improvements in DOS were made in response to users' needs and following up on the good ideas brought to bear on these problems by a number of companies that made DOS add-ons and utility programs. In this section you will learn about those earlier ways of dealing with large hard drives.

Large sectors

Before DOS 4.0, you couldn't have more than 65,536 sectors in a DOS-addressable disk volume. One way to handle a disk with a storage capacity greater than 32MB without violating that limit is simply to make each sector larger than 512 bytes. DOS allows you to do this but requires some help. The sector size can vary, but it is customary to use an integer multiple of 512 bytes. People have used sector sizes of 1,024 bytes, 1,536 bytes, 2,048 bytes, and all the way up to 8,192 bytes.

One serious consequence of this strategy is a potential loss in efficiency in the use of your disk space. Any file takes up at least one sector and perhaps several sectors (if the cluster size is several sectors). This is true no matter how small the file. If you store many tiny files on a disk with very large sectors, you may waste much of the disk drive's space. Each of those tiny files has a cluster all to itself. The space in each cluster after the end of the file it holds is called *slack space*. Large sectors (and thus large clusters) make for lots of slack space. In Chapter 10, you can read more about cluster sizes and the inefficiencies they cause.

The other important consequence of using a larger-than-standard sector size is that you must use some non-DOS program to set the sector size to your chosen nonstandard value. Your computer operates just a bit less compatibly, which doesn't *often* cause any problems — but it can.

TECHNICAL SECRET

Engineers at Wyse Technology introduced a way for DOS to deal with disk drives larger than 32MB in their Version 3.21 of MS-DOS. Their technique was simply to allow the FORMAT program to write larger sectors (or at least what look to DOS like larger sectors). They used the same technique with Version 3.3. With Wyse MS-DOS Version 4.0, they changed to the IBM- and Microsoft-blessed method for dealing with large disk partitions, using only standard 512-byte sectors.

The sector size is stored in the boot record on any disks formatted by recent versions of DOS. Therefore, any version of Wyse's MS-DOS after 3.21 can recognize Wyse's large-sector-size way of dealing with large disks and can access them successfully. Other manufacturers' MS-DOS versions may not.

The actual physical sectors created by the hard disk controller when it applies the low-level format continue to have exactly 512 data bytes in them. These larger apparent sector sizes are simply logical sectors created out of smaller physical sectors by the special Wyse DOS version of the FORMAT program as it applies the high-level format.

COMPAQ introduced its special technique for dealing with large disk partitions, starting with its Version 3.31 of MS-DOS. COMPAQ did not say so at the time, but later it came out that this special technique was developed in close consultation with Microsoft. The technique used was the same one used later by IBM and Microsoft, starting with Version 4.0 of PC DOS and MS-DOS. (This was good news for COMPAQ customers because it meant that they did not have to do anything special to their disks to achieve full compatibility with later DOS versions.)

If you use some special driver program to modify DOS by setting up a larger-than-normal logical sector size, you run a risk. If you lose that driver program, you will be unable to access the data on your hard drives. Also, any such non-DOS solution carries with it the potential for a nasty interaction with some DOS application program that expects your operating system to be pure DOS.

Disk partitions

The other common way to evade the 32MB limit is to break up a larger hard drive into several logical volumes, each less than 32MB in total capacity. DOS Version 3.3 enabled you to do this in a Microsoft- and IBM-blessed manner. Before that, you could evade the limit only by using some additional software to augment the basic DOS procedures. The details of how DOS 3.3 (and all later versions) create logical drives is covered in Chapter 10.

What are the consequences of using logical drives? If your disk drive is initially all one volume, when you add files to it, the files go into whatever space is available. But after you divide your drive into partitions, those boundaries are not flexible. Thus, if you fill one partition, you cannot automatically "borrow" space from another partition. This means you must more thoughtfully manage what goes into each partition.

The constraints imposed by fixed-size disk partitions are not necessarily all bad. First, they may force you to organize your files better. Second, they can make your disk work faster because you have the files and the FAT tables and directories that refer to those files all contained in a partition that spans only a relatively few cylinders. This lets DOS access those files more quickly.

Disk partitioning may be inappropriate if, for example, you bought a large hard drive in order to have some place to put data files larger than 32MB. In this case, the large sector approach makes sense, as does the use of a single huge partition under DOS 4 and later versions. Either way, you can address the whole disk as a single partition.

Chapter 7: Bumping Up Against and Breaking Barriers

If you partition your disk by using a third-party add-on software solution, you normally can access the first partition of any physical drive by using only DOS. You can access the rest only when you have that special driver installed on top of DOS. If you use DOS 3.3 or later to partition your disk, you will not have this problem.

TIP Some popular DOS add-on programs that can do this partitioning are Disk Manager from OnTrack Software, SpeedStor from Storage Dimensions, the Priam EVDR.SYS driver, and Vfeature Deluxe from Golden Bow Software. You can also use the latter program to alter the sector size or even to make two physical drives appear, logically, as if they were one even larger drive. (This latter use is an instance of the technique mentioned earlier in this chapter that will eventually become a necessity if one wants to use hard disk volumes in excess of about 8GB on a PC.)

DOS 3.3 has been available a long time, and most of its bugs have been expunged or techniques for dealing with them are well known. Therefore, it is no longer appropriate to use third-party DOS add-on programs to partition new hard disks. Still, many people continue to do so, out of habit more than anything else. They make the systems they build needlessly dependent on those device drivers. If you have DOS 3.3 and your system uses one of those device drivers, you may want to make some changes.

Regardless of what method you use to partition a disk, you must do so before the disk volumes are (high-level) formatted. The details for this technique are in Chapter 9, which also describes what is involved if you decide to change from a third-party solution to one of the pure DOS solutions.

Evading the Physical Limits

At first the most constraining limit on DOS volume size was the logical one. When that was raised with the introduction of DOS 4, from 32MB to 2TB (2 terabytes), the logical limit became a non-problem. At that point the other limits — those imposed by the BIOS on the physical dimensions of a hard drive attached to a PC — became important.

Evading these physical limits turns out to be quite a bit harder than evading the logical size limits. You learn about the many effective techniques that have been devised to do so in this section.

Part I: The Hard Disk Companion

The pure software-evasion technique

OnTrack Software's Disk Manager disk-partitioning program includes a component called XBIOS. It can be used with any 16-bit hard disk controller (the kind with two fingers that plug into the two connectors in an ISA or EISA input/output bus slot). Using XBIOS expands Disk Manager's capability to work with large hard disks.

XBIOS is a program that adds itself to DOS. Disk Manager knows how to find and use it instead of the BIOS interrupt number 13h program for reading or writing to the hard disk. IBM based their original design of the hard disk interface for the PC/XT on a Western Digital disk controller, but they did not choose to support in their BIOS the full range of disk size parameters that Western Digital supported.

The Western Digital controller design allows up to 12 bits for the cylinder number, instead of the 10 bits allowed for by INT 13h. The XBIOS program, in effect, modifies the BIOS limit from only permitting cylinders numbered 0 to 1023 to permitting them in the range 0 to 4095; it does nothing to evade the BIOS (INT 13h) limits on head and sector numbers.

This solution works only if you are using Disk Manager to partition your hard disk. It also is a bit peculiar in that you must read the program from your disk. But after it is read and linked into DOS and Disk Manager, the program changes how DOS reads the disk. The engineers at OnTrack had to be very clever to make it possible to read the disk in one way to find XBIOS and then in another way to use that same disk thereafter.

As often happens when someone is that clever, some other software turns out to be incompatible with it. Shortly after Microsoft's Windows Version 3.0 started shipping, people reported that they were losing all the data on their hard disks. The problem turned out to be an unfortunate interaction between OnTrack's clever software and the version of SMARTDRV.SYS that shipped with Windows 3.0.

That problem has now been solved. Indeed, in time, vendors can work out all such incompatibilities with patches to one or the other program. The more dependable method of evading these limits is to use a specially built hard disk controller.

Sector mapping

Remember that DOS at its highest levels views a disk as just a long string of sectors into which it can store information. Only as it gets ready to ask the BIOS

Chapter 7: Bumping Up Against and Breaking Barriers

to command the drive to do the actual disk access does it convert the logical sector number into a three-dimensional set of numbers for the actual cylinder, head, and physical sector to be addressed.

The hard disk controller can do something similar in reverse. It can take all the disk space on the actual physical disk drive and convert it to a single long list of sectors. Then it can convert a location in that list back into a fictitious cylinder, head, and sector address that it presents to DOS. This is called *head and sector translation,* or *sector mapping.*

> **TECHNICAL SECRET**
>
> Suppose that you have a drive that in its physical reality has 7 heads, 1,781 cylinders, and 54 sectors per track. (These are the dimensions of the Micropolis 1664-7 ESDI drive.) Multiplying this out, you will find that there are a total of 673,218 sectors. (With each sector holding 512 bytes, and remembering that a megabyte is 1,024KB, or 1,048,576 bytes, this drive has a formatted capacity of 328.7MB.)
>
> Now suppose that the hard disk controller pretended when communicating with the BIOS that the drive it was controlling had the maximum BIOS legal values of 16 heads and 63 sectors per track. This would make it appear to have 16 times 63, or 1,008, sectors per cylinder. That, in turn, would imply that the fictitious disk drive would have only 667 and a fraction cylinders, which is well within the DOS limit of 1,024 cylinders.
>
> The mapping is actually done this way: The first 54 sectors are put on the first track (cylinder 0, head 0). The next 9 sectors, which DOS thinks are still on that same track, are instead put on the next track (cylinder 0, head 1). What DOS thinks of as the second track (its cylinder 0, head 1) starts on cylinder 0, head 1 (the first 45 sectors) and finishes 18 sectors into cylinder 0, head 2, and so on (see Figure 7-1).

Sector mapping (also sometimes called sector translation) appeared in hard disk controllers in another context, before evading the physical limits was an issue. Some early software written for the PC "knew" that all disk drives had 17 sectors per track (as MFM drives do). These programs would not operate correctly with RLL drives, which have about 26 sectors per track. One solution was for the hard disk controller manufacturers to put in sector mapping.

> **TECHNICAL SECRET**
>
> For this purpose, manufacturers make the controller fool DOS in a direction opposite to that in the preceding example. Specifically, these controllers present to DOS a fictitious MFM drive with 17 sectors per track and, therefore, about 1.5 times as many tracks as the real drive has. That might be

Part I: The Hard Disk Companion

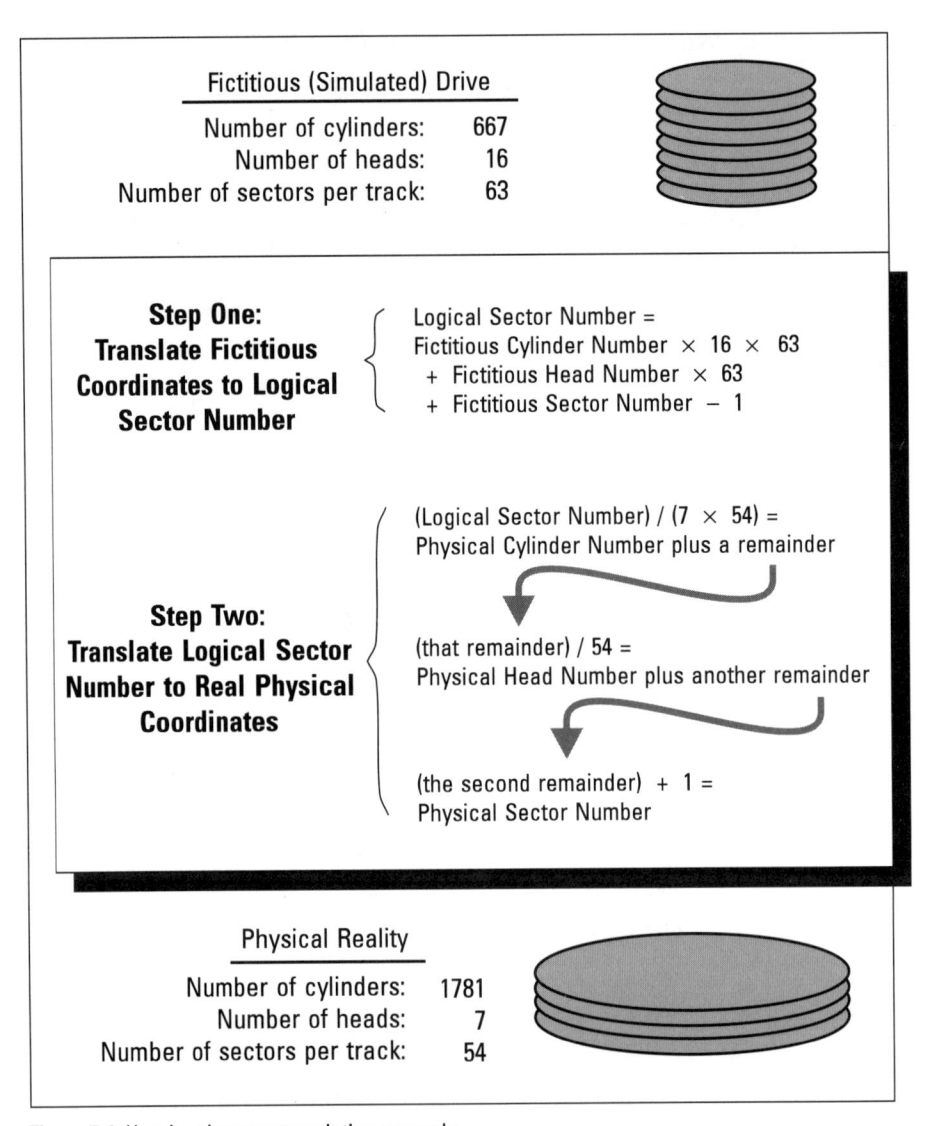

Fictitious (Simulated) Drive
Number of cylinders: 667
Number of heads: 16
Number of sectors per track: 63

Step One:
Translate Fictitious Coordinates to Logical Sector Number

Logical Sector Number =
Fictitious Cylinder Number × 16 × 63
+ Fictitious Head Number × 63
+ Fictitious Sector Number − 1

Step Two:
Translate Logical Sector Number to Real Physical Coordinates

(Logical Sector Number) / (7 × 54) =
Physical Cylinder Number plus a remainder

(that remainder) / 54 =
Physical Head Number plus another remainder

(the second remainder) + 1 =
Physical Sector Number

Physical Reality
Number of cylinders: 1781
Number of heads: 7
Number of sectors per track: 54

Figure 7-1: Head and sector translation example.

accomplished by pretending the drive had half again as many heads as it really had, or half again as many cylinders. As long as both those numbers stayed below the BIOS limits, it would not matter which way a disk controller designer chose to make the controller "lie."

Chapter 7: Bumping Up Against and Breaking Barriers

The advantage of having your hard disk controller lie in this manner is that your hard disk will appear to be a more standard, BIOS- and DOS-addressable disk. The drawback is that the BIOS, DOS, and all other programs don't know what the real disk dimensions are. For most of what DOS and DOS applications do, that does not matter. One case where it does matter is with sector-reinterleaving programs like SpinRite.

SpinRite and other sector-reinterleaving programs need to know exactly which sectors constitute a physical track on the real, underlying physical drive before they can reinterleave that track. Without real numbers for the drive dimensions, these programs simply cannot deliver all the benefits for which they were designed. (Which is not to say that they cannot still do some very useful things.)

Other controller-mapping strategies

Controllers are sometimes designed to do other kinds of mappings for a variety of reasons, one of which is to make the drive appear to have fewer defects than it really does. Another reason is to cram more data into less space.

TECHNICAL SECRET

The UltraStor 12F, and its caching sibling the 12C, is a typical modern ESDI controller (and a good choice to use with the Micropolis drive mentioned above). When you use it to do a low-level format, it will present you with many options.

One choice you have is whether to request Head Skewing. Head skewing adjusts the sector numbers from one track or cylinder to the adjacent ones, to allow for the time involved in head switching or in moving the heads from cylinder to cylinder (see Figure 3-3 and the discussion of head skewing in Chapter 3).

Spare Sector, another option, means that the controller will format the tracks of the drive with 55 sectors, but if all the sectors are good, it will only use the first 54. If any one sector on a track is bad, that one will be marked as such and ignored. The remaining sectors on that track will then have their physical sector numbers decreased by one (assuming 1:1 sector interleave).

That same controller also offers four choices for Sector Mapping: to make it present 17, 32, or 63 sectors per track, or the real number, which for the Micropolis 1664-7 drive is 54 sectors per track.

The reason for offering 17 sectors is clear: to make the drive appear to be a normal MFM drive. The reason for offering 63 sectors per track is also clear: 63 is the maximum number of sectors per track allowed according to the INT 13h design. Offering no translation allows programs access to the real, physical drive. The one strange option is 32 sectors per track. It turns out that some versions of DOS have an FDISK program that cannot deal with more than 32 sectors per track, so this option allows the maximum number of sectors that those versions of DOS can handle.

For drives with a capacity of more than 504MB, you must use Track Mapping, the next option, with DOS. That limit is what the official BIOS INT 13h interface design imposes. Track Mapping takes advantage of the head number loophole in the BIOS limits on disk size by artificially increasing the maximum head number enough to keep both sector and cylinder numbers in bounds, even for very large drives (although it still can only do this for drives no larger than 7.875GB total capacity).

Finally, the UltraStor 12F offers the option of 1,024 Cylinder Truncation, which merely means asking the controller to ignore any cylinders past number 1,023 that the drive may have. Using this option will make the controller present an acceptable drive to the BIOS but at the cost of not using a part of the drive's capacity.

The UltraStor 12F and 12C ESDI controllers are two good hard disk controllers that offer various kinds of mapping and translation strategies, and they are by no means the only ones. Many modern drives and controllers offer these features and in many different ways. Some do so to accommodate larger drives. Others translate in order to hide defects. And many of the latest designs absolutely must present the appearance of a drive with dimensions other than their real ones, simply because they cannot be described accurately by any single set of dimensions. (These latter drives are the ones that break the drive into zones — ranges of cylinder numbers — each having a different number of sectors per track.)

SCSI and IDE/ATA drives are examples of drives that do extensive sector mapping, and they often do it for several reasons. All modern SCSI and IDE/ATA drives are designed to appear perfect, and most of them use a zoned strategy to stuff the maximum possible amount of data into what is, in each design, a smaller space than in any previous design.

How can drives like this give the illusion that they are perfect? They do this by having a special extra pointer in each sector. If a given sector is good, that pointer will not be used. If it has some defect, this pointer will show where to find an alternate sector. These drives have several spare tracks and may have some spare sectors on each track. This approach permits these drives to appear to DOS as if they are perfect. CHKDSK, for example, will report no bad sectors at all for such a drive.

Sometimes (and this is the case for most IDE/ATA drives) this strategy is invoked only for defects that the manufacturer finds when the drive is first tested. Other drives (usually SCSI drives) are able to make "hot fixes," which means that they can reassign sectors on-the-fly, whenever the controller attached to the drive detects that a sector has gone bad.

Any drive that uses zone-bit recording always uses sector translation. This technique was mentioned in Chapters 2 and 3 as one used in some SCSI and IDE drives and sometimes on hard-disk cards to cram as many bytes on the drive as possible. The essence of this strategy is that the number of sectors per track is not constant from cylinder to cylinder. This *mandates* having the controller lie to DOS because everything in DOS assumes that whatever the number of sectors per track, at least it will be a constant for any one drive. For these drives, then, the controller must always do head and sector translation.

RAID and Related Strategies

Sector translation can enable you to use a disk that has too many cylinders or too many sectors per track, but it cannot help you if the total disk capacity exceeds the BIOS limit of 504MB or 7.875GB (which number you use depends on whether or not the head numbers are allowed to exceed 16). The XBIOS approach will enable you to use disks with up to 4,096 cylinders, which implies a maximum disk capacity of about 2GB or 32GB (again, depending on what is assumed about the maximum number of heads). Other vendors have created some specialized techniques like XBIOS, with different limits, but all of them are in the same general size range.

What if you want to use a disk with a really large capacity? And what if you need a single large volume that contains tens of gigabytes or more? You can't trick a PC into accepting such a large hard drive; there is no way to get a PC to accept a single hard disk drive that is this large. But you can attach multiple hard disks to a PC and thereby get almost any total storage capacity you want. Of the several ways to use this strategy, some are designed specifically to let you get the effect of a single, large hard drive, and others are more focused on enhancing the reliability of the disk subsystem in the PC.

Ever since the first XT, having either one or two hard disk drives attached to one disk controller in a PC has been completely standard. For nearly that long, it has been possible to have two controllers in a PC and, thus, a maximum of four hard disk drives.

Using two similar controllers has long been a possibility, but it is a rarely used option. Some, but not many, of the MFM, RLL, or ESDI disk controllers on the market are able to share a PC with another controller. For this sharing to work, only one of the controllers can have an active option ROM, and the two controllers must be addressed at different port address ranges.

The introduction of SCSI host adapters and SCSI hard drives presented some new possibilities. Every SCSI host adapter can be connected with up to seven SCSI slave devices. Each slave device could, in principle, serve a collection of up to eight logical devices. So one SCSI host adapter can, in theory, support up to 56 hard disk drives.

This possibility can't be achieved with most of the SCSI hard drives on the market because each of them has its own SCSI slave interface built in. But if someone were to build a suitable multiple-drive SCSI slave interface to ATA unit, you could connect up to eight IDE/ATA drives to it and up to seven of those interface units to a single SCSI host adapter. Furthermore, you can have more than one SCSI host adapter in a single PC. There seems to be no real limit on how many you can have, other than that you will run out of interrupt request levels (IRQs) and slots into which to plug them.

These multiple drive solutions all enable you to get a very much larger total disk storage capacity in your PC, but they do so by creating a large number of separate storage areas. At least at the hardware level, you have four key dimensions to specify whenever you want to access some data — the drive, cylinder, head, and physical sector numbers.

DOS, up until Version 5, only knew how to talk to two hard disk drives. DOS now is able to support up to seven physical drives. (And, of course, those drives may be divided up into 24 separate logical drives designated C through Z.) If you were to put 50 or more drives on your PC, DOS would have no way to assign drive letters to all of them.

The solution to this problem, and a way to get very large single logical DOS volumes, is to treat multiple physical drives as a single logical volume. Until recently, this solution was provided by using some third-party software drivers (such as VFeature Deluxe from Golden Bow Software). It will no doubt become one of the mainstream methods of attacking this problem after multigigabyte hard drives become common.

Another approach, and one that promises some additional benefits, is the group of schemes that go under the name RAID. This name is an acronym standing for Redundant Array of Inexpensive Disks. The whole notion is that it is cheaper and easier for manufacturers to build a multigigabyte storage subsystem by using a number of smaller drives rather than by trying to build one huge drive. Furthermore, by a careful choice of how the capacity of the overall system gets constructed from the individual drives, it is possible to produce an overall system that is more reliable than any of its component pieces. (This achievement is quite unusual. More often, when you combine parts, the whole is less reliable than any one of its parts.)

Five levels of RAID are formally defined. They range in complexity and in the specific features they offer. One strategy used in several of the levels is to split up each byte to be stored across several drives. By having the information stored in this way and by using some sufficiently competent error correction codes, it becomes possible to recover all the information with pretty high reliability — even if one of the drives completely dies.

Some of the RAID implementations further allow you to do a "hot swap" — to replace a dead disk drive while all the rest continue to work. Properly implemented and properly maintained, these schemes promise storage subsystems with an effectively infinite mean time between failures (MTBF).

So maybe the modern (post DOS 4) limit to the size of a logical volume (2TB) isn't quite so fantastically large after all. Certainly, we won't be seeing PCs with DOS logical volumes anywhere near that large for a while. But stop and think. Today we have 1GB drives (and they are actually quite common). And just 12 years ago, when the PC was introduced, the largest on-line magnetic storage system available for a PC (the single-sided floppy disk drives) held only 160KB. If that rate of progress continues, in less than ten more years we will be pushing the 2TB disk volume as hard as we used to be pushing the 32MB limit.

Error Messages

Earlier, you learned about the several layers of programs in your PC. Requests for action filter down from the top level and finally, at the bottom, get turned into commands to hardware. At any stage in this process, the module that is asked to do something could decide to respond to the requestor with some message (perhaps declaring success or failure, or explaining why it cannot do what it was asked to do). These messages are passed back up the same chain in reverse order (see Figure 7-2).

Any layer can generate an error message if it fails to understand the request it received from above. An error message also results if the hardware fails to operate correctly or if the layer in question cannot perform its task for some other reason.

Each level of program can react to an error message in several ways: it can ignore the message; it can decide to pose its request again in hopes that this time it might succeed; or it can decide to try something different.

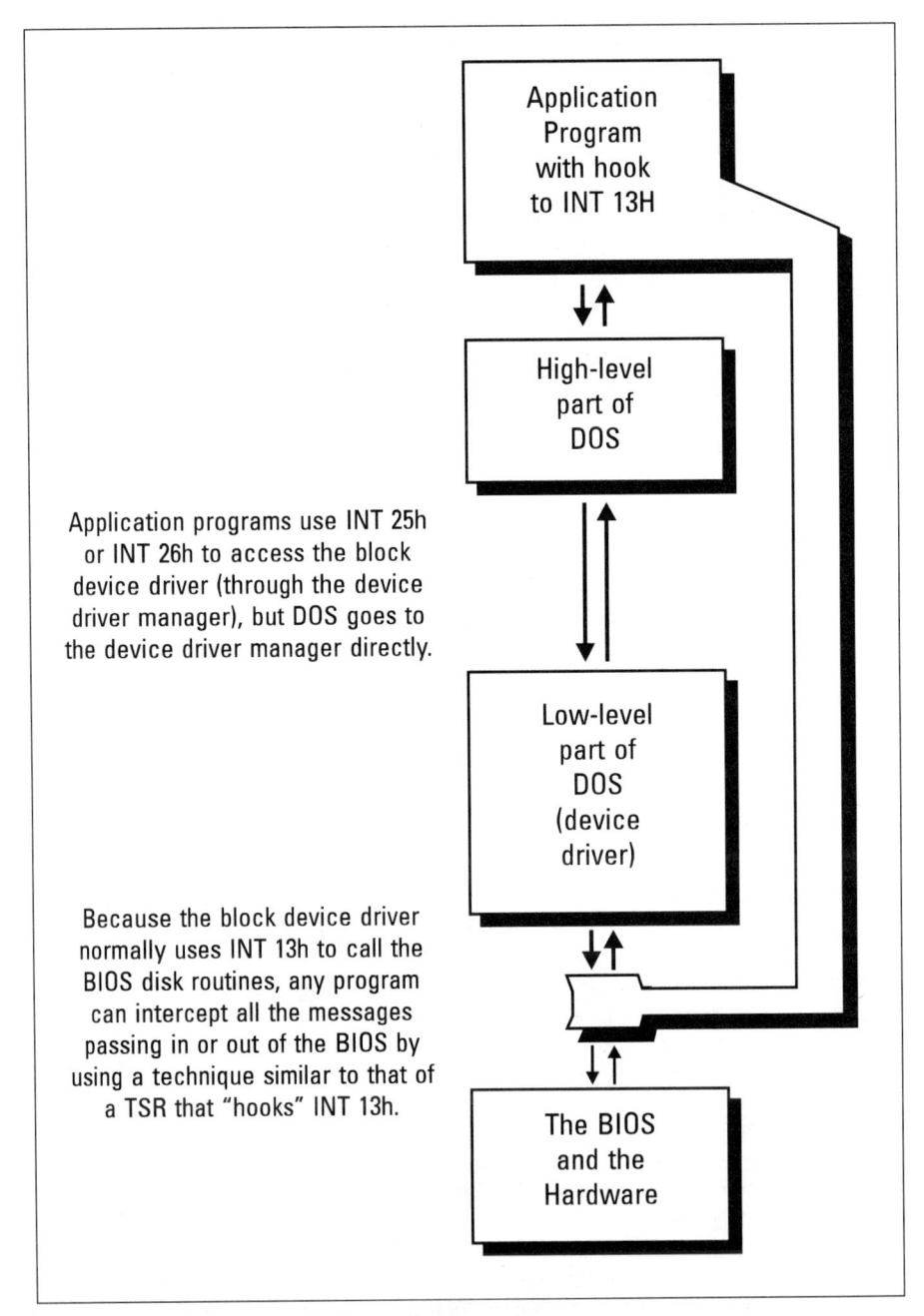

```
                                    ┌──────────────┐
                                    │ Application  │
                                    │   Program    │
                                    │  with hook   │
                                    │  to INT 13H  │
                                    └──────────────┘
                                          ↕
                                    ┌──────────────┐
                                    │  High-level  │
                                    │   part of    │
                                    │     DOS      │
                                    └──────────────┘
  Application programs use INT 25h        ↕
  or INT 26h to access the block    ┌──────────────┐
  device driver (through the device │  Low-level   │
  driver manager), but DOS goes to  │   part of    │
  the device driver manager directly.│    DOS      │
                                    │   (device    │
                                    │   driver)    │
                                    └──────────────┘
                                          ↕
  Because the block device driver
  normally uses INT 13h to call the
  BIOS disk routines, any program
  can intercept all the messages
  passing in or out of the BIOS by
  using a technique similar to that of
  a TSR that "hooks" INT 13h.
                                    ┌──────────────┐
                                    │   The BIOS   │
                                    │   and the    │
                                    │   Hardware   │
                                    └──────────────┘
```

Figure 7-2: Hooking an interrupt to intercept error messages.

Chapter 7: Bumping Up Against and Breaking Barriers

The actions most relevant to the discussion in this book are requests to the hard disk drive (or to its controller) to read or write data on the disk. These processes can fail in many ways. For each failure mode, there is an error message that the controller will send to the BIOS, which in turn will send it on to DOS, which may or may not send it on to you or your application program.

TECHNICAL SECRET

The drive may be asked to position the heads over a particular cylinder ("seek" to that cylinder). The controller may attempt this action and then find that it was unsuccessful. The usual recovery procedure from this error is to recalibrate the drive (seek to cylinder zero) and then try again to seek the desired cylinder.

The controller may be asked to read a particular sector. Two kinds of error can occur in this process. One is that the sector header cannot be found or, if found, its cyclical redundancy check (CRC) may be invalid. That message means it is not possible to be sure that you are where you thought you were on the drive. Again, a recalibration followed by a retry is an appropriate response.

The other kind of error in reading is that the controller may find the sector header, but the data it read may turn out to be inconsistent with the error correction codes (ECC) that were also read. This case further subdivides, depending on whether the ECC seem adequate to correct the data. Either way, a retry may be the simplest way to deal with this problem. At some point, if the ECC are adequate, it may be easier (and quicker) to use them to correct the data. If the controller uses the ECC, it must pass along the corrected data with a message that says it had to use ECC.

If the program receiving an error message chooses simply to repeat its request, when does it stop retrying? Most often the BIOS will ask the hard disk controller to retry several times to read a sector that it could not find. Then if it must, the BIOS will accept defeat and tell DOS that it didn't find the sector. At this point, DOS may ask the BIOS to ask the controller to try again. Then another round of retries starts. Because DOS may make that request of the BIOS several times, and each time the BIOS may force the controller to try again several times, the total number of retries quickly escalates to a large number. Hundreds of retries are not unusual.

Finally, DOS may decide to accept defeat. Two things may happen next. Most of the time, DOS will announce defeat with a brief message and then give its infamous choice, `Abort, Retry, or Ignore` (or `Abort, Retry, Ignore or Fail`, or `Abort, Retry, or Fail` — the exact phrase depends on the DOS version). Alternatively, if the request for that sector's data came from a modern, sophisticated application program, it may intercept the DOS message of defeat and do whatever that program's designers thought appropriate. They could even ask DOS to try again, thus forcing several hundred more retries.

There is one case where DOS is neither so diligent nor so informative. That is when the ECC seem adequate for reconstructing data initially read incorrectly. Then no retries are called for. DOS simply accepts the reconstructed data as gospel truth, without informing the application to which it delivers the data about the original error.

This case is most unfortunate. It hides from you what may be impending doom, only revealing it when a disaster is already upon you. Fortunately, even a DOS application can "go behind DOS" and intercept the error messages from the disk controller before they are masked.

This intercept is done, simply enough, by putting some code into the DOS application that loads an address inside itself into the interrupt vector table in the location for interrupt 13h (INT 13h). Then whenever DOS would have asked the BIOS to access the disk drive, it will instead ask the special bit of code in the application to do the job.

DOS will not know that the intercept is happening; it simply issues the INT 13h call. The CPU finds the address of the application code miniprogram instead of the previous INT 13h interrupt service routine and, therefore, the CPU calls the application program as if it were the ISR. The miniprogram doesn't have to know how to do any real disk access. Rather than performing the requested task, all the program has to do is call on the BIOS at whatever address the BIOS had originally inserted into the interrupt vector table at those locations.

Why put a program in the way if it doesn't do anything but pass along a request? Because doing that puts your program in the path along which the system returns any messages about the results of that request to the higher level programs. Your program will get those results before DOS has a chance to receive and perhaps ignore them (see Figure 6-12).

SpinRite and other disk-reinterleaving programs hook INT13h for exactly this reason (among others). These programs can then see any place on the disk where there is a struggle to get data back. They can then move the reconstructed data to some safer place before the problems become insurmountable.

Chapter 7: Bumping Up Against and Breaking Barriers

Summary

- A feature of the BIOS design in the original IBM PC, which has been copied to every PC made since then, limits the number of heads, cylinders, and sectors per track for a hard disk. These "official" limits imply that no hard disk attached to a PC can have a capacity in excess of 504MB.

- A widely used "cheat" allows head numbers all the way up to 255. That implies a hard disk size limit of 7.875GB.

- In addition to the physical size limitation, DOS imposes a logical size limitation. No disk volume (single drive letter) could contain more than 32MB for any of the standard versions of DOS prior to 3.3. This size limitation was raised in DOS Version 4.0 to 2TB (about 2.2 million million bytes).

- Before DOS 3.3, certain computer makers had customized DOS to allow their customers to use larger-than 32MB logical disk volumes. Some did this by making their FORMAT program create larger-than 512-byte logical sectors (the physical sectors stayed at their original 512-byte size). COMPAQ introduced a different strategy with its DOS 3.31, the same strategy used by Microsoft in MS-DOS Version 4.0 and all later versions, to allow very large disk volumes.

- DOS 3.3 allows partitioning a large physical drive into many modest-sized (32MB) logical volumes. This is a sufficient solution for most people's needs.

- Prior to DOS 3.3, various third-party disk-partitioning programs allowed users to create logical volumes beyond C that were larger than 32MB. These solutions were all made obsolete with the introduction of DOS 4. Many PCs still have the third-party drivers installed, unnecessarily. Owners of such a PC would be well served to redo their disk partitioning to eliminate those drivers.

- You can only fully use disks with more than 1,024 cylinders in a PC if you somehow evade the physical size limitation. This "evasion" can be done by using a BIOS addition or by using a translating disk controller. The latter approach is generally preferable because it is invisible to almost all software.

- More than one hard disk can be attached to a single PC. Two is common, but more are possible. The new RAID strategies allow using many disk drives to get both higher capacity and higher reliability.

- Most programs get the hardware in your PC to work by passing request messages down through several layers of software. Response messages return up the same chain. DOS, to keep users from seeing more than it thinks they need to know, filters out certain disk error messages. This filtering can be most unfortunate because it could lead to loss of data if you don't know about an impending disk failure at an early enough stage to move your data to safety.

- Any DOS program that wants to see those messages can get access to them by hooking interrupt 13h. SpinRite is one example of such a program; by using these programs, you can protect yourself against data loss from many kinds of premature disk death.

Now you know all the essential facts about how MS-DOS treats hard disks. In the next three chapters, you will learn how to prepare a hard disk for use under DOS, and to a lesser extent, what that process is like under the UNIX, OS/2, Windows NT, and Novell NetWare operating systems.

Chapter 8

Preparing a Hard Disk to Store Information Step One: The Physical (Low-Level) Format

In This Chapter
- Why a hard disk is useless until it has had some essential magnetic information written to its data-storage areas in a process called formatting the disk
- The three phases or steps in which this formatting is done (although you may not have to do all three steps yourself)
- How to do the first phase, called low-level formatting, with details on what that step does to the disk, and some rather weird variations used in low-level formatting by certain hard disk controllers

What Is Disk Formatting?

You now know how hard disks work and how MS-DOS works with them. Before any hard disk can work with DOS, though, you need to prepare the hard disk. As it comes from the factory, a hard disk is incapable of storing any information because it lacks any organizing magnetic marks on the platter surfaces.

Putting those organizing marks on the platter surface is the first of three steps in an overall process that must be taken before a disk is usable by DOS — the process called *formatting* a disk. This chapter describes the overall process and then explains in detail the first of the three necessary steps.

Remember that the hard disk controller looks for sectors of information. It expects each sector to be complete with sector headers containing address information and a valid cyclical redundancy check (CRC), plus a data area and the corresponding error correction codes (ECC). The hard disk controller anticipates that this information will be encoded according to its particular data-encoding method (such as MFM, RLL, or ARLL). But before the drive is "properly introduced" to the controller, no such information exists on the disk.

The first job in preparing a hard disk is to get the controller to record the skeleton of the data pattern for which it will look. This is called a *physical format* (or a *low-level format*). After the drive has the necessary structure into which to store information, you must take it through *partitioning* and *logical* (or *high-level*) *formatting* to make it usable with DOS.

A Three-Step Process (and an Analogy)

To understand the three-level process of preparing a hard disk, consider this analogy: A new hard drive is much like a brand new parking lot — each has a vast expanse of potential storage space. In a parking lot, you first put down marks to show people where to park their cars, analogous to providing a physical format on the disk. Then you may divide the lot with fences to separate different groups of drivers (such as customers and employees) just as you partition a hard disk.

Next, you might provide a valet parking service (just as DOS "parks" your files on a disk), which requires a place to keep keys. And you need a directory of the owners' names and the stall number where each car is parked, much like the directory created by a high-level format. In this way, you can know which stalls are empty and where to find each person's car.

Although most cars are about the same size, files on your disk may be large or small. Stretching the analogy a bit to fit this discussion, you could assume that sometimes a group of cars will come together, and the leader of the group will specify when the whole group will leave. The valet parking directory will show the location of only the group leader's car. Some other table showing which spaces are available and which are occupied will indicate which cars are in which groups. Figure 8-1 shows a whimsical representation of this analogy.

Chapter 8: Preparing a Hard Disk to Store Information: Step 1

Figure 8-1: An analogy to show how information is stored on a hard disk.

Three Ways to Do Physical Formatting

There are at least three ways to impose a low-level format on a hard disk, but whichever of these options you choose, in the end they amount to the same thing. The first way is to use a special program provided by the controller's manufacturer on a diskette. The second way is to run a program in the BIOS extensions ROM on the controller or in the motherboard BIOS ROM. The third way is to use a third-party program (which will, in turn, activate the BIOS ROM program).

Some controllers come with a disk that has a low-level formatting program on it. IBM included a program with this function on an Advanced Diagnostic diskette shipped with the Technical Reference Manual for each model of PC, and it is on the Reference Diskette shipped with each model of PS/2. (To access the special, advanced options menu on those Reference Diskettes, press Ctrl-A at the main menu.)

Some controllers use a program that is permanently on the card in its BIOS extension ROM (read-only memory) chip. Typically, you run this program by using the DOS program DEBUG. At DEBUG's hyphen prompt, type **G=C800:5** and press Enter. If your hard disk controller has its option ROM located at an address other than C8000h, substitute that address (omitting the final zero) in this command. In some cases, the final number is not 5. If so, this command will do nothing. If after you enter this command you simply get another hyphen prompt, press Q and then Enter. That will bail you out of DEBUG, taking you back to the DOS prompt. Now contact the controller manufacturer for further instructions if you want to use this approach.

You also might use some third-party disk set-up software such as Disk Manager or SpeedStor. They come with simple directions. You will want to notice, however, that the simplest way to run one of these programs may let it do more than you want. Use Disk Manager in its Manual mode, for example, to keep it from doing all parts of the disk preparation. (In Chapter 9, you will learn why you very likely do *not* want to let these programs do all this work.)

Each of these three methods simply asks the controller to place a physical format pattern on the disk. In response to that request, the controller moves the head assembly from the innermost cylinder to the outermost, one cylinder at a time. At each cylinder position, the controller switches on one head at a time, stepping through all the heads before going on to the next cylinder position. For each cylinder and head, it records a full track of information in the format it will need to find whenever it reads or writes additional data.

Chapter 8: Preparing a Hard Disk to Store Information: Step 1

> **TECHNICAL SECRET**
>
> By starting the low-level formatting at the inside cylinder, the controller provides the maximum amount of time before it gets to the outer cylinders, which is where DOS puts the most critical data on your drive — the file allocation tables and root directory. Without the information in them, you cannot get at any of the rest of your data. If, therefore, you discover part way through the low-level formatting process that you really did not want to format your drive, you can stop the process in time to save some of your data. (Redoing a low-level format wipes out all your data.)
>
> The original hard disk controllers for PCs did their low-level formatting in precisely the opposite manner, wiping out the most critical data immediately. The controller makers changed this after too many users came to too much grief and suffered too many near heart attacks. Be glad if you have a modern hard disk controller. Consider getting one if you don't.

This low-level format is done one track at a time. Usually, you can command the controller to do this for a single track, and sometimes for the whole drive. Some third-party software (such as Disk Manager) will allow you to do it for a range of cylinders as well. This just means these programs repeat the command for the controller to format a single track until the track under each head over the specified range of cylinders is formatted.

A very important point to remember is that *only* at the time of this low-level format does the controller write the sector headers. It also writes the data sections of the sectors (filling them with some dummy data and the corresponding ECC). The sector headers, of course, are read to find where to read or write data, but those headers are never again rewritten.

(If you are familiar with SpinRite, you may have thought: "Oh, yeah? SpinRite rewrites the sector headers. That is not the same as a low-level format because my data doesn't get wiped out." The fact is that SpinRite must ask the controller to redo the low-level format on a track if it is going to rewrite the sector headers. It simply manages to keep all your data in memory and replace it afterwards, so you think it didn't wipe out anything. Chapters 12 and 14 go over all this in more detail.)

Only the controller can do it

Only the controller can actually format the disk at this lowest level, which means that the controller's design dictates the way the format is carried out. Each controller design accomplishes low-level formatting differently. (If a controller lacks the capability to perform low-level formatting, no program can make the controller do it.)

Part I: The Hard Disk Companion

/ TECHNICAL SECRET /

All PC *floppy* disk controllers, on the other hand, perform low-level formatting in the same way (for disks of that size and capacity) — in part because there is only one standard set of integrated circuit chips used in the design of floppy disk controllers. More important, though, it reflects our need to be able to take a disk formatted on one PC and use it on any other PC. Because hard disks stay put, they do not share this requirement.

Some hard disks are removable. They work with only those PCs that have the same special hardware in them. You cannot take a Tandon AdPac removable disk pack, for example, and insert it into a MegaDrive system and expect the system to work.

Different controllers sometimes put the head, cylinder, and physical sector numbers into the sector headers in varying order. They may further differ on their choice of the formula by which they compute ECC, on where they put the bad sector flag, and on any other information they may put in the sector header. Finally, even for controllers of the same nominal sort (RLL, for example), they also may differ on precisely how they encode data. The result of all this individuality is that you must redo the low-level format on a drive each time you attach it to a new controller.

/ TECHNICAL SECRET /

At least you must redo the low-level format each time you attach the drive to a new kind of hard disk controller. Naturally, all the Tandon AdPac controllers, for example, must be sufficiently alike so that you can switch AdPac disk packs between them successfully. Being able to move data that way is the main selling point for any removable hard drive, creating a crucial limitation on the design of their controllers. Other makers, without those restraints, seem to change their low-level format patterns nearly every time they introduce a new model, and sometimes more often.

PerStor hard disk controllers are unusual in a couple of ways. For one thing, they are an exception to the generalization just stated. Another, related way, is that they store information with twice the density of normal MFM drives (even more densely than RLL drives). They number their physical sectors starting with zero (instead of one, as the BIOS normally expects) and then hide this fact from the BIOS. These tricks enable a PerStor controller to recognize the low-level format of a drive formatted by any other PerStor controller. You even can move a drive formatted on a PerStor XT controller to a PerStor AT controller.

Because they are so unusual, you may have to inform SpinRite if you are using it on a PerStor controller. You do this with a special command-line parameter. Then SpinRite will recognize the controller's quirks and deal with

Chapter 8: Preparing a Hard Disk to Store Information: Step 1

it accordingly. (You may be able to run SpinRite without this special command-line parameter, but if it complains in any way, try it again with the special parameter.)

CAUTION: Please understand: Redoing the low-level format on a hard drive utterly destroys previously recorded data. (The most insidious computer viruses order the hard disk controller to redo the low-level format on one or all of your hard drives.)

TECHNICAL SECRET

Some data-recovery specialists claim to be able to detect the residual magnetism in the disk surface. They say they can (at least sometimes) recover data even after the data have been written over, whether by a low-level format or by a simple copying of one file on top of another. This possibility worries the government enough that when national security is at stake, the government specifies that files should be erased by writing over them many times with many different (prescribed) data patterns. Still, for all normal purposes, after a file or a disk full of data is written over, that information is gone for good.

Generally, DOS does not destroy data with its high-level, or logical, format (although some versions of DOS do). This fact is what makes it possible to create utility programs that let you "unformat" (undo the high-level format of) a drive (more on this in Chapter 11).

Disk reinterleaving programs, such as SpinRite, introduced the capability to redo the low-level format on a drive without destroying the data stored there. *This is not the same as undoing the low-level format.* These programs refresh the sector header information, without requiring you first to back up the data on the disk and afterward redo the disk partitioning and high-level format, as well as restore the backed-up data.

In essence, disk reinterleaving programs do this by making a copy of the data on one track at a time. Then they ask the controller to reformat just that one track. They test the newly formatted track to be sure that it can safely hold the data and then put the original data back. This is not really an exception to the rule that the low-level format wipes out the data. These programs just keep a copy long enough to replace it after the reformatting is complete. The data they replace includes the DOS high-level format information, which lets you avoid both the reformatting and the backup/restore cycle.

Some weird alternative formats

Although almost every hard disk controller has its own idiosyncratic approach to performing a low-level format, some take a weirder tack than others. The following are some examples.

Certain disk/controller combinations

Some manufacturers who ship controllers and drives already matched together put the low-level format on their drives at the factory and do everything in their power to prevent anyone from redoing that low-level format. For these drive and controller combinations, it does not matter whether a program like SpeedStor asks it to do a low-level format in preparation for the initial storage of data, or whether SpinRite asks it to do so as a means of increasing the data-transfer rate or improving the integrity of data already stored; the controller simply will refuse to do the job. And if the controller won't do it for you, no one can.

> **TECHNICAL SECRET**
>
> The Hardcard series of products from Quantum does two things that led the company to refuse to allow other programs to redo their low-level formats. One is zone recording, in which Quantum puts more sectors per track on the outer tracks than on the inner ones. The other is spare-sector mapping, in which the company replaces defective sectors with some otherwise-unused sectors to make the drive appear to have no defects, at least when the drive is shipped from the factory. Engineers at Quantum think these special strategies justify denying anyone but them the right to do a low-level format on their drives.
>
> Most IDE and SCSI drives use similar strategies. They often also prevent any programs from redoing their low-level formats.
>
> Another interesting and strange example is what Toshiba does on the hard drives in its laptop computers. This strategy is called *head multiplexing*, a strategy employed to fit the maximum data possible on some small hard drives and yet make them look to the computer as if they are standard MFM drives. Toshiba found that it could put 34 sectors on each track. That strategy doubles the data on each track, but if the BIOS knew what had been done, it would not see the drive as standard.
>
> The engineers solved that problem by making the controller do something special. When the BIOS tells the controller to read a particular sector number for a particular head number, the controller translates the requested location into a real location by using the following translation rule: First, double the requested sector number and add one, if the head number is odd, to get the real sector number. Then divide the requested head number by two and discard any remainder to get the real head number. If, for example, you tell the computer to read sector 5 for head 0, it will actually read sector 10 for head 0. If you tell it to read sector 15 for head 1, it will actually read sector 31 for head 0.

Chapter 8: Preparing a Hard Disk to Store Information: Step 1

The most unusual aspect of this translation rule is that logical heads 0 and 1 share the top surface instead of each head having a surface to itself. Logical head 0 gets to use every other sector on the track and logical head 1 gets to use the rest. The disk appears, then, to have only 17 sectors per track, as any normal MFM drive does.

Of course, there is only one physical head for each surface. Toshiba simply pretends that the head is sometimes logical head n and at other times logical head $n+1$.

The low-level format for a track on the top surface, then, can only be done once for both logical heads 0 and 1. Toshiba thinks this unusual treatment means that it should deny all programs the right to do a low-level format on its laptop computer's hard drives. Unfortunately, it doesn't *prevent* a program from doing the low-level format, nor does it force the low-level format pattern to come out right for you. Programs that might want to do the low-level format on Toshiba laptop computer hard disks need to recognize this problem and avoid doing anything dangerous.

Some autoconfiguring hard disk controllers

Some autoconfiguring hard disk controllers take a slightly less weird formatting approach. They put the drive dimensions in a special place on the drive, somewhere within the normal data area but "out of sight." For example, they may put those dimensions in a special, tiny sector located on one of the data tracks, in addition to the usual sectors for that track.

These controllers may allow you to request a low-level format of any track you want. If you are imprudent enough to do so on the track containing their special disk dimension table, you will most likely wipe it out, possibly rendering the whole drive inaccessible.

TECHNICAL SECRET

More than one program author has been tripped up by the hard disk controllers that allow you to wipe out their knowledge of the disk's dimensions. Steve Gibson discovered this behavior early in his work in SpinRite, so he carefully designed SpinRite to watch out for these controllers. That makes it safe for you to use it with any controller.

One situation in which it is unsafe to use SpinRite is if you have partitioned your disk with a version of Priam's EVDR.SYS program earlier than Version 5.0. In that one case, you must be sure not to use SpinRite on your system — as the SpinRite documentation well notes.

Almost all other autoconfiguring controllers put the drive dimension information on some cylinder that is safely out of harm's way, where only the controller can access it, and then only for that one purpose. These controllers won't let you destroy their drive dimension table no matter what you request.

TECHNICAL SECRET

Perhaps the weirdest solution is what Western Digital uses on some of its controllers. These engineers noticed that a part of the master boot record is always left empty. This sector, which is also called the Partition Table, is the very first sector on the disk. (The nature and use of this sector is discussed in detail in the next chapter.) Western Digital decided to use that unused space.

The Western Digital controllers that use this strategy put the drive dimensions into the middle of this blank space in the master boot record. Then they make the controller hide that information from view. If you read or write that sector, the controller will make you think that area contains zeros. Only the controller can read or change the actual numbers stored there, and it will only do so for its purposes — not for yours. As long as no program tries to store information there, you will never know the controller is doing this.

Summary

- Formatting means preparing a disk for use. All disks must be formatted before DOS can store and retrieve information on them.
- Hard disks have to be taken through three separate steps before they are fully formatted and ready to use. The first is called the low-level, or physical, format. The second is partitioning, and the third is the high-level, or logical, format.
- A low-level format may be put on a disk in one of three ways: by running a hard disk-preparation program supplied by the disk controller manufacturer, by running a similar program that may be built into the BIOS extensions ROM on the controller card or on the PC's motherboard, or by using a third-party disk-preparation and management program.
- All three ways to do the low-level format actually use the same underlying process; each is merely a front-end to the disk controller's internal low-level formatting capability.
- Some hard disks come from the factory with a low-level format already written on them. These drives necessarily come with a matching controller. Examples include hard disks on an option card, SCSI drives, IDE/ATA drives, and a few ESDI, RLL, or MFM, drive/controller combination kits.
- The formatting on some preformatted disks can be destroyed if a user (or program) attempts to redo the low level format. Most preformatted hard disks protect themselves and will refuse to do an actual low-level format except in response to special commands only the factory knows how to issue.

In this chapter, you learned about the first step that must be taken to prepare a new disk drive for use with DOS. In the next chapter, you learn about the second step, called Partitioning.

Chapter 9

Preparing a Hard Disk to Store Information Step Two: Partitioning

In This Chapter

▶ What partitioning a hard disk means and why PC hard disks must be partitioned

▶ The regions into which a PC hard disk is divided by partitioning

▶ How DOS keeps track of hard disk partitions

▶ What an extended partition table is and when it is used

▶ How you can see what partitions and logical volumes your disk has now

▶ How you can change that partitioning

▶ An important warning about an all-too-easy-to-make mistake when using the DOS command FDISK

▶ What typical third-party disk-partitioning software does

▶ Why you may not want to use third-party disk-partitioning software

▶ A novel way to put your personal identification onto your hard disk where almost no one will find it, but you can easily do so any time you need to prove that your PC is yours

Why PC Hard Disks Need to Be Partitioned

After you finish the *low-level format,* the disk is ready to store information. In other words, the controller that put the low-level format on the disk is thereby enabled to find any specified location and write whatever it may be told to put there. It also can find and return that data on command.

The low-level format is enough, as far as the hard disk controller is concerned, but it is far from enough for the purposes of DOS. Before you store files on an MS-DOS computer, you must *partition* the disk and perform the *high-level format.* Referring back to the parking lot analogy, one might say that the parking stalls have been defined, but some fences still need to be erected and a valet-parking booth needs to be established.

Floppy diskettes don't have partitions. The designers of DOS could have avoided requiring partitions for hard disks, but they did require them mostly because of the high price of hard disk drives when PCs (and DOS) were very young, about a decade ago. Back then, the designers of DOS felt they had to accommodate users who might want to install more than one of the several competing operating systems, including Microsoft's and IBM's DOS, Softech's P-system, and Digital Research's CP/M-86. They did so by allowing each operating system to use a portion, or *partition,* of the very costly hard disk.

Hard disks today cost about 1 percent as much per megabyte as they did during DOS's infancy. Committing a disk to only one operating system is a whole lot less extravagant now than it was then, but the PC design still requires hard disk partitioning for compatibility with earlier BIOS and DOS versions.

Carving Up the Disk

Partitioning means dividing into parts. Most of your disk is divided into partitions in which you can store files of information. Your computer, however, will not know about or be able to use these parts unless there is a special, "introductory" section on the disk. This section, which comes at the very beginning of the disk (starting at cylinder number 0, head number 0, physical sector number 1), holds something called the *master boot record* (MBR). This one-sector long program is often referred to by the name of a data table it contains: the *partition table.*

The very end of the disk usually contains one or two other special-purpose parts. These parts are the *diagnostic cylinder* and, with some controllers, a "secret" cylinder for storing the drive dimensions.

Figure 9-1 shows these three major sections into which partitioning divides a disk (the master boot record, the middle part, and the diagnostic cylinder plus "secret" cylinder if any). The figure also shows some ways you can further subdivide the middle part.

The master boot record and partition table

The very first sector on a hard drive (cylinder 0, head 0, physical sector 1) is called the *master boot record,* or the *partition table.* This sector is called the partition table because it contains a data table that specifies regions, called partitions, into which the bulk of the hard disk is divided. The sector is also called the master boot record because it contains the program that reads this table, goes to the correct partition, and loads another boot sector from the very beginning of that partition.

Chapter 9: Preparing a Hard Disk to Store Information: Step 2

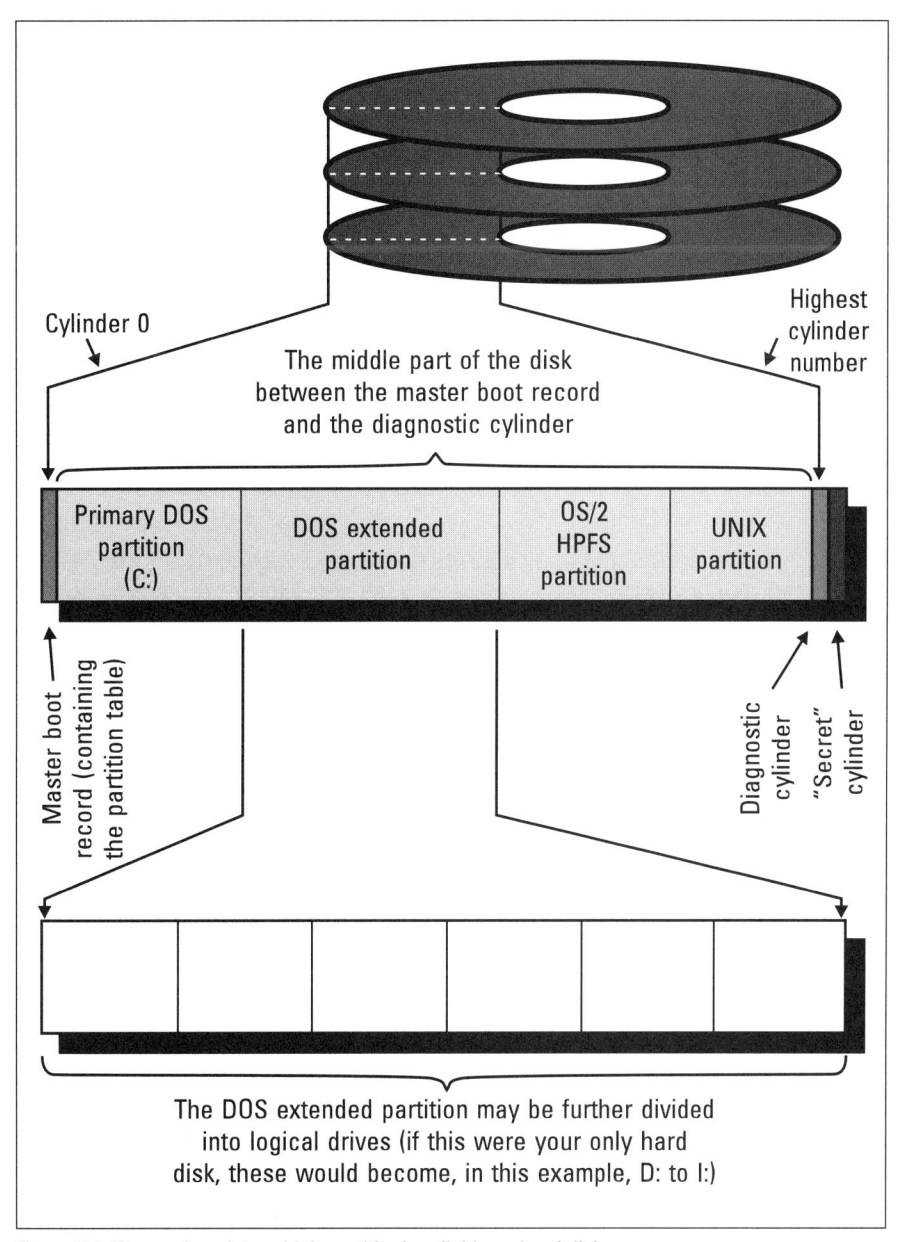

Figure 9-1: The regions into which partitioning divides a hard disk.

If this partition is a bootable DOS partition, the program portion of the boot sector at the start of the partition will be identical to the program portion of the boot sector on any DOS disk or diskette. If that partition is, for example, a UNIX partition, the boot sector will contain the standard UNIX boot program.

Part I: The Hard Disk Companion

> **TECHNICAL SECRET**
>
> The master boot record takes up only a single sector (cylinder 0, head 0, sector 1). DOS Version 2.x allocates only that one sector for the master boot record; the disk's first partition under that version of DOS starts in the very next sector (cylinder 0, head 0, sector 2). Beginning with Version 3.0, in recognition of the generally larger size of hard disks and to keep things simpler for itself, DOS "wastes" the rest of the first track. Thus, the first partition on disks that use modern DOS versions starts at cylinder 0, head 1, sector 1.
>
> There are some hard disk controllers that make use of this waste space; most do not. Western Digital, for example, has used this space with some models of its controllers to hold disk dimension information. Some antivirus programs put a copy of the MBR into another sector on that first track so they can later copy it back if the original MBR becomes infected. And some viruses copy the MBR to a sector midway down the track or put their own code there.
>
> If portions of that track are not used, you can put anything you like there; but check first to be sure that it is unused. The remainder of that track will not be used if all the following conditions are true:
>
> - Your controller does not use the rest of the track.
>
> - You don't use the portions of the track that are needed by any antivirus program you have.
>
> - You don't use any portions of the track that are likely to be overwritten by any virus your computer might contract.
>
> What might you put there? The last section of this chapter has some suggestions.
>
> If you have two physical hard disks, the master boot record program on the first one is what reads the data table on both of them. Still, both drives will have the full MBR program as well as its associated partition table. This means that you won't even find out about any accident that messes up the MBR program (but not the partition table) in the first sector of the second physical drive unless you go looking for the damage with some disk-snooping tool, such as the Norton Utilities Disk Editor program. On the other hand, such an accident will not harm you in any way, unless you should later attempt to use that hard disk as the first physical drive in a PC.

You can display the contents of this sector by using the DOS command DEBUG or any of a number of other programs. The Disk Editor program in the Norton Utilities (Version 5 and later) is a particularly good choice. One reason is that because it automatically starts up in a read-only mode, you will have less chance of damaging the MBR while you look at it. Another reason is that, if you turn off its read-only protection, this program can very easily be used to write a

Chapter 9: Preparing a Hard Disk to Store Information: Step 2

copy of the MBR to a file (or later on, if you know your hard disk's MBR is damaged, you can restore it from that file).

The MH-SAVE program on the *Hard Disk SECRETS* disk saves the entire first track of each hard disk, just in case your controller made some use of that "waste" space. The companion MH-RESTR program can put back on the hard disk the entire first track, just the MBR portion of the track, or just the "non-MBR" remainder of the track.

A DEBUG-style display of any file or region of memory looks something like that shown in Figure 9-2. This is the actual contents of a real MBR that was created by DOS 5 on my main computer's 1GB SCSI hard disk (a Micropolis model 1598-15).

```
Relative     Data bytes (in hexadecimal notation)              Data in ASCII
address

0000  FA 33 C0 8E D0 BC 00 7C-8B F4 50 07 50 1F FB FC   .3.....|..P.P...
0010  BF 00 06 B9 00 01 F2 A5-EA 1D 06 00 00 BE BE 07   ................
0020  B3 04 80 3C 80 74 0E 80-3C 00 75 1C 83 C6 10 FE   ...<.t..<.u.....
0030  CB 75 EF CD 18 8B 14 8B-4C 02 8B EE 83 C6 10 FE   .u......L.......
0040  CB 74 1A 80 3C 00 74 F4-BE 8B 06 AC 3C 00 74 0B   .t..<.t.....<.t.
0050  56 BB 07 00 B4 0E CD 10-5E EB F0 EB FE BF 05 00   V.......^.......
0060  BB 00 7C B8 01 02 57 CD-13 5F 73 0C 33 C0 CD 13   ..|...W.._s.3...
0070  4F 75 ED BE A3 06 EB D3-BE C2 06 BF FE 7D 81 3D   Ou...........}.=
0080  55 AA 75 C7 8B F5 EA 00-7C 00 00 49 6E 76 61 6C   U.u.....|..Inval
0090  69 64 20 70 61 72 74 69-74 69 6F 6E 20 74 61 62   id partition tab
00A0  6C 65 00 45 72 72 6F 72-20 6C 6F 61 64 69 6E 67   le.Error loading
00B0  20 6F 70 65 72 61 74 69-6E 67 20 73 79 73 74 65    operating syste
00C0  6D 00 4D 69 73 73 69 6E-67 20 6F 70 65 72 61 74   m.Missing operat
00D0  69 6E 67 20 73 79 73 74-65 6D 00 00 00 00 00 00   ing system......
00E0  00 00 00 00 00 00 00 00-00 00 00 00 00 00 00 00   ................
00F0  00 00 00 00 00 00 00 00-00 00 00 00 00 00 00 00   ................
0100  00 00 00 00 00 00 00 00-00 00 00 00 00 00 00 00   ................
0110  00 00 00 00 00 00 00 00-00 00 00 00 00 00 00 00   ................
0120  00 00 00 00 00 00 00 00-00 00 00 00 00 00 00 00   ................
0130  00 00 00 00 00 00 00 00-00 00 00 00 00 00 00 00   ................
0140  00 00 00 00 00 00 00 00-00 00 00 00 00 00 00 00   ................
0150  00 00 00 00 00 00 00 00-00 00 00 00 00 00 00 00   ................
0160  00 00 00 00 00 00 00 00-00 00 00 00 00 00 00 00   ................
0170  00 00 00 00 00 00 00 00-00 00 00 00 00 00 00 00   ................
0180  00 00 00 00 00 00 00 00-00 00 00 00 00 00 00 00   ................
0190  00 00 00 00 00 00 00 00-00 00 00 00 00 00 00 00   ................
01A0  00 00 00 00 00 00 00 00-00 00 00 00 00 00 00 00   ................
01B0  00 00 00 00 00 00 00 00-00 00 00 00 00 00 00 01   ................
01C0  01 00 04 3F 20 1E 20 00-00 00 E0 F7 00 00 80 00   ...? . .........
01D0  C1 DE 0A 3F E0 DE 00 F0-1E 00 00 08 00 00 00 00   ...?............
01E0  00 00 00 00 00 00 00 00-00 00 00 00 00 00 00 00   ................
01F0  01 1F 05 3F E0 DD 00 F8-00 00 00 F8 1D 00 55 AA   ...?..........U.
```

Figure 9-2: A typical master boot record (MBR). The contents of this disk sector (512 bytes) are shown here in a DEBUG-like format. The partition table data is near the end; the program occupies roughly the first half of the sector.

Part I: The Hard Disk Companion

This figure has three columns. The first column shows address numbers in hexadecimal notation. The second column gives the actual bytes stored at those addresses (also in hexadecimal notation). The third column shows the same data interpreted as ASCII characters.

The second and third columns each show 16 bytes of data per line. Thus the second column has 16 subcolumns, each with a single byte (represented as two hexadecimal symbols) in it. In the third column, any values that do not represent a printable ASCII character are indicated by a period. The address number in the first column of each line is the number of bytes that are in this sector before the first byte of data shown on that line.

Notice that there are 32 lines in the figure, with address column numbers from zero to 01F0h. When you add the number of bytes that are in the last line before the last byte (15, or Fh) to the address of that last line (1F0h), you get an address of 1FFh (or 511 decimal) for the last byte in the sector. Addresses from zero to 511 mean that there are 512 bytes shown here, which is exactly what one disk sector holds.

Also notice that the MBR program is contained within the first 14 lines — less than half of the sector — and that the last 80 bytes (five lines worth) are filled with the text of various messages this program may put on-screen. The partition table data is all contained in the last five lines of this figure, starting at address 01BEh. Almost half of the sector from address 1DAh (218 in decimal) through 1BDh (445 decimal) — a total of 227 bytes — are unused (filled with zeros).

The very last two bytes in the sector — which have the values 55h AAh and are at addresses 1FEh and 1FFh — are a "signature" that helps the bootstrap program (the program in the motherboard BIOS ROM that starts your computer) be sure that it is loading a plausible candidate for a boot record.

The bulk of the disk lies between the master boot record and the diagnostic cylinder. You can use this space as a single partition, or you may subdivide it into two, three, or four partitions. The partition table lists the starting and ending address (cylinder, head, and physical sector) for each of these partitions. Also, for each partition, it shows the operating system that gave it a high-level format. Finally, it shows which one of these partitions is active (bootable).

Figure 9-3 gives the details on what is stored where in the partition table. This example comes from another one of my hard disks, a 335MB Micropolis ESDI drive.

Chapter 9: Preparing a Hard Disk to Store Information: Step 2

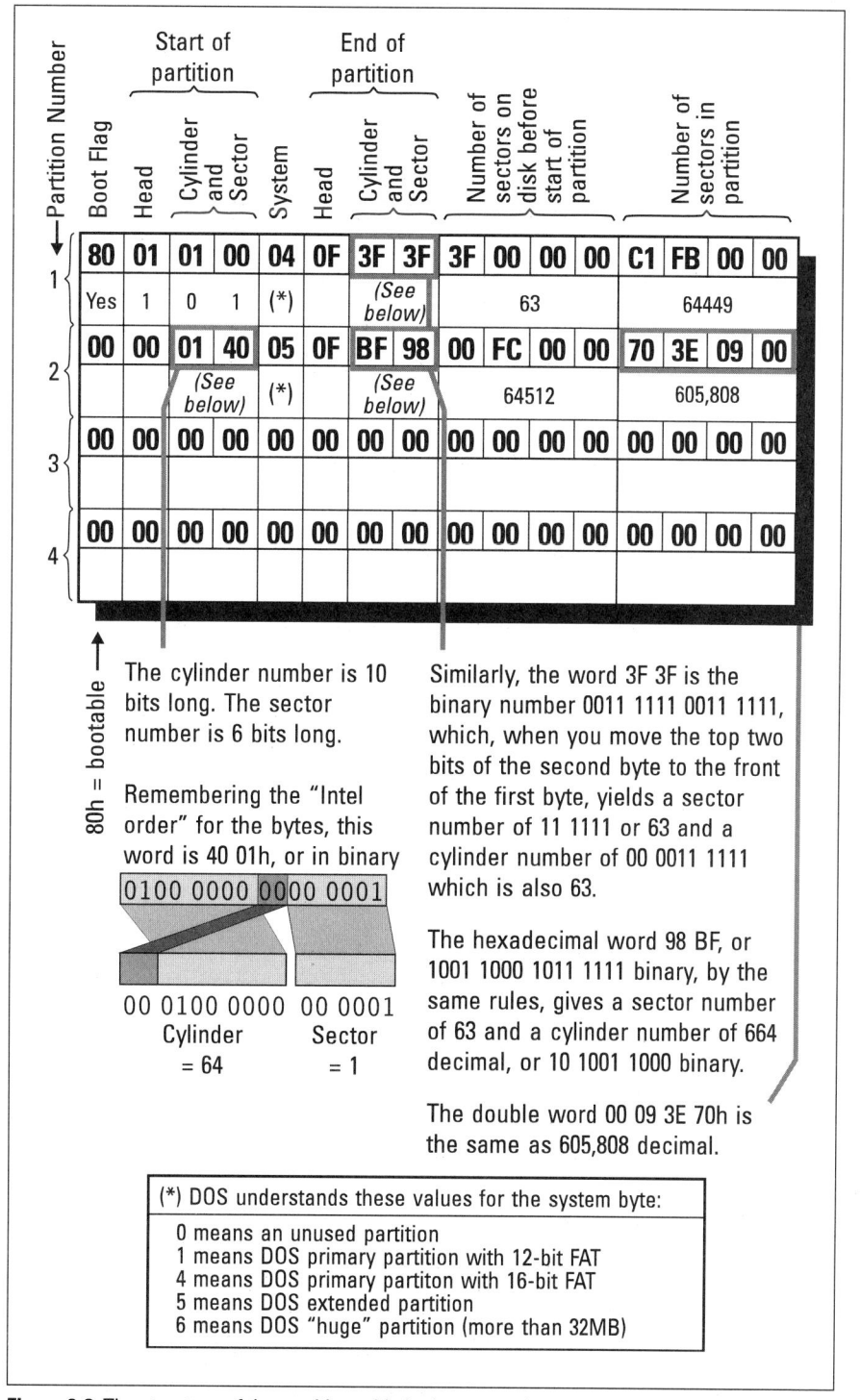

	Partition Number	Boot Flag	Head	Cylinder and Sector (Start)	Cylinder and Sector (Start)	System	Head	Cylinder and Sector (End)	Cylinder and Sector (End)	Number of sectors on disk before start of partition	Number of sectors on disk before start of partition	Number of sectors on disk before start of partition	Number of sectors on disk before start of partition	Number of sectors in partition	Number of sectors in partition	Number of sectors in partition	Number of sectors in partition
1		80	01	01	00	04	0F	3F	3F	3F	00	00	00	C1	FB	00	00
		Yes	1	0	1	(*)	(See below)	(See below)		63				64449			
2		00	00	01	40	05	0F	BF	98	00	FC	00	00	70	3E	09	00
				(See below)	(See below)	(*)		(See below)	(See below)	64512				605,808			
3		00	00	00	00	00	00	00	00	00	00	00	00	00	00	00	00
4		00	00	00	00	00	00	00	00	00	00	00	00	00	00	00	00

Start of partition | End of partition

80h = bootable

The cylinder number is 10 bits long. The sector number is 6 bits long.

Remembering the "Intel order" for the bytes, this word is 40 01h, or in binary
`0100 0000 0000 0001`

`00 0100 0000   00 0001`
Cylinder = 64   Sector = 1

Similarly, the word 3F 3F is the binary number 0011 1111 0011 1111, which, when you move the top two bits of the second byte to the front of the first byte, yields a sector number of 11 1111 or 63 and a cylinder number of 00 0011 1111 which is also 63.

The hexadecimal word 98 BF, or 1001 1000 1011 1111 binary, by the same rules, gives a sector number of 63 and a cylinder number of 664 decimal, or 10 1001 1000 binary.

The double word 00 09 3E 70h is the same as 605,808 decimal.

(*) DOS understands these values for the system byte:

0 means an unused partition
1 means DOS primary partition with 12-bit FAT
4 means DOS primary partiton with 16-bit FAT
5 means DOS extended partition
6 means DOS "huge" partition (more than 32MB)

Figure 9-3: The structure of the partition table in the master boot record.

Part I: The Hard Disk Companion

> ### A challenge for the reader
>
> After you understand how to read the data in the master boot record shown in Figure 9-3, you can test your understanding by figuring out what the partition table whose data is shown in Figure 9-2 would look like if it were to be displayed in the form used in Figure 9-3. Be sure that your numbers make sense for a SCSI drive. (Look back at the technical note in the section "Making the fictitious perfect drive" in Chapter 3 to see what the drive's apparent dimensions ought to be.) *Caution:* There is one non-DOS standard value in this partition table. The answer to this challenge and the meaning of that non-DOS standard entry are revealed at the end of this chapter.

TECHNICAL SECRET

The sector and cylinder numbers for the start and end of each partition are stored in a way that reinforces the INT 13h limits on the size of those numbers. (Remember, INT 13h is the BIOS interrupt that handles reading and writing to the disk. It limits cylinder numbers to the range 0 to 1,023, and sectors from 1 to 63. Also, at least officially, it limits heads to values from 0 to 15.)

Thus, this is one of the places that the BIOS imposes its disk size limit of 504MB. That limit, you will recall, came from the assumption of 512-byte sectors, and the INT13h "official limits" of no more than 1024 cylinders, 63 sectors per track, and 16 heads. Because head numbers can really be anything up to 255, both in the partition table and in INT 13h, this could be an 8GB limit. Raising the limit this way is only possible by "breaking one of the rules" of the INT 13h BIOS design.

The total number of sectors and the number of sectors from the start of the disk to the start of each partition are stored in 4-byte locations (32 bits each). This condition is compatible with the convention in DOS 4.0 and later versions for large hard disk partitions. Thirty-two bits for the sector numbers means one could, conceivably, have almost 2^{32} sectors. If each sector holds 512 bytes, the disk could then hold about 2TB (terabytes, or megamegabytes), or about 4,000 times as much as the maximum size disk permitted by the maximum sector, head, and cylinder numbers that the BIOS can accept.

The diagnostic cylinder

The diagnostic cylinder or, as IBM refers to it, the *customer engineering cylinder*, is one entire cylinder (all heads on one track). Normally, it is the last cylinder, closest to the spindle. IBM included this cylinder to have a place to conduct tests without messing up any of the data stored on the rest of the disk.

Chapter 9: Preparing a Hard Disk to Store Information: Step 2

TECHNICAL SECRET

Some controllers do not set aside a diagnostic cylinder. Because such a reserved cylinder was a standard part of the IBM drive design, many utility programs depend on its existence. SpinRite, for example, will check to see whether a particular drive has such a reserved, diagnostic cylinder and will use it if it does. It also correctly notes if that cylinder does not exist and refuses to attempt the operations that would have used it, thus keeping itself from accidentally overwriting any of the data on the drive.

The "secret" cylinder

The last part into which the system may carve up your disk is what might be called the "secret" cylinder. Not all disks have one, but if you have an autoconfiguring hard disk controller or an ESDI, IDE/ATA, or SCSI drive, it will very likely include such a cylinder in which the controller will store the drive's dimensions and possibly some other useful information. That cylinder, if it exists, is typically even farther in toward the spindle than the diagnostic cylinder.

Where Files Are Stored

The middle portion of the disk (which accounts for almost all of its capacity) is where a user's information is stored. The other regions before and after this portion are merely bookkeeping areas — but the information in the first section (the master boot record) is absolutely essential for accessing the data stored in the rest of the disk.

The active, or bootable, partition

Of the two, three, or four partitions into which you may divide the middle portion of your disk, you can boot from only one. The first byte in each line of the partition table is called the *boot flag*. Only one of those four bytes is permitted to be nonzero. That one is set to 80h to indicate that its partition is the active one. When you boot your computer, this flag is what tells the MBR program which partition to look in for a boot sector program.

Primary DOS partition

The active partition might have been created and formatted by any operating system that can run on a PC. If it is one that was formatted by DOS, it is called a *DOS primary partition*. (The labels on the partitions are placed there by using the DOS program FDISK or some corresponding program for another operating system.) Version 3.2 of DOS and all earlier versions ignore all the other partitions. DOS 3.3 or later, after it has booted from one partition, can access data stored in exactly one of the other partitions if you label it as a "DOS extended partition." The DOS extended partition itself cannot be bootable.

TECHNICAL SECRET

All versions of DOS before 4.0 could deal only with a logical volume size of up to 32MB. (A logical volume is what DOS identifies with a drive letter.) That size limit came, you will recall, from the limit on the logical sector number to a 16-bit number (thus less than 65,536) and the sector size of 512 bytes.

DOS 3.3 is limited to 32MB per logical volume, but it can have more than one of them per physical drive. You can have one volume that is the primary DOS partition (the one that can be bootable), plus any number you want in the single DOS extended partition.

For each partition, a number called the *system byte* is stored in the partition table to say what kind of partition it is. There are four possible values for this number for any partition that DOS can access. The values 1 or 4 say that this is a regular DOS partition — the only kind versions of DOS earlier than 3.3 could create. (The two different values indicate the size of the entries in the FAT table, which is explained in Chapter 10.) The value 5 indicates a DOS extended partition, which only Versions 3.3 and later can create. The value 6 is used for a "huge" DOS partition, a potentially bootable partition, created by DOS 4.0 or later, that exceeds 32MB. These system byte values are put in the partition table by FDISK. Other values may be put in the system byte positions by third-party disk partitioning software or by non-DOS operating systems (such as OS/2 or UNIX).

If you use a third-party disk-partitioning program to partition your hard disk, because it will put some special, non-DOS number into the system byte position for all but the DOS primary partition, you will have to have the special installable device driver that comes with that disk-partitioning program in order to access anything stored in one of those special partitions. (As an example, Disk Manager uses the device driver DMDRVR.BIN to obtain access to the logical drives it creates in the DOS extended partition.) Without one of those device drivers, DOS alone cannot get at anything stored in such a partition.

Chapter 9: Preparing a Hard Disk to Store Information: Step 2

> If an operating system other than DOS is used to format a partition, it will put its own identifying value into the system byte. Generally, that value will make that partition off-limits to all systems but itself. (Some operating systems that can read files in one another's partitions are the exceptions — a point more fully discussed later in this section.)

DOS extended partition

DOS treats the DOS extended partition almost as if it were a separate disk or a collection of separate disks. Its entries in the partition table (in the master boot record) look much like any other partition, but DOS uses them very differently. Because it looks like another disk or disks, you can make the DOS extended partition any size you want (up to 504MB, or perhaps up to 8GB), even if you are using DOS 3.3. The entries in the partition table are pointers to this region.

Normally, the master boot record program reads the first sector in the active partition and expects it to be a valid boot sector program. For a DOS extended partition, the master boot record program goes to the corresponding location, but instead of expecting to find and load a boot sector, it looks for another partition table. This subsidiary, or *extended partition table,* shows a further subdivision of the DOS extended partition into DOS *logical volumes.* If you are using DOS 3.3, it is these logical volumes that must be no larger than 32MB.

The partition table at the start of each DOS logical volume within the DOS extended partition is just like a master boot record partition table, with two exceptions: it doesn't contain the master boot record program, and its data table has only one or two entries. The first entry tells the size of the current DOS-accessible subpartition. The second entry points to the start of the next DOS logical volume (see Figure 9-4). The third and fourth entries are filled with zeros. The partition table for the last logical volume in the DOS extended partition will have zeros for its second entry also.

Other kinds of partition

In addition to the primary DOS partition and a DOS extended partition, you may choose to have one or two other partitions on your hard disk. These partitions could be used by some other operating system.

While you are booted under DOS, the other partitions are invisible. When you boot to the other operating system, it would have access to its own partition and very possibly not to the DOS partitions.

Part I: The Hard Disk Companion

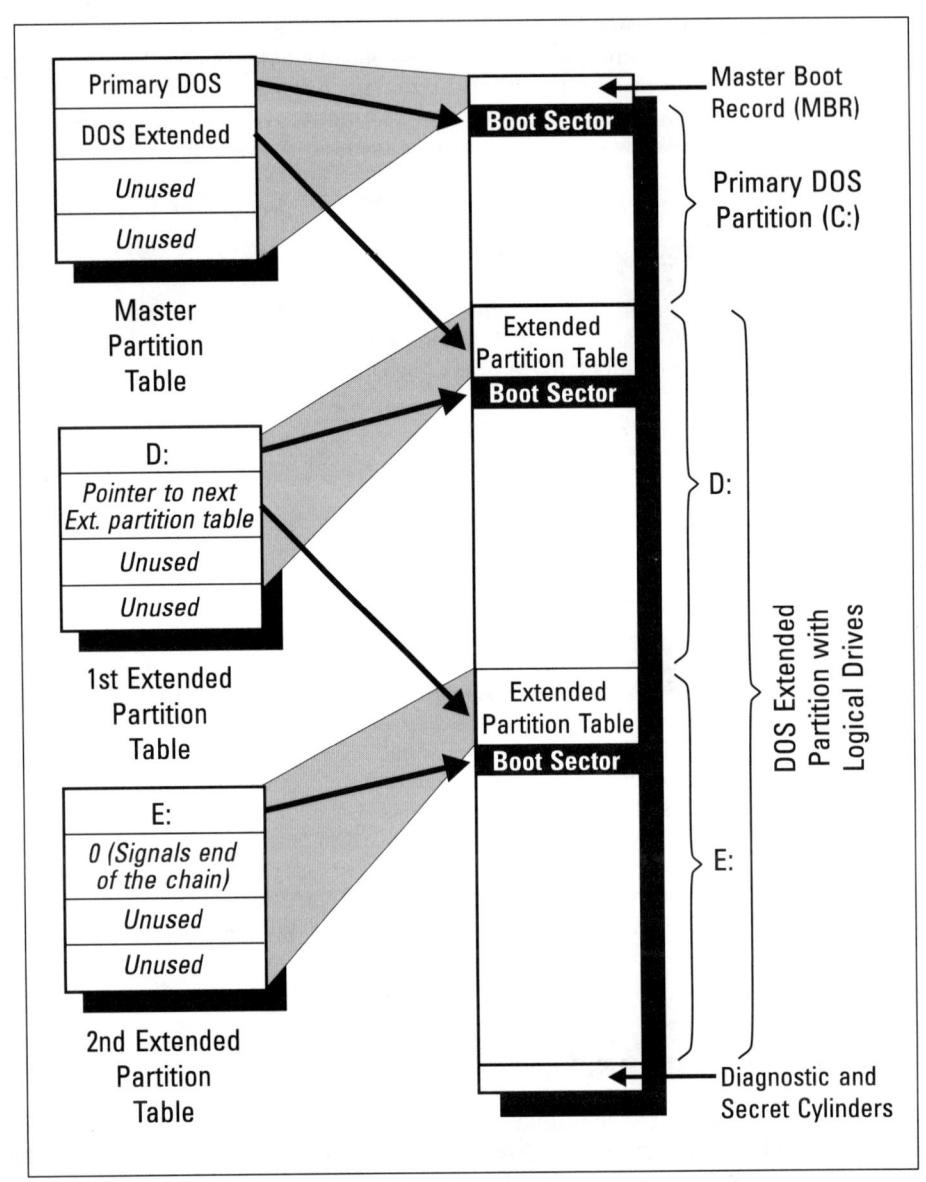

Figure 9-4: How the master and extended partition tables divide up the disk into logical volumes (drive letters).

Chapter 9: Preparing a Hard Disk to Store Information: Step 2

Non-DOS operating systems that can use the DOS primary and extended partitions

A couple of important operating systems other than DOS can access DOS partitions, both primary and extended. One is OS/2. The other is an announced but not yet released operating system that in many ways will be quite similar to OS/2. It is called Windows NT.

OS/2 actually can be put in a DOS logical volume — either the primary DOS partition or one of the logical volumes within an extended partition. Alternatively, OS/2 can be used to reformat one of the DOS logical volumes using an OS/2-specific file system call HPFS (High Performance File System). As long as OS/2 uses a FAT file system, its partition and all its files are accessible to DOS; in addition, all the DOS files are accessible to OS/2.

If you create any HPFS logical drives, they will be accessible only to OS/2. If you use DOS Version 5 or later, DOS will be able to access all the logical drives that use the FAT system, wherever they may be in the DOS extended partition. Earlier versions of DOS can only see FAT volumes that are located in front of the first HPFS volume.

Windows NT will support three file systems. You can install and run it in a FAT volume or in volumes formatted with its own NTFS. Windows NT will be able to read all the files in any FAT, HPFS, or NTFS volumes.

The Partition Table

DOS includes FDISK, a program for creating, examining, and altering these partition tables. In addition to working with DOS partitions, FDISK can reserve room for other partitions that other operating systems can later format and use, but it cannot do much with those partitions because it is designed for use with DOS.

You also can use FDISK to mark any of the four partitions in the master boot record (except the DOS extended partition if there is one) as the active, or bootable, one. In this way, FDISK can "turn off" DOS and "turn on" UNIX or another operating system residing in one of the other partitions.

Whenever you run FDISK on a new disk, you should first ask it to show you what partition information it can find, before authorizing it to make any changes. If the disk is newly low-level formatted, FDISK will not find a master boot record/partition table. Then it is appropriate to ask for FDISK's help in creating one.

Part I: The Hard Disk Companion

CAUTION

There are a couple of ways you can all too easily do yourself harm with FDISK. One is by forgetting to select the correct disk on which to have FDISK do its work. The other is by allowing FDISK to alter, *or even to reaffirm,* the partition table information on a disk with data already on it.

You will find more details on the second hazard in the next caution message in this chapter. There is, however, a simple way to avoid at least one possible problem: If you are going to use FDISK on a disk you are adding to your PC, first disconnect the existing hard disk. Then FDISK certainly will not wipe out your existing data. After you finish with FDISK, you can reconnect the original hard disk and the new disk, reboot, and proceed from there.

When you have more than one actual, physical hard disk in your PC, FDISK will include an option on its main menu to set which of the disks it will be looking at. If you don't choose this option, FDISK will look at the first disk (which it calls Drive 0 — normally your C drive). If you remember to ask FDISK to show you what it finds when it looks, what you see displayed may help you remember to be sure to set the working disk for FDISK to the correct value.

TECHNICAL SECRET

If you are working with a disk that already has a valid master boot record, be very careful. Altering the numbers in its partition table most likely will make all the data on the disk seem to disappear. It may be possible to get your data back (or at least most of your data) by restoring the partition table values, but only if you know exactly what all the values were.

If you alter these numbers by using a program that allows direct disk editing, you will change only the numbers in the partition table. Then you can reverse the effect of your work simply by putting back the original numbers. If you use FDISK to alter the partition table, it will usually erase the most critical part of the information in any partition it establishes, precluding any easy way back. (See "An important WARNING" later in this section for more details.)

One interesting example of how some other operating systems use partitions, and one you may encounter on PCs that normally are used as DOS machines, is the OS/2 Boot Manager. This program, introduced with OS/2, Version 2.0, occupies a 1MB partition all by itself. This partition is marked in the partition table as the active partition. When you boot a computer with the OS/2 Boot Manager installed, that program will get control of the machine.

Using a data table it stores within itself, the OS/2 Boot Manager presents a menu on-screen showing what operating systems are installed in the other partitions and allowing you to choose which one you'd like to have assume control of the PC this time. Once you make a choice (or after a timeout at which time Boot Manager makes a preselected default choice for you), Boot Manager will go to the indicated partition and load and run its boot sector.

Chapter 9: Preparing a Hard Disk to Store Information: Step 2   **251**

Steps to partitioning a new disk with FDISK

Assuming that you don't already have a DOS-bootable drive C, you will first have to boot your computer from a DOS diskette in drive A. Keep the DOS diskette handy because you will find yourself rebooting the computer from that diskette several or even many times before your PC is ready to boot from the hard drive.

If the hard disk is smaller than 32MB, the job is simple. First, you run FDISK, allowing it to use all the disk for DOS. You then proceed to the high-level format described in Chapter 10.

TECHNICAL SECRET

FDISK, in this case, does several things in one step. First, it creates the master boot record with its partition table. Next, it marks the first partition starting and ending points as the beginning and end of the space on the disk (except for the sector or track used for the master boot record and the diagnostic cylinder at the end). FDISK marks that partition as belonging to DOS and makes it the active partition. The other three entries in the partition table are filled with zeros to show that they are unused.

An important WARNING

There is a little-known aspect of FDISK's operation that could do your data grave harm unless you are aware of it. Remember this — it could save your data some day! The most insidious thing FDISK does is wipe out the first half dozen cylinders or so of each partition it creates. This action is what makes reversing the effects of FDISK so very difficult.

TECHNICAL SECRET

FDISK takes this action to make sure that the partition will not appear to be high-level formatted. If all it did was put numbers in the partition table, you could easily reverse its effect, but you also might find yourself with some leftover "junk" in your new partition that could, the DOS designers thought, cause you some trouble sometime.

How to get full use of a large hard disk

You could use less than all the disk for DOS if, for example, you wanted to reserve a portion of the disk for another operating system — this was, after all, the reason the notion of partitions and the FDISK program were invented. For a 32MB drive though, this solution is not very practical. Current versions of most other operating systems require well more than half this much disk space to do anything useful. Further, most DOS users today would find anything less than 16MB to be a cramped working space for DOS and their DOS applications and data files.

If the disk is larger than 32MB, you have up to three different options, depending on which DOS version you are using:

1. DOS Version 3.2 or earlier: the only way you can use all of your disk is by using a third-party disk-partitioning program. Your only other options are to upgrade to a later version of DOS or simply to ignore all the disk past the first 32MB (and who would want to do that?). Third-party disk-partitioning software is discussed more fully in the next section.

2. DOS Version 3.3: this version allows you to use most any size disk you want but does so by breaking up the large disk into several regions, each of which must be smaller than 32MB.

3. DOS 4.0 or later: you can use any size disk (at least up to 500MB) as a single large partition, or you may subdivide it. Before you decide whether and how to divide up a large disk under DOS 4.0 and later versions, please re-read the discussion in the section "Disk partitions" in Chapter 7.

If you choose to make a single large partition under DOS 4 or a later version, the process is the same as with a small disk (less than 32MB) under the earlier versions of DOS. Let FDISK do its thing with the default options and go on to the high-level format.

When you choose to have more than one volume on a single disk drive

If you choose to (or need to) subdivide your disk, you must take several steps. First, you run FDISK and ask it to create a primary DOS partition in some size smaller than the whole disk. DOS 3.3's FDISK command will not let you choose a size larger than 32MB. Next, you must make a DOS extended partition, assigning it the rest of the disk if you want to use all the disk for DOS. Do this even if you want eventually to have several smaller partitions.

TECHNICAL SECRET

In these steps, FDISK again creates the master boot record and its partition table. It fills in the first entry for the primary DOS partition, whatever size you chose to make that partition. It marks that partition as belonging to DOS. Then FDISK fills in the second entry of the partition table for the DOS extended partition. It puts zeros in every location in the last two entries (showing that they are unused).

FDISK in early versions of DOS would also mark the primary DOS partition it created as the active partition, allowing you to boot from that partition after it was properly high-level formatted. Later versions of DOS don't take this step automatically. You have to remember to ask FDISK to mark the active partition as a separate step unless you have committed the whole disk to being a single DOS partition.

Chapter 9: Preparing a Hard Disk to Store Information: Step 2

You don't have to create a primary DOS partition if all you want on this hard disk is a DOS extended partition. Remember, though, that you cannot boot your PC, using DOS, from a DOS extended partition. (You can boot OS/2 Version 2.0 from a logical drive in a DOS extended partition.) You might want to have only a DOS extended partition if this hard disk is going to be the second disk in your PC. Then its drive letters will all follow those for the DOS partition and the logical drives in the DOS extended partition on the first disk.

In some versions of DOS, FDISK asks you how many cylinders to assign to each partition it creates. In other versions, it asks you for the sizes of those partitions in megabytes. If your version is one of the latter, you may have trouble getting exactly the sizes you ask for because, except for the first partition, FDISK always assigns some whole number of cylinders to each partition it creates. The first partition starts just after the master boot record, either in the very next sector (DOS Versions 2.*x*) or at the start of the next track (DOS Versions 3.0 and later). The first partition, like all the others, ends at the end of some cylinder.

Now you must create logical DOS drives within that DOS extended partition, once more using FDISK. DOS 3.3's FDISK will again limit each of these logical drives to 32MB or smaller. In DOS 4 and later versions, FDISK will let you set these drives to any size you choose. You may create as many logical DOS drives (of any sizes you like) as will fit. Any of the DOS extended partition you do not allocate to a DOS logical drive will remain unavailable for use by DOS.

TECHNICAL SECRET

At this step, FDISK is creating the partition tables within the DOS extended partition, one for each subpartition, or *logical DOS disk*. Each of these tables has one line for that subpartition, and all but the last one have a second line that points to the next of these extended partition tables. That second line shows a partition size that is however much of the total extended partition still unaccounted for by this and the previous DOS logical disks. The last two (or for the final subpartition table, the last three) entries are filled with zeros.

After you build the master boot record, including its partition table, you can format the primary DOS partition. If you have a DOS extended partition, after you have created DOS logical disk drives within it, you can format each of them. To the DOS FORMAT program, each of these partitions or DOS logical disks looks almost exactly like a floppy diskette. The only difference is that FORMAT knows it is a nonremovable disk and what size it is.

Third-party disk-partitioning software

If you have a disk drive larger than 32MB and are using DOS Version 3.2 or earlier, you must upgrade your DOS version, use some third-party disk-partitioning software, or ignore the rest of your drive beyond 32MB.

Third-party programs can manage all three parts of the process: low-level format; partitioning; and high-level format, for which they require a DOS disk. Several different vendors produce these programs; you will have to consult the documentation that came with a particular program to learn how it operates. Each is easy to use if you operate it in its default mode. If you want to have more control, you can follow each package's instructions for working in an interactive mode. The previous discussion should help you understand the principles and, therefore, help you make the necessary choices correctly.

Important reminder: Third-party disk partitioners provide a non-DOS solution to a problem that versions of DOS prior to DOS 3.3 could not solve, making disks partitioned by these programs inherently *incompatible* with standard DOS procedures. You must install a device driver through your CONFIG.SYS file to get at all but the very first partition created by these programs (and that one is often very small). Booting from a copy of your DOS distribution disk will not work.

These programs will install the needed device driver for you, but you must make sure that you have suitable back-up copies for safety purposes somewhere other than on your hard disk. The backups should be bootable and include any device drivers needed, with configuration files properly modified for a floppy drive. Test this *safety boot diskette* after you have created it, to make sure that it allows you to access your hard drive.

A recommendation

If you upgrade to DOS 3.3 or later, don't continue to use third-party disk-partitioning software. When you install your new version of DOS, upgrade your disk partitions, too. To make this change, you first must back up your data. Next, boot from the new DOS disk and then use the new DOS's version of FDISK, which renders your old data inaccessible. Delete any DOS extended partitions and the primary DOS partition. (You may have to use the third-party disk-partitioning program that created the partitions to remove them.) Re-create the partitions (primary DOS and DOS extended) at whatever sizes you choose. Then run FORMAT (also from the new DOS). This last step will prepare the partitions and also install the new DOS on drive C.

When you upgrade, remember the following:

- The needed command for a bootable primary DOS partition is **FORMAT C: /S /V**. On all other partitions, you can use **FORMAT d: /V**, where *d* is replaced by the appropriate drive letter.

- Be sure that you update all your DOS files by copying from the floppy disk to the hard disk (use the command **COPY *.*** and make sure that you copy to a subdirectory, normally C:\DOS). Finally, restore all other programs and data files.

- When you restore your programs and data, you can put them back in the original directories, or you can take advantage of the opportunity to reorganize your hard disk.

- Watch out for the lazy system installer, whether it be a dealer or a friend, who may continue to use partitioning software after upgrading your system to DOS 3.3 or higher. Ask whoever put your system together to remove that unnecessary software or do so yourself.

A Suggestion (Only for Brave Readers!)

Unless you are using one of the 2.*x* versions of DOS, your hard disk has some space between the master boot record and the beginning of the first partition. (Typically, this space includes all but the first sector of the first track on the drive.)

Some disk controllers use some or all of that otherwise waste space. Some antivirus programs use one sector of it. And some computer viruses will overwrite one sector in that region. Other than these uses, though, the space is there and available for use in any way you choose (other than for normal DOS files because DOS cannot see that space). Here is one novel suggestion for how you might put it to use.

Sometimes a stolen computer is recovered by the police. But if the owner cannot prove ownership of the computer, the police may not give it back. A large hard disk might be removed from the PC, so etching a driver's license number inside the PC system unit case (which is a good idea) wouldn't help identify that drive.

If, however, that stolen computer was yours, and if the thief had not yet redone the low-level format on your hard disk (even if the DOS partition was formatted to remove all programs and other incriminating information), you could still prove the disk was yours if you had put your name, address, phone number, and any other identification information you chose into one or more sectors in the waste space on the first track. (You may want to add multiple copies of that information; then if one of the sectors is later overwritten, such as by a virus or an antivirus program, the remaining copies will still be available for identification purposes.)

This little precaution could get you back your valuable hard disk some day. If you are thinking of using this suggestion, however, please be very careful. Check and double-check what you are about to do before you do it. Use a tool like the Norton Disk Editor to look at each sector on the first track of your hard disk. Make sure that the track is completely empty or, if it is not, be sure that you know where it is being used and which sectors are unused. Then put your identification information only in the unused sectors.

Another Recommendation

Many people who get a new computer, a new hard drive, or a new version of DOS are delighted to learn that now, for the first time, they can format their hard disk into a single, large DOS volume. So they do that. And only later do they learn some of the reasons that doing so was not necessarily a really wise action.

You know, on the other hand, by having read what was said in Chapter 1, in the section "Good organization helps both you and DOS," that there is more to consider than merely the maximum size logical volume that DOS and the BIOS can accept. It is often much more important to partition your drive into multiple logical drives, just to keep your own sanity.

DOS may not have much trouble with 1,000+ directories and over 21,000 files, but not many users are handy at navigating such a directory structure. Even DOS slows down when it has to plow through all those subdirectories looking for a file. (You may smile with disbelief when you read those numbers. They are the actual, current figures that I found on the 1GB Micropolis hard drive on my main PC. If you get a much larger hard drive than you have ever had before, soon you, too, will be astonished by the number of files on it.)

Furthermore, as is explained in the section "Slack Space" in Chapter 10, you may lose the use of a substantial fraction of your hard disk if your logical volume sizes are too large. Anything over 128MB needs to be justified quite carefully.

All of these remarks don't mean that you definitely would be making a mistake to make your hard drive into one large logical volume (a C drive and no other lettered drives) — merely that before you decide to do this you would be well advised to study the alternatives and think about the ways you are comfortable using your computer. You might come up with a much better way to partition your hard drive.

The answer to the challenge

Here is the answer to the challenge presented earlier in this chapter: The approximately 1GB SCSI drive whose MBR is shown in Figure 9-2 has been partitioned into three parts. The raw capacity of this drive is about 1GB (1024MB). The formatted capacity turns out to be just under 991MB.

The first part is a primary DOS partition (the system byte's value is 4). It starts at head=1, cylinder=0, sector=1, as is usual, and it ends at head=63, cylinder=30, sector=32. Remember, this is a SCSI drive, and so, like all SCSI drives, it must do sector translation. Again, as is typical of a SCSI drive, it presents to DOS an apparent drive having 1MB capacity per cylinder by having heads go from 0 to 63 and sectors from 1 to 32. The sector count in this partition is 63,456 and there are 32 sectors before it begins.

The second partition in the table is the bootable one. It is very small and is located near the end of the drive. The system byte's value is 0Ah, which is not a valid value according to DOS. This partition contains OS/2's Boot Manager. It starts at head=0, cylinder=990, sector=1 and goes to head=63, cylinder=990, sector=32. The total sector count for this partition is 2,048 (1MB), and there are 2,027,520 sectors before it begins.

This disk drive initially runs the OS/2 Boot Manager program. It then can boot DOS, or it can boot OS/2. You may wonder where OS/2 is on this disk. (You know that DOS is going to be in the primary DOS partition, which is the C drive.) In this instance OS/2's system files were installed into a logical drive located within the DOS extended partition. That logical drive could have been formatted either with the OS/2 HPFS file structure (in which case only OS/2 could access it) or with the FAT structure (in which case both DOS and OS/2 could get at all the files in that logical drive).

The last line (the third line of the partition table is filled with zeros to represent an unused line) in the table describes the rest of this disk. It is a DOS extended partition (the system byte's value is 5). It starts at head=0, cylinder=31, sector=1 and ends at head=63, cylinder=989, sector=32. This partition has 1,964,032 bytes and there are 63,488 bytes before it begins.

A good check on your work is to see that the number of bytes in each partition plus the number of bytes before it add up to the number of bytes before the next partition. Naturally, you have to go through the partitions in order of their placement on the disk rather than their order in the partition table. In this case, the order would be the first line, then the last line, and finally, the second line.

Part I: The Hard Disk Companion

Summary

- Hard disks need to be partitioned because, when PCs were young, hard disks cost a lot and no one knew which operating system would be dominant. They still need to be partitioned, even though neither of those facts is still true, simply because the notion of partitions is deeply embedded in the PC's design.
- DOS creates and uses two kinds of partition: a primary DOS partition that can only hold one logical volume and a DOS extended partition that can hold multiple logical volumes (and even some OS/2 volumes). You need at least Version 3.3 of DOS to support a DOS extended partition.
- All DOS versions prior to 4.0 (with a few exceptions, such as COMPAQ DOS Version 3.31) cannot use a logical drive that is more than 32MB in size. Later versions can have almost arbitrarily large partitions (up to the size limited by the BIOS, which is ordinarily either 504MB or about 8GB).
- The DOS program FDISK lets you see what partitions and logical drives are on your disk now, and you can use it to change them. FDISK can be a very dangerous program, though. Read the cautions in this chapter before you use FDISK!
- If your DOS version is 3.3 or later, you don't need to use third-party disk-partitioning programs (like Disk Manager or SpeedStor), and you probably would be well-served not to do so.

In this and the preceding chapter, you learned all about the first two steps that must be taken to prepare a new disk drive for use with DOS. In the next chapter, you learn about the final step, called applying the high-level, or logical format.

Chapter 10

Preparing a Hard Disk to Store Information Step Three: The Logical Format

In This Chapter

▶ All about the third and final step in preparing a hard disk for use by DOS

▶ How DOS organizes information in a DOS logical volume

▶ What the DOS program FORMAT does to prepare a volume

▶ How the DOS format differs from the format created by UNIX, OS/2 in an HPFS partition, and Windows NT in an NTFS partition

What Is a Logical Format?

After you have given the disk its low-level format and have partitioned it, you are ready for the high-level format. In terms of the parking lot analogy, you now have the stalls painted (the controller has written the sectors to the disk) and the fences built (the partition table or tables created by FDISK). All that remains is to create the valet parking support structure so that cars (files) can be parked automatically for you. The DOS program FORMAT will create this last structure. This section describes that program's several functions, as well as explains what a disk's file allocation table (FAT) is.

The Logical Organization of a DOS Partition

You have learned about preparing a disk with a low-level format and the division of a disk into a master boot record, one or more partitions (of which the only ones DOS can see are one primary DOS partition and one DOS extended

Part I: The Hard Disk Companion

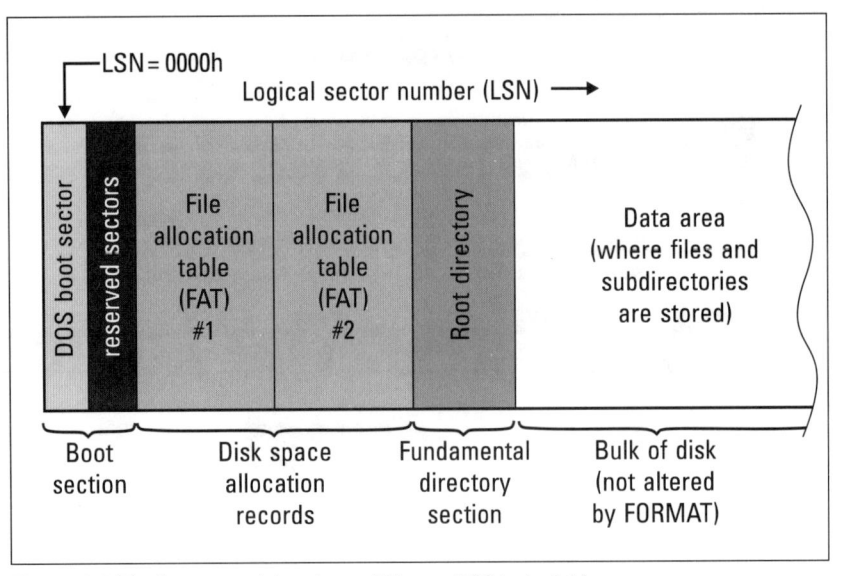

Figure 10-1: The four essential regions within any DOS logical drive.

partition), and a diagnostic cylinder (plus, possibly, a secret cylinder). Next, you must use the DOS FORMAT program to create more subdivisions within the DOS partition and within each DOS logical disk inside the extended partition (if you have any logical drives defined). Only then is the disk ready for DOS to use.

DOS divides every disk into four areas. It divides every primary DOS partition and every DOS logical volume on a hard disk into the same four areas. These areas are the boot sector, the file allocation tables (FATs), the root directory, and the data area (see Figure 10-1).

At this high level, DOS looks at all the disk space on each of these drives as a single long list of logical sectors. Only when DOS gives commands down to the lower levels of DOS and ultimately to the BIOS does that view translate into the real, physical addresses.

The DOS boot record

The *DOS boot record* is the first sector in a DOS logical volume. It is the same in all the volumes that have been formatted by the same version of DOS. Because the DOS boot record is exactly one sector long, and because it contains a program that runs as an essential part of the boot process, it is sometimes called the *boot sector* (see Figure 10-2).

Chapter 10: Preparing a Hard Disk to Store Information: Step 3

```
Relative
address     Data bytes (in hexadecimal notation)                    Data in ASCII

0000   EB 3C 90 4D 53 44 4F 53-35 2E 30 00 02 04 01 00    .<.MSDOS5.0.....
0010   02 00 02 E0 F7 F8 3E 00-20 00 40 00 20 00 00 00    ......>. .@. ...
0020   00 00 00 00 80 00 29 D9-17 00 00 4E 4F 20 4E 41    ......)....NO NA
0030   4D 45 20 20 20 20 46 41-54 31 36 20 20 20 FA 33    ME    FAT16   .3
0040   C0 8E D0 BC 00 7C 16 07-BB 78 00 36 C5 37 1E 56    .....|...x.6.7.V
0050   16 53 BF 3E 7C B9 0B 00-FC F3 A4 06 1F C6 45 FE    .S.>|.........E.
0060   0F 8B 0E 18 7C 88 4D F9-89 47 02 C7 07 3E 7C FB    ....|.M..G...>|.
0070   CD 13 72 79 33 C0 39 06-13 7C 74 08 8B 0E 13 7C    ..ry3.9..|t....|
0080   89 0E 20 7C A0 10 7C F7-26 16 7C 03 06 1C 7C 13    .. |..|.&.|...|.
0090   16 1E 7C 03 06 0E 7C 83-D2 00 A3 50 7C 89 16 52    ..|...|....P|..R
00A0   7C A3 49 7C 89 16 4B 7C-B8 20 00 F7 26 11 7C 8B    |.I|..K|. ..&.|.
00B0   1E 0B 7C 03 C3 48 F7 F3-01 06 49 7C 83 16 4B 7C    ..|..H....I|..K|
00C0   00 BB 00 05 8B 16 52 7C-A1 50 7C E8 92 00 72 1D    ......R|.P|...r.
00D0   B0 01 E8 AC 00 72 16 8B-FB B9 0B 00 BE E6 7D F3    .....r........}.
00E0   A6 75 0A 8D 7F 20 B9 0B-00 F3 A6 74 18 BE 9E 7D    .u... .....t...}
00F0   E8 5F 00 33 C0 CD 16 5E-1F 8F 04 8F 44 02 CD 19    ._.3...^....D...
0100   58 58 58 EB E8 8B 47 1A-48 48 8A 1E 0D 7C 32 FF    XXX...G.HH...|2.
0110   F7 E3 03 06 49 7C 13 16-4B 7C BB 00 07 B9 03 00    ....I|..K|......
0120   50 52 51 E8 3A 00 72 D8-B0 01 E8 54 00 59 5A 58    PRQ.:.r....T.YZX
0130   72 BB 05 01 00 83 D2 00-03 1E 0B 7C E2 E2 8A 2E    r..........|....
0140   15 7C 8A 16 24 7C 8B 1E-49 7C A1 4B 7C EA 00 00    .|..$|..I|.K|...
0150   70 00 AC 0A C0 74 29 B4-0E BB 07 00 CD 10 EB F2    p....t).........
0160   3B 16 18 7C 73 19 F7 36-18 7C FE C2 88 16 4F 7C    ;..|s..6.|....O|
0170   33 D2 F7 36 1A 7C 88 16-25 7C A3 4D 7C F8 C3 F9    3..6.|..%|.M|...
0180   C3 B4 02 8B 16 4D 7C B1-06 D2 E6 0A 36 4F 7C 8B    .....M|.....6O|.
0190   CA 86 E9 8A 16 24 7C 8A-36 25 7C CD 13 C3 0D 0A    .....$|.6%|.....
01A0   4E 6F 6E 2D 53 79 73 74-65 6D 20 64 69 73 6B 20    Non-System disk
01B0   6F 72 20 64 69 73 6B 20-65 72 72 6F 72 00 0A 52    or disk error..R
01C0   65 70 6C 61 63 65 20 61-6E 64 20 70 72 65 73 73    eplace and press
01D0   20 61 6E 79 20 6B 65 79-20 77 68 65 6E 20 72 65     any key when re
01E0   61 64 79 0D 0A 00 49 4F-20 20 20 20 20 20 53 59    ady...IO      SY
01F0   53 4D 53 44 4F 53 20 20-20 20 53 59 53 00 80 55 AA    SMSDOS    SYS..U.
```

Figure 10-2: The DOS boot record. This sample DOS boot record was taken from the logical drive C (the DOS primary partition) of the hard disk whose master boot record is shown in Figure 9-2.

The DOS boot record serves two purposes: It is a program that will load the operating system, a step required to boot the computer (hence the name), and it contains a data table of critical information about this disk partition. Later in this chapter, you learn the meaning of each of the numbers stored in the boot record data table (in the section "Interpretation of the DOS boot record data table").

All DOS boot records created by the same version of DOS are the same in their structure. They each hold some data within them that describes the disk they live on. These numbers, of course, must be different on disks of different capacities or on disks that differ in other ways that affect how DOS or the BIOS has to access them. But except for this variation in data table contents, the DOS boot record on a PC DOS 3.3 diskette, for example, is the same as the DOS boot record on a primary DOS partition of a hard disk. In such a case, the DOS boot record is also the same on any of the logical drives created within a DOS extended partition, provided only that those logical drives also have been formatted by PC DOS Version 3.3.

> **TECHNICAL SECRET**
>
> For a DOS diskette, the boot record is at the physical address cylinder 0, head 0, sector 1. On hard disks under DOS 2, the first partition's boot record is at cylinder 0, head 0, sector 2. (The master boot record, also known as the partition table, occupies cylinder 0, head 0, sector 1.) In later versions of DOS (3.0 and above), in which all but the first sector of the track containing the master boot record goes unused, the boot record is at cylinder 0, head 1, sector 1.
>
> Similarly, in the DOS extended partition (which can exist only for DOS Versions 3.3 and above), each DOS logical volume starts at head 1, sector 1 of the first cylinder of that part of the disk. (All partitions, including the DOS extended partition, and all logical disk drives start on a cylinder boundary.) The extended partition table is at head 0, sector 1 of that cylinder, and the rest of the sectors on that track (head 0, sectors 2 to whatever) are skipped.
>
> A DOS boot record starts with a jump instruction. Then comes a data table, most of whose values are copied into an area of RAM called the BIOS parameter block for this drive. Finally, there is the actual boot program that will use those numbers to find the operating system files in this partition, if it is to boot from this partition. Of course, only the primary DOS partition (which will be drive C) can be bootable. Thus, none of the other partitions or logical volumes need the actual boot program. Still, all DOS partitions or logical volumes have the same DOS boot record for simplicity.
>
> Every DOS boot record ends with the two bytes 55h AAh. This is called a *signature,* and it is used several places in DOS data structures. The master boot record, for example, ends with this same signature.

The data area

Although the data area is not the next part of the partition, it is the next part you need to explore. After you understand how the data area is used, you can more easily understand why the other two sections exist and how they are constructed.

At one level, DOS keeps track of information a file at a time. At a slightly lower level, it keeps track of it either a character at a time (when the file is coming from or going to a character device) or a sectorful at a time (when it is coming from or going to a block device, such as a disk drive).

You would think that because DOS keeps track of data a sector at a time when it is on its way to a disk drive, it would use the same unit to keep track of it after it arrives. It doesn't. Instead, DOS uses another unit, called either a cluster or an allocation unit.

Clusters

A *cluster* is a small group of sectors. A cluster may have only one sector in it, or it may have two sectors, or four, or any integral power of 2. The number of sectors DOS puts in a cluster depends on two things: the size of the disk drive and the version of DOS. Why does DOS use clusters, and how does it decide how large to make them?

Every place where data can be stored on the disk is in one of three states: available; in use by a file or subdirectory; or damaged and, therefore, not fit for data storage. DOS must keep track of the status of every sector in the data area of each DOS drive. Further, DOS must keep track of which file "owns" each place on the disk that is in use. If a file is too large to fit into one of those places, it is stored in pieces. DOS then has to be able to link together the right pieces to make up the whole file whenever some program requests the data.

The system keeps a permanent record of this information on disk with the files whose locations it describes. To speed up access to your files, it also keeps a copy of at least a good deal of this information in RAM for the disk that DOS is currently accessing.

Keeping that information in RAM, however, uses up some significant portion of the precious first 640KB of system RAM, so the designers of DOS had to compromise by separating disk file information into two parts — the file directory information, which tells everything about the files but gives only a snippet about where they reside, and disk space allocation information, which tells everything about the status of every part of the disk data storage area.

In the parking lot analogy, the file directory information is equivalent to the list of whose car is where and what it looks like. The disk space allocation information is equivalent to the list of which stalls are occupied, which are vacant, which are damaged, and, for groups of cars, which ones are in each group.

On the disk, some of the file directory information is kept in the *root directory;* the rest is kept in *subdirectories.* The disk space allocation information is kept in a *file allocation table* (FAT).

When accessing the disk to get a single file, DOS needs to keep in RAM only the file directory information about that one file, or, at most, information about a few files in the same subdirectory. To know where on the disk it may find that file and where it may put additional information for that or a new file, DOS must keep in RAM the disk space allocation information for much or all of the disk.

If you are only getting information out or putting information into one file, DOS can do so quickly. When it needs to access a new file, it takes just a bit longer, for it must get the directory information about that file off the disk.

By simplifying the disk space allocation information and divorcing it from the lengthy details about the files that are using the space, the designers of DOS made it possible to minimize the RAM used by DOS while it is getting at and creating files. When DOS needs to know a file's name, size, time of creation, or other facts, it can look up that information elsewhere.

Still, even the space allocation information is a lot of data to keep in RAM. If DOS tried to keep track of the status of every individual sector on a very large hard disk, it would use all of RAM just for that purpose, leaving no room for your applications. This is where clusters come into the story.

A cluster is some convenient number of consecutively numbered sectors. By dividing the disk space into these larger units, DOS has fewer units to track. By reducing the maximum value of a cluster number to something much less than the total number of sectors, DOS realizes a second space savings, as you will learn in the section "How big is your FAT?"

TECHNICAL SECRET

DOS Versions 1 and 2 divide the data storage area on any disk into no more than about 4,000 storage units, or clusters. Each cluster is numbered, starting at 2. Yes, that's right. For this one purpose, DOS numbers things starting not with 0, nor with 1, but with 2! Actually, there are cluster entries in the FAT, or at least places for entries, for clusters 0 and 1. They are used for a special signature byte called the *media descriptor byte* and for some padding bytes. (If you look at any hard disk, you will see that the first byte in each FAT is F8h and the next two or three bytes — depending on whether this is a 12-bit or 16-bit FAT table — are FFh. The F8h is the media descriptor byte for any hard disk. Other values are used for floppy diskettes of various sizes. The FFh bytes are the padding bytes.)

Starting with DOS Version 3, the number of possible clusters has grown to more than 65,000. Version 4 and later versions of DOS have the same maximum cluster number, but it calls them allocation units rather than clusters. This designation and maximum number continues with later DOS versions.

Only having to keep track of some 4,000, or even a bit more than 65,000, clusters substantially simplifies the system for DOS, compared to keeping track of every sector. Remember that early versions of DOS (before Version 4) allowed up to 65,536 sectors on one disk drive — the famous 32MB logical size limit. Starting with DOS Version 4, that maximum number has been increased to a whopping 4 billion according to one rule — the new DOS logical size limit — but only to just over a million by another rule — the BIOS INT13h limit.

Slack space

DOS saves a lot of valuable space in RAM by keeping track of the disk space allocated to files in chunks called clusters. There is a tradeoff. By not allocating disk space by the byte, DOS must waste some of that space. Every file, no matter what its actual size, must be allocated a portion of the disk that is a whole number multiple of a cluster.

The space at the end of the last cluster allocated to a file that is not filled with data belonging to that file is called *slack space*. Some files have a large amount of slack space. A single-byte file, for example, will waste all but that one byte of the one cluster that is allocated to it. Some other files have very little or no slack space. That is, a file might just happen to have exactly one or some other number of cluster's worth of data.

On average, if the files on your hard disk have sizes that are more or less randomly distributed, you will be wasting just about half a cluster of space per file. If your disk has a cluster size of four sectors (2,048 bytes), for example, you waste about as many kilobytes as you have files. Therefore, every thousand files on your disk will waste approximately one megabyte of disk space.

That may sound like a lot, but it is little enough to "spend" to save significant amounts of RAM and time usage by DOS. Consider that the files on my hard disk average about 50KB in size, so those same thousand files that waste 1MB actually occupy around 50MB. In other words, I'm only wasting 2 percent of my disk space in this way.

Your penalty in waste space may be larger than that — possibly much larger. If your hard disk is large and has been partitioned as a single volume, or if you have created some inappropriately sized logical volumes, your cluster size could be much larger than 2KB. If it is, your total slack space could also be much increased.

In the next section, you learn how DOS chooses the cluster size and how you can influence that choice. This will, in turn, set the amount of slack space you can expect to waste on your disk.

The file allocation table

DOS puts the status information on all clusters on a DOS partition or DOS logical drive in the file allocation table (FAT). A FAT is simply a table of numbers, one per cluster, that tells the status of those clusters. One special value designates those clusters that are available for data storage, and another value indicates a damaged cluster that the system should not use. Yet another number indicates a file that fits entirely within this cluster, or that a file that overlaps other clusters ends in this one. A few values are reserved (in case future DOS designers get any bright ideas for additional features in a FAT). Any other valid number points to a cluster where the file contained in this cluster continues (see Figures 10-3 and 10-4).

Part I: The Hard Disk Companion

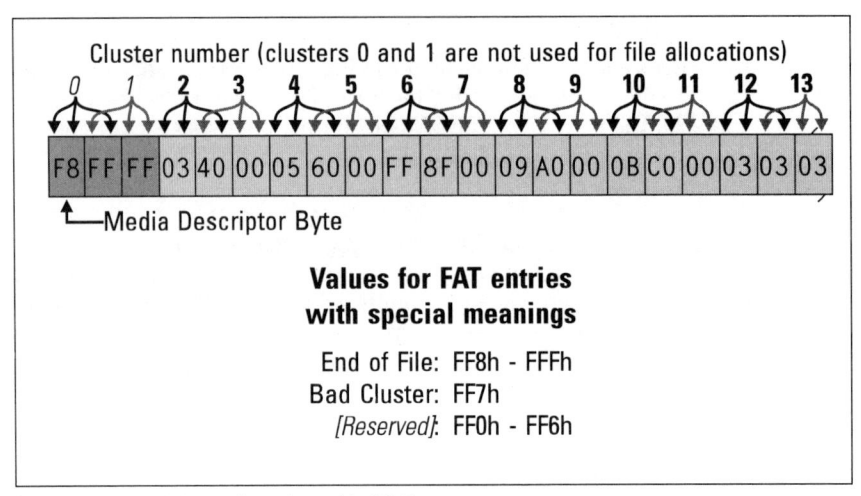

```
Cluster number (clusters 0 and 1 are not used for file allocations)
  0   1   2   3   4   5   6   7   8   9  10  11  12  13
|F8|FF|FF|03|40|00|05|60|00|FF|8F|00|09|A0|00|0B|C0|00|03|03|03|
 ↑
 └─Media Descriptor Byte
```

Values for FAT entries with special meanings

End of File: FF8h - FFFh
Bad Cluster: FF7h
[Reserved]: FF0h - FF6h

Figure 10-3: A 12-bit file allocation table (FAT).

The FAT contains chains of clusters that show where the system has put each file stored on the disk. It also shows which spaces are available for DOS to use when it has new information to record. Finally, the FAT's record of damaged areas on the disk prevents the system from storing data there.

You may have seen the DOS program CHKDSK display a message that it has found a number of lost clusters in a number of chains. You will learn how a chain of clusters may become lost in the section "How clusters become 'lost' and related problems."

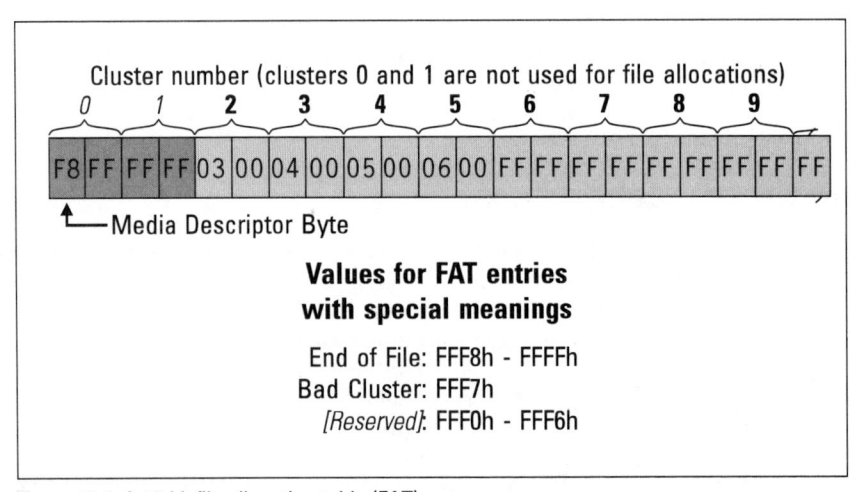

```
Cluster number (clusters 0 and 1 are not used for file allocations)
  0   1   2   3   4   5   6   7   8   9
|F8|FF|FF|FF|03|00|04|00|05|00|06|00|FF|FF|FF|FF|FF|FF|FF|FF|FF|
 ↑
 └─Media Descriptor Byte
```

Values for FAT entries with special meanings

End of File: FFF8h - FFFFh
Bad Cluster: FFF7h
[Reserved]: FFF0h - FFF6h

Figure 10-4: A 16-bit file allocation table (FAT).

Chapter 10: Preparing a Hard Disk to Store Information: Step 3

TECHNICAL SECRET

A couple of extra numbers at the start of the first sector of the FAT mark the beginning of the FAT and show what kind of disk this is. The first of these bytes is called the media descriptor byte. The other two or three special bytes are filled with ones (and thus have the hexadecimal value FF).

The media descriptor byte also appears in the DOS boot record's data table. Unfortunately, it does not give much useful information. Still, if it is not F8h, you know the disk is not a hard disk.

The two kinds of FAT

FATs come in two types: 12-bit and 16-bit. Prior to DOS Version 3, there were only 12-bit FATs. Later versions use both kinds. This distinction refers to the size of the numbers stored in the FAT for each cluster. For most purposes, you don't need to know what size FAT entries your disk has.

CAUTION

There is one very important exception to that statement. You do need to know the size of your FAT entries if you are upgrading from a 12-bit FAT to a new version of DOS that uses a 16-bit FAT. In this case, you must back up your data before you upgrade, or you will lose access to your data.

If you use some utility program to look at the FATs on your hard disk, be prepared to work some to understand what you see. Some utility programs, such as the very fine Disk Editor in the Norton Utilities (Version 5 or later), let you see each kind of information that the utility program can display in any of several formats.

TECHNICAL SECRET

Disk Editor can show you a FAT in terms that will easily make sense to you after you have read the description of a FAT in this section. It also can let you see what is really recorded on this disk. That display may be much harder to decipher.

If the logical volume whose FAT you are examining is of a size that makes the DOS program FORMAT choose to create 16-bit FATs, the job is not so difficult. All you have to know is that each cluster entry is a pair of bytes and that the bytes are arranged on the disk in "Intel order," with the least significant byte first. (The two principal standards for how to store a multibyte number in successive memory locations are the Intel order, which puts the least significant byte at the lowest memory address, and the Motorola address, which puts the most significant byte there. These names come from the fact that the Intel microprocessors, including the 80x86 family of chips used in PCs, all use the former strategy; the Motorola chips, including the 68x00 family used in Macintosh computers, use the latter strategy.)

Part I: The Hard Disk Companion

If you are looking at 12-bit FAT, on the other hand, things can be a lot more confusing. Look at Figure 10-3 again. Look carefully. You will see that the three nibbles (half-bytes) that make up one cluster entry are not recorded on the disk sequentially. Thank heavens (and Peter Norton) that the Disk Editor knows all about this and can easily display a FAT in a format that you will understand, whether it is a 12-bit or a 16-bit FAT.

The good news is this: DOS creates FATs. It maintains them. And almost never is it essential for you even to think about them. They simply are a part of what DOS keeps track of to help it do its job without unduly bothering you.

TECHNICAL SECRET

All DOS versions before 3.0 used 12-bit numbers in their FATs exclusively, and that was the source of their limit of no more than about 4,000 clusters. Raising 2 to the 12th power yields 4,096. Subtracting the special values that can't be used to point to other clusters yields a maximum of 4,078 clusters. All versions of DOS use 12-bit FAT entries for every floppy diskette.

When DOS 3 or later is high-level formatting a hard disk, it examines the size of the disk (the total number of sectors in the logical volume). It then decides whether it can get away with only 4,000 clusters without making the cluster size too large. If it can, it uses a FAT with 12-bit numbers. If not, it uses 16-bit numbers in the FAT. This larger size for the FAT entries means that you can have up to 65,518 clusters.

You may have noticed the vague term "too large" in the preceding paragraph. The exact rule that DOS uses to choose the cluster size and which size of FAT entries to use is not well documented. Further, DOS does not provide any way for you to tell it what you would prefer. Its FORMAT program does whatever it was built to do, and you just have to live with it. One thing you can do to influence it, though, is to choose your partition sizes carefully. Any partition larger than about 16MB will get a 16-bit FAT and as small a cluster size as possible. Smaller partitions are likely to get a 12-bit FAT; the resulting cluster size may meet DOS's notion of not "too large," but not yours.

Also, notice that if you choose to create partitions that are larger than 32MB, the clusters will necessarily be larger than one sector each. If the partition is very large, the clusters become very large, too. If you have a 260MB partition, for example, your clusters will be 8KB each. Table 10-1 shows the relationships among volume size, cluster size, FAT entry size, and DOS version.

Chapter 10: Preparing a Hard Disk to Store Information: Step 3

Size of Disk Volume (MB)	Size of Clusters (KB)	File Allocation Table Entry Size (bits)	DOS Versions
Up to 32	4	12	2.x
Up to 8	2	12	3.0+
8 to 15	4	12	3.0+
16 to 32	2	16	3.x
16 to 127	2	16	4.0+
128 to 255	4	16	4.0+
256 to 511	8	16	4.0+
512 to 1023	16	16	4.0+

Table 10-1: Cluster sizes for various size disks or logical drives and versions of DOS.

How big is your FAT?

Whatever kind of FAT your disk has, it occupies only a small fraction of the disk that it describes. Because it is so critical to the proper accessing of the files on the disk and it is small, DOS keeps two copies of the FAT on most disks for greater reliability.

TECHNICAL SECRET

If you have a 12-bit FAT, DOS will place two cluster-status numbers in every three bytes because three bytes are 24 (3x8) bits. This means that the size of your FAT under DOS 1 or 2 can be no more than about 6KB (4,000 entries times 1.5 bytes each). For DOS 3 and all later versions, the maximum size of the FAT is larger because you can have more clusters and thus more entries in the FAT, and because if you have a 16-bit FAT, each cluster number will take up two bytes instead of only 1.5 bytes. For these more recent versions of DOS, the maximum FAT size is 128KB.

Although it's easy to let DOS use enough RAM for a copy of a 6KB FAT, you couldn't permit it to store all of a 128KB FAT there. For that reason, DOS 3 and later versions are a bit more clever about what part of the FAT they must keep in RAM and what they will get from the disk when they need it.

Whenever DOS allocates a new cluster to a file or notices that a cluster has been released (because a file was erased), it updates both copies of the FAT. If DOS gets an error when reading the first FAT, it will try to read the second FAT. If that succeeds, DOS will use the information it got, but it may not tell you that it had to use the second FAT, and it won't attempt to repair the damaged first FAT.

The DOS program CHKDSK allows you to find out about discrepancies between the two copies of the FAT. Other than these two uses for it, though, DOS ignores the second FAT — one reason that it makes sense to run CHKDSK regularly, to reveal problems if they do arise.

DOS never fixes any problem it may notice with the FATs. At most, it will alert you, after which it may very well "give up." You have to fix the problem with the aid of some utility program before DOS can go on about its business. CHKDSK can fix some sorts of problems with the FAT. Unfortunately, all too often, its way of fixing them leaves much to be desired. See the discussion about this point in the section "Using DOS's CHKDSK First" in Chapter 16.

The root directory

The root directory, an orderly table of facts about files, is the final separate region of a DOS partition or logical drive that the FORMAT program creates. It is here that DOS begins to store the file directory information, connecting the filename with its location on the disk.

Each directory entry takes up 32 bytes. The first 11 bytes give the file's name (8 bytes) and extension (3 bytes). The next byte stores the file's attributes. Ten bytes are reserved, which means that Microsoft says not to use them. They will customarily be filled with zeros. Then comes the time and date at which a program opened the file with permission to change its contents (2 bytes for the date and 2 for the time). This part of the entry is followed by the cluster number at which DOS began storing this file's contents (2 bytes). The last 4 bytes store the file's size in bytes (see Figure 10-5).

In this figure, each byte is represented by a box. Each directory entry (32 bytes) is represented by one row of boxes. Inside each box at the bottom is the hexadecimal value of the number stored there. When that value represents an ASCII character, that character is printed above the hex value.

The attribute byte is interpreted by DOS bit-by-bit. Figure 10-5 shows the meaning of each of the six attribute bits that DOS uses. Some network operating systems use one or both of the remaining bits.

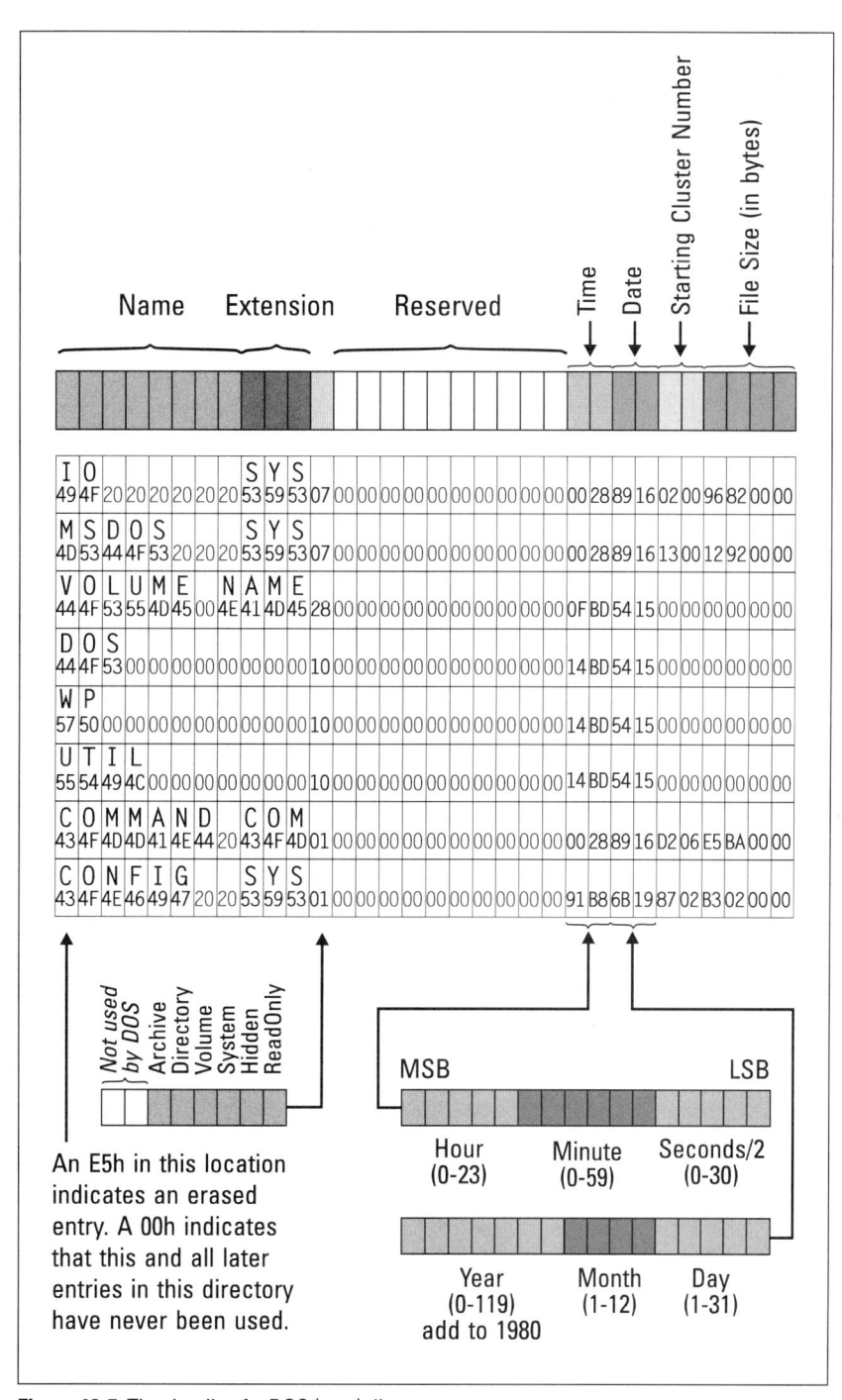

Chapter 10: Preparing a Hard Disk to Store Information: Step 3

| Name | Extension | Reserved | Time | Date | Starting Cluster Number | File Size (in bytes) |

```
I O       S Y S
49 4F 20 20 20 20 20 20 53 59 53 07 00 00 00 00 00 00 00 00 00 00 00 28 89 16 02 00 96 82 00 00

M S D O S   S Y S
4D 53 44 4F 53 20 20 20 53 59 53 07 00 00 00 00 00 00 00 00 00 00 00 28 89 16 13 00 12 92 00 00

V O L U M E   N A M E
44 4F 53 54 4D 45 00 4E 41 4D 45 28 00 00 00 00 00 00 00 00 00 00 00 0F BD 54 15 00 00 00 00 00 00

D O S
44 4F 53 00 00 00 00 00 00 00 00 10 00 00 00 00 00 00 00 00 00 00 00 14 BD 54 15 00 00 00 00 00 00

W P
57 50 00 00 00 00 00 00 00 00 00 10 00 00 00 00 00 00 00 00 00 00 00 14 BD 54 15 00 00 00 00 00 00

U T I L
55 54 49 4C 00 00 00 00 00 00 00 10 00 00 00 00 00 00 00 00 00 00 00 14 BD 54 15 00 00 00 00 00 00

C O M M A N D   C O M
43 4F 4D 4D 41 4E 44 20 43 4F 4D 01 00 00 00 00 00 00 00 00 00 00 00 28 89 16 D2 06 E5 BA 00 00

C O N F I G   S Y S
43 4F 4E 46 49 47 20 20 53 59 53 01 00 00 00 00 00 00 00 00 00 00 00 91 B8 6B 19 87 02 B3 02 00 00
```

Not used by DOS
Archive
Directory
Volume
System
Hidden
ReadOnly

An E5h in this location indicates an erased entry. A 00h indicates that this and all later entries in this directory have never been used.

MSB ... LSB

Hour (0-23) Minute (0-59) Seconds/2 (0-30)

Year (0-119) add to 1980   Month (1-12)   Day (1-31)

Figure 10-5: The details of a DOS (root) directory.

Part I: The Hard Disk Companion

The date and time at which the file was last changed are each stored in a two-byte binary number. The figure also shows how those bits are broken down. The most significant bit (MSB) is to the left and the least significant bit (LSB) is to the right in all three byte detail diagrams (for attribute, time, and data bytes).

Notice that the directory entry states only where the file begins, not where the entire file resides. To find the rest of the file, DOS must consult the FAT, starting with the cluster where the file begins (and ends, if it's a small file) and following the chain of clusters until it reaches the file's end.

The root directory has a fixed size, which depends on your version of DOS and the size and type of your disk drive. A common number for a hard drive is 512 entries.

Subdirectories

If you have more than 512 files (or whatever number can fit in your disk's root directory), you have to store their directory information in a subdirectory, a concept introduced with DOS 2.0. A subdirectory is nothing more than a special file. That is, although it is stored like a file, its contents are interpreted as an extension to the root directory.

> **TIP:** One of several reasons why it is a very good idea to keep everything out of the root directory that can be put elsewhere is that if you attempt to put more files into the root directory than will fit, DOS will tell you it can't do so. The message it gives you, however, is misleading. It tells you there is no more room on the disk, not that there is no more room in the root directory. Remember that among the several files that must be in the root directory are the hidden system files (if this is a bootable disk) and the volume label (if you have given this disk volume a name). So the best rule is: If it doesn't have to be in the root directory, get it out of there!

The first-level subdirectories are listed as files in the root directory. They contain listings of other files and perhaps other, second-level subdirectories, and so on. Figure 10-6 shows two views of the directory and subdirectory structure on a hypothetical hard disk.

At the top of this figure is what you would see if you ran the DOS program TREE (from DOS, Version 5). The lower part of the figure shows a somewhat whimsical representation of the directories on a disk as rooms in a warehouse for data. The backslash character by itself (\) is the DOS name for the root directory.

The tree of subdirectories can go about as many levels deep as you want. The limit is that the path from the root directory to any file must not be more than 64 characters long, including a backslash character (\) to separate each directory name from the next and one backslash at the end of the path.

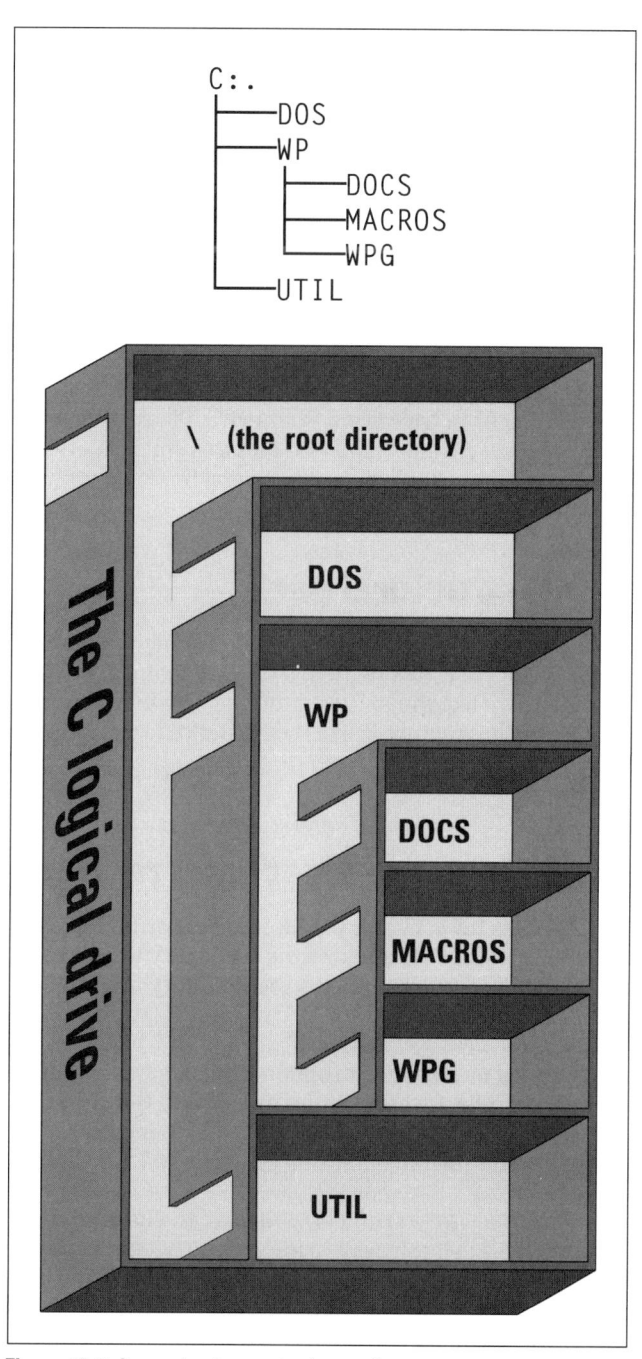

Chapter 10: Preparing a Hard Disk to Store Information: Step 3

```
C:.
 ├──DOS
 ├──WP
 │   ├──DOCS
 │   ├──MACROS
 │   └──WPG
 └──UTIL
```

Figure 10-6: A couple of ways to view a directory tree.

The volume label

One other special "file" that may be found in a root directory is the disk's *volume label,* which you can use to store the name you want to associate with this disk partition or logical volume. The system lists this label like a file, but it has the special volume attribute bit turned on, and its size and cluster number are both zero.

> **TIP** You don't have to give partitions or volumes a name, but it is a good idea. Starting with Version 3.2 of DOS, the FORMAT program has a very valuable feature: If you ask it to reformat a hard disk that has a volume name, it will refuse to do the job unless you can tell it what that volume name is. This feature helps keep you from accidentally wiping out your C drive. (It will help you, but it won't prevent you from wiping out your drive. Please remember not to use the FORMAT program casually, and don't let this small safety feature lull you into not keeping good backups of your hard disk!)

Recap of the structural parts

At last, you have learned about all the elements that must be on a disk to allow DOS to use it. In terms of the parking lot analogy, the painted stripes on the pavement are like the low-level format. The fences are like the partitions. The valet parking structure is like the FAT and directories. The disk volume label is like a sign over the entrance.

How clusters become "lost" and related problems

DOS updates the FAT and the directory information independently of each other. Normally, DOS updates the FAT every time it adds new information to a file on the disk. It only updates the directory information when it finishes work with that file.

If something interrupts a program while it's writing a file to the disk, the FAT entries will reflect where on the disk to find the data for that file, but there won't yet be a directory entry for the file to indicate where it starts. The standard name for the clusters marked in the FAT for that file is a *lost chain.*

One common way you end up with lost chains is when a program becomes confused and the only way to interrupt it seems to be by rebooting the computer. That step stops what the computer was doing, but it also prevents the program from cleaning up after itself. Lost chains are almost an inevitable consequence. This is one reason that it is generally not a good idea to stop programs by turning off or rebooting your computer.

Chapter 10: Preparing a Hard Disk to Store Information: Step 3

The way to find lost chains is by running the DOS program CHKDSK without any command line switches. You can type **CHKDSK C:**, but don't type **CHKDSK C: /F**, or at least, don't do so at first.

If CHKDSK reports only lost clusters, then it is safe, and usually a good idea, to rerun it on the same drive, and this time do specify the /F option. When asked if you want to convert the lost chains to files, answer **Yes**. After CHKDSK is through, you will find one or more files in the root directory with names like FILE0000.CHK, FILE0001.CHK, and so on. Look at the contents of these files. (The LIST program on the *Hard Disk SECRETS* disk is a wonderful way to look at these files.) If you find a file you had lost and were looking for, rename the file and move it to the proper directory. Otherwise, simply delete these files so that you can reuse the space they occupy on your disk.

Any time you recover a lost chain to a file, don't assume that what you get is one entire file, complete and correct in every detail. In particular, if you find that you have recovered a program, do not run that program. The odds that it is damaged are way too high. Replace the program from a backup or from the original distribution disk. If the file you recover is a spreadsheet, word processing document, or database file, you may have to examine it quite closely, using the application that created it. Frequently, you will find that you have a big chunk of what you lost, but that is missing several sectors of information and has within it some other sectors of totally irrelevant material taken from some other (erased or lost) file.

Some other ways DOS can mess things up

If the file to which data was being written already existed, then a directory entry also exists. But the file length in the directory entry does not get updated until DOS finishes with the file (when the application program adding to this file "closes" the file). If something interrupts the program before it gets around to closing its files, another kind of error will be built into the directory-FAT structure. CHKDSK will notice this discrepancy and report that the file length is invalid. Unfortunately, its fix for this error is almost surely *not* what you would like it to do. (It will simply lop off the apparently excess length, when in all likelihood that is your most recently saved data.)

Keeping CHKDSK from doing you such a "favor" is one reason never to run that program with the /F option until you have let it find out what it thinks is wrong with your disk. If it finds some files with invalid lengths, you may well want to find some alternative utility program to help you deal with that condition. The Norton Utilities and PC Tools (from Central Point Software) are two of the most popular general-purpose utility packages that are useful for this sort of work.

The last of the common errors that CHKDSK can report is the existence of files that *cross-linked* at some cluster. This report simply means that the chains of clusters for these two files both contain a common number; that is, both files claim to have a portion of their data stored in the same place.

> **TIP** The cause of a cross-linked error is not altogether obvious. What is clear is that DOS, or some program that bypassed DOS, became confused and wrote invalid information into the FAT. The only good solution is to erase both the files that are cross-linked and replace them from back-up copies. Before you do this, however, it is prudent to get a "second opinion" from some other utility program. CHKDSK may be the program that was confused. It also is a good idea to reboot your computer before seeking that second opinion so that DOS gets a fresh copy of the FATs from the disk.

The Rest of What FORMAT Does

The DOS program FORMAT does more than just set aside space for each of the four regions of a DOS logical volume. It also must initialize the values in three of them, and it makes at least a cursory check of the integrity of the fourth region. Finally, and most unfortunately, it may do one more thing (depending on which brand and version of DOS you are using) that could ruin your day! Read on to learn what it is and when you might thus inadvertently do yourself in.

Disk initialization

The boot sector receives a copy of the standard DOS boot program and a data table appropriate to this partition or logical volume. The FAT has its first byte set to the media descriptor byte, and the next two or three bytes have all their bits set to ones. The rest of the FAT is filled with zeros.

A simple-minded disk test

FORMAT then reads the whole of the data space. It records in the FAT any clusters in which it finds one or more bad sectors that either it couldn't read or that the low-level format program marked as bad. Finally, FORMAT enters a zero into every location of the root directory. If the disk is to be bootable, it copies the system files to the disk and makes appropriate entries in the root directory and FAT for those files.

Most versions of DOS write nothing to the data area when the FORMAT program is run (aside from the system files if you are making the disk bootable). In the next chapter, in a section titled "Destructive FORMAT programs," you will learn about some versions of DOS that do (and read a warning about what to do if you have one of them on your PC).

Chapter 10: Preparing a Hard Disk to Store Information: Step 3

Interpretation of the DOS boot record data table

Now, at last, you can understand all the numbers contained in the DOS boot record's data table. Thirteen to 50 of these numbers (depending on the version of DOS) are copied to the BIOS parameter block for this drive. All of them are available to DOS programs through interrupt calls (see Figure 10-7).

/ **TECHNICAL SECRET** /

The data area in the boot sector in Figure 10-7 contains the following information:

- The first eight bytes of the data table (starting with the fourth byte in the sector) contain the name of the original equipment manufacturer (OEM) name and DOS version number for the FORMAT program that created this boot sector. This field does not go into the BIOS parameter block.

- The second field (2 bytes) is the number of bytes per sector (which can be anything at all, up to 65,536 bytes). All PC hard disks use 512 bytes per physical sector; therefore, if they use some other value for the logical sector size, it is likely to be a multiple of 512 bytes.

- The third field (a single byte) is the number of sectors per cluster. The product of these first two numbers tells how many bytes are in one cluster.

- The fourth field (two bytes), the number of reserved sectors, is really the number of sectors in this partition before the first FAT begins. Because logical sectors begin at number zero, the number of reserved sectors is the first sector in the first FAT. Ordinarily, this has the value one, meaning that only the boot sector precedes the FAT, although the designers of DOS have allowed for a format that might reserve more sectors between the boot record and the first FAT.

- The next two fields (one and two bytes, respectively), the number of FATs and the number of entries in the root directory, are self-explanatory.

- The field for total number of sectors in volume is only used for DOS volumes smaller than 32MB in size. Because it is only a two-byte number, it cannot express the number of sectors in a larger volume (assuming the logical sector size is the DOS standard value of 512 bytes). For DOS logical volumes more than 32MB in size, a zero appears in this field. The actual size for these "huge" partitions is put in a later field that only occurs in DOS boot records created by DOS 4 or later versions.

- In the next field, the media descriptor byte for any hard disk is F8 hexadecimal.

- The next field is the number of sectors per FAT.

- The boot sector data table under DOS 2 ends with one more field for the number of sectors in a track. In DOS 2.x, this entry is a one-byte number, and thus its value cannot be more than 255.

- DOS 3 increased the size of the sectors per track field and added two new fields — the number of heads and a number called hidden sectors. The number of heads is the number of platter surfaces on which data gets recorded (as you may have guessed). The number of hidden sectors is the total number of physical sectors on the drive before the start of this partition. (Notice the difference between the reserved sectors and the hidden sectors. The former says how many sectors *within this partition* to skip to get to the beginning of the first FAT. The latter says how many sectors *on the drive* to skip to get to the beginning of this partition.)

- DOS 4 increased the size of the hidden sectors field from two to four bytes. This increase will allow truly gigantic disks! Version 4 also added a four-byte field for the total number of sectors for DOS logical volumes greater than 32MB in size.

- DOS 5 added several more fields. These fields include one for the BIOS physical address for the disk containing this partition or logical drive, an extended boot record signature, a volume serial number, a volume name, and a file system identification string.

The BIOS physical address for the disk may confuse you. The normal value for the first physical hard disk is 80h. If you have a second hard disk, it will have address 81h. Starting with DOS Version 5.0, you may have up to seven physical hard disks, so their addresses will go up 86h.

DOS calls the volume within the DOS primary partition on the first physical drive C. If you have a DOS primary partition on a second physical drive, it is called D. This process continues through all your physical disks, but only if they have DOS primary partitions.

The logical volumes within a DOS extended partition on the first drive get drive letters next. (If you have two physical drives and both have a DOS primary partition, these drive letters will start with E.) Then drive letters are assigned to the logical volumes within the DOS extended partition on the next physical drive. Again the process continues until DOS runs out of logical drives to give letters to (or until it gets to Z).

Normally, the boot sectors in logical volumes within an extended partition have the same BIOS physical address as the DOS primary partition on the same drive.

Chapter 10: Preparing a Hard Disk to Store Information: Step 3   279

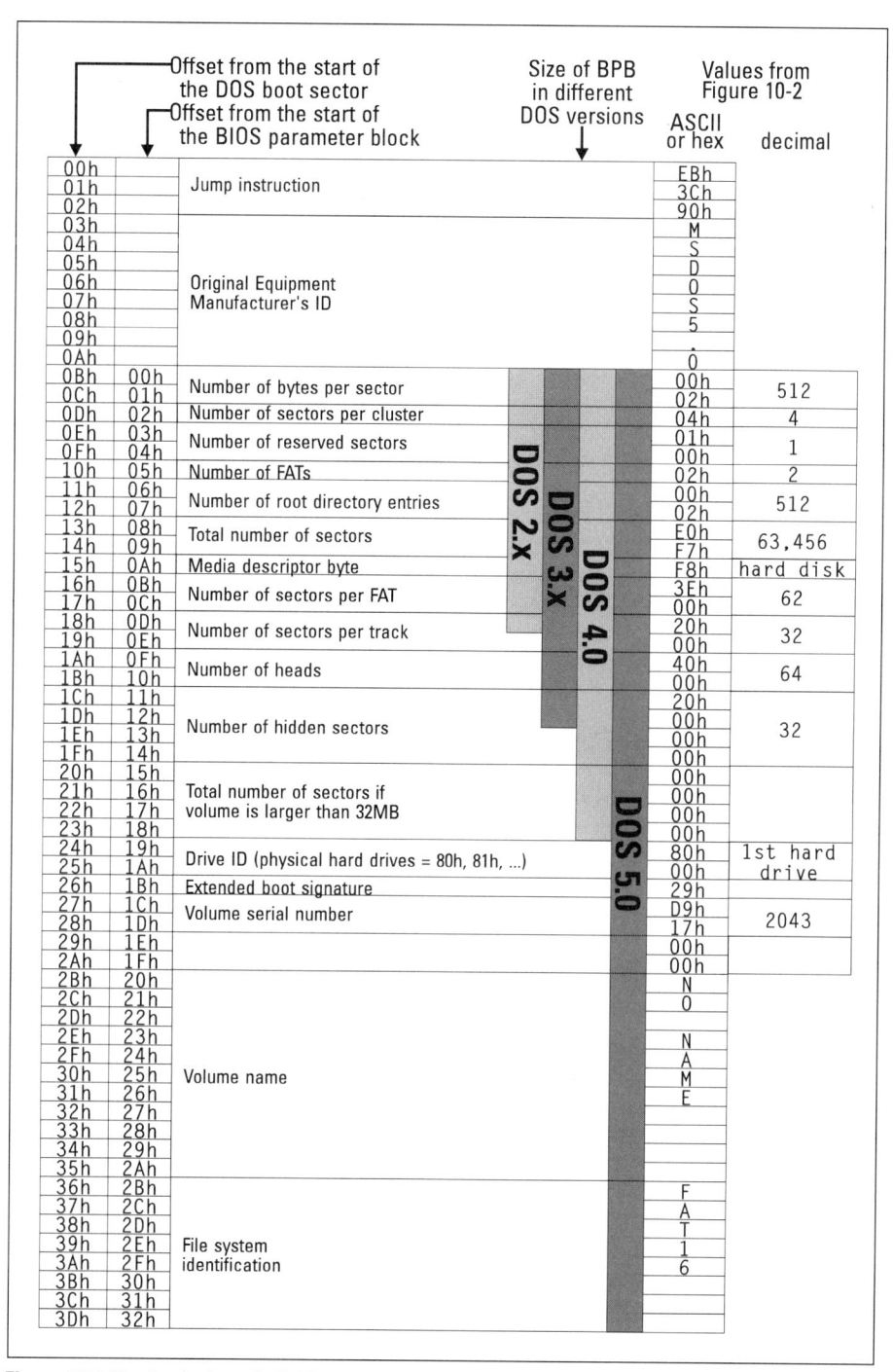

Offset from start of DOS boot sector	Offset from start of BIOS parameter block	Field	Size of BPB in different DOS versions	ASCII or hex	decimal
00h		Jump instruction		EBh	
01h				3Ch	
02h				90h	
03h		Original Equipment Manufacturer's ID		M	
04h				S	
05h				D	
06h				O	
07h				S	
08h				5	
09h				.	
0Ah				0	
0Bh	00h	Number of bytes per sector		00h	512
0Ch	01h			02h	
0Dh	02h	Number of sectors per cluster		04h	4
0Eh	03h	Number of reserved sectors	DOS 2.x	01h	1
0Fh	04h			00h	
10h	05h	Number of FATs		02h	2
11h	06h	Number of root directory entries		00h	512
12h	07h			02h	
13h	08h	Total number of sectors		E0h	63,456
14h	09h			F7h	
15h	0Ah	Media descriptor byte	DOS 3.x	F8h	hard disk
16h	0Bh	Number of sectors per FAT		3Eh	62
17h	0Ch			00h	
18h	0Dh	Number of sectors per track		20h	32
19h	0Eh		DOS 4.0	00h	
1Ah	0Fh	Number of heads		40h	64
1Bh	10h			00h	
1Ch	11h	Number of hidden sectors		20h	32
1Dh	12h			00h	
1Eh	13h			00h	
1Fh	14h			00h	
20h	15h	Total number of sectors if volume is larger than 32MB		00h	
21h	16h			00h	
22h	17h			00h	
23h	18h			00h	
24h	19h	Drive ID (physical hard drives = 80h, 81h, ...)	DOS 5.0	80h	1st hard drive
25h	1Ah			00h	
26h	1Bh	Extended boot signature		29h	
27h	1Ch	Volume serial number		D9h	2043
28h	1Dh			17h	
29h	1Eh			00h	
2Ah	1Fh			00h	
2Bh	20h	Volume name		N	
2Ch	21h			O	
2Dh	22h				
2Eh	23h			N	
2Fh	24h			A	
30h	25h			M	
31h	26h			E	
32h	27h				
33h	28h				
34h	29h				
35h	2Ah				
36h	2Bh	File system identification		F	
37h	2Ch			A	
38h	2Dh			T	
39h	2Eh			1	
3Ah	2Fh			6	
3Bh	30h				
3Ch	31h				
3Dh	32h				

Figure 10-7: The beginning of a DOS boot sector, showing the data that is kept there, and indicating which of those items are copied to the BIOS parameter block.

How the floppy diskette format process is different

The DOS program FORMAT usually does more to a floppy diskette than it does to a hard disk. In particular, it must do more if you are putting the initial format on a floppy diskette. On a hard disk, the low-level format and partitioning must be done before FORMAT will be able to do anything. On a floppy diskette, FORMAT does the whole job. (That is, it does both the low-level and the high-level formatting. There are no partitions on a floppy diskette, so there is no need to create a partition table.)

Beginning with Version 5 of DOS, the FORMAT command was modified to make it a bit safer to use. Its default mode of operation, if the disk you ask it to format has been formatted previously, is a safe format: FORMAT skips the low-level-formatting step, and before it initializes the FATs and root directory, it saves a copy of them on the disk. Thus, you can recover files from that disk up until you actually store information belonging to some other file in the sectors your old file had been in. When you do that, you overwrite the actual file data, making recovery of that file impossible.

These improvements in FORMAT's safety apply to floppy disks just as they do to hard disks. If you are formatting a previously formatted floppy disk with DOS 5 or a later version, it will do just what it would do on a hard disk, and no more.

Alternatives to the DOS high-level format

The discussion in Chapters 8 and 9 of low-level formatting and partitioning applies to disks used with DOS and to those used with other PC operating systems. The controller lays down the low-level format, so the operating system cannot change it. The BIOS reads the partition table, so it must be the same no matter which operating system you install on your disk. Because the high-level format within each partition is put there by the operating system that will be using that partition, its form can vary wildly from one operating system to another.

UNIX and OS/2 are currently the other popular operating systems for single PCs. A lot of local-area networks (LANs) use Novell NetWare, which amounts to a special operating system for the file server PC in those LANs. Novell supplies only the file server's operating system; the workstation PCs hooked to the file server run DOS or OS/2. Microsoft has announced a new operating system, Windows NT, that will compete with UNIX, OS/2, and NetWare.

Because these operating systems understand and use the same partitioning method used by DOS, they can share a disk with DOS in the manner described in Chapter 9. Equally, they could be the only operating system on a PC's disk.

Chapter 10: Preparing a Hard Disk to Store Information: Step 3

UNIX

UNIX does its high-level format very differently from DOS, making a partition that has been formatted by UNIX completely mysterious to DOS. This condition is true even though the DOS designers have borrowed more and more notions about how an operating system ought to be built from the design of UNIX. When you examine the details, UNIX does many things about dealing with a hard disk in a manner that is quite similar to what DOS does but with just enough difference to keep the two systems from reading each other's disk partitions.

> **TECHNICAL SECRET**
>
> Here are a few of the ways in which UNIX (or Xenix) does things differently from DOS:
>
> - UNIX defines areas on the disk in terms of *blocks* and *inodes*. These areas are similar to sectors and clusters, but UNIX will check them for ECC errors every time they are read or written. If any errors occur, the data automatically will be moved to some new location. For this operation to work, you must set aside some spare tracks when you format the partition. When you run the UNIX format program, it will offer to do this task for you and suggest a number of spare tracks to use, based on the size of the partition.
>
> - UNIX keeps track separately of the disk space occupied by files belonging to each user of the system. Each user is limited to some number of files and number of megabytes of total storage, independent of what any other user has taken.
>
> - UNIX defines more attributes that a file may have, such as various permissions and the notion of linking more than one filename to the same data.
>
> - UNIX defines a *dirty bit* for files. If a file is somehow not correctly written to the disk and its directory entry is not properly updated, the system will notice this fact and demand that you run the equivalent of CHKDSK the next time you start the system.

OS/2 and the HPFS

OS/2 operates a bit strangely. It can make its disks look just like DOS disks, which lets it share those disks or partitions with DOS. It also can allocate disk space by using the high performance file system (HPFS), a new and improved method that is completely incompatible with the DOS FAT method of disk space allocation. You can make some of your OS/2 drives FAT format and some HPFS format, allowing DOS access to the former (but not to the latter) when you reboot your PC by using DOS.

Part I: The Hard Disk Companion

TECHNICAL SECRET

DOS descended from both CP/M and UNIX, with more of the UNIX features included in each new version of DOS. As a child of DOS, OS/2 not surprisingly has much in common with UNIX. Here are a few ways in which OS/2 does things in an HPFS partition differently than in a normal DOS partition:

- An HPFS partition does not have FAT tables. Directory information is kept in many different places, closer to the file locations on the disk. This feature means that there may be less time wasted by moving the disk head between files and the directory entries describing them. The new directory format allows you to use long filenames (up to 256 characters).

- The HPFS file system allocates disk space directly in sectors (no more multisector clusters with their resulting inefficiency). Unfortunately, it does not automatically test data integrity and move data to safety.

- An HPFS partition can be really large; that is, its maximum logical size can be really large. Because OS/2 uses the BIOS, INT 13h still limits it to a maximum physical disk size of 504MB or 8GB, depending on whether you "cheat." See the discussion of "RAID and related strategies" in Chapter 7 for a way to beat this limit.

- OS/2 radically extends the notion of file attributes. OS/2's HPFS uses disk caching extensively, including deferred-write caching. This feature is risky, as is explained in Chapter 5.

If you turn off power (or power fails, or your computer gets "hung") before your information is written to the disk, your files will not be updated correctly. To help guard against disaster, OS/2 keeps track of the state of its disk cache and will alert you the next time you boot up OS/2 if you should make that mistake (or have that misfortune).

Windows NT and the NTFS

Windows NT will extend the notion, introduced with OS/2, of "grandfathering" an older operating system's file systems. Windows NT will be able to read and write files in a FAT logical volume, an HPFS logical volume, or in its own, new NTFS volumes.

TECHNICAL SECRET

The NTFS file system incorporates most of the advantages of OS/2's HPFS, UNIX's file system, and has some new features of its own. The NTFS is designed for maximum file integrity, so it includes the hot fix feature of UNIX, and also a transaction-based model, to ensure that an entire file is written or none of it is written.

Chapter 10: Preparing a Hard Disk to Store Information: Step 3

> Naturally, with something that is (at the time this book is being written) only "vaporware," one cannot be sure just how wonderful it will be in practice until after it is a released product.

Novell NetWare

Novell's NetWare uses a special format for its file servers for a couple of reasons. Having a proprietary format allows Novell to optimize the disk usage for its special needs, and it helps ensure file security.

NetWare provides several barriers to accessing files stored on its servers by requiring passwords and permissions. This security would be worthless if one could get at those files by rebooting the file server PC off a DOS floppy disk and then using standard DOS commands to read or copy the hard disk's files. With NetWare's unique high-level format for the file server, however, you can't boot off a DOS disk to get at those files.

TECHNICAL SECRET

NetWare is famous for its COMPSURF program. The standard NetWare installation procedure takes you through all the steps of preparing a hard disk, from low-level to high-level formats, with partitioning in the middle. This procedure has led some people to think that Novell is doing all the levels of disk preparation in some special way.

That is not really true. NetWare simply hides most of the steps from you. Of necessity, it first asks the controller to do the usual low-level format. Next, the COMPSURF program tests the disk as an extension of the normal controller tests after doing a low-level format. Conducting many more tests assures NetWare that it has found all the bad spots on the server's hard disks. In fact, COMPSURF does for a NetWare partition something very much like what SpinRite does for a DOS logical volume, at least in terms of testing the disk's integrity. The major difference is that COMPSURF *only* does so *before* the data are put on the disk.

Finally, with Version 3.x of NetWare, Novell has replaced COMPSURF with a new Surface Test routine (in the Disk Options of the INSTALL program). This new routine allows the user to do a non-data-destructive surface test at any time. The only restriction is that the disk must be dismounted from the network first.

After it finishes testing the newly low-level formatted disk, NetWare's installation procedure creates a standard partition table and then does the high-level format — the only part that is unique to NetWare.

How Bad Spots Are Found and Avoided

During the low-level format process, the disk controller tests each sector, at least superficially. The manufacturers would like you to believe that this assures you that the sectors are able to store and retrieve data faithfully. Although the controller will set the bad sector flag in the header of any sector it notices as bad, occasionally a bad sector will pass the controller test and be marked as good.

Some controllers only check to see that the sector headers can be read without a CRC error. They don't even check to see that the sector headers contain the right information, and they don't check the data areas of the sectors at all.

The low-level format program also may allow you to enter bad track or bad sector numbers. If you enter bad tracks, the controller will set the bad sector flag in each sector of the tracks you specify, whether or not it found them to be bad. Similarly, if you enter bad sector numbers, those sectors will be flagged as bad, no matter what the controller's test reported.

The DOS high-level format program (FORMAT) retests all the data area in each DOS partition or DOS logical drive that it is formatting. (This test is a little bit better, but it still is just a read test and will not catch many marginal sectors.) The FORMAT program then records in the FAT a special value for each cluster that contains one or more bad sectors. Notice that, because DOS cannot keep track of any unit of disk storage smaller than the cluster, whole clusters are marked bad and rendered unavailable for data storage.

TECHNICAL SECRET

Another tricky point may have occurred to you. What if the sector you want to read is bad in its header? In that case, you cannot read which sector it was. How do you know which one is the bad one? The answer is that you (or, more accurately, the BIOS) can only read a sector by asking the controller for it by number. If the controller comes back with an error, you know that the sector whose number you asked for is a bad one (or else that your disk's head positioner is malfunctioning).

Any sector (with a bad sector header) may not be able to receive an appropriate mark in its bad sector flag. Still, FORMAT will catch it — although only after many attempts to read it — which is the source of the grinding noises you may hear when FORMAT is testing a disk after it applies the high-level format.

No other DOS program ever marks clusters as bad. Because you normally only format a disk once, if a region goes bad after you have been using it, DOS will not help you find that bad spot, which creates a situation that can have dire consequences. You'll learn more about this situation in the next chapter.

Chapter 10: Preparing a Hard Disk to Store Information: Step 3

Summary

▶ An operating system imposes its own organization upon a disk volume during a high-level, or logical, format. DOS does this with the FORMAT program.

▶ A DOS format can be done only on a hard disk volume that has been previously created by using FDISK (or its equivalent in some other PC operating system), and that can be done only if the disk has previously been low-level, or physically, formatted. This condition is in contrast to the case for floppy diskettes, for which the DOS program FORMAT can do the whole job.

▶ FORMAT divides a DOS logical volume into four regions. First is the boot section. Next are the file allocation tables (FATs). Third is the root directory. The rest of the disk is the data area, where you store your files.

▶ Subdirectories are merely files with a special format that are used in a special way by DOS.

▶ Alternative PC operating systems such as UNIX, OS/2, Windows NT, and Novell NetWare use different strategies to format the disk volumes they use. The UNIX and NetWare formats are completely incompatible with DOS. OS/2 and Windows NT can use DOS logical volumes and also can create and use DOS-incompatible volumes.

▶ Except for the NetWare COMPSURF program, none of the PC operating systems does a thorough job of checking the disk surface integrity as it is formatting a volume. DOS users can accomplish this level of testing by using SpinRite, with the added advantage that SpinRite testing can be done any time, without damage to the data stored in a volume — quite unlike testing with NetWare's COMPSURF (and, in recent versions, the Surface Test routine).

Now you know all about how healthy hard disks work. Next, you will learn how hard disks sometimes die, how to prevent untimely deaths, and how to try to resuscitate expired drives.

Chapter 11

How Hard Disks Die

In This Chapter

▶ The many ways that your hard disk can "die"

▶ How to differentiate between hardware failures and the hard disk deaths that are merely a result of some messed up information

▶ Some versions of DOS that have a dangerous FORMAT program

▶ An apparent slow death of your hard disk that is really a simply correctable degradation of its performance

▶ What you can hope for, realistically, in the way of data recovery from a failed hard drive

▶ The what, why, and how of creating effective backups for your valuable data

Failure Modes

Your hard disk can fail for a number of reasons. Some are a consequence of human error, such as dropping a hard disk, which is almost guaranteed to seriously damage it. Random hardware failures also can do in your drive, as can external events, such as power surges. Some drives fall victim to a creeping "illness" that you will find described in detail later in this chapter.

Given the degree to which most PC users depend on their hard disks, a disk crash is likely to induce terror and panic. This is not the best state of mind for troubleshooting a bad drive (or anything else)! Know this: You often can recover your data after a disk failure. There, that should dispel some of your fear and lower your panic level.

Because your hard disk is part of a larger subsystem of your PC, a failure of any component in that subsystem will look like a failure of the hard drive. The important hardware parts to consider are the configuration CMOS memory, the hard disk controller, the cables connecting the controller to the drive and the drive to the power supply, and the drive electronic and mechanical parts (see Figure 11-1).

You also must consider the various pieces of stored information that are required for access to any hard drive. These include the drive type and dimension data stored in the configuration CMOS memory, the partition tables

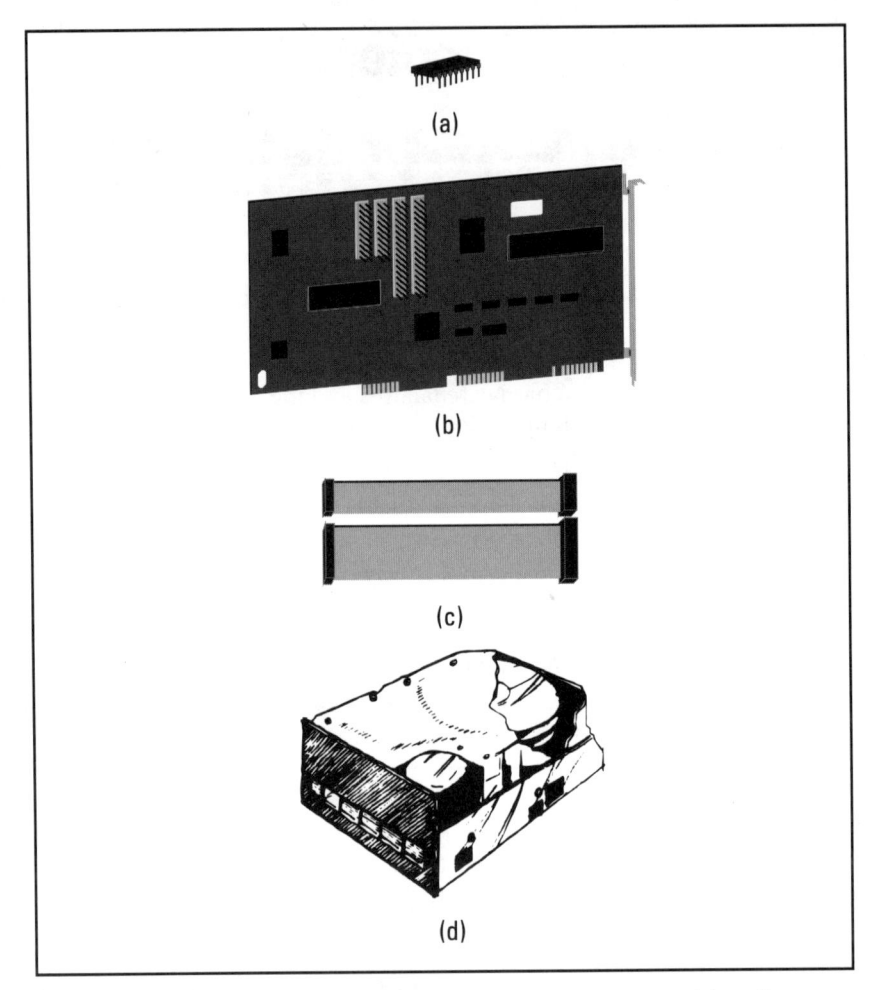

Figure 11-1: The essential hardware parts of a PC's hard disk subsystem: (a) configuration CMOS memory chip, (b) controller, often on an option card, (c) cables, and (d) disk drive.

and BIOS parameter table data stored in the master boot record and the DOS boot record, the file allocation and directory information stored in the DOS volume (in the FATs and the root directory and various subdirectories) — see Figure 11-2. Booting your computer requires that all these hardware and information "parts" function correctly.

There are several quite subtle issues involved in how all these information parts in a PC are used to access the hard disk. The configuration CMOS stores the drive's dimensions. The dimensions are implied by the numbers in the partition table (stored within the master boot record). Those same dimensions

> **Essential information "parts"
> required for access to a file**
>
> Drive type (or dimensions) in
> CMOS configuration memory
>
> Hard disk parameter table entries
>
> Partition table entries
> (contained in master boot record)
>
> BIOS parameter table entries
> (contained in DOS boot record)
>
> File allocation tables
>
> Directories and subdirectores
>
> Data in file
>
> **Additional information
> "parts" required for booting**
>
> Master boot record program
>
> DOS hidden system files
>
> CONFIG.SYS file and all the
> device drivers mentioned in it
>
> Command interpreter program
> (COMMAND.COM)
>
> AUTOEXEC.BAT file and all
> the programs mentioned in it

Figure 11-2: The essential information "parts" of a PC's hard disk subsystem.

also are stored in the BIOS parameter block for each logical volume, which gets its information from the DOS boot record for that volume. An autoconfiguring hard disk controller records another set of drive dimensions somewhere on the disk; normally, only the controller can access this set of dimensions.

What if these different sets of drive dimensions don't all have the same values? Whether that is a problem depends on many things. Most autoconfiguring hard disk controllers don't much care what drive type (and therefore what set of implied drive dimensions) is stored in the configuration CMOS memory. Well, these controllers don't care as long as the size shown in the CMOS is smaller than the actual size of the drive. (If the drive and controller are not capable of sector translation, the individual dimensions for number of heads, number of cylinders, and number of sectors per track must each be smaller than or equal to the corresponding real numbers. If the drive or controller does sector translating, it may only care that the total capacity be no larger than the drive's actual capacity.)

Some autoconfiguring controllers will use the actual dimensions of the drive, and thus give you its full capacity, even if the drive type you chose was for a much smaller drive. Other autoconfiguring controllers, especially those on IDE/ATA drives, may give you only as much capacity as the drive type you selected, even though the actual drive may have much more capacity it could give you. To solve this problem, you can choose a better fitting drive type or get a different kind of controller or a BIOS with the right size among those in its drive type table.

In some other cases, the computer relies on the configuration CMOS numbers to boot the system but then doesn't use those numbers any time thereafter. Instead, all subsequent accesses to the hard disk use the dimensions shown in the BIOS parameter block. In those systems, both sets of numbers (CMOS and BIOS parameter block) need to be correct for the PC to work normally. If only the CMOS numbers are wrong, you will find that you can boot from a floppy diskette and then access the hard drive normally, but you will be unable to boot from the hard drive.

Here is an even more subtle way things can go amiss: You may find that you cannot boot from your hard drive, but you can use it just fine after you boot from a floppy diskette. Upon checking, you may discover that the drive dimensions shown by the CMOS drive-type entry and those in the DOS boot record are both correct. What you may have forgotten to check is whether the *bootable* flag byte (also called the *active* flag) in the master boot record is set correctly.

These are just some examples of how the proper function of your PC depends on many different pieces of information. When you consider all these different places that must have just the right information stored in them, it is not so surprising that most failures of hard drives turn out not to be actual hardware failures, but rather data failures. After the messed up data is restored to its previous content, the "drive failure" disappears.

One way to help detect which part has failed is to use some diagnostic test programs. A great number of them are on the market. One you will read about in more detail in Part II of this book is SpinRite. Although it's not marketed as a hard disk testing utility, SpinRite offers one of the best tests of the hardware and controller electronics.

Many other disk utility programs claim to offer disk testing, but most of them do a much more cursory job. An inexpensive one that does a fair job and is very easy to use is CheckIt from Touchstone Software Corporation (2130 Main Street, Suite 250, Huntington Beach, CA 92648-9927; 800-531-0450, 714-969-7746).

How to distinguish hardware failures from information pattern failures

If your hard drive is reporting errors such as `Sector not found reading drive C`, `Read [or write] error on drive C`, or `Cannot find system files`, it is probable that your controller, cables, and hard disk hardware are all fine. Your problem is with the information on the disk, not with the disk. Often, the easiest solution to that sort of difficulty is to run SpinRite.

If you get an error message such as `Invalid drive specification` or `General failure reading drive C`, on the other hand, that may indicate a more serious, hardware-related problem. Even here, though, the source of the problem may only be some messed up information recorded on the drive's surface. Think about all the steps necessary to prepare a disk for DOS; if any of the patterns recorded during those steps become damaged, the disk can be rendered totally inaccessible until you repair the damage. When you encounter such problems, it makes sense to try the easiest and least expensive remedies first.

The worst cases to diagnose are when a PC just won't do anything. If you try to boot from your hard disk and the whole system hangs, without giving you any error messages, it could be a symptom of quite a few different possible problems. You simply have to go through the list in an orderly and systematic manner until you find what the problem is and fix it (or, if you should be so unlucky, until you find what the problems are and fix each one of them in its turn).

Simple things that sometimes go wrong

Look at your hard disk. Listen to it. Does it sound any different? Does the light emitting diode (LED) light up in the normal fashion? Does the drive get as warm as usual? (To test how warm your disk becomes, you may have to let your PC run for a couple of hours before you open up the PC's system unit case and feel the outside of the drive.)

To know whether the temperature you feel on the hard disk is unusual, you must have previously opened the case and felt the drive when there was no problem so that you know its normal temperature. (This procedure is akin to taking your temperature, weighing you, and checking your pulse each time you visit the doctor's office — even if there seems to be nothing wrong with you; it's called "taking your baseline measurements.")

CAUTION

Following some simple precautions can make the difference between safe exploration and utter destruction of your PC. Heed the following warnings:

- Before you open your PC, be sure to disconnect it from the power line. Don't just flip off the power switch. Unplug the power cord where it enters the PC's chassis. Also unplug the power cord for the monitor and any other peripheral devices you have attached to your PC (or disconnect the data cables that connect your PC to those devices). You can do substantial damage to your PC, and possibly to yourself, if you ignore these precautions.

- Also, touch the power supply of the PC before touching anything else inside the system unit. This will ensure that you and the PC are at the same voltage. Do this *every time* you are about to reach inside.

- Do not move your PC while it is turned on. In particular, do not tilt the case. Your hard drive is spinning all the time your PC is on, making it a gyroscope. Tilting a spinning gyroscope puts a terrible strain on its bearings.

- After doing some work inside your PC, you may choose to plug it in and operate it for a brief test before you put the cover back on. That's fine. You probably can even get away with plugging in or unplugging the cables that go from your PC to various peripheral devices while the PC is turned on. (Please touch the outer grounded shell of the connector to the PC system unit case before plugging in such a cable.) But *never* unplug or plug in any of the cables inside your PC (such as the cables from the power supply to the drive or from the drive to the controller) while it is turned on.

- Do not put the cover back on while the PC is turned on. It is too easy to drop a screw inside and short out something.

If the cable from the power supply to the hard drive becomes disconnected from the hard drive, the drive absolutely won't work. The light on it will not light, and the drive will not get warm. Such an eventuality is easy to overlook but simple to remedy, by just unplugging the power cable and then plugging it firmly back in. (Yes, it often is hard to unplug those cables once they have been firmly plugged in. You just have to use some muscle. If you find yourself in this situation, be careful not to flex the printed circuit card on which the stationary part of the connector is mounted. You could break some of the traces on the printed circuit card if you do not exercise caution.)

Chapter 11: How Hard Disks Die   293

> ### A useful suggestion
>
> Before disconnecting and replacing the cables, you should sketch out where and how to hook up the cables. If you hook up the cables incorrectly, you probably will do no damage, but your hard disk surely won't work. You also must be very careful to get the connector orientation just right. Some cables are "keyed," which will prevent them from being plugged in incorrectly, but most are not.
>
> Unplugging the cables and then plugging them back in again can help because doing so wipes their contacts. The friction can remove oxides or grease that might have been preventing good electrical connection. Because the wiping action is what counts, you can just barely remove the connectors and then replace them, working with only one connector at a time. That way, you are less likely to connect one incorrectly.
>
> This *reseating* also helps ensure that the cable connector is pushed all the way onto its mating connector on the option card, motherboard, or peripheral device. A connector that is pushed in only part of the way is another common problem.
>
> Be somewhat careful when you push cables back in place. You won't need to exert much more force than you did to remove that same cable. The absolute amount will vary from one type or size of connector to another, but generally the push-on force is about the same as the pull-off force.

The data cables (usually some flat *ribbon* cables) can come loose as well, causing the drive to fail. Again, you should unplug the cables and then plug them back in. Do this at each end of each cable. This practice is the only sure way to diagnose such a problem. If loose cables are not the problem, try replacing the cables with new ones.

Very rarely, one or more wires in a cable will actually be broken. Even a bent connector pin at one end is enough to bring down the cable. If this happens to one of your hard drive cables, replace it. Fortunately, you often can see the damage in a cable (if you look very carefully), and it is one of the cheapest components to replace.

Another thing to watch out for in many PCs is whether the ribbon cables are jammed into far too little space. This "jamming" can impede air flow, causing the PC to become too warm inside, or the crowded cables can end up rubbing against the back side of an option card. Contact with an option card is unfortunate because most of those cards are covered with very sharp wire ends on their back sides. These wires can actually cut the insulation in the ribbon cable and short one or more of the conductors to some inappropriate portion of the option card's circuitry. A simple fix is to push a piece of thin cardboard (such as a 3" x 5" index card) between the cable and the sharp side of the option card.

Slow death by growing misalignment

Hard disks are mechanical wonders. They move their heads around by millionths of an inch at a time and expect to get them repositioned precisely where they first were, a difficult chore at best. Over time, a head-positioning mechanism in a hard drive simply may not be able to put the heads back exactly where they should go.

From the point of view of the heads, the tracks of information recorded on the platter surface will appear to have slipped a bit to one side. The disk will work adequately as long as the slippage remains small, but as the slippage increases, it can cause the disk subsystem to malfunction.

Remember that your computer puts down the sector header information only when the low-level format is done. As the drive ages, the heads may move sideways relative to those recorded sector headers. (This movement won't happen if the drive uses an embedded or buried servo head-positioning strategy, but it can and often does happen with all other drive designs.)

If the heads do move sideways relative to the tracks, they will see a smaller and smaller fraction of the total track width, the signals coming from the heads will decrease, and the controller will have an increasingly difficult time reading the headers. This problem most likely will progress until one day your PC will deliver the dreaded message `Sector not found` (see Figure 11-3).

Figure 11-3: How head drift can cause drive malfunction.
(a) When a track is first recorded, it will certainly line up with the head that wrote it.
(b) Later, if that head drifts to one side, it may no longer be able to read information on that track reliably.
(c) Rewriting the data aligns the data — but not the sector headers — to the new path of the head. This can lead to `Sector not found` errors. Redoing the low-level format will restore the original, perfect alignment.

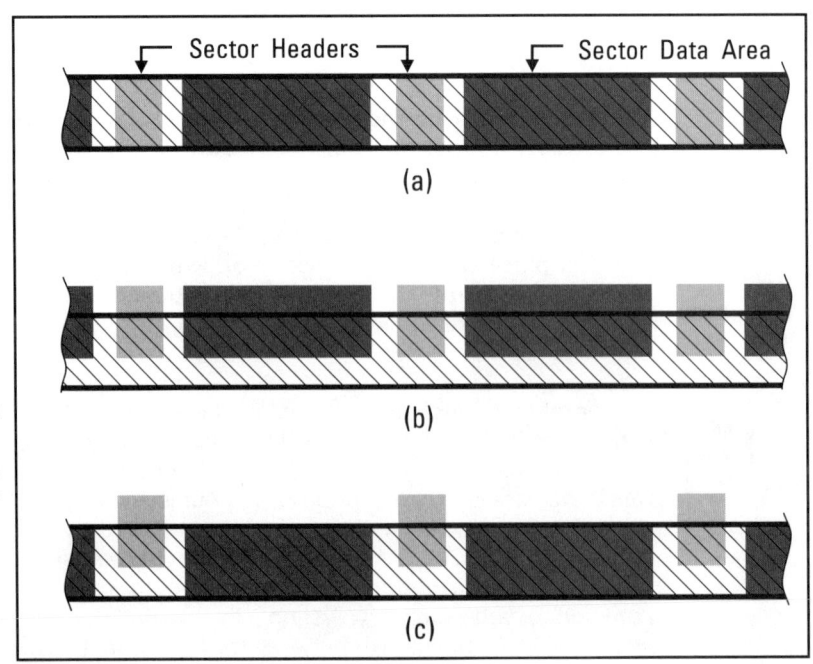

Chapter 11: How Hard Disks Die

If the drive was bumped while you were doing the low-level format, the head might have momentarily swerved to the side a bit. That would create a *wave* in the track it wrote. Depending on which way the head assembly drifts as it ages, this sector will be either the first or the last to show a problem (see Figure 11-4).

A read fault error can occur if the sector you are trying to read was written to only once, quite some time ago. The magnetic pattern could have become somewhat weakened or damaged over time so that eventually the signals picked up by the head may be too small to decipher correctly or will contain some bits of misinformation. At first, the error correction codes recorded with the information will suffice to get your data back, but eventually even that may not work.

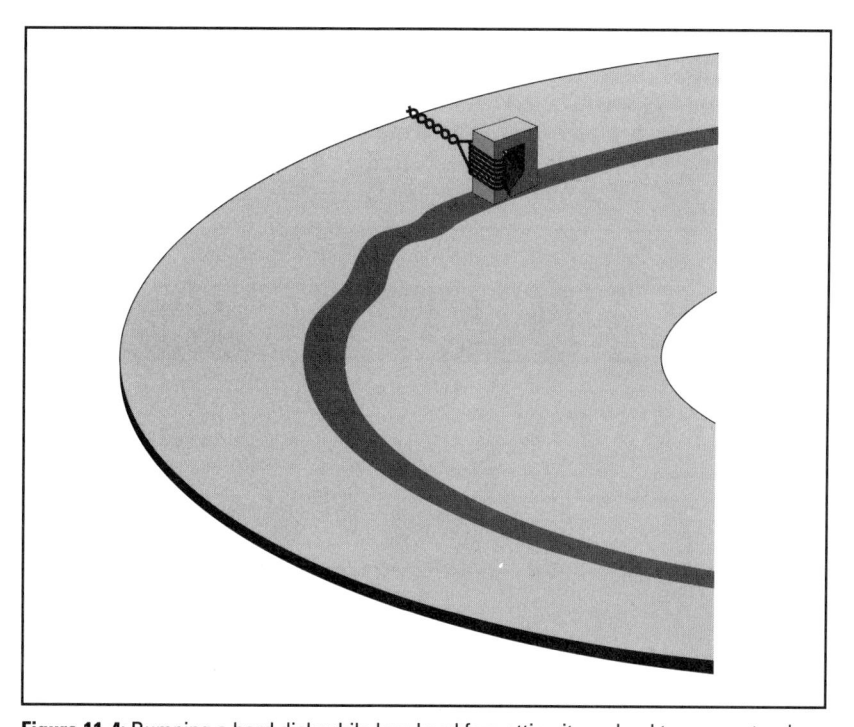

Figure 11-4: Bumping a hard disk while low-level formatting it can lead to a wavy track.

Part I: The Hard Disk Companion

TECHNICAL SECRET

The heads themselves are permanently magnetized. If you do not *park* the heads each time you turn off your PC, those permanent magnets may end up sitting down on top of some of your valuable data. When the drive starts up, the heads will scrub around a bit, at random, before starting to fly above the surface. This process can weaken, if not reverse, some bits recorded in the surface.

The notion of magnetic patterns getting weakened has been controversial. See the discussion in the section "A common misconception" in Chapter 13 for more on this point.

The system writes information into most sectors from time to time. As the drive alignment drifts, therefore, the data portion of the sector will be constantly rewritten under the current location of the heads. This means that gradually a sector that was labeled bad during the low-level format (due perhaps to a pinhole in the magnetic coating on the surface) may no longer contain any defect, while a good sector may have inherited a flaw (see Figure 11-5).

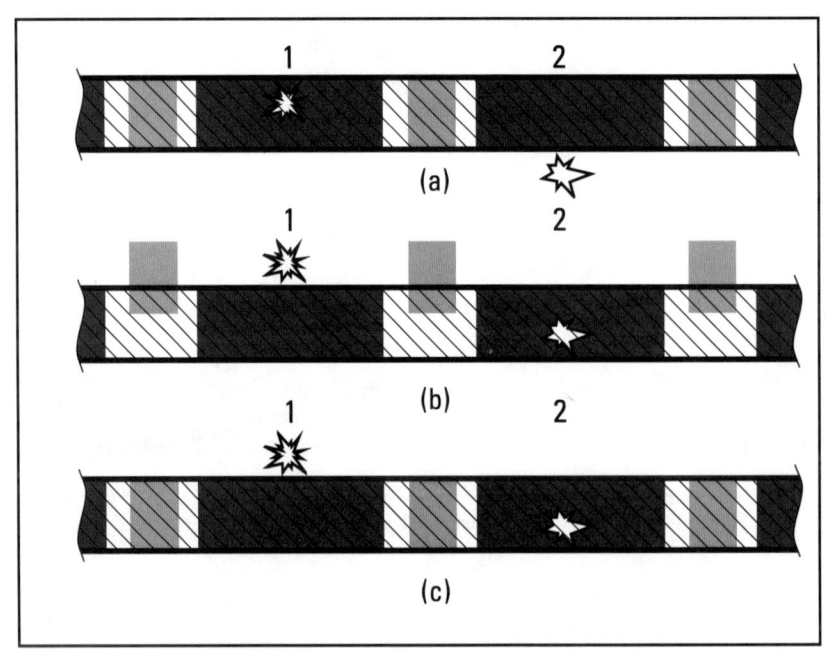

Figure 11-5: Pinhole surface defects can appear to come and go, making sectors appear to become good or become bad.
(a) Pinhole defect in drive makes sector #1 bad at time of low-level format.
(b) Drifting head moves data portions of sectors to one side, moving them off the first pinhole defect but over another one. Sector #1 is now good, but sector #2 is not unusable.
(c) Even redoing the low-level format (which puts the sector headers back into line with the data portions) will not help. Sector #2 is still not usable.

Redoing the low-level format resolves some of these problems by moving the sector headers and the data portions under the new head location. If you were getting `Sector not found` messages, this suggestion may eliminate them. But, as Figure 11-5 shows, not all of the problems that can creep in can be eliminated by a low-level format. It is important that you test the sectors carefully after you have redone the low-level format to make sure that you don't put data back into a bad sector.

For the cylinders of a drive that fall inside a DOS partition or DOS logical drive, disk reinterleaving programs like SpinRite provide the most convenient way to refresh the format, test the disk surface, and replace the data. If you run one of these programs before your heads drift so far that your data is unreadable, you have a good chance of never encountering such errors. Amazingly, even if you wait until DOS finds the drive almost unreadable, one of these programs sometimes can recover *all* your data and eliminate the drive's errors.

Part II of this book goes into great detail on what a particular one of these programs, SpinRite, does. In Part II you also learn on which drive and controller combinations it can do those things, and how they can help you recover from this sort of problem.

Data accidents

Some hard drive failures arise due to accidents, such as when a power surge causes a bit to flip from one to zero or vice versa. The most common human errors that induce drive failure include erasing COMMAND.COM or copying over it with a different version of the same program; erasing all the files in your root directory; or mistakenly executing the command *FORMAT C:* despite DOS's warning that you are about to wipe out a fixed disk.

The following error messages are typical indicators of a data accident: `Probable Non-DOS disk`; `Bad or missing Command Interpreter`; `Bad or missing xxxx` (where *xxxx* is some filename mentioned in your CONFIG.SYS file in a `DEVICE=` line or in a line by itself in your AUTOEXEC.BAT file); `Bad Partition Table`; `Disk boot failure`; `Disk error reading FAT x` (where *x* is 1 or 2); `Error loading operating system`; `Invalid partition table`; or `Missing operating system`. Depending on the version of DOS you use and whether it's been customized by a hardware manufacturer, you may get slightly different messages, but their general import will be the same.

Happily, some data accidents are transient, vanishing with a simple reboot of your computer. On the other hand, a persistent problem means that you need to find and repair the damaged information.

Part I: The Hard Disk Companion

A source of data accidents you may not have considered

Another kind of data error can occur if you imprudently turn your PC back on immediately after turning it off. For all PCs, the best advice is never to turn it on while it is in the middle of the process it goes through after you turn it off.

Yes, there is a succession of events that happen after you turn off your PC's power switch. The voltages coming out of the power supply die away to zero. The hard disk stops turning. Things cool off, and in that process they change their physical size slightly.

These events take place over different intervals of time. The voltages from the power supply drop essentially to zero within a few seconds. The hard disk may take several seconds to stop turning. The various parts of your PC may take many minutes to return to room temperature.

The consequences of turning on your PC too soon can depend on exactly when within these processes you do so. IBM engineers decided that it was not a good idea to let their customers turn on any of their PCs until after a certain time had elapsed. They built a time-delay relay into the power supplies that they included in all the PCs they made. Some clone PC makers have done this also, but most of them have not. If your PC's power supply doesn't have a time-delay relay in it, you will do yourself and your PC a favor if you develop a strong habit of waiting at least 30 seconds after turning it off before you try turning it back on.

If you turn off a PC equipped with such a time-delay relay in its power supply, and if you turn it right back on again, nothing at all will happen. Your PC will act as if it is still turned off. You must turn it off and wait until after the relay times out (at which time you might hear a soft click if you listen very closely). This time delay is usually several seconds. Any time after that, you can turn the PC back on again without any surprises.

What might go wrong if you turn on a PC that is not equipped with a time-delay protection feature immediately after turning it off? Two sorts of problem have been common.

First, this action can be very hard on the hard drive. If it is spinning down and the heads are just about to land — or have just landed — on the platter surface and then you reapply power to the drive, some not-so-nice things can happen. Some of them will lead to data damage, and the worst of them actually can harm some piece of the internal hardware and render the whole drive useless.

The other commonly seen problem is that the information in the configuration CMOS memory may become scrambled. In some PC clones, this is not just a possibility — they *always* scramble their CMOS contents whenever they are turned on too quickly after turning them off.

If you scramble your CMOS contents but have been prudent enough first to use MH-SAVE and prepare yourself a safety recovery floppy diskette, you can recover from this problem really easily. If your hardware is damaged, you will end up having to replace the damaged piece (once you figure out which one it is).

How to fix damaged data, and some popular disk utility packages that make it easier

Many things can go wrong with data in your PC. Here are a few examples with some suggestions for how you might recover from those problems:

- If you know you reformatted your hard disk by typing **FORMAT C:**, you need to find a way to "unformat" the drive. Paul Mace made his fortune by marketing the first program to do this: the Mace Utilities (which are now available from Fifth Generation Systems, 10049 N. Reiger Road, Baton Rouge, LA 70809-4559; 504-291-7221). The Norton Utilities package (created and sold by the Peter Norton Computing Division of Symantec, 2500 Broadway, Suite 200, Santa Monica, CA 90404; 310-319-2000) also includes this capability, as does PC Tools (Central Point Software, 15220 N.W. Greenbrier Parkway, #200, Beaverton, OR 97006; 503-690-8090). Starting with Version 5, DOS includes Central Point's UNDELETE program, which also can handle this problem. In all cases, these utilities work best if you use them first to save some key data that they can use in doing the recovery.

    If you have used the DOS 6 DoubleSpace program to compress some of your drives, there is a variation of this problem you need to know about. You can add a /FORMAT option on the DBLSPACE.EXE command line that will wipe out the files in a compressed drive. That action cannot be reversed by using UNDELETE.

- If you deleted or copied over the correct version of COMMAND.COM, simply copying it onto your hard disk from your original DOS disk should set things straight. If you deleted all the files in your root directory, you can restore them from back-up files. If those don't exist, you can use one of the programs mentioned in the previous paragraph to "unerase" the files, a capability Peter Norton pioneered.

- If your disk won't boot or has a bad partition table, programs like the Norton Disk Doctor, DiskTool, or Disk Editor may solve the problem (all these programs are included in the recent versions of the Norton Utilities). Another approach is to use KFDISK to repair partition-table damage and the DOS command SYS to refresh the hidden system DOS files. KFDISK is one of several programs included in the HTHF package from Kolod Research (1898 Techny Court, Northbrook, IL 60062-5474; 708-291-1586). Using a commercial program to remedy these problems offers two advantages: these programs operate automatically, and most of them allow you to undo any functions they performed that weren't helpful.

- If you decide to use only DOS commands to recover, you should seek counsel from an experienced user — there are many wrong ways to use the DOS commands and only one right way.

If you decide to try using FDISK to repair partition table damage, for example, you could wipe out the most essential information on your disk. That consequence is because, in addition to changing the entries in the partition table, many versions of FDISK routinely clear out the first several cylinders whenever they are used to create a partition.

If you are using MS-DOS 5 or a later version, you can use the undocumented command FDISK /MBR to restore the master boot record/partition table without altering the partition table numbers and without wiping out any of the valuable data stored in your DOS partition or extended partition.

Destructive FORMAT programs

The FORMAT program can completely initialize a floppy diskette, doing both a low-level and a high-level format. The only exception is when you use the DOS 5 or 6 FORMAT command in its safe or quick modes. On a hard disk, in most DOS versions, FORMAT initializes only the boot record, FAT, and root directory. This makes it possible, at least partially, to "unformat" the disk.

Some versions of the DOS FORMAT program do a bit more to your hard disks. AT&T's DOS up through Version 3.1, COMPAQ's DOS up through Version 3.2, and some versions of MS-DOS from Burroughs, for example, have FORMAT programs that supplement the usual functions by initializing the data area of the partition or DOS logical drive. This difference prevents even an unformatting program like that offered by Mace or Norton Utilities from recovering the data in that partition or DOS logical drive. To avoid such a catastrophe, you should strongly consider upgrading to a new version of DOS if you are using one of these obsolete versions.

If you are not yet using DOS 5 or 6, you also may want to consider replacing your FORMAT program with something like the Norton Utilities Safe Format program or the PC Tools program PCFORMAT. If a low-level format already exists, these programs will do only the high-level format, even on floppy diskettes (unless you specifically request a destructive format), allowing an unformat program to recover data.

Starting with Version 5, when you use the MS-DOS FORMAT program to reformat a disk that contains data, it routinely saves information to allow recovery of those files if they have not been overwritten. The various third-party utility programs also offer this feature.

On the other hand, if you want to sell your computer, you may truly want to erase your hard disk to protect your privacy. In that case, rather than just deleting your files (using the DOS command DEL or ERASE) or even using the DOS command FORMAT, you should use one of the programs offered by the utility packages: Mace has DESTROY and Norton has WIPEFILE and WIPEDISK or, in the latest versions, WIPEINFO. The PC Tools PCSHELL program includes a Clear File command for the same purpose.

If you are using DOS 5 or a later version, you can force FORMAT to erase the entire disk by using its /U option. This option will do the job pretty well, but WIPEINFO is able to do an even better job if you are really concerned.

Sudden death by drive hardware failure

The most common hard drive hardware failure occurs when the drive sticks, refusing to turn. (One disk repair depot estimates that 60 percent of the drives they service have this problem.)

Stiction

The name for this failure mode is *stiction,* short for *static friction.* (Static friction is the force it takes to get an object at rest on another object to start sliding. "Static" here refers to not moving; stiction has nothing to do with static electricity. Generally the sliding friction, which is the force it takes to keep it moving, is quite a bit smaller.) What happens is that the heads become stuck to the platters after you turn off your PC. When you turn it back on, the drive's motor may not be strong enough to dislodge the heads. If you do break the platter free, the drive may work fine until you turn off the power again.

There are several reasons that drive heads get stuck to the platters in this way. One reason is that some drives are lubricated with a shellac or lacquer. When they get hot, this coating liquifies. When the drive is turned off, the heads come to rest on the surface before the coating solidifies. When the drive cools down, the coating acts like a glue holding the heads to the platter.

TECHNICAL SECRET

If you are daring, you can sometimes fix this problem, temporarily, by using a simple trick. Turn off and unplug your PC. Open the system unit. Remove the hard disk. (Don't try to open the hard disk's sealed chamber. Doing so will only destroy any remaining usefulness of the drive.) Remember to draw a picture to help you plug in the cables again correctly.

At this point, you can try a number of things to make the drive capable of spinning once more. Here they are in ascending order of brutality to the drive:

- First, you can try simply holding the drive in your hands and giving it a sharp rotary jerk. You want to rotate the drive housing in the same direction that the platters normally turn. If you do this vigorously enough, inertia in the platters will keep them from turning while the housing will make the head assembly move around the axis of rotation. That can break the bond between heads and platters.

Once you think you may have accomplished breaking the bond, you can temporarily hook up the drive to your PC with the cover off. (It is okay to set the drive upside down on the PC frame if you want; just be sure that the cables are on correctly. Also, be sure that the disk won't slip and fall off the frame. Putting a piece of cardboard between the disk drive and the PC's frame will help ensure against short circuits.) Power up the PC and see if this time the disk will start turning.

- If that "fix" didn't work, you are ready to try the next more daring (and more brutal) method. Lay the disk down with the electronic circuit card on top. (This is upside down from the normal mounting position for the drive.) You will likely see a hole in the card, through which you can see the end of the spindle. (This hole may be covered up with a plastic cover. You can gently pry off the cover.) If you can gently but firmly twist that shaft with a screwdriver or pair of pliers, you may be able to get the disk turning freely again. If you succeed in turning the platters, again hook up the drive to your PC temporarily and test it.

- If you still haven't solved the problem, there is one more thing you can try. This is a real, last gasp effort. You have nothing to lose at this point, so you might as well try it. With the drive hooked up to the PC and power on, lift one corner about an inch or two and then let it drop on the table or PC case. If you are lucky this time, the drive will start to spin.

After you have the disk turning, one way or another, you'd best *immediately* back up all the files that you can. You may not get another chance. Definitely don't turn off your PC until you have finished backing up everything you want to save.

Spindle-bearing failure

Sometimes the spindle bearing will completely seize up, preventing the drive from turning. Drive manufacturers tell you that they lubricate hard drives for life. That is quite true: after the spindle-bearing fails, the life of that drive is over! Approximately 15 percent of all hard drives meet their end this way. The symptoms for spindle-bearing failure resemble those for stiction, except that you cannot get the spindle to turn at all, making it very difficult to retrieve your data.

Sometimes you will get a warning that the drive's spindle bearings are about to go. The very first hard drive I owned started squealing about a week after I got it. I took it back to the dealer and asked about the noise. The technician there replaced the drive and told me how very lucky I was to get a warning.

If a drive's bearings are failing more subtly, you still may be able to discern the impending failure. Each time you run a program that tells you how fast the disk is turning (and SpinRite is one such program), notice precisely what the speed is. Most hard drives turn at 3600 rpm, though a few turn as fast as 5400 rpm. Whatever the speed is, it should always be very nearly the same. If you start noticing unusually large speed variations from one time you test it to the next, your drive's spindle bearings could be on their way out. (Alternatively, the spindle motor control circuit could be failing — though that is a much less likely cause.)

The only way to recover data from a drive whose spindle bearing has seized is to open it up and somehow get the spindle to turn, definitely not something you can do at home. An expensive solution is to take your drive to a data-recovery service. If you have been backing up frequently, you can save a lot of money by just replacing the hard drive and loading your software and data from the backups.

Drive electronics failures

About another 20 percent of drive hardware failures result from failed electronics mounted on the drive. The drive and the heads may still function well, but the electronics might be unable to read or write data to the drive. If the electronics of the drive-motor controller fail, the drive won't turn, or it won't turn at the right speed. To diagnose this problem, you can replace the electronics board with a functioning one from a very similar drive. (A repair facility may have a spare.)

Temperature-related problems

Often drives have temperature-related problems. Some of them will not work correctly unless they are fully warmed up. Others will die as soon as they warm up. Sometimes this condition can be fixed by redoing the low-level format — usually most conveniently done by using a disk reinterleaving program. Other times the drive is really sick and will need substantial repairs.

The drive may be about to fail due to a slow distortion or wear of the mechanical parts, which change shape just enough to function after they have warmed up. In such cases, you should back up your data and then have the disk either repaired or replaced.

One fairly common temperature-related problem happens when a part on the circuit board goes bad. It may function okay as long as the board is cool, but once the drive warms up it will fail, possibly because it starts to turn too quickly or because the data processing circuitry may not function correctly. In this case, you may be able to get your data off the disk by separating the circuit card from the drive body as far as you can. (Gently please! You don't want to disconnect the wires going into the sealed enclosure.) The circuitry may then stay cool enough to keep on working for just long enough to let you back up your files. Then the board, at least, will have to be repaired or replaced.

Part I: The Hard Disk Companion

If the disk can start the boot process but then has trouble finding the system files, however, your problem may lie in the information stored in the DOS partition. Running a disk reinterleaving program like SpinRite may move the data tracks back under the heads and strengthen the recorded information enough to make the drive work correctly.

If that does not work, you should boot your computer from your safety boot diskette. (See Chapter 1 for details on how to create such a diskette.) If you don't yet have a safety boot diskette for this computer, you can use any bootable DOS diskette *with the same version of DOS on it as is on your hard disk*. If you then can access your hard disk, the data damage is fairly minor, and Norton Disk Doctor usually can repair it.

If the drive can't even begin the boot process, you may have a problem with the readability of information outside the DOS partition, indicated by error messages such as `Invalid partition table`, `Error loading operating system`, or `Missing operating system`. If you have an identically partitioned drive in your system of the same type and size, you can copy the good drive's partition table to the bad drive. (Some popular utility programs allow you to save your hard disk's partition table to a file on a disk. They also give you a simple way to use that disk to repair any damage done to your hard disk's partition table.)

DISK: The MH-SAVE program on the *Hard Disk SECRETS* disk can be used to save the partition table as well as data from many other crucial places on your hard disk. The companion MH-RESTR program can be used to put the data back any time they get messed up.

TIP

Freeze your data

You need to repair (or replace) a drive that overheats. One way to retrieve your data before taking the drive in to the shop is to chill it thoroughly. Literally take the drive out of your PC and put it in your refrigerator or freezer for several hours; then hook it up to the PC. Soon after you turn the PC back on, when the drive first starts to function, copy off as much data as you can. After the drive overheats, turn off the PC, put the drive back in the freezer for a while, and then try again.

Put only the drive in the freezer. You don't want the main PC to become cold because condensation of moisture on it while it warms up could lead to other problems.

Wrap the drive tightly in plastic before you chill it. If you can leave the cables attached to the drive and hanging out of the wrapping and still cut off almost all air flow into the drive, you then can leave the wrapping in place while you start running the drive. This precaution will help keep moisture from condensing on the drive's electronics board. Alternatively, do your work in an air-conditioned or other low-humidity room.

If all else fails, you may have to recover the old-fashioned way: Back up all your data. Do the low-level format as if this were a new drive. Use FDISK to reinstall the partitioning information. Do the high-level format (with the FORMAT program). Reinstall your software. (This takes long enough that it is not usually the best thing to do, if some simpler remedy would suffice. If you cannot find a simpler remedy, though, this is one thing to try.)

If your drive works when cold but fails after it warms up, the mechanism may be drifting. If so, the techniques just described may help. On the other hand, your drive may be seriously overheating, due to either a bearing problem (the drive may stop turning after it warms up) or a problem with the electronics.

Head crashes

Though often mentioned as a cause of disk failure, damaging head crashes rarely occur. Every time you turn off your PC, the heads "softly crash," but thanks to their good design, they rarely do any damage to the magnetic coating on the disk surface as they land.

You can further guard against damage by parking the heads, which positions these soft crashes in an area in which you do not have any important data stored. *Always* use a park program before turning off power to a hard drive, unless it is a self-parking drive. (See Chapter 16 for a discussion of safe and unsafe park programs.)

Steve Gibson created a head-parking program, called PARK.COM, that is safe to use on any hard drive. He feels so strongly that one should always use such a program that he has made his available not only to purchasers of SpinRite, but to anyone who wants to download a copy from his company's bulletin board. And he graciously permitted its inclusion on the *Hard Disk SECRETS* disk included with this book.

You also should park the heads if your PC will be idle for a while, in case the computer is accidentally bumped or knocked to the floor. One advantage of using the Gibson Research park program from your *Hard Disk SECRETS* disk is that it doesn't require you to shut off or reboot your PC afterwards, as some programs do.

Even with the best of head-parking practices, your hard disks may some day suffer a damaging head crash. The disk may suddenly flail its heads around violently for no obvious reason, or an earthquake may knock the computer to the floor while it is running. The good news is that the heads are not likely to gouge out more than about 20 percent of the disk surface, allowing you to back up the remaining 80 percent.

> ### Some simple mistakes to avoid
>
> When installing an electronics card on a hard disk, you should beware of screwing it down too firmly, thereby distorting the frame. This distortion can then make the disk platters rub against the inside of the sealed housing, preventing them from turning.
>
> Similarly, when mounting the drive back into your PC, be careful not to distort the drive frame or sealed housing. In a PC or XT (and in some ATs), the disk is screwed to the computer's case. Use very short screws, or make sure that there is enough space behind the hole so that the screw does not bear on the sealed chamber (see Figure 11-6). Don't ever put more than two screws into the frame and then never from opposite sides.
>
> If you must mount a drive with screws going in from both sides, put them in *very loosely* on one side. You can use a product such as Loctite to keep those loosely engaged screws from falling out over time. The screws on the other side can be tightened down normally, which is to say firmly but not very firmly. (Loctite brand adhesive comes in three strength formulations. You will probably want to use the formulation that has the lowest strength. You want to be able to remove those screws someday; you simply don't want them rattling out.)
>
> In most ATs and 386 computers, the hard disks have rails screwed to each side; these rails slide into some channels in the PC's frame. Clips screwed into the front of the computer's case keep the drives from sliding out of those channels.
>
> This is a nice way to keep the drive from being stretched by being mounted too firmly. The only worry here is to be sure that you don't use overlong screws to fasten the rails to the drive. They must not be long enough to touch the sealed chamber of the hard drive.

The bad news is that the gouged-up magnetic coating goes somewhere else inside the drive. It may clog up the ventilation holes, stick to the read/write heads, or it may seem to be safely out of the way for a while and later come back to haunt you. You may be able to use a disk that has suffered a major head crash, but you shouldn't rely on it for the long term.

Controller death

Hard disk controller boards also rarely fail, but when they do, it can be dramatic. Your PC, for example, may return a message along the lines of `Invalid drive`, `General failure reading drive C`, or `Drive not ready` when you execute a command that requires access to the hard disk.

If unplugging the cables connecting the hard disk to its controller and plugging them in again doesn't resolve the problem, you can try removing the controller card from the PC and then putting it back. While you have the card out of the PC, it may be a good idea to clean off the contacts on the card where it plugs into the motherboard. (Please remember to turn off the PC and unplug it before

Chapter 11: How Hard Disks Die 307

Mounting holes

(a)

DANGER

(b)

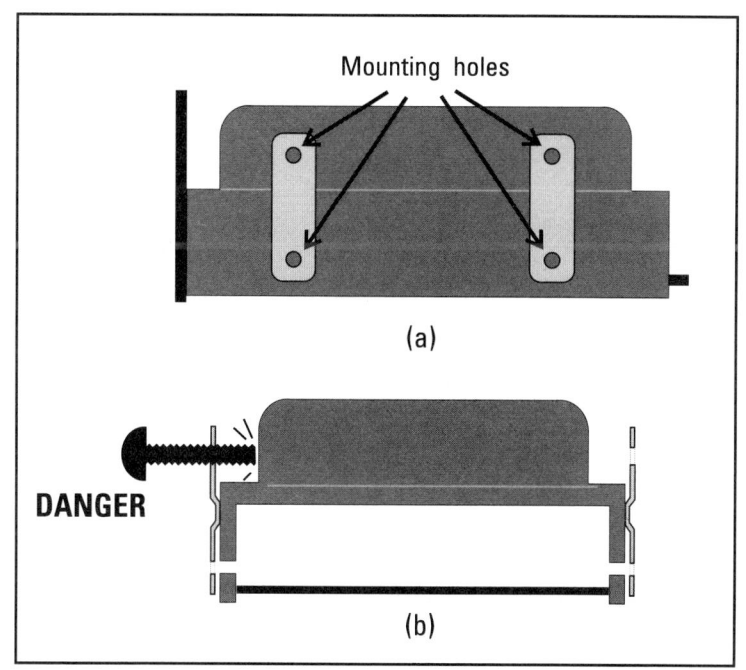

Figure 11-6: An error to avoid when mounting a hard drive (a) side view, (b) rear view.

you open the case. Also remember to touch the PC power supply or frame just before *each* time you reach inside the system unit.) If this doesn't work either, you may have a failed controller card or disk, or you may have suffered a data accident.

Diagnostic programs can help you decide whether your drive or your controller has failed. Sometimes they even get it right! You can also try replacing one or the other to see whether that eliminates your problem. (If you are unsure which one to try replacing first, think about this: A set of cables will cost about $10. A new controller will cost more, but certainly less than $100. A new drive will set you back several hundred dollars, and if you replace it, you will have lost access to all the data on your old drive in the process.)

Your hard disk must have just the right patterns of information recorded on it for your controller to read and write data to it. Remember that each controller is likely to put down its low-level format information in a slightly different way. If you replace your controller with a new one, you very likely will have lost access to all the data on your hard disk, even if the disk itself has not been damaged. The one exception is if you use a new controller that is the same model and revision level as the old controller, which should let you get at your data. Only replace your controller as a last option. Also hope you have a good, current set of backups. You are likely to need them.

You now have a description of the many ways in which your hard disk can die. Before leaving this topic, though, there is one more situation to consider. This is a misleading symptom that may make you erroneously conclude that your disk is dying.

A form of degradation that does NOT signal impending hard disk death — file fragmentation

When you first use a hard disk, it will seem wonderfully fast, particularly when compared to a floppy diskette. If, after some months or years of use, you notice that it has slowed down appreciably, the culprit most likely is file fragmentation.

Whenever you write a file to your hard disk, DOS first looks in the FAT for available clusters. If the first file takes 10 clusters, DOS will assign to it the first 10 clusters on the disk. If the next file takes 6, it gets the next 6, and so on. If all you ever did was write new files to the disk, sequential files would reside in adjacent clusters.

Of course, most users will also remove files and add to existing ones from time to time. Let's look at how each of those actions affects a file's placement on the disk.

If, after putting several files on the disk, you remove the third file, it will leave a hole. If you then write a new file to the disk that is larger than the third file, DOS will allocate part of the new file to that hole and place the rest of it far away, *fragmenting* the file into two pieces. You also will fragment an existing file any time you add data to it if there isn't enough room for the added data between the original end of that file and the beginning of the one just beyond it.

When DOS goes to retrieve a file from the disk, it looks in the directory to locate the first cluster of the file's information. Then it consults the FAT to track down the rest of that file's information. If all the clusters for that file are close together, the controller can read them quickly. The more scattered the clusters are, the longer it will take to read them.

TECHNICAL SECRET

When DOS 3.0 came out, much was made of a special built-in feature that was supposed to help reduce file fragmentation and overwriting of deleted files. This feature simply was a pointer DOS maintains that says where in the FAT it last found an available cluster. When DOS wants another cluster, it will begin its search through the FAT right after that point. If the disk is fairly full, this process does help DOS find a new cluster more quickly. It also will tend to prevent putting a new file into the holes left behind after a file is erased.

Chapter 11: How Hard Disks Die

This strategy, however, cannot do anything to prevent file fragmentation that comes from adding to an existing file. It also does less than you may imagine to prevent fragmentation of new files. Because DOS keeps this pointer in memory, it must return to the beginning of the FAT each time you reboot your computer. Serious file fragmentation builds up over months or years despite this feature of DOS.

After months of use, most of a hard disk's data files and many of its program files commonly are fragmented. This process will continue to reduce your disk's efficiency and over time may even make your hard disk slower than your floppy diskette drives, but it does not signal incipient data loss or disk failure. Unlike the creeping misalignment problem, no matter how fragmented your files become, you will always be able to access your data, albeit slowly. The extra head motion needed to access fragmented files, however, will hasten your hard disk's demise.

In addition to making your disk work more slowly, file fragmentation can add to the difficulty you will have if you have to recover erased files. Essentially, once a file is deleted you have lost the FAT's record of what clusters it used to occupy. The directory entry tells you how many clusters the file occupied and which cluster it started in. If the file was not fragmented, you could recover it (if it were not overwritten) by simply starting at the specified starting cluster and recovering the correct number of clusters. But if it were fragmented, that strategy would not give you the right clusters. You'd have the right number of them, but some of them would be ones that had belonged to some other file.

This situation might not be a problem, especially if you have been using either a file deletion tracking system or a delayed erasure strategy. (The former is called Delete Tracker in DOS 5 or 6. This strategy keeps track of the clusters a file was occupying each time a file is deleted. The latter is new to DOS with Version 6 and is called Delete Sentry. This strategy moves the files you tell DOS to delete into a special trashcan directory — and then doesn't actually delete them until either they are some specified number of days old or until the pending deleted files take up some specified fraction of your disk space.)

The obvious solution to this creeping inefficiency is to defragment your files. You *could* do it the hard way: copy your files to floppies, erase them from the hard disk or format the partition, and then restore the files to the hard disk. Alternatively, you can use a special file-defragmenting program.

All the popular disk utilities mentioned in the section "How to fix damaged data, and some popular disk utility packages that make it easier" include such a program. Another very good file defragmenter is PC-Kwik Power Disk from the PC-Kwik Corporation (15100 SW Koll Parkway, Suite L, Beaverton, OR 97006; 800-274-5945, 503-644-5644). The Power Disk program is especially good for very large volumes (in excess of 200MB). Starting with Version 6, DOS includes its own DEFRAG program, which is a licensed version of the Norton Speed Disk program.

Part I: The Hard Disk Companion

The DOS 6 program DEFRAG is not nearly as flexible as Norton's Speed Disk. DEFRAG (see Figure 11-7) only offers two strategies for optimization: Full optimization and Unfragment files only. In the first case, DEFRAG moves enough data to make all the files contiguous and also pushes them as far toward the front of the disk as possible; it doesn't particularly care what order they are in. In the Unfragment files only case, DEFRAG simply makes sure that each file is contiguous. The files may be left most anywhere that DEFRAG finds convenient, and the empty space may be scattered in among all the files.

Speed Disk, on the other hand, offers a wealth of options. In addition to five different optimization strategies, it also offers options to choose which files it should not move, and in which order it should place the files it does move. Further, Speed Disk can be used to examine the map of files on the disk to see which ones are fragmented — and how badly.

On the other hand, DEFRAG can do something that no other defragmenter on the market can do. At least in their present versions, all the commercial and shareware defragmenters are unable to work with DoubleSpace compressed volume files (CVFs). DEFRAG can. (Each of these commerical programs will add this feature in its next version, no doubt.)

When you run DEFRAG on an uncompressed volume, you see a map of the drive showing which regions are in use and which are free. As it is defragmenting the disk, you get to watch as it reads information from one place, writes it to another, and then erases it from the original place. This process is repeated over and over until all the pieces that needed to be moved have been moved.

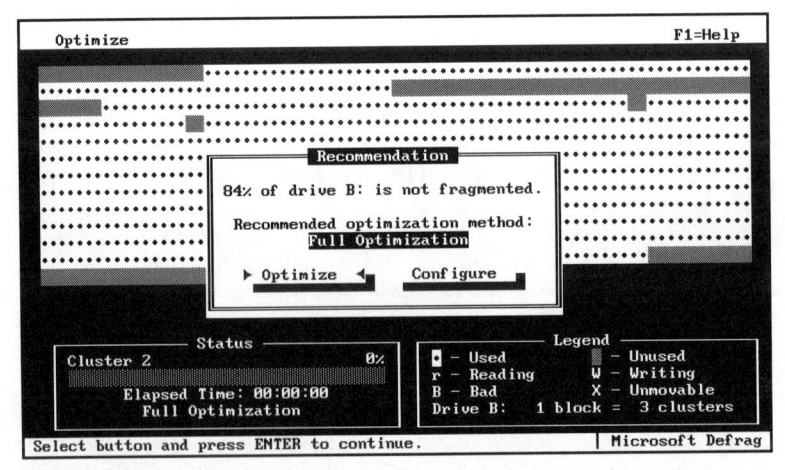

Figure 11-7: The new DEFRAG program from MS-DOS.

There are three ways you can run DEFRAG on a CVF. First, you can directly invoke **DEFRAG** and specify the drive letter that DoubleSpace assigned to that CVF. Second, you can run DBLSPACE with a command line option **/DEFRAGMENT** and specify the drive letter. Third, you can run DBLSPACE.EXE in its interactive mode and choose the DEFRAG option on a menu after you have specified the disk you want to work with.

With any of the methods you use to run DEFRAG inside a DoubleSpace volume, you won't get to see the track map or much of anything else. DEFRAG simply does its work quietly and then exits.

DoubleSpace seems to be a little more fussy about having its CVF files defragmented frequently. Run **CHKDSK** on the host volume, then run **DBLSPACE /CHKDSK** on the compressed volume, and finally run **DEFRAG** on the compressed volume. Do this often and your system will not only give you maximum performance, it will be substantially more stable (and your data will, therefore, be just that much safer).

That Laundry List of Failure Modes Is Fine, but I'd Rather You Just Told Me How to Fix My Ailing Hard Disk

Perhaps you are getting tired of reading all about the many ways a disk *can* die. You simply want to know which way *yours* just died. You want to find a list of symptoms, match up what you have seen with some entry in that list, and then read exactly what is wrong and how to remedy it.

I am very much sympathetic with that goal. In fact, in preparing to write this chapter, I attempted to create such a universal hard disk troubleshooting flow chart. I proved to myself that it was not nearly as simple as I had hoped. So far, I have not managed to build a chart that applies except in quite particular circumstances (such as with a certain brand of BIOS, a certain type of hard disk, and a certain version of DOS).

Why this assignment is tough

There are some very good reasons why this is a tough task — so tough that mostly it is not a feasible one. To understand those reasons, consider the symptoms you may see and what their sources are.

First, there are the pure hardware symptoms. These can range from the very obvious to the totally obscure. One, for an example of the obvious, is a shrieking sound that can emanate from the hard disk just before the spindle bearing seizes up. An example of the opposite extreme is the total failure of your PC to do anything (which might be caused by a dead short across the hard disk platter motor — or by any of a vast variety of other things). In between are the hardware failures that give what are, at best, ambiguous hints of what is wrong. Many controller failures fall into this category.

The possible ways in which a hard disk can fail depends a lot on what sort of system it is. What data encoding strategy is it using (MFM or RLL)? Which interface standard does it adhere to (ST412/ST506, IDE/ATA, ESDI, SCSI, PCMCIA, or something else)? What sort of controller is it connected to (autoconfiguring or not, sector translating or not, and so on)? Naturally, the error messages you get will vary along with the kinds of failure that they could be reporting.

Then there are the pure information failures. These failures cause another variety of symptoms, mostly in the form of error messages that appear on your PC's monitor. There are many possible sources of these error messages. A few of the more obvious ones are described in the next several paragraphs.

Some error messages that are symptoms of a hard disk problem will come from the boot program in the BIOS ROM on the motherboard. These messages appear only when you try to boot your computer. Another group come from the programs in the hard disk controller option card's BIOS ROM extensions. These messages could appear during a boot, or they could come at any time when you access your hard disk.

What brand of BIOS chip do you have? Each BIOS maker uses a different set of error messages to report difficulties. The version of that BIOS may matter as well. Many times, the BIOS has been further modified by a motherboard manufacturer and will have new messages in it that are proprietary to that manufacturer.

The master boot record program was put on your hard disk by some operating system's disk-initialization program. (The DOS program to do this job is FDISK.) Which brand and version of which program was used to put the MBR on your hard disk? Do you know? The exact wording of its error messages depends on which version of which program it is.

The DOS boot record program is put on each DOS volume by the FORMAT program. You could well have used a different version of DOS when you did this. If you upgraded your DOS version from 4.0 to 5.0, for example, you probably did not redo the partitioning. That means that you'll have a DOS Version 4.0-created master boot record but a DOS Version 5.0-created DOS boot record in each DOS volume. Again, the wording and meanings of the error messages will depend on which version you used to install each of these programs that are so critical to hard disk access.

In addition to these system-level programs that can indicate problems they are having with accessing your hard disk, many device drivers, TSR programs, and application programs have their own sets of error messages relating to file or disk access problems.

Are you getting the idea that there is a lot of diversity in the PC marketplace and that this diversity leads to many possible sets of error messages? That notion is absolutely correct. It may be impossible to create a chart that will allow you to unambiguously identify the source of your problem just from the original symptoms of difficulty. You may get some good hints, but then you very likely will have to try some further experiments also.

When you can make an explicit troubleshooting chart

In a few situations, preparing a detailed flow chart that lists all possible error conditions and what to do to solve the problem behind each one does make sense.

Any time a single manufacturer puts together the whole system, including all the hardware and software parts of it, that manufacturer is in a pretty good position to know what all the possibilities for failures are and what symptoms their systems will display in each case. The manufacturer also can prescribe recommended solutions in each case.

If you use only "pure" IBM-manufactured PCs and run only IBM software on them (a *most* unusual situation), there is an IBM diagnostic tool that may resemble what you seek. IBM publishes a multivolume manual of maintenance and repair procedures. These books include many flow charts to guide you through the troubleshooting process. Just about every possible case is covered.

The only difficulty you may have with this solution (aside from the implausibility of running only IBM-created software) is that you will spend a lot of money buying the necessary set of manuals. And if your PCs are not totally pure, the chances are unfortunately good that you will, from time to time, encounter problems that this flow-chart-reading approach will fail to solve.

The flow chart manual covering all the cases can be a feasible solution if you have a large number of very pure IBM PCs to maintain, but it may well not be a good investment otherwise.

An approach that may help

In general, if you have a problem, try to simplify the situation so that you can better discern what is going on. In the case of PC hard disk problems, this simplification means several things. Try to identify the source of any error messages you see. You may need to examine the various ROMs and the key programs on your disk to see what messages they contain.

You can use the DOS program DEBUG to display the content of the ROMs, if you know what address range they occupy. (Once you start DEBUG, at its hyphen prompt, type the command in the form *d sector:offset* to display 128 bytes of memory starting at the specified address. Then enter just the *d* command with no arguments to display the next 128 bytes. Continue in this manner until you have seen all the information in that ROM.)

You can use the LIST program from the *Hard Disk SECRETS* disk to examine the messages in program files. See Appendix B for information on how to use that program.

To help pin down the source of your problem, try booting from your safety boot diskette. Or try renaming the AUTOEXEC.BAT and CONFIG.SYS files on your hard disk and then rebooting. If you are using DOS 6 you have a third option: simply tap function key F5 during the message `Starting MS-DOS`. DOS is then forced to ignore your CONFIG.SYS and AUTOEXEC.BAT files. (I use the names AE and CF as temporary holding names for those two files.) If you boot off a diskette or if you boot from the hard disk without your usual AUTOEXEC.BAT and CONFIG.SYS files, you will see how your PC works in its simplest configuration. By seeing whether or not your problem goes away in this case, you can tell if it is one that relates mostly to the software environment you have created on your PC or to the hardware and system-level software that provides the foundation for that computing environment.

Watch the screen as your PC boots. Think about the meaning of each message you see and the context in which it occurs. After you see something you recognize as normally occurring during the processing of your CONFIG.SYS file, for example, you know that the boot process has succeeded most of the way. Any remaining problem is most likely one caused by something in your software environment.

A message like `Missing operating system` comes from the master boot record. This can mean any of several things, including that the configuration CMOS entry for the first hard disk type is wrong, the partition table data in the MBR has been altered, or the DOS boot record in the DOS primary partition is missing. It clearly does not indicate a problem with the software loaded after DOS itself is loaded. Nor does it indicate a hardware failure (which would have prevented loading and executing the master boot record program).

If you are not seeing anything that indicates that the PC is booting even part of the way, reboot. This time, watch very carefully to see whether the hard disk activity light flickers on at all. If not, then (unless someone wired that light incorrectly) your controller is never telling the disk to do anything. And if you don't tell it to do something, it will very cheerfully do nothing. That is a very clear indication of a hardware-level problem.

TIP The LED that shows you activity on your hard disk may be mounted on the disk itself (usual in an XT) or on the front panel of the system unit (usual in ATs and higher models). If yours is on the front panel, you need to know that it is connected to your motherboard or hard disk controller option card by a two-wire ribbon cable. The connector that it plugs into may have four pins. There are two right ways to plug it in (and four wrong ways). If you notice that it is not working, but your hard disk does seem to work, suspect that connection. Observing the usual precautions about opening up a PC system unit, check where the cable goes. Maybe it has fallen off the connector entirely. Try plugging it in first one way and then another until you find one of the right ways. Now write that way down so you can find it more quickly the next time.

After you have an idea of the area in which the problem lies, you usually can tackle it fairly directly. If you have a hardware problem, swap parts until you get to where you can boot from your safety boot diskette and then can access your hard drive. If you get that far, you have solved almost any hardware-level problem. If you get error messages from the master boot record or the DOS boot sector program, focus on fixing the data tables and programs that those programs use or load.

Approaching problems this way, by reasoning from symptoms to causes, depends on a good understanding of the way in which all the parts of your system function. That approach is what this book teaches you. It sometimes means you have to work hard and think carefully, which may not be as nice as just looking up a fixed repair procedure in some flow chart, but at least this approach applies no matter what combination of brands of components went into making your PC.

Data Recovery — The Hope Versus the Reality

Anyone who has lost data wants a way to recover the data. You can sometimes resurrect lost data from a hard drive, but it is not always feasible.

Much depends on how you lost your data. If you had a minor data accident, it may be simple for you to recover your data. If one of your drive cables came loose or you need to remove and reinsert your controller card in the slot connector on your PC's motherboard, attending to that will take just a few minutes.

If, on the other hand, a destructive head crash gouged off some of the magnetic coating on the platters, the data stored in that part of the coating is irretrievably gone.

An in-between case is when the spindle bearing seizes so that it won't turn. All your files are on the disk platters, but you can't read them. Someone who has the necessary equipment and knowledge (and the use of a suitable "clean" room) may be able to coax the drive into working again, allowing access to your data. This process could work, but it can be very expensive, sometimes costing much more than the drive itself.

This case is one where the possible may very well not be the same as the feasible. Whether it is feasible depends on the value you place on your data and perhaps on the age of your backups. One company that offers this sort of last-gasp-chance data-recovery service is Workman and Associates (1925 East Mountain Street, Pasadena, CA 91104; 818-791-7979). OnTrack (maker of the Disk Manager program) also runs a hard disk data-recovery service.

A far simpler way to lose data is by mistakenly erasing files. It may be possible to unerase them, but the task may turn out to be too difficult and complex to be feasible. Some utility programs, if used in advance, can make unerasing files much more feasible: These include the Norton Utilities FR /SAVE, or, in the newest version of the Norton Utilities, the IMAGE program, and PC Tools' MIRROR program. A version of MIRROR is also included with MS-DOS 5 and PC DOS 5. That same functionality is in UNDELETE in Version 6 of DOS.

An even tougher situation arises when you overwrite as well as delete valuable files. A mere unerase program cannot help you in this case — you have to resort to some very specialized (and again, expensive) data-recovery services. This presents another strong argument for implementing a regular back-up strategy.

Backups: What, Why, and How

Anyone who has been around PCs for more than a very short time undoubtedly has heard of backups. Not everyone understands what that really means. Even fewer know all the many different ways that you can create and maintain backups, the diverse uses to which they may be put, and the tools available to help in this process. This section will help you join the select company of well-informed PC users.

Three kinds of backups

There are three fundamentally different approaches to creating a back-up copy of vital PC data. They are the full backup (or total backup), the incremental backup, and the differential backup.

Full backups

A *full backup* is just that: a copy of all of the information on your hard disk onto some medium for safe storage. Many people use a tape drive to create full backups on a regular basis. That is a good approach to backing up, but you can improve on it.

It certainly is simple to throw a tape in the drive and run a batch file at the end of the day each Friday, for example. This approach, however, is not going to protect you from losing work you did during the week in which your PC's hard disk dies. Also, you will either have to recycle your back-up tapes (which leads to some vulnerabilities discussed a little later in this chapter), or you will quickly run out of room to store them and dollars to pay for them.

Incremental backups

Most of the information stored on your hard disk does not change very often at all. Most programs never change. Many data files change only infrequently. You may have many documents stored on your hard disk since you created them months ago. You may need them there for reference, but you never intend to change them. So why back them up every week, or however often you normally make a full backup? That practice really is unnecessary.

What *is* necessary is to make a copy of all the new or changed files on your disk. Fortunately, DOS provides you with a simple means of seeing which files those are.

Each time a program asks DOS to open a file and give that program permission to both read and write information in that file, DOS sets a flag for that file to indicate what it has done. This flag is one bit in the *attribute byte* stored in the directory entry for this file. The name of the bit in question is the *archive bit* (see Figure 10-4). *Note:* DOS sets that flag if it has opened the file for a program with permission granted to the program to make changes. DOS does not know whether any changes actually were made.

Many back-up programs can use this bit to choose which files to back up and which to ignore. The DOS programs BACKUP and XCOPY can be told to use that information also. Furthermore, these programs can either reset that flag after they have backed up a file, or they can leave it alone. You decide which they will do when you invoke the program.

Up until Version 6, the DOS commands BACKUP and RESTORE were widely regarded as barely able to do their jobs. The third-party programs, like FAST-BACK or Norton Backup, got all the praise. In Version 6, MS-DOS now includes a licensed version of the Norton Backup called MSBACKUP.

A simple *incremental-backup* plan is to run some such program and let it copy to a back-up medium all the files that have their archive bits turned on; then turn off those archive bits.

If you want two back-up sets, you do it almost as simply. First, make a set of backups by using the archive bit to tell your program which files to copy, but instruct it not change the settings of those bits. Then rerun the program to make a second set of backups, only this time let it turn off the archive bits as it goes.

This method is a very good way to make backups. One weakness of it is that you will find yourself backing up many files that were opened by some program that merely inspected the contents but did not make any changes. If those are large database files, you can quickly become overwhelmed with multiple back-up copies of the same data.

This simple approach to incremental backups also will make copies of all the temporary and BAK files you may have littering your hard drive. Some back-up programs let you explicitly screen out those files, although there are limits as to how accurately that instruction can be programmed into them.

Perhaps the optimal way to use an incremental-backup strategy involves some active participation of the user at the time you make each backup. You can use a program such as XtreeGold to show you a list of all the files whose archive bits are turned on. Then you can select which of them to back up and which to ignore. Xtree can turn off the archive bits for the latter group, and it or some other program can be used to back up the rest of the files.

The principal advantage of an incremental-backup approach is that you will save a very much smaller number of bytes each time you go through a back-up process. Therefore, because it will take much less time to do successive backups, you can afford to do those back-up processes much more often. Also, you will use fewer tapes or disks to store your backups, precisely because you have backed up less information.

Differential backups

A third approach to backups is called a *differential backup*. The idea in this approach is to make a full backup once in a while. Then each time you do another backup, you copy each file that was changed since the last full backup.

The differential backup is midway between the other two strategies. When your hard disk dies, if you have a recent enough full backup, you can simply restore from it to a new hard drive and be back in business. If you used only rare full backups supplemented by frequent incremental backups, you could still recover fully, but at a price. You first would have to restore from the most recent full backup and then restore from each of the intervening incremental backups in order. Along the way, you will have to delete all the files you had deleted to keep the restored set of your hard disk files as an accurate copy of what you had on the day that each incremental backup was created.

With the differential approach, you have nearly the simplicity of the full backup and a portion of the economy of the incremental backup. Each time you do a backup, you will be saving all the files that changed since the last full backup, not merely those since the last backup. When you restore from your backups to a new hard disk, you need only restore from the most recent full backup and one (the most recent) incremental backup.

What makes a good backup strategy "good?"

To be good, a backup strategy must first of all be one you will use — regularly. Almost any approach is fine *if* you use it; still, some are better than others.

How often should you back up?

How often should you back up your work? Here is a simple rule of thumb: If the pain of re-creating the data that would be lost if your computer failed in the next few minutes exceeds the pain of making a backup, then make a backup.

For some people, this means doing an incremental backup every day; for others, it means backing up every hour. You still will find it helpful to make occasional full backups, to make it quicker and easier to restore files, but you can make your full backups a whole lot less often and still be completely safe. You may also want to keep a spare set of your incremental and full backups in another building. This will protect you against loss of both your computer and its back-up data set. It is appropriate to create the second set of backups more rarely than the primary set because the hazards of theft, fire, or flood are less likely than data corruption.

A good backup strategy

So what is the definition of a good backup strategy? A combination of full and incremental backups will work well for most offices. You could perform the full backups every quarter or six months, storing a spare set elsewhere. To get away with this, you will want to add to the incremental backup set at least every day or so.

After you fill an incremental disk or tape, catalog it and make it read-only. For easy access, you can store the incremental backups close to the PC, or you can lock them up for greater security. Don't rerecord on these backup media — after they are filled, use them only to restore files when needed. One way to enforce this policy is to use WORM (Write Once, Read Mostly optical disk) drives. Because you cannot rewrite the disks in these drives, they provide permanent, unalterable copies of your files at each stage of their evolution.

One case where a different approach to backing up may be needed

Used this way, your backups become an archive of all your past work. That gives them another value and you another reason to create and preserve them faithfully.

Infrequent full backups and very frequent incremental backups gives a lot of security at very little effort — while the backups are being made. It will cost the most effort when it is necessary to restore the backed up information, but this is not so bad because hard disk deaths occur very much more rarely than times when you should be creating a backup.

The one situation in which this approach fails miserably is that of a large database file which has a few bytes added to it or changed each day. If you backed up the whole file each day onto incremental backups you would use up almost as much time and back-up media as if you had done a full backup daily. If, on the other hand, you waited and only did your backups once a week, you would make yourself vulnerable to losing up to a full week's work.

In this case, the differential backup is most applicable. You can make just a few differential backup copies and recycle them because you only will be depending on the most recent one (plus the most recent full backup) when your hard disk dies.

There is an even better approach to use in this case. It involves a bit of effort to set up, but it can lead you to making backups very much more often (thus reducing your vulnerability to losing data). It also will let you keep an accurate picture of how all your changeable files looked at each time you did a backup, and still use no more time or back-up media than if you had only small files to back up.

The key to this approach is to use a program that examines a copy of your large database file as it was at the time of the last incremental backup and compares it to the working copy of that database as it is now. From these two files, this program will prepare a *difference* file. Later on, when you need to restore the database as it is now, you simply "apply" the difference file to the copy of the database as it was (by using the program that created the difference file), and the result is a copy of the database file as it is now.

By applying each difference file in turn to a copy of the original database (stored on your most recent full backup), you can recover today's database in complete accuracy from a full backup you made many days ago. You merely need to go through a lot of steps to do so — the same as if you were restoring from a full backup and a lot of incremental backups.

One program you can use to do this job is DeltaFile by Hyperkinetix. Another is RT-Patch. DeltaFile creates a differences file with the re-creation engine built in. RT-Patch uses a separate re-creation program and only stores the difference information in each data file it generates. (DeltaFile comes from Hyperkinetics, 18001 Irvine Boulevard, Suite H, Tustin, CA 92680; 800-873-9993. RT-Patch comes from PocketSoft, 7676 Hillmont, Suite 195, Houston, TX 77040; 713-460-5600.)

Another use for good backups

Most people make backups to protect their data against the possibility of a disk failure, but backups can be very useful for other reasons. If you catalog your back-up disks or tapes and keep them forever, you can quickly find the back-up copy of a file you have long since deleted from your hard drive. Occasionally, that can be even more important than restoring the total contents of a hard drive after it dies.

One good program to use for disk cataloging is Rick Hillier's CATDISK, a shareware program that you may find on a local BBS, or you can contact Mr. Hillier at 9820 Toynbee Crescent, Kitchener, Ontario, Canada, N2N1R9; 519-570-3523.

Is Disk Mirroring a Substitute for Backups?

For many years, the common practice on many large computer systems is to have redundant disk drives. These drives are managed by a special mirroring disk controller. All data are written to both disks at the same time. Then, if one disk dies, the controller can still read and write data using the other disk. The best mirroring systems permit the user to remove and replace the failed drive without interrupting the computer operation. Once the new drive is installed, the controller automatically makes it contain a full copy of the information on the other drive.

This strategy can give a computer's hard disk subsystem what amounts to an infinite Mean Time Between Failures (MTBF). That sounds like perfection. Of course, it does require some human intervention to replace hard drives when they die.

Recently, mirroring controllers for PCs have started appearing on the market. Does this mean that you could get one of these controllers and an extra hard drive and then forget all about the nuisance of doing backups? Not a chance! You still need to make regular backups and keep copies of them off-site to protect against catastrophic disasters (such as a major fire) that might take out your entire computer system.

Mirroring systems do allow you to do your backups while the computer is busy doing other tasks because you can be backing up from one drive, which you have disconnected from the main mirroring controller, while the computer is merrily computing away using the other drive. Then when you are done with your backups, you can reconnect that hard drive and let the controller bring it up to date. Backups, then, can be more convenient and less an interruption in the day's work. The added reliability, plus this convenience, makes this an appropriate strategy for "mission critical" applications.

Some Stern Warnings and Strong Suggestions

- Make no mistake: all hard disks die. It is only a matter of when. (All floppy disks die also; don't become a victim of over-reliance on data stored there.)

- Store a spare copy of your backups off-site. This precaution will protect you against loss of data should your primary set of backups (which should be stored close to your computer for convenience) and your computer both be lost, perhaps through a fire or by theft.

- Test and periodically retest your backup strategy. The strategy is acceptable only if *every* file you back up can be restored to your PC's hard disk without a single byte being in error.

- Avoid panic. If you do panic, try not to let the panic motivate you to "do something — anything — just do something now!" Instead, use that panic to help motivate you to take steps to protect yourself from data loss in the future.

- Remember the good advice you have read here (in Chapter 1 and elsewhere) on how to keep from hurting your PC when you need to work on what's inside it. Mainly, turn off power before doing anything inside the system unit. Unplug all connections to peripheral devices and pull the power cord out of the back of the power supply. Touch the PC power supply or frame before each time you reach inside.

- Now might be a very good time to reread Chapter 1. Pay special attention to the discussion there about backups and about the safety boot diskette. Now that you know how many ways your hard disk can die, you may be more motivated to take appropriate precautions ahead of time.

Summary

- Many, perhaps most, hard disk deaths are not necessarily forever. You often can recover your data, and you may be able to return your hard disk to full function.

- Your first job, when faced with a malfunctioning disk subsystem, is to decide whether you have a hardware problem or a glitch in the stored information used to access your disk files.

- Some disk errors are caused by mechanical misalignment between the heads and the tracks of recorded information. Running a program such as SpinRite often can completely eliminate these problems.

- Bad PC practices (such as shutting off or rebooting your computer at any time other than when it is waiting at the DOS prompt, or turning it on again immediately after shutting it off) are frequent causes of data accidents. Naturally, a power failure can also cause these problems. These causes may produce a variety of consequences, ranging from losing some clusters of space on your disk to becoming unable to access that disk at all.

- Understanding how hard disks work is your most powerful tool in diagnosing and repairing disk failures. Almost all data-glitch problems can be remedied. Many (although, not as many) hardware failures also can be fixed.

- File fragmentation is a natural consequence of using a PC for any length of time. It can lead to a substantial degradation of the PC's performance. Defragmenting your hard disk may boost your PC's apparent speed considerably and increase the difficulty of file recovery.

- When all is said and done, fixing disk problems to recover data is *much* harder than simply restoring those files from a recent backup copy.

- There are many different backup strategies. The most important single consideration is that you choose one you can and will use.

- Test your back-up strategy comprehensively once and then retest it on a sampled basis frequently. A backup is worthless if you cannot flawlessly restore the files you need.

Now you know all you need to know about how hard disks in PCs work, how they die, and what to do about it. In Part II, you learn all about a very special hard disk utility program, SpinRite, that can help your hard disks live as long as possible. SpinRite also may help you recover data from a hard disk that no other program can read.

PART II

The SpinRite Companion

Page

327 **Chapter 12**
Reinterleaving Software: A New Category of Utility Program

343 **Chapter 13**
Preventing the Slow Death of Your Hard Disk

365 **Chapter 14**
Details of SpinRite's Operation

389 **Chapter 15**
SpinRite's Evolution

407 **Chapter 16**
Advanced User's Guide to SpinRite

Chapter 12

Reinterleaving Software: A New Category of Utility Program

In This Chapter

▶ How sector interleave was adjusted in the good old days

▶ How SpinRite revolutionized the PC industry, spawning a whole new category of utility software

The Good Old Days

In 1987, personal computers were not nearly as efficient as they are now. Among other things, we now have some revolutionary new utility software, including the one that is the focus of this part of *Hard Disk SECRETS*. Steve Gibson was bothered by the effort one had to go through to adjust precisely an arcane hard disk parameter called the *sector interleave*. He knew that getting the right value meant that his PC would work *much* faster. Pained by how hard it was to set the sector interleave value by using the methods available, Gibson was shocked to discover that almost no PCs then in use had it set correctly.

When Gibson started his testing there were no easy tools available for checking the appropriateness of the interleave setting. He wrote a small test program he called SPINTEST.COM, which he later released as freeware. This program simply measures how long it takes to transfer 200 tracks worth of data. If the interleave is set too tightly, the time required will be very much greater than if the interleave is set correctly or a bit too loosely. He tried his test program on a wide variety of PCs — essentially all the PCs he could get his hands on in his own establishment, at his friends' homes and offices, and in computer stores.

Gibson devised a better method for setting the interleave, from which came the product SpinRite. What he did not foresee was the revolutionary effect that program would have as the beginning of a new category of utility software for PCs.

To understand this revolution, you first must know what things were like back "in the good old days" before SpinRite. (Some of this is a recap of what you learned in Part I. Here, though, the emphasis is on the problem faced by early PC users, the ways in which that problem and ways to deal with it evolved over time, and how Steve Gibson's SpinRite program solved it for all of us once and for all.)

Disks on PCs store information in chunks called *sectors* (usually with 512 bytes per sector). The sectors are arranged around the disk in rings called *tracks*. As the disk turns, the read/write head passes over the track, reading or writing information (see Figure 12-1). For a more detailed description of each of these ideas, see Chapter 2.

Any useful collection of information, called a *file,* is stored in one or more sectors. If you have a file that takes up several sectors, it might seem (naively) that the sensible way to store it would be in successive sectors along a track. Then the pieces could be put down in order and picked up in order.

Although fine in theory, this method often fails in execution because your PC may not be able to write or read one sector immediately after it has written or read another one. There is some minimum "digestion time" that must pass between reading (or writing) one sector and the next. Often, it will turn out that while the PC is waiting for that digestion time to go by, the next sector, or even more than one sector, also will go past the read/write head.

If that happens, you must wait until the disk turns around the rest of that revolution before the sector you want comes into view again. This drastically reduces the speed at which a file may be read or written because you only read or write one sector on each revolution of the disk.

A clever solution to this problem is to arrange the sectors of information around the track in a more sophisticated manner. Instead of having sector number 2 placed right after sector number 1, it may be placed several sectors farther down the track. If you do it just right, the added time it takes for sector 2 to come into view under the read/write head after the PC has finished with sector 1 will be just a bit more than the digestion time. Then when the PC is ready for sector 2, voila! There it is. (See Figure 12-2, and refer to the discussion in Chapter 3 in the section "Improvement of Hard Disk Performance by Sector Interleaving and Head Skewing.") Although the idea of sector interleave proves simple enough, setting it correctly before the advent of SpinRite was no mean feat.

Chapter 12: Reinterleaving Software

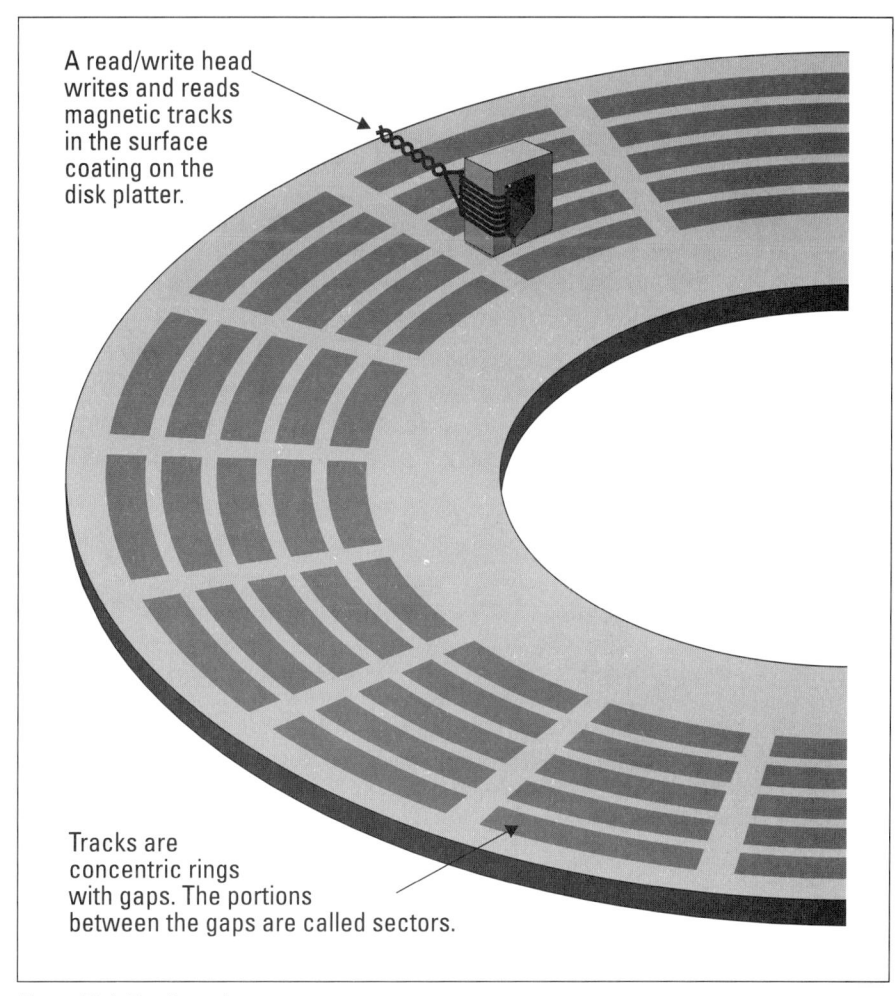

A read/write head writes and reads magnetic tracks in the surface coating on the disk platter.

Tracks are concentric rings with gaps. The portions between the gaps are called sectors.

Figure 12-1: Tracks and sectors.

The Old Method

I want to give you a feeling for what it used to be like for anyone who tried to set up a PC, and in particular, anyone who tried to get it set up optimally. The following paragraphs cover what that user had to go through.

There are three major steps in preparing a new hard disk for use in a PC. They are low-level formatting, partitioning, and high-level formatting (see Chapters 8 through 10 for the details).

Part II: The SpinRite Companion

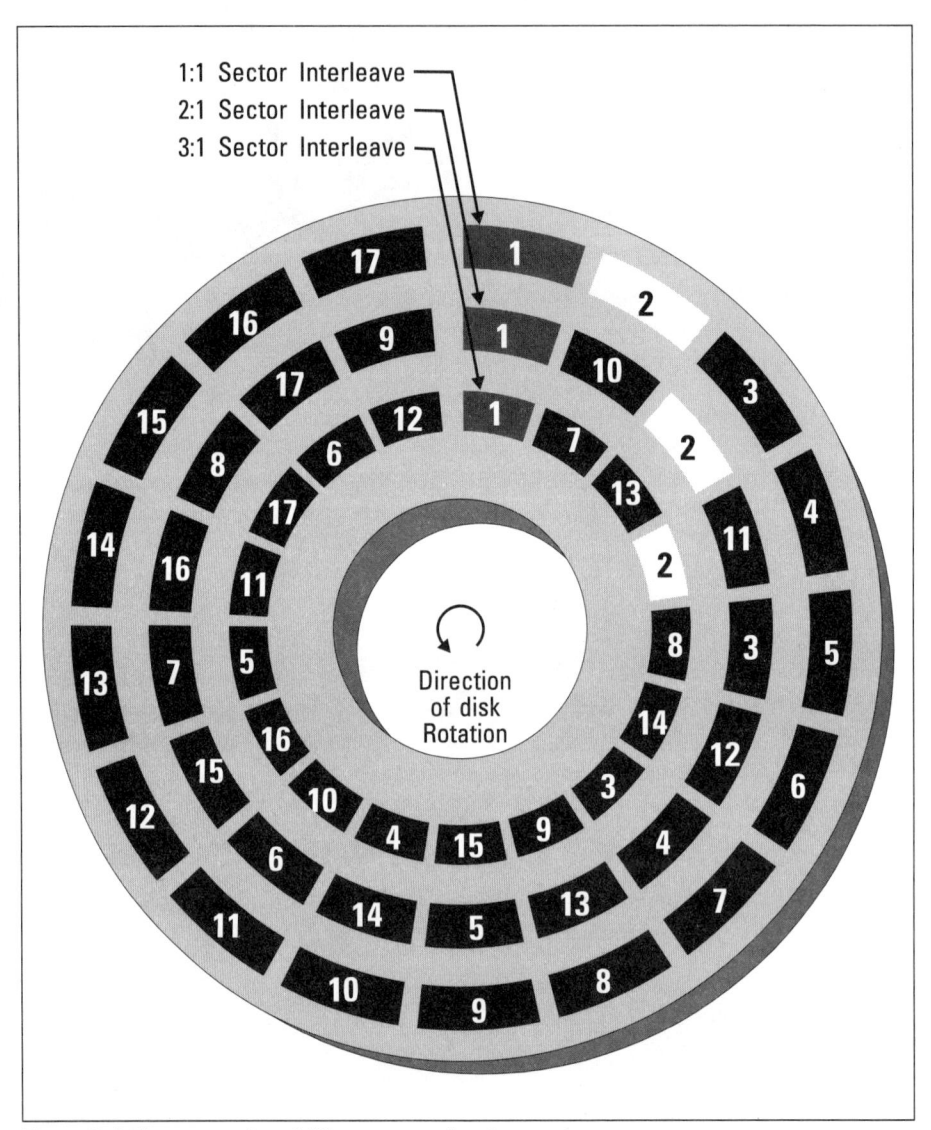

Figure 12-2: Three examples of different sector interleave values.

The person who puts the system together must perform the first of these steps because it can only be done after the drive is connected to the controller in the PC. The other two steps, partitioning and high-level formatting, may be redone from time to time as the PC's user reorganizes how the disk is used. But until quite recently, almost no one ever repeated the low-level format step.

Actually, this description only applies to installing a hard drive that does not have its controller built onto it at the factory. Those drives, which include all IDE/ATA and SCSI drives, plus all hard disks on an option card and the newest PCMCIA card drives, have their low-level format performed at the factory. Often only the factory is able to redo that low-level format. Fortunately, therefore, those drives are correctly interleaved every time.

The sector interleave value is established by the low-level format. You can't change the interleave without going back to that step. Before SpinRite, most PC users never considered taking that step, even if they knew what it was all about (and most users did not). On the other hand, until all three steps are complete, DOS cannot use the hard disk. You, therefore, cannot easily test to see whether you have the sector interleave value correct until after the last of these steps is complete.

Back up your data

People who wanted to set the interleave correctly on a PC whose hard disk had been in use some time were faced first with one absolutely essential step: backing up all the data on that disk. Backing up was necessary because to reset the interleave meant redoing the low-level format on that disk drive. And redoing the low-level format, after all, totally wiped out all the data stored there.

It's easy now, but back then...

Modern drives often come with their controller attached and the sector interleave value set to the optimum value by the manufacturer. (In particular, this is true of IDE/ATA and SCSI drives.) That circumstance makes it really easy for the modern PC system assembler.

Back in the mid-1980s, life was much tougher. All the most popular hard disk drives were either MFM or RLL encoded, ST412/ST506 interface designs. These drives required a separate controller card, and the system assembler — often a retail computer dealer, consultant, repair person, or even an end-user — was faced with mating a controller and a drive that were made by different companies.

Merely getting the two working together and some sort of usable low-level formatting accomplished was regarded as a major accomplishment. The whole notion of getting the sector interleave set to the optimum value did not even cross most of those system assemblers' minds.

Redo the sector interleave

Next, the ambitious PC user or technician would have to redo the low-level format. Typically, this meant running some special set-up program or, more often, using the DOS program DEBUG to access the low-level format program built into the BIOS extension option ROM on the hard disk controller card.

Redo the partitioning and high-level format

Some controllers would let you redo the low-level format only on selected tracks. Others simply did it for the whole disk or not at all. Most people who tried to redo their PC's hard disk sector interleave were unclear about all that, so they simply redid the low-level format on the whole disk.

If you reformatted the whole disk, you then had to redo the partitioning, using FDISK, and the high-level format, using the DOS program FORMAT. By now, your whole morning was pretty well shot.

Restore your data

Even after all that, you would only be able to boot your computer — not do very much useful with it. Next, you probably would have restored at least some of your files so that you would have some utility programs you could use for testing.

XTs and ATs

Initially, all hard disks in PCs required an option card with a BIOS extension ROM because the motherboard BIOS ROM in an XT knew nothing about hard disks. When IBM introduced the AT, its motherboard BIOS ROM had the necessary routines to support a hard disk. The only way to low-level format the hard disk in an AT was to use the IBM Advanced Diagnostics set-up disk.

An aspect of most low-level format programs in the option ROMs was the capability to set the sector interleave. Sometimes these programs would ask the person running the program what value to use. More often, you had to know enough to set up the right value in some register of the PC before running the format routine. That program would simply assume that you wanted its default value unless you had known about and taken that critical first step.

Chapter 12: Reinterleaving Software

Test to see whether you chose the right interleave value

Now your PC was ready to use again. Was it improved? This was the earliest opportunity for you to find out.

Testing involved measuring the time it took to copy some large files from one place to another on the disk. (If you copied either to or from a diskette, the much slower speed of the diskette drive would mask what you were hoping to measure.) This file-transfer time was, at best, a rough indication of the correctness of the sector interleave value because a file copy operation involves more than just flowing data on or off the disk. There are also many times when the heads must be moved to the FAT area, back to the data area being read, then to the area being written, and so on, over and over again.

By now, most of the afternoon also was shot. And you still might not have been finished!

Do it again (and again) until you get it right

Thus, to set the interleave correctly, using only the tools included in DOS, you had to do the low-level formatting, the partitioning, and then the high-level formatting of the disk, after which you tested to see whether you had the interleave set correctly. A wrong interleave meant you had to repeat the entire tedious process, which only the most perfectionistic of PC users ever bothered to do.

An Early Attempt to Make It Easy

A fellow named Mark Kolod created a collection of programs to help those perfectionistic PC users. His HOPTIMUM program allowed the user to check a hard disk and find the optimum value for its sector interleave. His HFORMAT program then made it possible to redo the low-level format and, in the process, to set the sector interleave to the optimum value. A third program in his collection, HTEST, tested the capability of your hard disk to store and retrieve data reliably.

TECHNICAL SECRET

HOPTIMUM dramatically shortened the process of finding the optimum interleave value. Instead of redoing the low-level format on the entire disk, it simply directed the hard disk controller to redo the low-level format on one or a few tracks with some specified sector interleave value. Then it tested how rapidly it could read or write data to that track. It repeated this process for several other sector interleave values. Finally, HOPTIMUM showed you which interleave value yielded the highest average data-transfer rate (the number of bytes per second you can read or write).

Because these tests could be done somewhere past the first few cylinders of the disk, they could be done without destroying the partitioning and high-level format information. They would destroy any data you might have stored on the cylinders you used, though. The programs did not make you do the tests on a safely empty cylinder, but they allowed you to do so if you knew where one was, and if you remembered to tell it to use that empty cylinder. This capability and the use of only one or a few cylinders for the tests made it possible to choose the optimum sector interleave value in only a few minutes, instead of the few hours that typically were needed before.

These programs contained the kernel of what was needed, but they required that you knew a lot about how your PC worked, and they did their work in a destructive fashion, destroying any data that resided on the track being tested or reformatted. (HTEST did have a nondestructive, read-only test, but it didn't report nearly as much about the integrity of the disk.)

A Better Way

One of Steve Gibson's key insights was how to do this work without destroying data on the hard disk. In fact, using his new approach, you could do these steps without losing even one byte of it. Further, he realized the importance of making his program do all this very technically sophisticated work without requiring a matching sophistication in its users.

The essential insight

What was Gibson's key insight? In retrospect, it is simplicity itself: First, read all the data on a single track and store it someplace safe. Test that one track and redo its low-level format. When you are finished, put the data back.

That is the whole plan, in its essence. Of course, reality has a way of complicating things a bit.

A few pitfalls along the way

Gibson's original plan was simply to read a track's data, redo its low-level format, and then put the data back. Doing just that is not safe, though. It is essential to do at least some testing as you go.

If a sector on the track has a bad spot as a result of a pinhole defect in the magnetic coating on the platter, that sector will still be bad after redoing the low-level format. If you change the sector interleave value, this sector will no longer have the same sector number. If you simply restore the data to each sector according to its sector number, the bad sector may get some important data put into it (see Figure 12-3).

If you noticed that the sector was marked as bad, you could just avoid placing any data in it. That might work, but because errors have a way of creeping in when you least expect them, it would be, at best, an imprudent way to do things.

The only safe way to proceed is by following these four steps:

1. Read and save the data for a given track.
2. Redo the low-level format for that track with the optimal sector interleave value.
3. Test every sector in that track very carefully.
4. If the sectors are all perfect, put the data back. If one or more of the sectors are flawed, store the data from them somewhere else and make whatever other adjustments are needed to let DOS find the data.

Help like this you can do without

There is a shareware program available on many bulletin board systems and on CompuServe called the Interleave Adjustment Utility, or IAU (formerly called ILEAVE). This program is dangerous. Don't use it.

The author, Dave Bushong, assumed that anyone using IAU would have an XT-class PC with a hard disk controller that could only declare an entire track bad or good. Modern hard disk controllers allow the user to mark individual sectors as good or bad.

IAU does some of what SpinRite does but with one horrible exception. It does *no* data-integrity testing at all. (It also is not nearly as capable at reading data from disks with problems.) IAU simply lifts the data from the track, redoes the low-level format for that track to set the sector interleave to the desired value, and then plops the data back down again.

If you use IAU on a disk with some defects, most likely you will lose some of your data. The IAU author tells the user to make very good backups before starting to use IAU. And if you lose some of your data, he is not prepared to help you get it back. You've been warned!

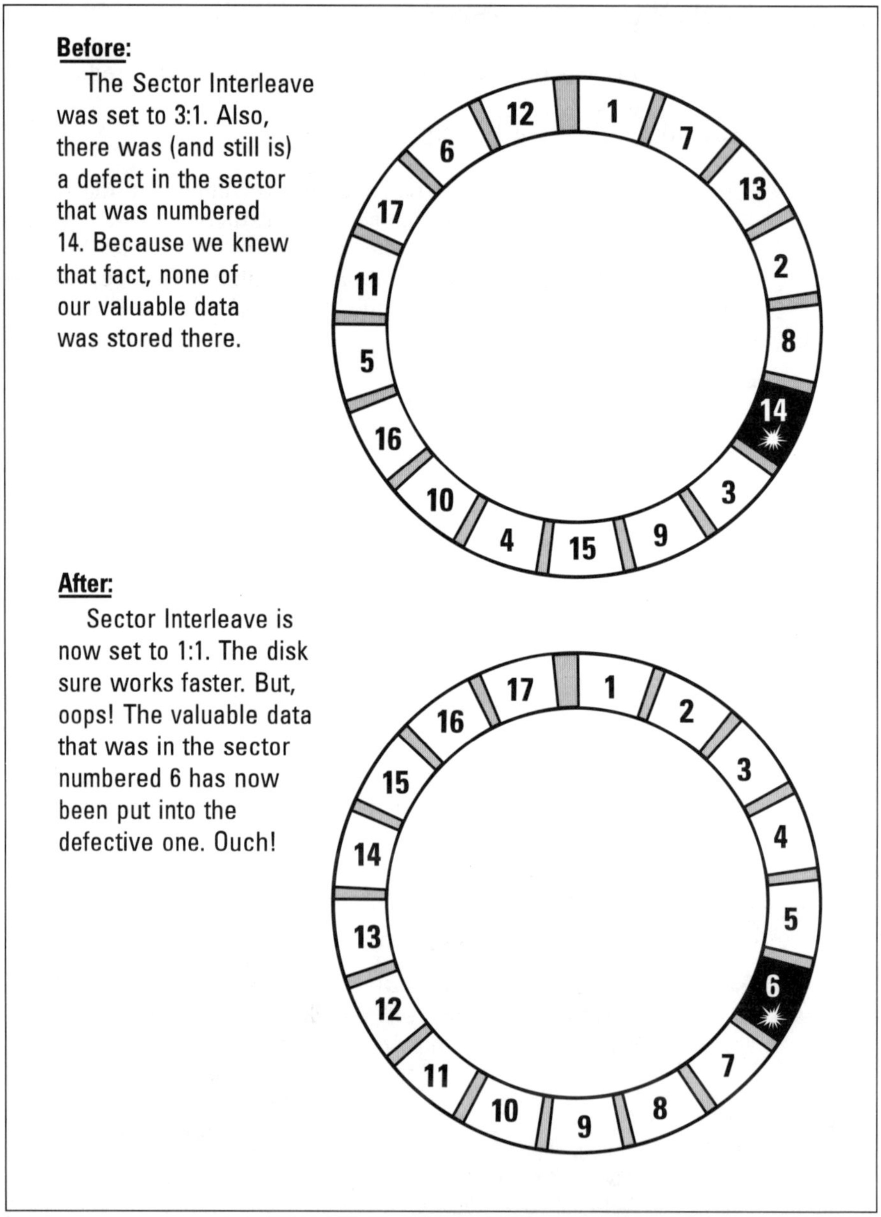

Part II: The SpinRite Companion

Before:

The Sector Interleave was set to 3:1. Also, there was (and still is) a defect in the sector that was numbered 14. Because we knew that fact, none of our valuable data was stored there.

After:

Sector Interleave is now set to 1:1. The disk sure works faster. But, oops! The valuable data that was in the sector numbered 6 has now been put into the defective one. Ouch!

Figure 12-3: The problem with reinterleaving without data-integrity testing.

As the development of SpinRite progressed, Gibson realized that his task was much more complicated than he had first imagined. He began with the intention of making a program to allow easy, safe resetting of the sector interleave value. In the end, he was *forced* to make a program that is at least as useful for data recovery and for ensuring the integrity of future data storage.

The Side Benefits (Now the Main Point of These Programs)

Gibson tested hard drives thoroughly to learn all the many ways they can fail. He did this to be sure that his new program would not trip up on any opportunities to fail and cause an accidental data loss. He was flabbergasted to find out just how many different ways hard disks can fail. The subtleties of the interactions between all the different brands and types of hard disks and hard disk controllers with the many different brands of IBM PC-compatible computers were mind boggling. Developing SpinRite took a lot longer than he had expected.

After all that research, SpinRite emerged a much more capable program than the one Gibson initially envisioned. The additional benefits fall into three categories: refreshing sector header information, recovering unreadable data, and moving data to safety.

Refreshing the sector headers

A very scary error message to get from your PC is `Sector not found`. You know your data is out there, but your PC simply cannot find it.

Before DOS can read or write any data, it must find the correct sector in which to look for or put that data. It does so by reading the sector headers (see Figure 12-4).

TECHNICAL SECRET

Before the disk controller can read or write any data, it must first move the head assembly to the correct cylinder and activate the correct head. Then it reads the header on each sector of that track until it finds the one it is looking for, or until the entire track has gone past the head.

The sector headers contain all three address numbers: cylinder, head, and physical sector number. If the controller sees all three right numbers, it can be sure it has positioned the head assembly correctly and switched on the right head and that it has found the right sector on the track.

Part II: The SpinRite Companion

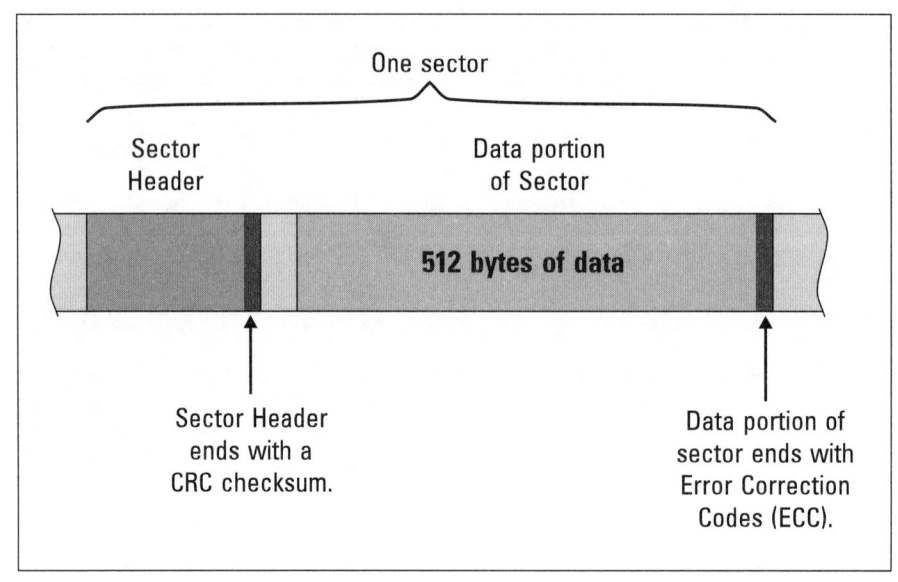

Figure 12-4: The anatomy of a hard disk sector.

Three things can make a sector header unreadable: a physical defect in the magnetic coating in that part of the disk surface; a data accident that may have damaged the data stored in the sector header but may not have done any damage to the magnetic coating; or the head assembly may have drifted slightly to one side so that it no longer tracks over the sector header enough to read it accurately.

If the magnetic coating is damaged where the sector header information should be stored, it will be impossible to record data there. Most such coating defects are on the drive from the day it is manufactured, but new ones can occur, such as when something jars the disk and makes the head bounce on the surface hard enough to gouge out a bit of the magnetic coating.

TECHNICAL SECRET

The controller reads all the information in a sector header and then checks to see whether what it read was valid. It uses a cyclical redundancy check (CRC) strategy to do this validation. (See Chapter 2 under "A Problem of Imperfection and Some Solutions" for an explanation of what a CRC is.) If the CRC value the controller reads from the header does not agree with the value it computes, it will reject that sector as unreadable.

A data accident may also render a sector header unreadable. If anything changes even one bit of the information stored in the header, the controller will reject that sector as unreadable. Such an accident may occur if the head comes

Chapter 12: Reinterleaving Software

to rest over that sector header when you turn off power to your PC. When you turn on your PC again, the head may jerk around a bit before the platter starts turning. Further, a brief surge of current may pass through the head winding, causing a magnetic field that may reverse some bits recorded in the sector header. Even the residual magnetization of the head may be enough to alter those bits, even without a current surge.

A misalignment also may cause the sector header to become unreadable, simply because it is too far to one side of the path that the read head is currently following (see Figure 12-5).

You can solve each of these problems by having SpinRite refresh the low-level format, which is the only way to rewrite the sector headers. The rewriting realigns the sector headers under the present head path and repairs any changes induced by a data accident. Only physical damage to the surface cannot be repaired this way, but SpinRite can detect it and relocate data to some safer spot.

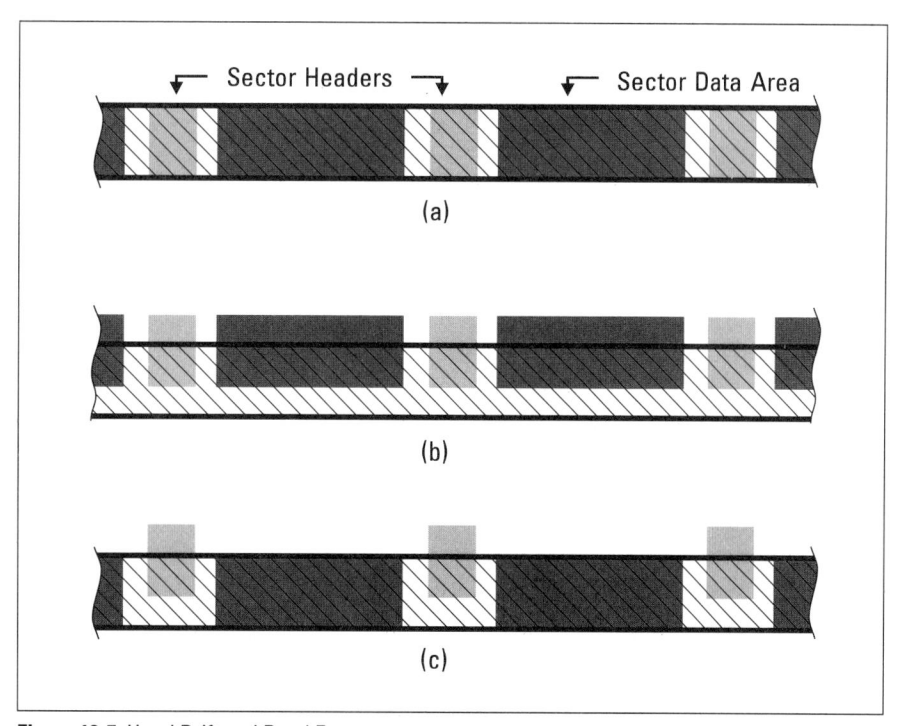

Figure 12-5: Head Drift and Read Errors.
The path of the read/write head is indicated by the shaded region between the two heavy lines.
(a) At first, the sector headers and data sections are created by the head under its path.
(b) Later on, the head path may drift to one side enough to make reading data difficult.
(c) Rewriting the data puts that portion of the sector back on track, but the sector headers remain dangerously to one side. Using SpinRite, you can redo the low-level format and get the sector headers into line, as in (a).

Recovering "unreadable" data

Another horrible error message is `Read fault`, which means that DOS cannot read some sector. It may give you a portion of your file, or it may refuse to give you any of your file, even though the error affects only a minute part of a single sector.

Sometimes, DOS or the BIOS will force the controller to attempt to reread the sector several or even many times, but eventually they will give up. SpinRite is both more persistent and often more clever in how it rereads a sector, and so it frequently succeeds where DOS and the BIOS have failed.

SpinRite can very often read the whole file accurately. If it cannot, at least it will give you back all but the very few bytes that actually were damaged. Chapter 14 includes a description of just how SpinRite performs this sort of magic.

Moving data to safety

The third category of side benefits a program like SpinRite provides is moving data to safety. When your disk develops weak places, SpinRite will relocate the data. SpinRite looks for indications of problems that DOS normally hides from users.

The controller will tell the BIOS when it has difficulty reading a sector, in particular whenever it needs to use the ECC stored in the sector with the data. (When it cannot read all the data accurately, the controller uses the error correction codes to deduce what the sector data used to be; see the section "A better solution: error correction" in Chapter 2 for details on how ECC works.) It also will report any sector that it is unable to read or reconstruct.

If the controller says it has successfully reconstructed the data by using ECC, DOS accepts the data as reported without informing us of any difficulties. Though you may receive the right data this time, you may not be so lucky the next time.

SpinRite goes through incredible gyrations in trying to get an accurate reading of the data in the sector without using ECC. If ever it gets one perfect reading of the data, it will use that reading. If it must use ECC to correct the data, it will, finally, accept that solution, but it will move the data to prevent possible future data loss.

SpinRite's persistence in reading data despite great difficulties and its insistence on relocating data from suspicious sectors are what makes it so good at keeping your data safe.

Incidental testing of RAM and other parts of your computer

Although SpinRite was designed primarily to help you improve or maintain your hard disk's performance, it also can serve as a pretty good test of much of the rest of your PC. To be sure that it is safe to move any data around on your hard disk, SpinRite performs some rather extensive tests on a portion of your main system RAM and the direct memory access (DMA) chips.

Running SpinRite also gives your whole system quite a workout. Before it is finished, SpinRite easily can move many gigabytes (GB) of data on and off the disk. (This includes both the data you have stored there and all the test patterns that SpinRite writes and reads on each track it tests.)

In fact, SpinRite keeps your PC so busy that often the CPU is not given enough time to update the DOS clock. (The DOS clock is the time of day as kept in DOS, which is displayed whenever you type the DOS command **TIME**.)

You may observe this effect by noticing how accurately your PC knows the time before you run SpinRite and checking again after it finishes, but before you reboot the machine. (Rebooting in many PCs causes them to reread the real-time clock and that clock's time-keeping accuracy is not affected by how busy the CPU is.) The DOS clock may lose many minutes in just a few hours — far more than it is likely to lose or gain normally.

Because it exercises your PC so heavily, you could use SpinRite as another diagnostic tool to test how well a PC is working. Certainly, if there are any problems in the hard disk subsystem of the PC, SpinRite will flush them out.

Part II: The SpinRite Companion

Summary

- Setting a hard disk's sector interleave to the optimum value can only be done after it is mated to a hard disk controller. The choice of controller can profoundly influence the optimum interleave value.
- The only way to adjust the sector interleave is to redo the low-level format on the disk.
- The old method for adjusting the interleave was tedious, at best. It required the user to back up all the disk's contents, redo the low-level format, repartition the disk, redo the high-level format, and restore the data.
- SpinRite revolutionized the industry first by providing an easy way to reset the sector interleave to its optimum value. It did this by working its way across the disk, lifting up the data and redoing the interleave on the track, and then replacing the data. In the user's perception, the sector interleave value was reset without destroying any data at all.
- To do its job safely, SpinRite has to test very thoroughly the disk tracks it has reinterleaved before putting the data back. If there are any bad places in that track, data that otherwise would have been put in those places must be relocated to some other, safer place.
- This side benefit of SpinRite has become the main reason to use it now because modern disk drives often come mated with a controller and already set to the optimum sector interleave value.

In the next chapter, you learn more about the preventable slow deaths of hard disks and what role SpinRite and other similar programs play in preventing those failures.

Chapter 13
Preventing the Slow Death of Your Hard Disk

In This Chapter

- A common misconception many people have regarding disk data storage
- Why refreshing the low-level format can be useful even if your sector interleave value is already at its optimum value
- What can cause bad spots on a disk and how you can find them
- How to tell a hard disk controller where on a disk there are bad spots that should not be used (and also how to set the interleave value you prefer)
- The difference between the factory surface tests and what you can do on the hard disk in your PC by using digital testing techniques
- The details on all the test patterns used by SpinRite and its procedure for using those tests

How to Catch Problems Before They Become Problems

Hard disk calamities can strike instantaneously, such as if an earthquake or a clumsy colleague knocks your PC on the floor, or if your hard disk controller suffers a violent electronic breakdown. Other, less dramatic problems build up over time until they finally show themselves by preventing your hard disk from working.

The only defense against the swift, sudden death of your hard disk is to have good backups. On the other hand, you often can catch the problems that creep up on you before they become disasters.

This chapter focuses on some slow death mechanisms and how SpinRite can help *forestall* those deaths. (See Chapter 2 for a detailed explanation of how hard disks are built and how they work. Chapter 11 goes into a lot of detail about ways disks die and how to recover from those events.)

A common misconception

A commonly held misconception purports that hard disks store data digitally. Although this would be wonderful, it is not actually the case. The CPU sends digital data (bits of information — that is to say, a whole lot of ones and zeros) to the hard disk controller, and the controller returns digital data. But all hard disk drives store data as analog signals in the sense that the information is encoded in the form of magnetic field patterns that vary from place to place on the disk.

The advantage that truly digital data has over analog is that, in digital form, noise usually can be ignored. (*Noise* means any deviation from the ideal pattern.) As long as the noise is not "too loud," it will not overwhelm the data, and the digital information can be reconstructed with complete reliability. Errors creep in whenever the noise exceeds a critical level.

Some complex electronics called the *write circuitry* create the magnetic field patterns that represent your data. The *read circuitry,* some other electronics that are at least as fancy, detect the patterns. The read/write heads lay down the patterns and pick them up. The head-positioning assembly positions these heads over the spinning platters. (See Chapters 2 and 4 for details.)

Sometimes, one or more of these parts of your hard disk drive (write electronics, head positioner, and so on) may temporarily alter their performance, impairing the disk's capability to read data without affecting its storage capability. The head-positioning assembly may not always return the heads to precisely the same places; the motor that turns the platters, bringing the magnetic field patterns under the heads, may not always turn at the same speed.

Other alterations have a more permanent effect. The magnetic field patterns may weaken or may become rearranged a bit, causing the data they represent to become more and more difficult to read.

TECHNICAL SECRET

The notion of magnetic field patterns on a hard disk "weakening" over time has become a controversial one. Some people have noted that permanent magnets are just that: for all practical purposes, they keep their magnetization forever. Therefore, they say, data patterns once recorded on the disk platter surface should stay there, full strength, until new data are recorded over them. That is mostly true. Experience suggests that sometimes something happens to the patterns to make them appear to be weaker. What might that be?

As the read/write head sweeps over the platter surface, it records a swath of data called a track. Later, it will again sweep over that part of the platter surface to detect that data. The band of magnetized surface is as wide as the head.

Suppose that at some time the head passes over one edge of the track, and while it does so puts out a magnetic field that reverses the magnetization in the platter surface from what was recorded previously. Now assume that the next time the head flies over the center of the original track. Only a portion of the width of the original track is as it was when it first was recorded. The rest has been altered by that one off-center pass. The signals picked up by the head will be sort of what they were supposed to be, only much weaker. Perhaps enough weaker that they cannot reliably be read. This is just one way the recorded data patterns, in effect, can become weaker.

Although some of these problems reflect an underlying defect in the disk, others are merely alterations of the data stored there. If your disk is damaged, you must retrieve your data somehow (if you can) and store it elsewhere. If your data was merely altered, you again must retrieve the data, but you then can put them back where they came from, only without the errors.

Benefits of rewriting the data

You can deal with some problems decisively and easily. If the magnetic signals representing your data become weakened or have some "confusing dirt" signals mixed in, you may be able to repair the damage by rewriting the data. If the sector happens to reside on a damaged part of the disk surface, you must move the data.

TECHNICAL SECRET

If the signals representing the data are all correctly placed, but simply a bit weaker than normal, rewriting the data will return them to full strength. If a few of the magnetic field transitions have been altered, the pattern of transitions will represent some slightly altered bits of information (see Chapter 2 for more details). This means that you must solve the problem of reading the data before you rewrite them.

There are two very different cases of altered data patterns. If altered data lies in the sector header, the problem can be detected by using the cyclical redundancy check (CRC) number stored in that header. If the altered data lies in the data portion of the sector, the error will be caught by use of the error correction codes (ECC) stored with the data. (Both are discussed in Chapter 2.)

The CRC enables catching problems with the sector header information. If the data as read are not consistent with the CRC, however, you know only that an error exists. All that can be done is to try to read that sector header again and again, hoping to get it right. Worse, when the data in that sector are rewritten, the sector header will not be rewritten, so its defect will remain.

It is easier to cope with an error in the data section. The ECC numbers stored with the data not only allow detection of errors, but they often can be used to reconstruct the original information.

After you have recovered the data, you can replace them without error, provided the sector is not physically damaged. This rewriting of the data will completely remove most of the problems that commonly occur. You can deal with the other, more permanent problems by moving your data to some other sector that does not have any physical damage.

Another advantage of rewriting the data is that the process cures at least part of the problem of head misalignment. If the head-positioning mechanism has drifted, rewriting the data will align the data under the new position of the head, making the data easier to read. Rewriting data will not realign the sector header, though. A program like SpinRite can either redo the low-level format for the track — which will eliminate the problem of head misalignment — and then rewrite your data for you, or it will move your data to a safer place. Either way, it cures many problems that simple data rewriting will not.

Benefits of refreshing the low-level format

A head alignment problem, or a data glitch in the sector header, requires more than just rewriting the data portion of the sectors. Otherwise, the sector header information will continue to be difficult or impossible to read reliably.

The sector headers are written only during a low-level format, even though they must be read before each time the data in that sector is accessed. If you can read the data in a bad sector even once, you can move them to a safer place. Even better, if you can rewrite the sector header, you may remove any damage entirely, making the location a safe place for your data once more.

Chapter 13: Preventing the Slow Death of Your Hard Disk

On most disk controller and drive combinations, SpinRite is able to redo the low-level format, thereby rewriting all the sector headers. SpinRite's extensive testing of the disk before restoring the data will catch all the residual problems caused by defects in the disk surface.

> **TECHNICAL SECRET**
>
> Neither SpinRite nor the other programs like it can do a low-level reformat on all drive and controller combinations. Mostly the problem is with controllers that "lie" about the dimensions of the drive. SpinRite must know the real number of heads, cylinders, and sectors per cylinder to do low-level reformatting safely.
>
> When you run SpinRite (or any of its competitors), it will report to you if it is unable to learn the real disk dimensions. One of the most important things that SpinRite does is to be very, very sure it knows what your drive and controller are doing and whether it is being lied to.
>
> Some controllers must lie about these numbers (and some others may do so). They *translate* or *map* real locations on the drive to equivalent locations on a fictitious drive with some other dimensions. These controllers are called *translating controllers*. This is explained in more detail in the section "Sector mapping" in Chapter 7.
>
> Any drive/controller combination that uses sector mapping to translate sectors must prohibit all programs from redoing their low-level format (except for programs that can temporarily turn off this mapping — as SpinRite can for some controller/drive combinations). Still, even if it cannot redo the low-level format, SpinRite can do a lot for these drives by testing and refreshing the data portions of the sectors.

Just how SpinRite does its testing is an interesting story. Understanding this story will make it clear why you are better off relying on SpinRite than on the table of defects the manufacturer may have pasted on the drive.

Surface Analysis — Finding the Bad Tracks, Sectors, and Clusters

Disk manufacturers routinely run a *surface analysis* once on every hard disk, meaning that they test the disk to see which places on the platter surfaces can store data reliably. Using SpinRite, you can perform your own surface analysis whenever you want. SpinRite's tests differ from the manufacturers' tests; for your purposes, SpinRite's tests are better.

Part II: The SpinRite Companion

It is impossible for drive manufacturers to make a large hard drive that is completely free of flaws. Small drives (up to 30MB capacity) may be perfect, but larger ones may have up to 0.1 percent of the disk surface flawed. Of course, that means they are more than 99.9 percent perfect. That sounds pretty good — and it is. Still, they are not *really* perfect.

Most of the flaws consist of tiny pinholes in the magnetic coating on the disk platters — places where the coating is thinner than usual. These areas simply don't have enough magnetic material to hold the field patterns reliably, making them unsafe places to store data.

The manufacturers test each drive before it is shipped and they include with each of their drives a label or a slip of paper that lists any defects they found. Years ago, the conventional wisdom was that one should not use any portion of a track that contained a defect. This policy might make sense if the defect were a micro-boulder sticking up out of the surface. Positioning the head over that track would mean it would have to bounce over that micro-boulder with each revolution of the disk, possibly damaging the head and further ruining the disk surface when the head crashed down on the other side of the boulder.

Fortunately, such defects are exceedingly rare. Today's conventional wisdom says it is okay to use any of the disk surface except the immediate neighborhood of each defect. The former approach led to the term *bad track*, meaning any track with at least one bad spot on it. Now we use the term *bad sector*, meaning the portion of that track that holds the defect.

TECHNICAL SECRET

If you really thought you had micro-boulders to contend with, you would declare *bad cylinders,* not just bad tracks, because the head positioner puts the heads over all the tracks of a cylinder at once. (A cylinder is comprised of all the tracks under the heads for a given position of the head assembly.) Even the most conservative experts have not proposed declaring entire cylinders as bad. The original reason for marking whole tracks as bad more likely had to do with some limitations on the way disks are tested by the manufacturers. These limitations are discussed in the section "Why this is less helpful than it appears," later in this chapter.

Older-style XT controllers have two commands to low-level format a track. One command sets up the interleave you specify and marks all the sectors as good (INT 13h, Function 5). The other command formats all the sectors the same but marks every one of them as bad (INT 13h, Function 6).

More modern disk controllers allow you to tell them, at the time you request that they low-level format a track, which individual sectors in the track to mark as good and which to mark as bad. (SpinRite will do this task for you,

Chapter 13: Preventing the Slow Death of Your Hard Disk

but the intention of the disk and controller manufacturers was that you, the user or system integrator, would do it manually. The low-level format program usually gives you an opportunity to type in the track and sector numbers you wish to mark as bad.) They also support a more flexible approach to sector numbering. Instead of telling them simply an interleave factor, you give them a table of sector numbers (and associated good or bad sector flags), which lets you number the sectors in any fashion you want.

A program that wants to set up a given sector numbering pattern and to mark certain of those sectors as good or bad will call INT 13h, Function 5. This interrupt call is the same one that commands the controller to "format a track that is good" in an XT. The difference is that for AT and PS/2 computers, the ES:BX register points to a 512-byte buffer. The entries in this buffer are pairs of bytes, one pair for each sector around the track. The first number in each pair is 0 if the sector is good and 80h if that sector is bad. The second byte in each pair gives the physical sector number (see Figure 13-1).

Because DOS manages the disk in terms of a unit larger than the sector (the *cluster* or *allocation unit*), we also have the term *bad cluster,* meaning a cluster with one or more bad sectors in it. (Chapter 10 gives details on clusters and the file allocation table used to keep track of them.)

What the Factory Tells You

Drive manufacturers carefully test their drives just after finishing the drive construction, before sending them to a distributor or other customer. In this section you learn how they test the drives, the way they report the results, and why this may not be very helpful to you. (Of course, you are glad that they do test the drives. At least that means that they won't ship any real duds!)

How they test

There are two different ways that manufacturers of drives can perform these preshipping tests. The one most commonly used until recently was to substitute an analog test board for the normal, digital electronics board mounted on the drive. Then, after the tests were finished, the digital board would be installed. More recently, disk manufacturers have started using a testing protocol that allows them to have the final, digital electronics board installed on the drive during the tests.

Part II: The SpinRite Companion

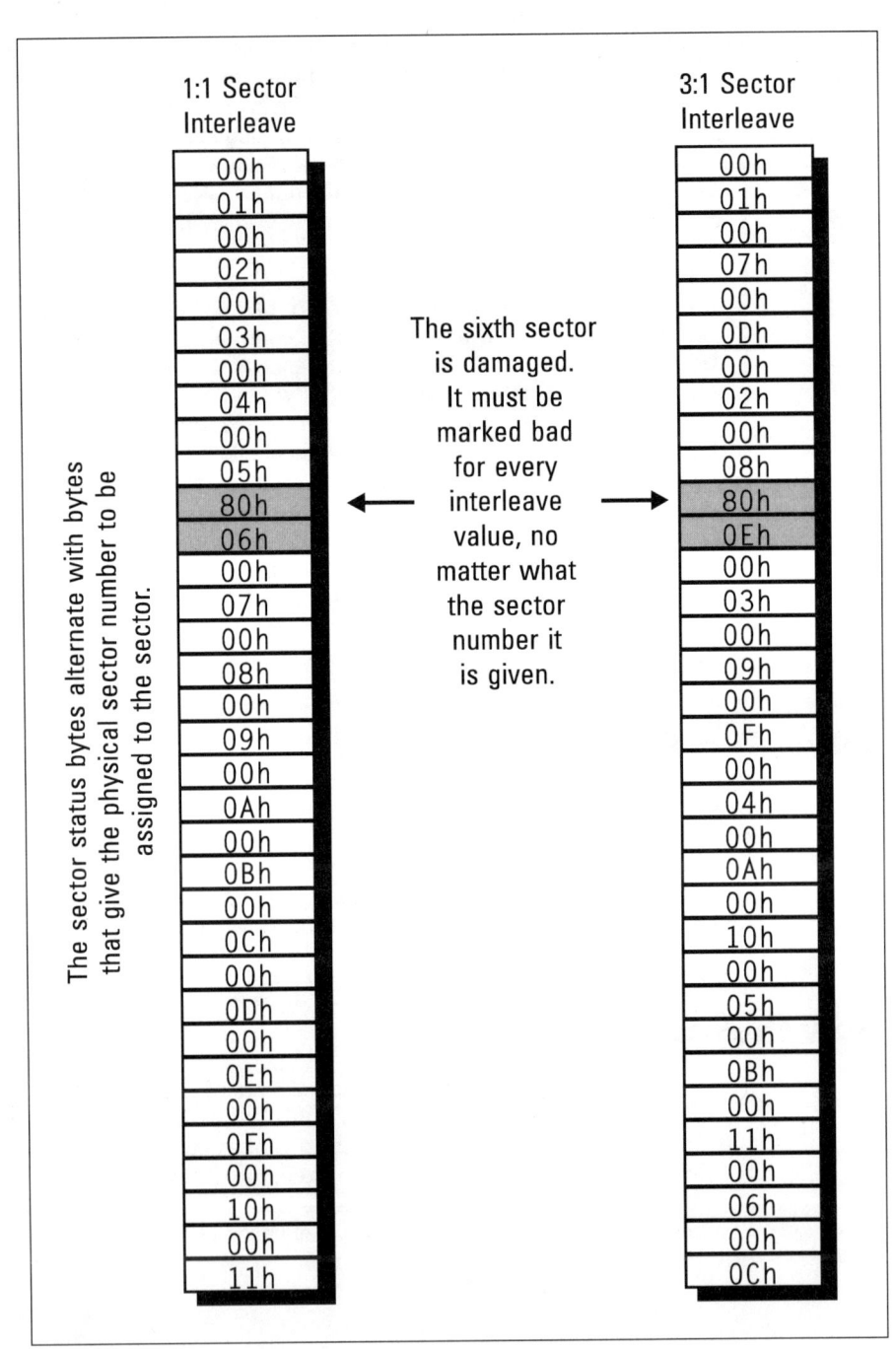

1:1 Sector Interleave		3:1 Sector Interleave
00h		00h
01h		01h
00h		00h
02h		07h
00h		00h
03h		0Dh
00h		00h
04h		02h
00h		00h
05h		08h
80h	← The sixth sector is damaged. It must be marked bad for every interleave value, no matter what the sector number it is given. →	**80h**
06h		**0Eh**
00h		00h
07h		03h
00h		00h
08h		09h
00h		00h
09h		0Fh
00h		00h
0Ah		04h
00h		00h
0Bh		0Ah
00h		00h
0Ch		10h
00h		00h
0Dh		05h
00h		00h
0Eh		0Bh
00h		00h
0Fh		11h
00h		00h
10h		06h
00h		00h
11h		0Ch

The sector status bytes alternate with bytes that give the physical sector number to be assigned to the sector.

Figure 13-1: A sample of the table of bytes used to tell an AT-style (16-bit) hard disk controller how to interleave a track and which sectors on that track are to be marked as bad.

The manufacturer can also perform two *kinds* of tests. One test checks how accurately and consistently the head-positioning mechanism can put the heads in any desired location. The other test is designed to find all the places on the platter surfaces that are not able to hold a recorded magnetic signal adequately.

The first test may involve having the head seek to various tracks while measuring with a laser interferometer exactly where the heads go. This test is performed in a clean room with the sealed housing's cover removed. The second test can be done with the housing installed, in a normal laboratory environment. This test mainly involves writing patterns to the surface and reading them back.

If the manufacturer is running analog tests, the surface analysis will consist of recording standard amplitude sine waves (smoothly varying signals) and seeing how loud they appear when they are played back. Weak signals during the reading indicate thin spots in the platter, and those spots are logged as defective.

If the manufacturer is running tests with the digital electronics board installed, some test points will have been included in the board's design to allow the head signals to be picked up before some of the digital signal processing has been done. Again, the strength of those signals will tell the manufacturer where the weak spots (defects) are on the surface.

How they report defects

Notice that these tests do not record data bits, at least not of the same kind that your controller will be putting on the disk when you are using it. The tests are not specific to the kind of data-encoding technology that will later be used with the drive. (See Chapter 2 for a discussion of data encoding.)

One result of this limitation is that the manufacturer cannot tell you in which sectors these defects will finally appear, only the cylinder and head combination (that is, the track) that contains each defect and how far around the track those defects are from an index position. By making some assumptions about how your data will be encoded (usually by assuming either MFM or 2,7 RLL), they then translate the angle from the index in degrees into an assumed number of *bytes from index*. The track number and that calculated position in bytes from index (abbreviated BFI) is what is written on the defect list shipped with the drive.

An MFM or RLL drive will only have a list of defects written on paper, either on a label on the drive or on a sheet of paper enclosed with the drive. Most IDE/ATA or SCSI drives have their defects noted in a table that is recorded on the drive and which can be accessed by the hard disk controller. (That table is one of the kinds of information that may be put in a "secret cylinder" if that drive/controller combination has one.)

An ESDI drive and controller also can store defect information this way. Remember, though, that usually the low-level format is first done after the drive and controller are mated by a system assembler and not at the factory. The person doing the low-level format, therefore, will have to enter the defects manually (by reading from the paper list) before the controller can record them on the drive.

Defects are listed on the paper list as a set of numbers for the cylinder, head, and bytes from index of each defect. You need to know the drive model number, and what that suggests about the data-encoding technology being assumed, before you can derive any meaning from these numbers. Of course, if all you want to do is mark bad tracks, you can just use the numbers for the cylinder and head at which the defects were found and ignore the bytes-from-index values.

You could mark entire tracks as bad, but most people don't want to lose all that disk storage space needlessly. In fact the best strategy may be to act as if the drive had no defects when you initially set it up. Then later on you can let SpinRite, or a similar program, find and mark any defective sectors as bad. Why this is a better approach is discussed in the next section.

Why this is less helpful than it appears

The defect lists supplied by the manufacturers are not always what you need. Sometimes they can be very helpful; other times, you would be better off just ignoring them.

What makes the difference? If the manufacturer's tests were performed with the drive's final electronics board installed, the results should be considerably more meaningful than if an analog board was used. Further, if the drive uses an embedded, buried, or hybrid servo strategy for head positioning, its defect list will be much more relevant.

The defect list that the manufacturer includes with any MFM or RLL drive or any other drive that uses a stepper-motor head positioner or an open-loop (external) servo head-positioning system may as well be ignored — if, that is, you will do a very good job of testing that drive yourself by using SpinRite.

Why might the manufacturer's defect information be untrustworthy? There are several possible reasons.

Chapter 13: Preventing the Slow Death of Your Hard Disk

If the drive's final electronics board has identical circuits for positioning the heads and for turning the spindle to those on the test electronics board, the defects will probably appear to be where the manufacturer said they were. If the spindle motor turns just a tad slower with the final board than with the test board, all the defects will appear to be a bit farther along each track than the manufacturer said.

Even that circumstance assumes that the clock rate at which the data encoder turns data bits into magnetic field transitions is exactly the same as that assumed by the tester. Not only do individual clocks tend to vary, but some controllers will intentionally alter their clock rates in certain circumstances. They speed up their clocks, for example, when they are asked (by the system assembler — who could be you) to produce a spare sector at the end of each track. This variance is another reason not to count on those bytes-from-index numbers.

To make matters worse, if the head positioner functions differently when you use the drive from how it was working when the manufacturer tested it, the tracks on the drive will not lie exactly where the tester assumed they would. In this case, even the bad-track information will be wrong.

Before it was possible to do a thorough digital test, computer users had to rely on the manufacturer's analog test results. With SpinRite, you no longer need to rely on these dubious results, which many system assemblers were ignoring anyway.

Digital Surface Testing

What makes a digital test good? Exactly how does it work? Are digital tests as sensitive as analog ones? These questions are among those answered in the rest of this chapter.

SpinRite performs meticulous digital testing. SpinRite checks the disk's capability to store virtually every conceivable data pattern and then reports which sectors contain the defects it finds. It expedites these tasks without requiring much sophistication on the part of its user.

Worst-case paradigm

Considering that there are an astronomical number of possible magnetic-field-transition patterns that could be recorded on your hard disk, programs such as SpinRite test only the "worst-case" scenarios. The program designers deduce which test patterns will give your disk subsystem the toughest workout and then use them.

What makes a case "worst"

Look at the pattern of magnetic field transitions in Figure 13-2(a). The data are encoded by where the transitions occur and where they do not. When the disk turns, the pattern moves under the read head. Voltage pulses are generated each time a field transition goes under the head. Figure 13-2(b) shows an idealized view of these pulses.

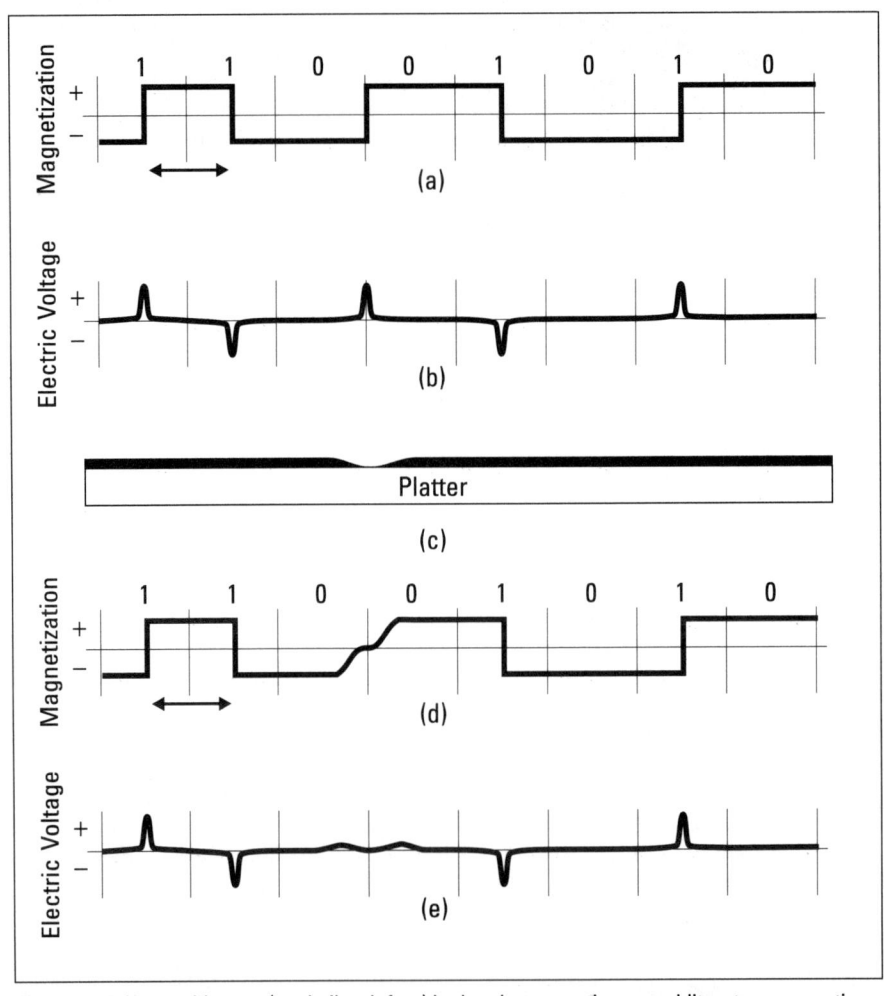

Figure 13-2: How a thin spot (or similar defect) in the platter coating can obliterate a magnetic field transition, thus causing a data error.
(a) Normal MFM field pattern to record the data byte 11001010.
(b) Resulting voltage pulses as pattern passes under read head.
(c) A thin spot in platter coating.
(d) If this defect is where a field transition should go, it will make the sharp field change into a blurry one.
(e) The resulting voltage pulse is smeared and reduced in size so far that it cannot be read.

Chapter 13: Preventing the Slow Death of Your Hard Disk

If a microscopic weakness in the disk coating exists at any of a number of special places on the disk, one of which is shown in Figure 13-2(c), you will notice this defect because a signal you otherwise would see will be missing. Figures 13-2(d) and 13-2(e) show the resulting magnetization and voltage pulses from the read head. On the other hand, if the weakness occurs in a place where there normally wouldn't be a pulse anyway, you may not detect the flaw. Where the significant places are depends on exactly what data pattern has been recorded on the disk.

/ **TECHNICAL SECRET** /

A defect in the surface won't necessarily alter the signals from every possible pattern that could be recorded there, yet it may well alter some of them. The only patterns that get altered are those that involve recording a transition where the defect happens to be.

This fact points up the impossibility of a really thorough digital test that is read-only. Many programs, including the Norton Utilities and PC Tools, have a function to test or verify a disk that just reads whatever patterns happen to be on the disk already. This means that they cannot find weak spots if there happen to be no field transitions at these places.

If the defect lies just to one side of one of these special spots, the write head might be able to record any data pattern in which there is a transition on either side of the spot but not a pattern in which there are transitions on both sides of the spot. Depending on how the write and read electronics function, other data patterns may also be particularly hard to record and read back reliably.

Disk surface tests

You can do an effective test of the disk surface for these microscopic defects only if you can be sure that the patterns you put down and attempt to read back will reveal the presence of those defects. Patterns that meet this requirement are called *worst-case* patterns. Later in this chapter, the specific patterns used by SpinRite are described, along with how it uses those patterns to reveal even the most subtle defects.

An important first step

Before testing the disk-surface integrity, it is clearly very important to ascertain that every other aspect of the drive is functioning properly. This assurance includes testing some parts of the PC outside the disk subsystem to verify that any defects you find on the surface are real and not just phantom defects stemming from some general system problem. You may have a flaky head positioner or read or write circuitry, for example, or even an intermittent problem with some of your computer's main memory. Before it embarks on its surface analysis, SpinRite extensively tests all parts of the PC that it will be using.

How the Encoding Technology Affects the Choice of Worst-Case Patterns

The first key to good digital surface analysis is to put down the magnetic-field transitions in every possible place on the disk. Next, a program should put down combinations of adjacent transitions that stress the write and read circuitry to the fullest.

Look back at Figure 2-7. This figure shows four different ways to encode the same byte of data. Notice that the places where the magnetic field changes from plus to minus or from minus to plus form a very different pattern in each of these four cases.

To test the platter surface thoroughly, you need to choose different data for each kind of data-encoding scheme. These different encoding schemes place different demands on the data-decoding circuitry. If the drive uses MFM data-encoding, the pulses come with only two possible spacings. When the drive uses 2,7 RLL, six possible pulse spacings exist. We therefore need two different groups of test patterns: one for MFM and one for RLL.

TECHNICAL SECRET

What about SCSI, ESDI, and IDE? Rather than types of data recording, these acronyms refer to specifications for the interface between the drive and the computer. Most SCSI, ESDI, and IDE drives use 2,7 RLL as their data-encoding technique. A few use MFM, and some others use a variation of RLL called, variously, ARLL or ERLL (which stand for advanced or enhanced RLL). Chapter 2 briefly describes these alternative forms of data encoding. For all such drives, either SpinRite's MFM or its RLL test patterns work just fine.

SpinRite's Digital Tests

For this book, Steve Gibson has flung open the door to reveal his hitherto hidden algorithms, to detail for us exactly how SpinRite tests your hard disk. In this and in the remaining chapters of this book, you'll learn more abut how SpinRite works than you can currently learn about any other commercial program's testing procedure. That Gibson has agreed to share his methodology is a measure of his faith in how well chosen it is. It also allows you to examine his procedures and assure yourself that indeed he does know what he is doing.

Things get pretty technical from this point. If I lose you on some detail, just skip over it. You can get a good sense of what SpinRite does, even if you don't grasp all the nuances of its methods.

If you find yourself puzzled by some of the jargon or basic concepts, you may have to return to Part I of this book.

The test patterns

To test the disk, SpinRite uses five basic patterns of data — a different five patterns depending on which data-encoding style that disk uses (MFM or 2,7 RLL). Before it begins pattern testing, SpinRite figures out which kind of data encoding your drive uses.

Figures 13-3 and 13-4 show all 10 patterns. The first line for each test pattern is the byte string SpinRite sends to DOS. The program repeats this pattern as many times as necessary to fill one whole track. The next line shows this pattern expressed as the sequence of bits (ones and zeros) that is sent to the disk.

TECHNICAL SECRET

For the very simplest patterns, it is easy to see how the bit sequence follows from the byte string. Each pair of hexadecimal symbols represents one byte (8 bits) of data. If the test pattern repeats every byte, you need merely write those bytes in bit form to get the bit sequence.

After you reach the fourth test pattern, things become more interesting. To get from that byte string to its bit sequence, you must know that DOS stores a string of bytes on the disk in pairs, called *words* (16-bits). It puts the *least significant byte* of each word first (called "Intel order"). Thus, DBB6h will be stored with the B6h byte before the DBh byte.

The pattern of magnetic field transitions, rather than the byte string or its corresponding bit sequence, is what matters. Below each bit sequence is a graph of the magnetic field transitions that are stored on the disk.

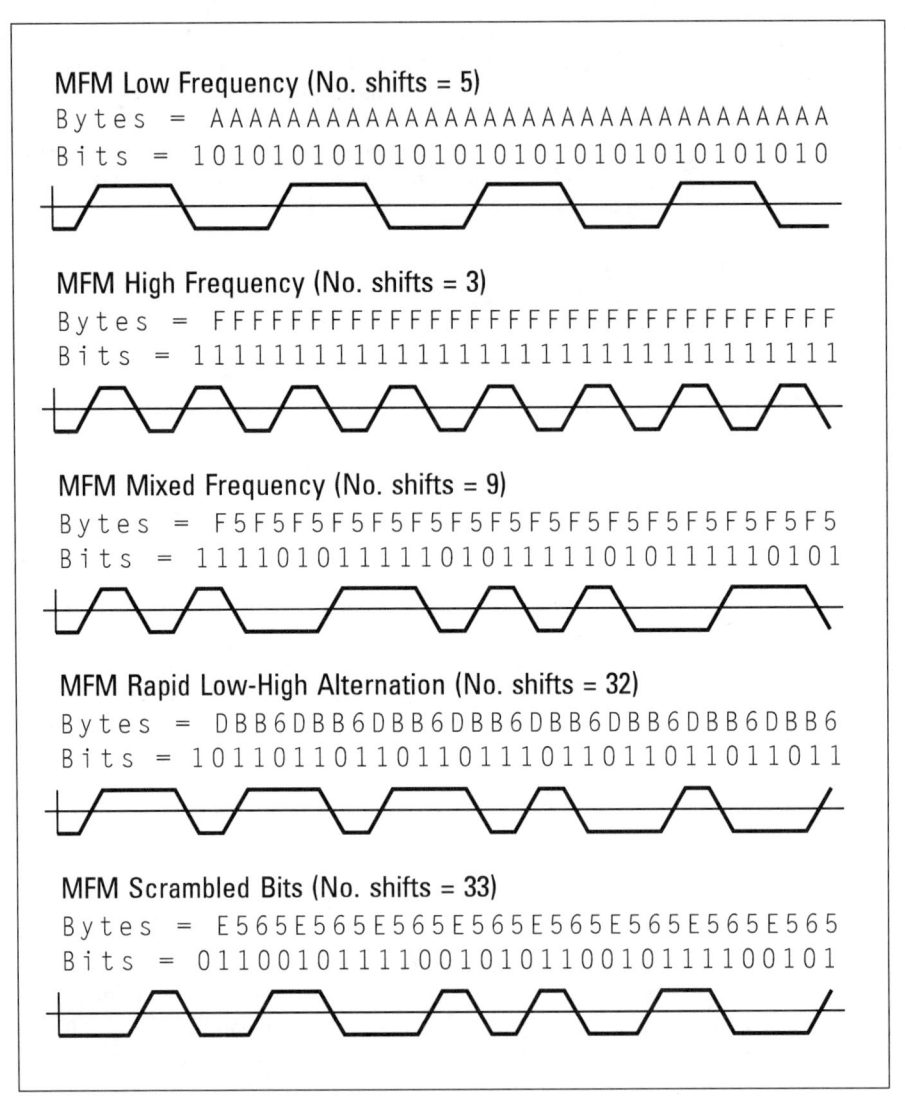

MFM Low Frequency (No. shifts = 5)
Bytes = AAAAAAAAAAAAAAAAAAAAAAAAAAAAAA
Bits = 101010101010101010101010101010

MFM High Frequency (No. shifts = 3)
Bytes = FFFFFFFFFFFFFFFFFFFFFFFFFFFFFF
Bits = 111111111111111111111111111111

MFM Mixed Frequency (No. shifts = 9)
Bytes = F5F5F5F5F5F5F5F5F5F5F5F5F5F5F5
Bits = 111101011110101111010111110101

MFM Rapid Low-High Alternation (No. shifts = 32)
Bytes = DBB6DBB6DBB6DBB6DBB6DBB6DBB6DBB6
Bits = 10110110110110110110110110110011

MFM Scrambled Bits (No. shifts = 33)
Bytes = E565E565E565E565E565E565E565E565
Bits = 01100101110010101100101111001 01

Figure 13-3: The SpinRite data test patterns for MFM drives. Each test pattern is shown in full in the line labeled Bytes =. There are many more bits and field transitions than can fit on the third and fourth lines for each test pattern, but these samples give a good feel for what those patterns are like.

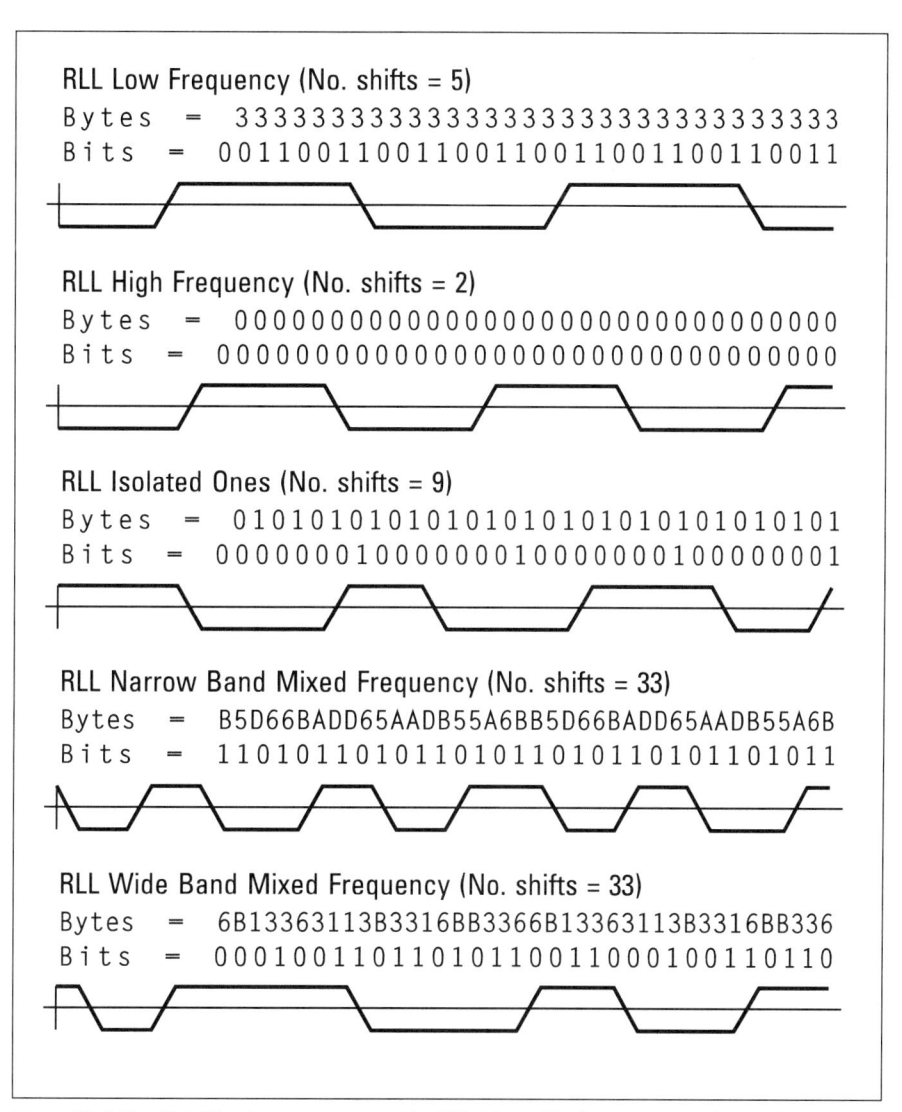

Chapter 13: Preventing the Slow Death of Your Hard Disk

```
RLL Low Frequency (No. shifts = 5)
Bytes  =    3333333333333333333333333333333333
Bits   =    0011001100110011001100110011001100110011
```

```
RLL High Frequency (No. shifts = 2)
Bytes  =    0000000000000000000000000000000000
Bits   =    0000000000000000000000000000000000000000
```

```
RLL Isolated Ones (No. shifts = 9)
Bytes  =    010101010101010101010101010101010101
Bits   =    000000010000000100000001000000010000001
```

```
RLL Narrow Band Mixed Frequency (No. shifts = 33)
Bytes  =    B5D66BADD65AADB55A6BB5D66BADD65AADB55A6B
Bits   =    11010110101101011010110101101011
```

```
RLL Wide Band Mixed Frequency (No. shifts = 33)
Bytes  =    6B13363113B3316BB3366B13363113B3316BB336
Bits   =    0001001101101011001100010011 0110
```

Figure 13-4: The SpinRite data test patterns for RLL drives. The last two cases have a byte pattern that does not repeat for a full 10 bytes (80 bits). All the others repeat much more often. Again, this figure shows only a tiny, but typical, sample of the full pattern of field transitions.

TECHNICAL SECRET

You can verify the patterns of magnetic field transitions shown in Figures 13-3 and 13-4 by applying the rules for MFM and RLL encoding given in Chapter 2 in the section "Data-Encoding Strategies." In particular, see Figures 2-7 and 2-8. You will find that in a few cases, the pattern you come up with may differ from that in Figure 13-4 for the first few bits. This difference occurs because the encoding depends partly on the bit or bits that came just before the ones you are encoding. The patterns shown in the figure are what you would find in the middle of the track as the test pattern repeats itself over and over.

Finally, notice that for each test pattern, Figures 13-3 and 13-4 show a number of shifted repetitions to be used (`No. of shifts` in the figure). This idea is explained in the section "How the patterns are used" later in this chapter.

Why these patterns were chosen

Applying test data patterns to the hard disk surface and reading them back can reveal much more than defective spots on the disk surface. If the program designer chose the patterns appropriately, these tests also will reveal any problems the disk or controller may have, such as problems with the head-positioning mechanism, the circuitry used to keep the disk turning at a constant speed, the clock-data separator, or the write precompensation circuits. (These parts are described in the section "Bit Size" in Chapter 2, and in Chapter 4.)

After consulting with hard disk drive and controller design engineers and other experts, Steve Gibson chose these patterns and then tested them extensively to be sure that they really were doing the job.

Low-frequency test

The first test for either MFM or RLL drives is a data pattern that produces magnetic field transitions spaced as widely apart as possible. This procedure measures the disk drive's constancy of rotation and the capability of the read circuitry to find data bits in the presence of whatever speed drift or flutter may occur.

High-frequency test

Next, SpinRite uses a data pattern that produces magnetic field transitions spaced as closely together as possible — a good way to test the entire system's capability to work at top speed. This pattern also tests the effectiveness of the write-precompensation circuits.

Chapter 13: Preventing the Slow Death of Your Hard Disk

MFM mixed-frequency test

For MFM drives, the third test mixes regions of maximum and minimum frequency to measure the capability of certain circuits to follow changes. (These circuits track the rate at which the voltage pulses emerge from the head.) Because some of those circuits help keep the disk turning at a constant speed, the test also evaluates that aspect of the drive.

Rapid low-high alternation test

The fourth MFM test resembles the mixed-frequency test, differing only in the length of each region of high or low frequency. It tests the same aspects of the drive but in slightly different ways.

Scrambled-bits test

Steve Gibson named the final MFM test scrambled bits. The test consists of a pseudo-random pattern of transitions, which means that the pattern is the same every time you run it, but it contains lots of variety. (A truly random pattern would be different each time, but not in a dependable way, which means it would vary in its capability to detect problems.)

Isolated-ones test

Silence is hard to hear. Likewise, recording a pattern of almost all zeros is often challenging for a hard drive, particularly for an RLL drive. (See the discussion of data encoding in Chapter 2 for more on this point.) After conducting a low-frequency and a high-frequency test, SpinRite imposes this important test on RLL drives.

RLL narrow-band and wide-band mixed frequency tests

The last two RLL test patterns are long; they do not repeat for 80 bits. Through these chaotic signals, SpinRite measures the capability of the read/write amplifiers to follow rapid fluctuations.

How the patterns are used

All the test patterns repeat after some length. The MFM and RLL high-frequency bit sequences are all ones and all zeros, respectively, which means that these patterns repeat every bit. The MFM low-frequency bit sequence alternates ones with zeros, which means that it repeats every 2 bits. The RLL low-frequency bit sequence repeats every 4 bits. The rest of the patterns repeat every 8 bits, except the last two RLL tests, which only repeat every 80 bits.

For each pattern, SpinRite first fills the entire track with repetitions of that pattern. It then reads back the pattern. It has found a defect if even a single bit differs from what was written. SpinRite will accept only data that were read correctly without the aid of ECC.

Applying all five tests gives a good workout to the read and write circuitry and catches *some* surface defects. To catch *all* the defects, SpinRite must reapply the patterns in all possible locations. If you choose the deepest level of pattern testing in SpinRite (Depth 4), the program will apply each pattern more than once, shifting the pattern by one bit position between each application. The number of shifts used varies with the pattern (see Figures 13-3 and 13-4).

TECHNICAL SECRET

The number of shifts used for each pattern depends on a couple of things. The patterns that repeat every few bytes are shifted at least enough bits so that they return to where they started. The two patterns that do not repeat for 80 bits are shifted only 32 times. Because these patterns were chosen mostly to test the read/write circuitry, more shifts don't help.

Pattern testing at Depth 3 works similarly but uses about half as many shifted versions of each pattern. Though this level of testing is not thorough enough to catch all defects, it takes only half as long to run as Depth 4. When you allow SpinRite to test at its maximum depth (using all the patterns a maximum number of times), it will catch all data-affecting defects and will detect any dysfunction that could affect your data in any other aspect of the disk drive and controller's operation. Although SpinRite cannot guarantee that your disk is truly perfect, the disk should act as if it is. For most of us, that condition is good enough.

Which Way Is Best?

Advocates of relying on the manufacturer's analog surface testing often point out that analog testing is inherently more sensitive than digital testing. After all, the digital circuitry on the drive, which SpinRite or any program running in your PC has to use in its digital testing, is built to discard noise. The analog test circuits sense noise-like variations in signal strength as their means of seeing anomalous spots on the disk surface. Although this is true, it is irrelevant. PC users don't care what the precise "signal-to-noise" ratio is for the head signals. They want to know that they can rely on their disk drives to work without any loss of data.

Advocates of the digital testing done by other manufacturers point out that laser interferometers and multichannel recorders are expensive testing devices

Chapter 13: Preventing the Slow Death of Your Hard Disk

not available to every PC user. Again, this is not necessarily relevant if you do have available a means of adequately testing your hard disk. Adequacy here means that you are able to detect any flaw that would prevent it from doing what you normally ask it to do, namely, store your data reliably.

You may be overreacting if you mark spots on your disk as bad simply because the manufacturer said they were. Just because you can measure something doesn't mean it's important. You wouldn't declare yourself sick just because your temperature is a tenth of a degree off normal. Analog test data has its own limitations, as we discussed in the section "Why this is less helpful than it appears," earlier in this chapter. Even the digital tests may not be relevant if the manufacturer did not assume the same number of sectors per track and data-encoding strategy that you will be using. By testing the drive after it has been low- and high-level formatted and by using actual digital data patterns, SpinRite can report and pinpoint the location of any defect that affects data-storage integrity. Reporting errors in their data context is one of SpinRite's greatest strengths.

Another of SpinRite's great strengths is its capability to discover and return to service once-defective sectors that are no longer flawed. This feature is one way SpinRite is unique among programs that perform nondestructive low-level reformatting. (Chapter 11 explains how it is possible for a bad spot to become good, as well as one way in which good spots can become bad, in the section "Slow death by growing misalignment.")

TECHNICAL SECRET

Some people shy away from storing data in a once-defective area. Although Steve Gibson believes that this is not a proper concern, SpinRite will allow you to disable that feature if you choose to do so.

Summary

- Hard disks are complex mechanical and electronic devices. Sometimes they fail catastrophically; more often, they die gradually and not necessarily permanently.
- Surface analysis is the key to finding those places on your disk's platter surface that are not able to store data reliably. Manufacturers perform one kind of surface analysis on each disk drive at the factory. You can do another, possibly even more relevant, test in your own PC by using SpinRite.
- SpinRite uses a suite of test patterns that exercise your hard disk subsystem to the maximum possible extent and, in the process, is able to flush out almost any conceivable disk defect that could affect the reliability with which that disk drive will store your data.

You have a pretty good idea now of what SpinRite does. In the next chapter, you learn the details of how it does those things.

Chapter 14
Details of SpinRite's Operation

In This Chapter
▶ All the details of how SpinRite does its work, including how it checks your PC to be sure that it is up to the arduous work SpinRite must do

▶ More about this program's algorithms than has been revealed publicly about any other commercially successful PC utility program

Getting Ready to Work

To avoid making any mistakes, SpinRite runs a comprehensive check before it does anything to the data on your hard disk. This section describes the checking process SpinRite goes through.

SpinRite checks its own health

SpinRite first checks to see that it has not been tampered with or damaged in any way — a surprisingly uncommon precaution among PC programs. The program comes on the disk in a compressed form and contains its own decompressing program. SpinRite runs a checksum test on the original, compressed program. If it does not come up with the right value, it will refuse to operate. After SpinRite decompresses itself into your PC's main system memory, it again executes a checksum test, which also must provide the correct value or else the program will refuse to run.

These tests will catch a number of problems. The first test assures you that the program on your disk is not damaged. Passing the second checksum test assures you, and SpinRite, that your PC's system RAM (its main memory) is working correctly, at least in that part of RAM where the program resides. Finally, it ensures that no computer virus has attached itself to SpinRite; it would be close to impossible for a virus to attach itself in a way that would not produce an error in one or the other of the checksum tests.

Part II: The SpinRite Companion

Choosing what to do and where

After SpinRite is sure it is in good shape, it displays its main menu. From here, you can choose which test to do and set various options for how SpinRite will function. After completing a test, SpinRite returns to the main menu so that you can generate a report, either on your printer or in a disk file.

If you interrupt a SpinRite operation or if you had interrupted one the last time you ran SpinRite, your first option is to resume that interrupted operation (even if you turned off the computer). The details of how SpinRite does this are discussed in the last section of this chapter.

The first main menu option, Quick Surface Scan, is a good place to start. It checks out the disk subsystem and shows you the readability of your data. As its name implies, it doesn't take a long time. Most of the time you will use the second option, Begin SpinRite Analysis, to test your disk thoroughly.

After choosing a test, you next must indicate which disk, or actually which DOS logical volume, SpinRite should examine. (If you are unsure about the difference between a disk and a DOS logical volume, refer to Chapter 9.) SpinRite then assures itself that the rest of your PC is functioning properly before proceeding with a surface scan or a deeper disk analysis.

Making sure that the system memory is good enough

SpinRite uses more of your PC's system memory than just the area in which its program code resides. Unlike some programs, it has no regions of zeros within its code that are later used for buffers. (This characteristic helps keep it safe from viral infection.) Consequently, SpinRite must allocate several regions in the PC's system memory as temporary storage places for data. It then tests those regions very carefully to be sure of their integrity.

SpinRite's scratch pads

SpinRite's buffers, or scratch-pad areas, serve several purposes. One of two track buffers serves to hold the data read from the track, and the other provides an area for the program to construct test data patterns. SpinRite writes these patterns to the track and then compares what it reads back against them. As it finishes testing sectors, the program assembles full clusters of data in another buffer area, returning the data to the disk when the buffer is full. The buffer's size depends on how large the clusters are on your hard disk.

SpinRite also keeps a status byte for each sector in the current track, plus one for any sectors that may have been left in the cluster buffer when it finished the preceding track. These status bytes tell SpinRite where it should put the sectors (back where they came from or elsewhere) and which messages to put in the Detailed Technical Log file.

Chapter 14: Details of SpinRite's Operation

A two-sector (1,024 byte) area serves double duty. When SpinRite needs to work with information from the file allocation table, it reads two consecutive sectors from the first FAT into this buffer. (See Chapter 10 for an explanation of FATs.)

> **TECHNICAL SECRET**
>
> The reason for keeping two sectors in SpinRite's buffer is that if the FAT has 12-bit entries, one of those entries could overlap a sector boundary. Smaller hard disk logical volumes or those formatted by earlier versions of DOS typically have FATs with 12-bit entries. Having both of the sectors in the buffer makes it easier to work with that information.

At other points in its operation, SpinRite uses this 1,024-byte buffer as a place to receive raw data from the disk. When the controller reports difficulty reading a sector, SpinRite can request that it pass on all the information it was able to read, including both the data and the ECC bytes.

> **TECHNICAL SECRET**
>
> To store data plus ECC requires a buffer at least a little bit larger than is needed to hold just the standard 512 bytes of data. An entire extra sector is far more than is needed; that is okay. Different controllers use different numbers of ECC bytes, but none uses anywhere near 512 of them.

In addition, the program maintains an interleave buffer and a system stack. Before each track is reformatted, SpinRite prepares a table of sector status and sector numbers in the interleave buffer (see Figure 13-1). It uses the system stack to keep track of various pointers and other numbers it needs to do its work.

Checking the scratch pads

After it has allocated these different memory areas, SpinRite checks them. The power-on self test (POST) routine in the BIOS of most (but not all) computers has already tested this system memory, a process that occurs when you see those memory numbers counting up on your screen as your PC is first booting. Though the POST catches most memory errors, Gibson had SpinRite take the test much further, so you can be sure that at least one portion of your system RAM is in the absolute pink of health.

Testing the hard disk controller

As the gateway between your hard disk and your PC's main memory, the hard disk controller is an essential element in your system. Before messing with the data on your hard disk, SpinRite tries to assure itself that the controller is working perfectly. Because controllers vary so much, the most SpinRite feasibly can do is to command the controller to run its own built-in diagnostic routines.

Part II: The SpinRite Companion

Then SpinRite asks the controller to check the health of the scratch-pad RAM that it has on itself. Only if the controller reports no errors in either of these tests will SpinRite proceed to work with your hard disk.

Catching active caching

Disk caching can greatly increase the speed with which you get data on and off your hard disk, but it also can prevent a program from knowing just how long it takes the disk to do anything. To run its precise timing tests, SpinRite must be sure that no caching software or hardware will get in the way. (For more details on a variety of caching programs and hardware and how they work, see Chapter 5.)

/ TECHNICAL SECRET /

The caching test is simple. SpinRite first reads sector A on the disk. Then it reads sector B, located far away from A. Finally, it goes back and reads sector A again. Any caching program worth its salt will have kept a copy of A, so the time delay between reading B and rereading A will appear to be almost zero. This is a sure sign of disk caching.

Earlier versions of SpinRite were totally blocked by any active caching scheme. Version 1.1 of SpinRite II can turn off hardware caching for some controllers. Version 2 is able to get behind almost any caching scheme so that it can do all its work. (The next chapter has more details on this subject.)

SpinRite will notify you if it detects that you are using disk caching, and (depending on the version of SpinRite) it may refuse to do any low-level reformatting of your disk. Fortunately, it can still deliver its other major benefits: data-integrity testing and data recovery. If you can, you should always turn off disk caching before running SpinRite. If you installed some disk speed-up program through a line in your CONFIG.SYS or AUTOEXEC.BAT file, boot from a "clean" DOS floppy and then run SpinRite. (See the section "The SpinRite Clean Boot Diskette Approach" in Chapter 16 for more details.)

Watching for device driver weirdness

DOS at its highest levels thinks of your hard disk as simply a long string of sectors in which to store data. The BIOS level, which must use a more physically accurate picture, specifies the location of data three-dimensionally, using three separate numbers for the cylinder, head, and physical sector.

Chapter 14: Details of SpinRite's Operation

A built-in part of DOS that translates from logical addresses to physical ones and back is called the *block device driver*. You may install a replacement block device driver. If you use Disk Manager from OnTrack, or SpeedStor from Storage Dimensions, for example, you are replacing the DOS-resident block device with their special device. (See the section "Physical Size Limits Imposed by the BIOS" in Chapter 7 for more details on installable block devices and why you might be using them.)

To assure itself that your controller's block device operates in a standard mode, SpinRite first asks the BIOS what the drive's dimensions are. Then it sends several *read logical sector* requests to the device driver and watches the *read physical sector* commands into which they are translated. If the translations agree with what SpinRite thinks they should be, it knows the device driver is doing its job in the standard manner.

TECHNICAL SECRET

The drive dimensions, according to the BIOS, are easy to get. Just ask the BIOS, using INT 13h, Function 8. What you get back may not be the real, physical dimensions of the drive, but they are what the BIOS believes and what the device driver must assume. Later, SpinRite will check to see whether these dimensions are the same as the real, physical ones.

SpinRite hooks INT 13h so that it can see all commands that are sent to the BIOS that way. Then it uses INT 25h to request sector reads. It asks for many different sectors, each 100 logical sectors apart. From watching what the device driver asks for from the BIOS (through INT 13H), SpinRite easily can tell whether the driver is using a strange translation algorithm.

If your system's device driver produces a "funny" translation, SpinRite cannot do low-level reformatting, though it still can and will do data testing and data recovery. (Actually, Gibson says he has never seen a device driver of this sort. He included this test for completeness. He says that if he finds the test is never needed, he may remove it from later versions of the program.)

When passed, these tests satisfy SpinRite that it can safely proceed with a surface scan. If you had selected the deeper disk analysis, SpinRite would have carried out some additional tests.

The Quick Surface Scan

The quick surface scan is a read-only test; SpinRite doesn't write or move any information on your disk. This test verifies the readability of your disk or confirms that the unreadable portions are safely locked out and marked as bad clusters in the FAT so that DOS won't use them.

Part II: The SpinRite Companion

This test is a good one to start with the first time you use SpinRite on a particular disk or PC. If this test goes smoothly, you can be fairly certain that SpinRite will work just fine with that PC and hard disk.

In doing a quick surface scan, SpinRite reads every track in the DOS logical volume. If it cannot get an entire track's data correctly in one step, it reads each sector individually, comparing its findings with what the FAT says about the disk's condition. The program reports on-screen and in the Detailed Technical Log file the details about every bad sector in the logical volume.

TECHNICAL SECRET

The difference between full-track reads and single-sector reads is dramatic. When SpinRite switches from doing full-track reads to doing single-sector reads, you will notice three things if you look and listen carefully. First, you will notice that SpinRite dwells on the bad locations much longer than it does on good ones. Second, you may notice that the head is constantly being repositioned as SpinRite attempts to read a difficult sector. This routine partially explains why it can successfully read data when other programs give up. Finally, you may notice a funny *chunk-chunk* sound every few tracks. That is when SpinRite goes back to the start of the logical volume to read another couple of sectors from the FAT.

You can examine the quick surface scan results on the Track Map, a screen display that graphically represents the entire DOS logical volume, showing a symbol for every few tracks. Initially, the symbols are blank, with a question mark showing where SpinRite is currently working. A period (.) on the Track Map represents one or more tracks that were tested and deemed perfect, as far as this test could tell. Deeper pattern testing may reveal problems, but for now you may consider that a safe place for your data.

The letter B indicates a sector that is part of a cluster already marked as bad in the FAT. No data is stored there now and — without a lot more testing first — it wouldn't be safe to store any there in the future.

Any other letter marks a place that the controller reported some difficulty reading the data. The letter C means a sector that the controller could not read but for which the ECC sufficed to deduce the sector's contents. The letter U indicates that SpinRite couldn't read the sector, even with the help of the ECC. This indicator means that some data was lost. An uppercase letter signals that one of your files was using the sector in question. A lowercase letter indicates that none of your data lies in the sector yet.

After completing the quick surface scan, SpinRite allows you to return to the main menu, where you can create a report in a file or on your printer.

Further Testing Before Doing Anything Serious

If you choose Begin SpinRite Analysis, SpinRite will conduct more tests, in addition to performing the system diagnostics already described. These tests are described in this section.

Seek and maybe you'll find a problem

SpinRite first checks to be sure that the head-positioning assembly is working correctly, by measuring four numbers to determine the seek performance of your drive.

Seeking means moving the heads to the correct cylinder. Before the drive can accomplish this task, the BIOS has to compose and deliver the appropriate command, which takes a little bit of time. It is not much time, but if you are going to be as fussy as Steve Gibson, you will want to measure this *BIOS overhead*.

SpinRite measures the BIOS overhead by asking the controller to tell the drive to seek the same cylinder many times. Because it has nothing to do, the controller will immediately return from each such command with a message saying that it is finished. The time taken to do these commands, therefore, must be the time it took the BIOS to compose and deliver them.

Next, SpinRite checks to see how quickly the drive can move the heads from one track to the adjacent one. This test is followed by testing the time it takes to move the heads from the outermost cylinder to the innermost one (a *full-stroke seek*). Finally, it checks the average time to do many seeks to "randomly" chosen cylinders.

In these last two tests, SpinRite uses the full range of cylinders for that physical hard drive. Some other programs only test seek times within the DOS logical volume. If you want to compare the results with those published by manufacturers of hard drives, you must test the full range of head motion, because when manufacturers conduct their tests, the drives don't have partitions or logical volumes.

After each time SpinRite commands the drive to seek to some cylinder, it checks to see whether that is where the heads actually went. If the drive seeks more than a thousand times without error, SpinRite is assured that it can position the heads where it needs to, every time.

When you may not want to do this test

If your drive passes this seek test many times without incident, you may want to turn off this aspect of SpinRite's testing. Chapter 16 explains how you can turn it off, in the section "When to perform the seek test."

Scoping Out the Drive — It's All a Matter of Timing

Chapter 13 pointed out that SpinRite or any similar program chooses a set of test data patterns based on the drive's data-encoding scheme. SpinRite deduces whether your drive is MFM or RLL by performing exquisitely accurate timing tests, which also reveal your drive's sector-interleave value, data-transfer rate, and several other important numbers.

To produce these measurements, SpinRite looks at the time between reading one sector and another. Because the program depends on these numbers to base its decision on how to handle the drive, they must be precise.

How and what SpinRite times is an interesting story.

Checking revolutions per minute: First, SpinRite measures the average time the controller takes to go from reading sector #1 on a certain track to reading that same sector again. This measurement gives it the disk's revolutions per minute (RPM).

Getting the intersector times right: Next, SpinRite measures the interval between reading sector #1 and reading each other sector on the track. This requires using a more complicated process than you might think.

TECHNICAL SECRET

Many things can corrupt or bias the times that are measured. Occasionally, for example, there may be misreads of a sector. The controller automatically will try to read that sector again. If it succeeds, it will give back the data without comment, but it will have taken longer than normal by at least one full revolution time for the disk.

Interruptions by the PC's *timer tick* also can produce timing errors. Approximately 18 times each second, DOS triggers INT 8. Any process that needs to be sure to do its job in a timely manner may hook that interrupt. Then it will get a chance to have the PC do its work 18 times each second. DOS uses these opportunities to update its time-of-day counter.

Chapter 14: Details of SpinRite's Operation

Depending on what other programs you have hooking that interrupt and what they do when they get control of the PC, the intersector times reported to SpinRite may be anywhere from a little bit to wildly wrong. This is yet another reason you should use SpinRite only in a "clean" system.

Because any single timing measurement is suspect, SpinRite uses many of them for each number it wants to find. It does not simply average those many measurements, however; it is far more clever than that. SpinRite measures time in multiples of some arbitrary, small time. That internal unit of time, which Gibson calls one *click,* is about 1.5 microseconds. It takes a typical hard drive about 11,000 clicks to turn one full revolution.

That full revolution time is measured by asking repeatedly for sector #1 of the same track. The average of all plausible values it reads becomes a second important unit of time for SpinRite. (A sector misread would at least double the value. Clearly that time should not be averaged in with the others.)

Next comes the interval between reading one sector to reading any other sector on that same track. Here is where SpinRite becomes very fancy, in order to be sure to reject all the instances of a timing measurement that are somehow messed up.

The BIOS told SpinRite how many sectors there were on a track. This may not be the real number. SpinRite assumes it is correct at first, but then it tests to find out what the truth really is:

- For every sector number from #1 to whatever the BIOS said was the maximum number of sectors per track, SpinRite measures an *intersector time.* That is, it reads sector #1 and then sector #N, and it notes the time between those two operations.

- For each sector pair (1 and N), SpinRite begins by getting 16 measurements of the intersector time. Many of these are pretty good values, but some may be wildly wrong. SpinRite picks the four measurements in the middle of the pack. (That is, it ignores six smaller times and six larger times.) It averages those four times and then sets up a *measurement window* around that average time.

- For any drive, the maximum time between sectors will be about the same as the full revolution time. For drives turning at 3,600 revolutions per minute, that time is about 16 milliseconds. In SpinRite's units, this time is about 11,000 clicks. The minimum intersector time will occur between adjacent sectors on a drive with the largest number of sectors. If the drive has no more than 55 sectors, that time will be at least 300 microseconds, which is about 200 clicks.

Part II: The SpinRite Companion

- SpinRite assumes that all valid measurements of an intersector time must lie within 200 clicks of the average it computed from that first set of measurements. This computation is the measurement window it uses to validate the intersector times for that particular sector number. Now it measures that intersector time repeatedly until it gets 16 measurements that are valid by that criterion. The average of these 16 measurements is a really good estimate of the true intersector time.

This whole process is repeated for every value of sector number (symbolized by N in the preceding paragraphs), from 2 to the maximum sector number according to the BIOS. Armed with these very accurate intersector timings, SpinRite is ready to identify a couple of important facts about the drive.

After it has completed these intersector-timing measurements, SpinRite uses them to deduce the data-encoding technique. It also uses them to get the actual, physical drive dimensions, the sector-interleave value, and the data-transfer rate for this drive.

SpinRite sets up a table of all possible differences between these numbers. It looks for the time difference that corresponds to adjacent sectors. If all the sectors really were on one track, that would be the smallest time difference in the table. Because the controller may be doing sector translation, SpinRite cannot depend on such a simple strategy.

Whatever the true adjacent sector time is, it will show up many times in the table. Also, multiples of two, three, and four times that number will show up. SpinRite looks for a number that satisfies both these tests.

Breaking the code

After SpinRite knows how long it takes for the disk to turn from one sector to the adjacent one, it can get the true number of sectors per track by dividing that adjacent-sector time into the time for a full revolution.

Notice that if the controller created a spare sector at the end of the track or if the end-of-track gap is unusually large, the computed number may come out a bit higher than the BIOS-reported number, though not by much. If the two numbers agree to within plus or minus two, SpinRite will accept the controller as nontranslating. Then it can do low-level reformatting.

If the true number of sectors per track is 17, you have an MFM controller and drive. Twenty-six sectors per track means that you have an RLL controller and drive. At 54 sectors per track, SpinRite calls it an ERLL controller and drive.

SpinRite assumes that the encoding is MFM if the number of sectors is less than 22. For 22 through 30 sectors, it reports RLL. Any more than that and it reports ERLL (and uses the RLL test patterns).

Checking your interleave

Similarly, it is possible to compute the current sector interleave value. Just divide the time to go from sector #1 to sector #2 by the adjacent-sector time.

SpinRite makes all these measurements on a track near the center of the DOS logical volume. This explains something that has puzzled some SpinRite users. Suppose that you had run SpinRite previously and asked it to change your sector interleave. Now suppose that you had interrupted SpinRite in the middle of its work. What interleave would it report when you next started it?

The answer depends on whether you had interrupted SpinRite before or after the halfway point. If you interrupted it early, the central track would still have its sector interleave set to the old value, which is what SpinRite would measure and report. If you interrupted it a bit later, SpinRite would see and report the new value.

Other calculations

Finally, SpinRite measures the time to read a full track's worth of sectors (using the number of sectors on a logical track, as reported by the BIOS). From this result, it calculates the maximum data-transfer rate your disk will support with its present setting of sector interleave. It also reports the number of revolutions required to transfer a full (logical) track of data. If your controller is doing sector translation, this latter number may be misleading.

Suppose that you have an actual sector interleave of 1:1 and an actual sector count of 54. Further suppose that your controller says to the BIOS that it has 63 sectors per track. You can read a physical track in a single revolution, but it will take more than one revolution to read all 63 sectors of a logical track.

SpinRite's Disk Analysis

Having assured itself that your PC's system memory, disk controller, and disk head-positioning mechanisms are working perfectly, SpinRite can proceed to the serious work for which it was designed, knowing what data-encoding technology is in use and whether the controller is doing any sector translating. If its tests say it is safe to proceed, SpinRite will now attempt to read every byte of data in your DOS logical volume, test every sector, and replace the data. It may also, if you want (and if it can do so safely), redo the low-level format for each track, thus curing the maximum possible number of disk errors and setting the sector interleave to whatever value you choose.

What interleave is best?

Well, there is one more test to do. Although SpinRite knows the current sector interleave value, it still must find out what impact changing that number would have. It will then be able to recommend the optimum value and let you choose the value you want. The program skips this test only if you have told it you don't want low-level reformatting, or if your drive or controller will not permit SpinRite to carry out that operation.

SpinRite discovers the impact of different sector interleave values by reformatting, eight times, a track in the diagnostic cylinder, which resides outside any disk partition. (See Chapter 9 for a description of this cylinder.)

TECHNICAL SECRET

For these tests to be meaningful, the track being tested must have no defects. SpinRite first tests the track at head #0 of the diagnostic cylinder. If the track is perfect, and if SpinRite can get stable timings for reading that track, it will use it.

If the first track won't do, SpinRite tries head #1, and so on. It keeps this up until it finds a perfect track to use. If none of the tracks in the diagnostic cylinder are perfect, SpinRite will do the same thing it would do if there were no diagnostic cylinder: refuse to do any low-level reformatting.

After SpinRite has found a suitable track, it reformats it with a 1:1 sector interleave. It reads all the sectors on the track in sector number order several times. From the time required to do this, SpinRite computes a maximum data-transfer rate for this interleave setting. This process is repeated for sector interleave values from 2:1 to 8:1.

SpinRite displays the results of the interleave tests, highlighting the optimum interleave (the one leading to the highest data-transfer rate). Although SpinRite recommends the optimum interleave setting, the user is free to choose another.

Setting the interleave

After the user has chosen the desired interleave, SpinRite reads a track, reformats it with the new sector interleave value, tests it, and then restores the data. If SpinRite finds any bad sectors in the testing step, it repeats the reformatting, marking those sectors as bad in their headers before putting back the data.

The user may select one of four levels of testing. SpinRite can reformat the disk without performing any tests, but you normally should do this only if you are not changing the interleave. Chapter 16 includes a discussion of how to choose the appropriate level of pattern testing (including one special case in which no testing before reinterleaving is appropriate).

When SpinRite can't reformat your drive

In the following situations, SpinRite cannot safely redo the low-level format on your drive:

- If your controller has buffering that cannot be turned off or circumvented
- If the controller "lies" about the drive dimensions (does sector translation)
- If there is no diagnostic cylinder (or all the diagnostic cylinder tracks are flawed)

You also can tell SpinRite that you don't want it to do any low-level reformatting by selecting an option on the Alter SpinRite's Operation submenu.

Data-Integrity Testing and Data Recovery

Even if SpinRite does not redo the low-level format, you still can use the program to recover data that are unreadable by normal means and move that data to safety. It also can discover defects in the disk before any data is rendered unreadable and again move it out of harm's way.

Reading the data

SpinRite is exceptionally good at reading data. When the going gets tough, SpinRite becomes very clever. At the point where most programs give up, SpinRite is just starting its real efforts.

When it's easy: The BIOS accepts commands to read a string of consecutive sectors, and when it can, SpinRite uses this fast and easy technique.

When it's difficult: This easy technique doesn't work, and the controller will inform the BIOS of its difficulty. To whatever program issued the request, the BIOS in turn either presents the data but reports to DOS that the controller had to use ECC to reconstruct what the data probably were (a correctable error); or it reports a noncorrectable error, which means that even with the ECC, the controller could not deduce what should have been read.

TECHNICAL SECRET

There is a small chance, when the ECC are used, that the correction will be wrong. If the error in the data was confined to a few adjacent bits, the ECC will suffice to correct it perfectly. If there are some wrong bits in two or more regions of the sector, the ECC could imply an erroneous fix. This result does not occur as often as the truly correctable errors. That it can ever occur is another reason for SpinRite to pay very close attention to all uses of ECC and, whenever it can, refuse to accept data obtained that way.

Any program that uses DOS to read from the disk will not learn about correctable errors because DOS hides them from the application, reporting only noncorrectable errors. When a noncorrectable error occurs (and when it does, DOS gives back *no* data), most programs either give up or try again exactly as they tried before. Neither approach is likely to produce the data.

When the BIOS reports any error, correctable or not, SpinRite immediately begins to read the track a sector at a time. Although it may get most of the sectors this way with little effort, at least one sector is likely to present a problem.

When DOS or almost any other program reads a sector, it simply sends the heads to the correct cylinder, switches on the correct head, and then waits for the sector it wants to come into view. SpinRite knows better. Because a misalignment of the heads often causes misreads, the capability to align the heads just slightly off the track to one side or the other often helps a lot. Some older, very expensive disk drives and some of the latest servo-controlled ESDI and SCSI drives support commands to do just that. Typical PC hard disks do not.

To get around this limitation, SpinRite takes advantage of a property shared by all mechanical systems, which is that any positioning mechanism will not go to exactly the same place if it approaches that place in a different way each time. The name for this phenomenon is *backlash,* or *hysteresis.* SpinRite uses this technique to achieve slightly off-track head alignments.

Each time before it asks the BIOS to read a recalcitrant sector, SpinRite will request that it move the heads to a cylinder one side or the other from the one it wants and then back again. By varying the off-track direction or distance, SpinRite can induce various off-track alignments when the heads return, after which it again tries to read the sector. This method often works.

When SpinRite first started using this technique, most PC hard disks were not very smart. Now, many of the newer drives for PCs are quite smart. They will do things very much like this on their own, to see whether they can coax data out of a tough-to-read sector, before they first report failure reading that sector. In those drives (mostly IDE/ATA and SCSI models), SpinRite's strategy is unlikely to help, but it never hurts to try.

If the controller still cannot read the sector perfectly, but the use of the ECC will allow the data to be reconstructed, SpinRite will accept that. If the sector has a noncorrectable error, SpinRite can command the controller to forget about trying to correct the data and just turn over what it found, errors and all. Most noncorrectable errors affect only a few bits of data. Out of 4,096 bits, maybe as few as 12 (less than two bytes) are messed up. Most people often would prefer to get back all but two bytes of a file, rather than lose the file entirely. In addition, SpinRite will point out which sector of which file was flawed so that you can more easily repair the damage.

Low-level reformatting

After SpinRite has safely stored your data in one of its track buffers, it is ready to reformat the track. Amazingly, this step often repairs all the defects, restoring a previously flawed track to full health. In its next step, SpinRite tests to see whether this restoration happened.

Dealing with damaged files

An executable file (a program, also sometimes called a *binary file*) must be totally accurate. If it is not accurate, it may not run at all or it may malfunction in some terrible way. You therefore must not accept an almost-right version of any program. Data files may or may not be acceptable with almost all the bytes correct.

If you find that one of your program files is unreadable in any degree, the correct thing to do is replace that program from a good back-up copy. There is no other safe way to proceed. If you get a data file with some minor damage in it, you may be able to repair that damage, or you may be able just to accept it without causing any serious problems later on.

How you should proceed to attempt a repair of the damage depends entirely on what kind of data file it is. A document file can often be fixed simply by loading it into the word processor that created it and running a spelling check. (If the damage is to the formatting, you may have to print it or view it in an on-screen print preview mode to discover where the problem is.) After you spot the damage, normally you can easily fix it.

A damaged database or spreadsheet file can either be much easier or much tougher to deal with. The Norton Utilities program, File Fix, is one example of the specialized programs available to test and repair certain kinds of damage to specific formats of database or spreadsheet files.

Pattern testing

SpinRite's pattern testing was described in Chapter 13. Depending on the level of testing you have chosen, it will apply 82 test patterns, or 43, or 5, or it may skip pattern testing altogether. The deeper the level of pattern testing you choose, the more thoroughly SpinRite examines your disk to catch all surface defects and drive dysfunctions. The level of testing you choose is important. Any is better than none; more is even better. The trade-off is that each level takes progressively longer to complete. Only with the deepest level can you be completely sure to catch all surface defects and all drive dysfunctions.

If it receives a correctable error even once while pattern testing, SpinRite will declare the sector in question a bad place to store data. But the many times and clever ways it tries to read your original data means that they almost always can be recovered. That SpinRite has no tolerance for even a correctable error during pattern testing means that your data will not be put in jeopardy after testing is completed.

Recording problems

SpinRite informs you of every problem it encounters, reporting bad sectors in three ways: on-screen and, if you choose, in a disk or printed report; in the Detailed Technical Log; and in the sector headers.

On the screen and in the report

SpinRite shows you a lot of information on-screen as it does its work. When its testing is complete, you can ask SpinRite to create a report, either as a printed copy or in a disk file, showing everything that appeared on-screen during its operation.

The first way in which SpinRite reports bad sectors is via the Track Map display. If it found an error when reading your original data, or if the FAT shows those clusters marked as bad, SpinRite will display one of the symbols described in the section "The Quick Surface Scan" earlier in this chapter. If during pattern testing it finds one or more defects, it will display the number it found (1 to 9; if it found nine or more defects it will show that by a 9).

For all but the smallest drives, the Track Map is not big enough to show a different symbol for each track. One symbol often shows the status of four or more tracks. What if those tracks deserve different symbols? The order of precedence SpinRite uses reflects the seriousness of the problems detected.

The worst problems are difficulties in reading your original data. Next most serious are difficulties in reading sectors that happen not to have any data you care about (but which soon may). Defects that show up in pattern testing come next. Of lowest precedence is showing where there are clusters marked as bad in the FAT.

Every sector on each track for a given Track Map location earns a symbol. These symbols are U or u for noncorrectable errors (U if that sector is part of a file and u if not). Correctable errors get a C or a c, again depending on whether that sector is currently in use. A sector that proves defective upon pattern testing gets a 1. Sectors that are part of a marked bad cluster get a B.

The symbols for all the sectors corresponding to that Track Map location are combined to derive the symbol for the Track Map. A U beats a C beats a u beats a c. If the worst sector has a 1, the Track Map will show a number (1 to 9) that tells how many sectors there were with a 1 in those tracks. If a B is the worst sector's symbol, that is what will show.

In the Detailed Technical Log

The symbols give a good overview of the health of your drive but don't provide you with all the details you might want to know. The Detailed Technical Log, a new feature with SpinRite II, records those details.

While it is running, SpinRite always makes available the last 1,000 lines of the Detailed Technical Log. You can review them on-screen by using your cursor pad keys (Home, End, and the arrow keys). If you don't tell it otherwise, SpinRite will write the same information to a file named SPINRITE.LOG in the root directory of the logical volume it is testing.

In the sector headers

Finally, SpinRite makes sure that any sector it finds bad is marked as such in its sector header. It does this task for all but 8-bit XT-class hard disk controllers (which don't allow doing this) by doing an extra track reformatting. Figure 13-1 shows how the sector header flags are used to mark bad sectors.

TECHNICAL SECRET

If a controller board has only one *tongue* on the slot that plugs into the PC's bus, it is an 8-bit controller. If it has two tongues, it is a 16-bit controller. Eight-bit controllers can be used in any PC. They are not able to transfer data as rapidly as 16-bit controllers. Only PC's with the full ISA bus, like the AT, can accept those 16-bit controllers. Because those controllers are faster, almost all ISA PCs use them.

With few exceptions, the 8-bit controllers do not allow marking individual sectors as bad. All the 16-bit controllers do.

Part II: The SpinRite Companion

Because SpinRite rewrites sector headers by performing a second low-level reformatting of the track, it can't mark the header as bad if low-level reformatting has been suppressed, either by user request or hardware limitations.

Putting the data back

In the final step, SpinRite restores your data. If the entire track has received a clean bill of health, which is usually the case, SpinRite places the data back where it came from.

Moving data to safety

DOS keeps track of data on a hard disk only in clusters, so if SpinRite detects that a sector is bad, it must move the data from all the sectors of that cluster.

SpinRite keeps track of the status of each sector on the track. It puts each sector's data into the cluster buffer and updates the status of that group of sectors. When the cluster buffer is full, SpinRite either puts the data back where they came from or moves them, depending on the status of the group of sectors.

One exception is if the data are a part of a hidden or system file, possibly signaling a copy-protected file, in which case SpinRite will not move the data. Instead, SpinRite will report its findings in the Detailed Technical Log and recommend that you move that file if you can safely do so.

> **TIP**
> Users of the popular disk-compression programs Stacker and SuperStor may know that these products create the illusion of a large hard disk volume by putting a compressed version of the files that go on that disk into a special, large file on one of your real hard disks. That file is marked with the system, hidden, and read-only attributes. DOS Version 6 includes a similar compression product, DoubleSpace. It works in almost precisely the same manner (differing mainly in how it gets loaded by the operating system when you boot your PC).

Always run SpinRite only on the *host* volume (the real drive that holds the compressed volume file), not on the drive letter that represents the compressed volume file. If you forget and try to run it on a compressed volume, it will tell you that the drive you have asked it to work on is not a standard DOS drive, and, therefore, it will simply decline to do anything on that volume.

Chapter 14: Details of SpinRite's Operation

If SpinRite is run on the host volume, it may report a problem and decline to fix it because it involves a portion of the disk occupied by that special file. The right way to deal with this situation involves the following steps:

1. Run CHKDSK on the host volume. Fix any problems it tells you about, which may mean running CHKDSK again and specifying the /F option (or you may use some other tools).

   Then run the corresponding test program for your compressed volume file (or files, if you have more than one compressed volume file on this host drive). For Stacker the program you want is called **SCHECK**. For DoubleSpace the command is **DBLSPACE /CHKDSK**. (Again, if this command yields any error messages, you may need to reissue the command specifying that you want the program to fix whatever trouble it found.)

   Finally, defragment the compressed volume(s). Stacker users use **SDEFRAG**. DoubleSpace users use the command **DBLSPACE /DEFRAGMENT**.

2. Unhide the compressed volume file. (This means turn off the hidden and system attribute bits.) You can turn off these attribute bits with the ATTRIB command in some versions of DOS, or you can use a third-party utility program such as the Norton Utilities or PC Tools.

3. Rerun SpinRite. This time, it will both find and fix the problem with the hard disk. You are not finished yet, though.

4. Reset the hidden and system attributes on the special file. Use the same utility program you used in the first step.

5. Rerun the same checking programs you used in step 1. This will clean up any messes that may have been left from SpinRite's moving a portion of the compressed volume file to a new location on the host disk.

WARNING: While Stacker, SuperStor, and the new DOS DoubleSpace all do on-the-fly file compression in a very similar manner, other products on the market work in a very different way. One that has been quite popular is Expanz. Another new product in this market is XtraDrive from IIT. Both of these products use techniques that make it quite dangerous to treat their drives with SpinRite or any other low-level disk repair or disk reinterleaving program.

Where should your data go?

When SpinRite must move a cluster of data, it scans the FAT for the first available cluster, starting at the beginning. This maximizes the chance that it will find one where it has already finished testing.

How will DOS find the data it moved?

Besides copying the data to the new location, SpinRite makes sure that DOS can find it by adjusting the pointers in the FAT appropriately (see Figure 14-1).

Part II: The SpinRite Companion

A portion of a directory

MYFILE   DOC

The Directory Entry points to a starting cluster in the FAT. The FAT has a chain of pointers to the rest of the file.

A small section of the File Allocation Table

End of file

(a)

A portion of a directory

MYFILE   DOC

When a cluster includes a bad sector, SpinRite sets its FAT entry to reflect that. The pointers must show DOS how to find the data in its new location.

A small section of the File Allocation Table

End of file

(b)

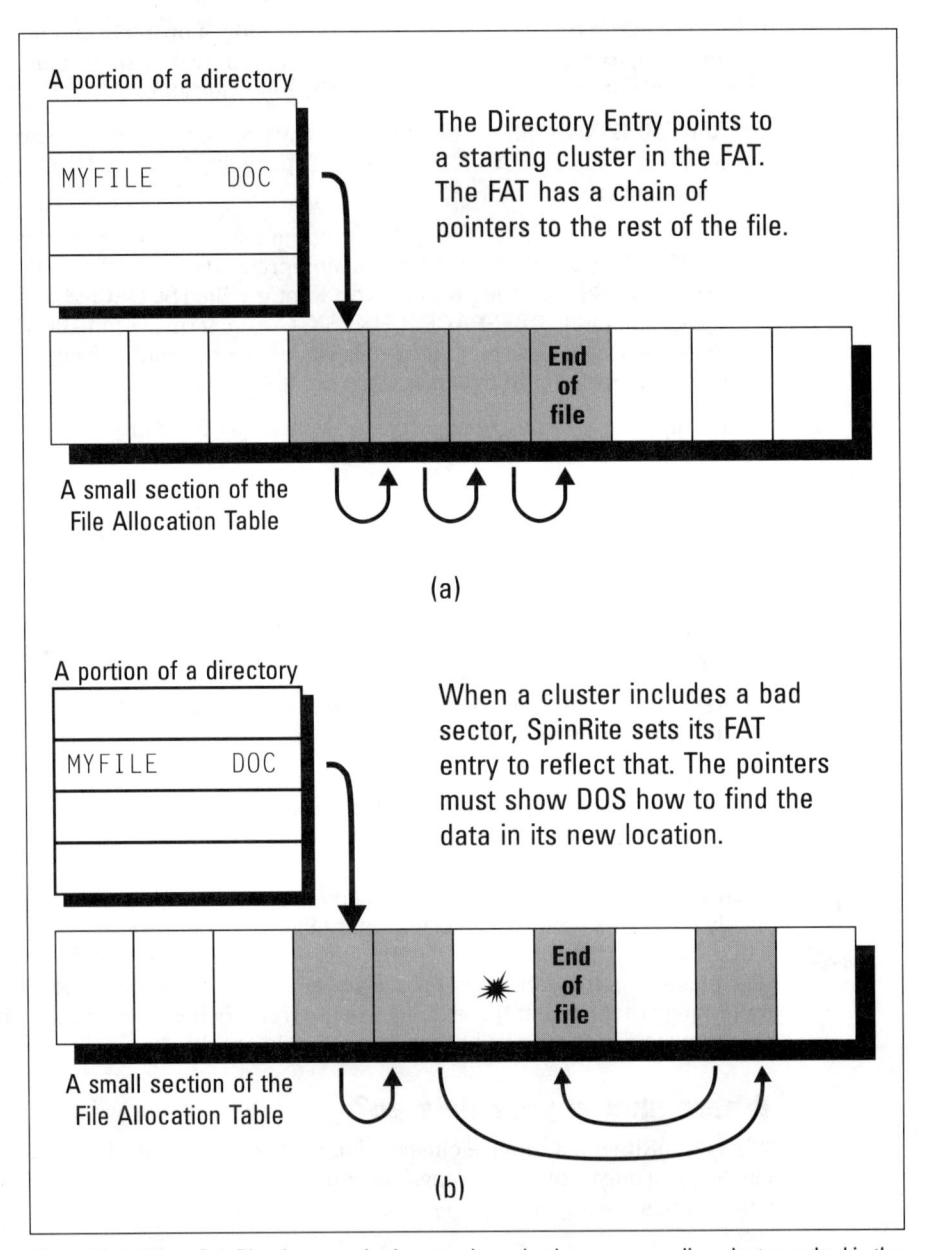

Figure 14-1: When SpinRite detects a bad sector, it marks the corresponding cluster as bad in the FAT. If the cluster was in use, the data stored there must be put elsewhere.

Figure 14-1 illustrates one of the following three cases that SpinRite encounters:

1. If the cluster is in the middle of a file, the data are moved and the FAT pointers adjusted. This case is the one shown in the figure.

2. If the cluster is the first one in the chain for a file, the directory entry pointing to it must also be adjusted.

3. If the cluster is the start of a chain that contains a directory, the pointer for that directory's parent directory also must be changed. This case is the most difficult one for SpinRite.

Moving data around this way does fragment the file a bit. (See the discussion in the section "A form of degradation that does NOT signal impending hard disk death — file fragmentation" in Chapter 11.) You can remedy this problem if you want by running a disk defragmenter after running SpinRite, but it is not usually worth the effort.

> **TIP** It never hurts to defragment your disk before you do something like running SpinRite. (Just as it never hurts to be very, very sure that your backups are in perfect order — but then that never hurts in any case!) What may be critical is that you run CHKDSK and defragment any compressed volumes that are contained in files on the disk drive you plan to treat with SpinRite. The on-the-fly file compression programs are sometimes a great deal less tolerant of mixed-up data than DOS, by itself, is.

Telling the user where the data went

Naturally, SpinRite records these actions in the Detailed Technical Log, alerting the user to where the defect was found, where SpinRite relocated the data, and the name of the affected file. Knowing which file was fragmented may help you decide whether it is worth defragmenting.

When the bad becomes good

Mostly, SpinRite is thought of as a program that finds defects and moves data out of harm's way. But it can also turn this trick inside out. Sometimes a sector marked as bad will test out as flawless. This is a case of a bad place spontaneously becoming good and fully usable. Yes, it happens!

If SpinRite is able to prove that a formerly defective sector is now in full health, it can return that sector to use for storing data. To be certain of its conclusion, it must use the deepest level of pattern testing. This feature is unique to SpinRite. Like most of SpinRite's features, you can turn this one off.

Part II: The SpinRite Companion

Interrupting SpinRite

To carry out a task as Herculean as a deepest level pattern test of a 300MB drive, SpinRite may require more than a day. The fact that it involves moving some 50,000MB of data on and off the disk should give you an idea of why it can take so long. Gibson realized that few PC users would want to interrupt their work that long, even for so important a task, so he made it easy to interrupt SpinRite.

What is stored and where

To allow for these interruptions, SpinRite retains in the diagnostic cylinder some data about what it was doing when it was interrupted.

When you press Esc, SpinRite first finishes with the track on which it is working before it reacts to your request to stop. It stores on every track of the diagnostic cylinder a record of what operation it was doing (for example, a quick surface scan of low-level format with depth 4 pattern testing), on which logical volume, and where it was in that process.

SpinRite also stores everything it has displayed on-screen since the program session began. This means that when you resume the interrupted operation, the Track Map will reappear just as it was right before the interruption. When SpinRite finally finishes its work, you can create a report file that contains all the information it would have if the job had been done in a single session, including any disk seek performance details or bad sectors found in an earlier

Be alert for an alert

All but a few PC hard disk controllers create a diagnostic cylinder. Some AT clones, however, have a motherboard BIOS that does not. If your controller did not create a diagnostic cylinder on your drive, SpinRite will be unable to store the information it needs to resume. You will be alerted to this fact during the initial phase of running SpinRite. Unfortunately, you will not receive a reminder when you interrupt SpinRite's operation. You simply will not be given the option of resuming that operation when you next run SpinRite. Instead, SpinRite will display its main menu and await your next command.

Be attentive when SpinRite is first testing your system. If your system lacks a diagnostic cylinder, you'll get this message: ATTENTION! SpinRite utilizes and requires the pre-defined auxiliary last track which is found on all true IBM compatible hard drives. This drive does not have the required last track. Consequently, SpinRite will be suppressing its low-level formatting of this drive. **If you get this message, you will not want to interrupt SpinRite quite so freely.**

session. Because the Detailed Technical Log entries are written to the disk file \SPINRITE.LOG as they are generated, they are not also stored in the diagnostic cylinder.

The information that is stored on the diagnostic cylinder takes up less than one track. SpinRite places a copy of it on each track in that cylinder, along with a checksum and a record of the version of SpinRite used. Therefore, you can resume an interrupted operation only if you run the same version of SpinRite. Further, if one copy of the stored information is corrupted, the checksum will reveal this fact, and SpinRite will use another copy in its stead.

When you resume

When you first start SpinRite, it checks the diagnostic cylinder of each physical drive, just in case you interrupted an operation on it. There can be only one such record there, so you can suspend and resume work on only one logical volume of each physical drive. If it finds a valid interruption record created by the same version of SpinRite, it will display a menu that offers to resume the interrupted operation. Before picking up where it left off, SpinRite will first run through the system diagnostics to be sure that your PC's system memory and controller are still working adequately.

Upon resuming, the only discernible difference will be a notation in the Detailed Technical Log window showing the date on which you resumed. That entry will be added to the end of the Detailed Technical Log file, SPINRITE.LOG. If there is no such file (for example, if you renamed or moved it between SpinRite sessions), it will create the file.

Part II: The SpinRite Companion

Summary

- ▶ SpinRite is one of the relatively few programs on the market that checks its own integrity each time it is run. This provides a high degree of protection against any illicit alteration of its code (including, but not limited to, alteration that a computer virus may cause).

- ▶ SpinRite is also very fussy about its working environment. It checks to be quite certain that your PC is working perfectly before it attempts to diagnose or fix anything on your PC's hard drive.

- ▶ Some aspects of how a drive or hard disk controller work can be learned simply by asking. SpinRite does not count on the accuracy of that information, however. It tests exhaustively to see for itself whether you are using disk caching, what data-encoding strategy is being used, and whether sector translation is in effect.

- ▶ SpinRite determines the present value of sector interleave on a typical track in the DOS logical volume being treated. It then evaluates the impact of changing that interleave and makes a suggestion. You can accept its recommendation, choose a different interleave value, or deny permission for SpinRite to alter the interleave value.

- ▶ SpinRite tries uncommonly hard to read even the most recalcitrant data. Often, it is able to read what no other program can. Then it moves data from any marginal or defective clusters to safer places on the disk and updates the many pointers that DOS uses to find your data.

- ▶ Finally, SpinRite is a very friendly program. If you want it to do all it can, most likely it will take a very long time. You can start it working and then interrupt it to do whatever you need to do. When you restart it, SpinRite will offer to resume working where it left off. In this way, you can let it do even the longest jobs without unduly interrupting your work.

This concludes my rundown on how SpinRite performs its magic. I hope this look under the hood makes you feel more confident in SpinRite's capabilities and that you found it interesting, besides!

Chapter 15
SpinRite's Evolution

In This Chapter
▶ The eight versions of SpinRite that have been published and a sneak preview of the next version
▶ Why you may want to upgrade to the latest SpinRite version or why you may not need to

A Short History of SpinRite

Steve Gibson introduced the original SpinRite in March, 1988. A significantly enhanced product, SpinRite II, debuted in October, 1989. In all, Gibson Research has marketed eight distinct versions of SpinRite, three of which were versions of SpinRite II as Table 15-1 outlines. (See Appendix A if you want to learn how Steve Gibson came to write SpinRite.)

The history of a program can be interesting, but what is really important to most people is how they can get optimum value from that program. Before you can learn how to do that with SpinRite, you must first determine which version you own.

Various versions

The following sections describe each of those versions and how they differ from one another, which may help you decide whether you want to upgrade your version. Also, knowing the limitations and problems others have encountered with earlier versions may help you avoid trouble.

Check the file date, time, and size of the version of SpinRite you have against those listed in Table 15-1. *Note:* The file date is not always the same as the date on which the program was released to the public. The time stamped on the file uniformly used to be midnight. Starting with SpinRite II, Version 1.1, Gibson used the time (hours and minutes) to encode the version number. He used the seconds part of the time to record a sub-version number. (Version 1.2 of the original SpinRite was not shipped to very many people, and at this time even Gibson Research is not certain what its file statistics were.)

Part II: The SpinRite Companion

SpinRite Versions

Product	Version	Size (bytes)	Date	Time
SpinRite I	1.0	44,209	02/20/88	12:00:00AM
	1.1	43,578	03/21/88	12:00:00AM
	1.2			
	1.2a	43,702	07/01/88	12:00:00AM
	1.2b	44,081	09/20/88	12:00:00AM
SpinRite II	1.0	46,060	10/12/89	12:02:52PM
	1.1	47,081	06/01/90	01:10:48AM
	2.0	47,473	03/01/91	02:00:12AM
SpinRite 3	3.1	??,???	01/01/93	03:10:??AM

Table 15-1: The names, sizes, and dates and times of all SpinRite versions.

As I write this book, the newest version, SpinRite 3, is not yet shipping to customers. I am told that its file size and date will be those shown in the table; the file size has not yet been determined.

SpinRite Version 1.0

Version 1.0 was the initial release of the program. Already a fully developed, essentially bug-free program, SpinRite 1.0 did the job for which it was designed (unlike some new releases of software today). Still, it was created by a mere human being, not an omniscient god. Before releasing it, Gibson had many people test it on a wide variety of PC systems, but he couldn't come close to testing it on the variety of machines on which end users ran the program. To no one's surprise, given this variety, some incompatibilities surfaced.

SpinRite Version 1.1

Although PC users initially reacted to SpinRite with enthusiasm, that reaction was tempered in some quarters by the discovery of some special situations in which the program could cause catastrophic data loss. After Gibson heard about these situations, he reacted quickly.

He released Version 1.1 of SpinRite just a few weeks after Version 1.0. Establishing the Gibson Research upgrade policy, Gibson announced that because this upgrade corrected a potentially serious oversight, he would ship a copy to all registered users. This upgrade was not only free, it came to the users without their having to request it. Gibson's goal was to rid the world of the potentially dangerous version.

The problem that Version 1.1 solved stemmed from SpinRites's interaction with certain unusual disk controllers that Gibson had not anticipated. Some early DTC autoconfiguring hard disk controllers save the drive dimensions in a special sector. The problem arises with where the controller places that sector and how it creates it. Seagate marketed a version of this controller, under their own brand name, that used the same strategy for saving the drive dimensions and, of course, caused the same problems for SpinRite.

These controllers put the drive dimensions into a sector with only 64 bytes of data (one-eighth the normal amount). That sector is given the number 63 (the maximum legal value), and it is put on the very first track of the drive after all the normal sectors. That is, its location is cylinder 0, head 0, sector 63.

When the BIOS asks the controller to redo the low-level format on that track, it does not automatically re-create that extra sector. No program other than the special disk initialization program in the controller's ROM can make it do so. All programs that attempted to control low-level formatting of a disk attached to such a controller encountered a serious problem. They could do the low-level format just fine, but the next time the computer was started, the controller had no idea how big the drive was. The user was unable to do anything useful with it.

This was a nuisance for people who were initially preparing a disk for use. It could be a disaster if they were trying to optimize its performance with SpinRite and had the disk full of valuable programs and data (especially if they did not have a good set of backups).

TECHNICAL SECRET

Other programs that have difficulties with this controller include certain versions of Disk Manager and SpeedStor. These programs can safely be used to create partitions on a drive after the controller has done the low-level format (although if you are using DOS Version 3.3 or later, you don't need them and, as I argued in Chapter 9, you should not use them). But if you use these programs in their normal manner, they will attempt to manage the whole initialization process and will fail dramatically.

The original SpinRite would redo the low-level format on every track in the DOS logical drive. It also would redo the low-level format on the track containing the master boot record (which is at cylinder 0, head 0, sector 0). SpinRite Version 1.1 solved the problem with these controllers by omitting the reformatting of the master boot record's track. All versions of SpinRite since then have not attempted to redo the low-level format on cylinder 0, head 0.

TECHNICAL SECRET

If your disk was formatted with DOS 3.0 or a later version, it does not use that initial track for anything but the master boot record. There is no increase in speed to be gained from resetting the sector interleave value for that one track. Giving this track up is, therefore, no great sacrifice. Even if you are using DOS 2.x, in which the rest of the track is used, the loss in efficiency will be minor.

Certain disk performance-testing programs, including Steve Gibson's own SPINTEST.COM and the Norton SI program, use that initial track very heavily in measuring the disk's data-transfer rate. If that track has a different sector interleave value than the rest of the disk, these programs will report a data-transfer rate that is not a fair measure of how the disk will work in normal use.

The Norton Utilities Calibrate program (at least in its initial release) only usually avoids low-level reformatting of the master boot record track; it does reformat the first track of the DOS partition. Unfortunately, if the disk was formatted with DOS 2.x, the master boot record track and the first track of the DOS partition are the same track, and Calibrate will then attempt to redo its low-level format.

Therefore, if an early version of Calibrate is used on a controller that creates this special sector in the first track and the disk was formatted with DOS 2.x, you will very likely have the same problem as you would have had if you had used the initial release of SpinRite.

Gibson wanted to help any SpinRite user who had lost data because of this problem. He contacted DTC, who told him there was no way to recover data from a disk after redoing the low-level format on its first track. Upon exploring their controller's ROM code, Gibson found a part of it that would allow re-creation of that special sector, complete with the drive dimensions. He shared his discovery with the DTC technical support department.

Gibson Research does not now assist its users directly with this problem. If you have a DTC controller and lose your data by using the original SpinRite, DTC should be able to help you. Of course, it would be better to upgrade your copy of SpinRite before that happens.

> ### OK to turn the PC on end?
>
> You may, as some people do, turn your desktop PC on end and place it on the floor to free up some space on the desk. This is generally an okay thing to do. (You would be better served if you set the PC on blocks, at least several inches up off the floor, to keep it away from the more dusty floor level. Also, please secure the PC firmly so that it cannot topple over. If that happens while the PC is on, it could be very, very bad for the hard drive.)
>
> When you turn your PC on end, you also turn the hard disk to a new orientation, of course. Often, users run SpinRite on the hard disk after it is in its new orientation, hoping to realign all the tracks with the new position of the head assembly. This is a good idea. But then you may wonder and worry about the master boot record. That track isn't reformatted by any version of SpinRite (since the very first version). Is this a problem? Possibly yes, but probably no.
>
> If you experience trouble accessing your hard disk at all, you could try turning off your PC and then putting it back up on the desktop. If you can then access your data, that suggests that the master boot record may have been unreadable in the other orientation and is readable now.
>
> If that happens to you, be sure that your backups are absolutely perfect and then reposition your PC where you want to use it, after which you should redo the low-level format the old way. (Remember, this means that you will have to follow up that step with partitioning [by using FDISK] and high-level formatting [by using FORMAT], plus reloading all your software from those backups. Now you know why the very first step must be verifying the integrity and total accuracy and completeness of your backups!)

Version 1.1 incorporated a few other minor changes. The original program, for example, did a test for compatibility between the drive and controller. Because this test turned out to be completely unnecessary, Gibson Research removed it from all later versions of the product.

SpinRite Version 1.2, 1.2A, and 1.2B

The other versions of the original SpinRite contained the usual assortment of minor improvements. Version 1.2 addressed one more discovery of a controller incompatibility: Omti made some autoconfiguring controllers that stored their drive dimensions in a special, hidden place, similar to what DTC had done.

TECHNICAL SECRET

> The Omti controllers also do something else in an unusual and interesting way — they automatically remap bad tracks. That means that if your drive has a defect on, say, cylinder 12, head 5, and you tell the controller it is a bad track, Omti will substitute some track out near the end of the drive. Thus, whenever the BIOS asks the controller to put some information into a sector at cylinder 12, head 5, it actually will go to the remapped track.

Part II: The SpinRite Companion

This feature is nice in that it makes your drive look as if it does not have any bad tracks. It is definitely not nice in that every time you try to access one of the tracks that was bad, the controller will have to send the drive searching way off to the end of the disk for its replacement. Even files that are unfragmented, according to DOS, may become scattered very widely on the disk.

Omti also used this capability to do its hiding of the disk dimensions. Whenever one of these controllers is in an autoconfiguring mode, it will take the track at head 0 of cylinder 100 for this purpose. It marks that track as one that is to be remapped. Then whenever the BIOS thinks it is reading or writing that track, it actually will be reading or writing the remapped track out near the end of the drive. Unfortunately, when you ask the controller to redo the low-level format on that track, it will comply. That actual physical track is reformatted, not the remapped one. (Ouch!)

Starting with Version 1.2, SpinRite knows enough to detect Omti controllers. It even can learn which model and revision-level controller it is dealing with, and whether that controller is in an autoconfiguring mode. (If the controller is not in autoconfiguring mode, it is not dangerous, no matter what the model.) When SpinRite is running on a system with one of the dangerous controllers, it will avoid redoing the low-level format on that special track.

Because these upgrades were of no significance to most users, Gibson Research offered them, without cost, only to those users who requested them.

SpinRite II Version 1.0

This version saw the dawn of a new generation of SpinRite. Significantly enhanced, the product retained its basic purpose and operation, but it augmented them with six major and several minor new features. In recognition of these changes, Gibson changed the name to SpinRite II. The most delightful new feature, from a user perspective, is that you no longer have to configure SpinRite for your PC, making it much easier to use.

TECHNICAL SECRET

DOS hides many things. Its purpose is to make life easy for users and application programs but not necessarily for application programmers. Without benefit of some special knowledge, it is not possible to make an application program talk directly to the hard disk controller.

The original SpinRite got around this problem in a clever way. You were asked to boot your computer from a DISKCOPY of the original SpinRite diskette, which used its own special "operating system" to get a view of your PC without DOS. It stored what it learned inside SPINRITE.COM.

Later, after you had rebooted your computer with DOS, SpinRite still would know how to access the hardware directly. The difficulty with this approach was that whenever you changed your PC's configuration, even if you just changed the video card, you had to reconfigure SpinRite before it would operate.

Gibson made SpinRite so sensitive to your computer's configuration for a very good reason. He was concerned that you might move the program to a new computer without telling it what you had done. Then it might make some mistakes, thinking it could access the new hardware the same way it had learned to do for the old computer. Thus, although it was an inconvenience, reconfiguring SpinRite whenever any part of your PC was changed provided a significant level of added protection.

By the time he created SpinRite II, Gibson had acquired considerable knowledge about undocumented DOS and BIOS features. He used that knowledge to make SpinRite II know how to find the routines it needs in the BIOS and the hardware despite the attempts of DOS at obfuscation. The earlier clever idea of booting off the SpinRite disk was no longer necessary.

The benefits of this improvement are two-fold. First, you can make a back-up copy of the SpinRite II files with the regular DOS COPY command. You no longer have to use DISKCOPY. Second, you can merely run SPINRITE.COM. You don't have to be concerned if you have changed some aspect of your PC. SpinRite II will detect those changes and accommodate them automatically.

The second major new feature was SpinRite II's capability to work with DOS logical drives of any size. Up until this version, it could operate only on 32MB or smaller logical drives. The new program understands large logical drives created by PC DOS or MS-DOS versions numbered 4.0 or later, by COMPAQ's DOS 3.31, and by the various third-party disk-partitioning programs, such as Disk Manager and SpeedStor.

TECHNICAL SECRET

Earlier versions of DOS limited logical drives to 32MB. (The reasons for this are discussed in Chapter 7 in the section "Logical Size Limits." Some popular ways to get around this limitation are discussed in the section "Evading the Logical Limits" in that same chapter.)

Essentially, the limit comes from restricting the number of sectors to 65,536 (64KB), with a fixed sector size of 512 bytes. Multiply these out and you get 32MB (or 33,554,432 bytes). SpinRite II can accommodate many more sectors, as well as sectors of almost any size.

Part II: The SpinRite Companion

Third, SpinRite II reports substantially more about what it finds and what it does with those findings. Some of the new information can be extremely useful.

TECHNICAL SECRET

SpinRite was designed to be a "no-brainer." That is, anyone can use it with little effort. Even in the first versions, it reported some things the user did not need to know. Gibson purposely limited the amount it reported to avoid intimidating users.

Many users wanted to be told more. Even more important, sometimes they *needed* to know more.

If SpinRite encounters an uncorrectable error while reading data from the disk, at least a couple of bytes of your data will inevitably be lost. With the earlier program, you could not easily find out which file had been damaged, let alone where in the file the damage could be found. The new SpinRite II Detailed Technical Log gives that information very explicitly. Armed with that knowledge, it is often quite easy to repair the damage or — if it is not easily repaired — replace the damaged file.

Fourth, although users of the original SpinRite were advised to remove any copy-protected programs before running SpinRite, SpinRite II users don't have that concern. Again, this makes SpinRite much more convenient to use.

When it discovers a disk defect, SpinRite moves the data from that sector to some safer place. To some copy-protected programs, such a change looks the same as an unauthorized copy. These programs will refuse to operate.

TECHNICAL SECRET

Most such copy-protected programs are concerned only with the location of certain special files. These files are typically marked with the DOS file attributes *hidden* or *system,* or both. SpinRite II checks the file attributes before moving any data. It will not move a sector if it is part of a hidden or system file, even if it finds a defect there. It will, of course, tell the user about the problem. The user then can solve it another way.

If SpinRite II tells you that it found a defect but did not move the data because it was part of a hidden file, you should then "deinstall" the copy-protected program and rerun SpinRite. This time, it will mark the defective sector as bad. Then, when you reinstall the copy-protected program, it will not be put back in the defective sector. (If you have more than one copy-protected program, you may have to investigate a bit to find out which one's hidden file is occupying the defective sector.)

Another source of hidden system files are disk-compression utilities, such as Stacker and SuperStor. If you have one of them installed on your system and SpinRite reports a problem with the disk in a place within one of their compressed volume files, there is a simple, four-step method for taking care of matters. This method is detailed in the section "Moving data to safety" in Chapter 14.

The fifth major new feature was the introduction of a hypertext on-line help system. This is a separate, stand-alone program by which one can learn more about what SpinRite does and how. It contains answers to commonly asked questions, information about how SpinRite works with drives using different interface designs (SCSI and ESDI, for example), and warnings about the few systems with which SpinRite still has some serious compatibility problems (such as the Priam EVDR.SYS driver). And it tells some trivia that Steve Gibson thought some of the users of his program might simply enjoy learning.

Sixth, SpinRite II now marks defective sectors as bad in their sector headers. All versions of SpinRite mark the FAT to show which clusters contain flawed sectors. That prevents DOS from using them. Still, this was not enough for some users, so when working with a 16-bit hard disk controller, the new SpinRite also records sector defects in their headers. Unfortunately, this improvement included a bug that necessitated creating SpinRite II Version 1.1, just a few months later.

TECHNICAL SECRET

You cannot selectively mark sectors as bad in their headers on XT-class hard disk controllers. You can only mark an entire track as bad or good. Selective sector marking can only be done on AT-style (16-bit bus interface) controllers. You can find out how sectors get marked bad in the section "Surface Analysis — Finding the Bad Tracks, Sectors, and Clusters" in Chapter 13; the process is illustrated in Figure 13-1. The original SpinRite was written to treat all disks equally, so it simply marked all sector headers as if the sectors were good.

To mark individual sectors as bad requires an extra step. The original SpinRite would go through four steps for each track. First, it read the original data and saved it. Next, it reformatted the track (marking all sectors as good). Third, it tested the track. Fourth, it restored the original data.

SpinRite II adds to this process. After testing, and before replacing the original data, it again reformats the track. This is the only way it can insert the bad sector marks into the sector headers. And this is where the problem was in SpinRite II Version 1.0.

Finally, SpinRite II has been improved in a number of other minor ways. These include cosmetic improvements to the screens and some internal changes of no interest to users.

SpinRite II Version 1.1

As soon as Gibson heard of a problem with SpinRite II Version 1.0, he got to work finding and fixing it. Again he mailed the fix, which was Version 1.1, to all registered users free of charge. (His commitment to supporting his users in this fashion has cost Gibson more than $50,000, but he says he regards it as money well spent.)

TECHNICAL SECRET

The bug in SpinRite II Version 1.0 only showed up when a user had a disk with a defective next-to-last sector on some track whose last sector was not defective. In that case, it marked the last sector as defective also. Further, it mistakenly set the sector number of that last sector to 0, rendering it inaccessible.

SpinRite next tried to put the original data back into that last sector. Because the sector number had been changed to zero, SpinRite could not find it. The program at that point simply locked up. The problem was simple enough to fix after its cause was found. Finding the cause required running the program on enough machines to encounter by chance a disk with that special combination of problems.

This problem did not happen often, and when it did, not much data was likely to be lost (at most a couple of sectors). Still, it was enough to prevent SpinRite from working further on that disk. Furthermore, Gibson says, *any* data loss is too much.

Version 1.1 includes a number of other improvements to the program, such as extending the range of controllers that it can work with, increasing its capability to recover "unreadable" data, and speeding up the program when dealing with massively defective drives. The hypertext help program was completely overhauled, and there were the usual number of minor tweaks to the screen displays and internal workings.

TECHNICAL SECRET

Some controllers contain track buffers. That feature can greatly speed up their operation. It also totally frustrated earlier versions of SpinRite. Those versions noted the buffering and declined to do anything with the drives attached to those controllers.

Version 1.1 knows how to turn off track buffering on many of those controllers. When it can turn off track buffering, SpinRite is capable of performing its full repertoire of services on the attached drives. If it cannot turn off track buffering, at least it can do data integrity testing and move endangered data

Chapter 15: SpinRite's Evolution

to safety. If those controllers also were doing sector translation, SpinRite still could not do any low-level reformatting, but now it at least could do all the data-integrity testing.

Data recovery was much enhanced by the addition of *head jiggling* during reading of the original data. This subject is discussed in the section "Reading the data" in Chapter 14. The program also now tries twice as many times before giving up on an unreadable sector.

Version 1.1 more than makes up for the extra time these steps take by some added efficiencies. If a cluster is marked bad in the FAT, there should be no valuable data stored there. Earlier versions of SpinRite ignored this fact and attempted to read data from these sectors anyway. Version 1.1 notes this and doesn't bother trying to read what is probably one or more badly flawed sectors. After it redoes the low-level format, it will test those sectors because they may have been repaired by the reformatting.

Another time-saver is that SpinRite now stops pattern testing of a sector at the earliest possible moment. No longer does it try its full repertoire of tests even if it has already found a defect in that sector.

SpinRite II Version 2.0

With the release of SpinRite II Version 1.1, Gibson Research claimed it could do defect analysis on "anything that spins." Although Gibson never intended this to mean that it would test Frisbees and phonograph records, he seriously intended it to be true for all PC hard drives.

Because the world of PCs is incredibly diverse, some weird combinations of PC, controller, and drive still caused SpinRite problems. Version 2.0 is able to work with all those weird systems which Gibson Research was aware of at the time SpinRite II Version 2.0 was written.

TECHNICAL SECRET

There is still one limit to this capability. SpinRite only works with drives that are accessed through INT 13h BIOS calls. Some drives, such as the Bernoulli Boxes made by the Iomega Corporation, use their own device drivers and do not go through INT 13h. SpinRite still cannot do anything at all for them.

Version 2.0 also incorporates a major new technological breakthrough. It now is able to perform all its functions, including both data-integrity testing and low-level reformatting, on most systems with disk caching.

Part II: The SpinRite Companion

> **TECHNICAL SECRET**
>
> In particular, Version 2.0 can perform all its functions with most hard disk controllers that contain a hardware cache. The one exception is any controller that implements a deferred-write caching strategy and that does not allow its cache to be turned off. (See the discussion of disk caching in Chapter 5 for an explanation of what this means.) Fortunately, such controllers are rare to nonexistent.
>
> SpinRite also is able to get behind most software disk-caching schemes. When it can, it will no longer report that caching is active, and it will do all its work with complete safety. When it cannot get behind software disk caching, Version 2.0 will at least do all its data-recovery and testing work.

You may think that this means you need not disable your disk cache before running SpinRite. Although you may get away with that with Version 2.0, Gibson does not recommend it.

In line with Gibson's earlier upgrade policy, this version is available upon request and free of charge to any registered user of SpinRite II. If you find SpinRite II won't do low-level formatting or defect analysis, or if it has any other problem working with your PC, call Gibson Research's technical support line and describe your system and your problem. Their solution may be to send you a more up-to-date version of SpinRite.

Should I upgrade?

All versions of SpinRite perform the same basic tasks. The later versions simply do them better, for more drives and controllers. If you have an early version and are happy with it, you need not upgrade. If you think you might run into one of the problems described above, though, perhaps you should upgrade.

From its inception, Gibson Research has had a policy of offering free upgrades within a given product generation. It even ships the upgrades free of charge, without waiting to be asked by users if the upgrade repairs some major bug. Users can upgrade from SpinRite II Version 1.0 or 1.1 to Version 2.0, at no cost. Registered users of any version of SpinRite can upgrade to SpinRite 3 for only $29. The list price of the new version is $129.

Because a major reason for owning and using SpinRite is to protect your data, most users have decided that upgrading is well worth the small amount of money it costs. This way, if ever any of their data becomes unreadable, they will have the very best chance of getting it back.

The future: SpinRite 3

As this book was being written, Steve Gibson was in seclusion, working on a new version of SpinRite. Before he disappeared from view, he told me that it would be called SpinRite 3 because it was going to be a totally new product. (He expected a level of improvement and extension of its capability at least as large as that between the original SpinRite and SpinRite II.)

The single most-requested improvement is some way to work with all IDE/ATA and SCSI drives. SpinRite II Version 2.0 already can work with some IDE/ATA drives, but customers demanded even more. The subtle issues involved include how best to work with a drive that does hot fixes, which refers to drives that will detect any accesses to a bad sector and remap them to spare sectors. Doing an excessively complete job of flushing out all the marginal sectors might merely cause the drive to use up its supply of spare sectors. Something better than that has to be done.

Gibson has a very strongly held principle: Commercial software should not be released before it is really and truly ready. So he has not and will not give any release date for the new version of SpinRite until he is ready to start shipping copies to customers. (He also has rarely done the sort of extensive outside beta testing common at many companies, believing that he can better control the testing process by keeping it in-house.)

News At Deadline - SpinRite 3 Update

Although the product is not yet shipping, Gibson Research has officially announced SpinRite 3. Steve Gibson gave me an advance peek at what it will be like. Here is a list of major new features in the product:

1. SpinRite 3 has a drastically simplified user interface. SpinRite always was an easy program to use, but now it is even easier. Most of the options that you used to select from a menu have been combined into one of the following seven "levels" of testing:

    Level 1: This level is a read-only test of the surface. It corresponds to the old Quick Surface Scan.

    Level 2: This level scans the surface as in level 1, but if it encounters a problem, it will immediately drop into the full data recovery and pattern testing routine. This level allows the quickest testing combined with the highest possibility of recovery of endangered data — fixing the damage, if possible, and moving the data to safety, if not. (It will not, however, find all the bad spots that would be found with one of the higher levels of scanning.)

Part II: The SpinRite Companion

Level 3: This level refreshes the surface. It does low-level reformatting, if possible, but does no testing. This level corresponds to the old reformat with no pattern testing option.

Level 4: This level corresponds to the previous pattern testing at Depth 2 (5 patterns tested).

Level 5: This level corresponds to the previous pattern testing at Depth 3 (43 patterns tested).

Level 6: This level corresponds to the previous pattern testing at Depth 4 (82 patterns tested).

Level 7: This level is identical to level 6 except, if it finds in testing that a sector previously marked as bad is now good, it will restore it to service.

2. The Track Map has been modified and renamed Examination-Recovery-Analysis. The major change is in the symbols and their meanings. The following chart shows the new symbols, which are now all capital letters, and what they correspond to in terms of the old symbols:

New Symbol	Old Symbol	Meaning
C	C or c	Corrected data here
E	U or u	Data here has errors that SpinRite cannot correct
D	1 to 9	New defect(s) found here
B	B	Was bad and still is bad
G		Was bad but now is good
.	.	Good, as it was before

The G symbol is only used for sectors that are being returned to service (which only happens during Level 7 operation). In some versions of SpinRite, this operation may be symbolized by an up-arrow. Most versions do not indicate these locations on the track map at all.

3. In a related change, SpinRite 3 has a much improved reporting capability. Now a single report replaces the former report file and Detailed Technical Log file, and you get better control over its location. In particular, you can direct the report to a file on a volume other than the one that SpinRite is testing. This practice can prevent some problems that earlier SpinRite versions have when working with a drive that is in really bad shape. In some of those cases, the attempt by SpinRite (pre-Version 3) to write to its log file actually worsens the condition of the drive.

A report can replace an earlier report, append to an earlier report, or replace the oldest one of a number of saved reports.

Chapter 15: SpinRite's Evolution

4. SpinRite 3 no longer depends so much on the diagnostic cylinder. It keeps a "fingerprint" record in a file with read-only, hidden, and system attributes in the root directory of each DOS logical volume that it treats. In this file, it stores the results of the various tests it has performed. This file enables SpinRite to skip some of those tests the next time SpinRite runs on the same volume, saving substantial amounts of the user's time. This file also stores the times of the last six treatments of the volume, what operation was done during each of those treatments, and a summary of the most significant results obtained in each of those treatments.

   Finally, the fingerprint file stores enough information to permit restarting an interrupted operation on the volume. By storing this last bit of information in the volume, SpinRite 3 is able to suspend an operation on any number of volumes and then resume whichever one you want.

5. SpinRite 3 can work on floppy diskettes. This feature is much requested and totally new. Because there are many copy-protected diskettes that use a very nonstandard pattern for the low-level format on one or more tracks, SpinRite 3 will not do any low-level formatting of floppies, but it will do all the rest of its magic: data recovery, pattern testing, and moving of endangered data to safety.

6. SpinRite 3 defaults to a mode in which it will treat all of the DOS logical volumes on your PC that it can, except the floppies. (SpinRite still is not able to treat a Bernoulli cartridge or any other drive that uses a non-DOS-standard means of access.)

7. Gibson Research has obtained access (under a nondisclosure agreement) to nearly all the formerly secret details of how all the IDE drive makers build their drives. This information has allowed them to develop literally hundreds of test patterns with which SpinRite can test every drive to the maximum extent possible.

   Some of these patterns are best for certain drives; other patterns are best for other drives. To be sure it tests each drive as well as possible, SpinRite 3 uses every one of its hundreds of test patterns on each drive. To keep each treatment of a drive to a manageable duration, the number of tests in a single treatment is limited, as in earlier versions, to 5, 43, or 82 patterns, depending on the level of testing chosen by the user.

   New, however, is that SpinRite 3's fingerprint file keeps track of which pattern it last used on a volume. The next time you run SpinRite 3 on the same volume, it will pick up where it left off and test with the next group of patterns. Eventually, SpinRite 3 will use every pattern on each drive on which it is allowed to do its testing many times.

8. In general, SpinRite 3 has a much improved support for IDE/ATA drives. Gibson is moving his product toward a view of disk drives that is based more on the notion of Logical Block Addresses, instead of the older physical

view in terms of heads, cylinders, and sectors. This new perspective means a move away from the original purpose of redoing the sector interleave; more and more drives are being built with an attached controller, and the interleave is getting set correctly at the factory. This progression in perspective parallels events in the development of the new SCSI 3 standard.

9. In keeping with this new orientation, Gibson has changed how SpinRite reports a disk's performance. SpinRite 3 measures and reports on a disk's Sector Access Velocity (SAV) and Data Transfer Rate (DTR). Essentially, the SAV measures how rapidly the drive can pass over the data you don't want to read on its way to the data you do want to read. The DTR, on the other hand, measures how rapidly you are able to read the data you want.

For a RAM disk that allows random access to any of your data in an instant, the SAV would be nearly infinite. In contrast, a tape drive requires that you read past the unwanted data at the same velocity as you traverse data you do want to read. For a tape drive, then, the SAV and the DTR are equal. Because a hard disk is a hybrid of random and sequential elements, it will have an SAV that is larger than the DTR, but not infinite.

10. When the data in a sector cannot be read without error, the usual strategies divide into three: (1) try reading that sector again and again; (2) accept the data as read, complete with errors, but correct the errors by use of the ECC; and (3) accept that the data cannot be read correctly.

In a totally new approach, which Gibson has named DynaStat, SpinRite 3 will repeatedly read and store erroneous reads for a damaged sector. Then, by combining these several readings statistically, it is able to get a more accurate version of the data in that sector than would be possible from any one (flawed) reading.

11. One change will have significant impact, though it cannot be seen by the user: Gibson has devised a new way of using the PC's hardware that permits him to do timing measurements with 64-bit precision and sub-microsecond resolution. All aspects of SpinRite that use timing measurements have been revised to use this new approach. The result is that the program works substantially faster and better than ever before.

12. Another change that users may notice in SpinRite Version 3 is that the main file is no longer called SPINRITE.COM. Instead it is SPINRITE.EXE. This change reflects the fact that the entire program has been recrafted to take advantage of the best of modern programming techniques. The only real significance this change will have for the users of SpinRite is that they must be careful to delete SPINRITE.COM. when they install the new SPINRITE.EXE. Otherwise, if they simply type SPINRITE at the DOS prompt, DOS will run the older SPINRITE.COM instead of the newer SPINRITE. EXE.

Chapter 15: SpinRite's Evolution 405

A Funny Thing Happened on the Way to Market

Just as Gibson Research was trying up the last loose ends on SpinRite 3.0, gearing up to start shipping copies by the tens of thousands, they received some very important news. Microsoft's MS-DOS 6 includes one component that will change how many PC users access their hard disks: DoubleSpace. This disk compression scheme and its associated proposed industry standard, Microsoft Real-time Compression Interface (MRCI), are just too important to ignore.

Reluctantly, Gibson announced that SpinRite 3.0 was being held up and in fact would never be shipped to customers. Instead another revision, SpinRite 3.1, is being prepared for release prior to the release of MS-DOS 6. This new SpinRite version will have "transparent support" for the DOS 6 compression scheme and also for the other industry leading on-the-fly file compression schemes.

When it finally does ship, the time stamp on the main SPINRITE.EXE file will be as shown in Table 15-1. The date stamp may be what is shown there, or it may be set later to reflect this newest delay.

Summary

▶ SpinRite is a mature product, having gone through one major enhancement and six minor upgrades since its introduction in March, 1988. The latest version is SpinRite II Version 2.0.

▶ All versions of the program do the same two essential jobs: (1) Reading hard-to-read data and moving any it finds to a safer place on the disk, and (2) redoing the low-level format within a DOS logical drive without destroying the data stored there and, in the process, resetting the sector interleave to its optimum value and realigning the tracks with the true paths of the heads. (Task number two is something that SpinRite can do with most disks and controllers, but not all.)

▶ Later versions of SpinRite do these jobs with a wider variety of disk/controller combinations, and in some cases they are able to do the data-recovery job a bit better.

▶ If the version of SpinRite you have works on your PC and hard disk, you do not necessarily need to upgrade it, although you may want to do so if you want to have the very best chance at data recovery in case of trouble. You certainly will want to upgrade if you anticipate going to newer hardware any time soon.

The next, and final, chapter in this book is mostly for power users. In it you learn several ways to use SpinRite that might not immediately be obvious to you. Even if you don't aspire to being a power user of SpinRite, you want to read the last two sections that discuss head parking programs and give you some valuable hints and tips.

Chapter 16
Advanced User's Guide to SpinRite

In This Chapter

▶ How to make SpinRite "dance and sing"

▶ How to make a SpinRite clean boot diskette and why and how to use it to make running SpinRite even safer

▶ All the options you have when running SpinRite interactively

▶ Your choices for batch mode operation and why sometimes you have to use SpinRite in its batch mode

▶ All about hard disk head parking — what it is, how to do it, and why you *always* should park the heads on your PC's hard disk each and every time you walk away from it

Become a SpinRite Power User

A *power user* of any program is someone who uses the program enough and understands it well enough to be able to take fairly full advantage of its features. It also implies someone who knows enough to know how or when not to use the product.

It is relatively easy to become a power user of SpinRite. That is not because it doesn't have a full set of features; rather it is because that feature set is easily explained and simply understood. This chapter tells you all you will need to know about SpinRite to become a master user and the SpinRite guru to your friends and coworkers.

If you merely want to run SpinRite with the least thought possible, you don't need the information in this book, let alone in this chapter. If, on the other hand, you want to learn everything you can about how to make SpinRite dance and sing, here are your dancing and singing lessons.

Part II: The SpinRite Companion

Get Out of Its Way!

The most important single thing you can do to help SpinRite help you is to let it have the machine to itself. You do need to have DOS running, but you don't need that nifty pop-up appointment calendar. In fact, you had better *not* have that pop-up calendar or any other nonessential resident software loaded into RAM while SpinRite is working.

You can copy the main SpinRite program file, SPINRITE.COM, to your hard disk and then run it from there. If you do so, please remember to rename your CONFIG.SYS and AUTOEXEC.BAT files and reboot your computer before you run SpinRite from the hard drive. Doing so will keep DOS from reading those files, and thus will let SpinRite run as nearly as possible in an "empty" machine. (See the next section for suggestions if you want to run SpinRite from a floppy diskette.)

If your CONFIG.SYS file loads some disk-partitioning software, such as DMDRVR.BIN (Disk Manager), SSTOR.SYS (SpeedStor), or HARDRIVE.SYS, you will have to create a special CONFIG.SYS file, which loads only that driver, and use it each time you run SpinRite from the hard drive.

If your disk was partitioned by using Disk Manager or SpeedStor or a similar product, the product's special device driver is required to get at all but the first partition (C:). If you fail to place a reference to it in your CONFIG.SYS file on the boot disk, you will find that D: and any other partitions on that drive will be unrecognized by DOS. ("Losing" a disk partition in this way is a common problem. Fortunately, recovering from that problem is easy after you realize what happened.)

If you are using DOS 3.3 or a later version, you probably do not need to continue using such a third-party disk-partitioning program. To stop using it, you will need to back up all your data, reformat the drive, and reinstall your data. See the section on using third-party disk-partitioning software under "The Partition Table" in Chapter 9 for details.

Likewise, if you use an on-the-fly file-compression program, such as Stacker or SuperStor, you may need to have that device driver loaded as well. More likely, you will not need, and should not load, the on-the-fly file-compression program (device driver), STACKER.COM, SSTOR.EXE.

DOS 6 includes a similar capability called DoubleSpace. The compression device driver, DBLSPACE.BIN, actually gets loaded before the CONFIG.SYS file is processed; therefore, you can't keep it from loading (except by booting from a disk that doesn't have that file, which is at best inconvenient). Don't worry; just realize that you cannot run SpinRite on one of the logical volumes created from one of the compressed volume files. (The differences between DoubleSpace and Stacker or SuperStor are explained more fully later in this section.) This information may surprise you; if so, read on to learn why it's true.

Chapter 16: Advanced User's Guide to SpinRite

You can run SpinRite on the host volume (the actual, physical disk partition or logical disk drive that contains the hidden system file created and maintained by the file-compression program). In fact, you should *only* run SpinRite on the host volume and not attempt to run it on the logical drive created by the disk-compression program.

All three of these on-the-fly file-compression programs (Stacker, SuperStor, and DoubleSpace) work in a very similar way. All three use a large file with read-only, hidden, and system attributes to store the information that makes up the contents of one of the newly created logical drives. The names used by the three manufacturers of these products differ somewhat, as the following table shows:

Company	*Compressed File Disk Name*	*Compressed File Name*
Stac	Host volume	STACVOL
Microsoft	Host volume	Compressed volume file (CVF)
Addstor	DOS disk	Container file

Stac calls the fictitious logical volume created from the STACVOL file the Stacker disk. Microsoft refers to this drive as "just another disk drive."

Here is how an on-the-fly file-compression program works: Suppose that you started with only one logical volume on your hard disk. It showed up as drive C. Then you got Stacker or SuperStor and had that program "double" the size of your disk. After doing so, you find that you have what appears to be a drive C with about twice the capacity of the original drive C, and you also appear to have a very small drive D.

That situation is the illusion. The reality is that you still have the same, single physical volume on your hard disk. But within that volume you have one very large file with its attributes set to hidden, system, and read-only. This file is created and maintained by the file-compression device driver. After the device driver (and perhaps an associated swap program) has done its job, that file appears to you and to DOS as if it were your drive C. The leftover space on your original drive C now appears as your drive D.

To boot your computer, some essential files must exist in the uncompressed portion of your hard drive. Specifically, these files are the hidden system files (IO.SYS and MSDOS.SYS, or IBMBIO.COM and IBMDOS.COM, depending on the brand of DOS you are using), CONFIG.SYS, the file-compression program (STACKER.COM or SSTORDRV.SYS), its associated swap program (SSWAP.COM or DEVSWAP.COM), and any device drivers that your CONFIG.SYS file specifies shall be loaded before the swap program runs.

Part II: The SpinRite Companion

All the rest of the files referenced in your CONFIG.SYS file, the command interpreter (normally COMMAND.COM, but it could be NDOS.COM or 4DOS.COM), the AUTOEXEC.BAT file — and all the files referred to in it — need to be compressed inside the big hidden system file that will become your new drive C.

As soon as the file-compression device driver loads, it will create a fictitious drive D out of the contents of the hidden system file. When the swap program runs, it will fool DOS into thinking of that new, fictitious drive as drive C and the original C as drive D.

DOS 6 and DoubleSpace do this same job, but they do it in a subtly different way. You need to understand the difference before you can understand how to use SpinRite correctly in a PC with DoubleSpaced drives.

The DBLSPACE.BIN file is the "engine" that does the file compression, and it also does file letter swapping. The system files (IO.SYS and MSDOS.SYS) load the DBLSPACE.BIN file before the CONFIG.SYS file is read. The drive letters are also swapped before looking for a CONFIG.SYS file.

If you DoubleSpace your drive C, you will find that all of the files you normally expect to find on it are inside the CVF file. The only exceptions are the hidden system files (IO.SYS, MSDOS.SYS, and now DBLSPACE.BIN), and possibly a copy of COMMAND.COM and 386SPART.PAR, if you have a permanent swap file for Windows. Once DOS has loaded all of its own pieces into RAM, the original drive C (the host volume) becomes some other drive letter and the CVF becomes C.

Because the swapping occurs before the CONFIG.SYS and AUTOEXEC.BAT files are read and acted on, both of those files must be inside the CVF. This all sounds quite complicated. Actually it is the simpler way to go. You can use a DOS 6 disk that has been DoubleSpace compressed almost exactly as you would any disk.

The few exceptions are (1) that you can't run SpinRite on such a disk, (2) that you must use DBLSPACE.EXE and its CHKDSK and DEFRAGMENT command options (or choose those commands from the Tools menu if you run the program in its interactive mode) instead of using the DOS programs CHKDSK and DEFRAG, and (3) that a CVF file cannot simply be converted back to an uncompressed disk.

The only reason you might need to load an on-the-fly file-compression program is that maybe some of the files you need to use while treating your disk with SpinRite are only to be found inside the compressed volume. The reasons you probably don't want to load that file-compression device driver are as follows:

- You never want any unnecessary device drivers loaded.
- You can put all the files you need to run SpinRite outside the compressed volume.

Chapter 16: Advanced User's Guide to SpinRite

- You want to run SpinRite on the host volume and not on the fictitious volumes created by that device driver.

- With some compression programs (and some of the ways they can be set up), the host volume actually disappears from view totally.

The easiest, safest way to run SpinRite in such a system is to boot from a specially prepared floppy diskette that does not load the file-compression device driver. Not only will that practice avoid some of the problems mentioned above, it also means you can, for sure, see the host volume that you want to use SpinRite on. The details of how to prepare the necessary floppy diskette are covered in the next section.

The SpinRite Clean Boot Diskette Approach

The easiest, and in some ways the safest, way to run SpinRite starts by your creating a special boot diskette for the purpose. Because this floppy diskette will load DOS and any essential hard disk access drivers but will not load anything extraneous, a good name for this method is the "SpinRite clean boot diskette approach."

The idea is to create a diskette that will allow you to boot your computer and to access the hard drives that you want to test and fix by using SpinRite. Figure 16-1 shows two views of the directory of such a diskette. In Figure 16-1(a), you see what the MS-DOS Version 5.0 DIR command would show you. In Figure 16-1(b), another utility program has been used that reveals all the files that are on the disk, including the two system files, and shows the DOS attributes for each one.

The two hidden files were put on the disk and given the attributes shown when the disk was formatted by using **FORMAT /S**. The other files were copied to the disk and then given the attributes shown for them by using the DOS command **ATTRIB +R -A A:*.***. (Making all these files read-only gives a small measure of protection against their being damaged. Write-protecting the whole diskette would provide even more protection.)

In addition to the files needed to boot DOS and to run SpinRite, the DOS command CHKDSK and the SpinRite head-parking program have been included. You will learn in the next section why you want to have CHKDSK handy. The next-to-last section of this chapter explains why including the PARK program is also a very good idea.

The example SpinRite clean boot diskette shown in Figure 16-1 is particularly simple. The CONFIG.SYS contents for this diskette are shown in Figure 16-2, and the AUTOEXEC.BAT file contents are shown in Figure 16-3.

Part II: The SpinRite Companion

```
Volume in drive B has no label
Directory of B:\

CONFIG    SYS        80  11-12-92   5:45p
COMMAND   COM     47845  11-12-92   5:43p
AUTOEXEC  BAT       138  11-12-92   5:47p
CHKDSK    EXE     16200  04-09-91   5:00a
SPINRITE  COM     47473  03-01-91   2:00a
PARK      COM       505  03-01-91   2:00a
        6 file(s)      112241 bytes
                       175104 bytes free
                            (a)

Volume in drive B has no label
Directory of B:\

IO        SYS     33430  11-12-92   5:43pm   SYS HID RO
MSDOS     SYS     37394  11-12-92   5:43pm   SYS HID RO
CONFIG    SYS        80  11-12-92   5:45pm           RO
COMMAND   COM     47845  11-12-92   5:43pm           RO
AUTOEXEC  BAT       138  11-12-92   5:47pm           RO
CHKDSK    EXE     16200   4-09-91   5:00am           RO
SPINRITE  COM     47473   3-01-91   2:00am           RO
PARK      COM       505   3-01-91   2:00am           RO
        8 File(s)      175104 bytes free
                            (b)
```

Figure 16-1: The SpinRite clean boot diskette approach to using SpinRite interactively (two versions of the disk directory).

You will notice that there are no device drivers loaded in the CONFIG.SYS file. None are needed for access to most hard disks. And the cardinal rule for creating the CONFIG.SYS and AUTOEXEC.BAT files for a SpinRite clean boot diskette is: If you don't need it, don't use it!

Now that you know why to create a SpinRite clean boot diskette, you may be wondering exactly what steps you need to take. The accompanying sidebar spells out all the steps for you.

```
FILES   = 20
BUFFERS = 20
```

Figure 16-2: The CONFIG.SYS file for the SpinRite clean boot diskette.

Chapter 16: Advanced User's Guide to SpinRite

```
@echo off
echo.
echo          Clean Boot Diskette - AUTOEXEC.BAT file
echo.
PATH=A:\
PROMPT CLEAN BOOT: Directory = $p $g
```

Figure 16-3: The AUTOEXEC.BAT file for the SpinRite clean boot diskette.

You also can use the SpinRite clean boot diskette approach to semiautomate running SpinRite in different ways for different purposes. In the next section, you will learn how to use the program interactively. The section after that explains how to use SpinRite from a batch file. You could add a menu and several SpinRite batch files to your SpinRite clean boot diskette, which would make it simple to command SpinRite to do whichever task you wanted (a very simple example is shown in this chapter in the section "An example of batch file usage").

What if you are using Stacker or SuperStor? Only run SpinRite on the host volume, not on the fictitious drives created by the file-compression program. The best way to be sure that you do this is simply not to load the file-compression device driver (and, of course, not to run the associated swap program) when you plan to run SpinRite. To make that approach work, you will have to be sure that you keep CHKDSK, SPINRITE, and any other program files you want to use with SpinRite in the uncompressed portion of your hard disk or on your SpinRite clean boot diskette.

If SpinRite finds problems on the disk in a region that is part of any hidden system file, it will point out that there is a problem there, but it will not move the data to any safer place. SpinRite limits itself in this way to prevent any possibility of moving a copy-protected program's key files and thus rendering that program unusable.

A detailed description of how to deal with this situation can be found in the tip in the section "Moving data to safety" in Chapter 14.

Part II: The SpinRite Companion

> ### How to create a SpinRite clean boot diskette
>
> 1. Boot your system as usual.
>
> 2. Put a blank floppy diskette into drive A.
>
> 3. Use the DOS command **FORMAT A: /S /V**. This command will format the diskette and put the essential DOS files on it. (The /V parameter is optional but nice; it causes FORMAT to prompt you for a volume label for this diskette.)
>
> 4. Copy CHKDSK.EXE (or CHKDSK.COM — the file extension depends on the version of DOS you are using) from the C:\DOS directory to the floppy diskette.
>
> 5. Copy SPINRITE.COM and PARK.COM from the SpinRite diskette to your new SpinRite clean boot diskette.
>
> 6. Examine the CONFIG.SYS file in the root directory of your C hard disk. See whether it has a line that says DEVICE= followed by DMDRVR.BIN or possibly SSTOR.SYS or HARDRIVE.SYS. There may be a path shown in front of the device driver name; for example, the line might be DEVICE=C:\DRIVERS\SSTOR.SYS.
>
> If you have such a line in your C drive's CONFIG.SYS file, you must create a CONFIG.SYS file for your floppy boot diskette. Use your favorite text editor. (If you use a word processor, be sure to save your work as a pure ASCII text file. If you are not sure you have done so, you can check your work by using the DOS command **TYPE**
>
> A:CONFIG.SYS when you finish. If you can read what it shows you and there are no extraneous "garbage" symbols, you have a pure ASCII file.)
>
> 7. Put the DEVICE= line in the CONFIG.SYS file on the floppy, but leave out the directory path — so that the line reads, for example, DEVICE=SSTOR.SYS. Also, remember to copy the device driver itself (the SSTOR.SYS or DMDRVR.BIN file, for example) to the floppy diskette.
>
> An optional enhancement would be to add an AUTOEXEC.BAT file that will run SpinRite with your own options automatically. (The command-line options for SpinRite are described later in this chapter.)
>
> Now try booting your computer from the floppy boot diskette (by putting the diskette in the drive and restarting the machine). You should get an A> prompt (or whatever your AUTOEXEC.BAT file on the floppy specified for the prompt). Do a **DIR** listing on each of your DOS logical volumes (drive letters). If you can do that and see all the files you are accustomed to seeing, you are set. Write-protect the floppy boot diskette so that it cannot easily have its files altered. Boot from this diskette whenever you want to run SpinRite.
>
> One more tip: Make a DISKCOPY of this diskette and keep it in some other building. That will help keep you from losing this valuable tool to fire, theft, or just ordinary human error.

Using DOS's CHKDSK First

SpinRite works with your hard disk on several levels. Sometimes, at the lowest level, it gets down and dirty with the bits, looking behind ECC to see what really can be read. At other times, it views your disk at a much higher level, above the organization imposed on your data by DOS. Here, it cares about the grouping of sectors into clusters and clusters into files, and here it must also find and sometimes change directory entries.

Chapter 16: Advanced User's Guide to SpinRite

To give SpinRite the best chance of doing wonderful things for you, it is important that you run the DOS program CHKDSK first.

Why CHKDSK is needed

Despite its name, CHKDSK, which stands for "CHecKDiSK," does not really test your disk. Its job is to check on the consistency of the DOS organization of the files in a DOS partition.

When you create a file on your disk, DOS must perform two independent functions — create a directory entry for that file and allocate space for it. It accomplishes the latter task by putting special markers in the file allocation table (FAT).

Chapter 10 gives many more details about this process. The section "How clusters become 'lost' and related problems" describes one way that it can go awry.

CHKDSK primarily looks to see whether the information about files contained in the directories is consistent with that in the FAT. You also can use it to check for file fragmentation. If CHKDSK finds a problem, you probably should fix it before you run SpinRite.

What CHKDSK can tell you

You can run CHKDSK in several ways. Depending on which method you choose, you may get different messages from it. The messages you need to attend to most closely are those you get when you run the program straight, without any command-line parameters.

At the DOS prompt, type **CHKDSK** and press Enter; or, after the name, you can add a logical volume designator (for example: **CHKDSK D:**). Either of these commands will tell CHKDSK to perform its most basic tests for consistency between the FAT and the directories.

The optional parameters are /V and /F. If you add /V to the end of the command line, CHKDSK will list all the files on the disk. If you add /F, it will attempt to fix anything it finds that it thinks is wrong. *You don't need the first parameter, and the second one can sometimes be positively dangerous because not all its "fixes" are right.*

One other option you might use with CHKDSK is to include a file specification — either an explicit one, or one including some wildcard characters — after the drive designation. For example, you might type **CHKDSK *.***. This command would tell CHKDSK to report on any fragmentation in the files on the current DOS default drive but only on those in the current DOS default directory. To check on fragmentation on *all* the files on that drive, you would have to repeat this form of the command in each subdirectory.

The most common message says CHKDSK found some number of lost clusters in some number of chains. The next most common message informs about report cross-linked files. Various other messages report on less common but potentially more serious problems.

What CHKDSK might do for you

CHKDSK can help you in several ways. Perhaps the most common benefit is recovering lost space on your hard disk. When chains of clusters become lost, the space they represent is literally unavailable. No file can use the space for new data storage, and you can't access any data that is already in that space. Whether you ask CHKDSK to convert the lost chains into files or simply let it erase them, the space they represent becomes accessible once again.

Often, the files CHKDSK recovers are not usable, especially if you let a lot of lost chains accumulate on your hard disk. After you have looked at the recovered files (named FILE*nnnn*.CHK, where *nnnn* is a number starting with 0000) and have seen whether any of them is your only copy of some important data, you may find yourself simply deleting them. But on the chance that one of them may contain an unexpected gem, I suggest you do let CHKDSK convert the lost chains to files each time.

The next major benefit that CHKDSK can deliver is when it is able to help you find a file you thought you had lost irretrievably. If you run an application program that creates a new file, put a lot of data into it, and then — before you are able to (or remember to) save that file and exit from the application program — your computer hangs, you may think all your hard work was lost forever. Sometimes that's not the case.

When this misfortune happens, you reboot your computer, go where you had planned to have the newly created file, and when you do a DIR command, you don't see any evidence of the file. Your heart sinks. But wait! You remember reading this section of *Hard Disk SECRETS,* so you run CHKDSK and it tells you it has found at least one lost chain. (For the following directions, I assume CHKDSK found only one lost chain, and if you run CHKDSK often enough, that is the most likely case.)

If — and this is a very important if — the *only* message from CHKDSK is about lost chains, you can simply rerun CHKDSK, this time adding the /F parameter. When it asks, you tell it to convert the lost chain to a file. Your file is now back from oblivion.

The file will not have the name you intended; you may never have gotten the chance to tell your application program what that name was going to be. Nor will the file be in the subdirectory you had intended. Instead, it will be in the root directory, and its name will be the uninformative FILE0000.CHK.

Look inside that file. If the recovered file seems to have the data you intended it to have, give it the name you intended and move it to the place you intended to keep it. The chances are very good that you have recovered a fully usable file.

An excellent tool for looking at these, or any files you want to examine, is the LIST program. You can find a copy of this shareware program on the *Hard Disk SECRETS* disk included with this book.

The length in the directory will be wrong because CHKDSK must round up the actual length to the next multiple of a complete cluster. Quite possibly, that will be fixed the next time you work on the file with your application program. Even if it isn't fixed, usually the few extra bytes of irrelevant stuff (which could be anything that has passed through the DOS disk buffers recently) at the end of your file will not be a serious problem.

What CHKDSK might do TO you

CHKDSK is pretty good at spotting certain problems with the file structure of your disk. It is much less capable for fixing most of them. About all it is safe to let CHKDSK do is fix chains of lost clusters. If CHKDSK reports many cross-linked files, unreadable subdirectories or FAT, or any of several other messages, you would be well advised to seek a second opinion. Run some other utility program that excels at disk file-structure analysis, such as the Norton Utilities Disk Doctor.

If you don't heed this advice, you may turn a problem into a disaster. CHKDSK can completely mess up your file structure far worse than it was if it should get a confused picture of what is wrong.

How to use CHKDSK safely

Here are the steps to safely use CHKDSK. Follow them, please, every time you plan to run SpinRite. Even better, follow them every time you boot up your computer. (Put **CHKDSK** on a line by itself in your AUTOEXEC.BAT file.)

1. Run CHKDSK without any parameters.

2. It may stop after reporting problems and ask your permission to fix them. Because you did not use the /F command-line parameter, you did not give it real permission, so it is okay to answer Yes at this stage. CHKDSK will act as if it were fixing things and then tell you what would have happened if it had. Don't worry, it didn't really do anything to the data on your disk.

Part II: The SpinRite Companion

Power user tricks need constant updating

The MS-DOS Version 5 CHKDSK will not stop to request confirmation when it finds errors, unless you have specified the /F "authorization to fix" parameter. That's too bad because the CHKDSK program also does not generate an ERRORLEVEL. The result is that there is no really easy way to check within your AUTOEXEC.BAT batch file to see whether CHKDSK found anything wrong and thus let you take care of the problem before going on to whatever else you want that batch file to do. There are ways around this problem, involving some fairly arcane batch file tricks.

The essential idea is to redirect the output of CHKDSK to a disk file and then examine that file with the FIND command, looking for the character string error (which will occur no matter what kind of error CHKDSK finds and will not occur if it finds none). Redirect the output of the FIND command to a file. If any errors were found, this output file will have some messages in it. Otherwise, it will be a zero length file. Use the DOS command COPY to copy it to another name. Because the COPY command won't copy zero-length files, this last file will exist if and only if CHKDSK found at least one error. All these steps, including detecting the existence or nonexistence of the final file, can be done in a batch file.

Finally, in DOS 6, CHKDSK is able to generate an exit code (which sets the ERRORLEVEL) so that you can test in a batch file whether CHKDSK found anything amiss on your disk. In this case, even though it won't stop and prompt you if it finds an error (and the /F parameter was not specified), you can force the batch file to stop and ask the user what to do next — or your choice of response to the existence of an error in the file allocation table and directory structure of your disk can be programmed in.

---

3. If CHKDSK reports no problems other than some lost chains of clusters, go to step 4. Otherwise, stop and get a second opinion from another disk utility. (If you are in a batch file at the time, you will have to press Ctrl-Break — possibly several times — until you get a prompt asking Terminate batch file (Y/N). Press Y.)

4. Rerun CHKDSK with the /F parameter. When it asks for permission to fix things, say Yes. This time, it will create a bunch of files in the root directory with names like FILE0000.CHK, FILE0001.CHK, and so on.

5. Look at the contents of these FILE*nnnn*.CHK files. (Use the LIST program from the *Hard Disk SECRETS* disk.) The files may turn out to be readable text, a gobbledygook of strange and unreadable symbols, or a mixture of the two.

6. If one of these files resembles a file you have been missing, rename it and move it to an appropriate subdirectory. If you don't recognize the file or its contents look like garbage, simply delete it.

7. At this point, you will have recovered some formerly inaccessible portion of your disk and maybe some valuable files as well. More important, you will have verified that nothing worse is wrong with your disk's file organization.

After completing these steps, you are ready to have SpinRite diagnose and treat your disk. If you stopped at step 3, you will have to do something else first to deal with the problems you have uncovered. For specific suggestions of what to do for each possible CHKDSK error message, refer to any good book on DOS or the manual of whatever other disk utility program you choose to use.

When You Can't Fix the Problems

Normally, you will not want to run SpinRite unless CHKDSK gives your disk a clean bill of health from its perspective. Exceptions to this rule include a situation in which your disk is unreadable in some critical areas. CHKDSK may tell you it cannot read the FAT or some subdirectory, or it may say it cannot change directories.

If you *cannot* find a way to fix these problems easily by using some other tool, SpinRite may do the job. *You run some risk by using SpinRite on a disk CHKDSK says is messed up, but sometimes there is no feasible alternative.* With a bit of luck, you may find that all your problems magically vanish after SpinRite's ministrations.

The Norton Utilities Calibrate program in Version 5.0 incorporates tests that do what CHKDSK does and go a little bit further. (For example, CHKDSK will ignore a circular chain of clusters in the FAT, though that clearly is not a proper situation. Calibrate will catch this problem.) Unfortunately, if those tests don't give your disk a complete okay, Calibrate will simply refuse to do anything. If your FAT is unreadable, its refusal could be most unfortunate. SpinRite's willingness to proceed anyway could be your data's only hope of salvation.

Interactive Use of SpinRite

Few DOS programs are easier to use than SpinRite. If you want, you can make it do its work automatically. Alternatively, you can intervene at various points to customize its operation. Assuming that you have booted off a clean SpinRite diskette, as suggested earlier in this chapter (but without any menu batch files), just type **A:SPINRITE** at the DOS prompt. That command will start the program. Now watch the bottom line of the screen for prompts that tell you when you have to press a key.

> **TIP** To receive SpinRite report files, you probably will want to have your DOS default drive and directory be something other than A:\. You could change the drive and directory (after booting from the clean diskette but before starting SpinRite) by typing **C:**, pressing Enter, and then typing **CD SPINRITE** and pressing Enter. (This assumes you have a C:\SPINRITE directory in which you want to keep your SpinRite report files.) Then type **A:SPINRITE** to start the program.

Part II: The SpinRite Companion

In this interactive mode of operation, SpinRite prompts you before it proceeds to the next step, giving you the option of modifying how it will execute that and following steps. You also can choose some options in the noninteractive, or batch, mode by specifying certain command-line parameters. In the interactive mode, you choose most of these options by selecting item 3, Alter SpinRite's Operation, from the main menu.

Whether to low-level reformat

The first option (Perform Low Level Formatting) on the Alter SpinRite's Operation submenu allows you to suppress low-level reformatting. One reason you might sometimes choose this option is if you have trouble giving your PC peace and quiet for the amount of time SpinRite requires to run all its tests. You may want to test your disk extensively without reformatting and then return and do a quick reformat. The first option gives you the control you'll need for this situation. This example is discussed further near the end of this chapter.

Should you let bad clusters become good?

The next option (Return Good Clusters To Active Use) lets you turn off another of SpinRite's features. A capability unique to SpinRite, this feature returns to full service sectors and clusters that were formerly marked as bad. It will do so only if you have allowed SpinRite to test the disk at the very deepest level and then only if it finds that the sectors in question are now performing perfectly. In that case, Gibson says, he sees no reason not to let you use the sectors — but you can turn off that feature here if it bothers you.

When to perform the seek test

SpinRite needs to be able to place the heads over the tracks of any cylinder it wants with absolute assurance. To this end, it tests the head-positioning mechanism extensively. This test is vital to perform the first time you run SpinRite on any drive.

If you have run SpinRite on a given drive many times without detecting any problem, you may want to skip this test. The third option (Perform Seek Reliability Testing) on this menu allows you to do so.

On a slow drive, it can take several minutes to do the seek test. If you run the test in interactive mode, you will have to be on hand to interact with the program at later stages of its operation, so you may want to skip this test. Likewise, if you have two DOS partitions on a single drive, remember that SpinRite tests the head-positioning mechanism for the whole drive at once, not just for a particular partition. If you use it on both partitions, one right after the other, you may well want to skip the seek testing for the second partition.

The remaining options on this menu are more often invoked when running SpinRite from a batch file. The section "Batch Mode Operation" later in this chapter covers these options.

Choose a pattern-testing depth

Because it is so important, SpinRite forces you to choose the pattern-testing depth every time you run the program, automatically bringing up a menu of pattern testing depths. You have four possible choices: none, a little, substantial, or complete pattern testing. In Chapter 13, you learned that these levels impose 0, 5, 43, or 82 test patterns on each sector in the DOS partition. The more testing you do, the more likely it is that SpinRite will detect every problem there may be with your disk and controller. The tradeoff is that more thorough tests take more time.

Only when the five basic patterns are applied in all their shifted variations will SpinRite be able to catch all surface defects. This is what Depth 4 (82 pattern) testing does.

The Depth 3 test (43 patterns) will catch most but not all defects. The Depth 2 test (5 patterns) will exercise the read/write circuitry and other aspects of the drive and controller but will have only a relatively poor chance of catching surface defects. (It still will do a better job than any read-only disk testing program such as Disk Test, which is the name of the relevant program in the Norton Utilities Version 4.5 or earlier, or Norton Disk Doctor, which is the name of the relevant program in the Norton Utilities Version 5 or later.)

The first time you run SpinRite on a new disk or controller, you should choose the deepest level of pattern testing, which applies the test patterns in all their shifted variations. Later on, you may not need that same level of assurance, so you may choose to run SpinRite at a lower level of pattern testing to save time.

Whenever you are going to change the sector interleave value on your disk, you definitely should choose the deepest level of pattern testing. SpinRite will default to Depth 4 testing in that case.

> **CAUTION:** Using Depth 4 pattern testing is important because when you change the sector interleave value, you are moving data from one location on the track to another. You may possibly be about to move some good data to a bad sector. Running the deepest pattern tests essentially prevents you from making that mistake.

When you are not changing the sector interleave value (and hence not running the risk of relocating data to a bad sector), SpinRite will default to Depth 3 pattern testing (43 patterns) to save you some time. Gibson provided Depth 2 (5 patterns) testing as a minimal test for those who aren't willing to spend very much time on testing.

Part II: The SpinRite Companion

You should choose the Depth 1 pattern testing (none) only if you have done some deeper-level testing on this partition recently. An example is the procedure recommended in the last section of this chapter for dealing with an environment in which your PC gets bumped or jiggled from time to time.

Create a report

Whenever SpinRite finishes one of its operations, you have an opportunity to create a report. In fact, you can even create a report on an operation you have just interrupted and then create another one when the operation is finished.

To create a report, you must return to the main SpinRite menu and select item 4, Print Full Operations Summary. Choosing this item brings you to a submenu, which presents the following options:

- Add a Title Block to the Report
- Send the Report to a Disk File
- Send the Report to a Printer

Adding a title block is optional, but it may help you remember why you ran this particular operation at this time. You may want to include the date, because that is not otherwise a part of the report, especially if you are going to print the report (rather than save it in a disk file, which would at least have a DOS file-creation date on it). Alternatively, if you run SpinRite from a batch file, you can have that batch file add a couple of lines to the report file for you, recording the current date and time.

If you choose the Send the Report to a Disk File option, the program will offer a default filename of SPINRITE.RPT. If you accept this name, SpinRite will write the file to the current DOS default drive and directory. This is the reason I suggested previously that you may want to be in a subdirectory where you keep such reports, before starting SpinRite.

TIP You are allowed to edit the suggested name, and you can even change the drive or directory to which the report will be sent. The program limits you to a total of 49 characters for the report name, including the path, but that should be adequate for most users. If you really want to put your report file in a subdirectory that is so deep that the pathname plus the filename exceed 49 characters, simply put it temporarily somewhere closer to the root, and after you exit SpinRite, move the report file to wherever you want to keep it.

Note two important differences between the SpinRite report file and its Detailed Technical Log file. The first has to do with where the file is placed and what it is called. The second is an important caution about overwriting the information.

Chapter 16: Advanced User's Guide to SpinRite

Although Spinrite proffers the name SPINRITE.RPT and suggests placing it in the current DOS default directory, you may choose whatever name and location you want for the report file. The program always calls the log file SPINRITE.LOG and always creates it in the root directory of the partition being tested.

If you accept the default name for the report file or choose one you had used previously, the new report file will replace the earlier one. On the other hand, SpinRite always appends to the Detailed Technical Log file. If you want to keep an on-going record of all operations performed by SpinRite, you will have to choose a series of unique names for the report files.

You also can choose to print the report and not save it in a disk file. Choosing the Send the Report to a Printer option will create a one- or two-page report with a *form-feed character* at the end of each page. Your printer must be able to print straight ASCII text, and it must be attached to a parallel printer port.

> **TIP:** You can print a report to a printer on a serial port, but you have to do it a special way. Select the option to send the report to a disk file, but when prompted for the name, use the DOS device name for the port (that is, **COM1:** or **COM2:**). If you have a PostScript printer that only understands PostScript code, your printer will be unable to print the report directly. In that case, use the option to create a disk file and print it later by using your word processor.

Something you can't do interactively

Although it might seem that the interactive mode of SpinRite would give you the absolute maximum amount of flexibility in controlling the program, there is one thing it can do in batch mode that it cannot do in interactive mode.

One way to manage the SpinRite report and log files

Here is a suggestion for some file-naming conventions that may help you keep track of what you have done with SpinRite. Each time you run SpinRite, accept the default name for the report, SPINRITE.RPT. As soon as you have finished that one process, exit SpinRite. Now rename the file to conform to some pattern you have chosen (and perhaps move it to some other directory). For example, you can name your files to show which partition was being tested, numbering them in serial order: SPINRITE.C01, SPINRITE.C02, SPINRITE.D01, and so on.

You may allow the SPINRITE.LOG file to grow in size each time you run SpinRite on that partition. Alternatively, after each operation, you can copy that file to the subdirectory that holds your SpinRite report files and give it a name that matches the associated report filename. For example, you can have log files SPINLOG.C01, SPINLOG.C02, SPINLOG.D01, and so on.

Remember to delete the original log file \SPINRITE.LOG after creating the copy of it. Otherwise, your next log file will include the log of the last session as well.

Part II: The SpinRite Companion

When you run it interactively, it offers you a list of partitions to test. They will be described as `C: on First Drive`, `D: on Second Drive`, and `E: on First Drive`. There may be up to ten partitions listed. It is entirely possible, although not highly likely, that you have more than ten DOS partitions. To get SpinRite to test one of them if it is not listed as a choice, you need to make that partition the DOS default drive and then run SpinRite in batch mode, which leads directly into the next topic.

Batch Mode Operation

Additional incentives to run SpinRite in its batch mode include the fact that you may not want to sit there waiting for each prompt if you plan to accept all of SpinRite's defaults anyway. Or, you may want to run SpinRite, not necessarily with its default actions, as a part of a larger batch file.

Your choices and their default values

The usual way to start SpinRite is to type **SPINRITE** and press Enter. (Of course, you may have to give a drive or path if SPINRITE.COM is not in the current directory or one listed in your current DOS PATH definition.) If you want, after typing **SPINRITE** and before pressing Enter, you can type some command-line options, which are words that tell the program how you want it to operate this time.

Remember to separate the program name from the first option, and each option from the next one, with one or more spaces. You may enter the options with any mixture of upper- and lowercase letters, in any order, but all on one line.

The command-line options fall into three groups. The first group includes commands that are fundamental to batch mode operation. The next set concerns various aspects of how SpinRite does its work. The last group simply affects how SpinRite appears or sounds.

In all cases, SpinRite assumes that you do not want the effect of any option you do not include. The one exception is the option to choose the depth of pattern testing. That option and its default value are described later in this section.

Fundamental command-line options

The most fundamental command-line option is BATCH. This option tells SpinRite that you want it to do its work without asking you for any further input.

The other fundamental option is AUTOEXIT. This option tells SpinRite that when it is finished, it should give control of your PC back to DOS. If you invoke SpinRite from within a batch file, this option allows the batch file to proceed with the rest of its actions. If you don't use AUTOEXIT, SpinRite will return to its main menu when it finishes its operations.

Functional command-line options

If you want to create a report file, you must include the option AUTOREPORT. This option will force the program to create a file named SPINRITE.RPT, which it will place in the DOS default drive and directory. The file will not include a title block. You cannot direct this report to the printer automatically. Of course, you can copy it to the printer in a subsequent line of a batch file.

The option to choose the depth of pattern testing is the only one that has alternative forms. You can specify DEPTH1, DEPTH2, DEPTH3, or DEPTH4, or you can opt not to specify a depth. These depth numbers correspond to using 0, 5, 43, or 82 test patterns on each sector. When you do not specify a depth, SpinRite will choose DEPTH4 if the operation it is about to do will include changing the interleave value; otherwise, it will choose DEPTH3.

SpinRite provides no option to choose the interleave value. SpinRite will automatically choose whatever it determines to be the optimum value if it is redoing the partition's low-level format.

You would not be wise to specify a depth of less than 4 unless you are sure SpinRite will not be resetting the sector interleave in your partition. SpinRite won't do that if one of the following conditions is true:

- If the sector interleave value is already set to the optimum
- If the hardware does not permit low-level formatting
- If you explicitly command it not to do low-level formatting (with the NOFORMAT option)

By not specifying a depth or by insisting on DEPTH4, you will be sure not to reset the sector interleave value without the full protection of the deepest level of pattern testing. (One exception to this rule is covered in the last section in this chapter.)

The LEAVEBAD command-line parameter tells SpinRite that you do not want it to return formerly bad sectors to full use, even if they test out perfectly. This option is the default unless you are testing at DEPTH4.

You can force SpinRite not to do any low-level reformatting by using the NOFORMAT option. You might want to choose this option if you are specifying DEPTH2 or DEPTH3 pattern testing. The section "When to perform the seek test" earlier in this chapter explains why you may not want to do so. Use the command-line option NOSEEKTEST to force SpinRite to skip that part of its testing.

There used to be a PERSTOR option, only available in the original SpinRite in its Version 1.1. Its purpose was to assure compatibility with some of the earlier PerStor hard disk controllers. More modern versions of SpinRite know how to recognize and adapt to those controllers without a need for you to specify a special command-line option.

The QUICKSCAN option forces SpinRite to do its read-only test of the partition, which is the minimum test it can do. QUICKSCAN will not move any data and is always safe to use, but it also prevents SpinRite from delivering the full benefits it has to offer.

The last of the functional command-line options is RESUME. This option tells SpinRite that if it finds an interrupted process, it should resume the process. If SpinRite resumes an interrupted operation, it will ignore all current command-line options other than RESUME and instead it will use the options that were chosen at the time that process was begun.

You can safely add the RESUME command-line option in a batch file, knowing it will finish off one interrupted operation each time that batch file is run. The rest of the command-line options in that batch file would take effect only if SpinRite had no interrupted operation to finish.

Cosmetic command-line options

Adding the word BLANKING to the command line will force SpinRite to blank the screen as soon as it starts a quick surface scan, pattern test, or low-level format operation. This condition is never necessary, but it will protect your monitor from possibly burning in a pattern from the SpinRite screen display. You can force SpinRite to unblank the screen at any time by pressing B. Pressing B again will reblank the screen. (The "blank" screen actually displays a small, moving box that announces that testing is under way.)

The NOCOLOR, NOSHADING, and NOSOUND options do just what you would expect. The first two may be useful if your computer has a gas plasma or liquid crystal display (common on laptop computers) or a monochrome monitor connected to a color display card. The last one suppresses the sound effects. Your coworkers may ask you to choose this one.

You can get a quick recap of these possibilities by using the SPINRITE ? command. You can get more extensive help by running the SPININFO program.

Chapter 16: Advanced User's Guide to SpinRite

An example of batch file usage

Figures 16-4 through 16-8 show much the same information as Figures 16-1 through 16-3 for a slightly different boot diskette (see Figure 16-4). In this case, the AUTOEXEC.BAT file runs a menu, and two other batch files help the user run CHKDSK and SpinRite.

```
 Volume in drive B has no label
 Volume Serial Number is 0AE8-1371
 Directory of B:\

CONFIG    SYS        76  11-14-92    4:25a
DMDRVR    BIN     10509  08-10-89   12:00p
COMMAND   COM     47845  04-09-91    5:00a
AUTOEXEC  BAT       147  11-14-92    4:58a
MENU      BAT       559  11-14-92    6:03a
CHK       BAT       478  11-14-92    6:03a
SR        BAT      2654  11-14-92    8:33a
CHKDSK    EXE     16200  04-09-91    5:00a
FIND      EXE      6770  04-09-91    5:00a
PARK      COM       505  03-01-91    2:00a
SPINRITE  COM     47473  03-01-91    2:00a
       11 file(s)      133216 bytes
                       151552 bytes free
                        (a)

 Volume in drive B has no label
 Directory of B:\

IO        SYS     33430   4-09-91    5:00am  SYS HID RO
MSDOS     SYS     37394   4-09-91    5:00am  SYS HID RO
CONFIG    SYS        76  11-14-92    4:25am          RO
DMDRVR    BIN     10509   8-10-89   12:00pm          RO
COMMAND   COM     47845   4-09-91    5:00am          RO
AUTOEXEC  BAT       147  11-14-92    4:58am          RO
MENU      BAT       559  11-14-92    6:03am          RO
CHK       BAT       478  11-14-92    6:03am          RO
SR        BAT      2654  11-14-92    8:33am          RO
CHKDSK    EXE     16200   4-09-91    5:00am          RO
FIND      EXE      6770   4-09-91    5:00am          RO
PARK      COM       505   3-01-91    2:00am          RO
SPINRITE  COM     47473   3-01-91    2:00am          RO
       13 File(s)       151552 bytes free
                        (b)
```

Figure 16-4: Running SpinRite from a clean boot diskette with a device driver and some special batch files (directory listing).

Part II: The SpinRite Companion

> **TIP**
>
> You can and perhaps should do better. The example batch files shown in this book are just that: examples. They may not be quite what you need to use on your PC. This is not a book on DOS and batch file programming, so I cannot go into all the possible ways in which you could elaborate or improve these batch files to make them more suitable for you. (For example, you could add a great deal more checking of the user input to assure that only valid entries are accepted.) If you don't understand what these batch files do or exactly how they do it, don't worry; you don't have to use them at all. Or, you can use them without understanding how they work. If you copy them faithfully (including every period and space exactly as shown), they should work just fine — even though possibly not as well as some more customized version would.

Notice that in this case, the CONFIG.SYS file loads a device driver, DMDRVR.BIN (see Figure 16-5). This program is the Disk Manager that allows access to all the DOS volumes in an extended partition created by Disk Manager — just an example of the sort of device driver you need to use on some PCs.

This AUTOEXEC.BAT batch file runs a MENU.BAT file (see Figure 16-6). These files demonstrate several things. First, by including an option to run CHKDSK and listing that option first, the batch file suggests that choosing this first might be a good idea. Indeed, that choice is a very good idea. On the other hand, this batch file technique doesn't force the user to follow the suggestion.

You are able to run SpinRite no matter what CHKDSK may have reported — and that capability can be vital at times — but please remember that it certainly is better not to do so if you can fix the problems with your disk's FAT and directory structure first.

These files set a minimal path, define a prompt, present a simple menu, and exit to DOS. Now you can type the name of one of two batch files to do the two items listed on that menu (CHK runs CHKDSK and SR runs SpinRite).

Both the CHK and SR batch files can take one or more parameters to tell them how to do their work. The first parameter in both cases must be the DOS logical volume that you want to test (in this example, only drives C and D are permitted).

```
FILES    =    20
BUFFERS  =    20
DEVICE   = A:\DMDRVR.BIN
```

Figure 16-5: The CONFIG.SYS file from this diskette.

Chapter 16: Advanced User's Guide to SpinRite

```
@echo off
echo.
echo   Clean Boot SpinRite Batch File
Diskette
echo              AUTOEXEC.BAT file
echo.
PATH=A:\
PROMPT Directory = $p $g
CLS
MENU
```
(a)

```
@echo off
rem                    MENU.BAT
echo.
echo   Choose one of the following menu options:
echo.
echo             CHK   -   Runs Checkdisk
echo.
echo             SR    -   Runs SpinRite
echo.
echo   You must also give at least the letter of the
echo   DOS logical volume that you wish to check.
echo   With the SR batch file you may specify a
echo   depth of testing and a directory in which to
echo   put the report and log files and an extension
echo   to give them.  Valid depth values are 0, 1, 2,
echo   3, or 4 (0 or unspecified = default depth).
echo.
echo.
echo   Sample:   SR  C  4  C:\SPINRITE  C01
echo.
```
(b)

Figure 16-6: The AUTOEXEC.BAT (a) and MENU.BAT (b) files from this diskette.

The CHK.BAT file also accepts up to three additional parameters, which it passes to CHKDSK without any validity checking or alteration (see Figure 16-7). You could, for example, add /F to tell CHKDSK to fix whatever it sees as needing fixing. (Please read carefully the section earlier in this chapter "What CHKDSK might do TO you" before you let it have this permission!)

```
@echo off
echo.
echo       CHK.BAT - Runs CheckDisk on C or D drive.
echo.
rem   If no drive was specified, return to the menu.
IF %1.==. goto alldone

IF %1==c goto DoC
IF %1==C goto DoC
IF %1==d goto DoD
IF %1==D goto DoD
rem   If you get here your drive choice was invalid.
goto alldone

:DoC
CHKDSK C: %2 %3 %4
goto alldone

:DoD
CHKDSK D: %2 %3 %4
goto alldone

:alldone
pause
rem   Return to the A drive and display menu once
more.
A:
CLS
MENU
```

Figure 16-7: The CHK.BAT file from this diskette.

The SR batch file accepts as its second parameter a single numeral to specify the depth of testing that SpinRite is to use (see Figure 16-8). The only valid values are 0, 1, 2, 3, and 4. In this batch file, 0 is used to signal that you don't want to tell SpinRite what depth to use; you want to let the program choose whatever it deems suitable. You don't have to have any second parameter. If you don't put a numeral here, or put in an invalid choice, the batch file does the same thing as if you entered a 0 for the default depth.

Chapter 16: Advanced User's Guide to SpinRite

```
@echo off
echo.
echo     SR.BAT - Runs SpinRite on your choice of drive
echo     (C or D) and with your choice of DEPTH and puts
echo     reports where you choose and named as you choose.
echo.
rem   If no drive is specified, simply quit.
IF %1.==. goto alldone

rem   Validate drive choice (and exit if it isn't C or D)
IF %1==c goto DoC
IF %1==C goto DoC
IF %1==d goto DoD
IF %1==D goto DoD
rem   If you get here your drive choice was invalid.
goto BadDrive

rem   Change to drive the user specified. Check for .log,
rem   .tmp, and .rpt files. If any one is found, give up.

:DoC
C:
cd \
IF exist \SPINRITE.LOG goto IsFile
IF exist \SPINRITE.RPT goto IsFile
IF exist \SPINRITE.TMP goto IsFile
goto GetDepth

:DoD
D:
cd \
IF exist \SPINRITE.LOG goto alldone
IF exist \SPINRITE.RPT goto alldone
goto GetDepth

:GetDepth
rem   Store starting time in SPINRITE.TMP file.
echo.                         >  SPINRITE.TMP
echo. | date | find "Current" >> SPINRITE.TMP
echo. | time | find "Current" >> SPINRITE.TMP
echo.                         >> SPINRITE.TMP

rem   Find out user's choice of depth (0 = default depth)
IF %2==0 goto DefDepth
IF %2==1 goto Depth1
IF %2==2 goto Depth2
IF %2==3 goto Depth3
IF %2==4 goto Depth4

:DefDepth
A:\SPINRITE BATCH AUTOREPORT AUTOEXIT
goto CleanUp
```

This figure continues on the next page.

Figure 16-8: The SR.BAT file from this diskette.

```
:Depth1
A:\SPINRITE BATCH DEPTH1 AUTOREPORT AUTOEXIT
goto CleanUp

:Depth2
A:\SPINRITE BATCH DEPTH2 AUTOREPORT AUTOEXIT
goto CleanUp

:Depth3
A:\SPINRITE BATCH DEPTH3 AUTOREPORT AUTOEXIT
goto CleanUp

:Depth4
A:\SPINRITE BATCH DEPTH4 AUTOREPORT AUTOEXIT
goto CleanUp

:CleanUp

rem    Add the date and time of completion.
echo.                              >> SPINRITE.RPT
echo.                              >> SPINRITE.RPT
echo. | date | find "Current" >> SPINRITE.RPT
echo. | time | find "Current" >> SPINRITE.RPT

rem    Then check to see if the user specified a location
rem    and extension for the SpinRite report and log
files.
rem    If so, create them; if not, exit.

IF %3.==. goto alldone
IF %4.==. goto alldone

COPY \SPINRITE.LOG %3\SPINLOG.%4
COPY \SPINRITE.TMP + \SPINRITE.RPT %3\SPINRITE.%4
IF exist %3\SPINLOG.%4 del \SPINRITE.LOG
IF exist %3\SPINRITE.%4 del \SPINRITE.RPT
IF exist %3\SPINRITE.%4 del \SPINRITE.TMP
goto alldone

:BadDrive
echo   You entered an invalid drive letter (must be C or D).
pause
goto alldone

:IsFile
echo   Processing of this drive will not be done by SpinRite.
echo     SPINRITE.LOG, SPINRITE.TMP, or SPINRITE.RPT exists
echo     in the root directory of %1:

:alldone
rem Return to A drive and display menu once more.
A:
CLS
MENU
```

This figure is continued from the previous page.

Figure 16-8 (continued): The SR.BAT file from this diskette.

Chapter 16: Advanced User's Guide to SpinRite

> **CAUTION:** The SR batch file is quite fussy about what parameters you enter and in what order. The first one must be the letter of the DOS logical volume to be treated. The second one, if it is present, must be the depth specifier. You must either specify a third and fourth parameter or not specify either.

The third and fourth parameters to the SR batch file are used to tell it where to put the log and report files and what extensions to append to their names. For example, you may specify C:\SPINRITE as the directory to contain those files and specify that the file extensions be D01 to indicate the first time you ran SpinRite on your drive D. That means that you would be creating the files C:\SPINRITE\SPINLOG.D01 and C:\SPINRITE\SPINRITE.D01. No error checking is done, so you must be sure that the directory path and file extension you specify are valid ones (and that the specified directory exists).

The SR batch file also shows one way to add the date and time to the report file. (The log file has the date and time put in it by SpinRite automatically.)

Finally, notice that as a small bit of protection, the SR batch file will not run if a SPINRITE.LOG file or a SPINRITE.RPT file already exists in the root directory of the drive it has been asked to test. If you are at all facile with batch file programming, you can, and probably should, do much more testing than that.

If you want to pursue this approach, the sky is the limit. You can add all manner of features to help make the batch files run more safely, even if they are invoked at 3 a.m. by someone who is more or less oblivious to any warning messages that might appear on the screen. A couple of small suggestions: You also might choose to log to some other directory than the root on the drive you are testing; just be sure that you select a directory that exists. You might also test for the existence of the report and log files in the final target directory with the specified extension before you begin running SpinRite.

Getting Around Some Limitations

Batch mode is useful, and if you have more than 10 DOS partitions, it is the only way you can use SpinRite on any of them past the first 10. All you need to do is log to the partition you want to test and then run SpinRite with the BATCH command-line option. Remember to add any other options you might want because you won't get another chance. If you don't include AUTOEXIT, however, you will get a chance to create a report after SpinRite finishes the operation and returns to its main menu.

What Is Head Parking?

Each time you read or write any information from or to the hard disk, the heads have to be positioned over the cylinder holding that information. Normally, the heads stay there until you tell them to move elsewhere.

Parking the heads moves them away from your valuable data. With some drives, this actually means moving the heads completely off the disk surfaces. For most drives, though, the manufacturer specifies a *landing zone*, which is a cylinder at or near the innermost reach of the head-positioning mechanism. Positioning the heads in the landing zone is what most disks do to park the heads. Figure 16-9 shows both strategies for head parking.

Moving the heads to a landing zone on the platter is easy. Building a mechanism that can safely move the heads all the way off the platters — and get them safely back onto the platters when you are ready to use the disk once more — is much tougher. Moving the heads all the way off is, however, much safer. Certain disk drives are built this way, especially some removable ones that are intended to survive relatively rough treatment when they are being transported from one PC to another. Tandon's AdPac is an example of such a drive.

Because parking the heads is usually nothing more than a seek to a specially chosen cylinder, you automatically unpark the disk the next time you ask it to seek to some other cylinder. And that is something you (or DOS) must do before it is possible to read or write data there.

The truth about hard disk head parking

In the early days of PCs, when hard disks were expensive, users were advised to protect their disks by "parking the heads" every time they shut down their computers. IBM did not want to intimidate users of its first PC/XT (which was introduced as a home computer). They actually provided a program to park the heads, but they called it SHIPDISK and only told customers that they needed to run that program before shipping the computer somewhere, not before each time the computer was turned off.

The best policy on parking the heads on the hard drives in your PC is to do it not only every time you turn the machine off, but any time you are going to leave the machine idle for more than a very few minutes. (You will learn why this is so in the section "Some horror stories" later in this chapter.)

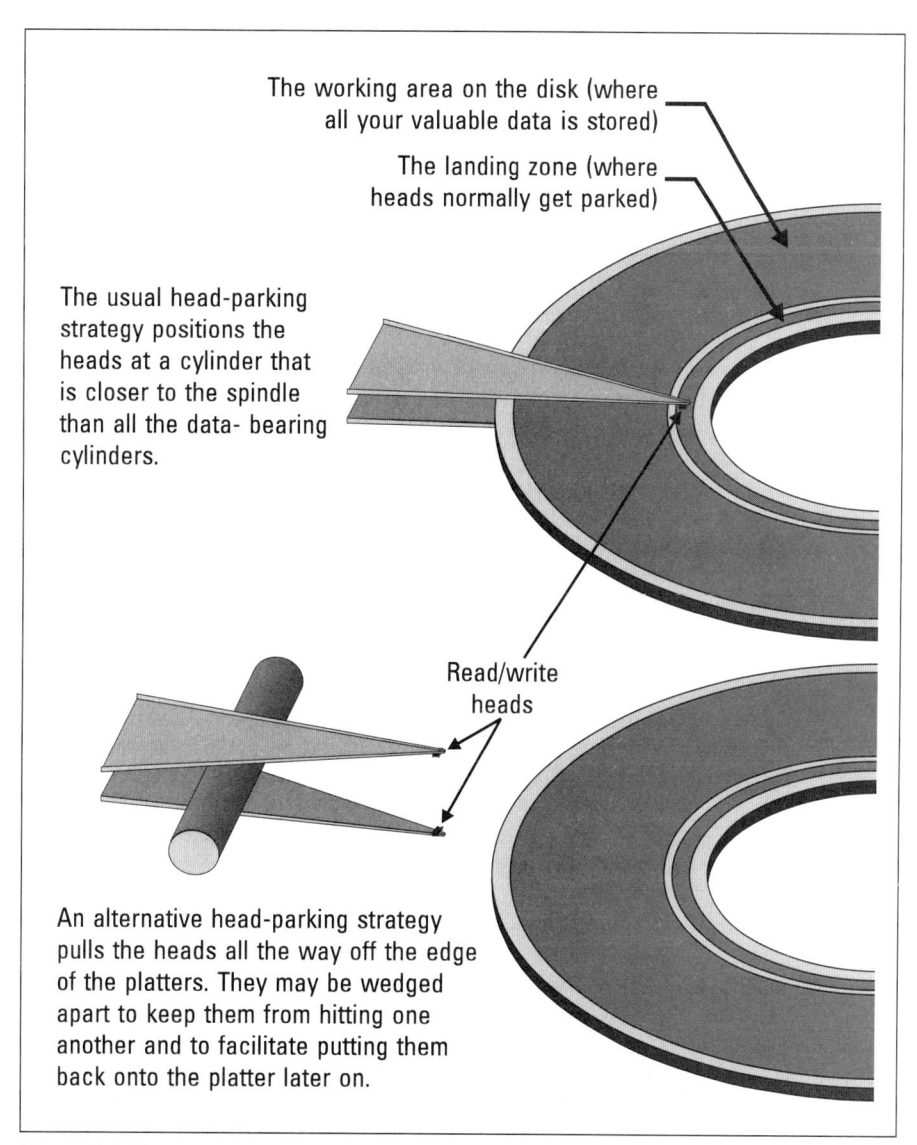

Figure 16-9: The two principal hard disk head-parking strategies.

Some horror stories

When SpinRite was under development, Gibson asked many people to help test it, keeping careful track of their experiences. One thing he noticed repeatedly was that their SPINRITE.RPT files would show whole regions of C symbols on

Part II: The SpinRite Companion

the Track Map. These results indicated regions of their disks where correctable errors were happening. Running SpinRite corrected those errors, but Gibson wondered what their source was. His testers informed him that the regions in question contained their most-used and most-valued files.

Upon further investigation, he concluded that the magnetic signals for data could become corrupted by having the heads land on them. When you turn off power to your PC, the hard disk stops turning. The heads, which have been surfing on a thin film of rushing air, sit down on the disk platter surface.

Almost all early PC hard disks used stepper-motor head positioners. (See the section on steppers and servos in Chapter 4 for more on these positioners.) With those drives, the heads sit down on whatever cylinder they last had been ordered to find.

When you turn on your PC, the disk starts to turn and the heads start to fly. But first the heads will very likely engage in some quite erratic behavior. They may jerk to one side. They also may have small surges of current go through their windings.

These unscheduled head activities will very possibly reverse one or more bits, or perhaps only weaken them. The details of what happens are not very well known. What is clear, though, is that whatever data damage does occur will happen wherever the heads find themselves. In the case of the early SpinRite testers' disks, that was often right on top of their most-used, and usually also their most-valuable, files.

Gibson's response was to write a program that would safely park the heads well away from the user's valuable data. The user must remember to run this program before shutting off the PC, but that is a significant improvement over not being able to protect your data at all. This program, or a descendent of it, is included with every copy of SpinRite.

Self-parking drives

More modern PC hard drives mostly use servo head positioners. These drives are nearly all self-parking, which means that when power is removed from the drive, it will automatically do one of three things: (1) Seek to a track very near the spindle; (2) force the heads all the way in toward the spindle (against some mechanical stop); or (3) pull the heads out all the way off the platters. If you are not sure whether yours is a self-parking drive, you should use a head-parking program, but be sure it is a safe program. (How to get a safe park program is explained later in this chapter.)

Chapter 16: Advanced User's Guide to SpinRite

Sometimes there is an easy way to determine whether your drive is self-parking: Listen to your drive. When you turn off power to the PC, if you hear it go "thunk," or maybe even "thunk" followed by "chunk," it is very likely a self-parking drive. (The thunk is the parking. The chunk could be the sound of a locking pin dropping into place to hold the heads safely against the spindle or off the platters.) You also can consult the manufacturer's manual on your hard drive, which you can get from the manufacturer or distributor of that brand of drive. (Computer retail dealers usually do not have these manuals, but you generally can get one from the manufacturer, for free, simply by asking.)

Some disks that are self-parking will park the heads only when you turn off the PC. Others will park the heads anytime you don't access the disk drive for more than some fixed time period. The latter strategy is much safer than the former, but, unfortunately, it also is much less frequently used by drive manufacturers.

Unless your hard disk parks itself each time you don't access the disk for a short time, you would do well to park it yourself anytime you plan to leave your PC for some time while it is turned on. This strategy guards against the possibility of someone accidentally jarring the computer or knocking it to the floor, which could force the heads to contact the disk surface briefly. If they are already safely parked in the landing zone, even if they do bang the surface, the heads will not damage your most recently accessed file.

Furthermore, a parked head may not crash when an unparked one would. Consider the facts. Parked heads are near the spindle (or off the platter altogether). The disk platters are much like cymbals, which flex when they are struck. Parked heads normally are resting where the platters cannot flex much, and so a head crash is less likely to occur even when the disk is jarred.

> **TIP:** Many people wonder whether it would be better to turn off the PC each time they are going to walk away from it, or whether they should leave it turned on. This issue has proven to be controversial. There are some good arguments on each side. Overall, the consensus of the experts seems to be that your PC will last longer and work better if you don't turn it off several times a day. Many experts even recommend never turning off a PC, or at least not unless it will be unused for several days (such as over a long holiday weekend). Whether or not you choose to turn off your PC at night, you still will want to park its hard drive's heads at lunch or any other time you walk away from the machine. Running a combination head-parking and screen-saving program will protect your data, your hard disk, and your monitor.

> **DISK:** The program DAZZLE on the *Hard Disk SECRETS* disk will both park your hard disks and put on your screen an amazing variety of patterns (which makes it a good screen saver). Depending on your computer's speed and the quality of its video display subsystem, you may find that this program becomes one of your favorites — not only for the security it helps provide for your data, but also for its entertainment value.

Conversely, it can be such a strong attractor/distractor that your visitors or colleagues may force you not to run it or to turn down the brightness of the monitor when you do. They may find themselves unable to talk or listen to you — instead finding themselves mesmerized by the ever-changing display on your PC's screen!

Head-parking programs

"OK, now I realize that I should park my drives. How do I do it?" The easy answer for SpinRite users is to run the PARK.COM program you will find on your SpinRite disk. There are many alternative park programs as well. Many IBM PCs come with a version of SHIPDISK.COM. Some PS/2s come with PARKHEAD.COM, and many bulletin boards boast a plethora of park programs.

Steve Gibson created what he believes is the safest of the safe park programs. He bundles this program with SpinRite, and every time you exit from SpinRite to DOS, he has it display a message reminding you to park your hard drive heads. The Gibson park program, PARK.COM, is included on the *Hard Disk SECRETS* disk. Gibson wants everyone to protect their data. To help, he has said anyone may freely give away copies of his program.

Gibson Research operates a bulletin board from which you or anyone may download a free copy of the SpinRite PARK.COM program. The number is 714-362-8848. Set your communications program to 8 data bits, 1 stop bit, and no parity. You may call at any speed up to 2400 bits per second.

Not all the head-parking programs are equal. The next several sections describe what distinguishes a good head-parking program from a less adequate one from those that are actually dangerous.

Safe park programs

A safe park program will not ask your disk drive to do anything it would not normally do in the course of everyday operation. In particular, it should ask the drive to seek to a cylinder that exists.

The hard disk parameter table for any drive contains an entry that ought to point to a safe place to park the heads. PS/2 computers have a special BIOS function to enable you to park the heads (INT 13h, Function 19h).

For most PCs, using one of these two approaches will succeed. For a few, it is necessary to choose the largest-numbered cylinder on the drive. (To get that cylinder, use the BIOS call "Get Drive Parameters," INT 13h, Function 8.)

Any program that picks some actual cylinder near the spindle and positions the heads there should be perfectly safe to use.

Impolite park programs

Many park programs are not very polite. After you run them, they will beep at you incessantly until you turn off power to the PC. Other park programs are not quite that bad but still are not what I regard as user friendly. These programs inform you that they have parked the heads and also that they have halted your PC. Now you can't use it for anything until you have either turned off power or pushed its reset button (if your PC has a reset button).

The reason these programs behave this way is clear: they want to keep you from inadvertently unparking the heads by accessing any file on the disk. The reason this response is not so wonderful is that you are very effectively punished for using one of these programs anytime you end up not wanting to turn off the PC. (How many times have you started to shut down your PC and then said to yourself, "Oops, I wasn't through. I need to do..."? If you are like most of us, that has happened many more times than once.)

> **TIP:** Don't ever turn off your PC and then turn it right back on again. If you have gone as far as actually clicking the power switch off, let the PC come to a full stop before you start it up again. Wait at least 20 or 30 seconds.

Some power supplies (including most that IBM used in its PCs) have a time-delay relay built into them to enforce this good advice. Most PC power supplies do not. You have to remember this good advice and follow it.

If you don't follow it, you may not notice anything bad happen right away, but you are putting quite a strain on the hard disk and perhaps some other parts of your PC. Also, in some PCs, switching off for just an instant will cause the data in their CMOS configuration memory to become scrambled. If you ever have that happen to you, the effort necessary to recover from that glitch will probably teach you the wisdom of following the advice in this tip.

Destructive park programs

Some park programs are positively dangerous to some drives. Avoid these programs. They depend on an assumption about hard disk drives that once was usually true but now is false more often than not.

On a drive with a servo-controlled head positioner, the assumption made by these programs can be fatal. If you run such a program on a vulnerable drive, you will hear it repeatedly slam the head assembly against the stop until eventually something breaks.

A typical hard disk with a stepper-motor head positioner often can have its heads moved in a bit farther than the highest numbered cylinder the manufacturer tells you about. Eventually, the positioner will hit a mechanical stop and go no farther. No damage is done by asking it to step in at that point. It simply will not move. (Your machine will make a disconcerting groaning sound, but the program will do no harm.)

Part II: The SpinRite Companion

When the only drives available for PCs used stepper motors, someone came up with what was supposed to be a very clever strategy. Rather than depending on the BIOS report to determine how many cylinders a drive actually had, the drive would be asked to go in until it could go no farther. That was supposed to be a clever strategy. Unfortunately, that clever programmer was outsmarted, and the resulting head-parking program became a horrible danger to some drives.

Hard disk controllers have a designed limit. They will not go to a cylinder number higher than what they have been told is the maximum cylinder count. Normally, that number is set by the BIOS, based on the numbers in the hard disk parameter table. But by creating a dummy hard disk parameter table, pointing to it with INT 41h or 46h, and using INT 13h, Function 9, you can fool the controller. You can tell it the drive has any number of cylinders you want. Then you can tell it to seek to any cylinder number up to that maximum number.

The controller may not check to see which cylinder it gets to when it seeks. (That behavior is commonplace with most ST412/ST506 controllers used with stepper-motor MFM and RLL drives.) The controller may only check the track that the heads are over when you next ask it to read or write some data. Even then, it will not tell you which cylinder it is on. It will simply give you an error if it cannot find the sector you want. Because it does check all three dimensions of sector addresses (cylinder, head, and physical sector number), that is a way for it to find out when the heads are over a wrong cylinder.

The authors of the dangerous park programs (and I don't know who they were) apparently used this technique to force the disk controller to move the heads in, many cylinders at a time, until the controller reported that an error had occurred the next time it tried to read a sector in the target cylinder. This message indicated it had failed to reach the target cylinder. Next, the program moved the head in by smaller steps. This pattern continued until the controller was unable to move in even one cylinder without an error, meaning that the head was parked at the mechanical stop.

This strategy depends on the controller being able to step the drive's head assembly a given number of cylinders further in, independent of where it is. That is exactly what older, stepper-motor drives attached to MFM or RLL controllers do. For them, and them only, this sort of park program is safe to use.

A servo-controlled drive can only seek to cylinders for which it has a pre-recorded servo track. You cannot ask it to go in several cylinders without it figuring out what cylinder number you are requesting. Asking it to find some cylinder past the range of those prerecorded ones causes great grief.

Chapter 16: Advanced User's Guide to SpinRite

First, the head will move to about where the drive thinks it should go. At least it will try to go there. In the case of seeking to a cylinder well past the last one, it will slam very hard into the mechanical stop. Now, not finding the servo information to indicate that it is where it should be, the drive controller will order a recalibration — a seek to the outermost cylinder. After it has done so, it will again attempt to find the requested cylinder. This process will repeat, moving the head all the way out and then slamming it all the way in (and then some), over and over until the drive breaks.

You have no easy way to be sure how any given park program was written, unless you have access to its source code or its programmer. The safest approach is to use a program you trust. The one that the manufacturer provided with your computer should be fine. SpinRite's PARK program on the *Hard Disk SECRETS* disk is also safe to use on any PC.

Resident park utilities

The one notable weakness of the best parking programs is that you must remember to use them. A resident park program takes care of this weakness automatically when you leave your computer idle for a while, and a self-parking drive does so when you turn off your PC.

Some computers run for hours without needing to access their hard disks. Then suddenly, they must. Then more hours go by until they do again. One example is a computer running a bulletin board program that does not get very many calls. It may be on 24 hours a day but only be used a few times each day. There is no operator present to park the disk, but the data on the disk would be much safer if its heads were parked all the times that the disk is not actually in use.

For such a computer, a timed-parking program can be a blessing. This is a park program that can be loaded into RAM as a terminate-and-stay resident (TSR) program. It will monitor the disk activity, parking the heads whenever the hard disk has not been accessed for several minutes.

Many such programs are available on various BBSs. They generally work as advertised, and they are fine if you have that special situation. Most PC users don't need them, however. Like all TSRs, they take up some of the precious first 640KB of system RAM. Worse, they may cause conflicts with other TSRs or with other programs you need to use.

The program TIMEPARK.COM on the *Hard Disk SECRETS* disk is this sort of TSR head-parking program. It works well with most bulletin board software, but it is also known to cause conflicts that can make a PC hang if it is resident and you attempt to run the TAPCIS program. (TAPCIS is a popular shareware program that is designed to help automate calls to CompuServe.)

Part II: The SpinRite Companion

Remember that even if you have a resident park utility installed, you still must park the heads manually before turning off power. Alternatively, you can be careful not to use the drive for the length of time it takes to trigger the automatic parking action of the resident utility and then turn off power (unless yours is a self-parking drive).

Hints and Tips

This section offers a reminder of some essential things to remember to do, along with a brief description of a special situation in which you might want to use SpinRite a bit differently than usual.

Some things to remember, always

First, back up your hard disk. Backups are always a good idea, but never so much so as when you are about to let some program work with your data at the low level used by SpinRite. You can get away without backing up before rerunning SpinRite, although the best advice is always to be fully backed up.

Next, run CHKDSK before you run SpinRite — every time. Only proceed to use SpinRite if you get a clean bill of health from CHKDSK or if you cannot fix the problems. (See the previous section "When You Can't Fix the Problems" for more on this situation.)

Third, run SpinRite in a clean system. That may mean booting the computer off a special clean SpinRite boot diskette. Or, you can just change your CONFIG.SYS and AUTOEXEC.BAT files appropriately each time. (See the section in this chapter called "The SpinRite Clean Boot Diskette Approach" for the details.)

Fourth, leave the PC undisturbed while SpinRite does its work. Even a gentle bump can make the heads bounce sideways briefly. If that should happen during a low-level format operation, it would create a wavy track.

An unusual way to use SpinRite

This section suggests a situation in which you might want to use SpinRite in a manner quite different from those described up to this point. Suppose that you want to use SpinRite on a disk that is in a PC which gets jostled fairly frequently. What do you do to avoid the creation of wavy tracks when SpinRite reformats the disk?

Chapter 16: Advanced User's Guide to SpinRite

If you just run SpinRite at the deepest level of pattern testing and with authorization to redo the low-level format, it will do all of its work with one track and then proceed to the next track, and the next, and so on. The actual moments at which the tracks are being low-level formatted are very brief and quite widely spaced in time.

It may not be feasible to protect your PC from being jostled for the whole time that SpinRite needs to completely surface test your disk (which could easily be many hours). But you might be able to protect it for just a few minutes.

Run SpinRite twice. First, let it do the deepest possible pattern testing, but *don't* let it do any low-level formatting. In the process, it will at least mark the bad spots in the FAT. (SpinRite cannot at that time mark the sector headers of the bad sectors because it is not redoing the low-level format.) Among other things, your hard-to-read data may be recovered and moved to safety. This process includes the full suite of pattern tests and could take all night.

When that process is complete, rerun SpinRite and this time tell it to do no pattern testing and let it redo the low-level format. At this time, it will realign the tracks to the path of the heads. Because this process takes only a few minutes, you can stand guard over your PC the whole time.

It might not be your disk

If you get a vast number of errors, especially correctable ones, consider the possibility that you may have a loose cable. Another possibility is that the hard disk controller is slightly crooked in its slot. Open the case, remove the cables, and then put them back in. Remove the controller and put it back in. And maybe your hard disk controller is flat out dead or dying. (See the section "Simple things that sometimes go wrong" in Chapter 11 both for some *important warnings* and some suggestions on how to fix these and some other problems.)

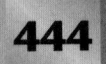

Part II: The SpinRite Companion

Summary

- SpinRite is very easy to use without any special instructions. It can do more for you if you understand all that you can command it to do, and it can do those things more easily if you learn how to use batch files to automate it (at least partially).
- Run CHKDSK before you run SpinRite. Run CHKDSK without any command-line parameters. (In particular, don't issue the command CHKDSK /F until after you have used the simpler CHKDSK by itself to see what it proposes to do to your data.) Fix any problems CHKDSK uncovers (if you can) before you run SpinRite. (Sometimes you cannot fix the problems, and then, just maybe, SpinRite may do it for you.)
- The best single thing you can do to help SpinRite work its wonders most effectively and with the least chance of any problems is to create a SpinRite clean boot diskette. The instructions for creating that diskette are in this chapter.
- *Always* park your hard disk's heads. Do so *every* time you stop using the hard disk for more than a very few minutes. Do so even though you are *not* planning on turning off your PC. (Also a good idea: run a screen saver program.)
- Beware of dangerous head-parking programs. The worst ones literally can kill a servo-controlled hard drive in minutes.
- One park program you can be sure is safe is Gibson's PARK.COM, a copy of which is on the *Hard Disk SECRETS* disk, and which is also available for free from the Gibson Research BBS.

Appendix A

Genesis of a Product: How SpinRite Was Born

"If you have drive — and I was lucky enough to be born with incredible drive and focus — you soon learn that you can teach yourself anything. Then you try anything. And you find you can do almost anything." That is Steve Gibson's explanation of how he got to be who he is today.

It helps to be born into a supportive family. Steve's father was educated as a mechanical engineer. He shared with his son a love for how things go together and how they work. Gibson developed a fascination with electronics at the age of five. For the next decade he immersed himself in activities like disassembling surplus radar gear and in reading every book or magazine he could find on the subject. From this and similar experiences, he gained a deep understanding of how things are assembled and how they really function. He calls this understanding essential to his ability to create innovative products.

The next major influence in Gibson's life was Harold Fearon, his electronics teacher at Aragon High School in San Mateo, California. In addition to teaching Steve many valuable lessons, Mr. Fearon gave him the opportunity to design the curriculum for and teach two years of advanced electronics classes. Also while in high school, Gibson found physics and computers — discoveries, he said, that "opened up my world."

During the next several years, Gibson found more mentors and role models, many at the Stanford Artificial Intelligence Laboratory. At the Stanford AI Lab, he worked on some cutting-edge projects in computer design, including the very first interface to the world's first laser printer.

He enrolled at the University of California. He did very well in his studies. In his sophomore year, however, he learned that if he tried to patent a novel processor he had invented, the Regents of the University of California would own all rights to it because he was a student at a tax-supported institution. Gibson thought this situation was unfair and, with financial difficulties at home and a summer employer wanting him to stay on, he left formal education.

Gibson continues a lifelong habit of "paying close attention to things and being intensely interested in them." He credits this habit with his ability to learn the many skills he has needed in his diverse jobs. He has served as a software and hardware designer, marketing director, and in other roles in several companies. He created his own advertising agency, but he finally found his niche as a creator of products for personal computers.

When Gibson bought his first Apple II computer, he missed the light pen he had used at the Stanford AI Lab. In 1982, a light pen wasn't available for microcomputers, which presented a business opportunity Steve could not resist. He created the Gibson LPS-II (Light Pen System for Apple II computers). Acclaimed by reviewers, the LPS-II sold very well.

One thing Gibson learned early in his business career was what he calls the "lesson of margin": If you have a good profit margin on your products, "you can eat well, drive whatever car you want, and generally have a lot of fun." Pursuing this aim has been a key part of his thinking in choosing all his product innovations.

To make and market the LPS-II, Gibson created Gibson Laboratories. Although this company was very successful, he did not enjoy the experience of managing it. After selling the company, he immediately sought another need he could fill with yet another innovative product.

Gibson began using an IBM PC with both a monochrome and a color graphics display. Horrified by the CGA's poor visual quality, he saw his next opportunity. He wrote a terminate-and-stay resident, or TSR, program called FlickerFree that would remain resident in the PC's memory to improve the CGA display's performance. Although not the first TSR program, it was one of the early ones. Creating it was no simple task.

Rather than establishing a large company again (and taking on the resulting management headaches), Gibson produced and sold FlickerFree from his home, with the help of only one employee. His product was very well received. He sold it to local dealers, at swap meets, and to computer user groups, soon saturating the regional market.

He asked the editor and publisher of *InfoWorld* (a weekly PC computer magazine) to let him write a weekly column in exchange for a free quarter-page advertisement in each issue. They agreed. Thanks to the success of both the column and the advertisement, the arrangement continues today, many years later. Gibson's *Tech Talk* remains one of the most popular and widely read columns in *InfoWorld*.

Appendix A: Genesis of a Product: How SpinRite Was Born

With FlickerFree selling very well, Gibson looked for a product to follow it. He thought he might create a simple hard disk reinterleaving program, a project that he initially estimated would take two weeks. It was not to be quite as simple a task as he thought. After more than a year of hard work, he released SpinRite Version 1.0 — a much more comprehensive disk utility program than he had initially imagined.

With the success of SpinRite, Gibson and his one assistant were unable to keep up with the telephone calls, let alone do all the other work of a small business. So Gibson Research acquired an office/warehouse and several more employees. As this book goes to press, Steve Gibson and his small band of workers are busily finishing up SpinRite 3.1 After they are done with that project, they will, no doubt, go on to create even more wonders for our benefit and enjoyment.

Appendix B
The Hard Disk SECRETS Disk

What Is on the Disk?

The disk that accompanies this book contains ten valuable programs, one great information file, and a small batch file to facilitate use of the information file. Some of the programs will help you protect your hard disk (and all the valuable data it contains). Others have been included to help you learn more about hard disks — the drive or drives you have in your PC and the vast range of drives available in the marketplace.

Here is a list of the main *Hard Disk SECRETS* collection. All of these files are in the root directory of the *Hard Disk SECRETS* disk. You learn what each one can do for you, and how to use it, in the sections that follow.

```
DAZZLE    EXE   169529   12-07-92    5:09a
HDINFO    BAT       32   12-22-92   11:45p
HDINFO    TXT   327124   12-15-92    6:13a
LISTR     COM    11895   10-07-92    7:07a
MH-ESDI   EXE    50526   12-07-92   11:29p
MH-IDE    EXE    50496   12-07-92   11:25p
MH-RESTR  EXE    75616   12-07-92   11:48p
MH-SAVE   EXE    79504   12-07-92   11:39p
MH-SYS    EXE    47936   12-07-92   11:54p
MOVEHDD   SYS      395   01-04-89    2:47p
PARK      COM      505   03-01-91    2:00a
TIMEPARK  COM      477   03-19-86    1:14p
```

In addition to these files in the disk's root directory, the disk has one subdirectory called LISTPGMS. The files in this subdirectory all normally come bundled with the shareware program LIST. They are also described in the following sections.

Part III: Appendixes

```
ARCE      COM    6798   04-12-92   4:10a
ARCE      DOC   12165   04-12-92   4:10a
COLOR     PAT     236   02-03-90   7:30a
DIALER    PAT     201   02-03-90   7:30a
FV        COM    8186   10-09-92   1:41a
FV        DOC    7360   10-09-92   1:41a
LICENSE          9769   10-07-92   7:07a
LIST      COM   25103   10-07-92   7:07a
LIST      DOC   99429   10-07-92   7:07a
LIST      HST   24751   10-07-92   7:07a
LISTMOD   DOC   19472   10-07-92   7:07a
MAILER           1507   10-07-92   7:07a
PROGRAMS         9999   10-09-92   7:07a
WHATSNEW        10669   10-07-92   7:07a
```

Before explaining all the wonderful things these programs can do for you, I want to explain just what your rights and responsibilities are regarding them. These valuable programs represent many hours of effort on the part of their authors.

Most of these files have been copyrighted by their authors. (The only exceptions are PARK.COM, TIMEPARK.COM, and the HDINFO.BAT batch file. Please note that although the HDINFO.BAT file is not copyrighted, the main text file, HDINFO.TXT, is.) The copyright means that the authors have control of how you may use the fruits of their labors — an ethical, moral, and legal matter.

Freeware

The very good news for you is that most of the authors have decided to grant you a very broad license for these files. With the exception of the programs in the LIST package and the DAZZLE program, the programs on the *Hard Disk SECRETS* disk are all freeware. By that I mean that the authors have declared that you are free to use their works and you are free to give copies of them to anyone else. You are not free, however, to sell the files or alter them in any way — which specifically includes any modification that would prevent others from seeing the author's copyright and any notices they may be designed to display.

Shareware

The LIST and DAZZLE packages are shareware programs. That means that the programs are — in all but one way — traditional, copyrighted, commercial programs. You have a copy of them on this disk, but that fact does not mean that you own the right to use these programs, except in the limited manner described here.

You are, on the other hand, perfectly free to give copies of these programs to anyone you choose. The only restrictions are that you must transfer all the files in the LIST collection *together* and that you cannot sell these programs (or include them with a commercial package) without the explicit, written permission of their authors.

You are permitted to try out these programs without charge so that you can find out before you commit to buying them if they really are going to be useful to you. You absolutely don't have to pay the author anything if you don't like the product, or even if you simply think you won't be using it. (Wouldn't it be nice if everything you ever bought came with that guarantee?)

If you decide that they are anything close to as wonderful as I think they are, you will be happy to send the authors the pittance they have requested as a registration fee. When you send them the registration fee, you give the authors two very important things you really do want them to have. First, you provide them money to continue writing valuable software. Second, you give them a tangible token of your appreciation for their work, which is often as important as what the money you send enables them to buy. Also, by supporting shareware as a marketing concept you are encouraging authors to continue distributing their work in that manner.

The Programs

Here is a brief description of each of the programs on the disk. In some cases, this is all you need to know about them. In other cases, you will find additional information in a documentation file on the disk or at the end of this appendix.

DAZZLE your eyes

The DAZZLE program is several things in one package: It is a wonderfully entertaining screen-saving program. It is a hard disk head parking program. It can be used as a meditation tool, to create graphic images you can use as Windows "wallpaper," or as an entertaining interactive toy.

DAZZLE is included on the *Hard Disk SECRETS* disk because it is the only PC screen-saving program that also parks the heads on your hard disks. This combination is very useful because any time you are going to leave your computer idle for a while your data and your screen will be protected. You data will be much safer if you first park the hard disk heads, and your screen will be protected from having a constant image burned into its phosphor when you put a constantly changing image on it.

Part III: Appendixes

DAZZLE understands most PC systems quite well. It is capable of automatically adapting to the requirements and using the possibilities inherent in your particular PC's disk and video display subsystems. If, however, DAZZLE is unable to correctly sense what your system can do, you can give it some command line parameters to govern how it works.

DAZZLE is most impressive on a PC with at least a VGA-quality video display system. The images it creates are so good that Radio Shack sells a videotape of them. If your PC does not have VGA video, DAZZLE will either give you a more restrained set of graphic images, or it will simply blank your PC's screen.

DAZZLE is not a self-activating screen saver. You need to execute it explicitly. The simplest way to run DAZZLE as a screen saver and disk head parker is with a small batch file. Here is the one I use:

```
@echo off
c:\setup\DAZZLE -rwbm
```

The parameters on the command line tell DAZZLE to do the following tasks:

1. Park the disk heads [r]
2. Use the Windows defaults (see DAZZLE.DOC for details on what the defaults are) [w]
3. Operate in "bashful" mode, in which it gives you no unnecessary messages [b]
4. Create its most splendiferous and rapidly changing display (use its "mad" mode) [m]

To run DAZZLE from within Windows, you can simply create a Program Manager icon that runs the batch file.

Run **DAZZLE** with a **-Z** on the command line one time, and you will find that it creates a DAZZLE.DOC file in the current directory. Read this file (using the LIST program) or print it out. Or if you want really easy access to the documentation, just keep reading this appendix.

As you will learn from reading the DAZZLE.DOC file, you can run and use DAZZLE in many different ways. Once you have learned some of the commands you need to make DAZZLE do the things it can do, you can get a quick reminder of its options by typing the **DAZZLE ?** command.

Recently, a new version of DAZZLE was introduced as a commercial product. Called RAZZLE-DAZZLE, it adds the capability to be a self-starting screen saver that you can use whether you normally work at the DOS prompt or in Microsoft Windows, Version 3.*x*. By running this program as a TSR in your

AUTOEXEC.BAT file, you will find that DAZZLE will spring into action, parking your hard drive(s) and displaying its screen show, any time you leave your computer idle. The program returns control of the PC when it notices any keystroke or mouse action. This product is available in most stores that sell computer software.

LIST, the much enhanced TYPE command

The DOS internal command TYPE allows one to view the contents of an ASCII text file, such as AUTOEXEC.BAT or CONFIG.SYS, on your PC's screen. TYPE has some severe limitations, however, that make it awkward to use for anything but very small files.

For example, TYPE simply prints every line of the file to the screen, one after another, without stopping until it comes to the end of the file. A long file will scroll off the screen before you can read it. Furthermore, all lines that are longer than 80 characters will be wrapped (the excess length is displayed on the following line on the screen). Sometimes, you don't know if you are looking at two separate lines or simply one long, wrapped line.

TYPE stops processing a file at the first occurrence of the Ctrl-Z character (ASCII value 1Ah). This end-of-file character can occur almost anywhere within some kinds of files. Finally, the TYPE command will only display a file if you tell it the full name of that file.

Many PC users quickly get quite tired of the limitations of the TYPE command. The person who got most usefully upset (from our perspective) is Vern Buerg. He decided to make something better. He wrote LIST.COM.

Over the years, LIST has been improved many times. Still, its core value is that it displays files on your screen with unparalleled convenience. You can give LIST a wildcard filename, or you can ask it to show you a "pick list" of filenames. While displaying a file, you can scroll a 23 line, 80 column window all around the file, moving up, down, left, or right. Or you can ask LIST to wrap lines (just as TYPE always does) so that you can view all of any long lines in a file without having to scroll left or right. LIST also provides a means to search for a string of characters, with options for a case-sensitive search or one that ignores capitalization.

When you are viewing a group of files, you can jump from one file to another and back again without losing your place in any of the files. You can display program files as easily as text files, using either a normal ASCII display or one that resembles what you see when you use the DOS DEBUG d(isplay) command. The resulting display of machine instructions may not mean much to

Part III: Appendixes

you. If you are able to decipher machine code, however, having the capability to display it is invaluable. Furthermore, even if you cannot make sense of most of the bytes in a program, you probably will see some text strings within them that will make sense to you. Sometimes this way is the easiest for finding out what a program you don't know anything about would be likely to do if you were to run it.

The basic LIST program

You now have the short version of what LIST can do for you. The full story is contained in the file LIST.DOC in the LISTPGMS subdirectory. You'll find it at the end of this appendix.

All you really need to know, in order to start using LIST, is that you invoke it by typing the command name, **LIST**, at the DOS command line. If you use no command line parameters, LIST displays a pick list of the files in the current directory. Use the cursor arrows to highlight the file you want to view and press Enter. Press the F1 function key to display several screens of help. If you type a filename on the command line or a string of filenames (separated by spaces) or a wildcard filename, LIST displays the first of the specified files. Press Ctrl-PgDn and Ctrl-PgUp to move back and forth among the files included in your list or wildcard specification.

Getting fancy

Vern Buerg has continued to add features to LIST until it has become quite a complex program. To accommodate people who needed only LIST's basic file display functions and who wanted to have a smaller program that would take up less RAM, Mr. Buerg created a small version of LIST.COM, called LISTR.COM. In fact, this version is the one in the root directory of the *Hard Disk SECRETS* disk. (The full version is in the LISTPGMS directory, along with LIST.DOC and several other files.) One of the limitations in the LISTR.COM version is that if you invoke it with no command line parameters by typing **LISTR**, instead of presenting you with a pick list of files, it will just prompt you for a new filename.

The main reason that I put only the small version, LISTR.COM, in the root directory is that this version is guaranteed never to do any damage to any file. The full program, LIST.COM, will not alter a file, but it can be used to delete files. Please read about this feature carefully in LIST.DOC before you use the full version of LIST.

The accompanying files

If you get the LIST program from Buerg software or if you download it from a bulletin board, you get a collection of related utilities included in the package (or in the ZIP file). ARCE.COM and FV.COM, in the LISTPGMS directory, are separate products with separate registration fees (but only if you decide you like them and plan to keep and use them).

ARCE extracts files from an ARC file — any file or group of files that have been compressed by the Seaware ARC program or by the Phil Katz PKARC program. (ARCE does not work with ZIP files created by Phil Katz's current offering, PKZIP.)

FV is a file viewing utility. Its purpose is to display the name and attributes of files contained within files of any of a wide range of archive and library file formats. Specifically, FV shows you the contents of files with extensions ARC, ZIP, PAK, DWC, LZH, LBR, and ZOO, and from self-extracting COM or EXE files created by any of the popular compression programs.

Other files in the LIST directory include COLORS.PAT and DIALER.PAT. You can use these DEBUG script files to modify the default colors for LIST and/or alter how LIST is set up to talk to a modem. See the LIST.DOC file for details on why and how to use these files.

Finally, LICENSE, LIST.HST, LISTMOD.DOC, MAILER, PROGRAMS, and WHATSNEW are all text documents that you easily can view using LIST.COM. With these files, you can learn something about the history of LIST, details on how to modify the program, other programs from Buerg Software, and how to register the programs you want to keep and use.

The Micro House utilities

Micro House is a publisher of both technical reference materials and programs. The company also has a great deal of experience in solving people's hard disk problems via the telephone. The Micro House principal reference products are *The Micro House Encyclopedia of Hard Drives, The Hard Disk Technical Guide, The Encyclopedia of Main Board,* and *The Network Interface Technical Guide.* The principal software products from Micro House are DrivePro and EZ-Drive.

The Hard Disk Technical Guide is a paperbound, single-volume work that gives a great deal of information about specific hard drives. After you learn all about how hard disks work from *Hard Disk SECRETS,* you can learn which companies make what models of hard drive with the particular dimensions and other parameters you may be seeking by looking in the *Hard Disk Technical Guide.*

The Hard Disk Encyclopedia contains much the same information, in even greater detail. When you purchase it, you buy a subscription for one copy of the three-volume encyclopedia, initially, and for updates at regular intervals.

The Encyclopedia of Main Boards is a six-volume paperback with several thousand 8 ½" x 11" pages giving details on all the different brands and models of PC motherboards. *The Network Interface Technical Guide* is a single paperback volume with about 1,000 pages of details on all the interface cards on the market.

Each of these reference works includes a brief introduction to the subject it covers, including diagrams of what typical parts look like, meant primarily to make sure that the reader understands the meanings the authors attach to the jargon and pictures contained in the books. Read other sources (like *Hard Disk SECRETS*) to learn the full details of how the listed devices actually work.

DrivePro, the principal Micro House software product, is a tool for hard disk installers that makes it possible to prepare and set up a new hard disk in a PC in a fraction of the time and with a fraction of the effort normally spent on those tasks. DrivePro is particularly useful for IDE drives but can work with MFM and RLL drives (ST506/ST412 interface), ESDI drives, and SCSI drives. It includes a database covering nearly all the hard drives sold for PCs since 1984.

EZ-Drive is essentially a subset of DrivePro that is specifically focused on making installation of new IDE drives a snap. It has some interesting options, one that gives you the effect of a custom-drive type for PC's whose motherboard BIOS doesn't offer that feature and another that helps defend against boot sector-infecting computer viruses.

Micro House also has developed a suite of helpful utility programs — the programs that are included on the *Hard Disk SECRETS* disk.

MH-ESDI and MH-IDE

MH-ESDI and MH-IDE are designed to enable you to learn more about the hard drives in your PC. These programs are essentially identical, except for their names and some of the text they display. The differences are because the programs get information from an ESDI or IDE (more precisely, an IDE/ATA) drive by asking the drive to identify itself. The calls to get this information are the same for both types of drive, but the interpretations of the answers from the drives do differ in some details.

You must know, therefore, whether yours is an IDE/ATA or an ESDI drive so that you can run the appropriate utility program. If you do not know what drive type you have, you won't do any harm by running the wrong program — but don't expect the program to inform you of your mistake. If you try running either of these programs on an SCSI or ST506/ST412 interface drive, the program simply will report that it cannot get the drive to provide the answers necessary for the program to display the information it is designed to display.

Like all the Micro House utilities, these programs will give you a brief help screen if you invoke them with **/?** or **/H** as the only parameter on the command line. They will accept three other parameters: **/M** or **/C** to force monochrome or color output and **/U** to force the program to use the disk dimensions in the hard disk parameter table (HDPT) instead of using an INT13h call to get them. Normally, you won't need to use any of these parameters when you run the program.

When you start either of these programs, you first get a screen of information telling you what the program can do for you. Press the Enter key to go the main report screen. At that point, press F1 for a description of each field on the report screen or press F2 to send a copy of the report to a file.

MH-SAVE and MH-RESTR

The preceding pair of programs simply tells you about your hard disk. This pair of programs can actually save you from losing access to your disk and its data.

MH-SAVE understands eight places where information that might be vital to disk access is kept in your PC. It can save any or all of those regions to a file. You can use MH-RESTR to put the data in that file back into the places it came from, offering the option of doing so for all eight places or for only a specified subset of the eight. Furthermore, MH-SAVE can do this job for both of your hard disk drives if you have two.

The eight places that MH-SAVE looks for critical data are

1. Normal configuration CMOS memory (one for the PC)

2. Extended CMOS memory (if your PC has one)

3. Master boot record and its included partition table (one per drive)

4. Remainder of the track at head 0, cylinder 0 (one per drive)

5. DOS boot record (one per logical volume)

6. File allocation tables (one per logical volume)

7. Root directory (one per logical volume)

8. Extended partition tables (one per logical volume within an extended DOS partition)

You probably recognize these locations, or most of them, from what you have read in *Hard Disk SECRETS*. If a few of the locations surprise you, read the following brief explanation of the more confusing items on this list.

Only PCs using the 80286, 386, or 486 processors have a configuration CMOS memory chip, normally. Not all of them have extended CMOS memory. MH-SAVE detects what configuration memory your PC has and saves all the information that is stored there (if you ask it to do so).

Most PCs store nothing on the track containing the master boot record except that one sector program and data file. A few use the additional sectors on that track to store some vital information. MH-SAVE can save all of that track, or not, at your option.

The two FATs in each logical volume should be identical. MH-SAVE checks to be sure that they are. If the FATs are identical, MH-SAVE saves one of them. If they are not identical, the program reports this fact and saves both of them.

By default MH-SAVE saves all the information it finds in all eight places on both the first and second physical hard drives in your PC. Because using the default can create a very large file of saved information, you have the option of selecting which parts of the information to save and which to ignore.

Notice that the information in places 1, 2, 3, 4, 5, and 8 ordinarily does not change except when you change your PC's hardware configuration, disk partitioning, or DOS version. On the other hand, the information in places 6 and 7 might very well change every day.

This information suggests a useful strategy: Run MH-SAVE and ask it to save all but the FATs and root directories. Put the resulting file of information on a couple of bootable DOS floppy diskettes along with MH-RESTR. Store one of the diskettes in a different building. The bootable floppy diskette will be enough to boot your PC and restore the information in most of the critical places. Then run MH-SAVE every day (perhaps in your AUTOEXEC.BAT file) and ask it to put the information from regions 6 and 7 into a file on another floppy diskette. This file, in conjunction with the files on the other special floppy, will enable you to recover from almost any hard disk disaster that only involves information corruption.

If you use either a DOS-provided or third-party tool to track deletions and keep a safety copy of the FAT and root directory on each logical volume, you can use those records and tools in place of the second use of MH-SAVE. No other available tools let you save all the regions 1–5 and 8 so easily as MH-SAVE.

MH-SYS

DOS includes a program called SYS. Its purpose is to transfer the essential DOS system files from one disk to another. Up until Version 5, the DOS SYS command only transferred the hidden system files (IO.SYS and MSDOS.SYS, if you were using MS-DOS, or IBMBIO.COM and IBMDOS.COM, if you were using PC DOS or DR DOS). Starting with Version 5, SYS also transfers COMMAND.COM. One of the key new features of MS-DOS 6 is its DoubleSpace compression. Essential to that program is another hidden system file DBLSPACE.BIN; starting with DOS 6, the SYS command also transfers that file.

One restriction to the DOS command SYS has annoyed many people. If you are logged to a drive that doesn't have the system files in its root directory, SYS will direct you to put a system disk in drive A, which might not be convenient. MH-SYS does everything the DOS command SYS does, and it removes this annoying restriction. In fact, MH-SYS allows you to move system files from any bootable disk to any disk no matter what drive you are logged onto. Furthermore, it moves the appropriate system files from the source disk, no matter what version of DOS the source disk may contain, and no matter what version of DOS is running on the PC at the time. Both of these capabilities extend beyond what the DOS command SYS can do.

Running MH-SYS is simplicity itself. Type its name at the command prompt, and it will prompt you for the source and destination drives. Alternatively, you can put the destination drive designation (C:, for example) or both source and destination drive designations on the command line. As usual, a /? command line parameter will result in a help screen to remind you of all these instructions.

MOVEHDD.SYS for when disk controllers put important data in an imprudent place

In Chapter 6, you learned that some autoconfiguring hard disk controllers create the hard disk parameter tables in either of two inappropriate places. Some put this information into a region of the interrupt vector table that is specified for "user defined" interrupts. Others put it into some RAM that is mapped into the CPU's memory address space in the same region as their on-board option ROM. The first choice, if you have two hard disks, is totally incompatible with the use of expanded memory. The second choice can prevent you from using as much as 16KB of upper memory that might otherwise be made available for programs to load high.

The solution to either of these (or any other imprudent location of the hard disk parameter tables) is to include in your CONFIG.SYS file a line reading `DEVICE=C:\DRIVERS\MOVEHDD.SYS` (of course you will have to replace *C:\DRIVERS* with whatever is the correct path to the directory containing MOVEHDD.SYS from the *Hard Disk SECRETS* disk on your system).

Place this line very early in your CONFIG.SYS file, before any line that refers to expanded memory (such as `DEVICE=C:\DOS\EMM386.EXE` or `DEVICE=C:\DRIVERS\EMM.SYS`). Then you can relax; this potential problem is gone. Next, try some experiments and see if you can get away with mapping memory into the same space as the hard disk controller's option ROM. Very often you can.

Steve Gibson's head parking program, PARK.COM

The PARK.COM program on the *Hard Disk SECRETS* disk is the head parking program that ships with SpinRite. This program will park the heads on both the first and second hard disks on any PC with total safety. Furthermore, it allows you to resume using the computer any time you want by pressing any key. This capability is far preferable to using a park program that insists you reboot your computer or, worse yet, that forces you to turn off the computer as soon as you have parked the hard disk heads.

Use this program, or DAZZLE, every time you are going to leave your computer for more than a few minutes. Your data will thank you for doing so. You will thank you for doing so the first time your disk gets bumped and your data survives unscathed!

Part III: Appendixes

TIMEPARK.COM, a head parking in time...

TIMEPARK.COM does only one thing, but it does that one thing very well. It watches disk accesses; when there have been none for approximately half an hour, TIMEPARK.COM parks the heads. If the PC is running an electronic remote bulletin board program, and it is seldom attended by anyone, this program can protect the hard disk during all but the times during which the bulletin board is being accessed by callers.

TIMEPARK.COM is a small TSR program. You can run it by including a line in your AUTOEXEC.BAT file that has the program's name and path on it, for example, `C:\UTILS\TIMEPARK`.

The Really Great Information File — HDINFO

Ray Martin is famous because of his hard disk information file. For several years he has been gathering information on as many models of disk drive as he can and publishing the list in a text file called HDINFO. Distributed via bulletin boards, this information file has become one of the standard reference sources for the industry.

To make using the file even easier, I have included on the *Hard Disk SECRETS* disk a small batch file, HDINFO.BAT, and the LISTR.COM program. Running the batch file causes LISTR to display the contents of the HDINFO.TXT file. You can scroll through the file, if you like, or you can jump to a particular line of interest by using LIST's search capabilities. Press the forward slash key (/) for a case sensitive search. Press the backslash key (\) for a case insensitive search. Then enter the text you want to find and press Enter. The display jumps to the first line with that text on it, with the line highlighted in one color and the search text in another. Press A to cause LIST to jump to the next line containing the same search text.

Shareware Documentation

The rest of this appendix consists of portions of the documentation for the DAZZLE and LIST shareware programs. The documentation has been formatted for presentation in this book, but the authors' own words have not been edited or rewritten. Full documentation for each program is included on the disk; for your convenience, most of the information is included here with a printed registration form for your use.

Appendix B: The Hard Disk SECRETS Disk

DAZZLE

The Ultimate Graphics Image Generator
Documentation for Revision 5.0i; 1992

©Copyright 1989-1992 Worldwide MicroTronics, Inc.

Please take the time to review this whole document as soon as possible in your use of DAZZLE. The program is far more configurable and flexible than it initially appears, and the great majority of questions that arise are addressed herein. The size of this document lends itself to being printed for easier review and reference.

Information in this document is subject to change without notice and does not represent a commitment on the part of Worldwide MicroTronics, Inc. The software described in this document is furnished under a license agreement. The software may be used or copied only in accordance with the terms of the agreement.

DAZZLE Overview

The only Screen Saver so stunning that it has been made into a Long Form Music Video!

Transform your color VGA- or EGA-equipped PC into a stunning source of computer-generated beauty. DAZZLE is a hypnotizing graphics image generator acclaimed in computer magazines as the best self-directing art program available. It fills the computer monitor with continually evolving displays that protect the screen from image burn. A popular diversion for waiting rooms, reception areas, and family rooms at home. Used in conjunction with your favorite music, there is no form of entertainment quite like it.

DAZZLE constructs breath-taking geometric images that can be used to complement desktop publishing materials, 35mm-slide and overhead design, or to create dynamic background animation for video production.

- Award-winning interactive color kaleidoscopic program that provides hours of changing visual viewscapes.

- Performance art for the eyes featuring a rich selection of drawing algorithms, fades, and special effects.

- Includes a self-directing mode which is an effective and entertaining attention-getter.

Part III: Appendixes

System requirements

- Personal computer using the 8088, 186, 286, 386, or higher processor.
- EGA, VGA, 8514/A graphics card, or compatible video graphics adapter and monitor.
- MS-DOS or PC DOS operating system version 3.1 or higher.

Enhancements

- R5.0 is the most significant "face lift" the program has ever received. The number of fades and drawing algorithms have been greatly expanded. A truly fresh interpretation of the DAZZLE vision.
- Configuration menu sets number of images and pause time in Auto mode.
- "/W" command line option for easier use with Windows (a windows screen saver is a separate product). Keyboard LEDs indicate program state and progress. The "/Z" option creates DAZZLE.DOC User's Manual. Enhanced interactive control.

Introduction

DAZZLE is an award-winning self-directing color image generator for DOS and Windows computers with EGA- or VGA-compatible color displays and adapters. Performance art for the eyes.

A source of beauty; sometimes subtle, sometimes vibrant, always changing. The image engine has numerous primary image drawing algorithms, most of which have at least two styles of presentation, many of which have multiple internal drawing variations. There is an assortment of fades, including split screens and pans, used by the imaging system for greater diversity of presentation. The entire color range of the detected video system is utilized for maximum variety and visual stimulation.

When the "Semi-Automatic" mode of DAZZLE is active, the user can play the program from the keyboard. Specifically selecting each pattern to draw, or letting the program select the pattern randomly. The selected pattern is generated for as long as the user holds the draw key. There are no limits on the mixing of image patterns. The user can then invoke a specific fade effect, or let the program select an effect randomly. The types of displays that can be generated in this fashion are far more varied, and personal, than anything that "Auto" mode ever produces.

Appendix B: The Hard Disk SECRETS Disk

There is a configuration menu that allows the customization of DAZZLE image generation. It also allows the selective disabling of various fades. This configuration information can be written to an editable text file, and either loaded again from the menu or loaded automatically at program invocation by specifying the filename on the DAZZLE command line.

An on-line HELP text window system is included in DAZZLE.

In the self-generating "Auto" mode the primary image algorithms are mixed randomly on the screen. An adjustable number of images are overlaid at a time, producing a very large assortment of possible displays. Each display remains for a while to be appreciated, then the screen is cleared via a fade algorithm, and another set of patterns is presented. Mathematically speaking, an exact pattern match might not occur for many weeks of continuous operation. Human perception is far less exacting and will discern repetition well ahead of these extremes, but the general effect is impressive and frequently surprising. Note that the starting patterns of the program will be different each time it is executed. If the program seems predictable, exit it and start it over again.

"PsL News" (713-524-6394) described DAZZLE as: the best kaleidoscope program we've seen yet. The beautiful use of colors, enhanced even further by the use of fading in and out, is, for want of a better word, awesome.

DAZZLE has received many other good press reviews, and has been awarded "Best New Graphics Program for 1990" (December 90 PsL News). There have since been complimentary reports too numerous to repeat here, my thanks to all who have been so supportive.

DAZZLE can be used in a variety of ways. At the office it keeps the screen from being burned by constant display of an unchanging prompt. Simply start the program when leaving your desk or answering the phone or otherwise diverted. One option is to start DAZZLE from a keyboard-locking program so that unauthorized access is prevented on your unattended computer until you return. Additional programs are available from Worldwide MicroTronics, Inc. that provide self-starting DOS and Windows Screen Saver capability, and optional password protection. This shareware version is NOT a self-activating memory-resident screen saver. The retail RAZZLE DAZZLE program provides full screen saver capability.

DAZZLE can be used to aid relaxation. In its slower cycling VGA modes (where this program REALLY shines) it is often soothing and helps one to shift conscious attention from the cares of the day. Various university and medical studies conducted on volunteers watching DAZZLE document a reduction of blood-pressure, general relaxation, and heightened alpha states in the brain. When overwhelmed with problems or pressures, it is often true that shifting one's focus from an immediate concern allows the objectivity needed to enhance decision-making and settle the nerves.

Part III: Appendixes

DAZZLE is a performing art realization on a computer platform. Used with your favorite music DAZZLE can be highly entertaining and regenerating. In its self-directing play mode it is great "living" mobile art.

Shareware

Shareware is a brave concept in software marketing that allows you to "try before you buy." Shareware authors retain all rights under their copyright, but allow free distribution of their programs within specified limits. Distributors of shareware — including on-line BBS and catalog outlets — usually do not charge for the shareware software itself. The distributors are charging for their own services in providing access to their resources. Registration payment directly to the author entitles the user to additional services, information, and newer products. It is a great deal for users, authors, and distributors alike. Please support this honor system marketing technique so that more great programs of increasingly professional quality can reasonably be provided via this system.

Copyright laws apply to both shareware and commercial software, and the copyright holder retains all rights, with a few specific exceptions clearly stated by the author. Shareware authors are accomplished programmers, just like commercial authors, and the programs are of comparable quality — in both cases there are good programs and bad ones! The main difference is in the method of distribution. The shareware author specifically grants the right to copy and distribute the software to all, except that Worldwide MicroTronics, Inc. requires that written permission be acquired before a commercial disk vendor may copy or distribute our products.

Shareware is a distribution method, not a type of software. You should find software that suits your needs and budget, whether it's commercial or shareware. The shareware system makes fitting your needs easier because you can try before you buy. And because the overhead is low, prices are low also. Shareware has the ultimate money-back guarantee — if you don't use the product, you don't pay for it.

You are encouraged to pass a copy of DAZZLE along to your friends for evaluation, BUT PLEASE DO NOT GIVE IT AWAY ALTERED OR AS PART OF ANOTHER SYSTEM. Please encourage them to register their copy if they find that they can use it. Businesses, BBSs, and catalog operations please note: distribution of Worldwide MicroTronics, Inc. shareware products, even free of charge, without clearly explaining to the recipient their legal requirement to register the program is strictly forbidden, and a violation of copyright law.

Usage limitation

Please note that this program is NOT FREE. You are entitled to use it for evaluation over a short time (not more than 15 days) to determine if it functions adequately for your needs, after which time a registration fee paid directly to Worldwide MicroTronics, Inc. is required by copyright law, and greatly appreciated by all of us. Any distribution or on-line fee paid by you to copy DAZZLE is (usually) not forwarded to Worldwide MicroTronics, Inc. by the distributor, and therefore would not constitute payment of a registration fee. The purchase price you paid for a book or magazine authorized to distribute this software does NOT constitute payment of mandatory registration fee. The images generated by this program are protected under copyright law.

Revision Control

Worldwide MicroTronics, Inc. is NOT responsible for revision control of DAZZLE through any source other than direct mailings from our office. If you request a copy from any other source, please be certain of the revision level that you are acquiring, and that it contains all related files and documentation.

Your registration fee for DAZZLE entitles you to one disk copy update of DAZZLE from us within the first year — at your option. It is assumed that all payments are registrations of existing copies, so disks are not automatically mailed unless the request for "order" or "update disk" is clearly identified in the letter. Many users prefer to retain their update option until the next newer release is available. PLEASE specify your floppy disk format when writing. Once you have received your update disk, additional disk updates are available at a reduced fee. Names on our mailing list will be maintained for at least 1 year from last contact unless materials are returned without a forwarding address.

Current registration fee and discounts

The registration fee for this version of DAZZLE is $15 ($20 US for customers outside the continental U.S.A. please). For those that wish to buy multiple registrations of the unmodified shareware product, the following discounts are currently allowed:

- Copies 1 through 3   Registration cost $15 each ($20 US foreign)
- Copies 4 through 8   Additional cost $12 each ($17 US foreign)
- Copies 9 or more   Additional cost $7 each ($12 US foreign)

Part III: Appendixes

Thus 12 copies would cost $133.00 (3 x $15 + 5 x $12 + 4 x $7). Discounts may be discontinued without prior notice. Multiple registrations make for a great gift idea to your computer using friends, and are wonderful around the office. This pricing is for independent registrations of multiple program copies. Worldwide MicroTronics, Inc, will provide a disk and documentation for each copy thus registered, and put the recipient of each copy on our mailing list.

A single registration fee will license one copy for use on any one computer at any one time. You must treat this software just like a book. An example is that this software may be used by any number of people and may be freely moved from one computer location to another, so long as there is no possibility of it being used at one location while it's being used at another. Just as a book cannot be read by two different persons at the same time.

Site licenses

Also available are MULTI-COPY or SITE LICENSES. The licensee receives one "master" copy of the program and all related documentation, additional master copies of disk and/or documentation available for an extra charge. These may be copied by the licensee for multiple users at the designated location (site) up to the number of licensed copies. The current offer is that $15 is paid for the master copy supplied from us, and you pay $5 for each additional copy that you make (subject to the terms of the Site License agreement). The number of authorized copies can be automatically extended by simply submitting the additional funds with a letter referencing the original site license.

Future products

Self-activating DOS and Windows Screen Saver RAZZLE DAZZLE is available at better computer software retail stores. All the features of the prior DAZLOGO program are now incorporated in the retail RAZZLE DAZZLE program.

A full computer security version of MT-DAZE is available from Harcom Security Systems Corp. For details, contact Worldwide MicroTronics, Inc.

Another derivative product for potential future release is DAZTUTOR. This allows users to experience a revolutionary Psycho-Ergonomic(tm) stress-less computer-aided memorization technique. Commit information to memory during a high-alpha state of relaxation without the duress and distraction associated with other memorization environments.

DAZZLE, the music video, is available on stereo VHS video cassette from your local Radio Shack, or from Miramar at (206) 284-4700.

Worldwide MicroTronics, Inc. is making available DAZZLE merchandise of a broad variety, including: Shirts, Mugs, Cards, Prints, Stick'EMs, and such.

Royalties

ALL COMMERCIAL RIGHTS TO THIS PROGRAM ARE RETAINED BY THE AUTHOR. The images generated by this program are intended for viewing on a computer executing a registered copy of this software, and may be extracted, projected, or otherwise translated onto other media only for personal enjoyment or non-commercial use within companies which have registered this software. Public display of DAZZLE images is permitted without royalty for registered copies that are used for trade shows, point of sales, and offices, where such usage is for entertainment or demonstration purposes, if no admission is charged, and the display is incidental to the business being conducted.

Disclaimer

Users of DAZZLE and related products must accept this disclaimer of warranty: "DAZZLE is supplied for non-exclusive usage as is. The author disclaims all warranties, expressed or implied, including, without limitation, the warranties of merchantability and of fitness for any purpose. The author assumes no liability for damages, direct or consequential, which may result from the use of these programs."

Distribution limitation

Anyone distributing DAZZLE for any kind of remuneration must first contact Worldwide MicroTronics, Inc. for authorization; use of the Distribution Authorization form below is recommended. This authorization will usually be automatically granted to distributors recognized by the (ASP) as adhering to its guidelines for shareware distributors (however Worldwide MicroTronics, Inc. must still be advised). Worldwide MicroTronics, Inc. shareware products, even free of charge, without clearly explaining to the recipient their legal requirement to register the program is strictly forbidden, and a violation of copyright law.

Part III: Appendixes

ASP Ombudsman

Worldwide MicroTronics, Inc. (formerly, MicroTronics) is an associate member of the Association of Shareware Professionals (ASP). ASP wants to make sure that the shareware principle works for you. If you are unable to resolve a shareware-related problem with an ASP member by contacting the member directly, ASP may be able to help. The ASP Ombudsman can help you resolve a dispute or problem with an ASP member, but does not provide technical support for members' products. Please write to the ASP Ombudsman at 545 Grover Road, Muskegon, MI 49442 or send a CompuServe message via CompuServe Mail to ASP Ombudsman 70007,3536.

Command Line Options

A number of options that control the action of the DAZZLE family of programs can be specified on the command line when the program is invoked, or can be encoded into a batch file for easy activation.

Main options menu

When you enter the command "DAZZLE -?" at the DOS prompt, you will be presented with the following display. The following options can be specified on the command line and are used to customize and control the action of "Dazzle". These options can also be specified in a batch (BAT) file for automatic activation.

-$ Display order information

-2 2-part palette, fixes flickering screens but slows drawing

-a Alternate Speed — uses faster color cycling speed

-b Bashful — no closing credits & pressing any key quits the program

-c Compatible mode — use the PC's BIOS for better compatibility

-d Delay — slows the drawing speed for faster PC's;"-d=xxxx" delays drawing speed by the specified value

-i Insecure — CRC checking is not performed when program starts

-m Mad — uses fastest color cycling speed...a real attention-getter

-q Quiet — no tones (this option has no effect on warning beeps)

-s Show — displays a single image then quits; "-s=xxxx" shows for the specified number of seconds then quits

-w Window — changes defaults for use with Windows

-x XT compatible — for use on 8088/8086 PC's with EGA or VGA

-z Create DAZZLE.DOC file on current disk path!

For example—if you want to start "DAZZLE" so that no tones are heard, no CRC checking is performed, and no closing credits are seen when you quit the program, type the following command:

   DAZZLE -q -i -b

Press any key to continue.

Additional options menu

When you press a key at the "Press Any Key" prompt, you will be presented with the following display. While "DAZZLE" is running, the [Tab] key will freeze the display until the [Space] bar is pressed. The [F1] key activates on-line help during the program. The [F2] key provides a menu of configuration options. The [Esc] key terminates the program.

Additional command line options

-e EGA — forces EGA display mode

-h Hide EGA border — forces a black border in EGA mode

-k Keyboard Typematic — keeps program from changing the typematic rate

-r Retract hard disk heads at program startup

-t Tall Video — forces the program to use standard BIOS aspect ratio

Limited use command line options

-+ Ignore TARGA+64, and empty keyboard buffer on exit

-4 Restrict the EGA mode to only 4 random colors

-f Fixed colors instead of randomized

-v VGA operation mode forced

Specifying Options

The Dazzle program accepts any combination of options on the initial command line that affect its mode of operation. The options may be preceded with either the "/" (slash) character or the "-" (minus) character. If you use the SwitchChar feature of MS-DOS, the "/" (slash) option marker character can be changed to any other key. At least one space must exist between the Dazzle command and the first option. For example, "DAZZLE -FC" instructs Dazzle to execute with Fixed colors and in Compatible mode. The options are not case-sensitive — uppercase and lowercase letters are treated identically. The options may either be concatenated into a single string or entered separately (-FC is treated the same as -F -C). The optional input file may be specified anywhere on the command line. For example, "DAZZLE -I MTDAZZLE.DZL" has the same effect as "DAZZLE MTDAZZZLE.DZL -I". Both commands instruct Dazzle to start up in Insecure mode and to load the configuration file MTDAZZLE.DZL before starting the image generation process. Note that Dazzle will automatically attempt to locate and load a configuration file named MTDAZZLE.DZL unless explicitly instructed otherwise with the "*" (asterisk) or "-*" (minus asterisk) command line options. The effects of each option are detailed below.

Compatibility options

Some of the options for DAZZLE are specifically related to increasing portability of the program to various computers and displays. The "2", "c", "d", "e", "k", "v", and "x" options default to the most desirable modes, but can be controlled by the user. VGA users also should refer to the "t" option for details.

/2 = 2 part palette update

Normally the entire color palette is updated at one time for each tick of the color cycling clock. If the CPU clock speed or the VGA palette register update rate is too slow, the upper part, or perhaps all of the display, will flicker badly during the display. To determine if this is due to palette updates, press and hold the "-" (minus) key during the running graphics display until it beeps (this is the slowest cycling clock rate).

If the display flickers only when the color changes, then palette update speed is a problem. Using the "2" option splits the VGA palette update request into two almost equal groups that are handled sequentially. This should remove, or at least significantly reduce, cycling induced flicker. This option should not be used if not needed, as it slows the entire display generation process. This option affects operation with VGA adapters only, since they allow longer 256 color palettes. Short 16 color palettes for EGA's are never divided into two separate updates.

/C = COMPATIBLE mode, use BIOS

Normally DAZZLE bypasses the video adapters BIOS code for maximum speed in color palette cycling. However, some rare adapters may have problems with this mode of operation. To cause DAZZLE to use the provided BIOS, the "C" option can be used. If your display flickers or distorts, or the color fails to cycle smoothly during the display, then try this option to determine if it corrects the problem. This option reduces program performance speed and should not be used if not needed.

/D = Delay, slow down drawing for faster PC's "-d=xxxx" delay xxxx units

This option serves both artistic and compatibility purposes. On faster computers the DAZZLE drawing algorithms can be too fast to appreciate as an evolving image. If the computer is too fast, or if you simply desire to induce a slower drawing speed for purely aesthetic reasons, this option can be used to delay the drawing process. If used simply as "/D", without specifying any delay units, the program will use a default delay amount. To adjust the amount of delay, a specific value can be provided after the "=" (equal) character. There is no exact relationship of the delay unit value and the impact on the drawing speed; it must be experimentally determined on each computer. The larger the number, the slower the drawing (TARGA+64 users note: this option works in reverse on this system; larger unit numbers produce faster drawing).

The delay unit value ranges from 1 (minimum) to 8191 (maximum), and can be entered without leading zeros. There must be no spaces or tabs between the "D", the "=", and the numbers for the delay units. This option can be concatenated with other non-numeric options. Thus "/AD=250W" is a legal command option string.

/E = EGA operation mode forced

Normally DAZZLE will automatically detect the video adapter hardware attached and adjust itself to use either the EGA or the VGA mode. This "/E" option allows VGA users to select and view the EGA mode of operation, which is 640x350x16 in format. As of revision 4.0 this option, like the "/V" option, will prevent DAZZLE from aborting if it thinks that it has detected an unacceptable video controller/monitor combination, though it will still give its usual error messages during startup. Refer to the "/V" option below for more information.

/K = Keyboard typematic unchanged

Revision 4.1a contains enhancements to make the program largely immune to some "keyboard acceleration" utilities that exist. These utilities cause the self-repeating "typematic" function of the keyboard to function far more rapidly. They come in two flavors:

- those that tell the keyboard to send keys more often
- those that trick DOS into thinking that more keys arrive than actually are sent by the keyboard

Part III: Appendixes

Without specifying this command line option, DAZZLE will set the "typematic" rate of the keyboard to it's minimum value for best program performance. When DAZZLE terminates, it puts the "typematic" speed back to a value typical of most DOS defaults; unfortunately I am not aware of a way to test the setting before changing it. Those that use a keyboard speed-up utility that stops having an effect after DAZZLE has been executed have the first type of such a utility. If you want the keys back to their quicker speed, you can re-execute your speed-up command. If you find this unacceptable, then use this command line option to force DAZZLE to keep from changing the "typematic" rate of the keyboard. The "/S", "/W", and the "/B" options automatically disable changing of the typematic rate.

/V = VGA operation mode forced

Normally DAZZLE will automatically detect the video adapter hardware attached and adjust itself to use either the EGA or the VGA mode. This option generally SHOULD NOT BE NECESSARY, OR USED. It should be unable to cause any damage, but is intended for rare compatibility conflicts where the startup code in DAZZLE falsely rejects the video controller/monitor combination as unacceptable. This option, like the "/E" option, will allow the error messages to be reported (so that you can write us of the problem), but will prevent the program from aborting itself. If the controller/monitor is really VGA compatible, or really EGA compatible if using the "/E" option, then normal image generation should be observed. Unlike the "/E" option, this option lacks artistic usage or impact. The VGA mode uses all 256 color palette registers for a far more subtle and interesting series of displays. The default VGA mode of DAZZLE uses a specially enhanced 320x400x256 mode that is not properly captured by many commercial products. The VGA modes require no more than 256KB of video memory.

/X = XT compatible mode, inferior but works

This option allows DAZZLE to execute on 8088- or 8086-based PC/XT type computers with EGA or VGA adapters and color displays. This option will be automatically initiated if the 808x style CPU is detected at program startup, but specifying the command line option avoids the warning message. The EGA performance on XT computers seems acceptable, but the VGA mode may be noticeably inferior to the performance of an 80x86-based computer. The faster the CPU clock, the better the overall performance and fluidity of DAZZLE.

Artistic options

These options adjust the image-generating algorithms used by the program. They are largely artistic in nature but allow customizing the presentation to various environments and requirements.

/4 = Restrict the EGA mode to 4 colors

The default EGA mode will use the full complement of available colors for the display. Using this option restricts the display to only 4 simultaneous colors at one time. This is used when the output from DAZZLE will be directed to another system that does not support more than 4 colors.

/A = ALTERNATE (faster) color cycling speed

The default color cycling mode is the slowest, with the most subtle shadings and transitions. This option increases the cycling rate used in shaping the palette contents. This effect is distinct from, but can complement, the "+" and "-" keys that can be used while the program is active.

/F = FIXED colors instead of randomized

Normally DAZZLE will randomize the color palette registers between each screen erase before starting the next image generation. This allows all the possible colors (up to a quarter million on VGA) to be used by the program. This option forces the palette to an identical state at all times.

/H = Hide EGA border

Some folks find the colored border on the EGA display distracting, and some displays do not perform retrace masking properly. This option will cause the border color in EGA modes to be forced to black at all times.

/M = MAD (fastest) color cycling speed

This option not only greatly accelerates the color palette contents rotation, but it also increases the number of image primitives that can be displayed in "Auto" mode at one time before the screen is erased. The effect is a far busier screen, a more intense visual experience. This is particularly suited to attention-getting in showrooms and other public displays, whereas the default mode is more practical for personal meditation and relaxation.

/S = SHOW mode, quick single image "-s=xxxx" Show mode, duration xxxx seconds

The "/S" option gives a single panel of images and then terminates automatically. This is most useful when DAZZLE is to be executed from within other programs or batch files. The image displayed is different each time.

The "/S=xxxx" option allows DAZZLE to execute for a specified length of time, after which it will terminate at the end of the next fade.

The duration value ranges from 1 (minimum) to 3600 (maximum), and can be entered without leading zeros. There must be no spaces or tabs between the "S", the "=", and the numbers for the duration. This option can be concatenated with other non-numeric options. Thus "/AS=250W" is a legal command option string.

/T = TALL video aspect ratio mode

Normally the EGA mode of DAZZLE uses a 16-color 640x350 resolution display with a modified aspect ratio (screen is mapped as if it had 640x700 resolution). The default VGA mode uses 256-color 320x400 resolution. The "/T" option causes the program to use the standard BIOS-supported screen resolution and aspect ratio in generating all images. The effect is somewhat faster image generation, but with a noticeably tall aspect ratio. As of revision 4.0 this option is functional with the VGA display mode, and causes it to use the BIOS-supported 320x200 video mode. Note that due to VGA hardware limitations, using this option will prevent the display of "dual page" effects (where a screen composed of a different image than the one being displayed is "panned" or "scrolled" onto the visible display area).

Other options

/$ = Display order information

Issuing this option when invoking DAZZLE will cause the program to output a convenient order form that can be quickly completed and sent to Worldwide MicroTronics, Inc. for product orders, information request, and shareware registration. To send this form directly to a printer, use the MS-DOS output redirection character ">" (greater-than) to specify the destination. For example, if you have a printer that can accept standard ASCII text on your computer port PRN:, then the command to use would be:

   DAZZLE -$ > PRN:

Complete the form and mail it to the indicated address. Enclose any indicated funds in U.S. Dollar instruments, payable to Worldwide MicroTronics, Inc.

/B = Bashful, no closing credits

DAZZLE will identify itself, including its revision level, when the program is started. The BASHFUL option will prevent closing credits when the program terminates (similar to the SHOW option), and additionally prevents DAZZLE from clearing the type ahead keyboard buffer when it exits. This allows usage of DAZZLE in a more classical "Screen Saver" mode, since whatever key is pressed to exit is not lost. This mode disables ALL key interpretation of DAZZLE. Even the "+" and the "-" keys will cause DAZZLE to terminate. The shareware version of DAZZLE does not initiate itself in a "Screen Saver" fashion under DOS or Windows; this flag is used by the retail Screen Saver drivers from Worldwide MicroTronics, Inc. This mode blocks the use of the keyboard LEDs to indicate the state condition of the executing DAZZLE program. DAZZLE has been successfully used within MS/Windows (copyright Microsoft), but use of this option will prevent window selection keystrokes. Use of the command line option "/W" was added in R4.2 for the windows environment as detailed below.

/I = Insecure, no antiviral checking

Before starting the image display process, DAZZLE will normally perform a test on the disk copy of itself in an attempt to assure that no unauthorized modifications ("hacks") have been made to the program after it was distributed from Worldwide MicroTronics, Inc. This is a safety feature added for YOUR protection! Please note that this is not a systemwide scan for virus infection — only the current disk copy of the DAZZLE.EXE file is checked, nor is the self-check completely exhaustive. Once you have used your copy of DAZZLE, after it has passed its antiviral test and you no longer wish to endure the delay at every invocation for this testing, you can use this command line option to bypass this safety feature. IF YOUR COPY OF DAZZLE FAILS THIS TEST, PLEASE NEVER USE THIS OPTION! INSTEAD WRITE TO US, AND TO THE SUPPLIER THAT GAVE YOU THE BAD COPY, AND LET US KNOW! A clean copy can be in your hands in a very short time, and might save your entire software investment (NOTE: Worldwide MicroTronics, Inc. only supplies disks to registered users.)

/Q = Quiet, no tones (no effect on beeps)

This option will block the tones that DAZZLE emits at various points in its operations. But warning beeps are generally not restricted. As of revision 4.1, DAZZLE uses programmed tones for most alerts and signals that it issues. These tones are of short duration, and change pitch depending on the condition being signaled. With the increase in operational options these tones are very helpful in determining the state the program is in. The one place where these tones are superfluous is the tiny tune in the closing credits, but this tune can be aborted with any key press.

/R = Retract hard disk heads at program startup

This option instructs DAZZLE to "park" your hard disk heads in a safe "landing zone" position. Retracting the disk heads is a safety precaution provided so that the possibility of disk damage from an unexpected loss of power to the computer while DAZZLE is executing. Older drives that do not automatically retract at the loss of power might benefit from retracting the heads before turning the power off. Retracting the heads, and removing electrical power, is also prudent before physically moving a computer. DAZZLE issues a standard BIOS "PARK DISK" (Int 13h, Function 19h) call to retract the disk; therefore, it is the BIOS in your own computer that performs the retraction. We can answer no questions about how this is done, nor warrant that the action taken is that which is desired. We are not responsible for direct or consequential problems or losses that may arise from using this option. We know of no reason to be concerned about using this option, but suggest not using it if you have any reason to doubt its impact on your computer. On some models of disk drives it is possible that an unusual sound will be made the next time the hard disk is accessed after having been parked. This is usually a "recalibration" step, and generally not a technical cause for concern.

/W = Window environment, changes defaults

This option was added to simplify use of DAZZLE within MS/Windows environments. It prevents the startup antiviral check (please see the "/I" option for a discussion of the risk involved), and all startup messages. This mode blocks the use of the keyboard LEDs to indicate the state condition of the executing DAZZLE program. It allows normal "switch" key commands to Windows for task switching. DAZZLE will still show the closing credits graphic image, but not the closing text messages. This option can be used, even if DAZZLE is not operating within Windows.

/Z = Create DAZZLE.DOC file

DAZZLE keeps the entire Users Manual within itself in an efficient manner that has minimal impact on total usage of the program. By specifying this option DAZZLE will create a new DAZZLE.DOC Users Manual file on your current default disk directory, which you can then print. Note that this file is formatted for generic text printers.

/+ = Ignore TARGA+64, and empty keyboard buffer on exit

This option forces the program to clear the keyboard buffer when exiting back to DOS, even if using the "/B" option. The TARGA portion of this option has essentially no effect on this shareware version of the program.

/! = Monitor Screen Saver driver interface

The retail versions of RAZZLE DAZZLE and related products allow execution as a self-activating Screen Saver under both DOS and Windows 3.x. This option allows the retail version of the program to monitor the Screen Saver driver interface so that it performs normally in that environment, which is the default mode invoked by DAZTSR.

Specifying the INPUTFILE

DAZZLE can accept the optional specification of an input file on the command line. This file must contain a text script that is consistent with the program's language specification. The specification of a path as well as a filename is acceptable. Be sure to separate the filename from options with at least one space.

As of R5.0, DAZZLE will automatically attempt to locate and load a configuration file named MTDAZZLE.DZL unless explicitly instructed otherwise with the "*" or "-*" command line options.

On-Line HELP

DAZZLE supports an on-line help menu system. You may press the "F1" function key to activate the help subsystem. This system is intentionally limited in size and scope to keep the program from growing too large, but it offers useful summaries of the newest and most pertinent features of DAZZLE. The graphics screen that was being displayed when help is activated is erased when help is exited.

Cursor keys within HELP

When within the help subsystem DAZZLE recognizes the various standard cursor keys. The "HOME" key jumps to the first page of help text. The "END" key jumps to the last page of help text. The "PgDn" key advances to the next page of help text; the "PgUp" returns to the previous page. The arrow keys also can be used. Note that the bottom right of the text window shows what page movement keys are valid at that point.

Exiting HELP

The text menu subsystems, including the help system, can be exited by pressing the same key that invokes that subsystem. Thus to exit help, press the "F1" key again.

LED Indications During DAZZLE

DAZZLE family of programs control the lighting of the Num Lock, Cap Lock, and Scroll Lock LEDs (Light Emitting Diodes) on the keyboard to indicate to the user the state of the program as it moves through the various conditions or "states" in normal operation. These LEDs (or lights) can be on, off, or blink; each represents a different condition as detailed below. Note that use of the "/W" or the "/B" command line options prevent the DAZZLE program from changing the keyboard LED indicators.

Scroll Lock LED

This light indicates 1 of 3 possible conditions for the program.

Part III: Appendixes

1) When off, the program is not in any pause state; something is actively being computed or displayed.

2) When blinking, the program is in an active countdown of a normal pause delay. When the delay expires, the program will proceed to the next action without any need for user intervention.

3) When on, the program is halted in a pause state, and will not proceed until the user takes some action. This can be induced by pressing either the "TAB" key or the "H" fade key. Refer to the details elsewhere for these specific keys to understand how to release the program from this state. This condition also occurs when any text menu is on the display; use the specified menu exit command to restore normal program execution.

Num Lock LED

This light indicates that the program is either computing or displaying a "Pan/Scroll Fade" process. If no activity is visible on the screen, then the program is building a new image on the "hidden" display so that it can be moved onto the active or "visible" display area. Refer to the "P" fade key for additional details.

Cap Lock LED

This light indicates that the program is computing a new VGA color palette to use on the active display. The duration of this period is directly dependent on the math speed of your computer. This indication was added to inform users when their program seems halted that valid computations are progressing unseen within the system. Refer to the "Shift-F10" key description for additional details.

Primary DAZZLE Modes

DAZZLE has two primary modes of operation. The original "Automatic" (a.k.a. "Auto") mode, which is fully self-generating; and a new "Semi-Automatic" (a.k.a. "Semi-Auto") mode, which allows interactive control of the image generation process. Some keys are only effective in the "Semi-Automatic" mode; others are active at all times.

Selecting modes

Selection between these two modes is done by pressing the "ALT" (Alternate) key and the "F9" function key. This combination is referred to as "Alt-F9". At program startup DAZZLE is always in "Auto" mode.

To enter "Semi-Auto" mode, press "Alt-F9". There is a short high-pitched tone. The display is cleared. The palette is reinitialized to a new setting (this may take a few seconds on a slow VGA machine). Then a short multi-tone chirp is emitted to indicate that "Semi-Auto" is ready for image drawing commands.

To return to "Auto" mode, press "Alt-F9". There is a short lower pitched tone. The display is cleared. The palette is reinitialized to a new setting. Then the self-generating engine begins creating random image displays.

Keys Active in All Modes

Some key commands that DAZZLE recognizes are active regardless of the current display mode. The meaning of some keys change slightly depending on the current display mode.

ESCAPE: Program termination

"The first and most important thing to learn about any program is how to get out of it." This key will do the job for you regardless of where you are in the program; just keep banging it till you get back to the DOS prompt. Note that when not in the various text menu screens, that "ENTER" also will terminate the program.

TAB: Freeze image

The "TAB" key can be pressed at any time when not in a text menu to "freeze" the current graphics image display. Once pressed, DAZZLE will remain in "freeze" mode until the "SPACE" key is pressed (the "n" key will also work). While in "freeze" mode, the "TAB" can be repeatedly pressed to toggle between color-cycling and color-static modes. The "Shift-F10" key can be used to change the palette of an image in "freeze" mode. This is most useful in stabilizing a specific display for image capture. Even an image in the midst of a fade or pan can be put into "freeze" mode. This key is also active in the "Semi-Automatic" mode, though here its usefulness is limited to halting a fade in mid-execution.

The Scroll Lock LED on the keyboard will be continuously lighted to indicate that "freeze" is active. Refer to the section on Scroll Lock LED above for more details.

F5: Dump screen image to disk file

Pressing the "F5" function key converts the display memory into an industry standard PCX disk image file. The program will name the file "DAZ_xxxx.PCX", where xxxx is replaced with a number from 0000 to 9999, depending on what filenames already exist on the current disk path. The image format will match the current video mode of the program. The program will resume normal display after the file is completely written. If a "Pan/Scroll" fade is in effect when "F5" is pressed, the "current" display will assume full screen position for the duration of the file creation; then the fade will return to normal action. Please note that all images from this program are copyrighted property of Worldwide MicroTronics, Inc.

".": Toggle quiet mode

Pressing the "." (period) key while the program is drawing will toggle the Quiet mode (refer to "/Q" command line option) on and off. This allows muting of the program sounds without having to terminate execution.

"+" and "-": Color cycling clock adjustment

The fluid changing of DAZZLE images is largely the result of a clock-driven rotation of the display's color palette. The user can adjust the rate of this clock at any time by using the "-" (minus) key or the "+" (plus) key. Pressing "-" reduces the clock rate; pressing "+" increases the clock rate. Note that DAZZLE defaults to maximum speed in VGA modes, and almost maximum rate in EGA modes. When either the maximum or the minimum clock rate is reached, the console emits a short tone. This process is distinct from, yet can complement, the palette control command line options (see descriptions for "/A" and "/M" options above).

"PgUp" and "PgDn" VGA color cycling step adjustment

The degree of color change that occurs at each event of the color clock can be adjusted on VGA displays using the "Page Up" (PgUp) and "Page Down" (PgDn) keys. The program starts in the minimum step condition when loaded. This effect is distinct from, yet strongly complements, the "+" and "-" key functions described above.

Shf-F10: Reinitialize the color palette

Pressing the "SHIFT" key and also the "F10" function key simultaneously (Shf-F10) causes the current color palette of the display to be reinitialized to a new random condition. There is a short tone at the start of the request, and another tone when the process is completed. In EGA modes the process is almost instantaneous. In VGA modes it can take up to a few seconds, and the Cap Lock LED will light while the new palette is being computed. Refer to the Cap Lock LED description for further details.

CTL-F10: Select new background color

Pressing the "CONTROL" key and also the "F10" function key simultaneously (CTL-F10) causes the background color of the current display to be changed to a new random value.

The fade control keys

DAZZLE allows the user to select which fades will be used. The actions of these keys vary slightly depending on the current mode. In "Auto" mode, pressing one of the fade keys sets which fade will be used next but allows the normal image generation process to continue. In the "Semi-Automatic" mode the fade keys induce the selected fade immediately.

The "Fade Enable Control" screen in the "Configuration" menu shows which key (without the "Alt", "Ctl", or "Shf" keys being used) can be pressed to select a specific fade algorithm.

Special fade control keys

The following behave a little differently, so they have been set aside for special discussion.

P : Pan/Scroll fade

Unlike the previous fade keys, this one has to be pressed at a certain time to have any effect in the "Automatic" mode. When DAZZLE is drawing in "Auto" mode, it is in the "Auto-DAZE" state (no LEDs are lit; see details above about LED usage). Once the last image has been drawn, it switches to the "Fade-Out" state (the Scroll Lock LED is lit). The first thing this latter state usually does is just pause for a while so that you can appreciate the incredible beauty of the display. The "P" key is only recognized in "Auto" mode if pressed while still in the "Auto-DAZE" state (before Scroll Lock lights). Once the last image has been drawn and the pause delay starts, this key will simply be ignored.

Part III: Appendixes

If a Pan/Scroll is in progress as indicated by the lighting of the Num Lock LED, then pressing the "P" key will assure that both a pan and also a scroll are presented.

In the "Semi-Automatic" mode this key will not induce a Pan/Scroll. Since that effect is not supported in the "Semi-Auto" mode, pressing "P" causes one of the other fades to be randomly selected and executed immediately.

H: Hold current display

This is distinct from, yet similar to, the "freeze" command that is called with the "TAB" key. This key is simply ignored in the "Semi-Auto" mode. In the "Auto" mode it lets the "Auto-DAZE" state (refer to Pan/Scroll description above) continue to normal completion, and will even let a Pan/Scroll proceed normally if one happens to have been selected by the "Fade-Out" state. But it causes the "Fade-Out" state to jam in the pause delay mode forever. Here the program will wait until you manually select a fade. Note that the fade that you select will commence immediately. The Scroll Lock LED will light solidly, indicating that user intervention is required to allow the program to proceed normally. Refer to the Scroll Lock LED description above for more details.

If you press "H" as soon as DAZZLE enters the pause delay mode, then any fade select key, the delay is effectively canceled — allowing you to immediately induce any fade you wish.

N : Next display now

This key has been made immediately effective in all modes. It stops any current image generation or fade, and begins a screen clear process. This is the fastest way to blank the screen.

Mouse clicks

DAZZLE will test for the presence of a Microsoft-compatible Mouse driver. If any mouse button is pressed (or if the screen is contacted when using a Touch Screen system that is Microsoft Mouse compatible), DAZZLE will usually interpret that action as being the same as pressing the "ENTER" key. Note that in the text menu subsystem of this current version a mouse click aborts the program.

Keys Active in "Semi-Auto" Mode

DAZZLE supports a whole set of commands to allow the user to control the image generation process of the program. Refer to "Selecting Modes" above for details on accessing the "Semi-Automatic" mode. Note that configuration options that disable a fade cause that fade to be unavailable in the "Semi-Auto" mode also. In addition to the keys described in the "Keys Active In All Modes" section above, the following keys can be used while in the "Semi-Auto" mode.

F8: Toggle continuous drawing mode

This key is similar to the F10 Draw Current Image key, except that "F8" will draw the selected image continuously until the next press of the "F8" key. All other keys maintain their normal function even while the continuous drawing mode is active. This mode is switched off when you exit 'Semi-Automatic' operation, but remains active through a fade or menu access. Review the section below with the F10 key description for more details.

F9: Select random image

If the user wishes to let DAZZLE randomly select the next image generating algorithm to be drawn, then press the "F9" function key. It selects another image each time it is pressed. Note that specific images can be selected as detailed below.

F10: Draw current image

Once an image algorithm has been selected by whatever means, the "F10" key is pressed to draw that image. The image will be drawn for as long as you hold down this key. You may release the key, and when you press it again it will simply resume where it left off if you have not pressed another key. It is suggested that you start an image with just a tap of this key, note what it is doing, and then decide how long you wish to hold it. Since there are no limits on image generation time with this key, you can let a really interesting pattern grow continuously, producing visual effects that "Auto" mode will never duplicate. This key will remember the image being played even if you perform a "fade." So if a great image gets too busy, you can "fade" it and press "F10" again and pick up where you left off.

Due to the behavior of the "typematic" key repeat built into the keyboard controller, it is possible for DAZZLE to get confused about when you release the "F10" key. If this happens, then the selected image will continue drawing after you release this key. Just a quick tap of this key again will bring it to a halt.

Alt-F10: Reinitialize current algorithm

This key allows the continued use of the same currently selected image algorithm. But it causes the image algorithm to be reinitialized to new random settings. This is most useful for changing between various modes of the same algorithm. Some images support use of exclusive-OR for "ghosting" or mosaic texturing, some can change shape, most will change color and screen location when this is pressed.

Specific image selection keys

It is possible to specify exactly which image algorithm you wish DAZZLE to use by pressing one of the Alt-keys 0 through 9, or A through Z. Press the "Alt" key, and a letter key or number key (use the numbers along the top of the keyboard, not the ones over on the side calculator pad). Each represents a specific image selection. The "Image Size" display in the "Configuration" menu lists the name of each algorithm, and the Alt-key that can be used to select that image.

In addition to the Alt-keys pattern selection, Ctl-keys A through Z can be used to select images that are detailed in the second "Image Size" display in the "Configuration" menu list of algorithms.

Configuration

DAZZLE allows the user to customize many of the characteristics of the image generation and fade actions. At any time you may press the "F2" function key to activate the configuration menu subsystem. This system offers useful enhancements and controls.

Cursor keys within CONFIGURE

When within the configure subsystem DAZZLE recognizes the various standard cursor keys. The "HOME" key jumps to the first entry field of the current screen. The "END" key jumps to the last entry field of the current screen. The "PgDn" key advances to the next screen; the "PgUp" returns to the previous screen. The arrow keys also can be used. Note that the bottom right of the text window shows what page movement keys are valid at that point.

Exiting CONFIGURE

The text menu subsystems, including the configure system, can be exited by pressing the same key that invokes that subsystem. Thus to exit configure, press the "F2" key again.

Image size control

These two screens allow the user to customize the images generated in the "Auto" mode of DAZZLE. When an image is called, it is allowed to draw on the display for a variable amount of time, the duration of which centers around the number entered in this menu. This number is multiplied by an internal value that reflects the size of the display and the resolution of the current active video mode. Therefore these numbers are relative and not absolute in their impact. Since the screen resolution varies from EGA to VGA, it is also true that the maximum value that can be entered changes between video modes. You may enter any large number; DAZZLE will reduce your input to the legal range for the current mode. The minimum value is 0, thus allowing the complete disabling of images as you desire. At least one image must have a non-zero value; a configuration file that fails this criteria may cause DAZZLE to abort during startup.

As the "Image Size" number is increased, the selected image is allowed to draw longer, producing either larger patterns, more patterns, and/or a greater variety of pattern variations.

The "KEY" field shows which Alt-key or Ctl-key (refer to "Specific Image Selection Keys" above) will select that specific image drawing algorithm. The "NAME" field shows the internal name of that image. The "SIZE" field shows the current relative size limit for that image. Note that the first Image Size screen is for use with Alt-key images, and the second Image Size screen is for use with Ctl-key images.

Fade enable control

This screen allows the user to selectively enable or disable specific fades. If disabled, the fade will be unavailable in either "Auto" or "Semi- Automatic" modes. If the user presses a fade command key (refer to "The Fade Control Keys" above) for a fade that has been disabled, then DAZZLE will randomly select an enabled fade to execute. Note that in addition to the listed fades, DAZZLE uses a "fade to black" process to clear the screen at the end of each fade.

Part III: Appendixes

The "KEY" field shows which key (without the "Alt", "Ctl", or "Shf" keys being used) will select that specific fade algorithm. The "FADE" field shows the internal name of that fade. The "ENABLE" field shows the current state for that fade.

Auto mode display customization

This menu shows two numbers: "Minimum images per display" and "Maximum images per display". These values control the number of images that will be overlaid on a single screen during the Auto Mode of operation. When set to small numbers only a few images will be mixed together on one display prior to the next fade. This reduces how busy the screen becomes. When set to large numbers, many images will be mixed together on a display prior to the next fade. This creates a much more complex display.

This menu also allows you to control how long the program pauses in an idle state before initiating a fade. This time is provided to allow a screen to be appreciated before it is removed.

The bottom of this menu states, "These numbers will be increased if in Alternate or Mad mode..." What specifically happens is that if the program is operating in the Alternate (faster color cycling) mode, then the number of overlaid images is increased by up to the number you entered as a minimum count. If the program is operating in the Mad (fastest color cycling) mode, then the number of overlaid images is increased by the number you entered as a maximum count.

File access menu

This screen allows the user to save or load a DAZZLE configuration file. There are three entry fields on this screen. Two additional function keys are also recognized only when viewing this screen.

Select mode

At this entry the user can select either to "Save" the current configuration information, or to "Load" an existing file. Press either the "S" key or the "L" key, then "ENTER".

Filename

At this entry the user can specify the file to be saved or loaded. Note that a default name is provided if one was not used at program invocation. To replace the name, simply begin typing it in, and press "ENTER" when completed. It is suggested that a file extension (the last three characters in the name, on the right of the period) of "DZL" be used. The following extensions are illegal: BAT, COM, EXE.

Beneath this field is an unmarked "File Status" field. If you attempt to load a nonexistent, file this will show "NOT FOUND". If you try to save over an existing file, this will show "EXIST", unless the file is protected from overwriting, in which case it will show "READ ONLY".

If you specify a wildcard character ("*" or "?") within this entry, then DAZZLE will automatically invoke a directory list to aid in your selection process.

Path

The current disk and directory path is displayed in this field. You may specify any variation of disk and path information that DOS would normally support. Each of the following are legal:

..	changes to previous directory
C:	changes to C drive
\MT	to MT directory on current disk
D:\	to root directory on D drive

F3: View disk directory

Pressing the "F3" function key invokes the disk directory display. Note that if you have begun an entry in any of the menu's fields, you must press "ENTER" before this key can take effect.

Once a disk directory is displayed you may use the various cursor keys to move around. Arrow keys work, and the "HOME" key jumps to the top of the display; the "END" key jumps to the bottom. The "PgUp" and "PgDn" keys can be used to move about more quickly. Press "ENTER" to select a specific file, or "F3" again to exit this display.

If you select a field that ends with a "\" (backslash) character, you are selecting a directory, and the display will be updated to reflect the contents of this new default path. The path field in the File Access Menu also will be updated to this new path.

Filenames displayed in lowercase letters are "Read Only".

F4: Execute Save/Load

Once the desired file has been specified, the "F4" function key can be pressed to execute the specified command. If the "F4" key is ignored, then you may still have a pending input entry; simply press "ENTER", then try the "F4" key again.

Part III: Appendixes

Usage within Windows

DAZZLE has been tested with both Windows 2.0 and Windows 3.x, both with excellent results. While a true Windows Application Interface is available from Worldwide MicroTronics, Inc., this version is very usable as is. DAZZLE can be left inactive in the background, and brought up on the screen where it was last interrupted with a simple Alt-TAB (or equivalent) key press. In Extended 386/486 system the DAZZLE image will start intact from an interruption; otherwise, the image may be corrupted when DAZZLE is first resumed, but it will correct itself once the next fade operation is completed.

As a basic starting point create DAZZLE.PIF with these entries:

Program Parameters : /W

Memory Required: 350KB, Memory Desired 350KB

Display Usage: Full Screen

Close Window on Exit

Allow Close on Exit

All other options should be disabled. Especially avoid any video monitor selections. If you are not using a 386/486 computer you may not be asked to set each of these options.

Configuration File Format

The file that is used by DAZZLE is an editable text file that follows a simple format. Each entry in the file must be on a separate line, and consist of a "Key ID" and a "Configuration Value". It is suggested that the user invoke DAZZLE in its default mode; use the File Access Menu to "Save" a copy of the program's configuration. That file should then be printed. With DAZZLE in the Configuration Menu mode, a printout of the configuration file, and a copy of this document in hand, the whole process should prove to be very clear.

Shift key tokens

A token in DAZZLE is a character that represents a condition. In order to represent within the configuration file the condition of the three shift keys — Alternate, Control, Shift — a group of tokens has been assigned as follows:

Alternate   ~ (Tilde character)

Control   ^ (Caret character)

Shift   ` (grave or backward-quote character)

Thus to specify the Alt-A key, the file entry would be "~A". To specify the Ctl-F key, the file entry would be "^F".

Special token

This file also contains a special token to allow the specification of menu configuration entries that do not match any shift key function. The "$" (dollar) token is used to mark such a field. The values for Auto Mode Display Customization are contained in this file as:

$I : the mInimum number of images on one display

$X : the maXimum number of images on one display

$F : Fade delay time in Auto mode

Key ID

A "Key ID" entry in the file consists of the key to be designated, with an optional shift key token prefix. Refer to "Shift key tokens" above for examples.

Configuration value

The value to be specified must be surrounded in square brackets; "[" and "]".

If the value is for an Image Size or configuration entry, then the use of an unsigned integer value is required. Unsigned meaning no "+" or "-" values. Integer meaning no fractions, decimal points, or exponents.

Therefore legal values are: "[25]" or "[0001]" or "[99]". Illegal values would include: "[-1]" or " 25]" or "[14.5]". If the value is for a fade entry, then the use of either a "Y" or an "N" character is required: "[Y]" or "[N]".

Comment lines

While reading (parsing) any line of text in the file, when a ";" (semicolon) is encountered DAZZLE stops reading that line. This allows the liberal insertion of various comments within the file. DAZZLE is very casual about parsing this file. It tolerates extra space and tab characters, so you can generally make the file look any way you like.

Part III: Appendixes

Version flag

The first non-comment line in the file should be the version flag. It consists of a "#" (hash) character followed by an unsigned integer of the DAZZLE version of the creating program. This is intended for future compatibility between upgrades and should not be changed.

Program Integrity

All reasonable effort has been made to assure that the use of this program on any compatible computer system can have no detrimental side effects. In addition to extensive Quality Assurance testing, the DAZZLE program contains an internal integrity check (read the section on the "/I" command line option above). If someone makes any code modifications to this program, it probably will be detected and the program will refuse to execute. Any persons making unauthorized modifications will be aggressively pursued and prosecuted. As of revision 5.0 the antiviral system uses a faster and better CRC checking algorithm.

Programmer's Comments

DAZZLE is written mostly in Borland C 3.0 (copyright Borland). Assembler code was used for direct video control.

Talented and accomplished people are always an asset. If you might be interested in contributing to a Worldwide MicroTronics, Inc. project, then please write, and if possible include a NON-CONFIDENTIAL sample of your work.

See the documentation files on the disk for additional Programmer's Comments.

Appendix B: The Hard Disk SECRETS Disk

Registration

Software products can be ordered from Worldwide MicroTronics, Inc. at the address below. Please include this completed form with your check. We do not take individual telephone orders, so please write.

Please PRINT your full name and address clearly.

Program name: DAZZLE
Revision: 5.0i
ID codes: r1=10509, r2=01000

Worldwide MicroTronics, Inc.
P.O.Box 8759
Spring, TX U.S.A. 77387-8759

Comments and inquiries about updates and other products are welcome at our mailing address. $15 ($20 US for non-U.S.A. sites) registration payable to Worldwide MicroTronics, Inc. required after 15 days usage, which makes you eligible for an update disk and puts you on our mailing list. Add $5 extra for a printed manual. DOS & Windows Screen Savers available for an additional cost. See DAZZLE.DOC for distribution limitations.

Check your MS-DOS floppy disk format: 5.25(__) 3.5(__)

DSHD [High Density] (__) DSDD [Low Density] (__)

When registering this shareware program, you will receive a credit for an update disk. Registered users receive our regular mailings providing the most current information about program enhancements and new products.

Check here if you want to receive a program disk now, instead of receiving a credit for your future use: (__)

RAZZLE DAZZLE, the full featured DOS & Windows screen saver, is available from better local computer software retail outlets. Check here if interested in quotes on over 100 copies of the Screen Saver product: (__)

DAZZLE, the music video on stereo VHS cassette, is available at your local Radio Shack or from Miramar (206) 284-4700. Check here to receive information about other merchandise (shirts, mugs, cards, prints, and so on): (__)

Please review the User's Manual and the software license for an abundance of useful information, DAZZLE Multi-Copy or Site License prices and legal limitations on the use of this program and its images.

LIST

A File Viewing and Browsing Utility
Documentation for Version 7.7, 1992

©Copyright Vernon D. Buerg 1983-92. All rights reserved.

LIST is a copyrighted program. LIST is NOT public domain.

LIST may be copied for personal use only subject to the restrictions set forth in the documentation.

Introduction

LIST is a user-supported program. It is not public domain. You may use LIST and give it to your friends, but you may not sell it or use it in business without obtaining a license. See the last page for information about licensing.

You use LIST to display files on your monitor, line by line with the aid of scrolling, positioning, and filtering commands.

LIST PLUS has many new commands which go beyond usual file viewing and browsing. We will explain how LIST is used, and then how the new file management commands are used.

Before going into all of the ways in which LIST can be used to display files, let's look at the three different varieties of LIST so that you understand the capabilities of each. Then, we'll go on and define certain terms like: redirection, piping, and filtering. In this way, you will better understand how you can use these things with LIST.

Installation

There are three varieties of the LIST program on the disk that you received (or in the file that you downloaded). This allows you to pick the version of LIST that is right for you, and to configure it to be exactly the way YOU want it to be.

Decide which of the LIST programs you would like to use and copy the COM file to your working disk, or into a subdirectory on your hard disk. Selecting a directory that is in your PATH will allow you to use LIST from anywhere on your system.

You may rename the program file to any convenient name, such as L.COM, READ.COM, LST.COM or leave it as LIST.COM. For example, place the distribution disk into drive A and enter the commands:

A:
COPY LIST.COM C:\L.COM

to copy the Plus version to the root directory of your C drive, renaming the program to L.COM in the process.

Printing the Manual

To print the documentation, set your printer for six lines per inch and 10 characters per inch. Then, use the DOS PRINT command. For example

PRINT LIST.DOC

You may also print out the documentation by using redirection and entering:

TYPE LIST.DOC > LPT1

Better yet, use LIST to print the manual. Enter

LIST LIST.DOC

then press the Ctrl and P keys at the same time.

Varieties of LIST.COM

LISTS.COM small version

- runs in about 30KB
- limited to smaller files (around 600KB)
- excludes the Alt-X (screen-saving) function
- excludes the Alt-G (goto DOS) function
- the Help screen is minimal

LISTR.COM regular version

- runs in about 80KB
- handles files up to 16MB
- excludes the Alt-V (file selection) function
- excludes the Alt-I (insert filename) function
- the Alt-W (windowing function) is minimal, that is you get two equal-sized windows; there is no ability to change window dimensions

LIST.COM PLUS version

- plus Alt-V file selection menu
- plus file management functions like copy and delete
- plus Alt-I hypertext-like file selection
- plus a help screen for the file selection Alt-V functions
- plus a second help screen for regular functions
- plus the Ctrl-T telephone dialer

A commercial version of LIST called LIST Enhanced

The main differences between LIST Plus and LIST Enhanced are:

- The File Selection menu has:
    - file tagging, including tag all, untag, retag, and so on
    - archive file extract and add/update commands
    - a sweep command to execute a specified program with all of the tagged files
    - a hardcopy (print) command for printing files with a user program
    - commands to change screen colors for all displayable items
    - shell to DOS
    - change video modes
    - a directory tree display command
    - the rename command that can rename directories
    - a command to create new directories

Appendix B: The Hard Disk SECRETS Disk

- The viewer part has:
  - the Alt-E command presents a menu offering up to 6 video modes including 132x25, 132x43, 80x43, and so on, if the video adapter supports that text mode
  - viewing of EBCDIC and ASCII files
  - handling of fixed-length record files like database files at two or more times the usual speed
  - optional number (on the left side) of each record
  - command line parameters to position to a given record number, or to the end of file
  - handling of files up to 32MB in size, larger upon request
  - the wrap option splits the line at a word boundary
- In general:
  - allocates memory more efficiently: can run in as little as 100KB with all functions
  - supports UltraVision video utility
  - options to use regular DOS input routines that take advantage of PCED, DOSKEY, or other keyboard utilities; or, to use an internal input routine which allows command line editing
  - a customization program that can be used to set any of the LIST options or toggle, and save them to a file, or read the options saved in a file; the customization program can define other printer names, can define all the names of archive programs used
  - a 170-page spiral bound manual
  - a 6-panel Quick Reference card of all commands
  - one year of free updates
  - telephone, FAX, and BBS support

LIST Enhanced may be purchased at computer stores or ordered directly from Buerg Software. Registered users of LIST receive a $20 discount.

The documentation file is marked with | before new and changed lines. It is marked with a double asterisk ** for LIST PLUS only features.

WARNING: LIST PLUS (LIST.COM) HAS THE ABILITY TO *DELETE* FILES FROM YOUR SYSTEM!!

IF YOU ELECT TO USE LIST PLUS, PLEASE READ THE SECTION ON THE FILE SELECTION MENU FOUND LATER ON IN THIS MANUAL.

Definition of DOS Terms

DOS redirection

The output of a DOS command can be "redirected" to a device other than the standard output device, which is in most cases, the monitor. This is done simply by entering the command, followed by a ">" and then the name of the desired device. For example, if you type

```
DIR > FILE.LST
```

you will see nothing on your screen and then suddenly your DOS prompt will reappear. What happened? The "output" of the DIR command was "redirected" to the file, FILE.LST.

In the same manner, you could enter the following command and send the contents of FILE.LST to your printer, like so:

```
TYPE FILE.LST > LPT1
```

The ">" symbol stands for redirection of output to another device. Broken down simply, the following command is saying:

DIR	>	FILE.LST
(send output of this)	(TO)	(This device, which is a file)

By the same token, you can also redirect "input" to a DOS command or a program like SORT by using the "<" symbol. Here is an example:

```
SORT < FILE.LST
```

This command would take the information in FILE.LST and "redirect" it into SORT. For more information on redirection, you may want to consult a DOS manual or other such reference.

DOS filters

FILTERS are commands, or programs, that read data from an input device, and then rearrange or "filter" the data before they then output the filtered information to an output device. DOS comes with several "filters", one of which is SORT. The following command would sort the file in alphabetical order:

```
SORT < FILE.LST
```

You are redirecting the file, FILE.LST, through the SORT filter and it is rearranging the file. Taking what you know about redirection and filters, you could now send your alphabetical list to yet another file by entering:

```
SORT < FILE.LIST > ALPHA.LST
```

which redirects FILE.LST into the SORT "filter" and then redirects the new output to the file ALPHA.LST. LIST also has some very helpful "filters" built right into it and we'll discuss these later on. Simply keep in mind that when you use a "filter" it will rearrange or alter the information into a form that is more presentable, or useful, to you.

DOS pipes

Pipes are quite similar, in some ways, to redirection. They are "connections" between two programs or two commands or a command and a program. Pipes take data that is output from one program and redirect it as input to a second program. The DOS symbol for a pipe is the vertical bar "|". To redirect the output from one program or command to another, you simply type the first command followed by a vertical bar and then followed by the second command. Here is an example of piping.

```
DIR | FIND "-88"
```

This command tells DOS to send the output of the DIR command, which you would normally see on the screen, and send it through the FIND filter. FIND would be searching each line for the string "-88". Only the files in the current directory that have a 1988 date stamp would be displayed on the screen! You can use more than one "pipe" in a command. Take this final example:

```
DIR | FIND "-88" | SORT/+14 > PRN
```

A "pipe" takes the output of the DIR command and converts it into input for the FIND filter. Then, a second "pipe" is used to send the output from FIND as input to the SORT filter. As a last step, output from SORT is redirected to the printer!

What would this command do? It would take the DIR of the current directory and pipe it through the FIND filter, looking for files created in 1988. Then the next pipe would SORT that information, sorting the files by SIZE (the 14th column of each line) and then send the output to the printer. For more information on PIPES, consult a DOS manual or other reference.

Now that you have a basic understanding of redirection, filtering, and piping, we will go on to discuss the command line of LIST.

Command Line

Command line syntax

The command line format is:

```
LIST [filespec...filespec] [/switches]
```

You may supply one or more file specifications (filespecs). LIST will display each file which has a filename matching one of the filespecs. If you do not supply one, LIST will prompt you for a filespec, or present you with a file selection menu.

Command line switches

Switch	Function
/?	Displays LIST usage information
/B	Tells LIST to use the BIOS for displaying data instead of using direct screen writes
/D	Forces display of the File Selection menu for the specified files, such as *.TXT for a menu display of only files with an extension of TXT
/E	Tells LIST to begin displaying the files from the end of each file instead of from the beginning
/K	Disables the mouse; both /M and /K mouse options are clonable
/Q	Toggles sounding of beeps; the same as Alt-Q
/V	Causes a verify operation to be performed after any Copy or Move operation; the /V option defaults to the value of the DOS VERIFY setting
/4	Places LIST into 443 (or 50) line display mode; this requires an EGA or VGA display adaptor
/S	Indicates viewing a piped or redirected file
/J	Sets Junk filter on
/7	Sets 7-bit display
/8	Sets 8-bit display
/*	Sets star filter on

/W	Sets Wrap on
/H	Sets Hex dump mode
/L	Sets pre-Loading on
/M	Allows use of a mouse for moving the cursor
/K	Disables mouse for cursor positioning
/Ftext	Begins a text search through all of the selected files and is case insensitive
/Ttext	Searches all files immediately for the 'text' and is case sensitive; the /Ftext and /Ttext options MUST be the last options on the command line; both cannot be used at one time
/#nnnn	Begins displaying the file at record 'nnnn'

The command line switch character is normally a slash, "/", but LIST will use whatever character that is defined to DOS as the command line switch character, such as a dash, "-". Depending on your needs, you could load LIST using any of these command line switches, such as:

(sets Word Wrap ON)

LIST MYFILE.TXT /J (turns on the JUNK filter)

The L, W, M, S, and /J command line switches may be used to disable the corresponding option by adding a minus symbol to them. For example, /-W or /W- will set wrap off.

The B, D, and Q switches are toggles; that is, specifying them reverses the default, or cloned, setting.

How to Use LIST

Starting LIST

To start LIST, you type the command **LIST**, at the DOS prompt, followed by the name(s) of the files that you want to see. For example:

C:>LIST CONFIG.SYS (displays file CONFIG.SYS)

C:>LIST *.DOC (displays all DOC files in current directory)

Part III: Appendixes

The "filename" is optional. If omitted, LIST PLUS will bring up a display of ALL files and subdirectories in the current directory. You may use the cursor keys to highlight the file that you would like to work on and press ENTER. Or, you may highlight any subdirectory entry and press ENTER to change to that subdirectory.

You may also use LIST to display piped or redirected files. A discussion of redirection, piping, and filtering is at the beginning of this manual.

To display a redirected file, use a < (less-than symbol) before the name of the file that was redirected and add the /S parameter to the LIST command.

For example, the output of the DIR command can be written to a file called XYZ, and then LIST can be instructed to read that file.

   dir a: >xyz
   list <xyz /s

To see a piped file, omit the filename, but supply the /S.

   dir a: | list /s

Or, to LIST a file within an ARC archive:

   ARC /p arcname.arc filename.ext | list /s

Or

   ARCE arcname filename.ext /p | list /S

Here, the ARC or ARCE program is invoked to extract the 'filename.ext' file. The /P switch for these programs sends the output to the standard output device, and this output is piped to LIST. Once the file is displayed on your screen, you may use the cursor positioning keys to move around and see different parts of the file. There are also commands to search for text, print, split the screen, display other files, change colors, change the way the data is displayed, and many other operations.

Exiting LIST

There are several ways to exit LIST depending on how you want the screen to look.

- The F10 command returns you to DOS with the DOS prompt on the bottom line. The last page that was displayed by LIST is left on the screen.

- The ESCape key also returns you to DOS without changing the screen. In

LIST PLUS, the ESCape key is also used to cancel an operation, or to exit file selection menu.

- The X command returns you to DOS and clears the screen. The DOS prompt is on the top line of the screen.

- The Alt-X command uses the screen-saving feature. It returns you to DOS and displays the screen that you had before LIST was run.

Entering commands

You enter commands by pressing a single key, or a combination of keys. There are often several ways to perform the same function with different keys. For example, D and PgDn both perform a scroll down one page function. This lets you pick the keys that you are most accustomed to.

When you press keys, they are entered into a keyboard buffer. Holding down a key can put many copies of that key into the buffer. This means that when you let up on a key, the program can still be processing input from the keyboard buffer. For example, by holding down the PgDn key, LIST scrolls down one page for each time the PgDn key is placed in the keyboard buffer. When you let up on the key, the buffer may not yet be empty and LIST will continue to page down. To make LIST stop when you let up on a key, you use the Alt-K key-ahead toggle.

Keyboard enhancement utilities, such as PCED, may also change the way that LIST reads the keyboard. With PCED, for example, pressing the ESCape key at a prompt is different. You do not see the / that DOS normally sends when you cancel an input line.

Display format

The monitor display is defined in terms of lines and columns. A typical monitor can display 25 lines of 80 columns each. LIST attempts to use the number of lines and columns for the monitor mode in use. For example, if the monitor is in 132 column mode, LIST displays 132 characters per line. If the monitor is set for other than 25 lines, such as 35, 43, or 50 lines, LIST displays that many lines per screen.

If you use the Alt-E command to change EGA/VGA modes, the EGA palette, cursor, and other settings are set to the DOS default values. LIST does not preserve fonts or palettes.

The top line of the display is called the Status line. The bottom line is called the Command line. The remaining lines are called the primary display window, and are usually lines two through 24.

Status line format

The Status line has two formats. The default format is:

LIST lllll nnnnnnn +sss mm/dd/yy hh:mm - filename

where

LIST	is the name of this program
lllll	is the line number of the first line in the primary display window (under the status line)
nnnnnnn	is the line number of the last record of the file; if the last record of the file has not been read, this field shows the percentage of the file that has been read
+sss	if displayed, this is the Scroll amount, in multiples of 10, corresponding to the number of columns that the display has been shifted to the right to view records longer than 80
mm/dd/yy	is the file's creation date (not today's date); or
dd-mm-yy	is the file's date in European format
hh:mm	is the file's creation time (not today's time)
filename	is the name of the file you are currently viewing

Note: The date and time shown on the top line is NOT the current date. It is the date and time that the file was created.

Command line format

Use the Alt-Z command to change the Command Line to this format:

LIST 70 2153 +20 09-02-89 18:12 LIST.DOC

By using the Alt-R ruler toggle, the top status line becomes:

++++++++10++++++++20++++++++30++++++++40++++++++50++++++++60++++++++70++

or, in Hex Dump (Alt-H) display mode:

Offset: 00 01 02 03 04 05 06 07 08 09 0A 0B 0C 0D 0E 0F —- DATA —-

The Command line has two formats. The default format is:

Command   Keys: ^v-><- PgUp PgDn F10=exit F1=Help

Appendix B: The Hard Disk SECRETS Disk

and the optional format after using the Alt-Z toggle is:

```
Command                 Toggles: h8kMpswTclJ F10=exit F1=Help
```

where

Command indicates the current process:

Command	function prompt; you are being asked to enter a command; enter the letter, or press the keys for the action to be performed
Reading	the file data is being read
Filter	the file data is being formatted for display
Looking	the Scan/Find text is being searched for
Scan	you are being asked to enter text to locate
Find	in the file, up to 31 characters may be entered
# lines?	you are being asked to enter a 1 to 5 digit number that is the amount of lines to skip
Line #?	you are being asked to enter a 1 to 5 digit line number to which the display is to be positioned

Message may be one of:

*** Text not found ***	the Scan/Text was not found in the file
*** Top of file ***	the first line of the file is being displayed
*** End-of-file ***	the last line of the file is being displayed
Toggles:	indicate status of toggles, lowercase means OFF, uppercase means the option is ON
H	indicates that the hex Dump display option is in use
b	the 'b' is replaced by a 7, 8, or * depending on which of those options is in effect
K	indicates that the Keyboard flush option is in use
M	indicates that tests for monitor retrace are not made

P	indicates that Print is in use
S	indicates file sharing option is in use
W	indicates that the Wrap mode is in effect
T	indicates that TAB characters are expanded
C	toggles continuous scrolling
L	indicates that the pre-loading option is on
J	indicates that line feeds are added to lone carriage return control characters, and backspaces are handled

A sample Command Line might look like this, after looking for a word that was not found:

```
Command *** Text not found *** Toggles: h*kMpswTclJ F10=exit F1=Help
```

Scrolling

You view different parts of the file by scrolling. That is, you use the cursor positioning keys up, down, left, and right to move the display one increment in that direction. For example, press the down arrow key to move the display one line in the file, that is display the next line in the file.

The PgDn and PgUp cursor keys move the display one full screen in either direction. Rather than press the up and down keys once for each line, you may use continuous scrolling.

Use the C key to toggle continuous scrolling on or off. The default is off. When toggled on, pressing the up or down arrow keys results in a moving display. For example, when you press the down arrow, the next line of the file is displayed automatically every second or so. It is like holding down the arrow key. To stop the continuous scroll, press the spacebar.

The speed of the continuous scroll can be adjusted by pressing the + (plus) or - (minus) key while the display is moving. The plus key makes the display move faster, and the minus key makes it move slower. You can save the speed value by using the cloning command (see "Configuring LIST, Cloning," later on in this documentation). The speed is independent of the computer speed and can be adjusted from approximately 50 lines per minute to 1000 lines per minute.

Summary of scrolling commands

Command	Function
right arrow	move display right 10 columns
left arrow	move display left 10 columns
down arrow	display next line of file
up arrow	display previous line of file
PgUp key	display previous "page," 23 (or 41) lines back
PgDn key	display next "page," 23 (or 41) lines ahead
C key	turns continuous scrolling on or off
spacebar or any key	interrupts continuous scrolling
+ (plus)	makes continuous scroll incrementally faster
- (minus)	makes continuous scroll slower

Positioning to lines

Each displayable line of the file is assigned a line number. The first line is assigned line number 1. The highest allowable line number is 16 million.

In order to determine the last line number of a file, the entire file must be read. For this reason, the first time that the END (bottom) command is issued, it will take longer to process. This is not necessary if the file has been completely read (see the Alt-L preloading option).

If the Wrap option is in effect, there is one line number required for each 80 bytes of the file's records. Thus, the line number does not represent the actual number of lines in the file.

If the hex dump option is in effect, there is one line number required for each 16 bytes of the file. For example, an 80-byte line will be displayed as 5 lines.

You may position to a specific line number by using the Ctrl-Home, or the # key. When Ctrl-Home is entered, you are prompted for the line number. Enter the line number. The display will now begin with that line number at the top of the screen.

To position forward or backward, you may use the + (plus), or - (minus) keys. You are prompted to enter the number of lines to be skipped. The display resumes at the line number shown on the top (status) line, plus or minus the number of lines that you specified.

When you change a filter option, such as Wrap, the line numbering changes. An attempt is made to retain the same file position, but the file may be repositioned at the top.

You may also reposition to the last "active" line by using the Alt-Y bookmark command. The last active line is one displayed after a Scan or Find command, or marked using the Alt-M or Alt-B commands, or the line set by the Ctrl-Y bookmark command. Up to ten bookmark lines may be saved by Ctrl-Y and recalled by Alt-Y

Summary of positioning commands

Command	Function
Ctrl-HOME, or #	Prompts for exact line number to display
+ (plus)	Prompts for the number of lines to skip for positioning further ahead in the file
- (minus)	Prompts for the number of lines to skip for positioning to an earlier line
Alt-Y	Reposition to the last bookmark
Ctrl-Y	Set new bookmark line number

Filtering

Filtering is the term used to describe the process that LIST uses to format file data for displaying on a monitor. After data is read from a file, it is filtered. The method of filtering depends upon the options in effect. LIST is fastest with no filter options set.

For a typical ASCII text file, the filter removes carriage return and line feed characters, and expands TAB characters. Because files contain different kinds of data, there are several commands to tell LIST how to display the data. The process that LIST uses to make the file data readable is called filtering. The filters in LIST can:

- replace non-text and control characters with blanks
- expand TAB characters
- display line drawing characters
- change 8-bit (W*) data to readable 7-bit text**
- display the hexadecimal values for each character
- remove "junk," such as control codes and backspaces

** W* is an abbreviation for WordStar (tm) formatted files which contain 'high-bit' characters. Using the '*' filter makes these files easier to read.

LIST was designed primarily to display ASCII files; that is, files which contain text, and not binary or control codes. Text characters, like A-Z and 0-9, are in the 7-bit range. Binary files like COM and EXE files contain the full range of 8-bit characters and the Alt-H (hex dump display) command is available for viewing them.

Characters above 127 (the 8-bit range) may be valid graphic characters, and may be displayed if the '8' command is in effect. To ensure that characters above ASCII value 127 are NOT displayed, use the '7' command to limit the display to characters in the 7-bit range.

Wrap filter

The file is displayed with one logical record on each display line: usually 80 characters. A logical record ends in a linefeed and may be up to 2048 characters long. If a record exceeds 80 characters, you may view the portion beyond the 80 columns by using the scroll right command, or by using the Wrap feature. The Wrap (W) command toggles ON or OFF the wrapping of lines longer than 80 characters. With Wrap on, lines are displayed in their entirety, 80 characters per display line. The scroll left (arrow) and right (arrow) functions are disabled when Wrap is ON.

Hi-bit filter

The 7, 8, and * (asterisk) commands determine whether characters above ASCII-127 are displayed. If the hi-bit option is off (7 command), the filter strips the high order bit from each character. If the hi-bit option is on (8 command), all characters, including graphic characters above ASCII-127, are displayed.

Star filter

The star (* or asterisk) command displays only ASCII characters below 128 (x'80'), but treats the special characters x'8A' and x'8D' as line-feed and carriage-return control characters. Any other characters above 127 are treated as spaces, and control codes below ASCII-26 are replaced by blanks.

Junk filter

The Alt-J command toggles the "junk" filter which ensures that carriage returns in the file also result in a new line. Also, backspace characters result in "backing up" the display by one position. This allows more readability of files that use backspacing to emphasize, or overwrite, characters.

Hex format filter

The hex dump option (Alt-H) causes the filtering to reformat the file data into a DEBUG-like display format. The largest file that can be displayed in Hex is 4 million bytes.

An attempt is made to retain the file position when switching from normal to hex-dump display, but due to filtering changing record lengths, the hex display may begin before the current record.

Tab expansion filter

The tab expansion option (Alt-T) causes LIST to insert spaces into a line. The default tab expansion interval is eight spaces, resulting in placing non-blank data in columns 1, 9, 17, 25, and so on. The Ctrl-I command can be used to change the tab interval from 1 to 99.

Summary of filtering commands

Command	Function
8	show all characters as is
7	strip the hi-bit from each character
*	use the star filter to remove control characters and some special word processor characters
Alt-J	use the "junk" filter
Alt-H	use the "hex" filter to display in hex dump format
Alt-T	expand TAB control characters
Alt-W	wrap long lines to fit on-screen
Ctrl-I	define TAB interval

Scanning for text

There are three ways to initiate a search for text. First is the Find (\ or F) command. Use this command to search for text without regard to the case (upper or lower) of the letters. Second is the Scan (/ or S) command. Use this command to search an exact match. That is, the search is case sensitive.

The third way to initiate a search for text is with the /F command line switch. With it, you supply the text to search for, and LIST begins the search before displaying the file, and before asking for commands. The search continues through all selected files until a match is found, or the last file has been searched. This search is case insensitive.

Each search begins at the line displayed on the top of the screen and proceeds in a forward direction until the end of file. You may start a search that goes backward rather than forward by using the ' (left quote) key instead of Find (\), or by using ' (right quote) instead of Scan (/).

To enter the Scan search text, type a slash (/) followed by up to 31 characters. The Scan text is displayed on the command line. The Scan is case sensitive. That is, lowercase Scan text will only match lowercase file text.

While the program is searching for the text, the bottom display line is changed to say "Looking". Pressing ANY key while the search is in progress will terminate the search and display the message 'Text not found' on the bottom line.

If the text is found, the line containing it is displayed as a high-intensity line (bright color) in the middle of the screen. The search text is displayed in reverse video colors on the highlighted line. The line where the found text is displayed depends on the setting of the "Find Row" (see Configuration section).

The display is scrolled left or right, as needed, so that the found text is visible.

If the text is NOT found, the command line is changed to say '*** Text not found ***', and the rest of the display remains unchanged.

To find the next occurrence of the same text, use the A)gain command, or press the F3 key. If you wish to continue the search through all of the remaining files, use the Alt-A command. To find the previous occurrence, press the F9 key.

If the a keyboard enhancement program, such as PCED, is installed, the up/down cursor keys may be used to recall and edit previously entered Scan/Find text.

In a shared file environment, if the file changes while being listed, the file position may become invalid. Use the HOME command to ensure proper file synchronization, or use the Alt-S (share files) command again.

Summary of scanning commands

Command	Function
/ or S	Scan for text with exact match
v or `	Scan for text going backward
\ or F	Find text with case insensitive search
^ or '	Find case insensitive text going backward
F3 or A	Find next occurrence of text
F9	Find previous occurrence of text
Alt-A	Scan for next occurrence of the text, and continue on to the next file until the text is found

Marking and extracting lines

There are two ways that lines can be extracted from a file:

- with the P (print) and Alt-P (print marked) commands
- with the Alt-D (dump data) and Alt-O commands

The lines to be extracted are either the current lines on the screen, or lines that you have marked with the Alt-M and Alt-B commands, or a line found by the Find or Scan commands.

To mark lines, you use either the Alt-M or Alt-B commands. The Alt-M command marks the top line on the screen, and Alt-B marks the bottom line on the screen. You can use either or both commands to mark the starting and ending lines (in the range of lines to be extracted). The marked lines are displayed in reverse video.

After you have marked a range of lines, you use the Alt-P (print) command to print all of the marked lines. Or, you can use the Alt-D (dump data) command to write those lines to a file. The Alt-D command asks you for a filename. If the file does not exist, a new one is created. If the file already exists, the extracted lines are added (appended) to the file. If no lines are marked, Alt-D either writes the current line (top line) or the highlighted line that was found by the Find or Scan commands.

For example, you would like to have LIST filter out all of the junk in a file and then write a new file. To do this, you might enter the following sequence of commands:

Command	Function
list TESTDATA	displays your TESTDATA file
Alt-J	filters out the junk
Alt-M	marks line 1 (top line)
END	positions to end of file
Alt-B	marks the bottom line (last line)
Alt-D	dumps data to a file
TESTDATE.NEW	you enter the new filename
Alt-X	quits and returns to DOS

Once you have marked a range of lines, use of Alt-M or Alt-B does not reset the entire line range. The first or last marked line may change, but both do not change. Using Alt-M again expands or contracts the range appropriately. If the new line for Alt-M/Alt-B is before the top mark, the top mark is moved. If the new line is after the bottom mark, the bottom mark is changed. If the new line is within the currently marked range, Alt-M moves the top mark—contracts the range—and Alt-B moves the bottom mark.

If no lines are marked, but there is a "found" line on the screen as the result of a search by Scan or Find, Alt-D and Alt-O will write the found line to the file.

Use the Alt-U command to unmark lines, especially after Alt-D (dump) to be sure.

Printing

The file may be PRINTed as it is displayed, in its entirety, or from a range of lines that you mark. If the printer is not on-line, you will receive an error message, and nothing will be printed.

The P command toggles the printer on or off. When first entered, the P command causes the current screen to be printed. As new lines are displayed, they too are printed. For example, pressing the down arrow will display and print the next line of the file.

Printing may be stopped by entering another P command. The PrtSc key may also be used, but the title and prompt lines will be printed with the lines of the file. Empty lines cause a line to be skipped on the printer. The capital letter P is displayed on the status line while printing if the bottom line is set to show TOGGLES.

Command	Function
Ctrl-P	prints the file in its entirety.
Ctrl-F	sends a form feed to the printer. The printer defaults to the LPT1 or PRN device.
Alt-P	prints only lines that have been marked.

Displaying multiple files

You can display more than one file at a time. LIST keeps track of up to 32 files at a time. You supply the filenames in the command line, through the Alt-F (get new filespec) command, through the Alt-I (insert filespec) command, and through the Alt-V file selection menu. The Alt-F command is disabled when viewing a piped file.

You can specify up to 16 filespecs on the command line. Each filespec can contain wildcards. Thus, several files can be selected via the command line. For example

   LIST *.DOC *.TXT

will display all files with an extension of DOC and TXT.

To display the next file, you use the Q or Ctrl-PgDn command. When the last file has been displayed, you can exit LIST by using the X, F10, ESCape, or Alt-X commands, depending on how you want the screen to look when LIST ends.

To display the previous file, you use the Z or Ctrl-PgUp (Ctrl and PgUp keys together). The 1 command restarts the displaying of files with the first file. LIST can keep track of up to 32 files at one time. The line number for each file is remembered.

The Alt-F asks you for a new filename, and you may enter a simple filename, or one that includes wild cards. These new filenames are added to the table of filenames that LIST keeps. Thus, you can use Alt-F for several different filenames, and use the Ctrl-PgDn and Ctrl-PgUp commands to move among them.

The Alt-I command allows you to select a filespec that is in the file you are viewing. You position the cursor to the filespec on the screen, and press Enter to add it to the list of files to display.

The Alt-V command displays a list of files in the current directory. You move the cursor to a file that you want to display, and press Enter to add that file to the list.

Summary of file review commands

Command	Function
Q	display next file, if any
Z	display previous file
1	display first selected file
Ctrl-PgUp	display previous file
Ctrl-PgDn	display next file
1	restart displaying with first file
Alt-F	prompt for new filename or filespec to display
Alt-I	insert a filespec that is displayed
Alt-V	select a file from a menu

Windows

LIST can display data in one or two parts of the screen called windows. The Alt-W command toggles this split screen mode. Entering Alt-W while the screen is split restores the display to a single, full-sized display.

In the regular version, the screen is split in the middle. The top half of the screen remains the same, and the bottom half becomes the part of the screen where files are displayed. Thus, the top window becomes a scratch pad.

In the LIST PLUS version, you are allowed to split the screen at any point. After entering Alt-W, you are asked to position the cursor to the spot where the screen will be split. By placing the cursor in column 1, you can adjust how many lines will be used by the top and bottom windows. This would be a vertical, or one window above the other, split.

By positioning the cursor to the top line with the HOME key, you can then use the left and right arrow keys to adjust how wide each of the windows is to be. This would be a horizontal, or side-by-side split.

You may display a different file in each window, and move between them. You use the Ctrl-V command to switch from one window to the other. You may also use the Review commands to display a different file in the second window. The Ctrl-V command has no effect unless you are viewing two or more files, that is a different file in each window.

Each window uses different colors. You can use the color commands to set the colors that you like, and then use the Alt-C command to save them.

Telephone dialer

LIST has a simple telephone dialer function. It allows you to point to a telephone number that is displayed on the screen, and to send dialing commands to your modem on COM1.

You use the Ctrl-T command to start the dialer. You position the cursor, with the arrow keys, to the start of the phone number and press Enter. The phone number may contain any character, but must end with a blank. If a highlighted line is displayed on the screen as a result of Find or Scan, the cursor is initially placed at the found text.

If the phone rings, you may pick up your telephone. Otherwise, you may press Enter to return to viewing the file, the spacebar to dial the number again, or Esc to hang up and stop dialing.

The Ctrl-H command hangs up the telephone.

If you are using a communications port other than COM1:, see the file DIALER.PAT for information on changing LIST to use COM2: or another COM port.

DOS Considerations

File sharing

LIST uses two techniques for allowing you to share files with other processes, such as programs running under multi-tasking systems, in other windows, or on networks.

The first technique is called "file closing" and is enabled by the Alt-S commands. This forces LIST to close the viewed file unless it needs to read from the file. If enough memory is available, the entire file may be loaded once and thus leave the file free for exclusive access by other processes.

The second technique is called "file sharing." It is a function of DOS and requires DOS version 3.0 or later. LIST opens the viewed files with a DENY NONE request. This allows other processes to read and write to the file if they do not request exclusive use of the file. If a file is not available to LIST because it is locked by another process, you will receive the error message "File not found" or "Access denied". There is no command to enable or disable this method of file sharing. It is implicit with the use of DOS version 3 and later.

Invoking DOS commands

If the "goto DOS" option is enabled, you may invoke DOS commands by using the Alt-G command. LIST reserves about 60KB of memory for its own use. This increases LIST's memory requirements to approximately 96KB when using Alt-G. The remaining memory is available to the DOS commands. Alt-G clears the screen and invokes the DOS command processor.

After you have finished entering DOS commands, use the DOS EXIT command to return to LIST.

To disable the "goto DOS" function, you must use DEBUG to alter the option byte described in the section about cloning. With it disabled, LIST requires less memory, about 66KB.

Screen saving

If the screen-saving option is enabled, LIST saves the contents of the current display screen when it starts. You can restore the original screen by exiting LIST with the Alt-X command.

Screen saving requires approximately 10KB more memory. This is sufficient to save 60 lines of 80 characters (EGA 8x6 mode). See the section about Configuring LIST and cloning for information about enabling and disabling the screen-saving feature.

The Alt-N command toggles the screen-saving feature. Its status is not displayed on the bottom Line. The small version is the only one which defaults to disabling screen saving.

File Selection Menu

LIST PLUS display

LIST PLUS has several new functions that greatly enhance the things that you can do. If you load the file LIST.COM (LIST PLUS) with no file specification, you would see something like this:

```
LIST - File Selection   1 of 40      Path: C:\*.*

^..
vWPW              WPSMALL       .DRS
vMAIN
vWORK
CONVERT  .EXE   WPWSTAR        .HLP
STANDARD .PRS   WP}WP{  .TV1
WP       .EXE   STORY          .DOC
WP       .FIL   FINDER  .LTR
WP       .MRS

List Copy Del Edit Move Path Ren Sort Viewarc 1-6 up F10=Exit
```

Note that the Command Line contains the following choices:

LIST, COPY, DEL, EDIT, MOVE, PATH, RENAME, VIEWARC, SORT, 1-6 up

Each of these commands may be executed from within LIST PLUS and are described below.

Movement keys

Use the arrow keys to move the cursor to a filename. The filename at the cursor is highlighted. The other cursor and filename selection keys are:

Movement Key	Movement
PgDn	displays the next page of files
PgUp	displays the previous page of files
HOME	positions to the first filename on the screen
END	positions to the last filename on the screen
Ctrl-HOME	positions to the first filename
Ctrl-END	positions to the last filename
F1	displays a Help screen
F10	exits to DOS in new directory
ESCape	exits to DOS in the original directory
Q	returns to viewing the last file, or returns to the File Selection menu
X	exits to DOS in the new directory this is the directory in which LIST is currently operating
| *	re-reads the directory to update the display
Alt-C	save settings (clone LIST.COM)
Alt-X	exits to DOS and displays the screen as it was before LIST was used
Alt-Z or / or F3	toggles bottom line display from a menu command line to statistics line:

To position quickly to a given filename, press the Shift key and the first letter of the filename at the same time. For example, to move the cursor to the filename LIST.COM, press Shift-L.

Changing directories

Any subdirectories contained in the current directory will have a down arrow next to them. If you highlight one of these and hit Enter, you will go to that directory. If the directory that you are in is a subdirectory itself, there will be an up arrow ... and selecting this will take you up. Thus, you can easily move around your hard disk from within LIST!

List file

This invokes LIST just as you would from DOS. Simply highlight the file that you wish to view, enter a carriage return, and you will be in LIST looking at the selected file. When you are finished, you may escape back to the original screen, with all of its options.

You may also open a window and then, using the Alt-V command, get another file directory and select another file to view. Using Alt-W, you can load more than two files.

Copy file

This function allows you to copy the selected file to a new subdirectory. Highlight the file you want to copy and press ENTER. You will be prompted for the new path to which you want to copy the selected file. Enter the path, press ENTER, and the file is copied to the directory you indicated.

Delete file

Allows you to delete any file in the current directory. Just highlight the file you want to delete and press D and ENTER. You will then be prompted to make sure that you want to delete this file. Enter Y if you do, and N if you do not.

Edit file

Invokes the EDIT program for the selected file. If you do not have an editor called EDIT, create a batch file called EDIT.BAT which calls your editor with the parameters that you like. For example

peii %1 /pc:\pe2.pro /q

Invoke file

Executes the selected file if it has an extension of BAT, COM, or EXE. LIST reserves about 80KB of memory and leaves the rest for use by the executed program. The I command is not listed on the menu. To cancel the command, press Enter at the "Options:" prompt. Otherwise, supply at least one space for the program options.

Move file

Move any file in the current directory to any other directory. Select the file that you want to move by highlighting it and hitting ENTER. You will then be prompted for a new path. Enter the path and the file is moved to it's new location.

Path changing

This function allows you to switch to ANY other directory on your system without having to exit LIST! Enter 'P' for Path, and type in the full path of the directory that you would like to change to, for example, C:\DNLD. You will find yourself in the selected directory and still within LIST. The "\" character may also be used to change to another drive and/or directory.

Rename

Using this function you can rename any file in the current directory. Highlight the file that you want to rename. You will then be prompted for the new filename. After you have entered a new filename, you will be prompted to make sure that you really want to rename this file. If so, then respond with a 'Y'; if you've changed your mind, just answer with an 'N' and the renaming procedure will be abandoned.

Sort filenames

Allows you to sort the files in the current directory by filename, extension, date, or size. Once you have completed the operation, you will find yourself back at the menu screen of LIST. The sort methods include F (by filename), E (by extension), D (by date), S (by size), and N (no sort). You may add a minus sign to the sort method to sort in descending, rather than ascending, order.

Attribute display/change

The A command can be used to display a file's attribute and to change them. There are four types of file attributes that can be changed. A letter is assigned to each one:

A   archive flag is on (file has not changed)

S   the file is a system file, such as MSDOS.SYS

H   the file is hidden

R   the file is read-only (cannot be deleted or changed)

The attribute command displays the status of the attributes in lowercase or uppercase letters. Lowercase means the attribute is off, and uppercase means the attribute is on, such as 'H' means the file is hidden, and 'h' means the file is not hidden. You may supply one or more of the attribute letters to change the current file's attributes.

1-9 up display

This function lets you set the display to anywhere from 1 to 9 filenames per line. In subdirectories with few numbers of files, you will begin to see not only filename, but file size, date, time, and attributes as well. You can customize this to suit your tastes. The 1-up display includes a display of the file attributes. These are:

A   archive bit is on, the file is unchanged

H   the file is hidden

R   the file is marked read-only

S   the file is a system file

ViewArc

This function will let you view the directory of an archive (ARC, ZIP, and so on) file, or self-extracting COM and EXE archive files. After you have viewed the desired file's directory, press ESCape to return to the file selection menu, or use the Alt-I (insert file) command to display a file within the archive file.

The directory listing is written to a temporary file in the current directory and is called FVFVFVFV.FV$. You may tell LIST to place the temporary file elsewhere by setting an environment variable called LIST. For example, to place all ViewArc and Alt-I extracted temporary files on drive D in the subdirectory called TEMP, use the DOS SET command prior to invoking LIST:

SET LIST=D:\TEMP

To view archive directories, the program FV.COM is required. It must be located in a directory included in your DOS PATH.

To display files within an ARChive file, the program ARCE.COM is required. It must be in your DOS PATH. For ZIP files, the program PKUNZIP must be in your PATH.

Files with a COM or EXE extension are assumed to be self-extracting LHARC (LZH) files.

Command Key Summary

Cursor keys

Cursor Key	Function
left arrow	scroll left 10 columns
right arrow	scroll right 10 columns
up arrow	up one (previous) line
down arrow	down one (next) line
Enter	continue to next page
END	position to end of file (bottom)
ESCape	Exit program unconditionally
HOME	restart from first line (top)
PgUp	scroll up one page, 23 lines
PgDn	scroll down one page, 23 lines

F- function keys

Function key	Function
F1	Displays the HELP screen
F3	Find NEXT occurrence of text after Scan or Find
F9	Find the PREVIOUS occurrence of text
F10	Exit to DOS

For changing display colors:

F2	Change background color for Find/Scan text
F4	Change foreground color for Find/Scan text
F5	Change background color for main body of display
F6	Change foreground color for main body of display
F7	Change background color for top and bottom lines
F8	Change foreground color for top and bottom lines

Appendix B: The Hard Disk SECRETS Disk

Letter keys

The Letter key commands are mnemonic. That is, the letter in some way, indicates what the command does.

Letter(s)	Function
A	Find next occurrence of 'text' (Again)
B	Skip to end of file (Bottom)
C	Toggles Continuous scrolling
D	Scroll Down one page
F	Find 'text' regardless of case
G	Get new filename/filespec (also Alt-F)
H	Display the Help screen
K	Toggles keyboard key-ahead
L	Scroll Left 10 columns
M	Toggles Monitor retrace testing to eliminate snow
N	Down one (Next) line
P	Toggles the printing of displayed lines
Q	Quits current file and displays next file, if any
R	Scroll Right 10 columns command, the 'R' command
S	Scan for exact text match, case dependent
T	Restart from first line (Top)
U	Scroll Up one page (23 lines)
W	Toggles the Wrap option for displaying long lines
X	Terminate, clear screen and eXit to DOS
Z	Display the previous file
7	Toggles the 7-bit filter
8	Toggles the 8-bit filter
*	Toggles the star filter
+	Position a given number of lines forward
-	Position a given number of lines backward
?	Displays the Help screen

Part III: Appendixes

space	Scrolls down one page
\text	Find any case 'text' going forward
/text	Scan exact case 'text' going forward
' or ^	Find any case 'text' going backward
' or v	Find exact case 'text' going backward

Control- keys

The Ctrl- key commands are entered by pressing the Ctrl key at the same time as you press one of the following letter keys:

Control Key	Function
Ctrl-HOME	Position to a specific line by number
Ctrl-PgDn	Display next file
Ctrl-PgUp	Display previous file
Ctrl-left	Reset display to column 1, that is scroll full left
Ctrl-right	Scroll full right (to the end of the current line)
Ctrl-A	Scroll full left
Ctrl-C	Display next page, scroll down
Ctrl-D	Scroll right 10 columns
Ctrl-E	Display previous line, scroll up 1 line
Ctrl-F	Send a form feed control character to the printer
Ctrl-H **	Hang up the telephone
Ctrl-N	Display previous file
Ctrl-P	Print the entire file
Ctrl-R	Display previous page, scroll up
Ctrl-S	Scroll left 10 columns
Ctrl-T **	Dial a telephone number
Ctrl-U	Display previous file
Ctrl-V **	Switch display windows
Ctrl-W	Display previous line, scroll up one line
Ctrl-Y **	Save current line number as bookmark line for a Y
Ctrl-X	Display next line, scroll down one line

Appendix B: The Hard Disk SECRETS Disk

Alt- keys

The Alt- key commands are entered by pressing the Alt key at the same time as you press one of the following letter keys:

Alt- letter	Function
Alt-A	Search for next occurrence of text, continue to next file until found
Alt-B	Mark bottom line of display
Alt-C	Copy options and setting to LIST.COM
Alt-D	Write marked lines, or found line, to a file
Alt-E	Toggle 25 or 43/50 line display with EGA or VGA
Alt-F	Enter additional filenames to display
Alt-G	Goto DOS temporarily to enter DOS commands
Alt-I **	Insert a filespec from the screen display
Alt-H	Toggle Hex display mode
Alt-J	Toggle the "junk" filter
Alt-L	Toggle preloading of files
Alt-M	Mark the line at the top of the display
Alt-N	Toggle the Alt-X screen-saving feature
Alt-O	Write marked lines, or found line, to the same file used by Alt-D
Alt-R	Toggle the display of a ruler line on top line
Alt-S	Toggle the file Sharing option
Alt-T	Toggle the TAB control character filer
Alt-U	Unmark lines marked by Alt-M and Alt-B
Alt-V **	Invoke the File Selection Menu
Alt-W	Toggle split screen
Alt-X	Exit to DOS and display the original screen
Alt-Y	Reposition to the last "active" line bookmark
Alt-Z	Toggles the command line in the bottom line. The default is to display the cursor key usage. Using Alt-Z changes the bottom line to show the option switches "Toggles:" settings.

Part III: Appendixes

Configuring LIST

Screen colors

The screen's lines may be in one of three different colors:

special color for the top status line and the bottom command line

normal color for the file's text windows

bright color for lines with Find/Scan text, and for the upside-down question mark in 7-bit mode

There is a pair of function keys assigned to each color. You use these function keys at any time to change the background and foreground colors temporarily, or use the Alt-C cloning command to make the colors permanent. Alt-C requires that the LIST.COM program file be on the current drive and in the current directory unless you are using DOS version 3.3 or later. With DOS 3.3, the program file may have any name and may reside in any subdirectory.

The border is not changed. The foreground color applies to the color of the characters. You may clone a second set of text colors for the second, and any other windows that you may create. The color attributes may be changed by using these function keys:

For the main body of text

    F5   background color

    F6   foreground color

For the top and bottom lines:

    F7   background color

    F8   foreground color

For the line with Find/Scan text:

    F2   background color

    F4   foreground color

Once you have decided upon the colors, use the Alt-C key combination to change the LIST.COM program file. This process is described below.

Appendix B: The Hard Disk SECRETS Disk

Cloning

The screen colors, the display retrace testing (M), the file sharing (S), ruler (Alt-R), and other options may be permanently set in the program COM file by using the Alt-C cloning function.

For cloning to take effect, the program should be called LIST.COM and on the current drive and in the current directory.

There are THREE versions of the LIST program file. One is the normal full program, which is LISTR.COM. The other, which is called LISTS.COM, is a slightly smaller file that excludes the Help screen. The third is LIST PLUS, found as LIST.COM. You may use any of the three COM files for cloning. After cloning, you may continue viewing the file. Several of the command toggles are also 'clonable'.

The values and toggles that are cloned are:

M	= Mono monitor, affects retrace testing. If you see "snow" on your color monitor, turn off this option
Alt-S	= file(s) are shared
W	= Wrap long lines
8/7/*	= display all 256 values, or 7-bit, or special case
K	= flush Keyboard each time a command is read
Alt-H	= hex dump display, like the DEBUG format
Alt-J	= toggle "junk" filter, add LF to CR, fix backspaces
Alt-L	= set on to force preloading (reading) of the entire file before any lines are displayed; default is OFF
Alt-N	= toggles screen-saving (see Alt-X) feature
Alt-R	= toggle columnar ruler on top line
Alt-T	= toggle expansion of TAB characters (also Ctrl-I)
Alt-V	= number of filenames per line and sort method
F2	= change background color for Find/Scan text
F4	= change foreground color for Find/Scan text
F5	= change background color for main body of display
F6	= change foreground color for main body of display
F7	= change background color for top and bottom lines
F8	= change foreground color for top and bottom lines

Note: Be sure you have no other copies of LIST.COM which are accessible (because of an APPEND type of utility). If you are familiar with the DOS utility DEBUG, you may want to modify LIST in that way. This is described in the next section.

Limitations

- The LIST.COM program requires about 64KB of memory. If more memory is available, it is used to store more of the file in memory. At least 80KB is required to use the DOS shell, and 9KB more is required if the screen-saving option (on by default) is enabled.
- The line number is currently limited to 16 million.
- The file size is limited to 16 million bytes for ASCII files and 4 million bytes for hex-dump files. Versions for larger files are available to licensed users.
- The review limit is 32 files for the regular and Plus versions. The bookmark limit is 10 entries.
- PC DOS Version 2.0 or later is required. DOS version 3.0 or later is required for file sharing.
- ANSI.SYS is NOT required.

DesqView, TopView, Double DOS, PCED, and IBM are all copyrighted, trademarked, and all that.

If you are using LIST and find it of value, your gift in any amount ($20 suggested) will be greatly appreciated. Please make checks payable in U.S. dollars to Vernon D. Buerg. Canadian and non-U.S. checks require excessive bank charges.

For use by corporations and other institutions, please contact me for a licensing arrangement. More information is supplied in the file LICENSE. Customizing and other special licensing are available upon request. Purchase orders and invoicing are acceptable.

The Buerg Utilities

The Buerg Utilities are NOT public domain; they are copyrighted work and may be distributed only pursuant to this license. Businesses, corporations, governments, and institutions must obtain a license for their use. Buerg Utilities are "user-supported" programs for personal use only.

Appendix B: The Hard Disk SECRETS Disk

Permission is hereby granted to reproduce and disseminate the Buerg Utilities so long as:

1. No remuneration of any kind is received in exchange; and
2. Distribution is without ANY modification to the contents of all accompanying documentation and/or support files, including the copyright notice and this license.

No copy of the Buerg Utilities may be distributed without including a copy of this license. Any other use, including bundling of any of the Buerg Utilities for your own distribution, is prohibited without express, written permission in advance from:

Vernon D. Buerg
139 White Oak Circle
Petaluma, CA 94952

CompuServe: 70007,1212

Forums: IBMAPP, IBMCOM, IBMHW, IBMNEW, IBMPRO, IBMSYS and HAMNET

Data/BBS: (707) 778-8944, -or- (707) 778-8841, 24-hour bulletin board systems

FAX: (707) 778-8728

Voice: (707) 778-1811, orders only

The registered version of LIST Plus is $37 plus appropriate postage. You receive a disk with the latest version, notification of updates, and a printed manual.

The commercial (retail) program LIST Enhanced is $99 plus shipping and may NOT be copied or distributed.

Copies of the "Buerg Utilites" disk set for personal use may be obtained on 5.25"/1.2MB or 3.5"/1.44MB diskettes for $60 plus shipping.

You may order with a credit card by phone at (707) 778-1811 from 10 a.m. to 7 p.m. Pacific time, Monday through Friday. The above products may be ordered by sending check, money, or credit card information with the following registration form:

Registration

Please add me as a supporter of LIST, version 7.7a:

Name_____

Company_____

Address_____

_____

City_____State_____ Zip_____

Amount$_____Copies_____Date_____

( )Check or money order payable to Vernon D. Buerg in U.S. funds

( )VISA ( )MasterCard   ( )5.25" disk ( )3.5" disk

Credit card number_____Exp date_____

Mail to: Vernon D. Buerg
            Buerg Software
            139 White Oak Circle
            Petaluma, CA 94952

Index

— A —

/$ parameter (DAZZLE), 474
/! parameter (DAZZLE), 476
- key with DAZZLE, 480
. key with DAZZLE, 480
+ key with DAZZLE, 480
/+ parameter (DAZZLE), 476
? parameter
    DAZZLE, 452
    Micro House utilities, 456
1-9 up command (LIST), 519
2, 7 RLL. *See* RLL data encoding
/2 parameter (DAZZLE), 470
/4 parameter (DAZZLE), 473
4DOS.COM, 24
8-bit controllers vs. 16-bit controllers, 381
12-bit file allocation table, 266, 267–269
16-bit controllers vs. 8-bit controllers, 381
16-bit file allocation table, 266, 267–269
/A parameter (DAZZLE), 473
"Abort, Retry . . ." message, 223
access time, 69
active flag, 290
active partition, 245
actuators, 39
    head-positioner drive circuit, 142–144
    manufacturer testing, 351
    stepper motor actuators, 39, 102–106
    voice coil actuators, 39, 107–112
addressing data
    Gray code, 114–116, 117
    layers of programs in a PC, 176–178
    logical structures, 97–98
    physical method, 96–97
Addstor, SuperStor, 408–411
advanced run-length limited (ARLL) data encoding, 60–61
Advanced SCSI Programming Interface (ASPI), 90
advanced write-through cache, 157
alignment. *See* misalignment
Alt key commands
    Alt-F10 (DAZZLE), 484
    in LIST, 523
American National Standards Institute, SCSI driver standard, 90
Amiga computers, 2
    PC Bridge Board, 171
amplifiers, 144
analog information
    analog testing vs. digital testing, 362–363
    data storage, 34, 344
    digital vs., 108–109
    servo signals, 122
    voice coil motor as analog, 108
ANSI SCSI driver standard, 90
ANSI.SYS, 190
antivirus programs
    in emergency toolkit, 30
    first track used by, 240
Apple Computer, 3
applications. *See* programs
ARCE.COM, 454–455
archived files, extracting and viewing, 455, 519
areal density of bits, 51, 141
ARLL data encoding, 60–61
ASCII file viewing, 453–454
ASPI (Advanced SCSI Programming Interface), 90
AT drive-type table, 197–199
ATA standard, 92
    PCMCIA specification and, 96
Atari computers, 2
"ATTENTION! SpinRite utilizes and requires the pre-defined auxiliary last track . . ." message, 386
autoconfiguring disk controllers, 195, 198–199
    low-level formatting and, 235–236
    "secret" cylinder, 245

Index

AUTOEXEC.BAT
  for safety boot diskette, 25, 28, 30–31
  for SpinRite, 408, 413, 428, 429
  TIMEPARK.COM, 460
  TSRs in, 184, 187
AUTOEXIT command line option (SpinRite), 425
auto-parking, 111–112
AUTOREPORT command line option (SpinRite), 425
azimuth alignment, 46

— B —

/B parameter (DAZZLE), 452, 474
background programs. *See* TSR programs
backlash, 378
backups, 316–321
  differential backups, 318–319
  disk mirroring vs., 321–322
  full backups, 317
  how often to back up, 319
  incremental backups, 317–318
  perfect, 19–20
  reinterleaving the old way and, 331
  strategy recommendations, 319–321
  warnings and suggestions, 322
"Bad or missing Command Interpreter" message, 297
"Bad or missing xxxx" message, 297
"Bad Partition Table" message, 297
bad sectors
  marking, 349, 381–382, 384
  turned good, 385, 420
bad track vs. bad sector, 348
basic input output system. *See* ROM BIOS
BATCH command line option (SpinRite), 424
batch files
  for CHKDSK, 428–430
  for DAZZLE, 452
  for SpinRite, 424–433
battery for CMOS chip, 196
BBSs. *See* bulletin board systems (BBSs)
benchmark programs, 160
bias oscillator signal, 34

bidirectional frequency modulation. *See* FM data encoding
binary files, 379
binary number, 51
BIOS extension ROM chips, 198–199
BIOS overhead, 371
BIOS parameter block, 190
BIOS program
  DOS and, 97, 170–171
  hard disk physical size limits, 209–210, 213–219
BIOS ROMs. *See* ROM BIOS
bit cell, 49
bit density (areal density), 51, 141
bit shifting, 50
bit size, 44–51
  coercivity, 47–49
  grain or domain size, 47
  head gap, 47
  magnetic repulsion and, 47
bits
  defined, 44, 51
  encoding strategies, 51–61
  length, 46
  width, 45
BLANKING command line option (SpinRite), 426
block devices
  character devices vs., 172–173
  default driver, 190, 209
  SpinRite driver testing, 369
Bold type in this book, 7
boot diskette. *See* clean boot diskette for SpinRite; safety boot diskette
Boot Manager strategy (OS/2), 29
boot record, 24, 260–262
  contents, 261–262
  data table, 261, 277–279
  functions, 261
  illustrated, 260, 261, 279
  signature, 262
  See also master boot record
boot sector. *See* boot record
bootable flag byte, 290
bootable partition, 245

Index 531

booting
    clean boot diskette for SpinRite, 411–414
    from floppy drives, 25
    head behavior during, 436
    information requirements for, 290
    start-up program, 198–199
    turning on PC after turning off, 298–299, 439
    See also safety boot diskette
Buerg Utilities, 526–527
Buerg, Vernon, 8, 454
buffers
    caching controllers vs. buffering controls, 162
    DOS disk buffers, 153, 164–167, 173–175
    SpinRite scratch pads, 366–367
    track buffers, 76
BUFFERS = statement, 164–167
    recommended settings, 165
bulletin board systems (BBSs)
    help using, 18
    PARK.COM from, 438
buried servo systems, 126–127
bus, input-output, 75, 81
Bushong, Dave, 335
byte, 44

— C —

/C parameter
    DAZZLE, 470–471
    Micro House utilities, 456
cables
    making certain of connection, 292–293
    power cables, 292–293
    ribbon cables, 85–86, 293
cache hit, 155
caching. *See* disk caching
caching controllers vs. buffering controls, 162
Calibrate (Norton Utilities), 419
CAM (Common Access Method), 90
"Cannot find system files" message, 291
cap lock LED with DAZZLE, 479
capacitor failure, 14
CATDISK, 321
Caution margin icon, 7
Central Point, UNDELETE, 21, 299

central processing unit (CPU) chip, 3, 171
centrifugal fan, 41
CGR (group-coded recording), 58
chain, device driver, 187, 190, 204
character devices vs. block devices, 172–173
CheckIt, 291
CHK.BAT (SpinRite), 428–430
CHKDSK
    batch file for, 428–430
    Calibrate (Norton Utilities) vs., 419
    cautions, 417
    cross-linked files, 276, 417
    DOS 6 improvement, 418
    /F parameter, 275, 415, 416, 418
    information from, 415–416
    lost chains and, 275, 416–417
    running before SpinRite, 414–419
    safe use of, 417–418
    on safety boot diskette, 26
    with SCSI drives, 91
    two copies of FAT and, 270
    /V parameter, 415
circuit boards. *See* controllers; drive electronics
clean boot diskette for SpinRite, 411–414
cleanliness, 41
click, 373
clock signals, 52, 57–58
clock-data separator, 87, 144
clusters, 263–264
    bad clusters, 276, 284
    bad clusters turned good, 385, 420
    defined, 263
    lost chains, 274–275, 416–417
    marking bad sectors, 349, 381–382, 384
    maximum number, 264
    media descriptor byte, 264, 267
    numbering, 264
    slack space, 265
CMOS. *See* configuration CMOS
code segment (CS), 185
coercivity, 47–49
cog in motors, 105
colors (screen) for LIST, 524–526
COLORS.PAT, 455

Index

COMMAND.COM, 24
    alternatives, 24
    replacing deleted or damaged file, 299
command keys
    DAZZLE, 479–484
    LIST, 520–523
command line
    DAZZLE options, 468–476
    LIST syntax and switches, 498–499, 502–504
    SpinRite options, 424–426
Common Access Method (CAM), 90
COMPAQ DOS Version 3.31, 212
complementary metal oxide semiconductor (CMOS). *See* configuration CMOS memory
COMPSURF program (NetWare), 283
CompuServe Information Service, 18
CONFIG.SYS
    BUFFERS = statement, 164–167
    DEVICE statement, 187
    DEVICEHIGH statement, 187
    INSTALL statement, 184, 187
    for safety boot diskette, 24, 25, 28, 30–31
    SHELL statement, 24
    for SpinRite, 408, 411–412, 414, 428
configuration CMOS memory
    acronym explained, 196
    AT drive-type table, 197–199
    contents lost, 31
    date and time setting, 196
    drive-type determination, 196–199
    invalid values, 196–197
    on safety boot diskette, 26
    turning on PC after turning off, 298–299
    utilities for saving and restoring, 26
configuring programs
    DAZZLE, 485–487, 488–490
    LIST, 524–526
construction of hard disks, 36–41
Control key commands. *See* Ctrl-key commands
controllers, 145–146
    8-bit vs. 16-bit, 381
    autoconfiguring disk controllers, 195, 198–199, 235–236
    caching controllers vs. buffering controls, 162
    card plugs, 83
    drive-type determination, 194–205
    failure, 306–308, 443
    high data density from separate controllers, 61
    low-level formatting, 231–236
    mapping strategies, 217–219
    matching to drives, 146
    SCSI host adapters vs., 146
    SpinRite testing, 367
    translating controllers, 347
    UltraStor 12f and 12C, 217–218
    what they do, 145–146
    See also drive-type determination; low-level formatting
Copy command (LIST), 517
copy protection and non-standard sectors, 71
CORETEST, SpinRite and incorrect results, 82
CPU chip, 3, 171
crashes, 140, 305–306
CRC error detection, 62
    rewriting data and, 346
    in sector header, 71
cross-linked files, 276, 417
crosstalk, 46
CS (code segment), 185
Ctrl-key commands
    Ctrl-F10 (DAZZLE), 481
    in LIST, 522
cursor keys with LIST, 520
customer engineering cylinder, 244–245
cyclical redundancy checks. *See* CRC error detection
cylinder truncation by UltraStor 12f and 12c, 218
cylinders, 39–41
    defined, 39
    diagnostic cylinder, 244–245
    "secret" cylinder, 245
    skew and performance, 23
    tracks per cylinder, 41
    See also head skewing

Index

— D —

/D parameter (DAZZLE), 471
daisy chain, 85
data
 noise vs., 344
 protecting, 19–21
 recovering, 315–316, 377–379
 relocating to safety, 340, 382–385
 repairing damaged data, 299–300
 rewriting, 345–346
 value of, 15
data accidents, 297–301
data area of logical drives, 262–265
 clusters, 263–264
 illustrated, 260
 slack space, 265
 subdirectories, 272–273
DATA.FIL, 28, 29
data recovery, 315–316, 377–379
data transfer rate, 69
 for ESDI drives, 87
 interleave best for, 376–377
data-encoding strategies, 51–61
 ARLL (advanced run-length limited), 60–61
 clock signals, 52, 57–58
 FM (frequency modulation), 55
 illustrated, 48, 54
 MFM (modified frequency modulation), 56–57
 NRZ (Non-Return-to-Zero), 55–56
 pulse approach, 52–54
 RLL (run-length limited), 57–60
 SpinRite determination, 374–375
 surface analysis and, 356
 See also specific strategies
data-recovery services, 316
DATE, 196
DAZTUTOR, 467
DAZZLE, 8, 461–491
 artistic options, 472–474
 command line options, 468–476
 compatibility options, 470–472
 configuration, 485–487, 488–490
 fade control keys, 481–482
 fade enable control, 485–486
 fees and licenses, etc., 465–468
 file access menu, 486–487
 head parking by, 437, 451
 help, 477
 image size control, 485
 INPUTFILE specification, 476
 keys active in all modes, 479–482
 keys active in "semi-auto" mode, 482–484
 keys with CONFIGURE, 485, 487
 LED indications during, 477–478
 modes, 478–479
 mouse clicks, 482
 music video, 467
 overview, 451–453, 461–464
 program integrity, 490
 programmer's comments, 490
 registration, 491
 requirements, 462
 revision control, 465
 usage limitation, 465
 Windows and, 488
DAZZLE.DOC file, 452
DBLSPACE.EXE command, 299
DBLSPACE/CHKDSK, 383
dead-reckoning positioners. *See* stepper motor actuators
death. *See* hard disk failure
DEBUG
 displaying master boot record, 240–242
 low-level formatting command, 230
 ROM BIOS date determination, 84
dedicated platter servo systems, 118–122
 fine positioning information, 120, 121
 Gray code, 119–121
 illustrated, 119, 120
 servo signals, 118–121
 tower tilt, 122
defect lists from manufacturers, 351–353
deferred-write cache, 157–159
 elevator cache, 159
 flushing the buffers, 158
 PC hangs and, 159
 SMARTDrive, 158–159, 163
DEFRAG, 310–311
defragmentation, 308–311
 performance and, 23
Del command (LIST), 517

Index

Delete Tracker, 309
deleting
    files with LIST, 454
    using DOS shells or Windows file managers, 21
DeltaFile, 321
DEPTHx command line option (SpinRite), 425–426
DESTROY, 301
Detailed Technical Log (SpinRite), 381, 385, 422–423
device driver chain, 187, 190, 204
device drivers
    default block device driver, 190, 209
    device driver chain, 187, 190, 204
    interrupt vector table and, 187, 190
    for partitions created by third-party software, 254
    SpinRite tests, 368–369
DEVICE statement, 187
DEVICEHIGH statement, 187
devices, block vs. character, 172–173
diagnosing hard disk failure, 311–315
diagnostic cylinder, 244–245
dialer (LIST), 513
DIALER.PAT, 455
differential backups, 318–319
digital information
    analog testing vs. digital testing, 362–363
    analog vs., 108–109
    data storage, 34, 344
    servo signals, 122
    stepper motor as digital, 108
direct-mapped cache, 161
directories
    changing in LIST, 516
    root directory, 270–272
    subdirectories, 272–273
    tree structure, 272–273
disabling hard disk to test the safety boot diskette, 27–28
"Disk boot failure" message, 297
disk caching, 151–167
    advanced write-through cache, 157
    benchmark program for setup, 160
    buffering controls vs. caching controllers, 162
    cache hit, 155
    deferred-write cache, 157–159
    direct-mapped cache, 161
    elevator cache, 159
    fully associative cache, 160
    hardware vs. software cache, 153, 162–164
    memory caching vs., 151
    options during setup, 159–160
    PC hangs and, 159, 164
    read cache, 154–156
    set-associative cache, 161–162
    SpinRite testing, 368
    track buffers, 76, 154
    write-through cache, 156
disk compression software
    safety boot diskette and, 30
    SpinRite and, 408–411
Disk Editor (Norton Utilities)
    disk snooping with, 175
    displaying FATs, 267–268
    on safety boot diskette, 27
"Disk error reading FAT x" message, 297
disk failures. *See* hard disk failure
disk included with this book. *See* Hard Disk SECRETS disk
disk initialization, 276
Disk Manager, 213
    DMDRVR.BIN, 30, 246
    low-level formatting, 230
    safety boot diskette and, 30
    SMARTDrive conflict with, 214
    SpinRite and, 408
    XBIOS, 214
Disk margin icon, 7
disk mirroring, 321–322
disk operating system. *See* DOS
disk test (FORMAT), 276, 284
display format for LIST, 501
DMDRVR.BIN, 30, 246
domain size, 47
DOS, 169–206
    acronym explained, 4
    alternative versions, 171

Index 535

alternatives to DOS high-level format, 280–283
BIOS program and, 97, 170–171
BIOS ROMs and, 97
block devices vs. character devices, 172–173
creating bootable diskettes, 24, 30–31
defined, 4
disk buffers, 153, 164–167
ECC and, 66–67
emulation programs, 171
file request processing steps, 178–179, 180–183
file storage and retrieval, 73
filters, 496–497
INT 25h and 26h interrupts bypassed by, 204
LIST "goto DOS" option, 514
LIST-related terminology, 496–497
with OS/2, 29
overview, 169–172
pipes, 497
redirection, 496
reference books, 5
upgrading to Version 3.3 or later, 254–255
volume size limits, 207–208, 210–213
DOS disk buffers, 153, 164–167
how they work, 173–174
recommended settings, 165
security risk from, 175
DOS extended partition, 247
creating with FDISK, 252–253
DOS for Dummies, 5
DOS logical drives. *See* volumes
DOS primary partition, 246–247
creating with FDISK, 251–253
DOS shells, 21
DOSSHELL, 21
double MIG heads, 135–136
Double-Sided Double-Density (DSDD) data encoding, 56
DoubleSpace, 299, 383, 405, 408–411
DR DOS. *See* DOS
drive electronics, 141–145
failure, 303

head-positioner drive circuit, 142–144
interface electronics, 145
spindle-motor drive circuit, 141–142
switches and amplifiers, 144–145
temperature-related problems, 303–304
"Drive not ready" message, 306
drive parameter block, 190
DrivePro, 31, 456
drivers. *See* device drivers
drive-type determination, 194–205
AT and higher PCs, 196–199
ESDI drives, 200
hard-disk cards, 200
IDE/ATA drives, 200–202
SCSI drives, 202–205
user-definable drive type, 197
XT and similar controllers, 194–195
DSDD data encoding, 56
Dual Boot strategy (OS/2), 29

— E —

/E parameter (DAZZLE), 471
ECC (error correction codes), 62–67
DOS and, 66–67
error messages and, 224
orchard model, 63–64
rewriting data and, 346
SpinRite monitoring of use, 378
"turning off," 67
Edit command (LIST), 517
electronic circuit boards. *See* controllers; drive electronics
elevator cache, 159
embedded servo systems, 124–125
illustrated, 125
Emergency toolkit, 29–30
encoding. *See* data-encoding strategies
Encyclopedia of Main Boards, The, 455
enhanced RLL data encoding, 61
Enhanced Small Device Interface drives. *See* ESDI drives
ERLL data encoding, 61
error correction, 34, 62–67
error correction codes. *See* ECC (error correction codes)

Index

error detection, 61–62
    cyclical redundancy checks (CRC), 62
    parity checking, 61–62
"Error loading operating system" message, 297, 304
error messages, 221–224
    "Abort, Retry . . .," 223
    "ATTENTION! SpinRite utilizes and requires the pre-defined auxiliary last track . . .," 386
    "Bad or missing Command Interpreter," 297
    "Bad or missing xxxx," 297
    "Bad Partition Table," 297
    "Cannot find system files," 291
    cross-linked files, 276, 417
    "Disk boot failure," 297
    "Disk error reading FAT x," 297
    "Drive not ready," 306
    "Error loading operating system," 297, 304
    "Error reading drive X," 62
    "General failure reading drive C," 291, 306
    "Invalid drive specification," 291, 306
    "Invalid partition table," 297, 304
    "I/O memory error at XXXXX," 62
    lost chains, 274–275, 416–417
    "Missing operating system," 297, 304
    "PARITY CHECK ONE" and "PARITY CHECK TWO" messages, 62
    "Probable Non-DOS disk," 297
    "Read fault," 340
    "Read [or write] error on drive C," 291
    "Sector not found," 291, 294–297, 337
"Error reading drive X" message, 62
Esc key with DAZZLE, 479
ESDI drives
    controllers, 61
    drive-type determination, 200
    ESDI standard, 87
    head positioner drive circuits for, 144
    RLL encoding on, 61
    sector interleave and performance, 77
    sectors per track, 77
    track buffer RAM requirements, 154
EVDR.SYS, 213, 235
exiting LIST, 500–501
expanded memory
    extended memory vs., 163
    second hard disks and EMS cards, 195
expert help, finding, 17–18
extended DOS partition, 247
    creating with FDISK, 252–253
extended memory vs. expanded memory, 163
extended partition table, 247
    illustrated, 248
external servo systems, 113–118
    alternatives to Gray code, 116, 118
    Gray code, 114–116, 117
    illustrated, 113
extracting lines using LIST, 510–511
EZ-Drive, 456

— F —

/F parameter
    CHKDSK, 275, 415, 416, 418
    DAZZLE, 473
F5 key with DAZZLE, 480
F8 key with DAZZLE, 483
F9 key with DAZZLE, 483
F10 key with DAZZLE, 483
fade control keys with DAZZLE, 481–482
fade enable control for DAZZLE, 485–486
failure. *See* hard disk failure
fan, 41
FATs. *See* file allocation tables (FATs)
FDISK
    cautions, 250, 251
    /MBR parameter, 300
    partition table and, 249–250
    partition table damage and, 300
    partitioning with, 251–253
    restoring master boot record, 300
    on safety boot diskette, 26
ferrimagnets, 35
ferromagnets, 35
FILE0001.CHK, etc., 275
file access, information requirements for, 287–290
file access menu (DAZZLE), 486–487
file allocation tables (FATs), 265–270
    12-bit FATs, 266, 267–269

16-bit FATs, 266, 267–269
   illustrated, 260
   overview, 263–264
   two copies of, 270
file compression on-the-fly, 30, 408–411
file fragmentation, 308–311
File Manager (Windows), 21
file managers
   delete confirmation feature, 21
   DOS shell programs, 21
   for Windows, 21
file request processing steps, 178–179, 180–183
file selection menu (LIST), 515–519
file sharing and LIST, 514
file viewing with LIST, 453–455
filtering in LIST, 506–508
filters (DOS), 496–497
firmware, 176
FlickerFree, 446–447
flip-flop length, minimum, 46–49
floppy disks
   booting from, 25
   clean boot diskette for SpinRite, 411–414
   DSDD disks, 56
   emergency programs on, 29–30
   failure, 19
   hard disk formatting vs., 280
   low-level formatting, 232
   safety boot diskette, 23–29, 30–31
   See also Hard Disk SECRETS disk
flux-sensing read heads, 132
flying height of heads, 37, 134–135, 139
FM data encoding, 55–56
   illustrated, 54
   See also NRZ data encoding
FORMAT
   destructive format, 300–301
   disk initialization by, 276
   disk test by, 276, 284
   /S option, 24
   on safety boot diskette, 26
   unformatting, 299
   /V option, 28
   See also logical formatting

formatting
   defined, 227–228
   floppy disks vs. hard disk, 280
   logical (high-level), 259–285
   low-level, 17, 227–236
   partitioning, 237–258
   safety boot diskette, 24, 25, 30–31
   three-level process, 228–229
   See also logical formatting; low-level formatting; partitioning
FR /SAVE (Norton Utilities), 316
freeware on *Hard Disk SECRETS* disk, 8, 450
freezing your hard drive, 304
frequency modulation. *See* FM data encoding
full backups, 317
full-stroke seek, 371
fully associative cache, 160
function keys
   with DAZZLE, 480, 483
   with LIST, 520
fundamental principles, 33–35
FV.COM, 454–455

— G —

"General failure reading drive C" message, 291, 306
GeoWorks, 170
Gibson LPS-II, 446
Gibson Research bulletin board, 438
Gibson, Steve, 305, 327, 356–357, 438, 445–447, 459
glass platters, 36
Golden Bow Software, Vfeature Deluxe, 213
Goodman, John M.
   mailing address, 9
   Memory Management for All of Us, 163, 178
Gookin, Dan, 5
grain size, 47
Gray code
   in dedicated platter servo systems, 119–121
   in external servo systems, 114–116
   illustrated, 117, 120
group-coded recording (CGR), 58

Index

— H —

h for hexadecimal notation in this book, 194
H key with DAZZLE, 482
/H parameter
    DAZZLE, 473
    Micro House utilities, 456
hard disk failure, 287–323
    backups, 316–321
    chances of recovery, 15–16
    data accidents, 297–301
    data recovery, 315–316
    diagnosing, 311–315
    file fragmentation, 308–311
    hard disk subsystem hardware, 287, 288
    hardware failure, 301–306
        controller death, 306–308
        drive electronics failure, 303
        head crashes, 305–305
        simple mistakes to avoid, 306
        spindle-bearing failure, 302–303
        stiction, 301–302
        temperature-related problems, 303–305
    hardware failure vs. information pattern failures, 291
    inevitability, 19, 23
    information required for file access and booting, 287–291
    misalignment, 294–297
    panic due to, 16
    preventive maintenance, 343–363
    reseating cables, 292–293
    safety boot diskette, 23–29
    simple things to check, 291–293
    troubleshooting chart, 313
    why computer components fail, 14–15
    See also preventive maintenance
hard disk parameter tables (HDPT), 190–194
    autoconfiguring disk controllers and, 195, 198–199
    drive-type determination, 194–205
    illustrated, 191–192
    interrupt vector table pointers, 190, 191, 192
    logical vs. physical drives, 190
Hard Disk SECRETS
    design conventions, 7
    how to use this book, 5–7
    knowledge required, 3–5
    mailing address for comments, 9
    margin icons, 7
    who the book is for, 1–2
Hard Disk SECRETS disk
    contents, 449–450
    DAZZLE, 8, 451–453, 461–491
    freeware, 8, 450
    freeware vs. shareware, 8
    HDINFO, 8, 460
    LIST, 8, 453–455, 492–528
    LISTPGMS subdirectory, 449–450
    margin icon, 7
    Micro House utilities, 455–459
    MOVEHDD.SYS, 195, 199, 459
    overview, 8
    PARK.COM, 305, 438, 459
    shareware, 8, 450–451
    TIMEPARK.COM, 441, 460 ·
    See also specific programs and files
Hard Disk Technical Guide, The, 455
hard disks
    basic construction, 36–41
    cutaway view, 36
    drive-type determination, 194–205
    fundamental principles, 33–35
    installing, 352
    logical vs. physical drives, 190
    mounting, 306, 307
    tape drives vs., 33–34
    value of, 14–15
hard magnets, 35
Hardcards, 93–94, 114
    low-level formatting and, 234
hard-disk cards, 93–94, 114
    drive-type determination, 200
hardware
    in hard disk subsystem, 287, 288
    information pattern failures vs. hardware failures, 291
hardware disk cache
    PC hangs and, 164
    software cache vs., 153, 162–164
    See also disk caching

Index

HDINFO files, 460
   viewing, 8
HDPT. *See* hard disk parameter tables (HDPT)
head assembly actuator. *See* actuators
head crashes, 140, 305–306
head drift, 294, 337–339
head gap, 42, 47, 134, 136
head multiplexing, 234–235
head parking. *See* parking heads
head skewing, 78–81
   altering, 81
   illustrated, 79
   overview, 78–80
   performance and, 23
   by UltraStor 12f and 12c, 217
   where information is stored, 80
   See also sector interleave
head translation. *See* sector mapping
headers, sector, 70–71, 127–128
   refreshing, 337–339, 346–347
head-positioner drive circuit, 142–144
heads. *See* inductive read/write heads
head-switching circuits, 144–145
help
   finding expert help, 17–18
   user groups, 18
Hewlett-Packard, Kittyhawk hard drives, 96
hex format filter (LIST), 507–508
hexadecimal notation, 194
hi-bit filter (LIST), 507
Hicks, Clint, 5
hidden files, 24
High Performance File System drives. *See* HPFS (High Performance File System) logical drives
high-density floppy drives, low-density diskettes with, 25
high-frequency test, 360
high-level formatting. *See* logical formatting
Hillier, Rick, 321
Historical Aside margin icon, 7
HOPTIMUM, 78, 333–334
hot fixes, 91–92
HPFS (High Performance File System) logical drives, 29, 249, 281–282

HTHF program, 81, 299
hybrid servo systems, 125–126
   settling time, 126
Hyperkinetix, DeltaFile, 321
hysteresis, 378

— I —

I command (LIST), 517
/I parameter (DAZZLE), 475
IAU (Interleave Adjustment Utility), 78, 335
IBM AT drive-type determination, 196–199
IBM clones, 3
IBM PC
   development of, 82–83
   SCSI devices with, 88–89
   XT hard disk controller with, 84
IBM XT
   development of, 82–83
   drive-type determination, 194–195
IBMBIO.COM, 24
IBMDOS.COM, 24
IDE paddle card, 92
IDE standard, 92–93, 95
IDE/ATA drives
   controllers, 51, 61
   defined, 200
   drive-type determination, 200–202
   head positioner drive circuits for, 144
   IDE standard, 92–93
   interface electronics, 145
   zone bit recording, 51
ILEAVE. *See* IAU (Interleave Adjustment Utility)
IMAGE, 316
image selection keys with DAZZLE, 484
incremental backups, 317–318
inductive read/write heads, 128–141
   amplifiers, 144
   flying height, 37, 134–135, 139
   future developments, 140–141
   head crashes, 140
   head gap, 42, 47, 134, 136
   head-switching circuits, 144–145
   how they work, 34–35, 36–41, 42–44, 101–127

Index

illustrated, 38, 40, 43, 48, 129
longitudinal recording, 129–136
numbering, 39, 40
permanent magnetization in, 128
servo-controlled head positioning, 113–127
skew and performance, 23
stepper motor actuators, 39, 102–110
stiction, 301–302
surfing, 37
vertical recording, 136–140
voice coil actuators, 39, 111–112
See also parking heads
information required for file access and booting, 287–291
    hardware failures vs. information pattern failures, 291
InfoWorld, 446
initialization of hard disk, 276
input-output bus, 75, 81
INSTALL statement, 184, 187
installable device drivers, 203–205
installing hard disks, 352
instruction pointer (IP), 185
INT 13h compatible SCSI host adapters, 203
integrated drive electronics/AT attachment drives. *See* IDE/ATA drives
integrated motherboards, 14
Intel order, 267, 357
interactive use of SpinRite, 419–424
interface electronics, 145
interleave. *See* sector interleave
Interleave Adjustment Utility, 78, 335
interrupt return (IRET), 185
interrupt service routines (ISRs), 184
    illustrated, 185
    TSRs and, 186–187
interrupt vector table, 184
    device drivers and, 187, 190
    hard disk parameter table (HDPT) pointers, 190, 191, 192
    illustrated, 185
    TSRs and, 186–187
interrupting SpinRite, 366, 386–387
interrupts, 179, 184
    defined, 179

DOS bypass of INT 25h and 26h interrupts, 204
error message intercepting, 221–222
hard disk parameter table pointers, 191, 192
hard disk physical size limits and, 209–210, 213–219
illustrated, 185
service routines (ISRs), 184, 185, 186–187
vector table, 184, 185, 186–187, 190
intersector time
    defined, 373
    testing (SpinRite), 372–374
"Invalid drive specification" message, 291, 306
"Invalid partition table" message, 297, 304
"I/O memory error at XXXXX" message, 62
IO.SYS, 24
IP (instruction pointer), 185
IRET (interrupt return), 185
isolated-ones test, 361
ISRs (interrupt service routines), 184
    illustrated, 185
    TSRs and, 186–187
Italic type in this book, 7

— J —

junk filter (LIST), 507

— K —

/K parameter (DAZZLE), 471–472
Katz, Phil, 455
key commands. *See* command keys
KFDISK, 299
Kittyhawk hard drives, 96
Kolod, Mark, 333
Kolod Research, 81, 299

— L —

label, volume, 274
LADDR (Layered Device Driver Architecture), 90
Layered Device Driver Architecture (LADDR), 90

Index 541

layers of programs in a PC, 176–179
  error messages and, 221–224
  firmware, 176
  illustrated, 177
  loaded at bootup, 176
LBA (logical block address), 91
  logical sectors vs., 98
lead screw, 106
least significant byte, order of storing, 267, 357
LEAVEBAD command line option (SpinRite), 425
LEDs
  with DAZZLE, 478–479
  for servos, 113–114
length
  bit cell, 49
  of bits, 46
  See also size
LICENSE, 455
Light Pen System for Apple II computers, 446
light-emitting diodes (LEDs)
  with DAZZLE, 477–478
  for servos, 113–114
LIST, 8, 492–528
  Buerg Utilities, 526–527
  changing directories, 516
  cloning, 525–526
  command key summary, 520–523
  command line syntax and switches, 498–499, 502–504
  configuration, 524–526
  display format, 501
  DOS considerations, 514–515
  DOS terms, 496–497
  entering commands, 501
  exiting, 500–501
  extracting lines, 510–511
  file selection menu, 515–519
  filtering, 506–508
  "goto DOS" option, 514
  installation, 492–493
  limitations and requirements, 526
  marking lines, 510–511
  movement keys, 516
  multiple file display, 511–512

overview, 453–455, 492
positioning commands, 505–506
printing, 511
printing the manual, 493
registration, 528
scanning for text, 508–509
screen colors, 524–526
screen saver, 514–515
scrolling, 504–505
starting, 499–500
status line format, 502
telephone dialer, 513
varieties of LIST.COM, 493–495
windows, 512–513
LIST.COM PLUS, 494
  file selection menu, 515–519
List command (LIST), 517
LIST Enhanced, 494–495
LIST.HST, 455
LISTMOD.DOC, 455
LISTPGMS subdirectory, 449
  contents, 450
LISTR.COM, 454, 494
logical block address (LBA), 91
  logical sectors vs., 98
logical drives. *See* HPFS (High Performance File System) logical drives; volumes
logical formatting, 259–285
  alternatives to DOS, 280–283
  boot record, 260–262
  data area, 260, 262–265
  destructive, 300–301
  disk initialization, 276
  disk test, 276, 284
  file allocation tables (FATs), 260, 265–270
  floppy disk formatting vs., 280
  root directory, 260, 270–272
  unformatting, 299
  See also FORMAT
logical sector number
  DOS limit, 208, 210–213
  evading the limits, 210–213
logical vs. physical hard disk drives, 190
longitudinal recording, 129–136
  bit density limitation, 133–134

Index

critical dimensions, 134–135
flux-sensing read heads, 132
illustrated, 131, 133, 134
MIG and double MIG heads, 135–136
thin-film heads, 130–131
vertical recording vs., 136–138
look aside read cache, 155–156
lost chains, 274–275, 416–417
loudspeakers, 107
low-density floppy drives, high-density diskettes with, 25
low-frequency test, 360
low-high alternation test, 361
low-level formatting, 227–236
    bumping the drive during, 295
    disk test during, 284
    Hardcards and, 234
    head multiplexing, 234–235
    how it works, 231
    nondestructive, 231, 233
    refreshing the format, 346–347
    by SpinRite, 231, 233, 346–347, 379, 420
    three ways to do it, 230–231
    Toshiba laptops and, 234–235
    when to reformat, 17
LPS-II, 446

— M —

/M parameter
    DAZZLE, 452, 473
    Micro House utilities, 456
McAfee Associates, 30
Mace Utilities, 299
Macintosh computers, 2
    SoftPC for, 171
magnetic field lines, 35, 42
magnetic flip-flop length, minimum, 46–49
magnetic flux, 35
magnetic materials vs. magnetizable materials, 35
magnetic recording
    bit size, 44–51
    cleanliness, importance of, 41
    data-encoding strategies, 51–61
    error correction, 34, 62–67

error detection, 61–62
fundamentals, 33–34
hard disk construction, 36–41
how the heads read and write, 42–44
"weakening" of magnetic fields, 344–345
magnetic transitions, defined, 50
magnetizable materials vs. magnetic materials, 35
MAILER, 455
maintenance. *See* preventive maintenance
manufacturer tests of hard disks, 347–348, 349–353
    defect lists, 351–352
    digital testing vs., 362–363
    head-positioning accuracy test, 351
    surface analysis, 351
marking bad sectors, 349, 381–382, 384
marking lines in LIST, 510–511
Martin Development Services, 8
Martin, Ray, 8, 460
master boot record, 238–244
    displaying, 240–242
    example, 241–242
    illustrated, 241, 243
    partition table, 243–244, 257
    restoring with FDISK, 300
    saving information, 21, 241
    signature, 262
MBR. *See* master boot record
/MBR parameter (FDISK), 300
measurement window, 373
media descriptor byte, 264, 267
memory. *See* RAM
memory caching, disk caching vs., 151
Memory Management for All of Us, 163, 178
memory-resident programs. *See* TSR programs
MENU.BAT (SpinRite), 428, 429
menus
    DAZZLE file access menu, 486–487
    LIST file selection menu, 515–519
    SpinRite main menu, 366
messages. *See* error messages
metal in gap (MIG) heads, 135–136
MFM data encoding, 56–57
    clock-data separator circuit, 144

Index

ECC with, 65
head positioner drive circuits for, 143
illustrated, 54
RLL vs., 86
sector interleave and performance, 77
sectors per track, 72–73
SpinRite test patterns, 358, 360–361
surface analysis and, 356
track buffer RAM requirements, 154
MH utility set, 8, 455–459
MH-ESDI.EXE, 456–457
MH-IDE.EXE, 456–457
MH-RESTR.EXE, 457–458
   restoring first track, 241
   restoring master boot record, 241
   on safety boot diskette, 26
MH-SAVE.EXE, 21, 197, 457–458
   data files too large, 26
   first track saved by, 241
   on safety boot diskette, 26
MH-SYS.EXE, 458–459
   on safety boot diskette, 26
Micro House, 8, 31, 455
   DrivePro, 456
   EZ-Drive, 456
   reference products, 455–456
   utilities, 455–459
Micro House Encyclopedia of Hard Drives, The, 455
micro-boulders, 348
Microsoft, DOS creation by, 4
Microsoft Real-time Compression Interface (MRCI), 405
Microsoft Windows. *See* Windows
MIG (metal in gap) heads, 135–136
minimum magnetic flip-flop length, 46–49
MIRROR, 21
   /PART option, 21
   /T*d* option, 21
mirroring vs. backups, 321–322
misalignment, 294–297
   refreshing the low-level format, 346–347
   rewriting data, 346
"Missing operating system" message, 297, 304

mistakes
   avoiding when working on hardware, 306, 307
   protecting against, 21
mixed-frequency tests, 361
modified frequency modulation. *See* MFM data encoding
most significant byte, order of storing, 267, 357
motherboards, 14
Motorola address, 267
mounting a drive, 306, 307
mouse clicks with DAZZLE, 482
Move command (LIST), 518
MOVEHDD.SYS, 195, 199, 459
MRCI (Microsoft Real-time Compression Interface), 405
MS-DOS. *See* DOS
MSDOS.SYS, 24
MT-DAZE, 466
multiple file display in LIST, 511–512
multipole motors, 103–105

— N —

N key with DAZZLE, 482
NDOS.COM, 24
negative feedback, 109–110
NetWare
   COMPSURF program, 283
   logical formatting, 283
   operating system, 172
   Surface Test routine, 283
Network Interface Technical Guide, The, 455
NeXT computers, 2
   SoftPC for, 171
NOCOLOR command line option (SpinRite), 426
NOFORMAT command line option (SpinRite), 425, 426
noise (in data), 344
noises
   during SpinRite quick surface scan, 370
   recalibration noises, 147–148
   when parking heads, 142–143
   when reading bad sectors, 148
   when running ordinary DOS programs, 148
Non-Return-to-Zero. *See* NRZ data encoding

Index

Norton Desktop for Windows, 21
Norton Utilities, 299
    Calibrate, 419
    Disk Editor, 27, 175
    in emergency toolkit, 30
    FR /SAVE, 316
    NDOS.COM, 24
    NU, 27
    SI, 82
    Speed Disk, 310
    WipeInfo, 175
NOSEEKTEST command line option (SpinRite), 426
NOSHADING command line option (SpinRite), 426
NOSOUND command line option (SpinRite), 426
Novell, NetWare, 172, 283
NRZ data encoding, 55–56
    illustrated, 54
    See also FM data encoding
NRZI data encoding, 56
NTFS volumes, 282–283
NU (Norton Utilities), 27
num lock LED with DAZZLE, 479

— O —

Official SpinRite II and Hard Disk Companion, The, 2
Official XTree MS-DOS, Windows, and Hard Disk Management Companion, 22
on-the-fly file-compression software, 30, 408
OnTrack Software, Disk Manager, 30, 213, 214
opening your PC, 4–5
    precautions, 27, 292
    simple mistakes to avoid, 306, 307
operating systems (non-DOS), 249
optical encoders for servos, 113–114
option ROM, 198–199
orchard model for ECC, 63–64
organizing the hard disk, 22
OS/2, 172
    Boot Manager strategy, 29
    DOS with, 29
    Dual Boot strategy, 29
    logical formatting, 281–282
    partitioning and, 249
    as programming environment, 170
    safety boot diskette for, 29
oxide coatings, bit size, 46–49

— P —

P key with DAZZLE, 481–482
panic, 16
"PARITY CHECK ONE" and "PARITY CHECK TWO" messages, 62
parity checking, 61–62
    ECC, 62–67
PARK.COM, 305, 438, 459
parking heads, 111–112, 305, 434–442
    banging noise during, 142–143
    data protection and, 296
    described, 434–435
    destructive programs, 439–441
    illustrated, 435
    impolite programs, 439
    programs, 438–442
    read/write head magnetization and, 128
    resident park utilities, 441–442
    safe programs, 438
    self-parking drives, 111–112, 436–438
    of servo-motor drives, 142–143
    startup and, 436
    using DAZZLE, 437, 451
    using PARK.COM, 459
    using TIMEPARK.COM, 460
/PART option (MIRROR), 21
partition table, 249–250
    extended partition table, 247
    FDISK and, 249–250
    illustrated, 244, 248
    repairing, 299, 300
    saving information, 21
    structure, 243–244, 257
    system byte, 246
    See also master boot record
partitioning, 237–258
    active or bootable partition, 245
    diagnostic cylinder, 244–245
    DOS extended partition, 247

Index 545

DOS primary partition, 246–247
  with FDISK, 249–253
  illustrated, 239
  large logical volume disadvantages, 256
  logical volumes, 212–213
  master boot record (MBR), 238–244
  more than 10 partitions with SpinRite, 423–424, 433
  organization and, 22
  rationale, 237–238
  "secret" cylinder, 245
  third-party programs, 213
  third-party software, 254–255
Path command (LIST), 518
PATH statement on safety boot diskette, 28
pattern testing (SpinRite), 357–362, 380, 421–422
PC Bridge Board, 171
PC DOS. *See* DOS
PC Tools, 299
PC user groups, 18
PC World DOS 5 Complete Handbook, 5
PC-Kwik Corp., 163
  Power Disk, 309
  Super PC-Kwik, 157, 163
PCMCIA standard, 94, 96
PCs
  acronym explained, 3
  historical development, 3
  layers of programs, 176–179
  opening, 4–5
  reference books, 5
  SCSI devices with, 88–89
  turning back on after turning off, 298–299
  usage in this book, 3–4
PCs for Dummies, 5
PCSHELL, Clear File command, 301
PE data encoding, 56
perfect backups, 19–20
performance
  access time, 69
  benchmark programs, 160
  cache hit rate, 155
  data transfer rate, 69
  defragmentation and, 23, 308–309

ESDI data transfer rate, 87
head and cylinder skew and, 23
organization and, 22
ribbon cables and, 86
sector interleaving and, 22–23, 75–78
SpinRite and performance-testing programs, 82
permanent magnets, 35
  read/write head magnetization, 128
PERSTOR command line option (SpinRite), 426
PerStor hard disk controllers, 232–233
PgUp and PgDn keys with DAZZLE, 480
phase-locked loop drives, 141, 142
phonograph record grooves, 38, 39
pinhole surface defects, 296
pinion, 105
pins, 85
pipes (DOS), 497
PKARC, 455
plated media drives, bit size, 46–49
platters
  basic construction, 36–37
  defects in coating, 354
  fan action, 41
  glass platters, 36
  grain or domain size, 47
  illustrated, 43, 45
  maximum number, 39
  numbering of surfaces, 39, 40
  speed of rotation, 101
  surface analysis, 347–363
  surface materials, 46–47
Plus Development Corp., 93
PocketSoft, RT-Patch, 321
positioning commands in LIST, 505–506
positioning heads. *See* servo-controlled head positioning
POST (power on self test), 198
power cables, reseating, 292–293
Power Disk, 309
power management features and hard disk life, 14–15
power on self test (POST), 198
power supply
  disconnecting from hard disk, 27

Index

hard disk connections, 83
power user, 407
PowerWrite, 157
preventive maintenance, 343–363
    low-level format refreshing, 346–347
    rewriting data, 345–346
    surface analysis, 347–363
    "weakening" of magnetic fields, 344–345
    See also surface analysis
Priam, EVDR.SYS, 213, 235
primary DOS partition, 246–247
    creating with FDISK, 251–253
printer port cards, 14
printing using LIST, 493, 511
"Probable Non-DOS disk" message, 297
programming environments, 170
PROGRAMS, 455
programs
    damaged files, 379
    DOS file request processing steps, 178–179, 180–183
    head parking, 438–442
    layers in a PC, 176–179
    lost chains, 275
PROMPT statement on safety boot diskette, 28
protection
    against user mistakes, 21
    data protection, 19–21
    perfect backups, 19–20
pulses
    data encoding approach, 52–54
    defined, 52
    pulse crowding, 50

— Q —

/Q parameter (DAZZLE), 475
Quantum Corp., 93
    Hardcards, 93–94, 114
QUICKSCAN command line option (SpinRite), 426

— R —

/R parameter (DAZZLE), 452, 475
rack, 105
rack and pinion actuators. *See* stepper motor actuators
rack-and-pinion gears, 105
Radio Shack, 3
RAID (Redundant Array of Inexpensive Disks), 220–221
RAM
    DOS disk buffers, 153
    extended vs. expanded memory, 163
    LIST requirements, 526
    memory cache vs. disk cache requirements, 151, 152
    read cache requirements, 154
    SpinRite tests, 365, 367
    testing, 341
    track buffer requirements, 154
    as volatile medium for data, 151, 153
    See also buffers; disk caching
rapid low-high alternation test, 361
Rathbone, Andy, 5
RAZZLE-DAZZLE, 452–453, 466
read ahead cache, 156
read amplifier circuitry, 144
read cache, 154–156
    look aside read cache, 155–156
    RAM requirements, 154
    read ahead cache, 156
    write-through cache vs., 156
read circuitry, 344
read fault error, 295
"Read fault" message, 340
"Read [or write] error on drive C" message, 291
read-only test (SpinRite), 369–370
read/write heads. *See* inductive read/write heads
recalibration noises, 147–148
records, phonograph, 38, 39
recovering data, 315–316, 377–379
redirection (DOS), 496
Redundant Array of Inexpensive Disks (RAID), 220–221
reformatting. *See* formatting
refreshing sector headers, 337–339, 346–347
refreshing the low-level format, 346–347

Index

register-compatible SCSI host adapters, 202–203
registering shareware, 8
    DAZZLE, 491
    LIST, 528
reinterleaving programs, 77–78, 327–342
    development, 327–337
    IDE and SCSI drives with, 93
    old method of reinterleaving, 329–333
    side benefits, 337–341
    See also SpinRite
remnant magnetization, 35
Ren command (LIST), 518
repairing damaged data, 299–300
repartitioning. *See* partitioning
reports from SpinRite, 380–382, 422–423
reseating cables, 292–293
RESUME command line option (SpinRite), 426
resuming interrupted SpinRite operations, 366, 387
revolutions per minute, testing, 372
rewriting data, 345–346
ribbon cables, 85–86
    reseating, 293
    for SCSI devices, 89
RLL data encoding, 57–60
    clock-data separator circuit, 144
    ECC with, 65
    head positioner drive circuits for, 143
    illustrated, 54, 59
    MFM vs., 86
    sector interleave and performance, 77
    sectors per track, 77
    SpinRite test patterns, 359, 360–361
    surface analysis and, 356
    track buffer RAM requirements, 154
RLL-capable drives, 60
ROM BIOS
    BIOS extension ROM chips, 198–199
    date of, 84
    defined, 66
    DOS and, 97
    ECC and, 66–67
    layers of programs in a PC, 176–179
    option ROM, 198–199
    overhead, 371
    start-up program and, 198–199
    video BIOS extension ROM, 198
    XT hard disk controller in PC and, 84
root directory, 270–272
    first-level subdirectories, 272
    illustrated, 260, 271
    volume label, 274
RT-Patch, 321
run-length limited. *See* RLL data encoding

— S —

/S parameter
    DAZZLE, 473
    FORMAT, 24
safety boot diskette, 23–29, 30–31
    AUTOEXEC.BAT file, 25, 28, 30–31
    CONFIG.SYS file, 24, 25, 28, 30–31
    configuration CMOS on, 26
    creating, 24, 25, 28–29
    creating after hard disk failure, 30–31
    customization files, 25
    DATA.FIL on, 28, 29
    formatting, 23–24
    optional files, 26
    for OS/2, 29
    system files, 23–24
    system requirements, 24
    testing, 27
saturated magnetization, 34
scanning for text in LIST, 508–509
SCHECK (Stacker), 383
scrambled-bits test, 361
screen colors for LIST, 524–526
screen savers
    DAZZLE, 8, 451–453
    LIST, 514–515
scroll lock LED with DAZZLE, 477–478
scrolling using LIST, 504–505
SCSI drives
    controllers, 51, 61, 202–203
    drive-type determination, 202–205
    head positioner drive circuits for, 144
    hot fixes, 91
    interface electronics, 145

Index

logical block addresses (LBA), 91
master and slaves, 88
RAID drives, 220–221
RLL encoding on, 61
SCSI standard, 88–92, 95
track buffer RAM requirements, 154
zone bit recording, 51
SCSI host adapters, 88–89, 202–204
   device driver standards and, 90
   installable device drivers, 203–205
   INT 13h compatible controllers, 203
   multiple slave drives, 220
   register-compatible controllers, 202–203
   SCSI controllers vs., 146
SCSI slave interface, 89
SCSI standards, 88–92, 95
   device drivers, 89–90
   SCSI-2 standard, 89
   SCSI-3 standard, 89
Seagate Technology, PC/XT hard disk standard, 84–86
Seaware ARC, 455
"secret" cylinder, 245
sector, 70–71
   bad sector, 348
   for copy-protected programs, 71
   defined, 37
   ECC in, 71
   FORMAT marking of bad sectors, 276
   headers, 70–71, 127–128, 337–339
   illustrated, 38, 70
   interleave, 22–23, 71–78, 80–82
   intersector time testing (SpinRite), 372–374
   larger than 512 bytes, 173, 211–212
   logical vs. logical block addresses (LBA), 98
   logical vs. physical, 98
   marking bad sectors, 349, 381–382, 384
   master boot record, 238–244
   maximum number of logical sectors, 208, 210–213
   noises when reading bad sectors, 148
   refreshing sector headers, 337–339
   size, 70
sector interleave, 71–78, 80–82
   altering, 81

DOS file storage and retrieval, 73
illustrated, 72
inconsistent values, 81–82
input-output bus and, 75, 81
optimum interleave, 75–78
overview, 71–73
performance and interleave value, 22–23, 75–78
ratios, 75
reinterleaving programs, 77–78
SpinRite analysis and setting, 375–377
SpinRite check, 375
track buffers and, 76
where information is stored, 80
See also head skewing
sector mapping
   evading physical limits on disk size, 214–217
   hot fixes, 91–92
   by IDE drives, 93, 201, 218–219
   illustrated, 216
   low-level reformatting and, 347
   by SCSI drives, 218–219
   translating controllers, 347
   by UltraStor 12f and 12c, 217–218
"Sector not found" messages, 291, 294–297, 337
sector translation. *See* sector mapping
security, 175, 301
seek errors, 223
seek tests, 271–272, 351, 420–421
seeking, 371
self-parking drives, 111–112, 436–438
servo, 110
servo feedback, 109–110
servo signals
   in buried servo systems, 126
   in dedicated platter servo systems, 118–121
   in embedded servo systems, 124
   in hybrid servo systems, 125–126
   in wedge servo systems, 123–124
servo-controlled head positioning, 113–127
   buried servo systems, 126–127
   dedicated platter servo systems, 118–122
   embedded servo systems, 124–125
   external servo systems, 113–118
   head-positioner drive circuit, 142–144

Index

hybrid servo systems, 125–126
manufacturer testing, 351
wedge servo systems, 123–124
set-associative cache, 161–162
settling time, 126
shareware, 464
  on *Hard Disk SECRETS* disk, 8, 450–451
  registering, 8
SHELL statement, 24
Shift-F10 key with DAZZLE, 481
SI (Norton Utilities), SpinRite and incorrect results, 82
sidebars, 7
signature, 262
size
  areal density of bits, 51
  bit cell length, 49
  bit size, 44–51
  DAZZLE image size, 485
  directory entries, 270
  grain or domain size, 47
  hard disk parameter tables, 191
  logical size limits from DOS, 207–208, 210–213
  maximum clusters, 264
  maximum logical disk size, 208
  maximum physical disk size, 210
  physical size limits from BIOS, 209–210, 213–219
  read/write head critical dimensions, 134–135, 138–140
  sectors, 70
  track buffer RAM requirements, 154
skew, head. *See* head skewing
slack space, 265
Slick, Beth, 22
slider, 132, 140
Small Computer System Interface drives. *See* SCSI drives
SMARTDrive, 158–159, 163
  OnTrack Disk Manager conflict with, 214
Socha, John, 5
softly magnetic materials, 35
SoftPC emulator program, 171
software disk cache

hardware cache vs., 153, 162–164
See also disk caching
Sort command (LIST), 518–519
speed. *See* performance
Speed Disk, 310
SpeedStor, 213
  low-level formatting, 230
  SpinRite and, 408
spindle-bearing failure, 302–303
spindle-motor drive circuit, 141–142
SpinRite, 365–447
  advanced tips, 407–443
  AUTOEXEC.BAT for, 408, 413, 428, 429
  bad sector marking, 349, 381–382, 384
  bad sectors turned good, 385, 420
  batch mode operation, 424–433
  CHKDSK, running before SpinRite, 414–419
  clean boot diskette for, 411–414
  command line options, 424–426
  CONFIG.SYS for, 408, 411–412, 414, 428
  controller tests, 367–368
  data recovery, 377–379
  data-encoding strategy determination, 374–375
  Detailed Technical Log, 381, 385, 422–423
  development, 327–337, 389–400, 445–447
  device driver tests, 368–369
  digital tests, 356–362
  disk cache tests, 368
  disk compression software and, 408–411
  ECC and, 67
  EVDR.SYS earlier than Version 5.0 and, 235
  future developments, 401–405
  genesis, 445–447
  high-frequency test, 360
  history of, 389–400
  IDE drives with, 93
  illustration of test patterns, 358–359
  INT 13h interrupt hooking, 224, 369
  interactive use, 419–424
  interleave analysis and setting, 375–377
  interleave check, 375
  interleave value variations from, 82
  interrupted operations, 366, 386–387
  isolated-ones test, 361

Index

jostling and, 442–443
low-frequency test, 360
low-level reformat limitations, 347
low-level reformatting (nondestructive), 231, 233, 346–347, 379, 420
main menu, 366
MFM mixed-frequency test, 361
more than 10 partitions and, 423–424, 433
moving data to safety, 382–385
PARK.COM, 459
pattern testing, 357–362, 380, 421–422
performance evaluation for sector interleave, 76
performance-testing programs and, 82
PerStor controllers and, 232–233
quick surface scan, 369–370
RAM tests, 365, 367
rapid low-high alternation test, 361
reminders, 442
reports, 380–382, 422–423
resuming interrupted operations, 366, 387
RLL narrow-band and wide-band mixed frequency tests, 361
running from clean boot diskette, 411–414
running from the hard disk, 408
scrambled-bits test, 361
scratch pads, 366–367
SCSI drives with, 93
sector mapping and, 217
seek tests, 271–272, 420–421
self-testing, 365
side benefits, 337–341
tests performed before surface testing, 355–356, 366–375
third-party partitioning software and, 408
timing tests, 372–374
Track Map, 370, 380–381
upgrading, 400
versions, 389–405
   SpinRite I Version 1.0, 390
   SpinRite I Version 1.1, 391–393
   SpinRite I Versions 1.2, 1.2A, and 1.2B, 393–394
   SpinRite II Version 1.0, 394–397
   SpinRite II Version 1.1, 398–399
   SpinRite II Version 2.0, 399–400
   SpinRite 3, 401–405
   table of versions, 390
   upgrading, 400
SPINRITE.LOG, 381, 423, 433
SPINRITE.RPT, 423, 433
SR.BAT (SpinRite), 428, 430–433
ST412/ST506 standard, 84–86, 95
   head positioner drive circuits and, 143
Stacker
   safety boot diskette and, 30
   SpinRite and, 408–411
STACKER.COM, 30
standards
   ATA, 92
   ESDI, 87
   IDE, 92–93
   PCMCIA, 94, 96
   SCSI, 88–92
   ST412/ST506, 84–86
   summary, 95
star filter (LIST), 507
starting LIST, 499–500
starting the PC. *See* booting
start-up program, 198–199
static electricity dangers to PC, 27
static friction, 301–302
status line format for LIST, 502
stepper motor actuators, 39, 102–106
   head-positioner drive circuit, 142–143
   how stepper motors work, 103–105
   illustrated, 106
   variations, 106
   voice coil motors vs. stepper motors, 108, 109, 111–112
stiction, 301–302
Storage Dimensions, SpeedStor, 213, 230, 408
subdirectories, 272–273
Substrate, 33
Super PC-Kwik, 163
   PowerWrite, 157
SuperStor and SpinRite, 408–411
surface analysis, 347–363
   defined, 347
   digital testing, 353–356

Index

disk test during low-level formatting, 284
manufacturer tests, 347–348, 349–353
preconditions for testing, 355–356
read-only test (SpinRite), 369–370
worst-case paradigm, 353–355, 356
Surface Test routine (NetWare), 283
surfing heads, 37
switches, head-switching circuits, 144–145
synchronous spindle motors, 141
syntax for LIST, 498
system byte, 246
system files on safety boot diskette, 23–24

— T —

/T parameter (DAZZLE), 474
tab expansion filter (LIST), 508
tab key with DAZZLE, 479
tables
    AT drive-type table, 197–199
    boot record data table, 261, 277–279
    extended partition table, 247–248
    file allocation tables (FATs), 265–270
    hard disk parameter tables (HDPT), 190–194
    interrupt vector table, 184, 185, 186–187, 190
    partition table, 243–244, 249–250, 257
    SpinRite versions, 390
    See also specific types of tables
Tandon AdPac removable disk packs, 232
Tandy computers, 3
TAPCIS, 441
tape drives vs. hard disks, 33–34
/T*d* option (MIRROR), 21
Tech Talk, 446
Technical Secrets
    margin icon, 7
    who needs them, 6
telephone dialer (LIST), 513
temperature of hard disk, 291–292, 303–305
terminate-and-stay-resident programs. *See* TSR programs
testing
    analog testing vs. digital testing, 362–363
    controller tests (SpinRite), 367–368
    device driver tests (SpinRite), 368–369

disk cache tests (SpinRite), 368
disk test by FORMAT, 276, 284
disk test during low-level formatting, 284
manufacturer tests, 347–348, 349–353, 362–363
pattern testing (SpinRite), 357–362, 380, 421–422
performance-testing programs and SpinRite, 82
POST (power on self test), 198
by reinterleaving programs, 341
safety boot diskette, 27–28
seek tests, 271–272, 351, 420–421
SpinRite self-testing, 365
surface analysis, 347–363
Surface Test (NetWare), 283
tests performed before SpinRite surface testing, 355–356, 366–375
timing tests (SpinRite), 372–374
See also SpinRite; surface analysis
thin-film heads, 130–131
    illustrated, 131
third-party disk partitioning software, 254–255
TIME, 196
TIMEPARK.COM, 441, 460
timer tick, 372
timing tests (SpinRite), 372–374
Tip margin icon, 7
Toshiba laptops and low-level formatting, 234–235
Touchstone Software Corp., 291
    CheckIt, 291
tower tilt, 122, 123, 126
track buffers, 76, 154
track density, 141
Track Map (SpinRite), 370, 380–381
track mapping by UltraStor 12f and 12c, 218
tracks, 37–41
    bad track, 348
    defined, 37
    illustrated, 38
    per cylinder, 41
    using empty first track, 240, 255–256
    width, 45–46
    zones, 51

Index

translating controllers, 347
tree directory structure, 272–273
troubleshooting chart, 313
TSR programs, 184, 186–187
    how they work, 186–187
    illustrated, 188–189
    MIRROR as, 21
    name derivation, 186
    on safety boot diskette, 25
turning on PC after turning off, 298–299, 439
TYPE, 453
Type conventions in this book, 7

— U —

/U parameter (Micro House utilities), 456
UltraStor 12f and 12C, 217–218
UNDELETE, 21, 299, 316
unformatting, 299
uninterruptible power supply (UPS), 159
UNIX, 172, 281
upgrading SpinRite, 400
UPS (uninterruptible power supply), 159
user groups, 18
user mistakes, protecting against, 21
user-definable drive type, 197

— V —

/V parameter
    CHKDSK, 415
    DAZZLE, 472
    FORMAT, 28
value of hard disks, 14–15
variable-length CGR, 58
vectors, interrupt, 184, 185, 186
vertical recording, 136–140
    critical dimensions, 138–140
    how it works, 136–138
    illustrated, 137, 139
    longitudinal recording vs., 136–138
Vfeature Deluxe, 213
video BIOS extension ROM, 198
Viewarc command (LIST), 519
viewing files with LIST, 453–455
VIRUSCAN, 30

viruses, 240
voice coil, 107, 108
voice coil actuators, 39, 107–112
    buried servo systems, 126–127
    dedicated platter servo systems, 118–122
    embedded servo systems, 124–125
    external servo systems, 113–118
    head-positioner drive circuit, 142–144
    how voice coil motors work, 107–110
    hybrid servo systems, 125–126
    illustrated, 110
    servo-controlled head positioning, 113–127
    stepper motors vs. voice coil motors, 108, 109, 111–112
    wedge servo systems, 123–124
volumes
    boot record, 24, 260–262
    creating with FDISK, 252–253
    data area, 260, 262–265
    defined, 190
    DOS size limits, 207–208, 210–213
    extended partition table, 247
    file allocation tables (FATs), 260, 265–270
    four essential regions, 260
    illustrated, 248
    large logical volume disadvantages, 256
    volume label, 274

— W —

/W parameter (DAZZLE), 452, 476
"weakening" of magnetic fields, 344–345
wedge servo systems, 123–124
    illustrated, 123
Western Digital controllers' use of first track, 236, 240
WHATSNEW, 455
width
    of bits, 45
    of tracks, 45–46
    See also size
Windows
    DAZZLE and, 488
    file managers, 21
    as programming environment, 170
    SMARTDrive, 158–159

Index

windows in LIST, 512–513
Windows NT, 172
    logical formatting, 282–283
    NTFS volumes, 282–283
    partitioning and, 249
    as programming environment, 170
WIPEDISK, 301
WIPEFILE, 301
WipeInfo (Norton Utilities), 175, 301
words (DOS), 357
Workman and Associates, 316
worst-case paradigm, 353–355, 356
    defining worst case, 354–355
    encoding technology effect on, 356
    illustrated, 354
wrap filter (LIST), 507
write amplifier, 144
write circuitry, 344
write precompensation, 50
write-through cache, 156
    advanced, 157
    read cache vs., 156
Wyse DOS Version 3.21, 211

— X —

XBIOS, 214
XT hard disk controller, 194–195
/XT parameter (DAZZLE), 472
XTreeGold, 21

— Z —

/Z parameter (DAZZLE), 452, 476
ZM data encoding, 56
zone bit recording, 51
zones of tracks, 51

Macworld Authorized Editions

Designed specifically for the Macintosh user, Macworld Books are written by leading *Macworld* magazine columnists, technology champions, and Mac gurus who provide expert advice and insightful tips and techniques not found anywhere else. Macworld Books are the only Macintosh books authorized by *Macworld*, the world's leading Macintosh magazine.

Macworld Guide To Microsoft System 7.1, 2nd Edition
by *Lon Poole*, Macworld *magazine's "Quick Tips" columnist*

The most recommended guide to System 7, updated and expanded!

**$24.95 USA/$33.95 Canada/£22.92 UK & EIRE,
ISBN: 1-878058-65-7**

Macworld Networking Handbook
by *David Kosiur, Ph.D.*

The ultimate insider's guide to Mac network management.

**$29.95 USA/$39.95 Canada/£27.45 UK & EIRE,
ISBN: 1-878058-31-2**

Macworld Guide To Microsoft Word 5
by *Jim Heid*, Macworld *magazine's "Getting Started" columnist*

Learn Word the easy way with this *Macworld* Authorized Edition. Now updated for Word 5.1.

**$22.95 USA/$29.95 Canada/£20.95 UK & EIRE,
ISBN: 1-878058-39-8**

Macworld Guide To Microsoft Excel 4
by *David Maguiness*

Build powerful spreadsheets quickly with this *Macworld* Authorized Edition to Excel 4.

**$22.95 USA/$29.95 Canada/£20.95 UK & EIRE,
ISBN: 1-878058-40-1**

Macworld Guide To Microsoft Works 3
by *Barrie A. Sosinsky*

Get inside the new Works so you can work more productively—the perfect blend of reference and tutorial.

**$22.95 USA/$29.95 Canada/£20.95 UK & EIRE,
ISBN: 1-878058-42-8**

Macworld Music & Sound Bible
by *Christopher Yavelow*

Finally, the definitive guide to music, sound, and multimedia on the Mac.

**$37.95 USA/$47.95 Canada/£34.95 UK & EIRE,
ISBN: 1-878058-18-5**

Macworld Complete Mac Handbook
by *Jim Heid*

The most complete guide to getting started, mastering, and expanding your Mac.

**$26.95 USA/$35.95 Canada/£24.95 UK & EIRE,
ISBN: 1-878058-17-7**

Macworld QuarkXPress Designer Handbook
by *Barbara Assadi and Galen Gruman*

Macworld magazine's DTP experts help you master advanced features fast with this definitive tutorial, reference and designer tips resource on QuarkXPress.

**$29.95 USA/$39.95 Canada/£27.45 UK & EIRE,
ISBN: 1-878058-85-1 — Available July 1993**

Macworld PageMaker Bible
by *Jo Ann Villalobos*

The ultimate insiders' guide to PageMaker 5, combining an authoritative and easy-to-use reference with tips and techniques. Includes 3 1/2" disk of templates.

**$39.95 USA/$52.95 Canada/£37.60 UK & EIRE,
ISBN: 1-878058-84-3 — Available July 1993**

For More Information Call 1-800-762-2974

InfoWorld SECRETS™ and Power Programming SECRETS™

SECRETS™ Books/disks offer a one-on-one session with an expert who reveals insider tips and techniques, undocumented features, and configuration and testing recommendations. The software includes ready-to-use utilities and applications that are strategically linked to the books' content. Power Programming SECRETS™ books/disks provide programming professionals with expert tips and techniques for successful and efficient application development. The included disk contains valuable templates and examples that users can easily customize to build their own applications.

Windows 3.1 SECRETS™
by Brian Livingston

Windows expert Brian Livingston reveals the secret power of Windows 3.0 and 3.1— and The Best in Windows Shareware.

$39.95 USA/$52.95 Canada/£37.60 UK & EIRE,
ISBN: 1-878058-43-6

PC SECRETS™
by Caroline M. Halliday

IDG's technical support expert shows you how to optimize your PC's performance — includes two disks of valuable utilities.

$39.95 USA/$52.95 Canada/£37.60 UK & EIRE,
ISBN: 1-87805849-5

Windows GIZMOS™
by Brian Livingston and Margie Livingston

The best Windows utilities, applications, and games — over 30 programs on 4 disks!

$39.95 USA/$52.95 Canada/£37.60 UK & EIRE,
ISBN: 1-878058-66-5

DOS 6 SECRETS™
by Robert D. Ainsbury

Reveals hundreds of insider SECRETS and expert techniques to put the full power of DOS at your fingertips. The definitive reference for optimizing your PC with new DOS features. Includes coverage of the latest DOS extensions and 2 disks of the best in DOS Shareware.

$39.95 USA/$52.95 Canada/£37.60 UK & EIRE,
ISBN: 1-878058-70-3

Hard Disk SECRETS™
by John M. Goodman, Ph.D., national bestselling author

The insider's guide to maximizing hard disk performance. Includes disk of FREE hard disk tune-up software.

$39.95 USA/$52.95 Canada/£37.60 UK & EIRE,
ISBN: 1-878058-64-9

Memory Management SECRETS™
by Brett Glass

InfoWorld's technical wizard Brett Glass reveals the hard-to-find and unusual secrets in this one-of-a-kind book/disk. Designed to help all users — beginning to advanced — install, configure, use, fine-tune, and understand memory management.

$34.95 USA/$44.95 Canada/£32.95 UK & EIRE,
ISBN: 1-878058-72-X

Paradox 4 Power Programming SECRETS™, 2nd Edition
by Gregory B. Salcedo and Martin W. Rudy

Learn advanced Paradox 4 programming techniques with this completely revised and updated bestseller. Includes disk of valuable Paradox add-in tools.

$44.95 USA/$59.95 Canada/£42.95 UK & EIRE,
ISBN: 1-878058-54-1

1-2-3 SECRETS™
by Rick Dobson

Let 1-2-3 expert Rick Dobson show you hundreds of undocumented tips, techniques and SECRETS to turbocharge 1-2-3 from simple spreadsheets to customized macro-driven applications.

$39.95 USA/$52.95 Canada/£37.60 UK & EIRE,
ISBN: 1-878058-73-8

Windows NT SECRETS™
by Brian Livingston

A sequel to Livingston's bestselling book *Windows 3.1 SECRETS*. Focused on Microsoft's hot new multiuser/multitasking operating environment, this is the only book power users need to understand and master Windows NT.

$39.95 USA/$52.95 Canada/£37.60 UK & EIRE,
ISBN: 1-878058-71-1 — Available Sept. 1993

For More Information Call 1-800-762-2974

PC World Handbook

AUTHORIZED PC WORLD EDITION

Expert information at your fingertips. Perfect for readers who need a complete tutorial of features as well as a reference to software applications and operating systems. All PC World Handbooks include bonus disks with software featuring useful templates, examples, and utilities that provide real value to the reader.

PC World DOS 6 Handbook, 2nd Edition
by John Socha, Clint Hicks, and Devra Hall

Completely revised and updated! Includes extended features of DOS and the 250 page command reference that Microsoft excludes. A complete tutorial and reference PLUS Special Edition of Norton Commander software.

**$34.95 USA/$44.95 Canada/£32.95 UK & EIRE,
ISBN: 1-878058-79-7**

PC World Excel 4 for Windows Handbook
by John Walkenbach and David Maguiness

Complete tutorial and reference by PC World's spreadsheet experts, with a FREE 32-page Function Reference booklet.

**$29.95 USA/$39.95 Canada/£27.45 UK & EIRE,
ISBN: 1-878058-46-0**

PC World Microsoft Access Bible
by Cary Prague and Michael Irwin

This authoritative tutorial and reference on Microsoft's new Windows database is the perfect companion for every Microsoft Access user.

**$39.95 USA/$52.95 Canada/£37.60 UK & EIRE,
ISBN: 1-878058-81-9**

PC World WordPerfect 6 Handbook
by Greg Harvey

Bestselling author and WordPerfect guru Greg Harvey brings you the ultimate tutorial and reference – complete with valuable software containing document templates, macros, and other handy WordPerfect tools.

**$34.95 USA/$44.95 Canada/£32.95 UK & EIRE,
ISBN: 1-878058-80-0 — Available July 1993**

Official XTree MS-DOS, Windows, and Hard Disk Management Companion, 3rd Edition
by Beth Slick

The only authorized guide to all versions of XTree, the most popular PC hard disk utility.

**$19.95 USA/$26.95 Canada/£18.45 UK & EIRE,
ISBN: 1-878058-57-6**

PC World Q&A Bible, Version 4
by Thomas J. Marcellus, Technical Editor of The Quick Answer

The only thorough guide with a disk of databases for mastering Q&A Version 4.

**$39.95 USA/$52.95 Canada/£37.60 UK & EIRE,
ISBN: 1-878058-03-7**

QuarkXPress for Windows Designer Handbook
by Barbara Assadi and Galen Gruman

Make the move to QuarkXPress for Windows, the new professional desktop publishing powerhouse, with this expert reference and tutorial.

**$29.95 USA/$39.95 Canada/£27.45 UK & EIRE,
ISBN: 1-878058-45-2**

PC World You Can Do It With DOS
by Christopher Van Buren

The best way to learn DOS quickly and easily.

**$19.95 USA/$26.95 Canada/£18.45 VAT UK EIRE,
ISBN: 1-878058-38-X**

PC World You Can Do It With Windows
by Christopher Van Buren

The best way to learn Window 3.1!

**$19.95 USA/$26.95 Canada/£18.45 VAT UK EIRE,
ISBN: 1-878058-37-1**

For More Information Call 1-800-762-2974

IDG BOOKS

Order Form

Order Center: (800) 762-2974 (8 a.m.-5 p.m., PST, weekdays) or (415) 312-0650

For Fastest Service: Photocopy This Order Form and FAX it to: (415) 358-1260

Quantity	ISBN	Title	Price	Total
	75-4	DOS For Dummies, 2nd Edition	$16.95	
	51-7	PCs For Dummies™	$16.95	
	53-3	Macs For Dummies™	$16.95	
	61-4	Windows For Dummies™	$16.95	
	77-0	WordPerfect 6 For Dummies™	$16.95	
	58-4	UNIX For Dummies™	$19.95	
	63-0	Excel For Dummies™	$16.95	
	60-6	1-2-3 For Dummies™	$16.95	
	86-X	Word for Windows For Dummies™	$16.95	
	78-9	C Programming For Dummies™	$19.95	
	76-2	OS/2 For Dummies™	$19.95	

Shipping & Handling Charges

Subtotal	U.S.	Canada & International	International Air Mail
Up to $20.00	Add $3.00	Add $4.00	Add $10.00
$20.01-40.00	$4.00	$5.00	$20.00
$40.01-60.00	$5.00	$6.00	$25.00
$60.01-80.00	$6.00	$8.00	$35.00
Over $80.00	$7.00	$10.00	$50.00

In U.S. and Canada, shipping is UPS ground or equivalent.
For Rush shipping call (800) 762-2974.

Subtotal _____

CA residents add applicable sales tax _____

IN residents add 5% sales tax _____

Canadian residents add 7% GST tax _____

Shipping _____

TOTAL _____

Ship to:

Name _____

Company _____

Address _____

City/State/Zip _____

Daytime Phone _____

Payment: ❑ Check to IDG Books (US Funds Only)   ❑ Visa   ❑ MasterCard   ❑ American Express

Card # _____ Exp. _____ Signature _____

Please send this order form to: IDG Books, 155 Bovet Road, San Mateo, CA 94402.
Allow up to 3 weeks for delivery. Thank you!

BOBMW93

International Data Group (IDG), and IDG Books Worldwide, Inc., an affiliate of IDG based in San Mateo, CA, are committed to directing the power of business and industry toward improving the environment.

▲▼▲

This book was printed on recycled paper, and can be recycled.

Disclaimer and Copyright Notice

Note

IDG Books Worldwide, Inc. warrants that the disk that accompanies this book is free from defects in materials and workmanship for a period of 60 days from the date of purchase of this book. If IDG Books receives notification within the warranty period of defects in material or workmanship, IDG Books will replace the defective disk. The remedy for the breach of this warranty will be limited to replacement and will not encompass any other damages, including but not limited to loss of profit, and special, incidental, consequential, or other claims.

5.25" Disk Format Available. The enclosed disk is in 3.5" 1.44MB format. If you don't have a drive that size or format and cannot arrange to transfer the data to the disk size you need, you can obtain the programs on 5.25" 1.22MB disks by writing: IDG Books Worldwide, Attn: *Hard Disk SECRETS* Disk, IDG Books, 155 Bovet Rd., Suite 310, San Mateo, CA 94402, or call 800-762-2974. Please allow 2-3 weeks for delivery.

IDG Books Worldwide, InfoWorld Publishing Inc., and the author specifically disclaim all other warranties, express or implied, including but not limited to implied warranties of merchantability and fitness for a particular purpose with respect to defects in the disk and the programs, contained therein, and/or the techniques described in the book, and in no event shall IDG Books Worldwide, InfoWorld, and/or the author be liable for any loss of profit or any other commercial damage, including but not limited to special, incidental, consequential, or other damages.

Licensing Agreement

Do not open the accompanying disk package until you have read and unless you agree with the terms of this licensing agreement. If you disagree and do not want to be bound by the terms of this licensing agreement, return the book for refund to the source from which you purchased it.

The entire contents of this disk are copyrighted and protected by both U.S. copyright law and international copyright treaty provisions. The individual programs on this disk are copyrighted by the authors of each program respectively. Each program has its own use permissions and limitations. You may copy any or all of these programs to your computer system. To use each shareware program, you must follow the individual requirements and restrictions detailed for each in the documentation contained in Appendix B of this book. Do not use a program if you do not want to follow its licensing agreement. Absolutely none of the material on this disk or listed in this book may ever be distributed, in original or modified form, for commercial purposes without written permission from the copyright owners.

Installation Instructions for the
Hard Disk SECRETS Disk

Attention: Before installing any of the programs from the distribution disks, read the Disclaimer and Copyright Notice on the preceding page.

Because the programs on the disk are in a fully ready-to-run form, you aren't required to install them to use them. You will find the programs easier to use, though, if you transfer them to your hard disk.

You can copy the files from the disk into whatever directory pleases you. I recommend that you put any of these files that you think you will use a lot in some directory that is on your DOS path. You can copy the others to a directory of their own, perhaps one you call HDSECRTS.

The two slight exceptions to this strategy are that the two files, HDINFO.BAT and HDINFO.TXT, need to be in the same directory, and LISTR.COM either needs to be in that directory or in one that is on your path. As an alternative to this arrangement, you can edit the HDINFO.BAT batch file.

The programs in the LISTPGMS subdirectory on the disk were put there merely to keep them together. This arrangement is most important if you plan to give copies of LIST and its associated programs to others — keeping them in a subdirectory makes it easy to remember which files to include when you make up your gifts for friends.

See Appendix B for complete information on the *Hard Disk SECRETS* disk.

IDG BOOKS WORLDWIDE REGISTRATION CARD

IDG BOOKS
THE WORLD OF COMPUTER KNOWLEDGE

Title of this book: _____

My overall rating of this book: ❏ Very good [1] ❏ Good [2] ❏ Satisfactory [3] ❏ Fair [4] ❏ Poor [5]

How I first heard about this book:

❏ Found in bookstore; name: [6] ❏ Book review: [7]
❏ Advertisement: [8] ❏ Catalog: [9]
❏ Word of mouth; heard about book from friend, co-worker, etc.: [10] ❏ Other: [11]

What I liked most about this book:
_____
_____

What I would change, add, delete, etc., in future editions of this book:
_____
_____

Other comments:
_____

Number of computer books I purchase in a year: ❏ 1 [12] ❏ 2-5 [13] ❏ 6-10 [14] ❏ More than 10 [15]

I would characterize my computer skills as: ❏ Beginner [16] ❏ Intermediate [17] ❏ Advanced [18] ❏ Professional [19]

I use ❏ DOS [20] ❏ Windows [21] ❏ OS/2 [22] ❏ Unix [23] ❏ Macintosh [24] ❏ Other: [25] _____
(please specify)

I would be interested in new books on the following subjects:
(please check all that apply, and use the spaces provided to identify specific software)

❏ Word processing: [26] ❏ Spreadsheets: [27]
❏ Data bases: [28] ❏ Desktop publishing: [29]
❏ File Utilities: [30] ❏ Money management: [31]
❏ Networking: [32] ❏ Programming languages: [33]
❏ Other: [34]

I use a PC at (please check all that apply): ❏ home [35] ❏ work [36] ❏ school [37] ❏ other: [38] _____

The disks I prefer to use are ❏ 5.25 [39] ❏ 3.5 [40] ❏ other: [41] _____

I have a CD ROM: ❏ yes [42] ❏ no [43]

I plan to buy or upgrade computer hardware this year: ❏ yes [44] ❏ no [45]

I plan to buy or upgrade computer software this year: ❏ yes [46] ❏ no [47]

Name: _____ Business title: [48] _____ Type of Business: [49] _____

Address (❏ home [50] ❏ work [51]/Company name: _____)

Street/Suite# _____

City [52]/State [53]/Zipcode [54]: _____

❏ **I liked this book!** You may quote me by name in future IDG Books Worldwide promotional materials.
My daytime phone number is _____

RETURN THIS REGISTRATION CARD FOR FREE CATALOG

☐ **YES!** Please keep me informed about IDG's World of Computer Knowledge. Send me the latest IDG Books catalog.

Fold Here

PLACE STAMP HERE

IDG Books Worldwide, Inc.
155 Bovet Road
Suite 310
San Mateo, CA 94402

Attn: Reader Response

IDG BOOKS
THE WORLD OF COMPUTER KNOWLEDGE